John C. Calhoun

CONSERVATIVE LEADERSHIP SERIES

EAGLE PUBLISHING, INC.

EAGLE BOOK CLUBS, INC.

CONSERVATIVE BOOK CLUB

REGNERY PUBLISHING, INC.

The Conservative Leadership Series is a joint project of Regnery Publishing, Inc., and Eagle Book Clubs, Inc., divisions of Eagle Publishing, Inc., to make the classics of conservative thought available in hardcover collector's editions.

John C. Calhoun:
Selected Writings and Speeches

Edited with Headnotes and an Introduction
by H. LEE CHEEK, JR.

 PUBLISHING, INC.
An Eagle Publishing Company • Washington, DC

ISBN: 0-89526-1790

Published in the United States by
Regnery Publishing, Inc.
An Eagle Publishing Company
One Massachusetts Avenue, NW
Washington, DC 20001

Distributed to the trade by
National Book Network
4720-A Boston Way
Lanham, MD 20706

Printed on acid-free paper
Manufactured in the United States of America

10 9 8 7 6 5 4 3 2 1

Books are available in quantity for promotional or premium use. Write to Director of Special Sales, Regnery Publishing, Inc., One Massachusetts Avenue, NW, Washington, DC 20001, for information on discounts and terms or call (202) 216-0600.

For Kathy B. Cheek, Mary Ann Braun,
and Howard "Red" and Ann Cheek

Soldiers All

CONTENTS

ACKNOWLEDGMENTS

RESEARCH SUPPORT from the Earhart Foundation and Lee University were of assistance to this editorial project.

Steve Ealy, Tim Goodman, Bob Paquette, Clyde Wilson, Tim Sifert, George Carey, Carey Roberts, Constantine Gutzman, Gary Gregg, James McClellan, and Jeff Nelson are colleagues who have aided my work at every juncture. My Lee University colleagues, Drs. Tom Metallo, Mary Waalkes, Matthew Melton, Richard Jones, and Chris Coulter, never let me neglect my Calhounian pursuits, even when there was substantial disagreement with my assessments. I owe a special thanks to Carey Roberts and Constantine Gutzman for helping me make some final emendations to the text.

One of the greatest blessings of being a teacher is to be graced with the presence of outstanding students. The overall enterprise that resulted in this volume was greatly augmented by the labors of three Lee University students—Allen Jervey, Robert Flowers, and Emily Noble.

Mr. Christopher B. Briggs is a gentleman and a scholar, and a talented series editor. I owe him many thanks.

My greatest debts are owed to my kind and disciplined wife, Kathy B. Cheek, my mother-in-law, Mary Ann Braun, and to Red and Ann Cheek, my parents who first shared with me the insights of Mr. Calhoun.

INTRODUCTION

⟨⟩ BACKGROUND

JOHN CALDWELL CALHOUN was born in 1782 near Abbeville, South Carolina. Calhoun's educational opportunities were limited, albeit advanced by the occasional tutelage offered by his brother-in-law, Reverend Moses Waddel. After his parents' death and a period of self-education, Calhoun entered Yale College, studying under the arch–Federalist Dr. Timothy Dwight. He proceeded to study law under Judge Tapping Reeve at the Litchfield Law School in Connecticut, the most prominent institution devoted to legal training during this period. Returning to his native South Carolina to practice law, a pursuit he considered "both dry and laborious," Calhoun married and served two terms in the South Carolina Legislature until elected to the U.S. House of Representatives in 1811. As a congressman, Calhoun continued to embody republican principles and acquired the reputation as a moral statesman who regarded republicanism and patriotism as synonymous: he supported the War of 1812; he revised Madison's original national bank proposal and backed limited internal improvements; and he continued to praise a free economy and a regime founded upon "reason and equity" that was surrounded by a world of "fraud, violence or accident."

President Monroe asked Calhoun to assume the helm at the War Department in 1817, where he served until 1825. Calhoun was generally considered too philosophical for such a practical post, but he accepted the appointment out of a republican sense of duty. In the course of two terms in office Calhoun completely reorganized and revitalized the War Department and its general staff, resolved its financial problems resulting from the war, and demonstrated a new, more compassionate approach to Native American affairs. Calhoun also began reforming West Point through a new spirit of openness in terms of admissions and administrative procedures. Calhoun has been described as the ablest war secretary the United States had before Jefferson Davis in 1853.

A broad spectrum of supporters encouraged Calhoun's candidacy for president in 1824 against his fellow cabinet members William H. Crawford and John Quincy Adams, Speaker of the House Henry Clay, and war hero and newly-elected senator, Andrew Jackson. Initially entering the presidential field, Calhoun realized he lacked adequate support and withdrew after Pennsylvania nominated Andrew Jackson. Accepting the vice-presidential nomination, Calhoun was elected by a large majority. The results in the presidential contest between Jackson and Adams were inconclusive in terms of the electoral and popular vote, and the election was "thrown" into the House of Representatives where Jackson's nemesis Clay served as speaker. In an unusual series of events, Clay came to Adams's aid, and the House vote secured the election for Adams. The president-elect proceeded to appoint Clay as secretary of state.

Many Americans considered the supposed arrangement between Clay and Adams a "corrupt bargain," including Calhoun, who believed it threatened the republican, constitutional regime of the United States. "Improperly acquired" power would doubtless be "improperly used," he opined. Soon after the election, Calhoun and either Adams or his representative engaged in a pseudonymous debate about the sources of political power, and the reader is treated to part of this vibrant exchange in this collection (Chapters V and VI). In the years that followed, Calhoun sought to distance himself even further from Adams, who, according to Calhoun, had abused presidential power, and Calhoun supported General Andrew Jackson in 1828. It was as part of this ticket, later tagged as the Democratic party, that Calhoun was elected vice-president in 1828.

The falling apart of the political union between Calhoun and Jackson is one of the most remarkable events in American politics. Calhoun had hoped Jackson would assume the republican mantel, but Calhoun's expectations were not fulfilled. The two men came into conflict over several issues, especially Jackson's support for high tariffs favoring Northern manufacturers at the expense of Southern agricultural interests, which Calhoun represented.

As a result of the disputes with Jackson, Calhoun resigned as vice-president and was elected to the Senate. In an attempt to moderate the crisis posed by tariff-related concerns and the "Force Bill" of 1833 (congressional legislation empowering Jackson to employ the armed forces of the United States to collect the disputed tariffs in, for example, Calhoun's home state of South Carolina), Calhoun questioned the benefit of preserving the Union by force.

Calhoun favored instead a "harmonious aggregate of the States" as the basis for political union.

To this point in his career as a statesman, Calhoun had made few statements regarding slavery, but troubled by the increasing national influence of abolitionist ideology and the looming threat of sectional conflict, Calhoun devoted the remainder of his life simultaneously to defending the South and to damping internecine conflict on American soil. Retiring from the Senate in 1843, he unsuccessfully pursued the presidency for the last time. In 1844, Calhoun was appointed secretary of state. In the same year, Calhoun helped contain a truly revolutionary secessionist "Bluffton Movement" composed of his fellow South Carolinians incensed over yet more high tariffs and agitated by the extension-of-slavery question raised by the possible annexation of Texas. Calhoun's success in moderating the conflict demonstrated his restraint in a crisis. Returning to the Senate in 1845, Calhoun served as a thoughtful critic of the war with Mexico and suggested the conflict would encourage further disharmony between the North and South.

Published after his death, Calhoun's two treatises on political theory and American constitutionalism, the *Disquisition* and *Discourse*, demonstrate his hope that America could avoid the pending conflict. Calhoun's persistent concern about the unequal treatment of the South would, he feared, lead to increased regional tensions and to civil war. His last years were spent attempting to unify the South and avoid strife. On March 31, 1850, Calhoun died in Washington, D.C.

In death, Calhoun became a source of inspiration for the Confederate government, its leaders, and the South. Calhoun's understanding of restraint within political order, albeit imperfect, remains one of the most important characteristics of his political thought and his achievement as a statesman. In Calhoun's interpretation, the interposing and amending power of the states implicit in the Constitution could only augment authentic popular rule by allowing for a greater diffusion of authority. Calhoun's purpose was the preservation of the original balance of authority and the fortification of the American political system against the destructive forces besetting it.

CALHOUN'S POLITICAL THOUGHT

THIS COLLECTION encourages the reader to view Calhoun as an original political thinker. Calhoun was both a lover of the American regime and of his native region. For Calhoun, the recovery of a proper mode of popular rule depended upon a return to the ideas of the Founding; such a project could not be accomplished without revisiting and expounding for a new day the "primitive principles" and experiences of the Founding generation. Calhoun devoted his life to this task, and his writings are the most profound examples of this attempt at recovery and self-understanding reframed for a nineteenth-century America consumed by new challenges.

For Calhoun, our political inheritance of liberty was established upon an appreciation of the necessary limitations on political life. Both the person and society, he argued, must exercise restraint when faced with the possibility of radical transformation. While change and social mobility were not the most commonly acknowledged aspects of Southern society, neither were such things, Calhoun argued, beyond the pale of possibility. But change had to occur slowly, he argued, if it were to last. As an articulate representative of agrarian republicanism during the early and mid-nineteenth century, Calhoun presented an Aristotelian mean as the basis of restraint in the operations of government. If government could not be restricted, he argued, the regime would necessarily lose its free character and the populace's role in governing would be greatly diminished. He firmly believed that government, with its potential to abuse power, must become more moderate, or suffer eventual demise, thus causing great harm to all inhabitants, great or small, of a regime.

According to Calhoun, the works of antiquity, the treatises of Christian authors, and the genius of the founding generation fostered the moral restraint needed in the American federal republic. Indeed, living within a society aware of its constraints, Calhoun also appreciated the limits of human experience, acknowledging the shortcomings of his own perspectives and holding all utopian schemes in disdain. The necessary balance between the need for popular participation in the government and the need to avoid the potential excesses of popular rule guided Calhoun's philosophical mission. In this regard, Calhoun's political theory should be understood as a reflective journey towards a recovery of genuine popular rule amidst the crises confronting a nation.

The contents of this volume will prove that Calhoun made a lasting contribution to American politics. His worldview serves as the philosophical foundation for a full-fledged theory of politics, one that is of significance to all students of politics and limited government. In presenting Calhoun's political writings in such a substantial manner, it is hoped that he might be appreciated by the modern—and indeed postmodern—world as a thinker of great importance.

NOTE ON THE TEXT

MOST OF the selections in this volume are taken from *The Works of John C. Calhoun*, edited by Richard K. Crallé (New York: D. Appleton and Company, 1888). The two exceptions are chapters eight and fourteen, which are respectively reprinted with permission from volume XI (pp. 250–56) and volume XII (pp.149–154) of *The Papers of John C. Calhoun* (Columbia, South Carolina: University of South Carolina Press), edited by Clyde N. Wilson. Calhoun's footnotes are indicated by standard symbols; Crallé's, by the same method but also labeled as his with a notation ("Crallé"). The editor's footnotes are indicated by numerals.

SELECTED BIBLIOGRAPHY

ᴄᴏPRIMARY SOURCES

Annals of Congress of the United States. Forty-two volumes. Washington, D.C.: Gales and Seaton, 1834–1856.

Calhoun, John C. *Calhoun: Basic Documents.* Edited by John M. Anderson. State College, Pennsylvania: Bald Eagle Press, 1952.

Calhoun, John C. *Correspondence of John C. Calhoun.* Edited by J. Franklin Jameson. Washington: Government Printing Office, 1900.

Calhoun, John C. *The Papers of John C. Calhoun.* Twenty-six volumes to date. Edited by Clyde Wilson, et al. Columbia: University of South Carolina Press, 1959–present.

Calhoun, John C. *The Works of John C. Calhoun.* Six volumes. Edited by Richard K. Crallé. New York: D. Appleton and Company, 1853–1855.

ᴄᴏSECONDARY SOURCES

Books

Bartlett, Irving H. *John C. Calhoun: A Biography.* New York, W. W. Norton and Company, 1993.

Butta, Giuseppe. *Democrazia e Federalismo: John C. Calhoun.* Messina: Edizioni, 2002.

Carpenter, Jesse T. *The South as a Conscious Minority, 1789–1861.* New York: New York University Press, 1930; reprint, Columbia: University of South Carolina Press, 1990.

Cheek, Jr., H. Lee. *Calhoun and Popular Rule.* Columbia and London: University of Missouri Press, 2001.

Coit, Margaret L. *John C. Calhoun: American Portrait.* Boston: Houghton Mifflin Company, 1950.

Coit, Margaret L., Editor. *Great Lives Observed: John C. Calhoun.* Englewood Cliffs, New Jersey: Prentice-Hall, 1970.

Current, Richard M. *John C. Calhoun.* New York: Washington Square Press, 1963.

Dodd, William E. *Statesmen of the Old South.* New York: The Book League of America, 1929.

Ericson, David F. *The Shaping of American Liberalism: The Debates Over Ratification, Nullification and Slavery*. Chicago: University of Chicago Press, 1993.

Freehling, William H. *Prelude to Civil War: The Nullification Controversy in South Carolina, 1816–1836*. New York: Harper and Row, 1965.

Marmor, Thedore R. *The Career of John C. Calhoun*. New York: Garland Publishing, 1988.

Meigs, William M. *The Life of John Caldwell Calhoun*. Two volumes. New York: Neale Publishing Company, 1917.

Merriam, Charles Edward. *American Political Ideas, 1865–1917*. New York: The Macmillan Company, 1929.

Morley, Felix. *Freedom and Federalism*. Indianapolis, Indiana: Liberty Fund, 1981.

Niven, John. *John C. Calhoun and the Price of Union*. Baton Rouge: Louisiana State University Press, 1988.

Peterson, Merrill D. *The Great Triumvirate: Webster, Clay, and Calhoun*. New York: Oxford University Press, 1987.

Spain, August O. *The Political Theory of John C. Calhoun*. New York: Bookman Associates, 1951.

Styron, Arthur. *The Cast-Iron Man: John C. Calhoun and American Democracy*. New York: Longmans, Green and Company, 1935.

Wilson, Clyde. *John C. Calhoun: A Bibliography*. Westport, Connecticut: Meckler, 1990.

Wiltse, Charles M. *John C. Calhoun: Nationalist, 1782–1828*. Indianapolis: Bobbs-Merrill Company, 1944.

Wiltse, Charles M. *John C. Calhoun: Nullifier, 1829–1839*. Indianapolis: Bobbs-Merrill Company, 1949.

Wiltse, Charles M. *John C. Calhoun: Sectionalist, 1840–1850*. Indianapolis: Bobbs-Merrill Company, 1951.

ARTICLES

Anderson, James L., and Hemphill, W. Edwin. "The 1843 Biography of John C. Calhoun: Was R.M.T. Hunter Its Author?" *Journal of Southern History*, Volume 38, Number 3 (August 1972), pp. 469–474.

Baskin, Darryl. "The Pluralist Vision of John C. Calhoun." *Polity*, Volume II, Number 1 (Fall 1969), pp. 49–65.

Cheek, Jr., H. Lee. "A Tenor of Discontent: Calhoun and His Critics." *Telos*, Number 118 (March 2001).

Cheek, Jr., H. Lee. "Calhoun, Sectional Conflict, and Modern America." *Journal of Libertarian Studies*, Volume 16, Number 2 (Spring 2002).

Davis, Jefferson. "Life and Character of the Hon. John Caldwell Calhoun." *North American Review*, Volume CXLV (September 1887), pp. 246–260.

Drucker, Peter. "A Key to American Politics: Calhoun's Pluralism." *Review of Politics*, Volume 10, Number 4 (October 1948), pp. 412–426.

Elwell, Margaret Coit. "The Continuing Relevance of John C. Calhoun." *Continuity: A Journal of History*, Volume 9 (Fall 1984), pp. 73–85.

Ericson, David F. "The Nullification Crisis, American Republicanism, and the Force Bill Debate." *The Journal of Southern History*, Volume LXI, Number 2 (May 1995), pp. 249–270.

Faulkner, Ronnie W. "Taking John C. Calhoun to the United Nations." *Polity*, Volume 15 (Summer 1983), pp. 473–491.

Ford, Lacy K. "Inventing the Concurrent Majority: Madison, Calhoun, and the Problem of Majoritarianism in American Political Thought." *The Journal of Southern History*, Volume LX, Number 1 (February 1994), pp. 19–58.

Ford, Lacy K. "Recovering the Republic: Calhoun, South Carolina, and the Concurrent Majority." *South Carolina Historical Magazine*, Volume 89, Number 3, (July 1988), pp. 146–159.

Ford, Lacy K. "Republican Ideology in a Slave Society: The Political Economy of John C. Calhoun." *The Journal of Southern History*, Volume LIV, Number 3 (August 1988), pp. 405–424.

Herzberg, Roberta. "An Analytic Choice Approach to Concurrent Majorities: The Revelance of John C. Calhoun's Theory of Institutional Design." *Journal of Politics*, Volume 54, Number 1 (February 1992), pp. 54–81.

Kirk, Russell. "Southern Conservatism: Randolph and Calhoun." Chapter in *The Conservative Mind: From Burke to Santayana*. Chicago: Henry Regnery, 1953, pp. 130–160.

Maier, Pauline. "The Road Not Taken: Nullification, John C. Calhoun, and the Revolutionary Tradition in South Carolina." *South Carolina Historical Magazine*, Volume 28, Number 1 (January 1981), pp. 1–19.

Putterman, Theodore L. "Calhoun's Realism?" *History of Political Thought*, Volume XII, Number 1 (Spring 1991), pp. 107–124.

Tabarrok, Alexander, and Tyler Cowen. "The Public Choice Theory of John C. Calhoun." *Journal of Institutional and Theoretical Economics*, Volume 148, Number 4 (December 1992), pp. 655–674.

Wilson, Clyde N. "Calhoun and Community." *Chronicles*, July 1985, pp. 17–20.

Wilson, Clyde N. "John Caldwell Calhoun." *Dictionary of Literary Biography*, Volume 3. Edited by Joel Myerson. Detroit: Gale Research Company, 1979, pp. 44–54.

Wilson, Clyde N. "Free Trade: No Debt: Separation from Banks: The Economic Platform of John C. Calhoun." Chapter in *Slavery, Secession, and Southern History*. Charlottesville: University Press of Virginia, 200.

CHAPTER I.

A DISQUISITION ON GOVERNMENT

Calhoun confided to his daughter Anna Maria that the impetus for composing the Disquisition *was to provide "a solid foundation for political science"[1] to assist future generations of Americans:*

> I finished yesterday, the preliminary work, which treats of the elementary principles of the Science of Government, except reading it over and making final corrections, previous to copying and publishing. It takes 125 pages of large foolscap closely written for me. I am pretty well satisfied with its execution. It will be nearly throughout new territory....[2]

In the Disquisition *Calhoun presented a theory of politics that is both original and in accord with the mainstream of the American political tradition. More than any other contemporary thinker of his period, Calhoun sought to explain the enduring qualities of American political thought in light of the troubled world of the mid-nineteenth century. In characterizing his* Disquisition *as "new territory" Calhoun was merely attempting to describe his treatise on the foundations of politics as his first and only systematic examination of these primary concerns. Unlike other theorists who had preceded and would follow Calhoun, both American and European, he did not seek to invent a new mode of philosophical speculation or a "grand theory" for the human sciences. Instead, he offered a refinement of classical, medieval and modern notions regarding the*

1. "To Mrs. T. G. Clemson," June 15, 1848, in Correspondence of John C. Calhoun, ed. J. Franklin Jameson, in *American Historical Association Annual Report for 1899,* Vol. 2 [Washington: U.S. Government Printing Office, 1900], p. 768 [hereafter cited as *Correspondence*].
2. Ibid.

relationship between government and the social order. First published in 1851, the Disquisition *remains one of the most important works in American political thought.*

IN order to have a clear and just conception of the nature and object of government, it is indispensable to understand correctly what that constitution or law of our nature is, in which government originates; or, to express it more fully and accurately,—that law, without which government would not, and with which, it must necessarily exist. Without this, it is as impossible to lay any solid foundation for the science of government, as it would be to lay one for that of astronomy, without a like understanding of that constitution or law of the material world, according to which the several bodies composing the solar system mutually act on each other, and by which they are kept in their respective spheres. The first question, accordingly, to be considered is,—What is that constitution or law of our nature, without which government would not exist, and with which its existence is necessary?

In considering this, I assume, as an incontestable fact, that man is so constituted as to be a social being. His inclinations and wants, physical and moral, irresistibly impel him to associate with his kind; and he has, accordingly, never been found, in any age or country, in any state other than the social. In no other, indeed, could he exist; and in no other,—were it possible for him to exist,—could he attain to a full development of his moral and intellectual faculties, or raise himself, in the scale of being, much above the level of the brute creation.

I next assume, also, as a fact not less incontestable, that, while man is so constituted as to make the social state necessary to his existence and the full development of his faculties, this state itself cannot exist without government. The assumption rests on universal experience. In no age or country has any society or community ever been found, whether enlightened or savage, without government of some description.

Having assumed these, as unquestionable phenomena of our nature, I shall, without further remark, proceed to the investigation of the primary and important question,—What is that constitution of our nature, which, while it impels man to associate with his kind, renders it impossible for society to exist without government?

The answer will be found in the fact, (not less incontestable than either of the others,) that, while man is created for the social state, and is accordingly so formed as to feel what affects others, as well as what affects himself, he is, at the same time, so constituted as to feel more intensely what affects him directly, than what affects him indirectly through others; or, to express it differently, he is so constituted, that his direct or individual affections are stronger than his sympathetic or social feelings. I intentionally avoid the expression, *selfish* feelings, as applicable to the former; because, as commonly used, it implies an unusual excess of the individual over the social feelings, in the person to whom it is applied; and, consequently, something depraved and vicious. My object is, to exclude such inference, and to restrict the inquiry exclusively to facts in their bearings on the subject under consideration, viewed as mere phenomena appertaining to our nature,—constituted as it is; and which are as unquestionable as is that of gravitation, or any other phenomenon of the material world.

In asserting that our individual are stronger than our social feelings, it is not intended to deny that there are instances, growing out of peculiar relations,—as that of a mother and her infant,—or resulting from the force of education and habit over peculiar constitutions, in which the latter have overpowered the former; but these instances are few, and always regarded as something extraordinary. The deep impression they make, whenever they occur, is the strongest proof that they are regarded as exceptions to some general and well understood law of our nature; just as some of the minor powers of the material world are apparently to gravitation.

I might go farther, and assert this to be a phenomenon, not of our nature only, but of all animated existence, throughout its entire range, so far as our knowledge extends. It would, indeed, seem to be essentially connected with the great law of self-preservation which pervades all that feels, from man down to the lowest and most insignificant reptile or insect. In none is it stronger than in man. His social feelings may, indeed, in a state of safety and abundance, combined with high intellectual and moral culture, acquire great expansion and force; but not so great as to overpower this all-pervading and essential law of animated existence.]

But that constitution of our nature which makes us feel more intensely what affects us directly than what affects us indirectly through others, necessarily leads to conflict between individuals] Each, in consequence, has a greater regard for his own safety or happiness, than for the safety or happiness of others; and, where these come in opposition, is ready to sacrifice the interests of others to his own. And hence, the tendency to a universal state of conflict, between individual and individual; accompanied by the connected passions of suspicion, jealousy, anger and revenge,—followed by insolence, fraud and cruelty;—and, if not prevented by some controlling power, ending in a state of universal discord and confusion, destructive of the social state and the ends for which it is ordained. This controlling power, wherever vested, or by whomsoever exercised, is GOVERNMENT.

It follows, then, that man is so constituted, that government is necessary to the existence of society, and society to his existence, and the perfection of his faculties. It follows, also, that government has its origin in this twofold constitution of his nature; the sympathetic or social feelings constituting the remote,—and the individual or direct, the proximate cause.

If man had been differently constituted in either particular;—if, instead of being social in his nature, he had been created without sympathy for his kind, and independent of others for his safety and existence; or if, on the other hand, he had been so created, as to feel more intensely what affected others than what affected himself, (if that were possible,) or, even, had this supposed interest been equal,—it is manifest that, in either case, there would have been no necessity for government, and that none would ever have existed. But, although society and government are thus intimately connected with and dependent on each other,—of the two society is the greater. It is the first in the order of things, and in the dignity of its object; that of society being primary,—to preserve and perfect our race; and that of government secondary and subordinate, to preserve and perfect society. Both are, however, necessary to the existence and well-being of our race, and equally of Divine ordination.

I have said,—if it were possible for man to be so constituted, as to feel what affects others more strongly than what affects himself, or even as strongly,—because, it may be well doubted, whether the stronger feeling or affection of individuals for themselves, combined with a feebler and subordinate feeling or affection for others, is not, in beings of limited reason and faculties, a constitution necessary to their preservation and existence. If reversed,—if their feelings and affections were stronger for others than for themselves, or even as strong, the necessary result would seem to be, that all individuality would be lost; and boundless and remediless disorder and confusion would ensue. For each, at the same moment, intensely participating in all the conflicting emotions of those around him, would, of course, forget himself and all that concerned him immediately, in his officious intermeddling with the affairs of all others; which, from his limited reason and faculties, he could neither properly understand nor manage. Such a state of things would, as far as we can see, lead to endless disorder and confusion, not less destructive to our race than a state of anarchy. It would, besides, be remediless,—for government would be impossible; or, if it could by possibility exist, its object would be reversed. Selfishness would have to be encouraged, and benevolence discouraged. Individuals would have to be encouraged, by rewards, to become more selfish, and deterred, by punishments, from being too benevolent; and this, too, by a government, administered by those who, on the supposition, would have the greatest aversion for selfishness and the highest admiration for benevolence.

To the Infinite Being, the Creator of all, belongs exclusively the care and superintendence of the whole. He, in his infinite wisdom and goodness, has allotted to every class of animated beings its condition and appropriate functions; and has endowed each with feelings, instincts, capacities, and faculties, best adapted to its allotted condition. To man, he has assigned the social and political state, as best adapted to develop the great capacities and faculties, intellectual and moral, with which he has endowed him; and has, accordingly, constituted him so as not only to impel him into the social state, but to make government necessary for his preservation and well-being.

But government, although intended to protect and preserve society, has itself a strong tendency to disorder and abuse of its powers, as all experience and almost every page of history testify. The cause is to be found in the same constitution of our nature which makes government indispensable. The powers which it is necessary for government to possess, in order to repress violence and preserve order, cannot execute themselves. They must be administered by men in whom, like others, the individual are stronger than the social feelings. And hence, the powers vested in them to prevent injustice and oppression on the part of others, will, if left unguarded, be by them converted into instruments to oppress the rest of the community. That, by which this is prevented, by whatever name called, is what is meant by CONSTITUTION, in its most comprehensive sense, when applied to GOVERNMENT.

Having its origin in the same principle of our nature, *constitution* stands to *government*, as *government* stands to *society*; and, as the end for which society is ordained, would be defeated without government, so that for which government is ordained would, in a great measure, be defeated without constitution. But they differ in this striking particular. There is no difficulty in forming government. It is not even a matter of choice, whether there shall be one or not. Like breathing, it is not permitted to depend on our volition. Necessity will force it on all communities in some one form or another. Very different is the case as to constitution. Instead of a matter of necessity, it is one of the most difficult tasks imposed on man to form a constitution worthy of the name; while, to form a perfect one,—one that would completely counteract the tendency of government to oppression and abuse, and hold it strictly to the great ends for which it is ordained,—has thus far exceeded human wisdom, and possibly ever will. From this, another striking difference results. Constitution is the contrivance of man, while government is of Divine ordination. Man is left to perfect what the wisdom of the Infinite ordained, as necessary to preserve the race.

With these remarks, I proceed to the consideration of the important and difficult question: How is this tendency of government to be counteracted? Or, to express it more fully,—How can those who are invested with the powers of government be prevented from employing them, as the means of aggrandizing themselves, instead of using them to protect and preserve society? It cannot be done by instituting a higher power to control the government, and those who administer it. This would be but to change the seat of authority, and to make this higher power, in reality, the government; with the same tendency, on the part of those who might control its powers, to pervert them into instruments of aggrandizement. Nor can it be done by limiting the powers of government, so as to make it too feeble to be made an instrument of abuse; for, passing by the difficulty of so limiting its powers, without creating a power higher than the government itself to enforce the observance of the limitations, it is a sufficient objection that it would, if practicable, defeat the end for which government is ordained, by making it too feeble to protect and preserve society. The powers necessary for this purpose will ever prove sufficient to aggrandize those who control it, at the expense of the rest of the community.

In estimating what amount of power would be requisite to secure the objects of government, we must take into the reckoning, what would be necessary to defend the community against external, as well as internal dangers. Government must be able to repel assaults from abroad, as well as to repress violence and disorders within. It must not be overlooked, that the human race is not comprehended in a single society or community. The limited reason and faculties of man, the great diversity of language, customs, pursuits, situation and complexion, and the difficulty of intercourse, with various other causes, have, by their operation, formed a great many separate communities, acting independently of each other. Between these there is the same tendency to conflict,—and from the same constitution of our nature,—as between men individually; and even stronger,—because the sympathetic or social feelings are not so strong between different communities, as between individuals of the same community. So powerful, indeed, is this tendency, that it has led to almost incessant wars between contiguous communities for plunder and conquest, or to avenge injuries, real or supposed.

So long as this state of things continues, exigencies will occur, in which the entire powers and resources of the community will be needed to defend its existence. When this is at stake, every other consideration must yield to it. Self-preservation is the supreme law, as well with communities as individuals. And hence the danger of withholding from government the full command of the power and resources of the state; and the great difficulty of limiting its powers consistently with the protection and preservation of the community. And hence the question recurs,—By what means can government, without being divested of the full command of the resources of the community, be prevented from abusing its powers?

The question involves difficulties which, from the earliest ages, wise and good men have attempted to overcome;—but hitherto with but partial success. For this purpose many devices have been resorted to, suited to the various stages of intelligence and civilization through which our race has passed, and to the different forms of government to which they have been applied. The aid of superstition, ceremonies, education, religion, organic arrangements, both of the government and the community, has been, from time to time, appealed to. Some of the most remarkable of these devices, whether regarded in reference to their wisdom and the skill displayed in their application, or to the permanency of their effects, are to be found in the early dawn of civilization;—in the institutions of the Egyptians, the Hindoos, the Chinese, and the Jews. The only materials which that early age afforded for the construction of constitutions, when intelligence was so partially diffused, were applied with consummate wisdom and skill. To their successful application may be fairly traced the subsequent advance of our race in civilization and intelligence, of which we now enjoy the benefits. For, without a constitution,—something to counteract the strong tendency of government to disorder and abuse, and to give stability to political institutions,—there can be little progress or permanent improvement.

In answering the important question under consideration, it is not necessary to enter into an examination of the various contrivances adopted by these celebrated governments to counteract this tendency to disorder and abuse, nor to undertake to treat of constitution in its most comprehensive sense. What I propose is far more limited,—to explain on what principles government must be formed, in order to resist, by its own interior structure,—or, to use a single term, *organism*,—the tendency to abuse of power. This structure, or organism, is what is meant by constitution, in its strict and more usual sense; and it is this which distinguishes, what are called, constitutional governments from absolute. It is in this strict and more usual sense that I propose to use the term hereafter.

How government, then, must be constructed, in order to counteract, through its organism, this tendency on the part of those who make and execute the laws to oppress those subject to their operation, is the next question which claims attention.

There is but one way in which this can possibly be done; and that is, by such an organism as will furnish the ruled with the means of resisting successfully this tendency on the part of the rulers to oppression and abuse. Power can only be resisted by power,—and tendency by tendency. Those who exercise power and those subject to its exercise,—the rulers and the ruled,—stand in antagonistic relations to each other. The same constitution of our nature which leads rulers to oppress the ruled,—regardless of the object for which government is ordained,—will, with equal strength, lead the ruled to resist, when possessed of the means of making peaceable and effective resistance. Such an organism, then, as will furnish the means by which resistance may be systematically and peaceably made on the part of the ruled, to oppression and abuse of power on the part of the rulers, is the first and indispensable step towards *forming* a constitutional government. And as this can only be effected by or through the right of suffrage,—(the right on the part of the ruled to choose their rulers at proper intervals, and to hold them thereby responsible for their conduct,)—the responsibility of the rulers to the ruled, through the right of suffrage, is the indispensable and primary principle in the *foundation* of a constitutional government. When this right is properly guarded, and the people sufficiently enlightened to understand their own rights and the interests of the community, and duly to appreciate the motives and conduct of those appointed to make and execute the laws, it is all-sufficient to give to those who elect, effective control over those they have elected.

I call the right of suffrage the indispensable and primary principle; for it would be a great and dangerous mistake to suppose, as many do, that it is, of itself, sufficient to form constitutional governments. To this erroneous opinion may be traced one of the causes, why so few attempts to form constitutional governments have succeeded; and why, of the few which have, so small a number have had durable existence. It has led, not only to mistakes in the attempts to form such governments, but to their overthrow, when they have, by some good fortune, been correctly formed. So far from being, of itself, sufficient,—however well guarded it might be, and however enlightened the people,—it would, unaided by other provisions, leave the government as absolute, as it would be in the hands of irresponsible rulers; and with a tendency, at least as strong, towards oppression and abuse of its powers; as I shall next proceed to explain.

The right of suffrage, of itself, can do no more than give complete control to those who elect, over the conduct of those they have elected. In doing this, it accomplishes all it possibly can accomplish. This is its aim,—and when this is attained, its end is fulfilled. It can do no more, however enlightened the people, or however widely extended or well guarded the right may be. The sum total, then, of its effects, when most successful, is, to make those elected, the true and faithful representatives of those who elected them,—instead of irresponsible rulers,—as they would be without it; and thus, by converting it into an agency, and the rulers into agents, to divest government of all claims to sovereignty, and to retain it unimpaired to the community. But it is manifest that the right of suffrage, in making these changes, transfers, in reality, the actual control over the government, from those who make and execute the laws, to the body of the community; and, thereby, places the powers of the government as fully in the mass of the community, as they would be if they, in fact, had assembled, made, and executed the laws themselves, without the intervention of representatives or agents. The more perfectly it does this, the more perfectly it accomplishes its ends; but in doing so, it only changes the seat of authority, without counteracting, in the least, the tendency of the government to oppression and abuse of its powers.

If the whole community had the same interests, so that the interests of each and every portion would be so affected by the action of the government, that the laws which oppressed or impoverished one portion, would necessarily oppress and impoverish all others,—or the reverse,—then the right of suffrage, of itself, would be all-sufficient to counteract the tendency of the government to oppression and abuse of its powers; and, of course, would form, of itself, a perfect constitutional government. The interest of all being the same, by supposition, as far as the action of the government was concerned, all would have like interests as to what laws should be made, and how they should be executed. All strife and struggle would cease as to who should be elected to make and execute them. The only question would be, who was most fit; who the wisest and most capable of understanding the common interest of the whole. This decided, the election would pass off quietly, and without party discord; as no one portion could advance its own peculiar interest without regard to the rest, by electing a favorite candidate.

But such is not the case. On the contrary, nothing is more difficult than to equalize the action of the government, in reference to the various and diversified interests of the community; and nothing more easy than to pervert its powers into instruments to aggrandize and enrich one or more interests by oppressing and impoverishing the others; and this too, under the operation of laws, couched in general terms;—and which, on their face, appear fair and equal. Nor is this the case in some particular communities only. It is so in all; the small and the great,—the poor and the rich,—irrespective of pursuits, productions, or degrees of civilization;—with, however, this difference, that the more extensive and populous the country, the more diversified the condition and pursuits of its population, and the richer, more luxurious, and dissimilar the people, the more difficult is it to equalize the action of the government,—and the more easy for one portion of the community to pervert its powers to oppress, and plunder the other.

Such being the case, it necessarily results, that the right of suffrage, by placing the control of the government in the community must, from the same constitution of our nature which makes government necessary to preserve society, lead to conflict among its different interests,—each striving to obtain possession of its powers, as the means of protecting itself against the others;—or of advancing its respective interests, regardless of the interests of others. For this purpose, a struggle will take place between the various interests to obtain a majority, in order to control the government. If no one interest be strong enough, of itself, to obtain it, a combination will be formed between those whose interests are most alike;—each conceding something to the others, until a sufficient number is obtained to make a majority. The process may be slow, and much time may be required before a compact, organized majority can be thus formed; but formed it will be in time, even without preconcert or design, by the sure workings of that principle or constitution of our nature in which government itself originates. When once formed, the community will be divided into two great parties,—a major and minor,—between which there will be incessant struggles on the one side to retain, and on the other to obtain the majority,—and, thereby, the control of the government and the advantages it confers.

So deeply seated, indeed, is this tendency to conflict between the different interests or portions of the community, that it would result from the action of the government itself, even though it were possible to find a community, where the people were all of the same pursuits, placed in the same condition of life, and in every respect, so situated, as to be without inequality of condition or diversity of interests. The advantages of possessing the control of the powers of the government, and, thereby, of its honors and emoluments, are, of themselves, exclusive of all other considerations, ample to divide even such a community into two great hostile parties.

In order to form a just estimate of the full force of these advantages,—without reference to any other consideration,—it must be remembered, that government,—to fulfill the ends for which it is ordained, and more especially that of protection against external dangers,—must, in the present condition of the world, be clothed with powers sufficient to call forth the resources of the community, and be prepared, at all times, to command them promptly in every emergency which may possibly arise. For this purpose large establishments are necessary, both civil and military, (including naval, where, from situation, that description of force may be required,) with all the means necessary for prompt and effective action,—such as fortifications, fleets, armories, arsenals, magazines, arms of all descriptions, with well-trained forces, in sufficient numbers to wield them with skill and energy, whenever the occasion requires it. The administration and management of a government with such vast establishments must necessarily require a host of employees, agents, and officers;—of whom many must be vested with high and responsible trusts, and occupy exalted stations, accompanied with much influence and patronage. To meet the necessary expenses, large sums must be collected and disbursed; and, for this purpose, heavy taxes must be imposed, requiring a multitude of officers for their collection and disbursement. The whole united must necessarily place under the control of government an amount of honors and emoluments, sufficient to excite profoundly the ambition of the aspiring and the cupidity of the avaricious; and to lead to the formation of hostile parties, and violent party conflicts and struggles to obtain the control of the government. And what makes this evil remediless, through the right of suffrage of itself, however modified or carefully guarded, or however enlightened the people, is the fact that, as far as the honors and emoluments of the government and its fiscal action are concerned, it is impossible to equalize it. The reason is obvious. Its honors and emoluments, however great, can fall to the lot of but a few, compared to the entire number of the community, and the multitude who will seek to participate in them. But, without this, there is a reason which renders it impossible to equalize the action of the government, so far as its fiscal operation extends,—which I shall next explain.

Few, comparatively, as they are, the agents and employees of the government constitute that portion of the community who are the exclusive recipients of the proceeds of the taxes. Whatever amount is taken from the community, in the form of taxes, if not lost, goes to them in the shape of expenditures or disbursements. The two,—disbursement and taxation,—constitute the fiscal action of the government. They are correlatives. What the one takes from the community, under the name of taxes, is transferred to the portion of the community who are the recipients, under that of disbursements. But, as the recipients constitute only a portion of the community, it follows, taking the two parts of the fiscal process together, that its action must be unequal between the payers of the taxes and the recipients of their proceeds. Nor can it be otherwise, unless what is collected from each individual in the shape of taxes, shall be returned to him, in that of disbursements; which would make the process nugatory and absurd. Taxation may, indeed, be made equal, regarded separately from disbursement. Even this is no easy task; but the two united cannot possibly be made equal.

Such being the case, it must necessarily follow, that some one portion of the community must pay in taxes more than it receives back in disbursements; while another receives in disbursements more than it pays in taxes. It is, then, manifest, taking the whole process together, that taxes must be, in effect, bounties to that portion of the community which receives more in disbursements than it pays in taxes; while, to the other which pays in taxes more than it receives in disbursements, they are taxes in reality,—burthens, instead of bounties. This consequence is unavoidable. It results from the nature of the process, be the taxes ever so equally laid, and the disbursements ever so fairly made, in reference to the public service.

It is assumed, in coming to this conclusion, that the disbursements are made within the community. The reasons assigned would not be applicable if the proceeds of the taxes were paid in tribute, or expended in foreign countries. In either of these cases, the burthen would fall on all, in proportion to the amount of taxes they respectively paid.

Nor would it be less a bounty to the portion of the community which received back in disbursements more than it paid in taxes, because received as salaries for official services; or payments to persons employed in executing the works required by the government; or furnishing it with its various supplies; or any other description of public employment,—instead of being bestowed gratuitously. It is the disbursements which give additional, and, usually, very profitable and honorable employments to the portion of the community where they are made. But to create such employments, by disbursements, is to bestow on the portion of the community to whose lot the disbursements may fall, a far more durable and lasting benefit,—one that would add much more to its wealth and population,—than would the bestowal of an equal sum gratuitously: and hence, to the extent that the disbursements exceed the taxes, it may be fairly regarded as a bounty. The very reverse is the case in reference to the portion which pays in taxes more than it receives in disbursements. With them, profitable employments are diminished to the same extent, and population and wealth correspondingly decreased.

The necessary result, then, of the unequal fiscal action of the government is, to divide the community into two great classes; one consisting of those who, in reality, pay the taxes, and, of course, bear exclusively the burthen of supporting the government; and the other, of those who are the recipients of their proceeds, through disbursements, and who are, in fact, supported by the government; or, in fewer words, to divide it into tax-payers and tax-consumers.

But the effect of this is to place them in antagonistic relations, in reference to the fiscal action of the government, and the entire course of policy therewith connected. For, the greater the taxes and disbursements, the greater the gain of the one and the loss of the other,—and *vice versa*; and consequently, the more the policy of the government is calculated to increase taxes and disbursements, the more it will be favored by the one and opposed by the other.

The effect, then, of every increase is, to enrich and strengthen the one, and impoverish and weaken the other. This, indeed, may be carried to such an extent, that one class or portion of the community may be elevated to wealth and power, and the other depressed to abject poverty and dependence, simply by the fiscal action of the government; and this too, through disbursements only,—even under a system of equal taxes imposed for revenue only. If such may be the effect of taxes and disbursements, when confined to their legitimate objects,—that of raising revenue for the public service,—some conception may be formed, how one portion of the community may be crushed, and another elevated on its ruins, by systematically perverting the power of taxation and disbursement, for the purpose of aggrandizing and building up one portion of the community at the expense of the other. That it *will* be so used, unless prevented, is, from the constitution of man, just as certain as that it *can* be so used; and that, if not prevented, it must give rise to two parties, and to violent conflicts and struggles between them, to obtain the control of the government, is, for the same reason, not less certain.

Nor is it less certain, from the operation of all these causes, that the dominant majority, for the time, would have the same tendency to oppression and abuse of power, which, without the right of suffrage, irresponsible rulers would have. No reason, indeed, can be assigned, why the latter would abuse their power, which would not apply, with equal force, to the former. The dominant majority, for the time, would, in reality, through the right of suffrage, be the rulers,—the controlling, governing, and irresponsible power; and those who make and execute the laws would, for the time, be, in reality, but *their* representatives and agents.

Nor would the fact that the former would constitute a majority of the community, counteract a tendency originating in the constitution of man; and which, as such, cannot depend on the number by whom the powers of the government may be wielded. Be it greater or smaller, a majority or minority, it must equally partake of an attribute inherent in each individual composing it; and, as in each the individual is stronger than the social feelings, the one would have the same tendency as the other to oppression and abuse of power. The reason applies to government in all its forms,—whether it be that of the one, the few, or the many. In each there must, of necessity, be a governing and governed,—a ruling and a subject portion. The one implies the other; and in all, the two bear the same relation to each other;—and have, on the part of the governing portion, the same tendency to oppression and abuse of power. Where the majority is that portion, it matters not how its powers may be exercised;—whether directly by themselves, or indirectly, through representatives or agents. Be it which it may, the minority, for the time, will be as much the governed or subject portion, as are the people in an aristocracy, or the subjects in a monarchy. The only difference in this respect is, that in the government of a majority, the minority may become the majority, and the majority the minority, through the right of suffrage; and thereby change their relative positions, without the intervention of force and revolution. But the duration, or uncertainty of the tenure, by which power is held, cannot, of itself, counteract the tendency inherent in government to oppression and abuse of power. On the contrary, the very uncertainty of the tenure, combined with the violent party warfare which must ever precede a change of parties under such governments, would rather tend to increase than diminish the tendency to oppression.

As, then, the right of suffrage, without some other provision, cannot counteract this tendency of government, the next question for consideration is— What is that other provision? This demands the most serious consideration; for of all the questions embraced in the science of government, it involves a principle, the most important, and the least understood; and when understood, the most difficult of application in practice. It is, indeed, emphatically, that principle which *makes* the constitution, in its strict and limited sense.

From what has been said, it is manifest, that this provision must be of a character calculated to prevent any one interest, or combination of interests, from using the powers of government to aggrandize itself at the expense of the others. Here lies the evil: and just in proportion as it shall prevent, or fail to prevent it, in the same degree it will effect, or fail to effect the end intended to be accomplished. There is but one certain mode in which this result can be secured; and that is, by the adoption of some restriction or limitation, which shall so effectually prevent any one interest, or combination of interests, from obtaining the exclusive control of the government, as to render hopeless all attempts directed to that end. There is, again, but one mode in which this can be effected; and that is, by taking the sense of each interest or portion of the community, which may be unequally and injuriously affected by the action of the government, separately, through its own majority, or in some other way by which its voice may be fairly expressed; and to require the consent of each interest, either to put or to keep the government in action. This, too, can be accomplished only in one way,—and that is, by such an organism of the government,—and, if necessary for the purpose, of the community also,—as will, by dividing and distributing the powers of government, give to each division or interest, through its appropriate organ, either a concurrent voice in making and executing the laws, or a veto on their execution. It is only by such an organism, that the assent of each can be made necessary to put the government in motion; or the power made effectual to arrest its action, when put in motion;—and it is only by the one or the other that the different interests, orders, classes, or portions, into which the community may be divided, can be protected, and all conflict and struggle between them prevented,—by rendering it impossible to put or to keep it in action, without the concurrent consent of all.

Such an organism as this, combined with the right of suffrage, constitutes, in fact, the elements of constitutional government. The one, by rendering those who make and execute the laws responsible to those on whom they operate, prevents the rulers from oppressing the ruled; and the other, by making it impossible for any one interest or combination of interests or class, or order, or portion of the community, to obtain exclusive control, prevents any one of them from oppressing the other. It is clear, that oppression and abuse of power must come, if at all, from the one or the other quarter. From no other can they come. It follows, that the two, suffrage and proper organism combined, are sufficient to counteract the tendency of government to oppression and abuse of power; and to restrict it to the fulfilment of the great ends for which it is ordained.

In coming to this conclusion, I have assumed the organism to be perfect, and the different interests, portions, or classes of the community, to be sufficiently enlightened to understand its character and object, and to exercise, with due intelligence, the right of suffrage. To the extent that either may be defective, to the same extent the government would fall short of fulfilling its end. But this does not impeach the truth of the principles on which it rests. In reducing them to proper form, in applying them to practical uses, all elementary principles are liable to difficulties; but they are not, on this account, the less true, or valuable. Where the organism is perfect, every interest will be truly and fully represented, and of course the whole community must be so. It may be difficult, or even impossible, to make a perfect organism,—but, although this be true, yet even when, instead of the sense of each and of all, it takes that of a few great and prominent interests only, it would still, in a great measure, if not altogether, fulfil the end intended by a constitution. For, in such case, it would require so large a portion of the community, compared with the whole, to concur, or acquiesce in the action of the government, that the number to be plundered would be too few, and the number to be aggrandized too many, to afford adequate motives to oppression and the abuse of its powers. Indeed, however imperfect the organism, it must have more or less effect in diminishing such tendency.

It may be readily inferred, from what has been stated, that the effect of organism is neither to supersede nor diminish the importance of the right of suffrage; but to aid and perfect it. The object of the latter is, to collect the sense of the community. The more fully and perfectly it accomplishes this, the more fully and perfectly it fulfils its end. But the most it can do, of itself, is to collect the sense of the greater number; that is, of the stronger interests, or combination of interests; and to assume this to be the sense of the community. It is only when aided by a proper organism, that it can collect the sense of the entire community,—of each and all its interests; of each, through its appropriate organ, and of the whole, through all of them united. This would truly be the sense of the entire community; for whatever diversity each interest might have within itself,—as all would have the same interest in reference to the action of the government, the individuals composing each would be fully and truly represented by its own majority or appropriate organ, regarded in reference to the other interests. In brief, every individual of every interest might trust, with confidence, its majority or appropriate organ, against that of every other interest.

It results, from what has been said, that there are two different modes in which the sense of the community may be taken; one, simply by the right of suffrage, unaided; the other, by the right through a proper organism. Each collects the sense of the majority. But one regards numbers only, and considers the whole community as a unit, having but one common interest throughout; and collects the sense of the greater number of the whole, as that of the community. The other, on the contrary, regards interests as well as numbers;—considering the community as made up of different and conflicting interests, as far as the action of the government is concerned; and takes the sense of each, through its majority or appropriate organ, and the united sense of all, as the sense of the entire community. The former of these I shall call the numerical, or absolute majority; and the latter, the concurrent, or constitutional majority. I call it the constitutional majority, because it is an essential element in every constitutional government,—be its form what it may. So great is the difference, politically speaking, between the two majorities, that they cannot be confounded, without leading to great and fatal errors; and yet the distinction between them has been so entirely overlooked, that when the term *majority* is used in political discussions, it is applied exclusively to designate the numerical,—as if there were no other. Until this distinction is recognized, and better understood, there will continue to be great liability to error in properly constructing constitutional governments, especially of the popular form, and of preserving them when properly constructed. Until then, the latter will have a strong tendency to slide, first, into the government of the numerical majority, and, finally, into absolute government of some other form. To show that such must be the case, and at the same time to mark more strongly the difference between the two, in order to guard against the danger of overlooking it, I propose to consider the subject more at length.

The first and leading error which naturally arises from overlooking the distinction referred to, is, to confound the numerical majority with the people; and this so completely as to regard them as identical. This is a consequence that necessarily results from considering the numerical as the only majority. All admit, that a popular government, or democracy, is the government of the people; for the terms imply this. A perfect government of the kind would be one which would embrace the consent of every citizen or member of the community; but as this is impracticable, in the opinion of those who regard the numerical as the only majority, and who can perceive no other way by which the sense of the people can be taken,—they are compelled to adopt this as the only true basis of popular government, in contradistinction to governments of the aristocratical or monarchical form. Being thus constrained, they are, in the next place, forced to regard the numerical majority, as, in effect, the entire people; that is, the greater part as the whole; and the government of the greater part as the government of the whole. It is thus the two come to be confounded, and a part made identical with the whole. And it is thus, also, that all the rights, powers, and immunities of the whole people come to be attributed to the numerical majority; and, among others, the supreme, sovereign authority of establishing and abolishing governments at pleasure.

This radical error, the consequence of confounding the two, and of regarding the numerical as the only majority, has contributed more than any other cause, to prevent the formation of popular constitutional governments,—and to destroy them even when they have been formed. It leads to the conclusion that, in their formation and establishment nothing more is necessary than the right of suffrage,—and the allotment to each division of the community a representation in the government, in proportion to numbers. If the numerical majority were really the people; and if, to take its sense truly, were to take the sense of the people truly, a government so constituted would be a true and perfect model of a popular constitutional government; and every departure from it would detract from its excellence. But, as such is not the case,—as the numerical majority, instead of being the people, is only a portion of them,—such a government, instead of being a true and perfect model of the people's government, that is, a people self-governed, is but the government of a part, over a part,—the major over the minor portion.

But this misconception of the true elements of constitutional government does not stop here. It leads to others equally false and fatal, in reference to the best means of preserving and perpetuating them, when, from some fortunate combination of circumstances, they are correctly formed. For they who fall into these errors regard the restrictions which organism imposes on the will of the numerical majority as restrictions on the will of the people, and, therefore, as not only useless, but wrongful and mischievous. And hence they endeavor to destroy organism, under the delusive hope of making government more democratic.

Such are some of the consequences of confounding the two, and of regarding the numerical as the only majority. And in this may be found the reason why so few popular governments have been properly constructed, and why, of these few, so small a number have proved durable. Such must continue to be the result, so long as these errors continue to be prevalent.

There is another error, of a kindred character, whose influence contributes much to the same results: I refer to the prevalent opinion, that a written constitution, containing suitable restrictions on the powers of government, is sufficient, of itself, without the aid of any organism,—except such as is necessary to separate its several departments, and render them independent of each other,—to counteract the tendency of the numerical majority to oppression and the abuse of power.

A written constitution certainly has many and considerable advantages; but it is a great mistake to suppose, that the mere insertion of provisions to restrict and limit the powers of the government, without investing those for whose protection they are inserted with the means of enforcing their observance, will be sufficient to prevent the major and dominant party from abusing its powers. Being the party in possession of the government, they will, from the same constitution of man which makes government necessary to protect society, be in favor of the powers granted by the constitution, and opposed to the restrictions intended to limit them. As the major and dominant party, they will have no need of these restrictions for their protection. The ballot-box, of itself, would be ample protection to them. Needing no other, they would come, in time, to regard these limitations as unnecessary and improper restraints;—and endeavor to elude them, with the view of increasing their power and influence.

The minor, or weaker party, on the contrary, would take the opposite direction;—and regard them as essential to their protection against the dominant party. And, hence, they would endeavor to defend and enlarge the restrictions, and to limit and contract the powers. But where there are no means by which they could compel the major party to observe the restrictions, the only resort left them would be, a [strict construction] of the constitution,—that is, a construction which would confine these powers to the narrowest limits which the meaning of the words used in the grant would admit.

To this the major party would oppose a liberal construction,—one which would give to the words of the grant the broadest meaning of which they were susceptible. It would then be construction against construction; the one to contract, and the other to enlarge the powers of the government to the utmost. But of what possible avail could the strict construction of the minor party be, against the liberal interpretation of the major, when the one would have all the powers of the government to carry its construction into effect,—and the other be deprived of all means of enforcing its construction? In a contest so unequal, the result would not be doubtful. The party in favor of the restrictions would be overpowered. At first, they might command some respect, and do something to stay the march of encroachment; but they would, in the progress of the contest, be regarded as mere abstractionists; and, indeed, deservedly, if they should indulge the folly of supposing that the party in possession of the ballot-box and the physical force of the country, could be successfully resisted by an appeal to reason, truth, justice, or the obligations imposed by the constitution. For when these, of themselves, shall exert sufficient influence to stay the hand of power, then government will be no longer necessary to protect society, nor constitutions needed to prevent government from abusing its powers. The end of the contest would be the subversion of the constitution, either by the undermining process of construction,—where its meaning would admit of possible doubt,— or by substituting in practice what is called "party-usage," in place of its provisions;—or, finally, when no other contrivance would subserve the purpose, by openly and boldly setting them aside. [By the one or the other, the restrictions would ultimately be annulled, and the government be converted into one of unlimited powers.)

*) this concept depublique fascist abducted + turned a leverage of criminal governance →

conservative reference to Conservatism; without legitimate reference to

Nor would the division of government into separate, and, as it regards each other, independent departments, prevent this result. Such a division may do much to facilitate its operations, and to secure to its administration greater caution and deliberation; but as each and all the departments,—and, of course, the entire government,—would be under the control of the numerical majority, it is too clear to require explanation, that a mere distribution of its powers among its agents or representatives, could do little or nothing to counteract its tendency to oppression and abuse of power. To effect this, it would be necessary to go one step further, and make the several departments the organs of the distinct interests or portions of the community; and to clothe each with a negative on the others. But the effect of this would be to change the government from the numerical into the concurrent majority.

Having now explained the reasons why it is so difficult to form and preserve popular constitutional government, so long as the distinction between the two majorities is overlooked, and the opinion prevails that a written constitution, with suitable restrictions and a proper division of its powers, is sufficient to counteract the tendency of the numerical majority to the abuse of its power,—I shall next proceed to explain, more fully, why the concurrent majority is an indispensable element in forming constitutional governments; and why the numerical majority, of itself, must, in all cases, make governments absolute. *A. $x/q \cong E/Q$*

The necessary consequence of taking the sense of the community by the concurrent majority is, as has been explained, to give to each interest or portion of the community a negative on the others. It is this mutual negative among its various conflicting interests, which invests each with the power of protecting itself;—and places the rights and safety of each, where only they can be securely placed, under its own guardianship. Without this there can be no systematic, peaceful, or effective resistance to the natural tendency of each to come into conflict with the others: and without this there can be no constitution. It is this negative power,—the power of preventing or arresting the action of the government,—be it called by what term it may,—veto, interposition, nullification, check, or balance of power,—which, in fact, forms the constitution. They are all but different names for the negative power. In all its forms, and under all its names, it results from the concurrent majority. Without this there can be no negative; and, without a negative, no constitution. The assertion is true in reference to all constitutional governments, be their forms what they may. It is, indeed, the negative power which makes the constitution,—and the positive which makes the government. The one is the power of acting;—and the other

The "negative" limits negational abuse

the power of preventing or arresting action. The two, combined, make constitutional governments. *To what forms, + sol. laws may legislative course?*

But, as there can be no constitution without the negative power, and no negative power without the concurrent majority;—it follows, necessarily, that where the numerical majority has the sole control of the government, there can be no constitution; as constitution implies limitation or restriction,—and, of course, is inconsistent with the idea of sole or exclusive power. And hence, the numerical, unmixed with the concurrent majority, necessarily forms, in all cases, absolute government.

It is, indeed, the single, or *one power*, which excludes the negative, and constitutes absolute government; and not the *number* in whom the power is vested. The numerical majority is as truly a *single power*, and excludes the negative as completely as the absolute government of one, or of the few. The former is as much the absolute government of the democratic, or popular form, as the latter of the monarchical or aristocratical. It has, accordingly, in common with them, the same tendency to oppression and abuse of power. *Democracy itself.*

Constitutional governments, of whatever form, are, indeed, much more similar to each other, in their structure and character, than they are, respectively, to the absolute governments, even of their own class. All constitutional governments, of whatever class they may be, take the sense of the community by its parts,—each through its appropriate organ; and regard the sense of all its parts, as the sense of the whole. They all rest on the right of suffrage, and the responsibility of rulers, directly or indirectly. On the contrary, all absolute governments, of whatever form, concentrate power in one uncontrolled and irresponsible individual or body, whose will is regarded as the sense of the community. And, hence, the great and broad distinction between governments is,—not that of the one, the few, or the many,—but of the constitutional and the absolute.

From this there results another distinction, which, although secondary in its character, very strongly marks the difference between these forms of government. I refer to their respective conservative principle;—that is, the principle by which they are upheld and preserved. This principle, in constitutional governments, is *compromise*;—and in absolute governments, is *force*;—as will be next explained.

It has been already shown, that the same constitution of man which leads those who govern to oppress the governed,—if not prevented,—will, with equal force and certainty, lead the latter to resist oppression, when possessed of the means of doing so peaceably and successfully. But absolute governments, of all forms, exclude all other means of resistance to their authority, than that of

force; and, of course, leave no other alternative to the governed, but to acquiesce in oppression, however great it may be, or to resort to force to put down
the government. But the dread of such a resort must necessarily lead the government to prepare to meet force in order to protect itself; and hence, of necessity, force becomes the conservative principle of all such governments.

On the contrary, the government of the concurrent majority, where the
organism is perfect, excludes the possibility of oppression, by giving to each
interest, or portion, or order,—where there are established classes,—the means
of protecting itself, by its negative, against all measures calculated to advance the
peculiar interests of others at its expense. Its effect, then, is, to cause the different interests, portions, or orders,—as the case may be,—to desist from attempting to adopt any measure calculated to promote the prosperity of one, or more,
by sacrificing that of others; and thus to force them to unite in such measures
only as would promote the prosperity of all, as the only means to prevent the
suspension of the action of the government;—and, thereby, to avoid anarchy,
the greatest of all evils. It is by means of such authorized and effectual resistance,
that oppression is prevented, and the necessity of resorting to force superseded,
in governments of the concurrent majority;—and, hence, compromise, instead
of force, becomes their conservative principle.

It would, perhaps, be more strictly correct to trace the conservative principle of constitutional governments to the necessity which compels the different
interests, or portions, or orders, to compromise,—as the only way to promote
their respective prosperity, and to avoid anarchy,—rather than to the compromise itself. No necessity can be more urgent and imperious, than that of avoiding anarchy. It is the same as that which makes government indispensable to
preserve society; and is not less imperative than that which compels obedience
to superior force. Traced to this source, the voice of a people,—uttered under
the necessity of avoiding the greatest of calamities, through the organs of a government so constructed as to suppress the expression of all partial and selfish
interests, and to give a full and faithful utterance to the sense of the whole community, in reference to its common welfare,—may, without impiety, be called
the voice of God. To call any other so, would be impious.

In stating that force is the conservative principle of absolute, and compromise of constitutional governments, I have assumed both to be perfect in their
kind; but not without bearing in mind, that few or none, in fact, have ever been
so absolute as not to be under some restraint, and none so perfectly organized
as to represent fully and perfectly the voice of the whole community. Such
being the case, all must, in practice, depart more or less from the principles by

which they are respectively upheld and preserved; and depend more or less for support, on force, or compromise, as the absolute or the constitutional form predominates in their respective organizations. *of law'd polarization*

Nor, in stating that absolute governments exclude all other means of resistance to its authority than that of force, have I overlooked the case of governments of the numerical majority, which form, apparently, an exception. It is true that, in such governments, the minor and subject party, for the time, have the right to oppose and resist the major and dominant party, for the time, through the ballot-box; and may turn them out, and take their place, if they can obtain a majority of votes. But, it is no less true, that this would be a mere change in the relations of the two parties. The minor and subject party would become the major and dominant party, with the same absolute authority and tendency to abuse power; and the major and dominant party would become the minor and subject party, with the same right to resist through the ballot-box; and, if successful, again to change relations, with like effect. But such a state of things must necessarily be temporary. The conflict between the two parties must be transferred, sooner or later, from an appeal to the ballot-box to an appeal to force;—as I shall next proceed to explain.

The conflict between the two parties, in the government of the numerical majority, tends necessarily to settle down into a struggle for the honors and emoluments of the government; and each, in order to obtain an object so ardently desired, will, in the process of the struggle, resort to whatever measure may seem best calculated to effect this purpose. The adoption, by the one, of any measure, however objectionable, which might give it an advantage, would compel the other to follow its example. In such case, it would be indispensable to success to avoid division and keep united;—and hence, from a necessity inherent in the nature of such governments, each party must be alternately forced, in order to insure victory, to resort to measures to concentrate the control over its movements in fewer and fewer hands, as the struggle became more and more violent. This, in process of time, must lead to party organization, and party caucuses and discipline; and these, to the conversion of the honors and emoluments of the government into means of rewarding partisan services, in order to secure the fidelity and increase the zeal of the members of the party. The effect of the whole combined, even in the earlier stages of the process, when they exert the least pernicious influence, would be to place the control of the two parties in the hands of their respective majorities; and the government itself, virtually, under the control of the majority of the dominant party, for the time, instead of the majority of the whole community;—where the theory of this form of government vests it. Thus, in the very first stage of the process, the government becomes the government of a minority instead of a majority;—a minority, usually, and under the most favorable circumstances, of not much more than one-fourth of the whole community.

But the process, as regards the concentration of power, would not stop at this stage. The government would gradually pass from the hands of the majority of the party into those of its leaders; as the struggle became more intense, and the honors and emoluments of the government the all-absorbing objects. At this stage, principles and policy would lose all influence in the elections; and cunning, falsehood, deception, slander, fraud, and gross appeals to the appetites of the lowest and most worthless portions of the community, would take the place of sound reason and wise debate. After these have thoroughly debased and corrupted the community, and all the arts and devices of party have been exhausted, the government would vibrate between the two factions (for such will parties have become) at each successive election. Neither would be able to retain power beyond some fixed term; for those seeking office and patronage would become too numerous to be rewarded by the offices and patronage at the disposal of the government; and these being the sole objects of pursuit, the disappointed would, at the next succeeding election, throw their weight into the opposite scale, in the hope of better success at the next turn of the wheel. These vibrations would continue until confusion, corruption, disorder, and anarchy, would lead to an appeal to force;—to be followed by a revolution in the form of the government. Such must be the end of the government of the numerical majority; and such, in brief, the process through which it must pass, in the regular course of events, before it can reach it. Jan. 6th 2021

This transition would be more or less rapid, according to circumstances. The more numerous the population, the more extensive the country, the more diversified the climate, productions, pursuits and character of the people, the more wealthy, refined, and artificial their condition,—and the greater the amount of revenues and disbursements,—the more unsuited would the community be to such a government, and the more rapid would be the passage. On the other hand, it might be slow in its progress amongst small communities, during the early stages of their existence, with inconsiderable revenues and disbursements, and a population of simple habits; provided the people are sufficiently intelligent to exercise properly, the right of suffrage, and sufficiently conversant with the rules necessary to govern the deliberations of legislative bodies. It is, perhaps, the only form of popular government suited to a people, while they remain in such a condition. Any other would be not only too complex and cumbersome, but unnecessary to guard against oppression, where the motive to use power for that purpose would be so feeble. And hence, colonies, from countries having constitutional governments, if left to themselves, usually adopt governments based on the numerical majority. But as population increases, wealth accumulates, and, above all, the revenues and expenditures become large,—governments of this form must become less and less suited to the condition of society; until, if not in the mean time changed into governments of the concurrent majority, they must end in an appeal to force, to be followed by a radical change in its structure and character; and, most probably, into monarchy in its absolute form,—as will be next explained.

Such, indeed, is the repugnance between popular governments and force,—or, to be more specific,—military power,—that the almost necessary consequence of a resort to force, by such governments, in order to maintain their authority, is, not only a change of their form, but a change into the most opposite,—that of absolute monarchy. The two are the opposites of each other. From the nature of popular governments, the control of its powers is vested in the many; while military power, to be efficient, must be vested in a single individual. When, then, the two parties, in governments of the numerical majority, resort to force, in their struggle for supremacy, he who commands the successful party will have the control of the government itself. And, hence, in such contests, the party which may prevail, will usually find, in the commander of its forces, a master, under whom the great body of the community will be glad to find protection against the incessant agitation and violent struggles of two corrupt factions,—looking only to power as the means of securing to themselves the honors and emoluments of the government.

From the same cause, there is a like tendency in aristocratical to terminate in absolute governments of the monarchical form; but by no means as strong, because there is less repugnance between military power and aristocratical, than between it and democratical governments.

A broader position may, indeed, be taken; viz., that there is a tendency, in constitutional governments of every form, to degenerate into their respective absolute forms; and, in all absolute governments, into that of the monarchical form. But the tendency is much stronger in constitutional governments of the democratic form to degenerate into their respective absolute forms, than in either of the others; because, among other reasons, the distinction between the constitutional and absolute forms of aristocratical and monarchical governments, is far more strongly marked than in democratic governments. The effect of this is, to make the different orders or classes in an aristocracy, or monarchy, far more jealous and watchful of encroachment on their respective rights; and more resolute and persevering in resisting attempts to concentrate power in any one class or order. On the contrary, the line between the two forms, in popular governments, is so imperfectly understood, that honest and sincere friends of the constitutional form not unfrequently, instead of jealously watching and arresting their tendency to degenerate into their absolute forms, not only regard it with approbation, but employ all their powers to add to its strength and to increase its impetus, in the vain hope of making the government more perfect and popular. The numerical majority, perhaps, should usually be one of the elements of a constitutional democracy; but to make it the sole element, in order to perfect the constitution and make the government more popular, is one of the greatest and most fatal of political errors.

Among the other advantages which governments of the concurrent have over those of the numerical majority,—and which strongly illustrates their more popular character, is,—that they admit, with safety, a much greater extension of the right of suffrage. It may be safely extended in such governments to universal suffrage: that is,—to every male citizen of mature age, with few ordinary exceptions; but it cannot be so far extended in those of the numerical majority, without placing them ultimately under the control of the more ignorant and dependent portions of the community. For, as the community becomes populous, wealthy, refined, and highly civilized, the difference between the rich and the poor will become more strongly marked; and the number of the ignorant and dependent greater in proportion to the rest of the community. With the increase of this difference, the tendency to conflict between them will become stronger; and, as the poor and dependent become more numerous in proportion, there will be, in governments of the numerical majority, no want of leaders among the wealthy and ambitious, to excite and direct them in their efforts to obtain the control.

The case is different in governments of the concurrent majority. There, mere numbers have not the absolute control; and the wealthy and intelligent being identified in interest with the poor and ignorant of their respective portions or interests of the community, become their leaders and protectors. And hence, as the latter would have neither hope nor inducement to rally the former in order to obtain the control, the right of suffrage, under such a government, may be safely enlarged to the extent stated, without incurring the hazard to which such enlargement would expose governments of the numerical majority.

In another particular, governments of the concurrent majority have greatly the advantage. I allude to the difference in their respective tendency, in reference to dividing or uniting the community. That of the concurrent, as has been shown, is to unite the community, let its interests be ever so diversified or opposed; while that of the numerical is to divide it into two conflicting portions, let its interests be, naturally, ever so united and identified.

That the numerical majority will divide the community, let it be ever so homogeneous, into two great parties, which will be engaged in perpetual struggles to obtain the control of the government, has already been established. The great importance of the object at stake, must necessarily form strong party attachments and party antipathies;—attachments on the part of the members of each to their respective parties, through whose efforts they hope to accomplish an object dear to all; and antipathies to the opposite party, as presenting the only obstacle to success.

In order to have a just conception of their force, it must be taken into consideration, that the object to be won or lost appeals to the strongest passions of the human heart,—avarice, ambition, and rivalry. It is not then wonderful, that a form of government, which periodically stakes all its honors and emoluments, as prizes to be contended for, should divide the community into two great hostile parties; or that party attachments, in the progress of the strife, should become so strong among the members of each respectively, as to absorb almost every feeling of our nature, both social and individual; or that their mutual antipathies should be carried to such an excess as to destroy, almost entirely, all sympathy between them, and to substitute in its place the strongest aversion. Nor is it surprising, that under their joint influence, the community should cease to be the common centre of attachment, or that each party should find that centre only in itself. It is thus, that, in such governments, devotion to party becomes stronger than devotion to country;—the promotion of the interests of party more important than the promotion of the common good of the whole, and its triumph and ascendency, objects of far greater solicitude, than the safety and prosperity of the community. It is thus, also, that the numerical majority, by regarding the community as a unit, and having, as such, the same interests throughout all its parts, must, by its necessary operation, divide it into two hostile parts, waging, under the forms of law, incessant hostilities against each other.

The concurrent majority, on the other hand, tends to unite the most opposite and conflicting interests, and to blend the whole in one common attachment to the country. By giving to each interest, or portion, the power of self-protection, all strife and struggle between them for ascendency, is prevented; and, thereby, not only every feeling calculated to weaken the attachment to the whole is suppressed, but the individual and the social feelings are made to unite in one common devotion to country. Each sees and feels that it can best promote its own prosperity by conciliating the good-will, and promoting the prosperity of the others. And hence, there will be diffused throughout the whole community kind feelings between its different portions; and, instead of antipathy, a rivalry amongst them to promote the interests of each other, as far as this can be done consistently with the interest of all. Under the combined influence of these causes, the interests of each would be merged in the common interests of the whole; and thus, the community would become a unit, by becoming the common centre of attachment of all its parts. And hence, instead of faction, strife, and struggle for party ascendency, there would be patriotism, nationality, harmony, and a struggle only for supremacy in promoting the common good of the whole.

But the difference in their operation, in this respect, would not end here. Its effects would be as great in a moral, as I have attempted to show they would be in a political point of view. Indeed, public and private morals are so nearly allied, that it would be difficult for it to be otherwise. That which corrupts and debases the community, politically, must also corrupt and debase it morally. The same cause, which, in governments of the numerical majority, gives to party attachments and antipathies such force, as to place party triumph and ascendency above the safety and prosperity of the community, will just as certainly give them sufficient force to overpower all regard for truth, justice, sincerity, and moral obligations of every description. It is, accordingly, found that, in the violent strifes between parties for the high and glittering prize of governmental honors and emoluments,—falsehood, injustice, fraud, artifice, slander, and breach of faith, are freely resorted to, as legitimate weapons;—followed by all their corrupting and debasing influences.

In the government of the concurrent majority, on the contrary, the same cause which prevents such strife, as the means of obtaining power, and which makes it the interest of each portion to conciliate and promote the interests of the others, would exert a powerful influence towards purifying and elevating the character of the government and the people, morally, as well as politically. The means of acquiring power,—or, more correctly, influence,—in such governments, would be the reverse. Instead of the vices, by which it is acquired in that of the numerical majority, the opposite virtues—truth, justice, integrity, fidelity, and all others, by which respect and confidence are inspired, would be the most certain and effectual means of acquiring it.

Nor would the good effects resulting thence be confined to those who take an active part in political affairs. They would extend to the whole community.

For of all the causes which contribute to form the character of a people, those by which power, influence, and standing in the government are most certainly and readily obtained, are, by far, the most powerful. These are the objects most eagerly sought of all others by the talented and aspiring; and the possession of which commands the greatest respect and admiration. But, just in proportion to this respect and admiration will be their appreciation by those, whose energy, intellect, and position in society, are calculated to exert the greatest influence in forming the character of a people. If knowledge, wisdom, patriotism, and virtue, be the most certain means of acquiring them, they will be most highly appreciated and assiduously cultivated; and this would cause them to become prominent traits in the character of the people. But if, on the contrary, cunning, fraud, treachery, and party devotion be the most certain, they will be the most highly prized, and become marked features in their character. So powerful, indeed, is the operation of the concurrent majority, in this respect, that, if it were possible for a corrupt and degenerate community to establish and maintain a well-organized government of the kind, it would of itself purify and regenerate them; while, on the other hand, a government based wholly on the numerical majority, would just as certainly corrupt and debase the most patriotic and virtuous people. So great is their difference in this respect, that, just as the one or the other element predominates in the construction of any government, in the same proportion will the character of the government and the people rise or sink in the scale of patriotism and virtue. Neither religion nor education can counteract the strong tendency of the numerical majority to corrupt and debase the people.

If the two be compared, in reference to the ends for which government is ordained, the superiority of the government of the concurrent majority will not be less striking. These, as has been stated, are twofold; to protect, and to perfect society. But to preserve society, it is necessary to guard the community against injustice, violence, and anarchy within, and against attacks from without. If it fail in either, it would fail in the primary end of government, and would not deserve the name.

To perfect society, it is necessary to develope the faculties, intellectual and moral, with which man is endowed. But the main spring to their development, and, through this, to progress, improvement and civilization, with all their blessings, is the desire of individuals to better their condition. For, this purpose, liberty and security are indispensable. Liberty leaves each free to pursue the course he may deem best to promote his interest and happiness, as far as it may be compatible with the primary end for which government is ordained;—while security gives assurance to each, that he shall not be deprived of the fruits of his exertions to better his condition. These combined, give to this desire the strongest impulse of which it is susceptible. For, to extend liberty beyond the limits assigned, would be to weaken the government and to render it incompetent to fulfil its primary end,—the protection of society against dangers, internal and external. The effect of this would be, insecurity; and, of insecurity,—to weaken the impulse of individuals to better their condition, and thereby retard progress and improvement. On the other hand, to extend the powers of the government, so as to contract the sphere assigned to liberty, would have the same effect, by disabling individuals in their efforts to better their condition.

Herein is to be found the principle which assigns to power and liberty their proper spheres, and reconciles each to the other under all circumstances. For, if power be necessary to secure to liberty the fruits of its exertions, liberty, in turn, repays power with interest, by increased population, wealth, and other advantages, which progress and improvement bestow on the community. By thus assigning to each its appropriate sphere, all conflicts between them cease; and each is made to co-operate with and assist the other, in fulfilling the great ends for which government is ordained.

But the principle, applied to different communities, will assign to them different limits. It will assign a larger sphere to power and a more contracted one to liberty, or the reverse, according to circumstances. To the former, there must ever be allotted, under all circumstances, a sphere sufficiently large to protect the community against danger from without and violence and anarchy within. The residuum belongs to liberty. More cannot be safely or rightly allotted to it.

But some communities require a far greater amount of power than others to protect them against anarchy and external dangers; and, of course, the sphere of liberty in such, must be proportionally contracted. The causes calculated to enlarge the one and contract the other, are numerous and various. Some are physical;—such as open and exposed frontiers, surrounded by powerful and hostile neighbors. Others are moral;—such as the different degrees of intelligence, patriotism, and virtue among the mass of the community, and their experience and proficiency in the art of self-government. Of these, the moral are, by far, the most influential. A community may possess all the necessary moral qualifications, in so high a degree, as to be capable of self-government under the most adverse circumstances; while, on the other hand, another may be so sunk in ignorance and vice, as to be incapable of forming a conception of liberty, or of living, even when most favored by circumstances, under any other than an absolute and despotic government.

The principle, in all communities, according to these numerous and various causes, assigns to power and liberty their proper spheres. To allow to liberty, in any case, a sphere of action more extended than this assigns, would lead to anarchy; and this, probably, in the end, to a contraction instead of an enlargement of its sphere. Liberty, then, when forced on a people unfit for it, would, instead of a blessing, be a curse; as it would, in its reaction, lead directly to anarchy,— the greatest of all curses. No people, indeed, can long enjoy more liberty than that to which their situation and advanced intelligence and morals fairly entitle them. If more than this be allowed, they must soon fall into confusion and disorder,—to be followed, if not by anarchy and despotism, by a change to a form of government more simple and absolute; and, therefore, better suited to their condition. And hence, although it may be true, that a people may not have as much liberty as they are fairly entitled to, and are capable of enjoying,—yet the reverse is unquestionably true,—that no people can long possess more than they are fairly entitled to.

Liberty, indeed, though among the greatest of blessings, is not so great as that of protection; inasmuch, as the end of the former is the progress and improvement of the race,—while that of the latter is its preservation and perpetuation. And hence, when the two come into conflict, liberty must, and ever ought, to yield to protection; as the existence of the race is of greater moment than its improvement.

It follows, from what has been stated, that it is a great and dangerous error to suppose that all people are equally entitled to liberty. It is a reward to be earned, not a blessing to be gratuitously lavished on all alike;—a reward reserved for the intelligent, the patriotic, the virtuous and deserving;—and not a boon to be bestowed on a people too ignorant, degraded and vicious, to be capable either of appreciating or of enjoying it. Nor is it any disparagement to liberty, that such is, and ought to be the case. On the contrary, its greatest praise,—its proudest distinction is, that an all-wise Providence has reserved it, as the noblest and highest reward for the development of our faculties, moral and intellectual. A reward more appropriate than liberty could not be conferred on the deserving;—nor a punishment inflicted on the undeserving more just, than to be subject to lawless and despotic rule. This dispensation seems to be the result of some fixed law;—and every effort to disturb or defeat it, by attempting to elevate a people in the scale of liberty, above the point to which they are entitled to rise, must ever prove abortive, and end in disappointment. The progress of a people rising from a lower to a higher point in the scale of liberty, is necessarily slow;— and by attempting to precipitate, we either retard, or permanently defeat it.

There is another error, not less great and dangerous, usually associated with the one which has just been considered. I refer to the opinion, that liberty and equality are so intimately united, that liberty cannot be perfect without perfect equality. *"perfect" means functional, not infallible*

That they are united to a certain extent,—and that equality of citizens, in the eyes of the law, is essential to liberty in a popular government, is conceded. But to go further, and make equality of *condition* essential to liberty, would be to destroy both liberty and progress. The reason is, that inequality of condition, while it is a necessary consequence of liberty, is, at the same time, indispensable to progress. In order to understand why this is so, it is necessary to bear in mind, that the main spring to progress is, the desire of individuals to better their condition; and that the strongest impulse which can be given to it is, to leave individuals free to exert themselves in the manner they may deem best for that purpose, as far at least as it can be done consistently with the ends for which government is ordained,—and to secure to all the fruits of their exertions. Now, as individuals differ greatly from each other, in intelligence, sagacity, energy, perseverance, skill, habits of industry and economy, physical power, position and opportunity,—the necessary effect of leaving all free to exert themselves to better their condition, must be a corresponding inequality between those who may possess these qualities and advantages in a high degree, and those who may be deficient in them. The only means by which this result can be prevented are, either to impose such restrictions on the exertions of those who may possess them in a high degree, as will place them on a level with those who do not; or to deprive them of the fruits of their exertions. But to impose such restrictions on them would be destructive of liberty,—while, to deprive them of the fruits of their exertions, would be to destroy the desire of bettering their condition. It is, indeed, this inequality of condition between the front and rear ranks, in the march of progress, which gives so strong an impulse to the former to maintain their position, and to the latter to press forward into their files. This gives to progress its greatest impulse. To force the front rank back to the rear, or attempt to push forward the rear into line with the front, by the interposition of the government, would put an end to the impulse, and effectually arrest the march of progress.

These great and dangerous errors have their origin in the prevalent opinion that all men are born free and equal;—than which nothing can be more unfounded and false. It rests upon the assumption of a fact, which is contrary to

universal observation, in whatever light it may be regarded. It is, indeed, difficult to explain how an opinion so destitute of all sound reason, ever could have
been so extensively entertained, unless we regard it as being confounded with
another, which has some semblance of truth;—but which, when properly
understood, is not less false and dangerous. I refer to the assertion, that all men
are equal in the state of nature; meaning, by a state of nature, a state of individuality, supposed to have existed prior to the social and political state; and in
which men lived apart and independent of each other. If such a state ever did
exist, all men would have been, indeed, free and equal in it; that is, free to do
as they pleased, and exempt from the authority or control of others—as, by supposition, it existed anterior to society and government. But such a state is purely
hypothetical. It never did, nor can exist; as it is inconsistent with the preservation and perpetuation of the race. It is, therefore, a great misnomer to call it *the
state of nature*. Instead of being the natural state of man, it is, of all conceivable
states, the most opposed to his nature—most repugnant to his feelings, and most
incompatible with his wants. His natural state is, the social and political—the
one for which his Creator made him, and the only one in which he can preserve and perfect his race. As, then, there never was such a state as the, so called,
state of nature, and never can be, it follows, that men, instead of being born in
it, are born in the social and political state; and of course, instead of being born
free and equal, are born subject, not only to parental authority, but to the laws
and institutions of the country where born, and under whose protection they
draw their first breath. With these remarks, I return from this digression, to
resume the thread of the discourse.

It follows, from all that has been said, that the more perfectly a government
combines power and liberty,—that is, the greater its power and the more
enlarged and secure the liberty of individuals, the more perfectly it fulfils the
ends for which government is ordained. To show, then, that the government
of the concurrent majority is better calculated to fulfil them than that of the
numerical, it is only necessary to explain why the former is better suited to combine a higher degree of power and a wider scope of liberty than the latter. I shall
begin with the former.

The concurrent majority, then, is better suited to enlarge and secure the
bounds of liberty, because it is better suited to prevent government from passing beyond its proper limits, and to restrict it to its primary end,—the protection of the community. But in doing this, it leaves, necessarily, all beyond it
open and free to individual exertions; and thus enlarges and secures the sphere
of liberty to the greatest extent which the condition of the community will

This is not + "true" only because it gives the white mind Laws to guide the Black mind is not aware to score Law; thine at

admit, as has been explained. The tendency of government to pass beyond its proper limits is what exposes liberty to danger, and renders it insecure; and it is the strong counteraction of governments of the concurrent majority to this tendency which makes them so favorable to liberty. On the contrary, those of the numerical, instead of opposing and counteracting this tendency, add to it increased strength, in consequence of the violent party struggles incident to them, as has been fully explained. And hence their encroachments on liberty, and the danger to which it is exposed under such governments.

So great, indeed, is the difference between the two in this respect, that liberty is little more than a name under all governments of the absolute form, including that of the numerical majority; and can only have a secure and durable existence under those of the concurrent or constitutional form. The latter, by giving to each portion of the community which may be unequally affected by its action, a negative on the others, prevents all partial or local legislation, and restricts its action to such measures as are designed for the protection and the good of the whole. In doing this, it secures, at the same time, the rights and liberty of the people, regarded individually; as each portion consists of those who, whatever may be the diversity of interests among themselves, have the same interest in reference to the action of the government.

Such being the case, the interest of each individual may be safely confided to the majority, or voice of his portion, against that of all others, and, of course, the government itself. It is only through an organism which vests each with a negative, in some one form or another, that those who have like interests in preventing the government from passing beyond its proper sphere, and encroaching on the rights and liberty of individuals, can co-operate peaceably and effectually in resisting the encroachments of power, and thereby preserve their rights and liberty. Individual resistance is too feeble, and the difficulty of concert and co-operation too great, unaided by such an organism, to oppose, successfully, the organized power of government, with all the means of the community at its disposal; especially in populous countries of great extent, where concert and co-operation are almost impossible. Even when the oppression of the government comes to be too great to be borne, and force is resorted to in order to overthrow it, the result is rarely ever followed by the establishment of liberty. The force sufficient to overthrow an oppressive government is usually sufficient to establish one equally, or more, oppressive in its place. And hence, in no governments, except those that rest on the principle of the concurrent or constitutional majority, can the people guard their liberty against power; and hence, also, when lost, the great difficulty and uncertainty of regaining it by force.

It may be further affirmed, that, being more favorable to the enlargement and security of liberty, governments of the concurrent, must necessarily be more favorable to progress, development, improvement, and civilization,—and, of course, to the increase of power which results from, and depends on these, than those of the numerical majority. That it is liberty which gives to them their greatest impulse, has already been shown; and it now remains to show, that these, in turn, contribute greatly to the increase of power.

In the earlier stages of society, numbers and individual prowess constituted the principal elements of power. In a more advanced stage, when communities had passed from the barbarous to the civilized state, discipline, strategy, weapons of increased power, and money,—as the means of meeting increased expense,—became additional and important elements. In this stage, the effects of progress and improvement on the increase of power, began to be disclosed; but still numbers and personal prowess were sufficient, for a long period, to enable barbarous nations to contend successfully with the civilized,—and, in the end, to overpower them,—as the pages of history abundantly testify. But a more advanced progress, with its numerous inventions and improvements, has furnished new and far more powerful and destructive implements of offence and defence, and greatly increased the intelligence and wealth, necessary to engage the skill and meet the increased expense required for their construction and application to purposes of war. The discovery of gunpowder, and the use of steam as an impelling force, and their application to military purposes, have for ever settled the question of ascendency between civilized and barbarous communities, in favor of the former. Indeed, these, with other improvements, belonging to the present state of progress, have given to communities the most advanced, a superiority over those the least so, almost as great as that of the latter over the brute creation. And among the civilized, the same causes have decided the question of superiority, where other circumstances are nearly equal, in favor of those whose governments have given the greatest impulse to development, progress, and improvement; that is, to those whose liberty is the largest and best secured. Among these, England and the United States afford striking examples, not only of the effects of liberty in increasing power, but of the more perfect adaptation of governments founded on the principle of the concurrent, or constitutional majority, to enlarge and secure liberty. They are both governments of this description, as will be shown hereafter.

But in estimating the power of a community, moral, as well as physical causes, must be taken into the calculation; and in estimating the effects of liberty on power, it must not be overlooked, that it is, in itself, an important agent in augmenting the force of moral, as well as of physical power. It bestows on a people elevation, self-reliance, energy, and enthusiasm; and these combined, give to physical power a vastly augmented and almost irresistible impetus.

These, however, are not the only elements of moral power. There are others, and among them harmony, unanimity, devotion to country, and a disposition to elevate to places of trust and power, those who are distinguished for wisdom and experience. These, when the occasion requires it, will, without compulsion, and from their very nature, unite and put forth the entire force of the community in the most efficient manner, without hazard to its institutions or its liberty.

All these causes combined, give to a community its maximum of power. Either of them, without the other, would leave it comparatively feeble. But it cannot be necessary, after what has been stated, to enter into any further explanation or argument in order to establish the superiority of governments of the concurrent majority over the numerical, in developing the great elements of moral power. So vast is this superiority, that the one, by its operation, necessarily leads to their development, while the other as necessarily prevents it,—as has been fully shown.

Such are the many and striking advantages of the concurrent over the numerical majority. Against the former but two objections can be made. The one is, that it is difficult of construction, which has already been sufficiently noticed; and the other, that it would be impracticable to obtain the concurrence of conflicting interests, where they were numerous and diversified; or, if not, that the process for this purpose, would be too tardy to meet, with sufficient promptness, the many and dangerous emergencies, to which all communities are exposed. This objection is plausible; and deserves a fuller notice than it has yet received.

The diversity of opinion is usually so great, on almost all questions of policy, that it is not surprising, on a slight view of the subject, it should be thought impracticable to bring the various conflicting interests of a community to unite on any one line of policy;—or, that a government, founded on such a principle, would be too slow in its movements and too weak in its foundation to succeed in practice. But, plausible as it may seem at the first glance, a more deliberate view will show, that this opinion is erroneous. It is true, that, when there is no urgent necessity, it is difficult to bring those who differ, to agree on any one line of action. Each will naturally insist on taking the course he may think best;— and, from pride of opinion, will be unwilling to yield to others. But the case is different when there is an urgent necessity to unite on some common course of action; as reason and experience both prove. When something *must* be done,— and when it can be done only by the united consent of all,—the necessity of the case will force to a compromise;—be the cause of that necessity what it may. On all questions of acting, necessity, where it exists, is the overruling motive; and where, in such cases, compromise among the parties is an indispensable condition to acting, it exerts an overruling influence in predisposing them to acquiesce in some one opinion or course of action. Experience furnishes many examples in confirmation of this important truth. Among these, the trial by jury is the most familiar, and on that account, will be selected for illustration.

In these, twelve individuals, selected without discrimination, must unanimously concur in opinion,—under the obligations of an oath to find a true verdict, according to law and evidence; and this, too, not unfrequently under such great difficulty and doubt, that the ablest and most experienced judges and advocates differ in opinion, after careful examination. And yet, as impracticable as this mode of trial would seem to a superficial observer, it is found, in practice, not only to succeed, but to be the safest, the wisest and the best that human ingenuity has ever devised. When closely investigated, the cause will be found in the necessity, under which the jury is placed, to agree unanimously, in order to find a verdict. This necessity acts as the predisposing cause of concurrence in some common opinion; and with such efficacy, that a jury rarely fails to find a verdict.

Under its potent influence, the jurors take their seats with the disposition to give a fair and impartial hearing to the arguments on both sides,—meet together in the jury-room,—not as disputants, but calmly to hear the opinions of each other, and to compare and weigh the arguments on which they are founded;—and, finally, to adopt that which, on the whole, is thought to be true. Under the influence of this *disposition* to *harmonize*, one after another falls into the same opinion, until unanimity is obtained. Hence its practicability;—and hence, also, its peculiar excellence. Nothing, indeed, can be more favorable to the success of truth and justice, than this predisposing influence caused by the necessity of being unanimous. It is so much so, as to compensate for the defect of legal knowledge, and a high degree of intelligence on the part of those who usually compose juries. If the necessity of unanimity were dispensed with, and the finding of a jury made to depend on a bare majority, jury-trial, instead of being one of the greatest improvements in the judicial department of government, would be one of the greatest evils that could be inflicted on the community. It would be, in such case, the conduit through which all the factious feelings of the day would enter and contaminate justice at its source.

But the same cause would act with still greater force in predisposing the various interests of the community to agree in a well organized government, founded on the concurrent majority. The necessity for unanimity, in order to keep the government in motion, would be far more urgent, and would act under circumstances still more favorable to secure it. It would be superfluous, after what has been stated, to add other reasons in order to show that no necessity, physical or moral, can be more imperious than that of government. It is so much so that, to suspend its action altogether, even for an inconsiderable period, would subject the community to convulsions and anarchy. But in governments of the concurrent majority such fatal consequences can only be avoided by the unanimous concurrence or acquiescence of the various portions of the community. Such is the imperious character of the necessity which impels to compromise under governments of this description.

But to have a just conception of the overpowering influence it would exert, the circumstances under which it would act must be taken into consideration. These will be found, on comparison, much more favorable than those under which juries act. In the latter case there is nothing besides the necessity of unanimity in finding a verdict, and the inconvenience to which they might be subjected in the event of division, to induce juries to agree, except the love of truth and justice, which, when not counteracted by some improper motive or bias, more or less influences all, not excepting the most depraved. In the case of governments of the concurrent majority, there is, besides these, the love of country, than which, if not counteracted by the unequal and oppressive action of government, or other causes, few motives exert a greater sway. It comprehends, indeed, within itself, a large portion both of our individual and social feelings; and, hence, its almost boundless control when left free to act. But the government of the concurrent majority leaves it free, by preventing abuse and oppression, and, with them, the whole train of feelings and passions which lead to discord and conflict between different portions of the community. Impelled by the imperious necessity of preventing the suspension of the action of government, with the fatal consequences to which it would lead, and by the strong additional impulse derived from an ardent love of country, each portion would regard the sacrifice it might have to make by yielding its peculiar interest to secure the common interest and safety of all, including its own, as nothing compared to the evils that would be inflicted on all, including its own, by pertinaciously adhering to a different line of action. So powerful, indeed, would be the motives for concurring, and, under such circumstances, so weak would be those opposed to it, the wonder would be, not that there should, but that there should not be a compromise.

But to form a juster estimate of the full force of this impulse to compromise, there must be added that, in governments of the concurrent majority, each portion, in order to advance its own peculiar interests, would have to conciliate all others, by showing a disposition to advance theirs; and, for this purpose, each would select those to represent it, whose wisdom, patriotism, and weight of character, would command the confidence of the others. Under its influence,— and with representatives so well qualified to accomplish the object for which they were selected,—the prevailing desire would be, to promote the common interests of the whole; and, hence, the competition would be, not which should yield the least to promote the common good, but which should yield the most. It is thus, that concession would cease to be considered a sacrifice,—would become a free-will offering on the altar of the country, and lose the name of compromise. And herein is to be found the feature, which distinguishes governments of the concurrent majority so strikingly from those of the numerical. In the latter, each faction, in the struggle to obtain the control of the government, elevates to power the designing, the artful, and unscrupulous, who, in their devotion to party,—instead of aiming at the good of the whole,—aim exclusively at securing the ascendency of party.

When traced to its source, this difference will be found to originate in the fact, that, in governments of the concurrent majority, individual feelings are, from its organism, necessarily enlisted on the side of the social, and made to unite with them in promoting the interests of the whole, as the best way of promoting the separate interests of each; while, in those of the numerical majority, the social are necessarily enlisted on the side of the individual, and made to contribute to the interest of parties, regardless of that of the whole. To effect the former,—to enlist the individual on the side of the social feelings to promote the good of the whole, is the greatest possible achievement of the science of government; while, to enlist the social on the side of the individual to promote the interest of parties at the expense of the good of the whole, is the greatest blunder which ignorance can possibly commit.

To this, also, may be referred the greater solidity of foundation on which governments of the concurrent majority repose. Both, ultimately, rest on necessity; for force, by which those of the numerical majority are upheld, is only acquiesced in from necessity; a necessity not more imperious, however, than that which compels the different portions, in governments of the concurrent majority, to acquiesce in compromise. There is, however, a great difference in the motive, the feeling, the aim, which characterize the act in the two cases. In the one, it is done with that reluctance and hostility ever incident to enforced submission to what is regarded as injustice and oppression; accompanied by the desire and purpose to seize on the first favorable opportunity for resistance:—

but in the other, willingly and cheerfully, under the impulse of an exalted patriotism, impelling all to acquiesce in whatever the common good requires.

It is, then, a great error to suppose that the government of the concurrent majority is impracticable;—or that it rests on a feeble foundation. History furnishes many examples of such governments;—and among them, one, in which the principle was carried to an extreme that would be thought impracticable, had it never existed. I refer to that of Poland. In this it was carried to such an extreme that, in the election of her kings, the concurrence or acquiescence of every individual of the nobles and gentry present, in an assembly numbering usually from one hundred and fifty to two hundred thousand, was required to make a choice; thus giving to each individual a veto on his election. So, likewise, every member of her Diet, (the supreme legislative body,) consisting of the king, the senate, bishops and deputies of the nobility and gentry of the palatinates, possessed a veto on all its proceedings;—thus making an unanimous vote necessary to enact a law, or to adopt any measure whatever. And, as if to carry the principle to the utmost extent, the veto of a single member not only defeated the particular bill or measure in question, but prevented all others, passed during the session, from taking effect. Further, the principle could not be carried. It, in fact, made every individual of the nobility and gentry, a distinct element in the organism;—or, to vary the expression, made him an *Estate of the kingdom.* And yet this government lasted, in this form, more than two centuries; embracing the period of Poland's greatest power and renown. Twice, during its existence, she protected Christendom, when in great danger, by defeating the Turks under the walls of Vienna, and permanently arresting thereby the tide of their conquests westward.

It is true her government was finally subverted, and the people subjugated, in consequence of the extreme to which the principle was carried; not, however, because of its tendency to dissolution *from weakness,* but from the facility it afforded to powerful and unscrupulous neighbors to control, by their intrigues, the election of her kings. But the fact, that a government, in which the principle was carried to the utmost extreme, not only existed, but existed for so long a period, in great power and splendor, is proof conclusive both of its practicability and its compatibility with the power and permanency of government.

Another example, not so striking indeed, but yet deserving notice, is furnished by the government of a portion of the aborigines of our own country. I refer to the Confederacy of the Six Nations, who inhabited what now is called the western portion of the State of New-York. One chief delegate, chosen by each nation,—associated with six others of his own selection,—and making, in all, forty-two members,—constituted their federal, or general government. When met, they formed the council of the union,—and discussed and decided all questions relating to the common welfare. As in the Polish Diet, each member possessed a veto on its decision; so that nothing could be done without the united consent of all. But this, instead of making the Confederacy weak, or impracticable, had the opposite effect. It secured harmony in council and action, and with them a great increase of power. The Six Nations, in consequence, became the most powerful of all the Indian tribes within the limits of our country. They carried their conquest and authority far beyond the country they originally occupied.

I pass by, for the present, the most distinguished of all these examples;—the Roman Republic;—where the veto, or negative power, was carried, not indeed to the same extreme as in the Polish government, but very far, and with great increase of power and stability;—as I shall show more at large hereafter.

It may be thought,—and doubtless many have supposed, that the defects inherent in the government of the numerical majority may be remedied by a free press, as the organ of public opinion,—especially in the more advanced stage of society,—so as to supersede the necessity of the concurrent majority to counteract its tendency to oppression and abuse of power. It is not my aim to detract from the importance of the press, nor to underestimate the great power and influence which it has given to public opinion. On the contrary, I admit these are so great, as to entitle it to be considered a new and important political element. Its influence is, at the present day, on the increase; and it is highly probable that it may, in combination with the causes which have contributed to raise it to its present importance, effect, in time, great changes,—social and political. But, however important its present influence may be, or may hereafter become,—or, however great and beneficial the changes to which it may ultimately lead, it can never counteract the tendency of the numerical majority to the abuse of power,—nor supersede the necessity of the concurrent, as an essential element in the formation of constitutional governments. These it cannot effect for two reasons, either of which is conclusive.

The one is, that it cannot change that principle of our nature, which makes constitutions necessary to prevent government from abusing its powers,—and government necessary to protect and perfect society.

Constituting, as this principle does, an essential part of our nature,—no increase of knowledge and intelligence, no enlargement of our sympathetic feelings, no influence of education, or modification of the condition of society can change it. But so long as it shall continue to be an essential part of our nature, so long will government be necessary; and so long as this continues to be necessary, so long will constitutions, also, be necessary to counteract its tendency to the abuse of power,—and so long must the concurrent majority remain an essential element in the formation of constitutions. The press may do much,—by giving impulse to the progress of knowledge and intelligence, to aid the cause of education, and to bring about salutary changes in the condition of society. These, in turn, may do much to explode political errors,—to teach how governments should be constructed in order to fulfil their ends; and by what means they can be best preserved, when so constructed. They may, also, do much to enlarge the social, and to restrain the individual feelings;—and thereby to bring about a state of things, when far less power will be required by governments to guard against internal disorder and violence, and external danger; and when, of course, the sphere of power may be greatly contracted and that of liberty proportionally enlarged. But all this would not change the nature of man; nor supersede the necessity of government. For so long as government exists, the possession of its control, as the means of directing its action and dispensing its honors and emoluments, will be an object of desire. While this continues to be the case, it must, in governments of the numerical majority, lead to party struggles; and, as has been shown, to all the consequences, which necessarily follow in their train, and, against which, the only remedy is the concurrent majority.

The other reason is to be found in the nature of the influence, which the press politically exercises.

It is similar, in most respects, to that of suffrage. They are, indeed, both organs of public opinion. The principal difference is, that the one has much more agency in forming public opinion, while the other gives a more authentic and authoritative expression to it. Regarded in either light, the press cannot, of itself, guard any more against the abuse of power, than suffrage; and for the same reason.

If what is called public opinion were always the opinion of the whole community, the press would, as its organ, be an effective guard against the abuse of power, and supersede the necessity of the concurrent majority; just as the right of suffrage would do, where the community, in reference to the action of government, had but one interest. But such is not the case. On the contrary, what is called public opinion, instead of being the united opinion of the whole community, is, usually, nothing more than the opinion or voice of the strongest interest, or combination of interests; and, not unfrequently, of a small, but energetic and active portion of the whole. Public opinion, in relation to government and its policy, is as much divided and diversified, as are the interests of the community; and the press, instead of being the organ of the whole, is usually but the organ of these various and diversified interests respectively; or, rather, of the parties growing out of them. It is used by them as the means of controlling public opinion, and of so moulding it, as to promote their peculiar interests, and to aid in carrying on the warfare of party. But as the organ and instrument of parties, in governments of the numerical majority, it is as incompetent as suffrage itself, to counteract the tendency to oppression and abuse of power;—and can, no more than that, supersede the necessity of the concurrent majority. On the contrary, as the instrument of party warfare, it contributes greatly to increase party excitement, and the violence and virulence of party struggles; and, in the same degree, the tendency to oppression and abuse of power. Instead, then, of superseding the necessity of the concurrent majority, it increases it, by increasing the violence and force of party feelings,—in like manner as party caucuses and party machinery; of the latter of which, indeed, it forms an important part.

In one respect, and only one, the government of the numerical majority has the advantage over that of the concurrent, if, indeed, it can be called an advantage. I refer to its simplicity and facility of construction. It is simple indeed, wielded, as it is, by a single power—the will of the greater number—and very easy of construction. For this purpose, nothing more is necessary than universal suffrage, and the regulation of the manner of voting, so as to give to the greater number the supreme control over every department of government.

But, whatever advantages simplicity and facility of construction may give it, the other forms of absolute government possess them in a still higher degree. The construction of the government of the numerical majority, simple as it is, requires some preliminary measures and arrangements; while the others, especially the monarchical, will, in its absence, or where it proves incompetent, force themselves on the community. And hence, among other reasons, the tendency of all governments is, from the more complex and difficult of construction, to the more simple and easily constructed; and, finally, to absolute monarchy, as the most simple of all. Complexity and difficulty of construction, as far as they form objections, apply, not only to governments of the concurrent majority of the popular form, but to constitutional governments of every form. The least complex, and the most easily constructed of them, are much more complex and difficult of construction than any one of the absolute forms. Indeed, so great has been this difficulty, that their construction has been the result, not so much of wisdom and patriotism, as of favorable combinations of circumstances. They have, for the most part, grown out of the struggles between conflicting interests, which, from some fortunate turn, have ended in a compromise, by which both parties have been admitted, in some one way or another, to have a separate and distinct voice in the government. Where this has not been the case, they have been the product of fortunate circumstances, acting in conjunction with some pressing danger, which forced their adoption, as the only means by which it could be avoided. It would seem that it has exceeded human sagacity deliberately to plan and construct constitutional governments, with a full knowledge of the principles on which they were formed; or to reduce them to practice without the pressure of some immediate and urgent necessity. Nor is it surprising that such should be the case; for it would seem almost impossible for any man, or body of men, to be so profoundly and thoroughly acquainted with the people of any community which has made any considerable progress in civilization and wealth, with all the diversified interests ever accompanying them, as to be able to organize constitutional governments suited to their condition. But, even were this possible, it would be difficult to find any community sufficiently enlightened and patriotic to adopt such a government, without the compulsion of some pressing necessity. A constitution, to succeed, must spring from the bosom of the community, and be adapted to the intelligence and character of the people, and all the multifarious relations, internal and external, which distinguish one people from another. If it do not, it will prove, in practice, to be, not a constitution, but a cumbrous and useless machine, which must be speedily superseded and laid aside, for some other more simple, and better suited to their condition.] *Same for screen plays!*

It would thus seem almost necessary that governments should commence in some one of the simple and absolute forms, which, however well suited to the community in its earlier stages, must, in its progress, lead to oppression and abuse of power, and, finally, to an appeal to force,—to be succeeded by a military despotism,—unless the conflicts to which it leads should be fortunately adjusted by a compromise, which will give to the respective parties a participation in the control of the government; and thereby lay the foundation of a constitutional government, to be afterwards matured and perfected. Such governments have been, emphatically, the product of circumstances. And hence, the difficulty of one people imitating the government of another. And hence, also, the importance of terminating all civil conflicts by a compromise, which shall prevent either party from obtaining complete control, and thus subjecting the other.

Of the different forms of constitutional governments, the popular is the most complex and difficult of construction. It is, indeed, so difficult, that ours, it is

perfected = functional, not flawless / flawless

cf. Lord Acton on 545. C. 1945

believed, may with truth be said to be the only one of a purely popular character, of any considerable importance, that ever existed. The cause is to be found in the fact, that, in the other two forms, society is arranged in artificial orders or classes. Where these exist, the line of distinction between them is so strongly marked as to throw into shade, or, otherwise, to absorb all interests which are foreign to them respectively. Hence, in an aristocracy, all interests are, politically, reduced to two,—the nobles and the people; and in a monarchy, with a nobility, into three,—the monarch, the nobles, and the people. In either case, they are so few that the sense of each may be taken separately, through its appropriate organ, so as to give to each a concurrent voice, and a negative on the other, through the usual departments of the government, without making it too complex, or too tardy in its movements to perform, with promptness and energy, all the necessary functions of government.

The case is different in constitutional governments of the popular form. In consequence of the absence of these artificial distinctions, the various natural interests, resulting from diversity of pursuits, condition, situation and character of different portions of the people,—and from the action of the government itself,—rise into prominence, and struggle to obtain the ascendency. They will, it is true, in governments of the numerical majority, ultimately coalesce, and form two great parties; but not so closely as to lose entirely their separate character and existence. These they will ever be ready to re-assume, when the objects for which they coalesced are accomplished. To overcome the difficulties occasioned by so great a diversity of interests, an organism far more complex is necessary.

Another obstacle, difficult to be overcome, opposes the formation of popular constitutional governments. It is much more difficult to terminate the struggles between conflicting interests, by compromise, in absolute popular governments, than in an aristocracy or monarchy.

In an aristocracy, the object of the people, in the ordinary struggle between them and the nobles, is not, at least in its early stages, to overthrow the nobility and revolutionize the government,—but to participate in its powers. Notwithstanding the oppression to which they may be subjected, under this form of government, the people commonly feel no small degree of respect for the descendants of a long line of distinguished ancestors; and do not usually aspire to more,—in opposing the authority of the nobles,—than to obtain such a participation in the powers of the government, as will enable them to correct its abuses and to lighten their burdens. Among the nobility, on the other hand, it sometimes happens that there are individuals of great influence with both sides, who have the good sense and patriotism to interpose, in order to effect a compromise by yielding to the reasonable demands of the people; and, thereby, to avoid the hazard of a final and decisive appeal to force. It is thus, by a judicious and timely compromise, the people, in such governments, may be raised to a participation in the administration sufficient for their protection, without the loss of authority on the part of the nobles.

In the case of a monarchy, the process is somewhat different. Where it is a military despotism, the people rarely have the spirit or intelligence to attempt resistance; or, if otherwise, their resistance must almost necessarily terminate in defeat, or in a mere change of dynasty,—by the elevation of their leader to the throne. It is different, where the monarch is surrounded by an hereditary nobility. In a struggle between him and them, both (but especially the monarch) are usually disposed to court the people, in order to enlist them on their respective sides,—a state of things highly favorable to their elevation. In this case, the struggle, if it should be long continued without decisive results, would almost necessarily raise them to political importance, and to a participation in the powers of the government.

The case is different in an absolute Democracy. Party conflicts between the majority and minority, in such governments, can hardly ever terminate in compromise.—The object of the opposing minority is to expel the majority from power; and of the majority to maintain their hold upon it. It is, on both sides, a struggle for the whole,—a struggle that must determine which shall be the governing, and which the subject party;—and, in character, object and result, not unlike that between competitors for the sceptre in absolute monarchies. Its regular course, as has been shown, is, excessive violence,—an appeal to force,—followed by revolution,—and terminating at last, in the elevation to supreme power of the general of the successful party. And hence, among other reasons, aristocracies and monarchies more readily assume the constitutional form than absolute popular governments.

Of the three different forms, the monarchical has heretofore been much the most prevalent, and, generally, the most powerful and durable. This result is doubtless to be attributed principally to the fact that, in its absolute form, it is the most simple and easily constructed. And hence, as government is indispensable, communities having too little intelligence to form or preserve the others, naturally fall into this. It may also, in part, be attributed to another cause, already alluded to; that, in its organism and character, it is much more closely assimilated than either of the other two, to military power; on which all absolute governments depend for support. And hence, also, the tendency of the others, and of constitutional governments which have been so badly constructed or become so disorganized as to require force to support them,—to pass into military despotism,—that is, into monarchy in its most absolute and simple form. And hence, again, the fact, that revolutions in absolute monarchies, end, almost invariably, in a change of dynasty,—and not of the forms of the government; as is almost universally the case in the other systems. ᴍonᴅᴇꜱ ꞯᵁ: ꞃ~ ꜱ ꞃ?

But there are, besides these, other causes of a higher character, which contribute much to make monarchies the most prevalent, and, usually, the most durable governments. Among them, the leading one is, they are the most susceptible of improvement;—that is, they can be more easily and readily modified, so as to prevent, to a limited extent, oppression and abuse of power, without assuming the constitutional form, in its strict sense. It slides, almost naturally, into one of the most important modifications. I refer to hereditary descent. When this becomes well defined and firmly established, the community or kingdom, comes to be regarded by the sovereign as the hereditary possession of his family,—a circumstance which tends strongly to identify his interests with those of his subjects, and thereby, to mitigate the rigor of the government. It gives, besides, great additional security to his person; and prevents, in the same degree, not only the suspicion and hostile feelings incident to insecurity,—but invites all those kindly feelings which naturally spring up on both sides, between those whose interests are identified,—when there is nothing to prevent it. And hence the strong feelings of paternity on the side of the sovereign,—and of loyalty on that of his subjects, which are often exhibited in such governments. ᴜ ᴋ ꜰil ᴍᴏᴺᴀᴿᶜʰⁱᵈ ꜰᴿᴏᴇᵗⁱ ——

There is another improvement of which it is readily susceptible, nearly allied to the preceding. The hereditary principle not unfrequently extends to other families,—especially to those of the distinguished chieftains, by whose aid the monarchy was established, when it originates in conquest. When this is the case,—and a powerful body of hereditary nobles surround the sovereign, they oppose a strong resistance to his authority, and he to theirs,—tending to the advantage and security of the people. Even when they do not succeed in obtaining a participation in the powers of the government, they usually acquire sufficient weight to be felt and respected. From this state of things, such governments usually, in time, settle down on some fixed rules of action, which the sovereign is compelled to respect, and by which increased protection and security are acquired by all. It was thus the enlightened monarchies of Europe were formed, under which the people of that portion of the globe have made such great advances in power, intelligence, and civilization.

To these may be added the greater capacity, which governments of the monarchical form have exhibited, to hold under subjection a large extent of territory, and a numerous population; and which has made them more powerful than others of a different form, to the extent, that these constitute an element of power. All these causes combined, have given such great and decisive advantages, as to enable them, heretofore, to absorb, in the progress of events, the few governments which have, from time to time, assumed different forms;—not excepting even the mighty Roman Republic, which, after attaining the highest point of power, passed, seemingly under the operation of irresistible causes, into a military despotism. I say, heretofore,—for it remains to be seen whether they will continue to retain their advantages, in these respects, over the others, under the great and growing influence of public opinion, and the new and imposing form which popular government has assumed with us.

These have already effected great changes, and will probably effect still greater,—adverse to the monarchical form; but, as yet, these changes have tended rather to the absolute, than to the constitutional form of popular government,—for reasons which have been explained. If this tendency should continue permanently in the same direction, the monarchical form must still retain its advantages, and continue to be the most prevalent. Should this be the case, the alternative will be between monarchy and popular government, in the form of the numerical majority,—or absolute democracy; which, as has been shown, is not only the most fugitive of all the forms, but has the strongest tendency of all others to the monarchical. If, on the contrary, this tendency, or the changes referred to, should incline to the constitutional form of popular government,—and a proper organism come to be regarded as not less indispensable than the right of suffrage to the establishment of such governments,—in such case, it is not improbable that, in the progress of events, the monarchical will cease to be the prevalent form of government. Whether they will take this direction, at least for a long time, will depend on the success of our government,—and a correct understanding of the principles on which it is constructed.

To comprehend more fully the force and bearing of public opinion, and to form a just estimate of the changes to which, aided by the press, it will probably lead, politically and socially,—it will be necessary to consider it in connection with the causes that have given it an influence so great, as to entitle it to be regarded as a new political element. They will, upon investigation, be found in the many discoveries and inventions made in the last few centuries.

Among the more prominent of those of an earlier date, stand the practical application of the magnetic power to the purposes of navigation, by the invention of the mariner's compass; the discovery of the mode of making gunpowder, and its application to the art of war; and the invention of the art of printing. Among the more recent are, the numerous chemical and mechanical discoveries and inventions, and their application to the various arts of production; the application of steam to machinery of almost every description, especially to such as is designed to facilitate transportation and travel by land and water; and, finally, the invention of the magnetic telegraph.

All these have led to important results. Through the invention of the mariner's compass, the globe has been circumnavigated and explored, and all who inhabit it, with but few exceptions, brought within the sphere of an all-pervading commerce, which is daily diffusing over its surface the light and blessings of civilization. Through that of the art of printing, the fruits of observation and reflection, of discoveries and inventions, with all the accumulated stores of previously acquired knowledge, are preserved and widely diffused. The application of gunpowder to the art of war, has for ever settled the long conflict for ascendency between civilization and barbarism, in favor of the former, and thereby guarantied that, whatever knowledge is now accumulated, or may hereafter be added, shall never again be lost. The numerous discoveries and inventions, chemical and mechanical, and the application of steam to machinery, have increased, many-fold, the productive powers of labor and capital; and have, thereby, greatly increased the number, who may devote themselves to study and improvement,—and the amount of means necessary for commercial exchanges,—especially between the more and the less advanced and civilized portions of the globe,—to the great advantage of both, but particularly of the latter. The application of steam to the purposes of travel and transportation, by land and water, has vastly increased the facility, cheapness and rapidity of both;—diffusing, with them, information and intelligence almost as quickly and as freely as if borne by the winds; while the electrical wires outstrip them, in velocity—rivalling, in rapidity, even thought itself.

The joint effect of all has been, a great increase and diffusion of knowledge; and, with this, an impulse to progress and civilization heretofore unexampled in the history of the world,—accompanied by a mental energy and activity unprecedented.

To all these causes, public opinion, and its organ, the press, owe their origin and great influence. Already they have attained a force in the more civilized portions of the globe sufficient to be felt by all governments, even the most absolute and despotic. But, as great as they now are, they have as yet attained nothing like their maximum force. It is probable, that not one of the causes, which have contributed to their formation and influence, has yet produced its full effect; while several of the most powerful have just begun to operate; and many others, probably of equal or even greater force, yet remain to be brought to light. When the causes now in operation have produced their full effect, and inventions and discoveries shall have been exhausted,—if that may ever be,— they will give a force to public opinion, and cause changes, political and social, difficult to be anticipated. What will be their final bearing, time only can decide with any certainty. That they will, however, greatly improve the condition of man ultimately,—it would be impious to doubt. It would be to suppose, that the all-wise and beneficent Being,—the Creator of all,—had so constituted man, as that the employment of the high intellectual faculties, with which He has been pleased to endow him, in order that he might develop the laws that control the great agents of the material world, and make them subservient to his use,—would prove to him the cause of permanent evil,—and not of permanent good. If, then, such a supposition be inadmissible, they must, in their orderly and full development, end in his permanent good. But this cannot be, unless the ultimate effect of their action, politically, shall be, to give ascendency to that form of government best calculated to fulfil the ends for which government is ordained. For, so completely does the well-being of our race depend on good government, that it is hardly possible any change, the ultimate effect of which should be otherwise, could prove to be a permanent good.

It is, however, not improbable, that many and great, but temporary evils, will follow the changes they have effected, and are destined to effect. It seems to be a law in the political, as well as in the material world, that great changes cannot be made, except very gradually, without convulsions and revolutions; to be followed by calamities, in the beginning, however beneficial they may prove to be in the end. The first effect of such changes, on long established governments, will be, to unsettle the opinions and principles in which they originated,—and which have guided their policy,—before those, which the changes are calculated to form and establish, are fairly developed and understood. The interval between the decay of the old and the formation and establishment of the new, constitutes a period of transition, which must always necessarily be one of uncertainty, confusion, error, and wild and fierce fanaticism.

The governments of the more advanced and civilized portions of the world are now in the midst of this period. It has proved, and will continue to prove a severe trial to existing political institutions of every form. Those governments which have not the sagacity to perceive what is truly public opinion,—to distinguish between it and the mere clamor of faction, or shouts of fanaticism,—

and the good sense and firmness to yield, timely and cautiously, to the claims of the one,—and to resist, promptly and decidedly, the demands of the other,— are doomed to fall. Few will be able successfully to pass through this period of transition; and these, not without shocks and modifications, more or less considerable. It will endure until the governing and the governed shall better understand the ends for which government is ordained, and the form best adapted to accomplish them, under all the circumstances in which communities may be respectively placed.

I shall, in conclusion, proceed to exemplify the elementary principles, which have been established, by giving a brief account of the origin and character of the governments of Rome and Great Britain; the two most remarkable and perfect of their respective forms of constitutional governments. The object is to show how these principles were applied, in the more simple forms of such governments; preparatory to an exposition of the mode in which they have been applied in our own more complex system. It will appear that, in each, the principles are the same; and that the difference in their application resulted from the different situation and social condition of the respective communities. They were modified, in each, so as to conform to these; and, hence, their remarkable success. They were applied to communities in which hereditary rank had long prevailed. Their respective constitutions originated in concession to the people; and, through them, they acquired a participation in the powers of government. But with us, they were applied to communities where all political rank and distinction between citizens were excluded; and where government had its origin in the will of the people.

But, however different their origin and character, it will be found that the object in each was the same,—to blend and harmonize the conflicting interests of the community; and the means the same,—taking the sense of each class or portion through its appropriate organ, and considering the concurrent sense of all as the sense of the whole community. Such being the fact, an accurate and clear conception how this was effected, in their more simple forms, will enable us better to understand how it was accomplished in our far more refined, artificial, and complex form.

It is well known to all, the least conversant with their history, that the Roman people consisted of two distinct orders, or classes,—the Patricians and the Plebeians; and that the line of distinction was so strongly drawn, that, for a long time, the right of intermarriage between them was prohibited. After the overthrow of the monarchy and the expulsion of the Tarquins, the government fell exclusively under the control of the patricians, who, with their clients and dependents, formed, at the time, a very numerous and powerful body. At first, while there was danger of the return of the exiled family, they treated the plebeians with kindness; but, after it had passed away, with oppression and cruelty.

It is not necessary, with the object in view, to enter into a minute account of the various acts of oppression and cruelty to which they were subjected. It is sufficient to state, that, according to the usages of war at the time, the territory of a conquered people became the property of the conquerors; and that the plebeians were harassed and oppressed by incessant wars, in which the danger and toil were theirs, while all the fruits of victory, (the lands of the vanquished, and the spoils of war,) accrued to the benefit of their oppressors. The result was such as might be expected. They were impoverished, and forced, from necessity, to borrow from the patricians, at usurious and exorbitant interest, funds with which they had been enriched through their blood and toil; and to pledge their all for repayment at stipulated periods. In case of default, the pledge became forfeited; and, under the provisions of law in such cases, the debtors were liable to be seized, and sold or imprisoned by their creditors in private jails prepared and kept for the purpose. These savage provisions were enforced with the utmost rigor against the indebted and impoverished plebeians. They constituted, indeed, an essential part of the system through which they were plundered and oppressed by the patricians.

A system so oppressive could not be endured. The natural consequences followed. Deep hatred was engendered between the orders, accompanied by factions, violence, and corruption, which distracted and weakened the government. At length, an incident occurred which roused the indignation of the plebeians to the utmost pitch, and which ended in an open rupture between the two orders.

An old soldier, who had long served the country, and had fought with bravery in twenty-eight battles, made his escape from the prison of his creditor,— squalid, pale, and famished. He implored the protection of the plebeians. A crowd surrounded him; and his tale of service to the country, and the cruelty with which he had been treated by his creditor, kindled a flame, which continued to rage until it extended to the army. It refused to continue any longer in service,—crossed the Anio, and took possession of the sacred mount. The patricians divided in opinion as to the course which should be pursued. The more violent insisted on an appeal to arms, but, fortunately, the counsel of the moderate, which recommended concession and compromise, prevailed. Commissioners were appointed to treat with the army; and a formal compact was entered into between the orders, and ratified by the oaths of each, which conceded to the plebeians the right to elect two tribunes, as the protectors of their order, and made their persons sacred. The number was afterwards increased to ten, and their election by centuries changed to election by tribes;—a mode by which the plebeians secured a decided preponderance.

Such was the origin of the tribunate;—which, in process of time, opened all the honors of the government to the plebeians. They acquired the right, not only of vetoing the passage of all laws, but also their execution; and thus obtained, through their tribunes, a negative on the entire action of the government, without divesting the patricians of their control over the Senate. By this arrangement, the government was placed under the concurrent and joint voice of the two orders, expressed through separate and appropriate organs; the one possessing the positive, and the other the negative powers of the government. This simple change converted it from an absolute, into a constitutional government,—from a government of the patricians only, to that of the whole Roman people,—and from an aristocracy into a republic. In doing this, it laid the solid foundation of Roman liberty and greatness.

A superficial observer would pronounce a government, so organized, as that one order should have the power of making and executing the laws, and another, or the representatives of another, the unlimited authority of preventing their enactment and execution,—if not wholly impracticable, at least, too feeble to stand the shocks to which all governments are subject; and would, therefore, predict its speedy dissolution, after a distracted and inglorious career.

How different from the result! Instead of distraction, it proved to be the bond of concord and harmony; instead of weakness, of unequalled strength;—and, instead of a short and inglorious career, one of great length and immortal glory. It moderated the conflicts between the orders; harmonized their interests, and blended them into one; substituted devotion to country in the place of devotion to particular orders; called forth the united strength and energy of the whole, in the hour of danger; raised to power, the wise and patriotic; elevated the Roman name above all others; extended her authority and dominion over the greater part of the then known world, and transmitted the influence of her laws and institutions to the present day. Had the opposite counsel prevailed at this critical juncture; had an appeal been made to arms instead of to concession and compromise, Rome, instead of being what she afterwards became, would, in all probability, have been as inglorious, and as little known to posterity as the insignificant states which surrounded her, whose names and existence would have been long since consigned to oblivion, had they not been preserved in the history of her conquests of them. But for the wise course then adopted, it is not improbable,—whichever order might have prevailed,—that she would have fallen under some cruel and petty tyrant;—and, finally, been conquered by some of the neighboring states,—or by the Carthaginians, or the Gauls. To the fortunate turn which events then took, she owed her unbounded sway and imperishable renown.

It is true, that the tribunate, after raising her to a height of power and prosperity never before equalled, finally became one of the instruments by which her liberty was overthrown:—but it was not until she became exposed to new dangers, growing out of increase of wealth and the great extent of her dominions, against which the tribunate furnished no guards. Its original object was the protection of the plebeians against oppression and abuse of power on the part of the patricians. This, it thoroughly accomplished; but it had no power to protect the people of the numerous and wealthy conquered countries from being plundered by consuls and proconsuls. Nor could it prevent the plunderers from using the enormous wealth, which they extorted from the impoverished and ruined provinces, to corrupt and debase the people; nor arrest the formation of parties, (irrespective of the old division of patricians and plebeians,) having no other object than to obtain the control of the government for the purpose of plunder. Against these formidable evils, her constitution furnished no adequate security. Under their baneful influence, the possession of the government became the object of the most violent conflicts; not between patricians and plebeians,—but between profligate and corrupt factions. They continued with increasing violence, until, finally, Rome sunk, as must every community under similar circumstances, beneath the strong grasp, the despotic rule of the chieftain of the successful party;—the sad, but only alternative which remained to prevent universal violence, confusion and anarchy. The Republic had, in reality, ceased to exist long before the establishment of the Empire. The interval was filled by the rule of ferocious, corrupt and bloody factions. There was, indeed, a small but patriotic body of eminent individuals, who struggled, in vain, to correct abuses, and to restore the government to its primitive character and purity;—and who sacrificed their lives in their endeavors to accomplish an object so virtuous and noble. But it can be no disparagement to the tribunate, that the great powers conferred on it for wise purposes, and which it had so fully accomplished, should be seized upon, during this violent and corrupt interval, to overthrow the liberty it had established, and so long nourished and supported.

In assigning such consequence to the tribunate, I must not overlook other important provisions of the Constitution of the Roman government. The Senate, as far as we are informed, seems to have been admirably constituted to secure consistency and steadiness of action. The power,—when the Republic was exposed to imminent danger,—to appoint a dictator,—vested, for a limited period, with almost boundless authority; the two consuls, and the manner of electing them; the auguries; the sibylline books; the priesthood, and the censorship;—all of which appertained to the patricians,—were, perhaps indispensable to withstand the vast and apparently irregular power of the tribunate;—while the possession of such great powers by the patricians, made it necessary to give proportionate strength to the only organ through which the plebeians could act on the government with effect. The government was, indeed, powerfully constituted; and, apparently, well proportioned both in its positive and negative organs. It was truly an iron government. Without the tribunate, it proved to be one of the most oppressive and cruel that ever existed; but with it, one of the strongest and best.

The origin and character of the British government are so well known, that a very brief sketch, with the object in view, will suffice.

The causes which ultimately moulded it into its present form, commenced with the Norman Conquest. This introduced the feudal system, with its necessary appendages, a hereditary monarchy and nobility; the former in the line of the chief, who led the invading army;—and the latter in that of his distinguished followers. They became his feudatories. The country,—both land and people,—(the latter as serfs,) was divided between them. Conflicts soon followed between the monarch and the nobles,—as must ever be the case under such systems. They were followed, in the progress of events, by efforts, on the part both of monarchs and nobles, to conciliate the favor of the people. They, in consequence, gradually rose to power. At every step of their ascent, they became more important,—and were more and more courted,—until at length their influence was so sensibly felt, that they were summoned to attend the meeting of parliament by delegates; not, however, as an estate of the realm, or constituent member of the body politic. The first summons came from the nobles; and was designed to conciliate their good feelings and secure their cooperation in the war against the king. This was followed by one from him; but his object was simply to have them present at the meeting of parliament, in order to be *consulted* by the crown, on questions relating to taxes and supplies; not, indeed, to discuss the right to lay the one, and to raise the other,—for the King claimed the arbitrary authority to do both,—but with a view to facilitate their collection, and to reconcile them to their imposition.

From this humble beginning, they, after a long struggle, accompanied by many vicissitudes, raised themselves to be considered one of the estates of the realm; and, finally, in their efforts to enlarge and secure what they had gained, overpowered, for a time, the other two estates; and thus concentrated all power in a single estate or body. This, in effect, made the government absolute, and led to consequences which, as by a fixed law, must ever result in popular governments of this form;—namely:—to organized parties, or, rather, factions, contending violently to obtain or retain the control of the government; and this, again, by laws almost as uniform, to the concentration of all the powers of government in the hands of the military commander of the successful party.

His heir was too feeble to hold the sceptre he had grasped; and the general discontent with the result of the revolution, led to the restoration of the old dynasty; without defining the limits between the powers of the respective estates.

After a short interval, another revolution followed, in which the lords and commons united against the king. This terminated in his overthrow; and the transfer of the crown to a collateral branch of the family, accompanied by a declaration of rights, which defined the powers of the several estates of the realm; and, finally, perfected and established the constitution. Thus, a feudal monarchy was converted, through a slow but steady process of many centuries, into a highly refined constitutional monarchy, without changing the basis of the original government.

As it now stands, the realm consists of three estates; the king; the lords temporal and spiritual; and the commons. The parliament is the grand council. It possesses the supreme power. It enacts laws, by the concurring assent of the lords and commons,—subject to the approval of the king. The executive power is vested in the monarch, who is regarded as constituting the first estate. Although irresponsible himself, he can only act through responsible ministers and agents. They are responsible to the other estates; to the lords, as constituting the high court before whom all the servants of the crown may be tried for malpractices, and crimes against the realm, or official delinquencies;—and to the commons, as possessing the impeaching power, and constituting the grand inquest of the kingdom. These provisions, with their legislative powers,—especially that of withholding supplies,—give them a controlling influence on the executive department, and, virtually, a participation in its powers;—so that the acts of the government, throughout its entire range, may be fairly considered as the result of the concurrent and joint action of the three estates;—and, as these embrace all the orders,—of the concurrent and joint action of the estates of the realm.

He would take an imperfect and false view of the subject who should consider the king, in his mere individual character, or even as the head of the royal family,—as constituting an estate. Regarded in either light, so far from deserving to be considered as the First Estate,—and the head of the realm, as he is,—he would represent an interest too inconsiderable to be an object of special protection. Instead of this, he represents what in reality is, habitually and naturally, the most powerful interest, all things considered, under every form of government in all civilized communities,—*the tax-consuming interest*; or, more broadly, the great interest which necessarily grows out of the action of the government, be its form what it may;—the interest that *lives by the government*. It is composed of the recipients of its honors and emoluments; and may be properly called, the government interest, or party;—in contradistinction to the rest of the community,—or, (as they may be properly called,) the people or commons. The one comprehends all who are supported by the government;—and the other all who support the government:—and it is only because the former are strongest, all things being considered, that they are enabled to retain, for any considerable time, advantages so great and commanding.

This great and predominant interest is naturally represented by a single head. For it is impossible, without being so represented, to distribute the honors and emoluments of the government among those who compose it, without producing discord and conflict:—and it is only by preventing these, that advantages so tempting can be long retained. And, hence, the strong tendency of this great interest to the monarchical form;—that is, to be represented by a single individual. On the contrary, the antagonistic interest,—that which supports the government, has the opposite tendency;—a tendency to be represented by many; because a large assembly can better judge, than one individual or a few, what burdens the community can bear;—and how it can be most equally distributed, and easily collected.

In the British government, the king constitutes an Estate, because he is the head and representative of this great interest. He is the conduit through which, all the honors and emoluments of the government flow;—while the House of Commons, according to the theory of the government, is the head and representative of the opposite—the great tax-paying interest, by which the government is supported.

Between these great interests, there is necessarily a constant and strong tendency to conflict; which, if not counteracted, must end in violence and an appeal to force,—to be followed by revolution, as has been explained. To prevent this, the House of Lords, as one of the estates of the realm, is interposed; and constitutes the conservative power of the government. It consists, in fact, of that portion of the community who are the principal recipients of the honors, emoluments, and other advantages derived from the government; and whose condition cannot be improved, but must be made worse by the triumph of either of the conflicting estates over the other; and, hence, it is opposed to the ascendency of either,—and in favor of preserving the equilibrium between them.

This sketch, brief as it is, is sufficient to show, that these two constitutional governments,—by far the most illustrious of their respective kinds,—conform to the principles that have been established, alike in their origin and in their construction. The constitutions of both originated in a pressure, occasioned by conflicts of interests between hostile classes or orders, and were intended to meet the pressing exigencies of the occasion; neither party, it would seem, having any conception of the principles involved, or the consequences to follow, beyond the immediate objects in contemplation. It would, indeed, seem almost impossible for constitutional governments, founded on orders or classes, to originate in any other manner. It is difficult to conceive that any people, among whom they did not exist, would, or could voluntarily institute them, in order to establish such governments; while it is not at all wonderful, that they should grow out of conflicts between different orders or classes when aided by a favorable combination of circumstances.

The constitutions of both rest on the same principle;—an organism by which the voice of each order or class is taken through its appropriate organ; and which requires the concurring voice of all to constitute that of the whole community. The effects, too, were the same in both;—to unite and harmonize conflicting interests;—to strengthen attachments to the whole community, and to moderate that to the respective orders or classes; to rally all, in the hour of danger, around the standard of their country; to elevate the feeling of nationality, and to develop power, moral and physical, to an extraordinary extent. Yet each has its distinguishing features, resulting from the difference of their organisms, and the circumstances in which they respectively originated.

In the government of Great Britain, the three orders are blended in the legislative department; so that the separate and concurring act of each is necessary to make laws; while, on the contrary, in the Roman, one order had the power of making laws, and another of annulling them, or arresting their execution. Each had its peculiar advantages. The Roman developed more fully the love of country and the feelings of nationality. *"I am a Roman citizen,"*—was pronounced with a pride and elevation of sentiment, never, perhaps, felt before or since, by any citizen or subject of any community, in announcing the country to which he belonged.

It also developed more fully the power of the community. Taking into consideration their respective population, and the state of the arts at the different periods, Rome developed more power, comparatively, than Great Britain ever has,—vast as that is, and has been,—or, perhaps, than any other community ever did. Hence, the mighty control she acquired from a beginning so humble. But the British government is far superior to that of Rome, in its adaptation and capacity to embrace under its control extensive dominions, without subverting its constitution. In this respect, the Roman constitution was defective;—and, in consequence, soon began to exhibit marks of decay, after Rome had extended her dominions beyond Italy; while the British holds under its sway, without apparently impairing either, an empire equal to that, under the weight of which the constitution and liberty of Rome were crushed. This great advantage it derives from its different structure, especially that of the executive department; and the character of its conservative principle. The former is so constructed as to prevent, in consequence of its unity and hereditary character, the violent and factious struggles to obtain the control of the government,—and, with it, the vast patronage which distracted, corrupted, and finally subverted the Roman Republic. Against this fatal disease, the latter had no security whatever; while the British government,—besides the advantages it possesses, in this respect, from the structure of its executive department,—has, in the character of its conservative principle, another and powerful security against it. Its character is such, that patronage, instead of weakening, strengthens it:—For, the greater the patronage of the government, the greater will be the share which falls to the estate constituting the conservative department of the government; and the more eligible its condition, the greater its opposition to any radical change in its form. The two causes combined, give to the government a greater capacity of holding under subjection extensive dominions, without subverting the constitution or destroying liberty, than has ever been possessed by any other. It is difficult, indeed, to assign any limit to its capacity in this respect. The most probable which can be assigned is, its ability to bear increased burdens;—the taxation necessary to meet the expenses incident to the acquisition and government of such vast dominions, may prove, in the end, so heavy as to crush, under its weight, the laboring and productive portions of the population.

I have now finished the brief sketch I proposed, of the origin and character of these two renowned governments; and shall next proceed to consider the character, origin and structure of the Government of the United States. It differs from the Roman and British, more than they differ from each other; and, although an existing government of recent origin, its character and structure are perhaps less understood than those of either.

CHAPTER II.

A DISCOURSE ON THE
CONSTITUTION AND GOVERNMENT
OF THE UNITED STATES

As a study of the "character and structure" of the republic, the Discourse *attempts to nourish the political tradition in such a way as to facilitate a recuperation of the body politic. The* Discourse *differs from the* Disquisition *in terms of focus rather than substance. In many regards, the* Discourse *amplifies aspects of Calhoun's thought that originated decades earlier.*

By turning to the fundamental law in the Discourse, *Calhoun attempted to sustain the philosophical and constitutional bedrock of American politics. The absence of an adequate interpretation of these core elements distressed the Carolinian. In response to a query from a "young man," Calhoun addressed the predicament: "You ask me a question not easy to answer. There is no satisfactory work extant on our system of government. The* Federalists *[sic] is the fullest and, in many respects, the best, but it takes many false views and by no means goes to the bottom of the system. The Virginia and Kentucky resolutions & the report to the Virginia Legislature by Mr. Madison on the Alien and Sedition acts take far deeper & correct views, but are less full."[1] The* Discourse *was Calhoun's final effort to fill this perceived void.*

Calhoun contemplated writing the Discourse *for many years, informing his nephew that if he were to undertake any literary project it would "be on the elementary principles of political science, preliminary to a discourse on the Constitution of the U. [United]*

---

1. John C. Calhoun, "To A. D. Wallace," December 17, 1840, in *The Papers of John C. Calhoun,* Clyde Wilson ed., Volume XV (Columbia: University of South Carolina Press, 1983), p. 389 [Hereafter cited as *Papers* throughout text].

States."[2] *Against the scholarly and political currents of his time, Calhoun refused to present his critique of the American political tradition in "the shape of [constitutional] commentaries"; instead, he sought to recover these foundational elements through "a philosophical discussion on its character and constitution in illustration of the elementary treatise."*[3] *In June 1849 he finished the* Disquisition, *the "elementary treatise," and was preparing to begin work on its sister volume, the* Discourse.[4] *At year's end his progress on the* Discourse *was the subject of much celebration: "The rough draft is finished," he proclaimed to his daughter.*[5] *Calhoun continued to revise the work during the early months of 1850, until his death on March 31, 1850.*[6] *Just hours before his passing, Calhoun asked his son John to read portions of the manuscript to him with the intent to make further revisions.*[7] *Unfortunately, Calhoun died before he could complete his final revision of the* Discourse. *The final preparations for publication were completed after Calhoun's death by Richard Kenner Crallé, his former chief clerk at the State Department and longtime associate. Through the efforts of Crallé, the* Discourse *was posthumously published (as was the* Disquisition*) in a limited edition in 1851 and in a more widely circulated version two years later. Although a journalist and man of letters himself, Crallé made no substantive emendations to his mentor's work, choosing only to add a few explanatory footnotes in reference to citations within the text, along with noting an omission of "illegible" marginalia from the published edition. Critics have subsequently devalued the* Discourse *in light of its purported textual, historical or philosophical shortcomings. Even though these assessments offer considerable insight into the work, the deeper, more profound interpretation of the American political tradition contained in the* Discourse *has been overlooked.*

OURS is a system of governments, compounded of the separate governments of the several States composing the Union, and of one common government of all its members, called the Government of the United States. The former preceded the latter, which was created by their agency. Each was framed by written constitutions; those of the several States by the people of each, acting

---

2. "To John A. Calhoun," April 2, 1845, in *Papers*, Vol. XXI, pp. 465–466.

3. *Correspondence*, p. 750.

4. Ibid., p. 768.

5. Ibid., p. 777. Earlier in his letter Calhoun noted that the manuscript totaled between 400 and 500 pages. In February he revised the number of draft pages from the earlier estimate to between 350 and 400 pages (*Correspondence*, p. 782).

6. *Correspondence*, p. 782.

7. William Meigs, *Life of John Calhoun*, Vol. II (New York: Stecher and Company, 1917), p. 455 and footnote 46, p. 461; for a somewhat less dramatic account, see Irving Bartlett, *John C. Calhoun* (New York: W.W. Norton and Company, 1993), p. 374.

separately, and in their sovereign character; and that of the United States, by the same, acting in the same character,—but jointly instead of separately. All were formed on the same model. They all divide the powers of government into legislative, executive, and judicial; and are founded on the great principle of the responsibility of the rulers to the ruled. The entire powers of government are divided between the two; those of a more general character being specifically delegated to the United States; and all others not delegated, being reserved to the several States in their separate character. Each, within its appropriate sphere, possesses all the attributes, and performs all the functions of government. Neither is perfect without the other. The two combined, form one entire and perfect government. With these preliminary remarks, I shall proceed to the consideration of the immediate subject of this discourse.

The Government of the United States was formed by the Constitution of the United States;—and ours is a democratic, federal republic.

It is democratic, in contradistinction to aristocracy and monarchy. It excludes classes, orders, and all artificial distinctions. To guard against their introduction, the constitution prohibits the granting of any title of nobility by the United States, or by any State.* The whole system is, indeed, democratic throughout. It has for its fundamental principle, the great cardinal maxim, that the people are the source of all power; that the governments of the several States and of the United States were created by them, and for them; that the powers conferred on them are not surrendered, but delegated; and, as such, are held in trust, and not absolutely; and can be rightfully exercised only in furtherance of the objects for which they were delegated.

It is federal as well as democratic. *Federal,* on the one hand, in contradistinction to *national,* and, on the other, to a *confederacy.* In showing this, I shall begin with the former.

It is federal, because it is the government of States united in a political union, in contradistinction to a government of individuals socially united; that is, by what is usually called, a social compact. To express it more concisely, it is federal and not national, because it is the government of a community of States, and not the government of a single State or nation.

That it is federal and not national, we have the high authority of the convention which framed it. General Washington, as its organ, in his letter submitting the plan to the consideration of the Congress of the then confederacy, calls it, in one place,—"the general government of the Union;"—and in

---

*1st Art. 9 and 10 Sec.

another,—"the federal government of these States." Taken together, the plain meaning is, that the government proposed would be, if adopted, the government of the States adopting it, in their united character as members of a common Union; and, as such, would be a federal government. These expressions were not used without due consideration, and an accurate and full knowledge of their true import. The subject was not a novel one. The convention was familiar with it. It was much agitated in their deliberations. They divided, in reference to it, in the early stages of their proceedings. At first, one party was in favor of a national and the other of a federal government. The former, in the beginning, prevailed; and in the plans which they proposed, the constitution and government are styled "National." But, finally, the latter gained the ascendency, when the term "National" was superseded, and *"United States"* substituted in its place. The constitution was accordingly styled,— *"The constitution of the United States of America;"*—and the government,— *"The government of the United States;"* leaving out "America," for the sake of brevity. It cannot admit of a doubt, that the Convention, by the expression "United States," meant the States united in a federal Union; for in no other sense could they, with propriety, call the government, *"the federal government of these States,"*—and *"the general government of the Union,"*—as they did in the letter referred to. It is thus clear, that the Convention regarded the different expressions,—"the federal government of the United States;"—"the general government of the Union,"—and,— "government of the United States,"—as meaning the same thing,—a federal, in contradistinction to a national government.

Assuming it then, as established, that they are the same, it is only necessary, in order to ascertain with precision, what they meant by *"federal government,"*— to ascertain what they meant by *"the government of the United States."* For this purpose it will be necessary to trace the expression to its origin.

It was, at that time, as our history shows, an old and familiar phrase,—having a known and well-defined meaning. Its use commenced with the political birth of these States; and it has been applied to them, in all the forms of government through which they have passed, without alteration. The style of the present constitution and government is precisely the style by which the confederacy that existed when it was adopted, and which it superseded, was designated. The instrument that formed the latter was called,— *"Articles of Confederation and Perpetual Union."* Its first article declares that the style of this confederacy shall be, "The United States of America;" and the second, in order to leave no doubt as to the relation in which the States should stand to each other in the confederacy about to be formed, declared,—"Each State retains its sovereignty, freedom and independence; and every power, jurisdiction, and right, which is not, by this confederation, expressly delegated to the United States in Congress assembled." If we go one step further back, the style of the confederacy will be found to be the same with that of the revolutionary government, which existed when it was adopted, and which it superseded. It dates its origin with the Declaration of Independence. That act is styled,—"The unanimous Declaration of the thirteen United States of America." And here again, that there might be no doubt how these States would stand to each other in the new condition in which they were about to be placed, it concluded by declaring,—"that these United Colonies are, and of right ought to be, free and independent States;" "and that, as free and independent States, they have full power to levy war, conclude peace, contract alliances, and to do all other acts and things which independent States may of right do." The "United States" is, then, the baptismal name of these States,—received at their birth;—by which they have ever since continued to call themselves; by which they have characterized their constitution, government and laws;—and by which they are known to the rest of the world.

The retention of the same style, throughout every stage of their existence, affords strong, if not conclusive evidence that the political relation between these States, under their present constitution and government, is substantially the same as under the confederacy and revolutionary government; and what that relation was, we are not left to doubt; as they are declared expressly to be *free, independent* and *sovereign* States." They, then, are now united, and have been, throughout, simply as confederated States. If it had been intended by the members of the convention which framed the present constitution and government, to make any essential change, either in the relation of the States to each other, or the basis of their union, they would, by retaining the style which designated them under the preceding governments, have practised a deception, utterly unworthy of their character, as sincere and honest men and patriots. It may, therefore, be fairly inferred, that, retaining the same style, they intended to attach to the expression,—"the United States," the same meaning, substantially, which it previously had; and, of course, in calling the present government,—"the federal government of these States," they meant by "federal," that they stood in the same relation to each other,—that their union rested, without material change, on the same basis,—as under the confederacy and the revolutionary government; and that federal, and confederated States, meant substantially the same thing. It follows, also, that the changes made by the present constitution were not in the foundation, but in the superstructure of the system. We accordingly find, in confirmation of this conclusion, that the convention, in their letter to Congress, stating the reasons for the changes that had been made, refer only to the necessity which required a different *"organization"* of the government, without making any allusion whatever to any change in the relations of the States towards each other,—or the basis of the system. They state that, "the friends of our country have long seen and desired, that the power of making war, peace, and treaties; that of levying money and regulating commerce, and the correspondent executive and judicial authorities, should be fully and effectually vested in the Government of the Union: but the impropriety of delegating such extensive trusts to one body of men is evident; hence results the necessity of a *different organization*." Comment is unnecessary.

We thus have the authority of the convention itself for asserting that the expression, "United States," has essentially the same meaning, when applied to the present constitution and government, as it had previously; and, of course, that the States have retained their separate existence, as independent and sovereign communities, in all the forms of political existence, through which they have passed. Such, indeed, is the literal import of the expression,—"the United States,"—and the sense in which it is ever used, when it is applied politically.— I say, *politically,*—because it is often applied, *geographically,* to designate the portion of this continent occupied by the States composing the Union, including territories belonging to them. This application arose from the fact, that there was no appropriate term for that portion of this continent; and thus, not unnaturally, the name by which these States are politically designated, was employed to designate the region they occupy and possess. The distinction is important, and cannot be overlooked in discussing questions involving the character and nature of the government, without causing great confusion and dangerous misconceptions.

But as conclusive as these reasons are to prove that the government of the United States is federal, in contradistinction to national, it would seem, that they have not been sufficient to prevent the opposite opinion from being entertained. Indeed, this last seems to have become the prevailing one; if we may judge from the general use of the term "national," and the almost entire disuse of that of "federal." National, is now commonly applied to "the general government of the Union,"—and "the federal government of these States,"—and all that appertains to them or to the Union. It seems to be forgotten that the term was repudiated by the convention, after full consideration; and that it was carefully excluded from the constitution, and the letter laying it before Congress. Even those who know all this,—and, of course, how falsely the term is applied,—have, for the most part, [slided into its use without reflection] But there are not a few who so apply it, because they believe it to be a national government in fact; and among these are men of distinguished talents and standing, who have put forth all their powers of reason and eloquence, in support of the theory. The question involved is one of the first magnitude, and deserves to be investigated thoroughly in all its aspects. With this impression, I deem it proper,—clear and conclusive as I regard the reasons already assigned to prove its federal character,—to confirm them by historical references; and to repel the arguments adduced to prove it to be a national government. I shall begin with the formation and ratification of the constitution.

That the States, when they formed and ratified the constitution, were distinct, independent, and sovereign communities, has already been established. That the people of the several States, acting in their separate, independent, and sovereign character, adopted their separate State constitutions, is a fact uncontested and incontestable; but it is not more certain than that, acting in the same character, they ratified and adopted the constitution of the United States; with this difference only, that in making and adopting the one, they acted without concert or agreement; but, in the other, with concert in making, and mutual agreement in adopting it. That the delegates who constituted the convention which framed the constitution, were appointed by the several States, each on its own authority; that they voted in the convention by States; and that their votes were counted by States,—are recorded and unquestionable facts. So, also, the facts that the constitution, when framed, was submitted to the people of the several States for their respective ratification; that it was ratified by them, each for itself; and that it was binding on each, only in consequence of its being so ratified by it. Until then, it was but the plan of a constitution, without any binding force. It was the act of ratification which established it as a constitution between the States ratifying it; and only between *them,* on the condition that not less than nine of the then thirteen States should concur in the ratification;—as is expressly provided by its seventh and last article. It is in the following words: "The ratification of the conventions of nine States shall be sufficient for the establishment of this constitution between the States so ratifying the same." If additional proof be needed to show that it was only binding between the States that ratified it, it may be found in the fact, that two States, North Carolina and Rhode Island, refused, at first, to ratify; and were, in consequence, regarded in the interval as foreign States, without obligation, on their parts, to respect it, or, on the part of their citizens, to obey it. Thus far, there can be no difference of opinion. The facts are too recent and too well established,—and the provision of the constitution too explicit, to admit of doubt.

That the States, then, retained, after the ratification of the constitution, the distinct, independent, and sovereign character in which they formed and ratified it, is certain; unless they divested themselves of it by the act of ratification, or by some provision of the constitution. If they have not, the constitution must be federal, and not national; for it would have, in that case, every attribute necessary to constitute it federal, and not one to make it national. On the other hand, if they have divested themselves, then it would necessarily lose its federal character, and become national. Whether, then, the government is federal or national, is reduced to a single question; whether the act of ratification, of itself, or the constitution, by some one, or all of its provisions, did, or did not, divest the several States of their character of separate, independent, and sovereign communities, and merge them all in one great community or nation, called the American people?

Before entering on the consideration of this important question, it is proper to remark, that, on its decision, the character of the government, as well as the constitution, depends. The former must, necessarily, partake of the character of the latter, as it is but its agent, created by it, to carry its powers into effect. Accordingly, then, as the constitution is federal or national, so must the government be; and I shall, therefore, use them indiscriminately in discussing the subject.

Of all the questions which can arise under our system of government, this is by far the most important. It involves many others of great magnitude; and among them, that of the allegiance of the citizen; or, in other words, the question to whom allegiance and obedience are ultimately due. What is the true relation between the two governments,—that of the United States, and those of the several States? and what is the relation between the individuals respectively composing them? For it is clear, if the States still retain their sovereignty as separate and independent communities, the allegiance and obedience of the citizens of each would be due to their respective States; and that the government of the United States and those of the several States would stand as equals and co-ordinates in their respective spheres; and, instead of being united socially, their citizens would be politically connected through their respective States. On the contrary, if they have, by ratifying the constitution, divested themselves of their individuality and sovereignty, and merged themselves into one great community or nation, it is equally clear, that the sovereignty would reside in the whole,—or what is called the American people; and that allegiance and obedience would be due to them. Nor is it less so, that the government of the several States would, in such case, stand to that of the United States, in the relation of inferior and subordinate, to superior and paramount; and that the individuals of the several States, thus fused, as it were, into one general mass, would be united *socially,* and not *politically.* So great a change of condition would have involved a thorough and radical revolution, both socially and politically,— a revolution much more radical, indeed, than that which followed the Declaration of Independence.

They who maintain that the ratification of the constitution effected so mighty a change, are bound to establish it by the most demonstrative proof. The presumption is strongly opposed to it. It has already been shown, that the authority of the convention which formed the constitution is clearly against it; and that the history of its ratification, instead of supplying evidence in its favor, furnishes strong testimony in opposition to it. To these, others may be added; and, among them, the presumption drawn from the history of these States, in all the stages of their existence down to the time of the ratification of the constitution. In all, they formed separate, and, as it respects each other, independent communities; and were ever remarkable for the tenacity with which they adhered to their rights as such. It constituted, during the whole period, one of the most striking traits in their character,—as a very brief sketch will show.

During their colonial condition, they formed distinct communities,—each with its separate charter and government,—and in no way connected with each other, except as dependent members of a common empire. Their first union amongst themselves was, in resistance to the encroachments of the parent country on their chartered rights,—when they adopted the title of,—"the United Colonies." Under that name they acted, until they declared their independence;—always, in their joint councils, voting and acting as separate and distinct communities;—and not in the aggregate, as composing one community or nation. They acted in the same character in declaring independence; by which act they passed from their dependent, colonial condition, into that of free and sovereign States. The declaration was made by delegates appointed by the several colonies, each for itself, and on its own authority. The vote making the declaration was taken by delegations, each counting one. The declaration was announced to be unanimous, not because every delegate voted for it, but because the majority of each delegation did; showing clearly, that the body itself, regarded it as the united act of the several colonies, and not the act of the whole as one community. To leave no doubt on a point so important, and in reference to which the several colonies were so tenacious, the declaration was made in the name, and by the authority of the people of the colonies, represented in Congress; and that was followed by declaring them to be,—"free and independent States." The act was, in fact, but a formal and solemn annunciation to the world, that the colonies had ceased to be dependent communities, and had become free and independent States; without involving any other change in their relations with each other, than those necessarily incident to a separation from the parent country. So far were they from supposing, or intending that it should have the effect of merging their existence, as separate communities, into one nation, that they had appointed a committee,—which was actually sitting, while the declaration was under discussion,—to prepare a plan of a confederacy of the States, preparatory to entering into their new condition. In fulfilment of their appointment, this committee prepared the draft of the articles of confederation and perpetual union, which afterwards was adopted by the governments of the several States. That it instituted a mere confederacy and union of the States has already been shown. That, in forming and assenting to it, the States were exceedingly jealous and watchful in delegating power, even to a confederacy; that they granted the powers delegated most reluctantly and sparingly; that several of them long stood out, under all the pressure of the revolutionary war, before they acceded to it; and that, during the interval which elapsed between its adoption and that of the present constitution, they evinced, under the most urgent necessity, the same reluctance and jealousy, in delegating power,—are facts which cannot be disputed.

To this may be added another circumstance of no little weight, drawn from the preliminary steps taken for the ratification of the constitution. The plan was laid, by the convention, before the Congress of the confederacy, for its consideration and action, as has been stated. It was the sole organ and representative of these States in their confederated character. By submitting it, the convention recognized and acknowledged its authority over it, as the organ of distinct, independent, and sovereign States. It had the right to dispose of it as it pleased; and, if it had thought proper, it might have defeated the plan by simply omitting to act on it. But it thought proper to act, and to adopt the course recommended by the convention;—which was, to submit it,—"to a convention of delegates, chosen in each State, by the people thereof, for their assent and adoption." All this was in strict accord with the federal character of the constitution, but wholly repugnant to the idea of its being national. It received the assent of the States in all the possible modes in which it could be obtained: first,—in their confederated character, through its only appropriate organ, the Congress; next, in their individual character, as separate States, through their respective State governments, to which the Congress referred it; and finally, in their high character of independent and sovereign communities, through a convention of the people, called in each State, by the authority of its government. The States acting in these various capacities, might, at every stage, have defeated it or not, at their option, by giving or withholding their consent.

With this weight of presumptive evidence, to use no stronger expression, in favor of its federal, in contradistinction to its national character, I shall next proceed to show, that the ratification of the constitution, instead of furnishing proof against, contains additional and conclusive evidence in its favor.

We are not left to conjecture, as to what was meant by the ratification of the constitution, or its effects. The expressions used by the conventions of the States, in ratifying it, and those used by the constitution in connection with it, afford ample means of ascertaining with accuracy, both its meaning and effect. The usual form of expression used by the former is:—"We, the delegates of the State," (naming the State,) "do, in behalf of the people of the State, assent to, and ratify the said constitution." All use, "ratify,"—and all, except North Carolina, use, "assent to." The delegates of that State use, "adopt," instead of "assent to;" a variance merely in the form of expression, without, in any degree, affecting the meaning. Ratification was, then, the act of the several States in their separate capacity. It was performed by delegates appointed expressly for the purpose. Each appointed its own delegates; and the delegates of each, acted in the name of, and for the State appointing them. Their act consisted in, "assenting to," or, what is the same thing, "adopting and ratifying" the constitution.

By turning to the seventh article of the constitution, and to the preamble, it will be found what was the effect of ratifying. The article expressly provides, that, "the ratification of the conventions of nine States, shall be sufficient for the establishment of this constitution, between the States so ratifying the same." The preamble of the constitution is in the following words;—"We, the people of the United States, in order to form a more perfect union, establish justice, insure domestic tranquillity, provide for the common defence, promote the general welfare, and secure the blessings of liberty to ourselves and our posterity, do ordain and establish this constitution for the United States of America." The effect, then, of its ratification was, to ordain and establish the constitution;—and, thereby, to make, what was before but a plan,—"The constitution of the United States of America." All this is clear.

It remains now to show, *by whom,* it was ordained and established; *for whom,* it was ordained and established; *for what,* it was ordained and established; and *over whom,* it was ordained and established. These will be considered in the order in which they stand.

Nothing more is necessary, in order to show by whom it was ordained and established, than to ascertain who are meant by,—"We, the people of the

United States;" for, by their authority, it was done. To this there can be but one answer:—it meant the people who ratified the instrument; for it was the act of ratification which ordained and established it. Who they were, admits of no doubt. The process preparatory to ratification, and the acts by which it was done, prove, beyond the possibility of a doubt, that it was ratified by the several States, through conventions of delegates, chosen in each State by the people thereof; and acting, each in the name and by the authority of its State: and, as all the States ratified it,—"We, the people of the United States,"—mean,—We, the people of the several States of the Union. The inference is irresistible. And when it is considered that the States of the Union were then members of the confederacy,—and that, by the express provision of one of its articles, "each State retains its sovereignty, freedom, and independence," the proof is demonstrative, that,—"We, the people of the United States of America," mean the people of the several States of the Union, acting as free, independent, and sovereign States. This strikingly confirms what has been already stated; to wit, that the convention which formed the constitution, meant the same thing by the terms,—"United States,"—and, "federal,"—when applied to the constitution or government;—and that the former, when used politically, always mean,—these States united as independent and sovereign communities.

Having shown, *by whom,* it was ordained, there will be no difficulty in determining, *for whom,* it was ordained. The preamble is explicit;—it was ordained and established for,—"The United States of America;" adding, "America," in conformity to the style of the then confederacy, and the Declaration of Independence. Assuming, then, that the "United States" bears the same meaning in the conclusion of the preamble, as it does in its commencement, (and no reason can be assigned why it should not,) it follows, necessarily, that the constitution was ordained and established *for* the people of the several States, *by* whom it was ordained and established.

Nor will there be any difficulty in showing, *for what,* it was ordained and established. The preamble enumerates the objects. They are,—"to form a more perfect union, to establish justice, insure domestic tranquillity, provide for the common defence, promote the general welfare, and secure the blessings of liberty to ourselves and our posterity." To effect these objects, they ordained and established, to use their own language,—"the constitution for the United States of America;"—clearly meaning by "for," that it was intended to be *their* constitution; and that the objects of ordaining and establishing it were, to perfect *their* union, to establish justice among *them*—to insure *their* domestic tranquillity, to provide for *their* common defence and general welfare, and to secure the blessings of liberty to *them* and *their* posterity. Taken all together, it follows, from what has been stated, that the constitution was ordained and established *by* the several States, as *distinct, sovereign communities;* and that it was ordained and established by them for *themselves*—for their common welfare and safety, as *distinct and sovereign communities.*

It remains to be shown, *over whom,* it was ordained and established. That it was not over *the several States,* is settled by the seventh article beyond controversy. It declares, that the ratification by nine States shall be sufficient to establish the constitution between the States so ratifying. "Between," necessarily excludes *"over;"*—as that which is *between* States cannot be *over* them. Reason itself, if the constitution had been silent, would have led, with equal certainty, to the same conclusion. For it was the several States, or, what is the same thing, their people, in their sovereign capacity, who ordained and established the constitution. But the authority which ordains and establishes, is higher than that which is ordained and established; and, of course, the latter must be subordinate to the former;—and cannot, therefore, be *over* it. "Between," always means more than over;—and implies in this case, that the authority which ordained and established the constitution, was the joint and united authority of the States ratifying it; and that, among the effects of their ratification, it became a contract between them; and, *as a compact,* binding on them;—but only as such. In that sense the term, "between," is appropriately applied. In no other, can it be. It was, doubtless, used in that sense in this instance; but the question still remains, *over whom,* was it ordained and established? After what has been stated, the answer may be readily given. It was *over the government* which it created, and all its functionaries in their official character,—and the individuals composing and inhabiting the several States, as far as they might come within the sphere of the powers delegated to the United States.

I have now shown, conclusively, by arguments drawn from the act of ratification, and the constitution itself, that the several States of the Union, acting in their confederated character, ordained and established the constitution; that they ordained and established it for themselves, in the same character; that they ordained and established it for their welfare and safety, in the like character; that they established it as a compact *between* them, and not as a constitution *over* them; and that, as a compact, they are parties to it, in the same character. I have thus established, conclusively, that these States, in ratifying the constitution, did not lose the confederated character which they possessed when they ratified it, as well as in all the preceding stages of their existence; but, on the contrary, still retained it to the full.

Those who oppose this conclusion, and maintain the national character of the government, rely, in support of their views, mainly on the expressions, "we, the people of the United States," used in the first part of the preamble; and, "do ordain and establish this constitution for the United States of America," used in its conclusion. Taken together, they insist, in the first place, that, "we, the people," mean, the people in their individual character, as forming a single community; and that, "the United States of America," designates them in their aggregate character, as the American people. In maintaining this construction, they rely on the omission to enumerate the States by name, after the word "people," (so as to make it read, "We, the people of New Hampshire, Massachusetts, &c.," as was done in the articles of the confederation, and, also, in signing the Declaration of Independence;)—and, instead of this, the simple use of the general term "United States."

However plausible this may appear, an explanation perfectly satisfactory may be given, why the expression, as it now stands, was used by the framers of the constitution; and why it should not receive the meaning attempted to be placed upon it. It is conceded that, if the enumeration of the States after the word, "people," had been made, the expression would have been freed from all ambiguity; and the inference and argument founded on the failure to do so, left without pretext or support. The omission is certainly striking, but it can be readily explained. It was made intentionally, and solely from the necessity of the case. The first draft of the constitution contained an enumeration of the States, by name, after the word "people;" but it became impossible to retain it after the adoption of the seventh and last article, which provided, that the ratification by nine States should be sufficient to establish the constitution as between *them;* and for the plain reason, that it was impossible to determine, whether all the States would ratify;—or, if any failed, which, and how many of the number; or, if nine should ratify, how to designate them. No alternative was thus left but to omit the enumeration, and to insert the "United States of America," in its place. And yet, an omission, so readily and so satisfactorily explained, has been seized on, as furnishing strong proof that the government was ordained and established by the American people, in the aggregate,—and is therefore national.

But the omission, of itself, would have caused no difficulty, had there not been connected with it a two-fold ambiguity in the expression as it now stands. The term *"United States,"* which always means, in constitutional language, the several States in their confederated character, means also, as has been shown, when applied geographically, the country occupied and possessed by them. While the term "people," has, in the English language, no plural, and is neces-

// sarily used in the singular number, even when applied to many communities or states confederated in a common union,—as is the case with the United States. Availing themselves of this double ambiguity, and the omission to enumerate the States by name, the advocates of the national theory of the government, assuming that, *"we, the people,"* meant individuals generally, and not people as forming States; and that *"United States"* was used in a geographical and not a political sense, made out an argument of some plausibility, in favor of the conclusion that, "we, the people of the United States of America," meant the aggregate population of the States regarded *en masse,* and not in their distinctive character as forming separate political communities. But in this gratuitous assumption, and the conclusion drawn from it, they overlooked the stubborn fact, that the very people who ordained and established the constitution, are identically the same who ratified it; for it was by the act of ratification alone, that it was ordained and established,—as has been conclusively shown. This fact, of itself, sweeps away every vestige of the argument drawn from the ambiguity of those terms, as used in the preamble.

They next rely, in support of their theory, on the expression,—"ordained and established this constitution." They admit that the constitution, in its incipient state, assumed the form of a compact; but contend that, "ordained and established," as applied to the constitution and government, are incompatible with the idea of compact; that, consequently, the instrument or plan lost its federative character when it was ordained and established as a constitution; and, thus, the States ceased to be parties to a compact, and members of a confederated union, and became fused into one common community, or nation, as subordinate and dependent divisions or corporations.

I do not deem it necessary to discuss the question whether there is any incompatibility between the terms,—"ordained and established,"—and that of "compact," on which the whole argument rests; although it would be no difficult task to show that it is a gratuitous assumption, without any foundation whatever for its support. It is sufficient for my purpose, to show, that the assumption is wholly inconsistent with the constitution itself;—as much so, as the conclusion drawn from it has been shown to be inconsistent with the opinion of the convention which formed it. Very little will be required, after what has been already stated, to establish what I propose.

That the constitution regards itself in the light of a compact, still existing between the States, after it was ordained and established; that it regards the union, then existing, as still existing; and the several States, of course, still members of it, in their original character of confederated States, is clear. Its seventh article, so often referred to, in connection with the arguments drawn from the preamble, sufficiently establishes all these points, without adducing others; except that which relates to the continuance of the union. To establish this, it will not be necessary to travel out of the preamble and the letter of the convention, laying the plan of the constitution before the Congress of the confederation. In enumerating the objects for which the constitution was ordained and established, the preamble places at the head of the rest, as its leading object,—"to form a more perfect union." So far, then, are the terms,—"ordained and established," from being incompatible with the union, or having the effect of destroying it, the constitution itself declares that it was intended, "to form a more perfect union." This, of itself, is sufficient to refute the assertion of their incompatibility. But it is proper here to remark, that it could not have been intended, by the expression in the preamble,—"to form a more perfect union,"—to declare, that the old was abolished, and a new and more perfect union established in its place: for we have the authority of the convention which formed the constitution, to prove that their object was to continue the then existing union. In their letter, laying it before Congress, they say,—"In all our deliberations on this subject, we kept steadily in our view, that which appears to us, the greatest interest of every true American, the consolidation of our union." "Our union," can refer to no other than the then existing union,— the old union of the confederacy, and of the revolutionary government which preceded it,—of which these States were confederated members. This must, of course, have been the union to which the framers referred in the preamble. It was this, accordingly, which the constitution intended to make more perfect; just as the confederacy made more perfect, that of the revolutionary government. Nor is there any thing in the term, "consolidation," used by the convention, calculated to weaken the conclusion. It is a strong expression; but as strong as it is, it certainly was not intended to imply the destruction of the union, as it is supposed to do by the advocates of a national government; for that would have been incompatible with the context, as well as with the continuance of the union,—which the sentence and the entire letter imply. Interpreted, then, in conjunction with the expression used in the preamble,—"to form a more perfect union,"—although it may more strongly intimate closeness of connection; it can imply nothing incompatible with the professed object of perfecting the union,—still less a meaning and effect wholly inconsistent with the nature of a confederated community. For to adopt the interpretation contended for, to its full extent, would be to *destroy* the union, and not to consolidate and perfect it.

※ "perfect" = fully functional

If we turn from the preamble and the ratifications, to the body of the constitution, we shall find that it furnishes most conclusive proof that the government is federal, and not national. I can discover nothing, in any portion of it, which gives the least countenance to the opposite conclusion. On the contrary, the instrument, in all its parts, repels it. It is, throughout, federal. It every where recognizes the existence of the States, and invokes their aid to carry its powers into execution. In one of the two houses of Congress, the members are elected by the legislatures of their respective States; and in the other, by the people of the several States, not as composing mere districts of one great community, but as distinct and independent communities. General Washington vetoed the first act apportioning the members of the House of Representatives among the several States, under the first census, expressly on the ground, that the act assumed as its basis, the former, and not the latter construction. The President and Vice-President are chosen by electors, appointed by their respective States; and, finally, the Judges are appointed by the President and the Senate; and, of course, as these are elected by the States, they are appointed through their agency.

But, however strong be the proofs of its federal character derived from this source, that portion which provides for the amendment of the constitution, furnishes, if possible, still stronger. It shows, conclusively, that the people of the several States still retain that supreme ultimate power, called sovereignty;—the power by which they ordained and established the constitution; and which can rightfully create, modify, amend, or abolish it, at its pleasure. Wherever this power resides, there the sovereignty is to be found. That it still continues to exist in the several States, in a modified form, is clearly shown by the fifth article of the constitution, which provides for its amendment. By its provisions, Congress may propose amendments, on its own authority, by the vote of two-thirds of both houses; or it may be compelled to call a convention to propose them, by two-thirds of the legislatures of the several States: but, in either case, they remain, when thus made, mere proposals of no validity, until adopted by three-fourths of the States, through their respective legislatures; or by conventions, called by them, for the purpose. Thus far, the several States, in ordaining and establishing the constitution, agreed, for their mutual convenience and advantage, to modify, by compact, their high sovereign power of creating and establishing constitutions, as far as it related to the constitution and government of the United States. I say, for their mutual convenience and advantage; for without the modification, it would have required the separate consent of all the States of the Union to alter or amend their constitutional compact; in like manner as it required the consent of all to establish it between them; and to obviate the almost insuperable difficulty of making such amendments as time and experience might prove to be necessary, by the unanimous consent of all, they agreed to make the modification. But that they did not intend, by this, to divest themselves of the high sovereign right, (a right which they still retain, notwithstanding the modification,) to change or abolish the present constitution and government at their pleasure, cannot be doubted. It is an acknowledged principle, that sovereigns may, by compact, modify or qualify the exercise of their power, without impairing their sovereignty; of which, the confederacy existing at the time, furnishes a striking illustration. It must reside, unimpaired and in its plentitude, somewhere. And if it do not reside in the people of the several States, in their confederated character, where,—so far as it relates to the constitution and government of the United States,—can it be found? Not, certainly, in the government; for, according to our theory, sovereignty resides in the people, and not in the government. That it cannot be found in the people, taken in the aggregate, as forming one community or nation, is equally certain. But as certain as it cannot, just so certain is it, that it must reside in the people of the several States: and if it reside in them at all, it must reside in them as separate and distinct communities; for it has been shown, that it does not reside in them in the aggregate, as forming one community or nation. These are the only aspects under which it is possible to regard the people; and, just as certain as it resides in them, in that character, so certain is it that ours is a federal, and not a national government.

The theory of the nationality of the government, is, in fact, founded on fiction. It is of recent origin. Few, even yet, venture to avow it to its full extent; while they entertain doctrines, which spring from, and must necessarily terminate in it. They admit that the people of the several States form separate, independent, and sovereign communities;—and that, to this extent, the constitution is federal; but beyond this, and to the extent of the delegated powers,—regarding them as forming one people or nation, they maintain that the constitution is national.

Now, unreasonable as is the theory that it is wholly national, this, if possible, is still more so; for the one, although against reason and recorded evidence, is possible; but the other, while equally against both, is absolutely impossible. It involves the absurdity of making the constitution federal in reference to a class of powers, which are expressly excluded from it; and, by consequence, from the compact itself, into which the several States entered when they established it. The term, "federal," implies a league,—and this, a compact between sovereign communities; and, of course, it is impossible for the States to be federal, in reference to powers expressly reserved to them in their character of separate States, and not included in the compact. If the States are national at all,—or, to express it more definitely,—if they form a NATION at all, it must be in reference to the delegated, and not the reserved powers. But it has already been established that, as to these, they have no such character—no such existence. It is, however, proper to remark, that while it is impossible for them to be federal, as to their reserved powers, they could not be federal without them. For had all the powers of government been delegated, the separate constitutions and governments of the several States would have been superseded and destroyed; and what is now called the constitution and government of the United States, would have become the sole constitution and government of the whole:—the effect of which, would have been to supersede and destroy the States themselves. The people respectively composing them, instead of constituting political communities, having appropriate organs to will and to act,—which is indispensable to the existence of a State,—would, in such case, be divested of all such organs; and, by consequence, reduced into an unorganized mass of individuals,—as far as related to the respective States,—and merged into one community or nation, having but one constitution and government as the organ, through which to will and to act. The idea, indeed, of a federal constitution and government, necessarily implies reserved and delegated powers,—powers reserved in part, to be exercised exclusively by the States in their original separate character;—and powers delegated, by mutual agreement, to be exercised jointly by a common council or government. And hence, consolidation and disunion are, equally, destructive of such government;—one by merging the States composing the Union into one community or nation; and the other, by resolving them into their original elements, as separate and disconnected States.

It is difficult to imagine how a doctrine so perfectly absurd, as that the States are federal as to the reserved, and national as to the delegated powers, could have originated; except through a misconception of the meaning of certain terms, sometimes used to designate the latter. They are sometimes called *granted* powers; and at others, are said to be powers *surrendered* by the States. When these expressions are used without reference to the fact, that all powers, under our system of government, are trust powers, they imply that the States have parted with such as are said to be granted or surrendered, absolutely and irrecoverably. The case is different when applied to them as trust powers. They them become identical, in their meaning, with delegated powers; for to grant a power in trust, is what is meant by delegating it. It is not, therefore, surprising, that they who do not bear in mind that all powers of government are, with us, trust powers, should conclude that the powers said to be granted and surrendered by the

States, are absolutely transferred from them to the government of the United States,—as is sometimes alleged,—or to the people as constituting one nation, as is more usually understood;—and, thence, to infer that the government is national to the extent of the granted powers.

But that such inference and conclusion are utterly unwarrantable,—that the powers in the constitution called granted powers, are, in fact, delegated powers,—powers granted in trust,—and not absolutely transferred,—we have, in addition to the reasons just stated, the clear and decisive authority of the constitution itself. Its tenth amended article provides that "the powers not delegated to the United States by the constitution, nor prohibited by it to the States, are reserved to the States respectively, or to the people."

In order to understand the full force of this provision, it is necessary to state that this is one of the amended articles, adopted at the recommendation of several of the conventions of the States, contemporaneously with the ratification of the constitution,—in order to supply what were thought to be its defects;—and to guard against misconceptions of its meaning. It is admitted, that its principal object was to prevent the reserved from being drawn within the sphere of the granted powers, by the force of construction,—a danger, which, at the time, excited great, and, as experience has proved, just apprehension. But in guarding against this danger, care was also taken to guard against others,—and among them, against mistakes, as to whom powers were granted, and to whom they were reserved. The former was done by using the expression, "the powers not delegated to the United States," which, by necessary implication means, that the powers granted are delegated to them in their confederated character;—and the latter, by the remaining portion of the article, which provides that such powers "are reserved to the States respectively, or to the people;"—meaning clearly by, "respectively," that the reservation was to the several States and people in their separate character, and not to the whole, as forming one people or nation. They thus repudiate nationality, applied either to the delegated or to reserved powers.

But it may be asked,—why was the reservation made both to the States and to the people? The answer is to be found in the fact, that, what are called, "reserved powers," in the constitution of the United States, include all powers not delegated to Congress by it,—or prohibited by it to the States. The powers thus designated are divided into two distinct classes;—those delegated by the people of the several States to their separate State governments, and those which they still retain,—not having delegated them to either government. Among them is included the high sovereign power, by which they ordained and established both; and by which they can modify, change or abolish them at pleasure. This, with others not delegated, are those which are reserved to the people of the several States respectively.

But the article in its precaution, goes further;—and takes care to guard against the term, "granted," used in the first article and first section of the constitution, which provides that, "all legislative powers herein *granted,* shall be vested in a Congress of the United States;"—as well as against other terms of like import used in other parts of the instrument. It guarded against it, indirectly, by substituting, "delegated," in the place of "granted;"—and instead of declaring that the powers not "granted," are reserved, it declares that the powers not "delegated," are reserved. Both terms,—"granted," used in the constitution as it came from its framers, and "delegated," used in the amendments,—evidently refer to the same class of powers; and no reason can be assigned, why the amendment substituted "delegated," in the place of "granted," but to free it from its ambiguity, and to provide against misconstruction.

It is only by considering the granted powers, in their true character of trust or delegated powers, that all the various parts of our complicated system of government can be harmonized and explained. Thus regarded, it will be easy to perceive how the people of the several States could grant certain powers to a joint,—or, as its framers called it,—a general government, in trust, to be exercised for their common benefit, without an absolute surrender of them;—or without impairing their independence and sovereignty. Regarding them in the opposite light, as powers absolutely surrendered and irrevocably transferred, inexplicable difficulties present themselves. Among the first, is that which springs from the idea of divided sovereignty; involving the perplexing question,—how the people of the several States can be partly sovereign, and partly, *not* sovereign,—sovereign as to the reserved,—and not sovereign, as to the delegated powers? There is no difficulty in understanding how powers, appertaining to sovereignty, may be divided; and *the exercise* of one portion delegated to one set of agents, and another portion to another: or how sovereignty may be vested in one man, or in a few, or in many. But how sovereignty itself—the supreme power—can be divided,—how the people of the several States can be partly sovereign, and partly *not* sovereign—partly supreme, and partly *not* supreme, it is impossible to conceive. Sovereignty is an entire thing;—to divide, is,—to destroy it.

But suppose this difficulty surmounted;—another not less perplexing remains. If sovereignty be surrendered and transferred, in part or entirely, by the several States, it must be transferred to somebody; and the question is, to whom? Not, certainly, to the government,—as has been thoughtlessly asserted by some; for that would subvert the fundamental principle of our system,—that sovereignty resides in the people. But if not to the government, it must be transferred,—if at all,—to the people, regarded in the aggregate, as a nation. But this is opposed, not only by a force of reason which cannot be resisted, but by the preamble and tenth amended article of the constitution, as has just been shown. If then it be transferred neither to the one nor the other, it cannot be transferred at all; as it is impossible to conceive to whom else the transfer could have been made. It must, therefore, and of course, remain unsurrendered and unimpaired in the people of the several States;—to whom, it is admitted, it appertained when the constitution was adopted.

Having now established that the powers delegated to the United States, were delegated to them in their confederated character, it remains to be explained in what sense they were thus delegated. The constitution here, as in almost all cases, where it is fairly interpreted, furnishes the explanation necessary to expel doubt. Its first article, already cited, affords it in this case. It declares that "all legislative power herein granted (delegated), shall be vested in the Congress of the United States;" that is, in the Congress for the time being. It also declares, that "the executive power shall be vested in the President of the United States;"—and that "the judicial power shall be vested in a Supreme Court, and such inferior courts, as Congress may, from time to time, ordain and establish." They are then delegated to the United States, by vesting them in the respective departments of the government, to which they appropriately belong; to be exercised by the government of the United States, as their joint agent and representative, in their confederated character. It is, indeed, difficult to conceive how else it could be delegated to them;—or in what other way they could mutually participate in the exercise of the powers delegated. It has, indeed, been construed by some to mean, that each State, reciprocally and mutually, delegated to each other, the portion of its sovereignty embracing the delegated powers. But besides the difficulty of a divided sovereignty, which it would involve, the expression, "delegated powers," repels that construction. If, however, there should still remain a doubt, the articles of confederation would furnish conclusive proof of the truth of that construction which I have placed upon the constitution; and, also, that not a particle of sovereignty was intended to be transferred, by delegating the powers conferred on the different departments of the government of the United States. I refer to its second article,—so often referred to already. It declares, as will be remembered, that,—"each State retains its sovereignty, freedom, and independence; and every power, jurisdiction, and right, which is not, by this confederation, expressly delegated to the United States in Congress assembled." The powers delegated by it were, therefore, delegated, like those of the present constitution, to the *United States*. The only difference is, that "the United States," is followed, in the articles of confederation, by the words,—"in Congress assembled,"—which are omitted in the parallel expression in the amended article of the constitution. But this omission is supplied in it, by the first article, and by others of a similar character, already referred to; and by vesting the powers delegated to the United States, in the respective appropriate departments of the government. The reason of the difference is plain. The constitution could not vest them in Congress alone;—because there were portions of the delegated powers vested also in the other departments of the government: while the articles of confederation could, with propriety, vest them in Congress;—as it was the sole representative of the confederacy. Nor could it vest them in the government of the United States; for that would imply that the powers were vested in the whole, as a unit;—and not, as the fact is, in its separate departments. The constitution, therefore, in borrowing this provision from the articles of confederation, adopted the mode best calculated to express the same thing that was expressed in the latter, by the words,—"in Congress assembled." That the articles of confederation, in delegating powers to the United States, did not intend to declare that the several States had parted with any portion of their sovereignty, is placed beyond doubt by the declaration contained in them, that,—"each State retains its sovereignty, freedom, and independence;" and it may be fairly inferred, that the framers of the constitution, in borrowing this expression, did not design that it should bear a different interpretation.

If it be possible still to doubt that the several States retained their sovereignty and independence unimpaired, strong additional arguments might be drawn from various other portions of the instrument;—especially from the third article, section third, which declares, that,—"treason against the United States, shall consist only in levying war against them or in adhering to their enemies, giving them aid and comfort." It might be easily shown that,—"the United States,"—mean here,—as they do everywhere in the constitution,—the several States in their confederated character;—that treason against them, is treason against their joint sovereignty;—and, of course, as much treason against each State, as the act would be against any one of them, in its individual and separate character. But I forbear. Enough has already been said to place the question beyond controversy.

Having now established that the constitution is federal throughout, in contradistinction to national; and that the several States still retain their sovereignty and independence unimpaired, one would suppose that the conclusion would follow, irresistibly, in the judgment of all, that the government is also federal. But such is not the case. There are those, who admit the *constitution* to be entirely federal, but insist that the *government* is partly federal, and partly national. They rest their opinion on the authority of the "Federalist." That celebrated work comes to this conclusion, after explicitly admitting that the constitution was ratified and adopted by the people of the several States, and not by them as individuals composing one entire nation;—that the act establishing the constitution is, itself, a federal, and not a national act;—that it resulted neither from the act of a majority of the people of the Union, nor from a majority of the States; but from the unanimous assent of the several States;—differing no otherwise from their ordinary assent than as being given, not by their legislatures, but by the people themselves;—that they are parties to it;—that each State, in ratifying it, was considered as a sovereign body, independent of all others, and is bound only by its own voluntary act;—that, in consequence, the constitution itself is federal and not national;—that, if it had been formed by the people as one nation or community, the will of the majority of the whole people of the Union would have bound the minority;—that the idea of a national government involves in it, not only authority over individual citizens, but an indefinite supremacy over all persons and things, so far as they are objects of lawful government;—that among the people consolidated into one nation, this supremacy is completely vested in the government; that State governments, and all local authorities, are subordinate to it, and may be controlled, directed, or abolished by it at pleasure;—and, finally, that the States are regarded, by the constitution, as distinct, independent, and sovereign.*

How strange, after all these admissions, is the conclusion that the government is partly federal and partly national! It is the constitution which determines the character of the government. It is impossible to conceive how the constitution can be *exclusively* federal, (as it is admitted, and has been clearly proved to be,) and the government *partly* federal and *partly* national. It would be just as easy to conceive how a constitution can be exclusively monarchical, and the government partly monarchical, and partly aristocratic or popular; and *vice versa*. Monarchy is not more strongly distinguished from either, than a *federal* is from a *national* government. Indeed, these are even more adverse to each other; for the other forms may be blended in the constitution and the government; while, as has been shown, and as is indirectly admitted by the work referred to, the one

---

*See Federalist, Nos. 39 and 40.

of these so excludes the other, that it is impossible to blend them in the same constitution, and, of course, in the same government. I say, indirectly admitted, for it admits, that a federal government is one to which States are parties, in their distinct, independent, and sovereign character; and that,—"the idea of a national government involves in it, not only an authority over individual citizens, but an indefinite supremacy over all persons and things, so far as they are objects of lawful government;"—and, "that it is one, in which all local authorities are subordinate to the supreme, and may be controlled, directed, and abolished by it at pleasure." How, then, is it possible for institutions, admitted to be so utterly repugnant in their nature as to be directly destructive of each other, to be so blended as to form a government partly federal and partly national? What can be more contradictious? This, of itself, is sufficient to destroy the authority of the work on this point,—as celebrated as it is,—without showing, as might be done, that the admissions it makes throughout, are, in like manner, in direct contradiction to the conclusions, to which it comes.

But, strange as such a conclusion is, after such admissions, it is not more strange than the reasons assigned for it. The first, and leading one,—that on which it mainly relies,—is drawn from the source whence, as it alleges, the powers of the government are derived. It states, that the House of Representatives will derive its powers from the people of "America;" and adds, by way of confirmation, "The people will be represented in the same proportion, and on the same principle, as they are in the legislatures of each particular State;"—and hence concludes that it would be national and not federal. Is the fact so? Does the House of Representatives really derive its powers from the people of America?—that is, from the people in the aggregate, as forming one nation; for such must be the meaning,—to give the least force, or even plausibility, to the assertion. Is it not a fundamental principle, and universally admitted—admitted even by the authors themselves,—that all the powers of the government are derived from the constitution,—including those of the House of Representatives, as well as others? And does not this celebrated work admit,—most explicitly, and in the fullest manner,—that the constitution derives all its powers and authority from the people of the several States, acting, each for itself, in their independent and sovereign character as States? that they still retain the same character, and, as such, are parties to it? and that it is a federal, and not a national, constitution? How, then, can it assert, in the face of such admissions, that the House of Representatives derives its authority from the American people, in the aggregate, as forming one people or nation? To give color to the assertion, it affirms, that the people will be represented on the same principle, and in the same proportion, as they are in the legislature of each particular State. Are either of these propositions true? On the contrary, is it not universally known and admitted, that they are represented in the legislature of every State of the Union, as mere individuals,—and, by election districts, entirely subordinate to the government of the State;—while the members of the House of Representatives are elected—be the mode of election what it may—as delegates of the several States, in their distinct, independent, and sovereign character, as members of the Union,—and not as delegates from the States, considered as mere election districts? It was on this ground, as has been stated, that President Washington vetoed the act to apportion the members, under the first census, among the several States; and his opinion has, ever since, been acquiesced in.

Neither is it true that the people of each State are represented in the House of Representatives in the same proportion as in their respective legislatures. On the contrary, they are represented in the former according to one uniform ratio or proportion among the several States, fixed by the constitution itself;* while in each State legislature, the ratio, fixed by its separate State constitution, is different in different States;—and in scarcely any are they represented in the same proportion in the legislature, as in the House of Representatives. The only point of uniformity in this respect is, that "the electors of the House of Representatives shall have the qualifications requisite for electors of the most numerous branch of the State legislatures;"† a rule which favors the federal, and not the national character of the government.

The authors of the work conclude, on the same affirmation,—and by a similar course of reasoning,—that the executive department of the government is partly national, and partly federal:—*federal,* so far as the number of electors of each State, in the election of President, depends on its Senatorial representation;—and so far as the final election, (when no choice is made by the electoral college,) depends on the House of Representatives,—because they vote and count by States:—and *national,* so far as the number of its electors depends on its representation in the Lower House. As the argument in support of this proposition is the same as that relied on to prove that the House of Representatives is national, I shall pass it by with a single remark.—It overlooks the fact that the electors, by an express provision of the constitution, are appointed by the several States;‡ and, of course, derive their powers from them. It would,

---

*1st Art, 2d Sec. of the Constitution.
†1st Art. 2d Sec. of the Con.
‡2d Art. 1st Sec. of the Con.

therefore, seem, according to their course of reasoning, that the executive department, when the election is made by the colleges, ought to be regarded as *federal;*—while, on the other hand, when it is made by the House of Representatives, in the event of a failure on the part of the electors to make a choice, it ought to be regarded as *national,* and not federal, as they contend. It would, indeed, seem to involve a strange confusion of ideas to make the same department partly federal and partly national, on such a process of reasoning. It indicates a deep and radical error somewhere in the conception of the able authors of the work, in reference to a question the most vital that can arise under our system of government.

The next reason assigned is, that the government will operate on individuals composing the several States, and not on the States themselves. This, however, is very little relied on. It admits that even a confederacy may operate on individuals without losing its character as such,—and cites the articles of confederation in illustration; and it might have added, that mere treaties, in some instances, operate in the same way. It is readily conceded that one of the strongest characteristics of a confederacy is, that it usually operates on the states or communities which compose it, in their corporate capacity. When it operates on individuals, it departs, to that extent, from its appropriate sphere. But this is not the case with a federal government;—as will be shown when I come to draw the line of distinction between it and a confederacy. The argument, then, might be appropriate to prove that the government is not a confederacy,—but not that it is a national government.

It next relies on the amending power to prove that it is partly national and partly federal. It states that,—"were it wholly national, the supreme and ultimate authority would reside in a majority of the people of the whole Union; and this authority would be competent, at all times, like that of a majority of every national society, to alter or abolish its established government. Were it wholly federal, on the other hand, the concurrence of each State in the Union would be essential to any alteration, that would be binding on all." It is remarkable how often this celebrated work changes its ground, as to what constitutes a national, and what a federal government;—and this, too, after defining them in the clearest and most precise manner. It tells us, in this instance, that were the government wholly national,—the supreme and ultimate authority would reside in the people of the Union; and, of course, such a government must derive its authority from that source. It tells us, elsewhere, that a federal government is one, to which the States, in their distinct, independent and sovereign character, are parties;—and, of course, such a government must derive its authority from them as its source. A government, then, to be partly one, and partly the other, ought, accordingly, to derive its authority partly from the one, and partly from the other; and no government could be so, which did not:—and yet we are told, at one time, that the constitution is federal, because it derived its authority, neither from the majority of the people of the Union, nor a majority of the States;—implying, of course, that a government, which derived its authority from a majority of the States, would be national; as well as that which derived it from a majority of the people:—and, at another, that the election of the President by the House of Representatives would be a federal act;—although the House, itself, is national, because it derived its authority from the American people. And now we are told, that the amending power is partly national, because three fourths of the States, voting as States, without regard to population, can, instead of the whole, amend the constitution; although the vote of a majority of the House of Representatives, taken by States, made the election of the President, to that extent, federal. If we turn from this confusion of ideas, to its own clear conceptions of what makes a federal, and what a national government, nothing is more evident than that the amending power is not derived from, nor exercised under the authority of the people of the Union, regarded in the aggregate,—but from the several States, in their original, distinct and sovereign character; and that it is but a modification of the original creating power, by which the constitution was ordained and established,—and which required the consent of each State to make it a party to it;—and not a negation or inhibition of that power,—as has been shown. In support of these views, it endeavors to show, by reasons equally unsatisfactory and inconclusive, that the object of the convention which framed the constitution was, to establish, "a firm *national* government." To ascertain the powers and objects of the convention, reference ought to be made, one would suppose, to the commissions given to their respective delegates, by the several States, which were represented in it. If that had been done, it would have been found that no State gave the slightest authority to its delegates to form a national government, or made the least allusion to such government as one of its objects. The word, *National,* is not even used in any one of the commissions. On the contrary, they designate the objects to be, to revise the federal constitution, and to make it adequate to the exigencies of the Union. But, instead of to these, the authors of this work resort to the act of Congress referring the proposition for calling a convention, to the several States, in conformity with the recommendation of the Annapolis convention;—which, of itself, could give no authority. And further,—even in this reference, they obviously rely, rather on the preamble of the act, than on the resolution adopted by Congress, submitting the proposition to the State governments. The preamble and resolution are in the following words:—"Whereas, there is a provision, in the articles of confederation and perpetual union, for making alterations therein, by the assent of a Congress of the United States and of the legislatures of the several States,—and whereas, experience has evinced that there are defects in the present confederation,—as a mean to the remedy of which, several of the States, and particularly the State of New-York, by express instruction to their delegates in Congress, have suggested a convention for the purpose expressed in the following resolution, and such convention appearing to be the most probable mean of establishing, in the States, a firm National Government,

Resolved, That, in the opinion of Congress, it is expedient that, on the second Monday of May next, a convention of delegates, who shall have been appointed by the several States, be held in Philadelphia, for the *sole* and *express* purpose of *revising the articles of confederation;* and reporting to Congress and the several legislatures, such *alterations* and *provisions therein* as shall render the *federal constitution* adequate to the exigencies of the government and the preservation of THE UNION."

Now, assuming that the mere opinion of Congress, and not the commissions of the delegates from the several States, ought to determine the object of the convention,—is it not manifest, that it is clearly in favor, not of establishing a firm national government, but of simply revising the articles of confederation for the purposes specified? Can any expression be more explicit than the declaration contained in the resolution, that the convention shall be held, "for the sole and express purpose of revising the articles of confederation?" If to this it be added, that the commissions of the delegates of the several States, accord with the resolution, there can be no doubt that the real object of the convention was,—(to use the language of the resolution,)—"to render the federal constitution adequate to the exigencies of the government and the preservation of the Union;" and not to establish a national constitution and government in its place:—and, that such was the impression of the convention itself, the fact, (admitted by the work,) that they did establish a federal, and not a national constitution, conclusively proves.

How the distinguished and patriotic authors of this celebrated work fell,—against their own clear and explicit admissions,—into an error so radical and dangerous,—one which has contributed, more than all others combined, to cast a mist over our system of government, and to confound and lead astray the minds of the community as to a true conception of its real character, cannot be accounted for, without adverting to their history and opinions as connected with the formation of the constitution. The two principal writers were prominent members of the convention; and leaders, in that body, of the party, which supported the plan for a national government. The other, although not a member, is known to have belonged to the same party. They all acquiesced in the decision, which overruled their favorite plan, and determined, patriotically, to give that adopted by the convention, a fair trial; without, however, surrendering their preference for their own scheme of a national government. It was in this state of mind, which could not fail to exercise a strong influence over their judgments, that they wrote the Federalist: and, on all questions connected with the character of the government, due allowance should be made for the force of the bias, under which their opinions were formed.

From all that has been stated, the inference follows, irresistibly, that the government is a federal, in contradistinction to a national government;—a government formed by the States; ordained and established by the States, and for the States;—without any participation or agency whatever, on the part of the people, regarded in the aggregate as forming a nation; that it is throughout, in whole, and in every part, simply and purely federal,—"the federal government of these States,"—as is accurately and concisely expressed by General Washington, the organ of the convention, in his letter laying it before the old Congress;—words carefully selected, and with a full and accurate knowledge of their import. There is, indeed, no such community, *politically* speaking, as the people of the United States, regarded in the light of, and as constituting one people or nation. There never has been any such, in any stage of their existence; and, of course, they neither could, nor ever can exercise any agency,—or have any participation, in the formation of our system of government, or its administration. In all its parts,—including the federal as well as the separate State governments, it emanated from the same source,—the people of the several States. The whole, taken together, form a federal community;—a community composed of States united by a political compact;—and not a nation composed of individuals united by, what is called, a social compact.

I shall next proceed to show that it is federal, in contradistinction to a confederacy.

It differs and agrees, but in opposite respects, with a national government, and a confederacy. It differs from the former, inasmuch as it has, for its basis, a confederacy, and not a nation; and agrees with it in being a government: while it agrees with the latter, to the extent of having a confederacy for its basis, and differs from it, inasmuch as the powers delegated to it are carried into execution by a government,—and not by a mere congress of delegates, as is the case in a confederacy. To be more full and explicit;—a federal government, though based on a confederacy, is, to the extent of the powers delegated, as much a government as a national government itself. It possesses, to this extent, all the authorities possessed by the latter, and as fully and perfectly. The case is different with a confederacy; for, although it is sometimes called a *government*,—its Congress, or Council, or the body representing it, by whatever name it may be called, is much more nearly allied to an assembly of diplomatists, convened to deliberate and determine how a league or treaty between their several sovereigns, for certain defined purposes, shall be carried into execution; leaving to the parties themselves, to furnish their quota of means, and to co-operate in carrying out what may have been determined on. Such was the character of the Congress of our confederacy; and such, substantially, was that of similar bodies in all confederated communities, which preceded our present government. Our system is the first that ever substituted a *government* in lieu of such bodies. This, in fact, constitutes its peculiar characteristic. It is new, peculiar, and unprecedented.

In asserting that such is the difference between our present government and the confederacy, which it superseded, I am supported by the authority of the convention which framed the constitution. It is to be found in the second paragraph of their letter, already cited. After stating the great extent of powers, which it was deemed necessary to delegate to the United States,—or as they expressed it,—"the general government of the Union,"—the paragraph concludes in the following words: "But the impropriety of delegating such extensive trusts to one body of men, (the Congress of the confederacy,) is evident; and hence results the necessity of a different organization." This "different organization," consisted in substituting a *government* in place of the Congress of the confederation; and was, in fact, the great and essential change made by the convention. All others were, relatively, of little importance,—consisting rather in the modification of its language, and the mode of executing its powers, made necessary by it,—than in the powers themselves. The restrictions and limitations imposed on the powers delegated, and on the several States, are much the same in both. The change, though the only essential one, was, of itself, important, viewed in relation to the structure of the system; but it was much more so, when considered in its consequences as necessarily implying and involving others of great magnitude; as I shall next proceed to show.

It involved, in the first place, an important change in the source whence it became necessary to derive the delegated powers, and the authority by which the instrument delegating them should be ratified. Those of the confederacy were derived from the governments of the several States. They delegated them, and ratified the instrument by which they were delegated, through their representatives in Congress assembled, and duly authorized for the purpose. It was, then, their work throughout; and their powers were fully competent to it. They possessed, as a confederate council, the power of making compacts and treaties, and of constituting the necessary agency to superintend their execution. The articles of confederation and union constituted, indeed, a solemn league or compact, entered into for the purposes specified; and Congress was but the joint agent or representative appointed to superintend its execution. But the governments of the several States could go no further, and were wholly deficient in the requisite power to form a constitution and government in their stead. That could only be done by the sovereign power; and that power, according to the fundamental principles of our system, resides, not in the government, but exclusively in the people,—who, with us, mean the people of the several States;—and hence, the powers delegated to the government had to be derived from them,—and the constitution to be ratified, and ordained and established by them. How this was done has already been fully explained.

It involved, in the next place, an important change in the character of the system. It had previously been, in reality, a league between the governments of the several States; or to express it more fully and accurately, between the States, *through the organs of their respective governments;* but it became a union, in consequence of being ordained and established between the people of the several States, by themselves, and for themselves, in their character of sovereign and independent communities. It was this important change which (to use the language of the preamble of the constitution) "formed a more perfect union." It, in fact, perfected it. It could not be extended further, or be made more intimate. To have gone a step beyond, would have been to consolidate the *States,* and not the Union;—and thereby to have destroyed the latter.

It involved another change, growing out of the division of the powers of government, between the United States and the separate States;—requiring that those delegated to the former should be carefully enumerated and specified, in order to prevent collision between them and the powers reserved to the several States respectively. There was no necessity for such great caution under the confederacy, as its Congress could exercise little power, except through the States, and with their co-operation. Hence the care, circumspection and precision, with which the grants of powers are made in the one, and the comparatively loose, general, and more indefinite manner in which they are made in the other.

It involved another, intimately connected with the preceding, and of great importance. It entirely changed the relation which the separate governments of the States sustained to the body, which represented them in their confederated character, under the confederacy; for this was essentially different from that which they now sustain to the government of the United States, their present representative. The governments of the States sustained, to the former, the relation of superior to subordinate—of the creator to the creature; while they now sustain, to the latter, the relation of equals and co-ordinates. Both governments,—that of the United States and those of the separate States, derive their powers from the same source, and were ordained and established by the same authority;—the only difference being, that in ordaining and establishing the one, the people of the several States acted with concert or mutual understanding;—while, in ordaining and establishing the others, the people of each State acted separately, and without concert or mutual understanding;—as has been fully explained. Deriving their respective powers, then, from the same source, and being ordained and established by the same authority,—the two governments, State and Federal, must, of necessity, be equal in their respective spheres; and both being ordained and established by the people of the States, respectively,—each for itself, and by its own separate authority,—the constitution and government of the United States must, of necessity, be the constitution and government of each;—as much so as its own separate and individual constitution and government; and, therefore, they must stand, in each State, in the relation of co-ordinate constitutions and governments. It is on this ground only, that the former is the constitution and government of all the States:—not because it is the constitution and government of the whole, considered in the aggregate as constituting one nation, but because it is the constitution and government of each respectively: for to suppose that they are the constitution and government of *each,* because of the *whole,* would be to assume, what is not true, that they were ordained and established by the American people in the aggregate, as forming one nation. This would be to reduce the several States to subordinate and local divisions; and to convert their separate constitutions and governments into mere charters and subordinate corporations: when, in truth and fact, they are equals and co-ordinates.

It, finally, involved a great change in the manner of carrying into execution the delegated powers. As a government, it was necessary to clothe it with the attribute of deciding, in the first instance, on the extent of its powers,—and of acting on individuals, directly, in carrying them into execution; instead of appealing to the agency of the governments of the States,—as was the case with the Congress of the confederacy.

Such are the essential distinctions between a federal government and a confederacy;—and such, in part, the important changes necessarily involved, in substituting a government, in the place of the Congress of the confederacy.

It now remains to be shown, that the government is a republic;—a republic,—or, (if the expression be preferred,) a constitutional democracy, in contradistinction to an absolute democracy.

It is not an uncommon impression, that the government of the United States is a government based simply on population; that numbers are its only element, and a numerical majority its only controlling power. In brief, that it is an absolute democracy. No opinion can be more erroneous. So far from being true, it is, in all the aspects in which it can be regarded, pre-eminently a government of the concurrent majority; with an organization, more complex and refined, indeed, but far better calculated to express the sense of the whole, (in the only mode by which this can be fully and truly done,—to wit, by ascertaining the sense of all its parts,) than any government ever formed, ancient or modern. Instead of population, mere numbers, being the sole element, the numerical majority is, strictly speaking, excluded, even as one of its elements; as I shall proceed to establish, by an appeal to figures; beginning with the formation of the constitution, regarded as the fundamental law which ordained and established the government; and closing with the organization of the government itself, regarded as the agent or trustee to carry its powers into effect.

I shall pass by the Annapolis convention, on whose application, the convention which framed the constitution, was called; because it was a partial and informal meeting of delegates from a few States; and commence with the Congress of the confederation, by whom it was authoritatively called. That Congress derived its authority from the articles of confederation; and these, from the unanimous agreement of all the States;—and not from the numerical majority, either of the several States, or of their population. It voted, as has been stated, by delegations; each counting one. A majority of each delegation, with a few important exceptions, decided the vote of its respective State. Each State, without regard to population, had thus an equal vote. The confederacy consisted of thirteen States; and, of course, it was in the power of any seven of the smallest, as well as the largest, to defeat the call of the convention; and, by consequence, the formation of the constitution.

By the first census, taken in 1790—three years after the call—the population of the United States amounted to 3,394,563, estimated in federal numbers. Assuming this to have been the whole amount of its population at the time of the call, (which can cause no material error,) the population of the seven smallest

States was 959,801; or less than one third of the whole: so that, less than one third of the population could have defeated the call of the convention.

The convention voted, in like manner, by States; and it required the votes of a majority of the delegations present, to adopt the measure. There were twelve States represented,—Rhode Island being absent;—so that the votes of seven delegations were required; and, of course, less than one third of the population of the whole, could have defeated the formation of the constitution.

The plan, when adopted by the convention, had again to be submitted to Congress,—and to receive its sanction, before it could be submitted to the several States for their approval,—a necessary preliminary to its final reference to the conventions of the people of the several States for their ratification. It had thus, of course, to pass again the ordeal of Congress; when the delegations of seven of the smallest States, representing less than one third of the population, could again have defeated, by refusing to submit it for their consideration. And, stronger still;—when submitted, it required, by an express provision, the concurrence of nine of the thirteen, to establish it, between the States ratifying it; which put it in the power of any four States, the smallest as well as the largest, to reject it. The four smallest, to wit: Delaware, Rhode Island, Georgia, and New Hampshire, contained, by the census of 1790, a federal population of only 336,948—but a little more than one eleventh of the whole: but, as inconsiderable as was their population, they could have defeated it, by preventing its ratification. It thus appears, that the numerical majority of the population, had no agency whatever in the process of forming and adopting the constitution; and that neither this, nor a majority of the States, constituted an element in its ratification and adoption.

In the provision for its amendment, it prescribes, as has been stated, two modes:—one, by two thirds of both houses of Congress; and the other, by a convention of delegates from the States, called by Congress, on the application of two thirds of their respective legislatures. But, in neither case can the proposed amendment become a part of the constitution, unless ratified by the legislatures of three fourths of the States, or by conventions of the people of three fourths,— as Congress may prescribe; so that, in the one, it requires the consent of two thirds of the States to propose amendments,—and, in both cases, of three fourths to adopt and ratify them, before they can become a part of the constitution. As there are, at present, thirty States in the Union, it will take twenty to propose, and, of course, would require but eleven to defeat, a proposition to amend the constitution; or, nineteen votes in the Senate,—if it should originate in Congress,—and the votes of eleven legislatures, if it should be to call a convention. By the census of 1840, the federal population of all the States,—including the three, which were then territories, but which have since become States,—was 16,077,604. To this add Texas, since admitted, say 110,000;—making the aggregate, 16,187,604. Of this amount, the eleven smallest States (Vermont being the largest of the number) contained a federal population of but 1,638,521: and yet they can prevent the other nineteen States, with a federal population of 14,549,082, from even proposing amendments to the constitution: while the twenty smallest, (of which Maine is the largest,) with a federal population of 3,526,811, can compel Congress to call a convention to propose amendments, against the united votes of the other ten, with a federal population of 12,660,793. Thus, while less than one eighth of the population, may, in the one case, prevent the adoption of a proposition to amend the constitution,—less than one fourth can, in the other, adopt it.

But, striking as are these results, the process, when examined with reference to the ratification of proposals to amend, will present others still more so. Here the consent of three fourths of the States is required; which, with the present number, would make the concurrence of twenty-three States necessary to give effect to the act of ratification; and, of course, puts it in the power of any eight States to defeat a proposal to amend. The federal population of the eight smallest is but 776,969; and yet, small as this is, they can prevent amendments, against the united votes of the other twenty-two, with a federal population of 15,410,635; or nearly twenty times their number. But while so small a portion of the entire population can prevent an amendment, twenty-three of the smallest States,—with a federal population of only 7,254,400,—can amend the constitution, against the united votes of the other seven, with a federal population of 8,933,204. So that a numerical minority of the population can amend the constitution, against a decided numerical majority; when, at the same time, one nineteenth of the population can prevent the other eighteen nineteenths from amending it. And more than this: any one State,—Delaware, for instance, with a federal population of only 77,043,—can prevent the other twenty-nine States, with a federal population of 16,110,561, from so amending the constitution as to deprive the States of an equality of representation in the Senate. To complete the picture:—Sixteen of the smallest States,—that is, a majority of them, with a population of only 3,411,672,—a little more than one fifth of the whole,—can, in effect, destroy the government and dissolve the Union, by simply declining to appoint Senators; against the united voice of the other fourteen States, with a population of 12,775,932;—being but little less than four fifths of the whole.

These results, resting on calculations, which exclude doubt, incontestably prove,—not only that the authority which formed, ratified, and even amended the constitution, regulates entirely the numerical majority, as one of its elements,—but furnish additional and conclusive proof, if additional were needed, that ours is a federal government;—a government made by the several States; and that States, and not individuals, are its constituents. The States, throughout, in forming, ratifying and amending the constitution, act as equals, without reference to population.

Regarding the Government, apart from the Constitution, and simply as the trustee or agent to carry its powers into execution, the case is somewhat different. It is composed of two elements: One, the States, regarded in their corporate character,—and the other, their representative population,—estimated in, what is called, "federal numbers;"—which is ascertained, "by adding to the whole number of free persons, including those bound to service for a term of years,—and excluding Indians not taxed,—three fifths of all others."* These elements, in different proportions, enter into, and constitute all the departments of the government; as will be made apparent by a brief sketch of its organization.

The government is divided into three separate departments, the legislative, the executive, and the judicial. The legislative consists of two bodies,—the Senate, and the House of Representatives. The two are called the Congress of the United States: and all the legislative powers delegated to the government, are vested in it. The Senate is composed of two members from each State, elected by the legislature thereof, for the term of six years; and the whole number is divided into three classes; of which one goes out at the expiration of every two years. It is the representative of the States, in their corporate character. The members vote *per capita,* and a majority decides all questions of a legislative character. It has equal power with the House, on all such questions,—except that it cannot originate "bills for raising revenue." In addition to its legislative powers, it participates in the powers of the other two departments. Its advice and consent are necessary to make treaties and appointments; and it constitutes the high tribunal, before which impeachments are tried. In advising and consenting to treaties, and in trials of impeachments, two thirds are necessary to decide. In case the electoral college fails to choose a Vice-President, the power devolves on the Senate to make the selection from the two candidates having the highest number of votes. In selecting, the members vote by States, and a majority of the States decide. In such cases, two thirds of the whole number of Senators are necessary to form a quorum.

The House of Representatives is composed of members elected by the people of the several States, for the term of two years. The right of voting for them,

*2d Art. 1st Sec. 6th clause of the Constitution.

in each State, is confined to those who are qualified to vote for the members of the most numerous branch of its own legislature. The number of members is fixed by law, under each census,—which is taken every ten years. They are apportioned among the several States, according to their population, estimated in federal numbers; but each State is entitled to have one. The House, in addition to its legislative powers, has the sole power of impeachment; as well as of choosing the President (in case of a failure to elect by the electoral college) from the three candidates, having the greatest number of votes. The members, in such case, vote by States;—the vote of each delegation, if not equally divided, counts one, and a majority decides. In all other cases they vote *per capita,* and the majority decides; except only on a proposition to amend the constitution.

The executive powers are vested in the President of United States. He and the Vice-President, are chosen for the term of four years, by electors, appointed in such manner as the several States may direct. Each State is entitled to a number, equal to the whole number of its Senators and Representatives for the time. The electors vote *per capita,* in their respective States, on the same day throughout the Union; and a majority of the votes of all the electors is requisite to a choice. In case of a failure to elect, either in reference to the President or Vice-President, the House or the Senate, as the case may be, make the choice, in the manner before stated. If the House fail to choose before the fourth day of March next ensuing,—or in case of the removal from office, death, resignation, or inability of the President,—the Vice-President acts as President. In addition to the ordinary executive powers, the President has the authority to make treaties and appointments, by, and with the advice and consent of the Senate; and to approve or disapprove all bills before they become laws; as well as all orders, resolutions or votes, to which the concurrence of both houses of Congress is necessary,—except on questions of adjournment,— before they can take effect. In case of his disapproval, the votes of two thirds of both houses are necessary to pass them. He is allowed ten days (Sundays not counted) to approve or disapprove; and if he fail to act within that period, the bill, order, resolution or vote, (as the case may be,) becomes as valid, to all intents and purposes, as if he had signed it; unless Congress, by its adjournment, prevent its return.

The judicial power is vested in one Supreme Court, and such inferior courts, as Congress may establish. The Judges of both are appointed by the President in the manner above stated; and hold their office during good behavior.

The President, Vice-President, Judges, and all the civil officers, are liable to be impeached for treason, bribery, and other high crimes and misdemeanors.

From this brief sketch, it is apparent that the States, regarded in their corporate character, and the population of the States, estimated in federal numbers, are the two elements, of which the government is exclusively composed; and that they enter, in different proportions, into the formation of all its departments. In the legislative they enter in equal proportions, and in their most distinct and simple form. Each, in that department, has its appropriate organ; and each acts by its respective majorities,—as far as legislation is concerned. No bill, resolution, order, or vote, partaking of the nature of a law, can be adopted without their concurring assent: so that each house has a veto on the other, in all matters of legislation. In the executive they are differently blended. The powers of this department are vested in a single functionary; which made it impossible to give to them separate organs, and concurrent action. In lieu of this, the two elements are blended in the constitution of the college of electors, which chooses the President: but as this gave a decided preponderance to the element of population,—because of the greater number of which it was composed,—in order to combat and to compensate this advantage,—and to preserve, as far as possible, the equipoise between the two, the power was vested in the House, voting by States, to choose him from the three candidates, having the largest number of votes, in case of a failure of choice by the college; and in case of a failure to select by the House, or of removal, death, resignation, or inability, the Vice-President was authorized to act as President. These provisions gave a preponderance, even more decided, to the other element, in the eventual choice. This was still more striking as the constitution stood at its adoption. It originally provided that each elector should vote for two candidates, without designating which should be the President, or which the Vice-President; the person having the highest number of votes to be the President, if it should be a majority of the whole number given. If there should be more than one having such majority,— and an equal number of votes,—the House, voting by States, should choose between them, which should be President:—but if none should have a majority, the House, voting in the same way, should choose the President from the five having the greatest number of votes; the person having the greatest number of votes, after the choice of the President, to be the Vice-President. But in case of two or more having an equal number, the Senate should elect from among them the Vice-President.

Had these provisions been left unaltered, and not superseded, in practice, by caucuses and party conventions, their effect would have been to give to the majority of the people of the several States, the right of nominating five candidates; and to the majority of the States, acting in their corporate character, the right of choosing from them, which should be President, and which Vice-President. The President and Vice-President would, virtually, have been elected by the concurrent majority of the several States, and of their population, estimated in federal numbers; and, in this important respect, the executive would have been assimilated to the legislative department. But the Senate, in addition to its legislative, is vested also with supervisory powers in respect to treaties and appointments, which give it a participation in executive powers, to that extent; and a corresponding weight in the exercise of two of its most important functions. The treaty-making power is, in reality, a branch of the law-making power; and we accordingly find that treaties as well as the constitution itself, and the acts of Congress, are declared to be the supreme law of the land. This important branch of the law-making power includes all questions between the United States and foreign nations, which may become the subjects of negotiation and treaty; while the appointing power is intimately connected with the performance of all its functions.

In the Judiciary the two elements are blended, in proportions different from either of the others. The President, in the election of whom they are both united, nominates the judges; and the Senate, which consists exclusively of one of the elements, confirms or rejects: so that they are, to a certain extent, concurrent in this department; though the States, considered in their corporate capacity, may be said to be its predominant element.

In the impeaching power, by which it was intended to make the executive and judiciary responsible, the two elements exist and act separately, as in the legislative department:—the one, constituting the impeaching power, resides in the House of Representatives; and the other, the power that tries and pronounces judgment, in the Senate: and thus, although existing separately in their respective bodies, their joint and concurrent action is necessary to give effect to the power.

It thus appears, on a view of the whole, that it was the object of the framers of the constitution, in organizing the government, to give to the two elements, of which it is composed, separate, but concurrent action; and, consequently, a veto on each other, whenever the organization of the department, or the nature of the power would admit: and when this could not be done, so to blend the two, as to make as near an approach to it, in effect, as possible. It is, also, apparent, that the government, regarded apart from the constitution, is the government of the concurrent, and not of the numerical majority. But to have an accurate conception how it is calculated to act in practice; and to establish, beyond doubt, that it was neither intended to be, nor is, in fact, the government of the numerical majority, it will be necessary again to appeal to figures.

That, in organizing a government with different departments, in each of which the States are represented in a twofold aspect, in the manner stated, it was the object of the framers of the constitution, to make it more, instead of less popular than it would have been as a government of the mere numerical majority—that is, as requiring a more numerous, instead of a less numerous constituency to carry its powers into execution,—may be inferred from the fact, that such actually is the effect. Indeed, the necessary effect of the concurrent majority is, to make the government more popular;—that is, to require more wills to put it in action, than if any one of the majorities, of which it is composed, were its sole element;—as will be apparent by reference to figures.

If the House, which represents population, estimated in federal numbers, had been invested with the sole power of legislation, then six of the larger States, to wit, New-York, Pennsylvania, Virginia, Ohio, Massachusetts and Tennessee, with a federal population of 8,216,279, would have had the power of making laws for the other twenty-four, with a federal population of 7,971,325. On the other hand, if the Senate had been invested with the sole power, sixteen of the smallest States,—embracing Maryland as the largest,—with a federal population of 3,411,672, would have had the power of legislating for the other fourteen, with a population of 12,775,932. But the constitution, in giving each body a negative on the other, in all matters of legislation, makes it necessary that a majority of each should concur to pass a bill, before it becomes an act; and the smallest number of States and population, by which this can be effected, is six of the larger voting for it in the House of Representatives,—and ten of the smaller, uniting with them in their vote, in the Senate. The ten smaller, including New-Hampshire as the largest, have a federal population of 1,346,575; which, added to that of the six larger, would make 9,572,852. So that no bill can become a law, with less than the united vote of sixteen States, representing a constituency containing a federal population of 9,572,852, against fourteen States, representing a like population of 6,614,752.

But, when passed, the bill is subject to the President's approval or disapproval. If he disapprove, or, as it is usually termed, vetoes it, it cannot become a law unless passed by two thirds of the members of both bodies. The House of Representatives consists of 228,—two thirds of which is 152;—which, therefore, is the smallest number that can overcome his veto. It would take ten of the larger States, of which Georgia is the smallest, to make up that number;—the federal population of which is 10,853,175: and, in the Senate, it would require the votes of twenty States to overrule it;—and, of course, ten of the larger united with ten of the smaller. But the ten smaller States have a federal population of only

1,346,575,—as has been stated,—which added to that of the ten larger, would give 12,199,748, as the smallest population by which his veto can be overruled, and the act become a law. Even then, it is liable to be pronounced unconstitutional by the judges, should it, in any case before them, come in conflict with their views of the constitution;—a decision which, in respect to individuals, operates as an absolute veto, which can only be overruled by an amendment of the constitution. In all these calculations, I assume a full House, and full votes;—and that members vote according to the will of their constituents.

If the election of the President, by the electoral college, be compared with the passage of a bill by Congress, it will be found that it requires a smaller federal number to elect, than to pass a bill;—resulting from the fact that the two majorities, in the one case, are united and blended together, instead of acting concurrently, as in the other. There are, at present, 288 members of Congress, of which 60 are Senators, and the others, members of the House of Representatives; and, as each State is entitled to appoint as many electors as it has members of Congress, there is, of course, the same number of electors. One hundred and forty-five constitute a majority of the whole; and, of course, are necessary to a choice. Seven of the States of the largest class, say, New-York, Pennsylvania, Virginia, Ohio, Tennessee, Kentucky and Indiana, combined with one of a medium size, say, New Hampshire, are entitled to that number;—and, with a federal population of 9,125,936, may overrule the vote of the other twenty-two, with a population of 7,061,668: so that a small minority of States, with not a large majority of population, can elect a President by the electoral college,—against a very large majority of the States, with a population not greatly under a majority. It follows, therefore, that the choice of a President, when made by the electoral college, may be less popular in its character than when made by Congress,—which cannot elect without a concurrence of a federal population of upwards of nine and a half millions. But to compensate this great preponderance of the majority based on population, over that based on the States, regarded in their corporate character, in an election by the college of electors, the provision giving to the House of Representatives, voting by States, the eventual choice, in case the college fail to elect, was adopted. Under its operation, sixteen of the smallest States, with a federal population of 3,411,672, may elect the President, against the remaining fourteen, with a federal population of 12,775,932:—which gives a preponderance equally great to the States, without reference to population, in the contingency mentioned.

From what has been stated, the conclusion follows, irresistibly, that the constitution and the government, regarding the latter apart from the former, rest, throughout, on the principle of the concurrent majority; and that it is, of course, a Republic;—a constitutional democracy, in contradistinction to an absolute democracy; and that, the theory which regards it as a government of the mere numerical majority, rests on a gross and groundless misconception. So far is this from being the case, the numerical majority was entirely excluded as an element, throughout the whole process of forming and ratifying the constitution: and, although admitted as one of the two elements, in the organization of the government, it was with the important qualification, that it should be the numerical majority of the population of the *several States,* regarded in their corporate character, and not of the whole Union, regarded as one community. And further than this;—it was to be the numerical majority, not of their entire population, but of their federal population; which, as has been shown, is estimated artificially,—by excluding two fifths of a large portion of the population of many of the States of the Union. Even with these important qualifications, it was admitted as the less prominent of the two. With the exception of the impeaching power, it has no direct participation in the functions of any department of the government, except the legislative; while the other element participates in some of the most important functions of the executive; and, in the constitution of the Senate, as a court to try impeachments, in the highest of the judicial functions. It was, in fact, admitted, not because it was the numerical majority, nor on the ground, that, as such, it ought, of right, to constitute one of its elements,—much less the only one;—but for a very different reason. In the federal constitution, the equality of the States, without regard to population, size, wealth, institutions, or any other consideration, is a fundamental principle; as much so as is the equality of their citizens, in the governments of the several States, without regard to property, influence, or superiority of any description. As, in the one, the citizens form the constituent body;—so, in the other, the States. But the latter, in forming a government for their mutual protection and welfare, deemed it proper, as a matter of fairness and sound policy, and not of right, to assign to it an increased weight, bearing some reasonable proportion to the different amount of means which the several States might, respectively, contribute to the accomplishment of the ends, for which they were about to enter into a federal union. For this purpose they admitted, what is called federal numbers, as one of the elements of the government about to be established; while they were, at the same time, so jealous of the effects of admitting it, with all its restrictions,—that, in order to guard effectually the other element, they provided that no State, without its consent, should be deprived of its equal suffrage in the Senate; so as to place their equality, in that important body, beyond the reach even of the amending power.

I have now established, as proposed at the outset, that the government of the United States is a democratic federal Republic;—democratic in contradistinction to aristocratic, and monarchical;—federal, in contradistinction to national, on the one hand,—and to a confederacy, on the other; and a Republic—a government of the concurrent majority, in contradistinction to an absolute democracy—or a government of the numerical majority.

But the government of the United States, with all its complication and refinement of organization, is but a part of a system of governments. It is the representative and organ of the States, only to the extent of the powers delegated to it. Beyond this, each State has its own separate government, which is its exclusive representative and organ, as to all the other powers of government;—or, as they are usually called, the reserved powers. However correct, then, our conception of the character of the government of the United States viewed by itself, may be, it must be very imperfect, unless viewed at the same time, in connection with the complicated system, of which it forms but a part. In order to present this more perfect view, it will be essential, first, to present the outlines of the entire system, so far as it may be necessary to show the nature and character of the relation between the two—the government of the United States and the separate State governments. For this purpose, it will be expedient to trace, historically, the origin and formation of the system itself, of which they constitute the parts.

I have already shown, that the present government of the United States was reared on the foundation of the articles of confederation and perpetual union; that these last did but little more than define the powers and the extent of the government and the union, which had grown out of the exigencies of the revolution; and that these, again, had but enlarged and strengthened the powers and the union which the exigencies of a common defence against the aggression of the parent country, had forced the colonies to assume and form. What I now propose is, to trace briefly downwards, from the beginning, the causes and circumstances which led to the formation, in all its parts, of our present peculiar, complicated, and remarkable system of governments. This may be readily done,—for we have the advantage, (possessed by few people, who, in past times, have formed and flourished under remarkable political institutions,) of historical accounts, so full and accurate, of the origin, rise, and formation of our institutions, throughout all their stages,—as to leave nothing relating to either, to vague and uncertain conjecture.

It is known to all, in any degree familiar with our history, that the region embraced by the original States of the Union appertained to the crown of Great

Britain, at the time of its colonization; and that different portions of it were granted to certain companies or individuals, for the purpose of settlement and colonization. It is also known, that the thirteen colonies, which afterwards declared their independence, were established under charters which, while they left the sovereignty in the crown, and reserved the general power of supervision to the parent country, secured to the several colonies popular representation in their respective governments, or in one branch, at least, of their legislatures,—with the general rights of British subjects. Although the colonies had no political connection with each other, except as dependent provinces of the same crown—they were closely bound together by the ties of a common origin, identity of language, similarity of religion, laws, customs, manners, commercial and social intercourse,—and by a sense of common danger;—exposed, as they were, to the incursions of a savage foe, acting under the influence of a powerful and hostile nation.

In this embryo state of our political existence, are to be found all the elements which subsequently led to the formation of our peculiar system of governments. The revolution, as it is called, produced no other changes than those which were necessarily caused by the declaration of independence. These were, indeed, very important. Its first and necessary effect was, to cut the cord which had bound the colonies to the parent country,—to extinguish all the authority of the latter,—and, by consequence, to convert them into thirteen independent and sovereign States. I say, "independent and sovereign," because, as the colonies were, politically and in respect to each other, wholly independent,— the sovereignty of each, regarded as distinct and separate communities, being vested in the British crown,—the necessary effect of severing the tie which bound them to it was, to devolve the sovereignty on each respectively, and, thereby, to convert them from dependent colonies, into independent and sovereign States. Thus, the region occupied by them, came to be divided into as many States as there were colonies, each independent of the others,—as they were expressly declared to be; and only united to the extent necessary to defend their independence, and meet the exigencies of the occasion:—and hence that great and, I might say, providential territorial division of the country, into independent and sovereign States, on which our entire system of government rests.

Its next effect was, to transfer the sovereignty which had, heretofore, resided in the British crown, not to the *governments* of, but to the *people* composing the *several* States. It could only devolve on them. The declaration of independence, by extinguishing the British authority in the several colonies, necessarily destroyed every department of their governments, except such as derived their authority from, and represented their respective people. Nothing, then, remained of their several governments, but the popular and representative branches of them. But a representative government, even when entire, cannot possibly be the seat of sovereignty,—the supreme and ultimate power of a State. The very term, *"representative,"* implies a superior in the individual or body represented. Fortunately for us, the people of the several colonies constituted, not a mere mass of individuals, without any organic arrangements to express their sovereign will, or carry it into effect. On the contrary, they constituted organized communities,—in the full possession and constant exercise of the right of suffrage, under their colonial governments. Had they constituted a mere mass of individuals,—without organization, and unaccustomed to the exercise of the right of suffrage, it would have been impossible to have prevented those internal convulsions, which almost ever attend the change of the seat of sovereignty;—and which so frequently render the change rather a curse than a blessing. But in their situation, and under its circumstances, the change was made without the least convulsion, or the slightest disturbance. The mere will of the sovereign communities, aided by the remaining fragments,—the popular branches of their several colonial governments, speedily ordained and established governments, each for itself; and thus passed, without anarchy,—without a shock, from their dependent condition under the colonial governments, to that of independence under those established by their own authority.

Thus commenced the division between the constitution-making and the law-making powers;—between the power which ordains and establishes the fundamental laws;—which creates, organizes and invests government with its authority, and subjects it to restrictions;—and the power that passes acts to carry into execution, the powers thus delegated to government. The one, emanating from the people, as forming a *sovereign community,*—creates the government;—the other, as a representative appointed to execute its powers, enacts laws to regulate and control the conduct of the people, regarded as *individuals.* This division between the two powers,—thus necessarily incident to the separation from the parent country,—constitutes an element in our political system as essential to its formation, as the great and primary territorial division of independent and sovereign States. Between them, it was our good fortune never to have been left, for a moment, in doubt, as to where the sovereign authority was to be found; or how, and by whom it should be exercised: and, hence, the facility, the promptitude and safety, with which we passed from one state to the other, as far as internal causes were concerned. Our only difficulty and danger lay in the effort to resist the immense power of the parent country.

The governments of the several States were thus rightfully and regularly constituted. They, in the course of a few years, by entering into articles of confederation and perpetual union, established and made more perfect the union which had been informally constituted, in consequence of the exigencies growing out of the contest with a powerful enemy. But experience soon proved that the confederacy was wholly inadequate to effect the objects for which it was formed. It was then, and not until then, that the causes which had their origin in our embryo state, and which had, thus far, led to such happy results, fully developed themselves. The failure of the confederacy was so glaring, as to make it appear to all, that something must be done to meet the exigencies of the occasion:—and the great question which presented itself to all was;—what should, or could be done?

To dissolve the Union was too abhorrent to be named. In addition to the causes which had connected them by such strong cords of affection while colonies, there were superadded others, still more powerful,—resulting from the common dangers to which they had been exposed, and the common glory they had acquired, in passing successfully through the war of the revolution. Besides, all saw that the hope of reaping the rich rewards of their successful resistance to the encroachment of the parent country, depended on preserving the Union.

But, if disunion was out of the question, consolidation was not less repugnant to their feelings and opinions. The attachments of all to their respective States and institutions, were strong, and of long standing,—since they were identified with their respective colonies; and, for the most part, had survived the separation from the parent country. Nor were they unaware of the danger to their liberty and property, to be apprehended from a surrender of their sovereignty and existence, as separate and independent States, and a consolidation of the whole into one nation. They regarded disunion and consolidation as equally dangerous; and were, therefore, equally opposed to both.

To change the form of government to an aristocracy or monarchy, was not to be thought of. The deepest feelings of the common heart were in opposition to them, and in favor of popular government.

These changes or alterations being out of the question, what other remained to be considered? Men of the greatest talents and experience were at a loss for an answer. To meet the exigencies of the occasion, a convention of the States was called. When it met, the only alternative, in the opinion of the larger portion of its most distinguished members, was, the establishment of a *national* government; which was but another name, in reality, for *consolidation*. But where wisdom and experience proved incompetent to provide a remedy, the necessity of doing something, combined with the force of those causes, which had thus far shaped our destiny, carried us successfully through the perilous juncture. In the hour of trial, we realized the precious advantages we possessed in the two great and prime elements that distinguish our system of governments,—the division of the country, territorially, into independent and sovereign States,—and the division of the powers of government into *constitution* and *law*-making powers. Of the materials which they jointly furnished, the convention was enabled to construct the present system,—the only alternative left, by which we could escape the dire consequences attendant on the others; and which has so long preserved peace among ourselves, and protected us against danger from abroad. Each contributed essential aid towards the accomplishment of this great work.

To the former, we owe the mode of constituting the convention;—as well as that of voting, in the formation and adoption of the constitution,—and, finally, in the ratification of it by the States: and to them, jointly, are we exclusively indebted for that peculiar form which the constitution and government finally assumed. It is impossible to read the proceedings of the convention, without perceiving that, if the delegates had been appointed by the people at large, and in proportion to population, nothing like the present constitution could have been adopted. It would have assumed the form best suited to the views and interests of the more populous and wealthy portions; and, for that purpose, been made paramount to the existing State governments: in brief, a consolidated, *national* government would have been formed. But as the convention was composed of delegates from separate independent and sovereign States, it involved the necessity of voting by States, in framing and adopting the constitution; and,—what is of far more importance,—the necessity of submitting it to the States for their respective ratifications; so that each should be bound by its own act, and not by that of a majority of the States, nor of their united population. It was this necessity of obtaining the consent of a majority of the States in convention, as, also, in the intermediate process,—and, finally, the unanimous approval of all, in order to make it obligatory on all, which rendered it indispensable for the convention to consult the feelings and interests of all. This, united with the absolute necessity of doing something, in order to avert impending calamities of the most fearful character, impressed all with feelings of moderation, forbearance, mutual respect, concession, and compromise, as indispensable to secure the adoption of some measure of security. It was the prevalence of these impressions, that stamped their work with so much fairness, equity, and justice—as to receive, finally, the unanimous ratification of the States; and which has caused it to continue ever since, the object of the admiration and attachment of the reflecting and patriotic.

But the moderation, forbearance, mutual respect, concession, and compromise, superinduced by the causes referred to, could, of themselves, have effected nothing, without the aid of the division between the constitution and the law-making powers. Feebleness and a tendency to disorder are inherent in confederacies; and cannot be remedied, simply by the employment or modification of their powers. But as governments, according to our conceptions, cannot ordain and establish constitutions;—and as those of the States had already gone as far as they rightfully could, in framing and adopting the articles of confederation and perpetual union, it would have been impossible to have called the present constitution and government into being, without invoking the high creating power, which ordained and established those of the several States. There was none other competent to the task. It was, therefore, invoked; and formed a constitution and government for the United States, as it had formed and modelled those of the several States. The first step was,—the division of the powers of government;—which was effected, by leaving subject to the exclusive control of the several States in their separate and individual character, all powers which, it was believed, they could advantageously exercise for themselves respectively,—without incurring the hazard of bringing them in conflict with each other;—and by delegating, specifically, others to the United States, in the manner explained. It is this division of the powers of the government into such as are delegated, specifically, to the common and joint government of all the States,—to be exercised for the benefit and safety of each and all;—and the reservation of all others to the States respectively,—to be exercised through the separate government of each, which makes ours, *a system of governments,* as has been stated.

It is obvious, from this sketch, brief as it is,—taken in connection with what has been previously established,—that the two governments, General and State, stand to each other, in the first place, in the relation of parts to the whole; not, indeed, in reference to their organization or functions,—for in this respect both are perfect,—but in reference to their *powers.* As they divide between them the delegated powers appertaining to government,—and as, of course, each is divested of what the other possesses,—it necessarily requires the two united to constitute one entire government. That they are both paramount and supreme within the sphere of their respective powers;—that they stand, within these limits, as equals,—and sustain the relation of co-ordinate governments, has already been fully established. As co-ordinates, they sustain to each other the same relation which subsists between the different departments of the government—the executive, the legislative, and the judicial,—and for the same reason. These are co-ordinates; because each, in the sphere of its powers, is equal to, and independent of the others; and because the three united make the government. The only difference is that, in the illustration, each department, by itself, is not a government,—since it takes the whole in connection to form one; while the governments of the several States respectively, and that of the United States, although perfect governments in themselves, and in their respective spheres, require to be united in order to constitute one entire government. They, in this respect, stand as principal and supplemental;—while the co-departments of each stand in the relation of parts to the whole. The opposite theory, which would make the constitution and government of the United States the government of the whole,—and the government of each, *because* the government of the whole,—and not that of *all,* because of *each,*—besides the objection already stated, would involve the absurdity of each State having only half a constitution, and half a government; and this, too, while possessed of the supreme sovereign power. Taking all the parts together, the people of thirty independent and sovereign States, confederated by a solemn constitutional compact into one great federal community, with a system of government, in all of which, powers are separated into the great primary divisions of the *constitution*-making and the *law*-making powers; those of the latter class being divided between the common and joint government of all the States, and the separate and local governments of each State respectively;—and, finally, the powers of both distributed among three separate and independent departments, legislative, executive, and judicial;—presents, in the whole, a political system as remarkable for its grandeur as it is for its novelty and refinement of organization.—For the structure of such a system—so wise, just, and beneficent,—we are far more indebted to a superintending Providence, that so disposed events as to lead, as if by an invisible hand, to its formation, than to those who erected it. Intelligent, experienced, and patriotic as they were, they were but builders under its superintending direction.

Having shown in what relation the government of the United States and those of the separate States stand to each other, I shall next proceed to trace the line which divides their respective powers; or, to express it in constitutional language,—which distinguishes between the powers delegated to the United States, and those reserved to the States respectively,—with the restrictions imposed on each. In doing this, I propose to group the former under general heads, accompanied by such remarks as may be deemed necessary, in reference to the object in view.

In deciding what powers ought, and what ought not to be granted, the leading principle undoubtedly was, to delegate those only which could be more safely, or effectually, or beneficially exercised for the common good of all the States, by the joint or general government of all, than by the separate government of each State; leaving all others to the several States respectively. The object was, not to supersede the separate governments of the States,—but to establish a joint supplemental government; in order to do that, which either could not be done at all, or as safely and well done by them, as by a joint government of all. This leading principle embraced two great divisions of power, which may be said to comprehend all, or nearly all the delegated powers; either directly, or as a means to carry them into execution. One of them embraces all the powers appertaining to the relations of the States with the rest of the world, called their foreign relations; and the other, of an internal character, embraces such as appertain to the exterior relations of the States with each other. It is clear that both come within the leading principle; as each is of a description which the States, in their separate character, are either incompetent to exercise at all, or if competent, to exercise consistently with their mutual peace, safety, and prosperity. Indeed, so strong and universal has this opinion been, in reference to the powers appertaining to their foreign relations, that, from the Declaration of Independence to the present time, in all the changes through which they have passed, the Union has had exclusive charge of this great division of powers. To the rest of the world, the States composing this Union are now, and ever have been known in no other than their united, confederated character. Abroad,—to the rest of the world,—they are but *one*. It is only at home, in their interior relations, that they are *many;* and it is to this twofold aspect that their motto, *"E pluribus unum,"* appropriately and emphatically applies. So imperious was the necessity of union, and a common government to take charge of their foreign relations, that it may be safely affirmed, not only that it led to their formation, but that, without it, the States never would have been united. The same necessity still continues to be one of the strongest bonds of their union. But, strong as was, and still is, the inducement to union, in order to preserve their mutual peace and safety *within,* it was not, of itself, sufficiently strong to unite the parts composing this vast federal fabric; nor, probably, is it, of itself, sufficiently strong to hold them together.

This great division of authority appertains to the treaty-making power; and is vested in the President and Senate. The power of negotiating treaties belongs exclusively to the former; but he cannot make them without the advice and consent of the latter. When made, they are declared to be the supreme law of the land. The reason for vesting this branch of the law-making power exclusively in the President and Senate, to the exclusion of the House of Representatives, is to be traced to the necessity of secrecy in conducting negotiations and making treaties;—as they often involve considerations calculated to have great weight,—but which cannot be disclosed without hazarding their success. Hence the objection to so numerous a body as the House of Representatives participating in the exercise of the power. But to guard against the dangers which might result from confiding the power to so small a body, the advice and consent of *two thirds* of the Senators present was required.

There is a very striking difference between the manner in which the treaty-making and the law-making power, in its strict sense, are delegated, which deserves notice. The former is vested in the President and Senate by a few general words, without enumerating or specifying, particularly, the power delegated. The constitution simply provides that, "he shall have power, by and with the advice and consent of the Senate, to make treaties; provided two thirds of the Senators present concur;"—while the legislative powers vested in Congress, are, one by one, carefully enumerated and specified. The reason is to be found in the fact, that the treaty-making power is vested, *exclusively,* in the government of the United States; and, therefore, nothing more was necessary in delegating it, than to specify, as is done, the portion or department of the government in which it is vested. It was, then, not only unnecessary, but it would have been absurd to enumerate, specially, the powers embraced in the grant. Very different is the case in regard to legislative powers. They are divided between the Federal government and the State governments; which made it absolutely necessary, in order to draw the line between the delegated and reserved powers, that the one or the other should be carefully enumerated and specified; and, as the former was intended to be but supplemental to the latter,—and to embrace the comparatively few powers which could not be either exercised at all,—or, if at all, could not be so well and safely exercised by the separate governments of the several States,—it was proper that the former, and not the latter, should be enumerated and specified. But, although the treaty-making power is exclusively vested, and without enumeration or specification, in the government of the United States, it is nevertheless subject to several important limitations.

It is, in the first place, strictly limited to questions *inter alios;* that is, to questions between us and foreign powers which require negotiation to adjust them. All such clearly appertain to it. But to extend the power beyond these, be the pretext what it may, would be to extend it beyond its allotted sphere; and, thus, a palpable violation of the constitution. It is, in the next place, limited by all the provisions of the constitution which inhibit certain acts from being done by the government, or any of its departments;—of which description there are many. It is also limited by such provisions of the constitution as direct certain acts to be done in a particular way, and which prohibit the contrary; of which a striking example is to be found in that which declares that, "no money shall be drawn from the treasury but in consequence of appropriations to be made by law." This not only imposes an important restriction on the power, but gives to Congress, as the law-making power, and to the House of Representatives as a portion of Congress, the right to withhold appropriations; and, thereby, an important control over the treaty-making power, whenever money is required to carry a treaty into effect;—which is usually the case, especially in reference to those of much importance. There still remains another, and more important limitation; but of a more general and indefinite character. It can enter into no stipulation calculated to change the character of the government; or to do that which can only be done by the constitution-making power; or which is inconsistent with the nature and structure of the government,—or the objects for which it was formed. Among which, it seems to be settled, that it cannot change or alter the boundary of a State,—or cede any portion of its territory without its consent. Within these limits, all questions which may arise between us and other powers, be the subject matter what it may, fall within the limits of the treaty-making power, and may be adjusted by it.

The greater part of the powers delegated to Congress, relate, directly or indirectly, to one or the other of these two great divisions; that is, to those appertaining to the foreign relations of the States, or their exterior relations with each other. The former embraces the power to declare war; grant letters of marque and reprisals; make rules concerning captures on land and water; to raise and support armies; to provide and maintain a navy; to make rules for the government and regulation of the land and naval forces; to regulate commerce with foreign nations and the Indian tribes; and to exercise exclusive jurisdiction over all places purchased, with the consent of the States, for forts, magazines, dockyards, &c.

There are only two which apply directly to the exterior relations of the States with each other; the power to regulate commerce between them,—and to establish post-offices and post-roads. But there are two others intimately connected with these relations;—the one, to establish uniform rules of naturalization, and uniform laws on the subject of bankruptcies, throughout the United States;—and the other, to secure, for a limited time, to authors and inventors, the exclusive right to their respective writings and discoveries.

In addition, there is a class which relates to both. They consist of "the power to coin money, regulate the value thereof, and of foreign coins, and to fix the standard of weights and measures,—to provide for the punishment of counterfeiting the securities and current coin of the United States; to provide for calling forth the militia, to suppress insurrections and repel invasions; to provide for organizing, arming and disciplining the militia, and for governing such parts of them as may be employed in the service of the United States; reserving to the States, respectively, the appointment of the officers, and the authority of training the militia according to the discipline prescribed by Congress." The two first relate to the power of regulating commerce; and the others, principally, to the war power. Indeed, far the greater part of the powers vested in Congress relate to them.

These embrace all the powers expressly delegated to Congress;—except, "the power to lay and collect taxes, duties, imposts and excises, to pay the debts and provide for the common defence and general welfare of the United States;—to establish tribunals inferior to the Supreme Court; to provide for calling forth the militia to execute the laws of the Union; to exercise exclusive jurisdiction over such district,—not exceeding ten miles square, as may, by cession of particular States, and the acceptance of Congress, become the seat of government of the United States; and to make all laws necessary and proper for carrying into execution the foregoing powers, and all other powers vested in the government of the United States, or in any department or officer thereof." It is apparent, that all these powers relate to the other powers, and are intended to aid in carrying them into execution; and as the others are embraced in the two great divisions of powers, of which the one relates to their foreign relations, and the other to their exterior relations with each other, it may be clearly inferred that the regulation of these relations constituted the great, if not the exclusive objects for which the government was ordained and established.

If additional proof be required to sustain this inference, it may be found in the prohibitory and miscellaneous provisions of the constitution. A large portion of them are intended, directly, to regulate the exterior relations of the States with each other, which would have required treaty stipulations between them, had they been separate communities, instead of being united in a federal union. They are, indeed, treaty stipulations of the most solemn character, inserted in the compact of union. And here it is proper to remark, that there is a material difference between the modes in which these two great divisions of power are regulated. The powers embraced by, or appertaining to foreign relations, are left to be regulated by the treaty-making power, or by Congress; and, if by the latter, are enumerated and specifically delegated. They embrace a large portion of its powers. But those relating to the exterior relations of the States among themselves, with

few exceptions, are regulated by provisions inserted in the constitution itself. To
this extent, it is, in fact, a treaty,—under the form of a constitutional compact,—
of the highest and most sacred character. It provides that no tax or duty shall be
laid on articles exported from any State; that no preference shall be given, by any
regulation of commerce or of revenue, to the ports of one State over those of
another; nor shall any vessel bound to, or from one State, be obliged to enter,
clear, or pay duties in another; that no State shall enter into any treaty, alliance,
or confederation; grant letters of marque and reprisal; coin money; emit bills of
credit; make any thing but gold or silver a tender in payment of debts, or pass
any law impairing the obligation of contracts:—that no State shall, without the
consent of Congress, lay any import or export duties, except what may be
absolutely necessary for the execution of its inspection laws; and that the net proceeds of all duties and imposts, laid by any State on imports or exports, shall be
for the use of the treasury of the United States; and all such laws shall be subject
to the revision and control of Congress; no State shall, without the consent of
Congress, lay any duty on tonnage; keep troops, or ships of war, in time of peace;
enter into any agreement or compact with another State or with a foreign power,
or engage in war, unless actually invaded, or in such imminent danger as will not
admit of delay; that full faith and credit shall be given, in each State, to the public acts, records, and judicial proceedings of any other State; that the citizens of
each State shall be entitled to all the privileges and immunities of citizens of the
several States; that a person charged in any State, with treason, felony, or other
crime, who shall flee from justice, and be found in another State, shall, on
demand of the executive authority of the State from which he fled, be delivered
up to be removed to the State having jurisdiction of the crime; that no person
held to service or labor in one State, under the laws thereof, escaping into
another, shall, in consequence of any law or regulation thereof, be discharged
from such service or labor; but shall be delivered up on claim of the party to
whom such labor may be due; that the United States shall guarantee to each State
in this Union a republican form of government, and shall protect each of them
against invasion,—and, on application of the legislature, or of the executive,
when the legislature cannot be convened, against domestic violence.

The other prohibitory provisions, and those of a miscellaneous character,
contained in the constitution as ratified, provide against Congress prohibiting
the emigration or importation of such persons as any of the States may choose
to admit, prior to the year 1808; against the suspension of the writ of *Habeas Corpus;* against passing bills of attainder, and *expost facto* laws; against laying a capi-
tation or other direct tax, unless in proportion to population, to be ascertained

by the census; against drawing money out of the treasury, except in consequence of appropriations made by law; against granting titles of nobility; against persons holding office under the United States, accepting any present or emolument, office or title, from any foreign power, without the consent of Congress; for defining and punishing treason against the United States; for the admission of new States into the Union; for disposing of, and making rules and regulations respecting the territory and other property of the United States; for the amendment of the constitution; for the validity of existing debts and engagements against the United States under the constitution; for the supremacy of the constitution, and the laws of the United States which shall be made in pursuance thereof, and all treaties made, or which shall be made under the authority of the United States; that the Judges in every State shall be bound thereby, any thing in the constitution or laws of any State to the contrary notwithstanding; and that members of Congress and of the State legislatures, and the executive and judicial officers of the United States, and of the several States, shall be bound by oath, or affirmation, to support the constitution; but that no religious test shall be required to hold office under the United States.

Twelve amendments, or, as they are commonly called, amended articles, have been added since its adoption. They provide against passing laws respecting the establishment of religion, or abridging its free exercise; for the freedom of speech and of the press; for the right of petition; for the right of the people to bear arms; and against quartering soldiers in any house against the consent of the owner; against unreasonable searches, or seizures of persons, papers, and effects; against issuing warrants, but on oath or affirmation; against holding persons to answer for a capital, or other infamous crime, except on presentment or indictment of a grand jury; for a public and speedy trial in all criminal prosecutions, by an impartial jury of the State and district where the offence is charged to have been committed; for the right of jury trial in controversies exceeding twenty dollars; against excessive bail and fines, and against cruel and unusual punishments; against so construing the constitution as that the enumeration of certain powers should be made to disparage or deny those not enumerated; against extending the judicial power of the United States to any suit, in law or equity, against one of the United States, by citizens of another State, or citizens or subjects of a foreign state; and for the amendment of the constitution in reference to the election of the President and Vice-President. In addition, the amended article, already cited, provides that the powers not delegated to the United States, nor prohibited to the States, are reserved to the States respectively or to the people.

It will be manifest, on a review of all the provisions, including those embraced by the amendments, that none of them have any *direct* relation to the immediate objects for which the union was formed; and that, with few exceptions, they are intended to guard against improper constructions of the constitution, or the abuse of the delegated powers by the government,—or, to protect the government itself in the exercise of its proper functions.

In delegating power to the other two departments, the same general principle prevails. Indeed, in their very nature they are restricted, in a great measure, to the execution, each in its appropriate sphere, of the acts, and, of course, the powers vested in the legislative department; and, in this respect, their powers are consequently limited to the two great divisions which appertain to this department. But where either of them have other vested powers, beyond what is necessary for this purpose, it will be found, when I come to enumerate them, that, if they have any reference at all to the division of power between the general government and those of the several States, they directly relate to those appertaining to one or the other of these divisions.

The executive powers are vested in the President. They embrace the powers belonging to him, as commander in chief of the army and navy of the United States, and the militia of the several States, when called into the actual service of the United States;—the right of requiring the opinion, in writing, of the principal officers in each of the executive departments, upon any subject relating to the duties of their respective offices; of granting reprieves and pardons for offences against the United States,—except in cases of impeachment; of making treaties, by and with the advice and consent of the Senate,—provided two thirds of the Senators present concur; of nominating and, by and with the advice and consent of the Senate, appointing ambassadors, other public ministers and consuls, judges of the Supreme Court, and all other officers of the United States, whose appointments have not been otherwise provided for, and which shall be established by law,—reserving to Congress the right to invest, by law, the appointment of such inferior officers as they may think proper,—in the President alone, in the courts of law, or in the heads of departments; of receiving ambassadors and other public ministers; of convening, on extraordinary occasions, both houses of Congress, or either of them; and, in case of disagreement between them, with respect to the time of adjournment, of adjourning them to such time as he may think proper; of commissioning all the officers of the United States. In addition, it is made his duty to give to Congress information of the state of the Union; and to recommend to their consideration, such measures as he may deem necessary and expedient; to take care that the laws are faithfully executed; and, finally, he is vested with the power of approving or disapproving bills passed by Congress, before they become laws,—which is called his veto. By far the greater part of these powers and duties appertain to him as chief of the executive department. The principal exception is, the treaty-making power; which appertains exclusively to the foreign relations of the States,—and, consequently, is embraced in that division of the delegated powers; as does, also, the appointment of ambassadors, other ministers and consuls, and the reception of the two former. The other exceptions are merely organic, without reference to any one class or division of powers between the two co-ordinate governments.

The judicial power of the United States is vested in the Supreme Court, and such inferior courts as Congress may, from time to time, ordain and establish. The judges hold their offices during good behavior; and have a fixed salary which can neither be increased nor diminished during their continuance in office. Their power extends to all cases in law or equity, arising under the constitution, the laws of the United States, and treaties made, or which shall be made under their authority; to all cases affecting ambassadors, other public ministers and consuls; to all cases of admiralty and marine jurisdiction; to controversies to which the United States shall be a party; to those between two or more States; between citizens of different States; between citizens of the same State, claiming lands under grants of different States; and between a State and the citizens thereof, and foreign states, citizens or subjects. The fact that, in all cases, where the judicial power is extended beyond what may be regarded its appropriate sphere, it contemplates matters connected directly with the foreign or external relations of the States, rather than those connected with their exterior relations with each other,—strikingly illustrates the position,—that the powers appertaining to the one or the other of these relations, and those necessary to carry them into execution, embrace almost all that have been delegated to the United States. Indeed, on a review of the whole, it may be safely asserted, not only that they embrace almost all of the powers delegated, but that all of the general and miscellaneous provisions (excluding those, of course, belonging to the organism of government, whether they prohibit certain acts, or impose certain duties,—as well as those intended to protect the government, and guard against its abuse of power,) appertain, with few exceptions, to the one or the other of these divisions. For, if the principle which governed in the original division or distribution of powers between the two co-ordinate governments, be that already stated; that is, to delegate such powers only as could not be exercised at all, or as well, or safely exercised by the governments of the States acting separately, and to reserve the residue,—it would be difficult to conceive what others could be embraced in them; since there are none delegated to either, which do not appertain to the States in their relations with each other, or in their relations with the rest of the world. As to all other purposes, the separate governments of the several States were far more competent and safe, than the general government of all the States. Their knowledge of the local interests and domestic institutions of these respectively, must be much more accurate, and the responsibility of each to their respective people much more perfect. This is so obvious, as to render it incredible, that they would have admitted the interference of a general government in their interior and local concerns, farther than was absolutely necessary to the regulation of their exterior relations with each other and the rest of the world;—or that a general government should have been adopted for any other purpose. To this extent, it was manifestly necessary;—but beyond this, it was not only not necessary, but clearly calculated to jeopard, in part, the ends for which the constitution was adopted;—"to establish justice, insure domestic tranquility, and secure the blessings of liberty."

Having, now, enumerated the delegated powers, and laid down the principle which guided in drawing the line between them and the reserved powers, the next question which offers itself for consideration is; what provisions does the constitution of the United States, or the system itself, furnish, to preserve this, and its other divisions of power? and whether they are sufficient for the purpose?

The great, original, and primary division, as has been stated, is that of distinct, independent, and sovereign States. It is the basis of the whole system. The next in order is, the division into the constitution-making and the law-making powers. The next separates the delegated and the reserved powers, by vesting the one in the government of the United States, and the other in the separate governments of the respective States, as co-ordinate governments; and the last, distributes the powers of government between the several departments of each. These divisions constitute the elements of which the organism of the whole system is formed. On their preservation depend its duration and success, and the mighty interests involved in both. I propose to take the divisions in the reverse order to that stated, by beginning with the last, and ending with the first.

The question, then, is,—what provision has the constitution of the United States made to preserve the division of powers among the several departments of the government? And this involves another; whether the departments are so constituted, that each has, within itself, the power of self-protection; the power, by which, it may prevent the others from encroaching on, and absorbing the portion vested in it, by the constitution? Without such power, the strongest would, in the end, inevitably absorb and concentrate the powers of the others in itself, as has been fully shown in the preliminary discourse;—where, also, it is shown that there is but one mode in which this can be prevented; and that is, by investing each division of power, or the representative and organ of each, with a veto, or something tantamount, in some one form or another. To answer, then, the question proposed, it is necessary to ascertain what provisions the constitution, or the system itself, has made for the exercise of this important power. I shall begin with the legislative department, which, in all popular governments, must be the most prominent, and, at least in theory, the strongest.

Its powers are vested in Congress. To it, all the functionaries of the other two departments are responsible, through the impeaching power; while its members are responsible only to the people of their respective States;—those of the Senate to them in their corporate character as States; and those of the House of Representatives, in their individual character as citizens of the several States. To guard its members more effectually against the control of the other two departments, they are privileged from arrest in all cases, except for treason, felony, and breach of the peace,—during their attendance on the session of their respective houses,—and in going to and returning from the same; and from being questioned, in any other place, for any speech or debate in either house. It possesses besides, by an express provision of the constitution, all the discretionary powers vested in the government, whether the same appertain to the legislative, executive, or judicial departments. It is to be found in the 1st art., 8th sec., 18th clause; which declares that Congress shall have power "to make all laws necessary and proper for carrying into execution the foregoing powers," (those vested in Congress,) "and all other powers vested, by the constitution, in the government of the United States, or in any department or officer thereof." This clause is explicit. It includes all that are usually called "implied powers;" that is,—powers to carry into effect those expressly delegated; and vests them expressly in Congress, so clearly, as to exclude the possibility of doubt. Neither the judicial department, nor any officer of the government can exercise any power not expressly, and by name, vested in them, either by the constitution, or by an act of Congress: nor can they exercise any implied power, in carrying them into execution, without the express sanction of law. The effect of this is, to place the powers vested in the legislative department, beyond the reach of the undermining process of insidious construction, on the part of any of the other departments, or of any of the officers of government. With all these provisions, backed by its widely extended and appropriate powers,—its security, resulting from freedom of speech in debate,—and its close connection and immediate intercourse with its constituents, the legislative department is possessed of ample means to protect itself against the encroachment on, and absorption of its powers, by the other two departments. It remains to be seen, whether these, in their turn, have adequate means of protecting themselves, respectively, against the encroachments of each other;—as well as of the legislative department. I shall begin with the executive.

Its powers are vested in the President. To protect them, the constitution, in the first place, makes him independent of Congress, by providing, that he "shall, at stated times, receive for his services, a compensation, which shall be neither increased nor diminished during the period for which he shall have been elected; and that he shall not receive, within that period, any other emolument from the United States, or any one of them."*

He is, in the next place, vested with the power to veto, not only all acts of Congress,—but it is also expressly provided that, "every order, resolution, or vote, to which the concurrence of the Senate and House of Representatives may be necessary, (except on a question of adjournment,) shall be presented to the President of the United States; and, before the same shall take effect, shall be approved by him; or being disapproved by him, shall be repassed by two thirds of the Senate and House of Representatives, according to the rules and limitations prescribed in the case of a bill."†

He is vested, in the next place, with the power of nominating and appointing, with the advice and consent of the Senate, all the officers of the government whose appointments are not otherwise provided for by the constitution; except such inferior officers as may be authorized, by Congress, to be appointed by the President alone, or by the courts of law, or heads of departments. I do not add the power of removing officers, the tenure of whose office is not fixed by the constitution, which has grown into practice; because it is not a power vested in the President by the constitution, but belongs to the class of implied powers; and as such, can only be rightfully exercised and carried into effect by the authority of Congress.

He has, in the next place, the exclusive control of the administration of the government, with the vast patronage and influence appertaining to the distribution of its honors and emoluments; a patronage so great as to make the election of the President the rallying point of the two great parties that divide the country; and the successful candidate, the leader of the dominant party in power, for the time.

---

*1st Art. 2d Sec. of Con.
†1st Art. 7th Sec. 7th clause of the Constitution.

He is, besides, commander in chief of the army and navy; and of the militia, when called into the service of the United States. These, combined with his extensive powers, make his veto (which requires the concurrence of two thirds of both houses to overrule it) almost as absolute as it would be without any qualification,—during the term for which he is elected. The whole combined, vests the executive with ample means to protect its powers from being encroached on, or absorbed by the other departments.

Nor are those of the judiciary less ample, for the same purpose, against the two other departments. Its powers are vested in the courts of the United States. To secure the independence of the judges, they are appointed to hold their offices during good behavior; and to receive for their services, a compensation which cannot be diminished during their continuance in office. Besides these means for securing their independence, they have, virtually, a negative on the acts of the other departments,—resulting from the nature of our system of government. This requires particular explanation. According to it, constitutions are of paramount authority to laws or acts of the government, or of any of its departments; so that, when the latter come in conflict with the former, they are null and void, and of no binding effect whatever. From this fact it results, that, when a case comes before the courts of the United States, in which a question of conflict between the acts of Congress or any department may arise, the judges are bound, from the necessity of the case, to determine whether, in fact, there is any conflict or not; and if, in their opinion, there be such conflict, to decide in favor of the constitution; and thereby, virtually, to annul or veto the act, as far as it relates to the department or government, and the parties to the suit or controversy. This, with the provisions to secure their independence, gives, not only means of self-protection, but a weight and dignity to the judicial department never before possessed by the judges in any other government of which we have any certain knowledge.

But, however ample may be the means possessed by the several departments to protect themselves against the encroachments of each other, regarded as independent and irresponsible bodies, it by no means follows, that the equilibrium of power, established between them by the constitution, will, necessarily, remain undisturbed. For they are, in fact, neither independent nor irresponsible bodies. They are all representatives of the several States, either in their organized character of governments, or of their people, estimated in federal numbers; and are under the control of their joint majority,—blended, however, in unequal proportions, in the several departments. In order, then, to preserve the equilibrium between the departments, it is indispensable to preserve that between the two majorities which have the power to control them, and to which they are all responsible, directly or indirectly. For it is manifest that if this equilibrium, established by the constitution, be so disturbed, as to give the ascendency to either, it must disturb, or would be calculated to disturb, in turn, the equilibrium between the departments themselves; inasmuch as the weight of the majority which might gain it, would be thrown in favor of the one or the other, as the means of increasing its influence over the government. In order, then, to determine whether the equilibrium between the departments is liable to be disturbed, it is necessary to ascertain what provisions the constitution has made to preserve it between the two majorities, in reference to the several departments; and to determine whether they are sufficient for the purpose intended. I shall, again, commence with the legislative.

In this department the two majorities or elements, of which the government is composed, act separately. Each has its own organ; one the Senate, and the other the House of Representatives: and each has, through its respective organ, a negative on the other, in all acts of legislation, which require their joint action. This gives to each complete and perfect means to guard against the encroachments of the other. The same is the case in the judiciary. There, the judges, in whom the powers of the department are vested, are nominated by the President, and, by and with the advice and consent of the Senate, appointed by him; which gives each element also a negative on the other; and, of course, like means of preserving the equilibrium established by the constitution between them. But the case is different in reference to the executive department.

The two elements in this department are blended into one, when the choice of a President is made by the electoral college;—which, as has been stated, gives a great preponderance to the element representing the federal population of the several States, over that which represents them in their organized character as governments. To compensate this, a still greater preponderance is given to the latter, in the eventual choice by the House of Representatives. But they have, in neither case, a veto upon the acts of each other; nor any equivalent means to prevent encroachments, in choosing the individual to be vested, for the time, with the powers of the department; and, hence, no means of preserving the equilibrium, as established between them by the constitution. The result has been,—as it ever must be in such cases,—the ascendancy of the stronger element over the weaker. The incipient measure to effect this was adopted at an early period. The first step was, to diminish the number of candidates, from which the selection should be made, from the five, to the three highest on the list; and,—in order to lessen the chances of a failure to choose by the electoral college,—to provide that the electors, instead of voting for two, without discriminating the offices, should designate which was for the President, and which for the Vice-President. This was effected in the regular way, by an amendment of the constitution. Since then, the constitution, as amended, has been, in practice, superseded, by what is called, *the usage of parties;* that is, by each selecting, informally, persons to meet at some central point, to nominate candidates for the Presidency and Vice-Presidency,—with the avowed object of preventing the election from going into the House of Representatives; and, of course, by superseding the eventual choice on the part of this body, to abolish, in effect, one of the two elements of which the government is constituted, so far, at least, as the executive department is concerned. As it now stands, the complex and refined machinery provided by the constitution for the election of the President and Vice-President, is virtually superseded. The nomination of the successful party, by irresponsible individuals makes, in reality, the choice. It is in this way that the provisions of the constitution, which intended to give equal weight to the two elements in the executive department of the government, have been defeated; and an overwhelming preponderance given to that which is represented in the House of Representatives, over that which is represented in the Senate.

But the decided preponderance of this element in the executive department, cannot fail greatly to disturb the equilibrium between it and the other two departments, as established by the constitution. It cannot but throw the weight of the more populous States and sections on the side of that department, over which their control is the most decisive; and place the President, in whom its powers are vested for the time, more completely under their control. This, in turn, must place the honors and emoluments of the government, also, more under their control; and, of course, give a corresponding influence over all who aspire to participate in them; and especially over the members, for the time, of the legislative department. Even those, composing the judiciary, for the time, will not be unaffected by an influence so great and pervading.

I come now to examine, what means the constitution of the United States, or the system itself provides, for preserving the division between the delegated and reserved powers. The former are vested in the government of the United States; and the latter, where they have not been reserved to the people of the several States respectively, are vested in their respective State governments. The two, as has been established, stand in the relation of coordinate governments; that is, the government of the United States is, in each State, the co-ordinate of its separate government; and taken together, the two make the entire government of each, and of all the States. On the preservation of this peculiar and important division of power, depend the preservation of all the others, and the equilibrium of the entire system. It cannot be disturbed, without, at the same time, disturbing the whole, with all its parts.

The only means which the constitution of the United States contains or provides for its preservation, consists, in the first place, in the enumeration and specification of the powers delegated to the United States, and the express reservation to the States of all powers not delegated; in the next, in imposing such limitations on both governments, and on the States themselves, in their separate character, as were thought best calculated to prevent the abuse of power, or the disturbance of the equilibrium between the two co-ordinate governments; and, finally, in prescribing that the members of Congress, and of the legislatures of the several States, and all executive and judicial officers of the United States, and of the several States, shall be bound, by oath or affirmation, to support the constitution of the United States. These were, undoubtedly, proper and indispensable means; but that they were, of themselves, deemed insufficient to preserve, undisturbed, this new and important partition of power between co-ordinate governments, is clearly inferrible from the proceedings of the convention, and the writings and speeches of eminent individuals, pending the ratification of the constitution. No question connected with the formation and adoption of the constitution of the United States, excited deeper solicitude,— or caused more discussion, than this important partition of power. The ablest men divided in reference to it, during these discussions. One side maintained that the danger was, that the delegated would absorb the reserved; while the other not less strenuously contended, that the reserved would absorb the delegated powers. So widely extended was this diversity of opinion, and so deep the excitement it produced, that it contributed more than all other questions combined, to the organization of the two great parties, which arose with the formation of the constitution; and which, finally, assumed the names of *"Federal"* and *"Republican."* In all these discussions, neither side relied on the provisions of the constitution of the United States, just referred to, as the means of preserving the partition of power between the co-ordinate governments; and thereby, of preventing either from encroaching on, and absorbing the powers of the other. Both looked to the co-ordinate governments, to control each other; and by their mutual action and reaction, to keep each other in their proper spheres. The doubt, on one side, was, whether the delegated, were not too strong for the reserved powers; and, on the other, whether the latter were not too strong for the former. One apprehended that the end would be, *consolidation;* and the other, *dissolution.* Both parties, to make out their case, appealed to the respective powers of the two; compared their relative force, and decided accordingly, as the one or the other appeared the stronger. Both, in the discussion, assumed, that those who might administer the two co-ordinate governments, for the time, would stand in antagonistic relations to each other, and be ready to seize every opportunity to enlarge their own at the expense of the powers of the other; and rather hoped than believed, that this reciprocal action and reaction would prove so well balanced as to be sufficient to preserve the equilibrium, and keep each in its respective sphere.

Such were the views taken, and the apprehensions felt, on both sides, at the time. They were both right, in looking to the co-ordinate governments for the means of preserving the equilibrium between these two important classes of powers; but time and experience have proved, that both mistook the source and the character of the danger to be apprehended, and the means of counteracting it; and, thereby, of preserving the equilibrium, which both believed to be essential to the preservation of the complex system of government about to be established. Nor is it a subject of wonder, that statesmen, as able and experienced as the leaders of the two sides were, should both fall into error, as to what would be the working of political elements, wholly untried; and which made so great an innovation in governments of the class to which ours belonged. It is clear, from the references so frequently made to previous confederacies, in order to determine how the government about to be established, would operate, that the framers of the constitution themselves, as well as those who took an active part in discussing the question of its adoption, were far from realizing the magnitude of the change which was made by it in governments of that form. Had this been fully realized, they would never have assumed that those who administered the government of the United States, and those of the separate States, would stand in hostile relations to each other; or have believed that it would depend on the relative force of the powers delegated and the powers reserved, whether either would encroach on, and absorb the other;—an assumption and belief which experience has proved to be utterly unfounded. The conflict took, from the first, and has continued ever since to move in, a very different direction. Instead of a contest for power between the government of the United States, on the one side, and the separate governments of the several States, on the other,—the real struggle has been to obtain the control of the former;—a struggle in which both States and people have united: And the result has shown that, instead of depending on the relative force of the delegated and reserved powers, the latter, in all contests, have been brought in aid of the former, by the States on the side of the party in the possession and control of the government of the United

States,—and by the States on the side of the party in the opposition, in their efforts to expel those in possession, and to take their place. There must then be at all times,—except in a state of transition of parties, or from some accidental cause,—a majority of the several States, and of their people, estimated in federal numbers, on the side of those in power; and, of course, on the side of the delegated powers and the government of the United States. Its real authority, therefore, instead of being limited to the delegated powers alone, must, habitually, consist of these, united with the reserved powers of the joint majority of the States, and of their population, estimated in federal numbers. Their united strength must necessarily give to the government of the United States, a power vastly greater than that of all the co-ordinate governments of the States on the side of the party in opposition. It is their united strength, which makes it one of the strongest ever established; greatly stronger than it could possibly be as a national government. And, hence, all conclusions, drawn from a supposed antagonism between the delegated powers, on the one hand, and the reserved powers, on the other, have proved, and must ever prove utterly fallacious. Had it, in fact, existed, there can now be no doubt, that the apprehensions of those, who feared that the reserved powers would encroach on and absorb the delegated, would have been realized, and dissolution, long since, been the fate of the system: for it was this very antagonism which caused the weakness of the confederation, and threatened the dissolution of the Union. The difference between it and the present government, in this respect, results from the fact, that the States, in the confederation, had but few and feeble motives to form combinations, in order to obtain the control of its powers; because neither the State governments, nor the citizens of the several States were subject to its control. Hence, they were more disposed to elude its requisitions, and reserve their means for their own control and use, than to enter into combinations to control its councils. But very different is the case in their existing confederated character. The present government possesses extensive and important powers; among others, that of carrying its acts into execution by its own authority, without the intermediate agency of the States. And, hence, the principal motives to get the control of the government, with all its powers and vast patronage; and for this purpose, to form combinations as the only means by which it can be accomplished. Hence, also, the fact, that the present danger is directly the reverse of that of the confederacy. The one tended to dissolution,—the other tends to consolidation. But there is this difference between these tendencies. In the former, they were far more rapid,—not because they were stronger, but because there were few or no impediments in their way; while in the latter, many and powerful obstacles are presented. In the case of the confederacy, the antagonistic position which the States occupied in respect to it,—and their indifference to its acts, after the acknowledgment of their independence, led to a non-compliance with its requisitions;—and this, without any active measure on their parts, was sufficient, if left to itself, to have brought about a dissolution of the Union, from its weakness, at no distant day. But such is not the case under the present system of government. To form combinations in order to get the control of the government, in a country of such vast extent,—and consisting of so many States, having so great a variety of interests, must necessarily be a slow process, and require much time, before they can be firmly united, and settle down into two organized and compact parties. But the motives to obtain this control are sufficiently powerful to overcome all these impediments; and the formation of such parties is just as certain to result from the action of political affinities and antipathies, as the formation of bodies, where different elements in the material world, having mutual attraction and repulsion, are brought in contact. Nor is the organization of the government of the United States, which requires the concurrence of the two majorities to control it,—though intended for the purpose,—sufficient, of itself, to prevent it. The same constitution of man, which would, in time, lead to the organization of a party, consisting of a simple majority,—if such had the power of control,—will, just as certainly, in time, form one, consisting of the two combined. The only difference is, that the one would be formed more easily, and in a shorter time than the other. The motives are sufficiently strong to overcome the impediments in either case.

In forming these combinations, which, in fact, constitute the two parties, circumstances must, of course, exert a powerful influence. Similarity of origin, language, institutions, political principles, customs, pursuits, interests, color, and contiguity of situations,—all contribute to facilitate them: while their opposites necessarily tend to repel them, and, thus, to form an antagonistic combination and party. In a community of so great an extent as ours, contiguity becomes one of the strongest elements in forming party combinations, and distance one of the strongest elements in repelling them. The reason is, that nothing tends more powerfully to weaken the social or sympathetic feelings, than remoteness; and, in the absence of causes calculated to create aversion, nothing to strengthen them more, than contiguity. We feel intensely the sufferings endured under our immediate observation;—when we would be almost indifferent, were they removed to a great distance from us. Besides, contiguity of situation usually involves a similarity of interests;—especially, when considered in reference to those more remote,—which greatly facilitates the formation of local combinations and parties in a country of extensive limits. If to this, we add other diversities,—of pursuits, of institutions, origin, and the like, which not unusually exist in such cases, parties must almost necessarily partake, from the first, more or less, of a local character: and, by an almost necessary operation, growing out of the unequal fiscal action of the government, as explained in the preliminary discourse, must become entirely so, in the end, if not prevented by the resistance of powerful causes. We accordingly find, that such has been the case with us, under the operation of the present government. From the first, they assumed, in some degree, this character; and have since been gradually tending more and more to this form, until they have become, almost entirely, sectional. When they shall have become so entirely,—(which must inevitably be the case, if not prevented,)—when the stronger shall concentrate in itself both the majorities which form the elements of the government of the United States,—(and this, it must shortly do,)—every barrier, which the constitution, and the organism of the government oppose to one overruling combination of interests, will have been broken down, and the government become as absolute, as would be that of the mere numerical majority; unless, indeed, the system itself, shall be found to furnish some means sufficiently powerful to resist this strong tendency, inherent in governments like ours, to absorb and consolidate all power in its own hands.

What has been stated is sufficient to show, that no such means are to be found in the constitution of the United States, or in the organism of the government. Nor can they be found in the right of suffrage; for it is through its instrumentality that the party combinations are formed. Neither can they be found in the fact, that the constitution of the United States is a written instrument; for this, of itself, cannot possibly enforce the limitations and restrictions which it imposes, as has been fully shown in the preliminary discourse. Nor can they be enforced, and the government held strictly to the sphere assigned, by resorting to a strict construction of the constitution;—for the plain reason, that the stronger party will be in favor of a liberal construction; and the strict construction of the minority can be of no avail against the liberal construction of the majority;—as has also been shown in the same discourse. Nor can they be found in the force of public opinion,—operating through the Press; for it has been, therein, also shown, that its operation is similar to that of the right of suffrage; and that its tendency, with all its good effects in other respects, is to increase party excitement, and to strengthen the force of party attachments and party combinations, in consequence of its having become a party organ and the instrument of party warfare. Nor can the veto power of the President, or the power of the Judges to decide on the constitutionality of the acts of the other departments, furnish adequate means to resist it,—however important they may be, in other respects, and in particular instances;—for the plain reason, that the party combinations which are sufficient to control the two majorities constituting the elements of the government of the United States, must, habitually, control all the departments;—and make them all, in the end, the instruments of encroaching on, and absorbing the reserved powers; especially the executive department,—since the provisions of the constitution, in reference to the election of the President and Vice-President, have been superseded, and their election placed, substantially, under the control of the single element of federal numbers. But if none of these can furnish the means of effective resistance, it would be a waste of time to undertake to show, that freedom of speech, or the trial by jury, or any guards of the kind, however indispensable as auxiliary means, can, of themselves, furnish them.

If, then, neither the constitution, nor any thing appertaining to it, furnishes means adequate to prevent the encroachment of the delegated on the reserved powers, they must be found in some other part of the system, if they are to be found in it at all. And, further;—if they are to be found there, it must be in the powers not delegated; since it has been shown that they are not to be found in those delegated, nor in any thing appertaining to them;—and the two necessarily embrace all the powers of the whole system. But, if they are to be found in the reserved powers, it must be in those vested in the separate governments of the several States, or in those retained by the people of the several States, in their sovereign character;—that character in which they ordained and established the constitution and government; and, in which, they can amend or abolish it;—since all the powers, not delegated, are expressly reserved, by the 10th Article of Amendments, to the one or the other. In one, then, or the other of these, or in both, the means of resisting the encroachments of the powers delegated to the United States, on those reserved to the States respectively, or to the people thereof,—and thereby to preserve the equilibrium between them, must be found, if found in the system at all. Indeed, in one constituted as ours, it would seem neither reasonable nor philosophical to look to the government of the United States, in which the delegated powers are vested, for the means of resisting encroachments on the reserved powers. It would not be reasonable; because it would be to look for protection against danger, to the quarter from which it was apprehended, and from which only it could possibly come. It would not be philosophical; because it would be against universal analogy. All organic action, as far as our knowledge extends,—whether it appertain to the material or political world, or be of human or divine mechanism,—is the result of the reciprocal action and reaction of the parts of which it consists. It is this which confines the parts to their appropriate spheres, and compels them to perform their proper functions. Indeed, it would seem impossible to produce organic action by a single power,—and that it must ever be the result of two or more powers, mutually acting and reacting on each other. And hence the political axiom,—that there can be no constitution, without a division of power, and no liberty without a constitution. To this a kindred axiom may be added;—that there can be no division of power, without a self-protecting power in each of the parts into which it may be divided; or in a superior power to protect each against the others. Without a division of power there can be no organism; and without the power of self-protection, or a superior power to restrict each to its appropriate sphere, the stronger will absorb the weaker, and concentrate all power in itself.

The members, then, of the convention, which framed the constitution, and those who took an active part in the question of its adoption, were not wrong in looking to this reciprocal action and reaction, between the delegated and the reserved powers;—between the government of the United States and the separate governments of the several States,—as furnishing the means of resisting the encroachments of the one or the other;—however much they may have erred as to the *mode* in which they would mutually act. No one, indeed, seems, at the time, to have formed any clear or definite conception of the manner in which, a division so novel, would act, when put into operation. All seem to have agreed that there would be conflict between the two governments. They differed only as to which would prove the stronger; yet indulging the hope that their respective powers were so well adjusted, that neither would be able to prevail over the other. Under the influence of this hope, and the diversity of opinion entertained, the framers of the constitution contented themselves with drawing, as strongly as possible, the line of separation between the two powers;—leaving it to time and experience to determine where the danger lay; to develop whatever remedy the system might furnish to guard against it;—and, if it furnished none, they left it to those, who should come after them, to supply the defect. We now have the benefit of these: Time and Experience have shown fully, where the danger lies, and what is its nature and character. They have established, beyond all doubt, that the antagonism relied on,—as existing in theory, between the government of the United States, on the one hand, and all the separate State governments, on the other, has proved to be, in practice, between the former, supported by a majority of the latter, and of their population, estimated in federal numbers,—and a minority of the States and of their population, estimated in the same manner. And, consequently, that the government of the United States, instead of being the weaker, as was believed by many, has proved to be immeasurably the stronger; especially, since the two majorities constituting the elements of which it is composed, have centred in one of the two great sections which divide the Union. The effect has been, to give to this section entire and absolute control over the government of the United States; and through it, over the other section, on all questions, in which their interests or views of policy may come in conflict. The system, in consequence of this, instead of tending towards dissolution from weakness, tends strongly towards consolidation from exuberance of strength:—so strongly, that, if not opposed by a resistance proportionally powerful, the end must be its destruction,—either by the bursting asunder of its parts, in consequence of the intense conflict of interest, produced by being too closely pressed together, or by consolidating all the powers of the system in the government of the United States, or in some one of its departments,—to be wielded with despotic force and oppression. The present system must be preserved in its integrity and full vigor; for there can be no other means,—no other form of government, save that of absolute power, which can govern and keep the whole together. Disregarding this, the only alternatives are,—a government in form and in action, absolute and irresponsible,—a consolidation of the system under the existing form, with powers equally despotic and oppressive,—or a dissolution.

With these preliminary remarks, I shall next proceed to consider the question,—whether the reserved powers, if fully developed and brought into action, are sufficient to resist this powerful and dangerous tendency of the delegated, to encroach on them? or, to express the same thing in a different form,—whether the separate government of a State, and its people in their sovereign character, to whom all powers, not delegated to the United States, appertain, can,—one or both,—rightfully oppose sufficient resistance to the strong tendency on the part of the government of the latter, to prevent its encroachment. I use the expression,—"a State and its people,"—because the powers not delegated to the United States, are reserved to each State respectively, or to its people; and, of course, it results that, whatever resistance the reserved powers can oppose to the delegated, must, to be within constitutional limits, proceed from the government and the people of the several States, in their separate and individual character.

The question is one of the first magnitude;—and deserves the most serious and deliberate consideration. I shall begin with considering,—what means the government of a State possesses, to prevent the government of the United States from encroaching on its reserved powers? I shall, however, pass over the right of remonstrating against its encroachments; of adopting resolutions against them, as unconstitutional; of addressing the governments of its co-States, and calling on them to unite and co-operate in opposition to them; and of instructing its Senators in Congress, and requesting its members of the House of Representatives, to oppose them,—and other means of a like character; not because they are of no avail, but because they are utterly impotent to arrest the strong and steady tendency of the government of the United States to encroach on the reserved powers; however much they may avail, in particular instances. To rely on them to counteract a tendency so strong and steady, would be as idle as to rely on reason and justice, as the means to prevent oppression and abuse of power on the part of government, without the aid of constitutional provisions. Nothing short of a negative, absolute or in effect, on the part of the government of a State, can possibly protect it against the encroachments of the government of the United States, whenever their powers come in conflict. That there is, in effect, a mutual negative on the part of each, in such cases, is what I next propose to show.

It results from their nature; from the relations which subsist between them; and from a law universally applicable to a division of power. I will consider each in the order stated.

That they are both governments, and, as such, possess all the powers appertaining to government, within the sphere of their respective powers,—the one as fully as the other,—cannot be denied. Nor can it be denied that, among the other attributes of government, they possess the right to judge of the extent of their respective powers, as it regards each other. In addition to this, it may be affirmed as true, that governments, in full possession of all the powers appertaining to government, have the right to enforce their decisions as to the extent of their powers, against all opposition. But the case is different in a system of governments like ours,—where the powers appertaining to government are divided,—a portion being delegated to one government, and a portion to another;—and the residue retained by those who ordained and established both. In such case, neither can have the right to enforce its decisions, as to the extent of its powers, when a conflict occurs between them in reference to it; because it would be, in the first place, inconsistent with the relation in which they stand to each other as co-ordinates. The idea of co-ordinates, excludes that of superior and subordinate, and, necessarily, implies that of equality. But to give either the right, not only to judge of the extent of its own powers, but, also, of that of its co-ordinate, and to enforce its decision against it, would be, not only to destroy the equality between them, but to deprive one of an attribute,—appertaining to all governments,—to judge, in the first instance, of the extent of its powers. The effect would be to raise one from an equal to a superior;—and to reduce the other from an equal to a subordinate; and, by divesting it of an attribute appertaining to government, to sink it into a dependent corporation. In the next place, it would be inconsistent with what is meant by a division of power; as this necessarily implies, that each of the parties, among whom it may be partitioned, has an equal right to its respective share, be it greater or smaller; and to judge as to its extent, and to maintain its decision against its copartners. This is what constitutes, and what is meant by, a division of power. Without it, there could be no division. To allot a portion of power to one, and another portion to another, and to give either the exclusive right to say, how much was allotted to each, would be no division at all. The one would hold as a mere tenant at will,—to be deprived of its portion whenever the other should choose to assume the whole. And, finally, because, no reason can be assigned, why one should possess the right to judge of the extent of its powers, and to enforce its decision, which would not equally apply to the other co-ordinate government. If one, then, possess the right to enforce its decision, so, also, must the other. But to assume that both possess it, would be to leave the umpirage, in case of conflict, to mere brute force; and thus to destroy the equality, clearly implied by the relation of co-ordinates, and the division between the two governments. In such case, force alone would determine which should be the superior, and which the subordinate; which should have the exclusive right of judging, both as to the extent of its own powers and that of its co-ordinates;—and which should be deprived of the right of judging as to the extent of those of either;—which should, and which should not possess any other power than that which its co-ordinate,—now raised to its superior,—might choose to permit it to exercise. As the one or the other might prove the stronger, consolidation or disunion would, inevitably, be the consequence; and which of the twain, no one who has paid any attention to the working of our system, can doubt. An assumption, therefore, which would necessarily lead to the destruction of the whole system in the end, and the substitution of another, of an entirely different character, in its place,—must be false.

But, if neither has the exclusive right, the effect, where they disagree as to the extent of their respective powers, would be, a mutual negative on the acts of each, when they come into conflict. And the effect of this again, would be, to vest in each the power to protect the portion of authority allotted to it, against the encroachment of its co-ordinate government. Nothing short of this can possibly preserve this important division of power, on which rests the equilibrium of the entire system.

The party, in the convention, which favored a national government, clearly saw that the separate governments of the several States would have the right of judging of the extent of their powers, as between the two governments, unless some provision should be adopted to prevent it. This is manifest from the many and strenuous efforts which they made to deprive them of the right, by vesting the government of the United States with the power to veto or overrule their acts, when they might be thought to come in conflict with its powers. These efforts were made in every stage of the proceedings of the convention, and in every conceivable form,—as its journals will show.

The very first project of a constitution submitted to the convention, (Gov. Randolph's,) contained a provision, "to grant power to negative all acts contrary, in the opinion of the national legislature, to the articles,—or any treaty, subsisting under the power of the Union; and to call forth the force of the Union, against any member of the Union, failing to fulfil its duties, under the articles thereof."

The next plan submitted, (Mr. Charles Pinckney's,) contained a provision that,—"the legislature of the United States shall have power to revise the laws that may be supposed to impinge the powers exclusively delegated, by this constitution, to Congress; and to negative and annul such as do." The next submitted, (Mr. Patterson's,) provided that, "if any State, or body of men in any State, shall oppose, or prevent the carrying into execution, such acts, or treaties," (of the Union,) "the federal executive shall be authorized to call forth the forces of the confederated States, or so much thereof, as shall be necessary, to enforce or compel obedience to such acts, or the observance of such treaties." The committee of the whole, to whom was referred Mr. Randolph's project, reported a provision, that the jurisdiction of the national judiciary should extend to all "questions, which involved the national peace and harmony." The next project, (Mr. Hamilton's,)—after declaring all the laws of the several States, which were contrary to the constitution and the laws of the United States, to be null and void,—provides, that, "the better to prevent such laws from being passed, the Governor, or President of each State, shall be appointed by the general government; and shall have a negative upon the laws, about to be passed in the State of which he is Governor or President." This was followed by a motion, made by Mr. C. Pinckney, to vest in the legislature of the United States the power, "to negative all laws, passed by the several States, interfering, in the opinion of the legislature, with the general interest and harmony of the Union; provided that two thirds of each house assent to the same."

It is not deemed necessary to trace, through the journals of the convention, the history and the fate of these various propositions. It is sufficient to say,—that they were all made, and not one adopted; although perseveringly urged by some of the most talented and influential members of the body, as indispensable to protect the government of the United States, against the apprehended encroachments of the governments of the several States. The fact that they were proposed and so urged, proves, conclusively, that it was believed, even by the most distinguished members of the national party, that the former had no right to enforce its measures against the latter, where they disagreed as to the extent of their respective powers,—without some express provision to that effect; while the refusal of the convention to adopt any such provision, under such circumstances, proves, equally conclusively, that it was opposed to the delegation of such powers to the government, or any of its departments, legislative, executive, or judicial, in any form whatever.

But, if it be possible for doubt still to remain, the ratification of the constitution by the convention of Virginia, and the 10th amended article, furnish proofs in confirmation so strong, that the most skeptical will find it difficult to resist them.

It is well known, that there was a powerful opposition to the adoption of the constitution of the United States. It originated in the apprehension, that it would lead to the consolidation of all power in the government of the United States;—notwithstanding the defeat of the national party, in the convention,—and the refusal to adopt any of the proposals to vest it with the power to negative the acts of the governments of the separate States. This apprehension excited a wide and deep distrust, lest the scheme of the national party might ultimately prevail, through the influence of its leaders, over the government about to be established. The alarm became so great as to threaten the defeat of the ratification by nine States,—the number necessary to make the constitution binding between the States ratifying it. It was particularly great in Virginia;—on whose act, all sides believed the fate of the instrument depended. Before the meeting of her convention, seven States had ratified. It was generally believed that, of the remaining States, North Carolina and Rhode Island would not ratify; and New-York was regarded so doubtful, that her course would, in all probability, depend on the action of Virginia. Her refusal, together with that of Virginia, would have defeated the adoption of the constitution. The struggle, accordingly, between the two parties in her convention, was long and ardent. The magnitude of the question at issue, called out the ablest and most influential of her citizens on both sides; and elicited the highest efforts of their talents.

The discussion turned, mainly, on the danger of consolidation from construction; and was conducted with such ability and force of argument, by the opponents of ratification, that it became necessary, in order to obtain a majority for it, to guard against such construction, by incorporating in the act of ratification itself, provisions to prevent it. The act is in the following words: "We, the delegates of the people of Virginia, duly elected in pursuance of a recommendation from the general assembly, and now met in convention, having fully and freely investigated and discussed the proceedings of the federal convention, and being prepared as well as the most mature deliberation hath enabled us to decide thereon, do, in the name and in behalf of the people of Virginia, declare and make known, that the powers granted under the constitution, being derived from the people of the United States, may be resumed by them, whensoever the same shall be perverted to their injury or oppression; and that every power not granted thereby, remains with them and at their will: that, therefore, no right, of any denomination, can be cancelled, abridged, restrained, or modified, by the Congress, by the Senate, or House of Representatives, acting in any capacity, by the President or any department, or officer of the United States, except in those instances in which power is given by the constitution for those purposes; and that among other essential rights, the liberty of conscience and of the press cannot be cancelled, abridged, restrained or modified by any authority of the United States.

"With these impressions,—with a solemn appeal to the Searcher of hearts for the purity of our intentions, and under the conviction, that, whatsoever imperfections may exist in the constitution ought rather to be examined in the mode prescribed therein, than to bring the Union into danger by delay, with the hope of obtaining amendments, previous to the ratification: We, the said delegates, in the name and behalf of the people of Virginia, do by these presents, assent to and ratify the constitution, &c."—concluding in the usual form.

Such is the recorded construction, which that great and leading State placed on the constitution, in her act of ratification. That her object was to guard against the abuse of construction, the act itself, on its face, and the discussions in her convention abundantly prove. It was done effectually, as far as it depended on words. It declares that all powers granted by the constitution, are derived from the people of the United States; and may be *resumed* by them when *perverted* to their injury or oppression; and, that every power *not granted,* remains with them, and at their will; and that no right of any description can be cancelled, abridged, restrained or modified by Congress, the Senate, the House of Representatives, the President, or any department, or officer of the United

States. Language cannot be stronger. It guards the reserved powers against the government as a whole, and against all its departments and officers; and in every mode by which they might be impaired; showing, clearly, that the intention was to place the reserved powers beyond the possible interference and control of the government of the United States. Now, when it is taken into consideration, that the right of the separate governments of the several States is as full and perfect to protect their own powers, as is that of the government of the United States to protect those which are delegated to it; and, of course, that it belongs to their reserved powers; that all the attempts made in the convention which framed the constitution, to deprive them of it, by vesting the latter with the power to overrule the right, equally failed; that Virginia could not be induced to ratify without incorporating the true construction she placed on it in her act of ratification; that, without her ratification, it would not, in all probability, have been adopted; and that it was accepted by the other States, subject to this avowed construction, without objection on their part;—it is difficult to resist the inference, that their acceptance, under all these circumstances, was an implied admission of the truth of her construction; and that it makes it as binding on them as if it had been inserted in the constitution itself.

But her convention took the further precaution of having it inserted, in substance, in that instrument. Those who composed it were wise, experienced, and patriotic men; and knew full well, how difficult it is to guard against the abuses of construction. They accordingly proposed, as an amendment of the constitution, the substance of her construction. It is in the following words: "That each State in the Union shall respectively retain every power, jurisdiction, and right, which is not, by the constitution, delegated to the Congress of the United States, or to the departments of the federal government." This was modified and proposed, as an amendment, in the regular constitutional form; and was ratified by the States. It constitutes the 10th amended article, which has already been quoted at length. It is worthy of note, that Massachusetts, New Hampshire, and South Carolina, proposed, when they ratified the constitution, amendments similar in substance, and with the same object:—clearly showing how extensively the alarm felt by Virginia, had extended; and how strong the desire was to guard against the evil apprehended.

Such, and so convincing are the arguments going to show, that the government of the United States has no more right to enforce its decisions against those of the separate governments of the several States, where they disagree as to the extent of their respective powers, than the latter have of enforcing their decisions in like cases. They both stand on equal grounds, in this respect. But as convincing as are these arguments, there are many, who entertain a different opinion;—and still affirm that the government of the United States possesses the right, fully, absolutely, and exclusively.

In support of this opinion, they rely, in the first place, on the second section of the sixth article, which provides that,—"This constitution, and the laws of the United States, which shall be made in pursuance thereof, and all treaties made, or which shall be made, under the authority of the United States, shall be the supreme law of the land; and the judges in every State shall be bound thereby, any thing in the constitution or laws of any State to the contrary notwithstanding."

It is sufficient, in reply, to state, that the clause is declaratory; that it vests no new power whatever in the government, or in any of its departments. Without it, the constitution and the laws made in pursuance of it, and the treaties made under its authority, would have been the supreme law of the land, as fully and perfectly as they now are; and the judges in every State would have been bound thereby, any thing in the constitution or laws of a State, to the contrary notwithstanding. Their supremacy results from the nature of the relation between the federal government, and those of the several States, and their respective constitutions and laws. Where two or more States form a common constitution and government, the authority of these, within the limits of the delegated powers, must, of necessity, be supreme, in reference to their respective separate constitutions and governments. Without this, there would be neither a common constitution and government, nor even a confederacy. The whole would be, in fact, a mere nullity. But this supremacy is not an absolute supremacy. It is limited in extent and degree. It does not extend beyond the delegated powers;—all others being reserved to the States and the people of the States. Beyond these the constitution is as destitute of authority, and as powerless as a blank piece of paper; and the measures of the government mere acts of assumption. And, hence, the supremacy of laws and treaties is expressly restricted to such as are made in pursuance of the constitution, or under the authority of the United States; which can, in no case, extend beyond the delegated powers. There is, indeed, no power of the government without restriction; not even that, which is called the discretionary power of Congress. I refer to the grant which authorizes it to pass laws to carry into effect the powers expressly vested in it,—or in the government of the United States,—or in any of its departments, or officers. This power, comprehensive as it is, is, nevertheless, subject to two important restrictions; one, that the law must be necessary,—and the other, that it must be proper.

To understand the import of the former, it must be borne in mind, that no power can execute itself. They all require means, and the agency of government, to apply them. The means themselves may, indeed, be regarded as auxiliary powers. Of these, some are so intimately connected with the principal power, that, without the aid of one, or all of them, it could not be carried into execution;—and, of course, without them, the power itself would be nugatory. Hence, they are called implied powers; and it is to this description of incidental or auxiliary powers, that Congress is restricted, in passing laws, necessary to carry into execution the powers expressly delegated.

But the law must, also, be proper as well as necessary, in order to bring it within its competency. To understand the true import of the term in this connection, it is necessary to bear in mind, that even the implied powers themselves are subject to important conditions, when used as means to carry powers or rights into execution. Among these the most prominent and important is, that they must be so carried into execution as not to injure others; and, as connected with, and subordinate to this,—that, where the implied powers, or means used, come in conflict with the implied powers, or means used by another, in the execution of the powers or rights vested in it, the less important should yield to the more important,—the convenient, to the useful; and both to health and safety;—because it is *proper they should do so.* Both rules are universal, and rest on the fundamental principles of morals.

Such is the true import of the term "proper," superadded to "necessary," when applied to this important question. And hence, when a law of Congress, carrying into execution one of the delegated powers, comes into conflict with a law of one of the States, carrying its reserved powers into execution, it does not necessarily follow that the latter must yield to the former, because the laws made in pursuance of the constitution, are declared to be the supreme law of the land: for the restriction imposed by the term "proper," takes it out of the power of Congress, even where the implied power is necessary, and brings it under the operation of those fundamental rules of universal acceptation, to determine which shall yield. Without this restriction, most of the reserved powers of the States,—and, among them, those relating to their internal police, including the health, tranquility, and safety of their people—might be made abortive, by the laws passed by Congress, to carry into effect the delegated powers; especially in regard to those regulating commerce, and establishing post-offices and post-roads.

The alterations finally made in this clause of the constitution, compared with it as originally reported by the committee on detail, deserve notice,—as shedding considerable light on its phraseology and objects. As reported by that committee, it was in the following words:—"The acts of the legislature of the United States, made in pursuance of this constitution, and all treaties made under the authority of the United States, shall be the supreme law of the several States, and of their citizens and inhabitants; and the Judges of the several States shall be bound thereby, in their decisions; any thing in the constitutions or laws of the several States to the contrary notwithstanding." After a long discussion of the plan of the constitution, as reported by this committee; and after many alterations were made, the whole, as amended, was referred to the committee of revision, or *"style,"* as it was also called. This particular clause had received no amendment; and, of course, was referred as reported by the committee on detail. The committee of revision, or style, reported it back as it now stands. On comparing the two, it will be found, that the word "constitution," which was omitted in the plan of the committee on detail, is added, as a part of the supreme law of the land; that the expression, "the acts of the legislature of the United States," is changed into "laws of Congress," and "land" substituted in lieu of, "several States and of their citizens and inhabitants." These modifications of phraseology were, doubtless, introduced to make the clause conform to what was believed to be the views of the convention, as disclosed in the discussion on the plan reported by the committee on detail, and to improve the manner of expression; for such were plainly the objects of referring the plan, as amended, to the committee of revision and style. "Constitution" was doubtless added, because, although a compact as between the States, it is a law,—and the highest law,—in reference to the citizens and inhabitants of the several States, regarded individually. The substitution of "Congress," for "the legislature of the United States," requires no explanation. It is a mere change of phraseology. For the substitution of "land," in place of the "several States and their citizens and inhabitants," no reason is assigned, so far as I can discover; but one will readily suggest itself on a little reflection. As the expression stood in the plan reported by the committee on detail, the supremacy of the acts of the legislature of the United States, and of treaties made under their authority, was limited to the "several States, and their citizens and inhabitants;" and, of course, would not have extended over the *territorial possessions* of the United States; or, as far as their authority might otherwise extend. It became necessary, therefore, to give them a wider scope; especially after the word, "constitution," was introduced in connection with, "laws of the United States;" as their authority never can extend beyond the limits, to which it is carried by the constitution. As far as this extends, their authority extends; but no further. To give to the constitution and the laws and treaties made in pursuance thereof, a supremacy coextensive with these limits, it became necessary to adopt a more comprehensive expression than that reported by the committee on detail; and, hence, in all probability, the adoption of that substituted by the committee of revision and style;—"the supreme law of the land," being deemed the more appropriate.

Such are the limitations imposed on the authority of the constitution, and laws of the United States, and treaties made under their authority, regarded as the supreme law of the land. To carry their supremacy beyond this,—and to extend it over the reserved powers, in any form or shape, or through any channel,—be it the government itself or any of its departments,—would finally destroy the system by consolidating all its powers in the hands of the one or the other.

The limitation of their supremacy, *in degree,* is not less strongly marked, than it is *in extent.* While they are supreme, within their sphere, over the constitutions and laws of the several States,—the constitution of the United States, and all that appertains to it, are subordinate to the power which ordained and established it;—as much so, as are the constitutions of the several States, and all which appertains to them, to the same creative power. In this respect, as well as their supremacy in regard to each other, in their respective spheres, they stand on the same level. Neither has any advantage, in either particular, over the other.

Those who maintain that the government of the United States has the right to enforce its decisions as to the extent of the powers delegated to it, against the decisions of the separate governments of the several States as to the extent of the reserved powers, in case of conflict between the two,—next rely, in support of their opinion, on the 2d sec. 3d art. of the constitution,—which is in the following words: "The judicial power shall extend to all cases, in law and equity, arising under this constitution, the laws of the United States, and treaties made, or which shall be made, under their authority;—to all cases affecting ambassadors, other public ministers and consuls;—to all cases of admiralty and maritime jurisdiction;—to controversies, to which the United States shall be a party;—to controversies between two or more States;—between a State and the citizens of another State;—between citizens of different States;—between citizens of the same State claiming lands under grants of different States, and between a State or the citizens thereof, and foreign states citizens or subjects."

It will be sufficient, in reply, to show, that this section contains no provisions whatever, which would authorize the judiciary to enforce the determination of the government, against that of the government of a State, in such cases.

It may be divided into two parts; that which gives jurisdiction to the judicial power, in reference to the *subject matter,* and that which gives it jurisdiction, in reference to the *parties litigant*. The first clause, which extends it, "to all cases in law and equity, arising under this constitution, the laws of the United States, and treaties made, or which shall be made under their authority," embraces the former; and the residue of the section, the latter.

It is clear on its face, that the object of the clause was, to make the jurisdiction of the judicial power, commensurate with the authority of the constitution and the several departments of the government, as far as it related to cases arising under them,—and no further. Nor is it less manifest that the word *"cases,"* being a well-defined technical term, is used in its proper legal sense;—and embraces only such questions as are of a judicial character;—that is, questions in which the parties litigant are amenable to the process of the courts. Now, as there is nothing in the constitution which vests authority in the government of the United States, or any of its departments, to enforce its decision against that of the separate government of a State; and nothing in this clause which makes the several States amenable to its process, it is manifest that there is nothing in it, which can possibly give the judicial power authority to enforce the decision of the government of the United States, against that of a separate State, where their respective decisions come into conflict. If, then, there be any thing that authorizes it, it must be contained in the remainder of the section, which vests jurisdiction with reference to the parties litigant. But this contains no provision which extends the jurisdiction of the judicial power to questions involving such conflict between the two co-ordinate governments,—either express or implied;—as I shall next proceed to show.

It will not be contended that either the government of the United States, or those of the separate States are amenable to the process of the courts; unless made so by their consent respectively; for no legal principle is better established than that, a government, though it may be plaintiff in a case, or controversy, cannot be made defendant, or, in any way, amenable to the process of the courts, without its consent. That there is no *express* provision in the section, by which, either of the co-ordinate governments can be made defendants, or amenable to the process of the courts, in a question between them, is manifest.

If, then, there be any, it must be *implied* in some one of its provisions: and it is, accordingly, contended, that it is *implied* in the clause, which provides that the judicial power shall extend, "to controversies to which the United States shall be a party." This clause, it is admitted, clearly extends the jurisdiction of the judiciary to all controversies to which the United States are a party, as plaintiff or defendant, by their consent. So far, it is not a matter of implication, but of express provision. But the inquiry is, does it go further, and, by implication, authorize them to make a State a defendant without its consent, in a question or controversy between it and them? It contains not a word or syllable that would warrant such an implication; and any construction which could warrant it, would authorize a State, or an individual, to make the United States a party defendant, in a controversy between them, without their consent.

There is, not only nothing to warrant such construction, but much to show that it is utterly unwarrantable. Nothing, in the first place, short of the strongest implication, is sufficient to authorize a construction, that would deprive a State of a right so important to its sovereignty, as that of not being held amenable to the process of the courts; or to be made a defendant, in any case or controversy whatever, without its consent;—more especially, in one between it and a coequal government, where the effect would necessarily be, to reduce it from an equal to a subordinate station.

It would, in the next place, be contrary to the construction placed on a similar clause in the same section, by an authority higher than that of the judicial, or of any other, or of all the departments of the government taken together. I refer to the last clause, which provides that the judicial power shall extend to controversies, "between a State or citizens thereof, and foreign states, citizens or subjects." It would be much more easy to make out something like a plausible argument in support of the position, that a State might be made defendant and amenable to the process of the courts of the United States, under this clause, than under that in question. In the former, the States are not even named. They can be brought in only by implication, and then, by another implication, divested of a high sovereign right: and this, too, without any assignable reason for either. Here they are not only named, but the other parties to the controversies are also named; without stating which shall be plaintiff, or which defendant. This was left undefined; and, of course, the question, whether the several States might not be made defendants as well as plaintiffs, in controversies between the parties, left open to construction;—and in favor of the implication, a very plausible reason may be assigned. The clause puts a State and its citizens on the same ground. In the controversies, to which it extends the judicial power, the State and its citizens stand on one side, and foreign states, citizens and subjects, on the other. Now as foreign states, citizens, or subjects may, under its provisions, make the citizens of a State defendants, in a controversy between them, it would not be an unnatural inference, that the State might also be included. Under this construction, an action was, in fact, commenced in the courts of the United States, against one of the States. The States took the alarm; and, in the high sovereign character, in which they ordained and established the constitution, declared that it should "not be so construed, as to extend to any suit in law or equity, commenced or prosecuted against one of the United States, by citizens of another State, or by citizens or subjects of any foreign state."[*]

If additional reasons could be thought necessary to sustain a conclusion supported by arguments so convincing, they might be found in the fact, that as long as the government has existed,—and as numerous as have been the questions between the United States and many of the several States,—the former never have attempted, in any of them, to bring the latter into the courts of the United States. If to this it be added, that all attempts made in the convention, to extend the judicial power, "to all questions, which involved the national peace and harmony;"—or which might have the effect of subjecting the several States to its jurisdiction, failed,—the conclusion against all constructive efforts, having the same objects in view, and based on any one of the clauses of this section, is irresistible.

It is, in the last place, contended,—that the Supreme Court of the United States has the right to decide on the constitutionality of all laws; and, in virtue of this, to decide, in the last resort, all questions involving a conflict between the constitution of the United States and laws and treaties made in pursuance thereof, on the one side, and the constitutions and laws of the several States, on the other.

It is admitted, that the court has the right, in all questions of a judicial character which may come before it, where the laws and treaties of the United States, and the constitution and laws of a State are in conflict or brought in question, to decide which is, or is not consistent with the constitution of the United States. But it is denied that this power is peculiar to it; or that its decision, in the last resort, is binding on any but the parties to it, and its co-departments. So far from being peculiar to it, the right appertains, not only to the Supreme Court of the United States, but to all the courts of the several States, superior and inferior; and even to foreign courts,—should a question be brought before them involving such conflict. It results, necessarily, from our system of government; where power is not only divided, but where constitutions and laws emanate from different authorities. Where this is the fact, it is the duty of the court to pronounce what is the law in the case before it;—and, of course,—where there is conflict between different laws,—to pronounce which is paramount. Now, as the constitution of the United States is, within its sphere, supreme over all others appertaining to the system, it necessarily results, that where any law conflicts with it, it is the duty of the court, before which the question arises, to pronounce the

[*]Amendments, Art. II.

constitution to be paramount. If it be the Supreme Court of the United States, its decision,—being that of the highest judicial tribunal, in the last resort, of the parties to the case or controversy,—is, of course, final as it respects them,—but only as it respects them. It results, that its decision is not binding as between the United States and the several States, as neither can make the other defendant in any controversy between them.

Others, who are forced by the strength of the argument to admit, that the judicial power does not extend to them, contend that Congress, the great organ of the government, has the right to decide, in the last resort, in all such controversies;—or in all questions involving the extent of their respective powers. They do not pretend to derive this high power from any specific provision of the constitution; they claim it to be a right incident to all governments, to decide as to the extent of its powers; and to enforce its decision by its own proper authority.

It is manifest, that they who contend for this right to its full extent, overlook the distinction, in this respect, between *single* governments, vested with all the powers appertaining to government, and *co-ordinate* governments, in a system where the powers of government are divided between two or more, as is the case with us. If it be admitted that the right belongs to both, and that co-ordinate governments, in this respect, stand on the same ground as single governments,—whatever right or power in such case, belongs to the one, must necessarily belong to the other: and, if so, the result must be, where they differ as to the extent of their respective powers, either a mutual negative on the acts of each other,—or the right of each to enforce its decision on the other. But it has already been established, that they have not the latter; and hence, under any aspect in which the question can be viewed, the same conclusion follows,—that where the two governments differ as to the extent of their respective powers, a mutual negative is the consequence.

The effect of this is, to make each, as against the other, the guardian and protector of the powers allotted to it, and of which it is the organ and representative. By no other device, could the separate governments of the several States, as the weaker of the two, prevent the government of the United States, as the stronger, from encroaching on that portion of the reserved powers allotted to them, and finally absorbing the whole; except, indeed, by so organizing the former, as to give to each of the States a concurrent voice in making and administering the laws; and, of course, a veto on its action. The powers not delegated are expressly reserved to the respective States or the people; that is, to the governments of the respective States and the people thereof; and by them only can they be protected and preserved. The reason has been fully explained in the discourse on the elementary principles of government. But the several States, as weaker parties, can protect the portion not delegated, only in one of two ways; either by having a concurrent voice in the action of the government of the United States; or a negative on its acts, when they disagree as to the extent of their respective powers. One or the other is indispensable to the preservation of the reserved rights,—and to prevent the consolidation of all power in the government of the United States, as the stronger. Why the latter was preferred by the convention which formed the constitution, may, probably, be attributed to the great number of States, and the belief that it was impossible so to organize the government, as to give to each a concurrent voice in its action, without rendering it too feeble and tardy to fulfil the ends for which it was intended. But, be this as it may, not having adopted it, no device remained, by which the reserved powers could be protected and preserved, but the one which they, in effect, did adopt,—by refusing to vest the government of the United States with a veto on the acts of the separate governments of the several States, in any form or manner whatever.

But it may be alleged, that the effect of a mutual negative on the part of the two co-ordinate governments, where they disagree as to the extent of their respective powers, will, while it guards against consolidation on one side,—lead to collision and conflict between them on the other;—and, finally, to disunion.

That the division of the powers of government between the two, without some means to prevent such result, would necessarily lead to collision and conflict, will not be denied. They are incident to every division of powers, of every description; whether it be that of co-ordinate departments, co-ordinate estates or classes, co-ordinate governments, or any other division of power appertaining to our system, or to that of any other constitutional government. It is impossible to construct one without dividing the powers of government. But wherever, and however power may be divided, collision and conflict are necessary consequences, if not prevented. The more numerous and complex the divisions, the stronger the tendency to both, and the greater the necessity for powerful and effectual guards to prevent them. It is one of the evils incident to constitutional governments of every form. But we must take things as they are, with all their incidents, bad or good. The choice between constitutional and absolute governments, lies between the good and evil, incident to each. If the former be exposed to collision and conflict between its various parts, the latter is exposed to all the oppressions and abuses, ever incident to uncontrolled and irresponsible power, in all its forms. With us the choice lies between a national, consolidated and irresponsible government of a dominant portion, or section of the country,—and a federal, constitutional and responsible government, with all the divisions of powers indispensable to form and preserve such a government, in a country of such vast extent, and so great a diversity of interests and institutions as ours. The advantages of both, without the evils incident to either, we cannot have. Their nature and character are too opposite and hostile to be blended in the same system.

But while it is admitted that collision and conflict may be necessarily incident to a division of powers, it is utterly denied, that the effects of the mutual negative between the two co-ordinate governments would contribute to either, or necessarily lead to disunion. On the contrary, its effects would be the very reverse. Instead of leading to either, it is an indispensable means to prevent the collision and conflict, which must necessarily arise between the delegated and reserved powers; and which, if not prevented, would, in the end, destroy the system, either by consolidation or dissolution. Its aim and end is to prevent the encroachment of either of the co-ordinate governments on the other. For this purpose it is the effectual, and the only effectual means that can be devised. By preventing such encroachments, it prevents collision and conflict between them. These are their natural offspring: collision follows encroachment,—and conflict, collision, in the order of events,—unless encroachment be acquiesced in. In that case, the weaker would be absorbed, and all power concentrated in the stronger.

But it may be alleged, that, in preventing these, it would lead to consequences not less to be dreaded;—that a negative on the part of the governments of so many States, where either might disagree with that of the United States, as to the extent of their respective powers, would lead to such embarrassment and confusion, and interpose so many impediments in its way, as to render it incompetent to fulfil the ends for which it was established. The objection is plausible; but it will be found, on investigation, that strong as the remedy is, it is not stronger than is required by the disease; and that the system furnishes ample means to correct whatever disorder it may occasion.

It may be laid down as a fundamental principle in constructing constitutional governments, that a strong government requires a negative proportionally strong, to restrict it to its appropriate sphere; and that, the stronger the government,—if the negative be proportionally strong, the better the government. It is only by making it proportionally strong, that an equilibrium can be established between the positive and negative powers—the power of acting, and the power of restricting action to its assigned limits. It is difficult to form a conception of a constitutional government stronger than that of the United States; and, consequently, of one requiring a stronger negative to keep it within its appropriate sphere. Combining, habitually, as it necessarily does, the united power and patronage of a majority of the States and of their population estimated in federal numbers, in opposition to a minority of each, with nothing but their separate and divided power and patronage, it is, to the full as strong, if not stronger, than was the government of Rome,—with its powerfully constituted Senate, including its control of the auspices, the censorship, and the dictatorship. It will, of course, require, in order to keep it within its proper bounds, a negative fully as strong in proportion, as the tribuneship; which, in its prime, consisted of ten members, elected by the plebeians, each of whom, (as has been supposed by some,—but a majority of whom, all admit,) had a negative, not only on the acts of the Senate, but on their execution. As powerful as was this negative, experiment proved that it was not too strong for the positive power of the government. If the circumstances be considered, under which the negative of the several States will be brought into action, it will be found, on comparison, to be weaker in proportion, than the negative possessed by the tribuneship; and far more effectually guarded in its possible tendencies to disorder, or the derangement of the system.

In the first place, the negative of the tribunes extended to all the acts of the Senate, and to their execution; and,—as it was a single government without limitation on its authority,—to all the acts of government. On the other hand, the negative of the governments of the several States extends only to the *execution* of such acts of the government of the United States, as may present a question involving their respective powers; which, relatively, are very few, compared to the whole. In the next place, every tribune, or, at least, the majority of the college, possessed the power; and was ordinarily disposed to exercise it, as they all represented the portion of the Roman people, which their veto was intended to protect against oppression and abuse of power on the part of the Senate. On the contrary, the habitual relation between the governments of the several States and the government of the United States for the time, is such, as to identify the majority of them, in power and interest, with the latter; and to dispose them rather to enlarge and sustain its authority, than to resist its encroachments,— which, from their position, they regard as extending,—and not as contracting their powers. This limits the negative power of the governments of the several States to the minority, for the time: and even that minority will have, as experience proves, a minority in its own limits, almost always opposed to its will, and nearly of equal numbers with itself, identified in views and party feelings, with the majority in possession of the control of the government of the United States;

and ever ready to counteract any opposition to its encroachments on the reserved powers. To this it may be added, that even the majority in this minority of the States, will, for the most part, be averse to making a stand against its encroachments; as they, themselves, hope, in their turn, to gain the ascendency; and are, therefore, naturally disinclined to weaken their party connections with the minority in the States possessing, for the time, the control of the government,—and whose interest and feelings, aside from party ties, would be with the majority of their respective States. Such being the case, it is apparent that there will be far less disposition on the part of the governments of the several States to resist the encroachments of the government of the United States on their reserved rights,—or to make an issue with it, when they disagree as to the extent of their respective powers,—than there was in the tribunate of the Roman republic to oppose acts, or the execution of acts, calculated to oppress, or deprive their order of its rights.

If to this it be further added, that the federal constitution provides,—not only that all the functionaries of the United States, but also those of the several States, including, expressly, the members of their legislatures, and all their executive and judicial officers,—shall be bound, by oath or affirmation, to support the constitution;—and that the decision of the highest tribunal of the judicial power is final, as between the parties to a case or controversy,—the danger of any serious derangement or disorder from the effects of the negative on the parts of the separate governments of the several States, must appear, not only much less than that from the Roman tribunate, but very inconsiderable. The danger is, indeed, the other way;—that the disposition on the part of the governments of the several States, to acquiesce in the encroachments of the government of the United States, will prove stronger than the disposition to resist; and the negative, compared with the positive power, will be found to be too feeble to preserve the equilibrium between them. But if it should prove otherwise,—and if, in consequence, any serious derangement of the system should ensue, there will be found, in the earliest and highest division of power, which I shall next proceed to consider, ample and safe means of correcting them.

I refer to that resulting from, and inseparably connected with the primitive territorial division of the country itself,—coeval with its settlement into separate and distinct communities; and which, though dependent at the first on the parent country, became, by a successful resistance to its encroachments on their chartered rights, independent and sovereign States. In them severally,—or to express it more precisely, in the people composing them, regarded as independent and sovereign communities, the ultimate power of the whole system resided, and from them the whole system emanated. Their first act was, to ordain and establish their respective separate constitutions and governments,—each by itself, and for itself,—without concert or agreement with the others; and their next, after the failure of the confederacy, was to ordain and establish the constitution and government of the United States, in the same way in every respect, as has been shown; except that it was done by concert and agreement with each other. That this high, this supreme power, has never been either delegated to, or vested in the separate governments of the States, or the federal government,—and that it is, therefore, one of the powers declared, by the 10th article of amendments, to be reserved to the people of the respective States; and that, of course, it still resides with them, will hardly be questioned. It must reside somewhere. No one will assert that it is extinguished. But, according to the fundamental principles of our system, sovereignty resides in the people, and not in the government; and if in them, it must be in them, as the people of the several States; for, politically speaking, there is no other known to the system. It not only resides in them, but resides in its plenitude, unexhausted and unimpaired. If proof be required, it will be found in the fact,—which cannot be controverted, so far as the United States are concerned,—that the people of the several States, acting in the same capacity and in the same way, in which they ordained and established the federal constitution, can, by their concurrent and united voice, change or abolish it, and establish another in its place; or dissolve the Union, and resolve themselves into separate and disconnected States. A power which can rightfully do all this, must exist in full plenitude, unexhausted and unimpaired; for no higher act of sovereignty can be conceived.

But it does not follow from this, that the people of the several States, in ordaining and establishing the constitution of the United States, imposed no restriction on the exercise of sovereign power; for a sovereign may voluntarily impose restrictions on his acts, without, in any degree, exhausting or impairing his sovereignty; as is admitted by all writers on the subject. In the act of ordaining and establishing it, they have, accordingly, imposed several important restrictions on the exercise of their sovereign power. In order to ascertain what these are, and how far they extend, it will be necessary to ascertain, in what relation they stand to the constitution; and to each other in reference to it.

They stand then, as to the one, in the relation of superior to subordinate—the creator to the created. The people of the several States called it into existence, and conferred, by it, on the government, whatever power or authority it possesses. Regarded simply as a constitution, it is as subordinate to them, as are their respective State constitutions; and it imposes no more restrictions on the exercise of any of their sovereign rights, than they do. The case however is different as to the relations which the people of the several States bear to each other, in reference to it. Having ratified and adopted it, by mutual agreement, they stand to it in the relation of parties to a constitutional compact; and, of course, it is binding between them as a *compact,* and not on, or over them, as a *constitution.* Of all compacts that can exist between independent and sovereign communities, it is the most intimate, solemn, and sacred,—whether regarded in reference to the closeness of connection, the importance of the objects to be effected, or to the obligations imposed. Laying aside all intermediate agencies, the people of the several States, in their sovereign capacity, agreed to unite themselves together, in the closest possible connection that could be formed, without merging their respective sovereignties into one common sovereignty,—to establish one common government, for certain specific objects, which, regarding the mutual interest and security of each, and of all, they supposed could be more certainly, safely, and effectually promoted by it, than by their several separate governments; pledging their faith, in the most solemn manner possible, to support the compact thus formed, by respecting its provisions, obeying all acts of the government made in conformity with them, and preserving it, as far as in them lay, against all infractions. But, as solemn and sacred as it is, and as high as the obligations may be which it imposes,—still it is but a *compact* and not a *constitution,—regarded in reference to the people of the several States, in their sovereign capacity.* To use the language of the constitution itself, it was ordained as a "constitution *for* the United States,"—not *over* them; and established, not *over,* but "*between* the States ratifying it:" and hence, a State, acting in its sovereign capacity, and in the same manner in which it ratified and adopted the constitution, may be guilty of violating it *as a compact,* but cannot be guilty of violating it as a *law.* The case is the reverse, as to the action of its citizens, regarding them in their individual capacity. To them it is a law,—the supreme law within its sphere. They may be guilty of violating it *as a law,* or of violating the laws and treaties made in pursuance of, or under its authority, regarded as laws or treaties; but cannot be guilty of violating it as a *compact.* The constitution was ordained and established *over them* by their respective States, to whom they owed allegiance; and they are under the same obligation to respect and obey its authority, within its proper sphere, as they are to respect and obey their respective State constitutions; and for the same reason, viz.: that the State to which they owe allegiance, commanded it in both cases.

It follows, from what has been stated, that the people of the several States, regarded as parties to the constitutional compact, have imposed restrictions on the exercise of their sovereign power, by entering into a solemn obligation to do no act inconsistent with its provisions, and to uphold and support it within their respective limits. To this extent the restrictions go,—but no further. As parties to the constitutional compact, they retain the right, unrestricted, which appertains to such a relation in all cases where it is not surrendered, to judge as to the extent of the obligation imposed by the agreement or compact,—in the first instance, where there is a higher authority; and, in the last resort, where there is none. The principle on which this assertion rests, is essential to the nature of contracts; and is in accord with universal practice. But the right to judge as to the extent of the obligation imposed, necessarily involves the right of pronouncing whether an act of the federal government, or any of its departments, be, or be not, in conformity to the provisions of the constitutional compact; and, if decided to be inconsistent, of pronouncing it to be unauthorized by the constitution, and, therefore, null, void, and of no effect. If the constitution be a compact, and the several States, regarded in their sovereign character, be parties to it, all the rest follow as necessary consequences. It would be puerile to suppose the right of judging existed, without the right of pronouncing whether an act of the government violated the provisions of the constitution or not; and equally so to suppose, that the right of judging existed, without the authority of declaring the consequence, to wit; that, as such, it is null, void, and of no effect. And hence, those who are unwilling to admit the consequences, have been found to deny that the constitution is a compact; in the face of facts as well established as any in our political history, and in utter disregard of that provision of the constitution, which expressly declares, that the ratification of nine States shall be sufficient to establish it *"between the States so ratifying the same."*

But the right, with all these consequences, is not more certain than that possessed by the several States, as parties to the compact, of interposing for the purpose of arresting, within their respective limits, an act of the federal government in violation of the constitution; and thereby of preventing the delegated from encroaching on the reserved powers. Without such right, all the others would be barren and useless abstractions,—and just as puerile as the right of judging, without the right of pronouncing an act to be unconstitutional, and, as such, null and void. Nor is this right more certain, than that of the States, in the same character and capacity, to decide on the mode and measure to be adopted to arrest the act, and prevent the encroachment on the reserved powers. It is a right indispensable to all the others, and, without which, they would be valueless.

These conclusions follow irresistibly from incontestable facts and well established principles. But the possession of a right is one thing, and the exercise of it another. Rights, themselves, must be exercised with prudence and propriety: when otherwise exercised, they often cease to be rights, and become wrongs. The more important the right, and the more delicate its character, the higher the obligation to observe, strictly, the rules of prudence and propriety. But, of all the rights appertaining to the people of the several States, as members of a common Union, the one in question, is by far the most important and delicate; and, of course, requires, in its exercise, the greatest caution and forbearance. As parties to the compact which constitutes the Union, they are under obligations to observe its provisions, and prevent their infraction. In exercising the right in question, they are bound to take special care that they do not themselves, violate this, the most sacred of obligations. To avoid this, prudence and propriety require that they should abstain from interposing their authority, to arrest an act of their common government, unless the case, in their opinion, involve a clear and palpable infraction of the instrument. They are bound to go further,—and to forbear from interposing, even when it is clear and palpable, unless it be, at the same time, highly dangerous in its character, and apparently admitting of no other remedy; and for the plain reason, that prudence and propriety require, that a right so high and delicate should be called into exercise, only in cases of great magnitude and extreme urgency. But even when, in the opinion of the people of a State, such a case has occurred;—that nothing, short of the interposition of their authority, can arrest the danger and preserve the constitution, they ought to interpose in good faith;—not to weaken or destroy the Union, but to uphold and preserve it, by causing the instrument on which it rests, to be observed and respected; and to this end, the mode and measure of redress ought to be exclusively directed and limited. In such a case, a State not only has the right, but is, in duty to itself and the Union, bound to interpose,—as the last resort, to arrest the dangerous infraction of the constitution,—and to prevent the powers reserved to itself, from being absorbed by those delegated to the United States.

That the right, so exercised, would be, in itself, a safe and effectual security against so great an evil, few will doubt. But the question arises,—Will prudence and propriety be sufficient to prevent the wanton abuse of a right, so high and delicate, by the thirty parties to the compact,—and the many others hereafter to be added to the number?

I answer, no. Nor can any one, in the least acquainted with that constitution of our nature which makes governments necessary, give any other answer. The highest moral obligations,—truth, justice, and plighted faith,—much less, prudence and propriety,—oppose, of themselves, but feeble resistance to the abuse of power. But what they, of themselves, cannot effect, may be effected by other influences of a far less elevated character. Of these, many are powerful, and well calculated to prevent the abuse of this high and delicate right. Among them may be ranked, as most prominent and powerful, that which springs from the habitual action of a majority of the States and of their population, estimated in federal numbers, on the side of the federal government;—a majority naturally prone, and ever ready,—in all questions between it and a State, involving an infraction of the constitution, to throw its weight in the scale of the former. To this, may be added another, of no small force. I refer to that of party ties. Experience, as well as reason shows, that a government, operating as ours does, must give rise to two great political parties,—which, although partaking, from the first, more or less of a sectional character, extend themselves, in unequal proportions, over the whole Union,—carrying with them, notwithstanding their sectional tendency, party sympathy and party attachment of such strength, that few are willing to break or weaken them, by resisting, even an acknowledged infraction of the constitution, of a nature alike oppressive and dangerous to their section. Both of these tend powerfully to resist the abuse of the right, by preventing it from being exercised imprudently and improperly. But I will not dwell on them, as they have been already considered in another connection. There are others, more especially connected with the subject at present before us, which I shall next consider.

The first may be traced to a fact, disclosed by experience, that, in most of the States, the preponderance of neither party is so decisive, that the minority may not hope to become the majority; and that, with this hope, it stands always ready to seize on any act of the majority, of doubtful propriety, as the means of turning it out of power and taking its place. Should the majority in any State, where the balance thus vibrates, venture to take a stand, and to interpose its authority, against the encroachment of the federal government on its reserved powers, it would be difficult to conceive a case, however clear and palpable the encroachment, or dangerous its character, in which the minority would not resist its action, and array itself on the side of the federal government. And there are very few, in which, with the aid of its power and patronage, backed by the numerous presses in its support, the minority would not succeed in overcoming the majority,—taking their place, and, thereby, placing the State at the foot of the federal government. To this, another of great force may be added. The dominant party of the State, for the time, although it may be in a minority in the Union for the time, looks forward, of course, to the period when it will be in a majority of the Union; and have at its disposal all the honors and emoluments of the federal government. The leaders of such party, therefore, would not be insensible to the advantage, which their position, as such, would give them, to share largely in the distribution. This advantage they would not readily jeopard, by taking a stand which would render them, not only odious to the majority of the Union, at the time, but unpopular with their own party in the other States,—as putting in hazard their chance to become the majority. Under such circumstances, it would require, not only a clear and palpable case of infraction, and one of urgent necessity, but high virtue, patriotism and courage to exercise the right of interposition;—even if it were admitted to be clear and unquestionable. And hence, it is to be feared that, even this high right, combined with the mutual negative of the two co-ordinate governments, will be scarcely sufficient to counteract the vast and preponderating power of the federal government, and to prevent the absorption of the reserved by the delegated powers.

Indeed the negative power is always far weaker, in proportion to its appearance, than the positive. The latter having the control of the government, with all its honors and emoluments, has the means of acting on and influencing those who exercise the negative power, and of enlisting them on its side, unless it be effectually guarded: while, on the other hand, those who exercise the negative, have nothing but the simple power, and possess no means of influencing those who exercise the positive power.

But, suppose it should prove otherwise; and that the negative power should become so strong as to cause dangerous derangements and disorders in the system;—the constitution makes ample provisions for their correction,—whether produced by the interposition of a State, or the mutual negative, or conflict of power between the two co-ordinate governments. I refer to the amending power. Why it was necessary to provide for such a power;—what is its nature and character;—why it was modified as it is,—and whether it be safe, and sufficient to effect the objects intended,—are the questions, which I propose next to consider.

It is, as has already been explained, a fundamental principle, in forming such a federal community of States, and establishing such a federal constitution and government as ours, that no State could be bound but by its separate ratification and adoption. The principle is essentially connected with the independence and sovereignty of the several States. As the several States, in such a community, with such a constitution and government, still retained their separate independence and sovereignty, it followed, that the compact into which they entered, could not be altered or changed, in any way, but by the unanimous assent of all the parties, without some express provision authorizing it. But there were strong objections to requiring the consent of all to make alterations or changes in the constitution. Those who formed it were not so vain as to suppose that they had made a perfect instrument; nor so ignorant as not to see, however perfect it might be, that derangements and disorders, resulting from time, circumstances, and the conflicting elements of the system itself, would make amendments necessary. But to leave it, without making some special provision for the purpose, would have been, in effect, to leave it to any one of the States to prevent amendments; which, in practice, would have been almost tantamount to leaving it without any power to amend;—notwithstanding its necessity. And, hence, the subject of making some special provision for amending the constitution, was forced on the attention of the convention.

There was diversity of opinion as to what the nature and character of the amending power should be. All agreed that it should be a modification of the original creative power, which ordained and established the separate constitutions and governments of the several States; and, by which alone, the proposed constitution and government could be ordained and established: or, to express it differently and more explicitly,—that amendments should be the acts of the several States, voting as States,—each counting one,—and not the act of the government. But there was great diversity of opinion as to what *number* of States should be required to concur, or agree, in order to make an amendment. It was first moved to require the consent of all the States. This was followed by a motion to amend, requiring *two thirds;* which was overruled by a considerable majority. It was then moved to require the concurrence of *three fourths,* which was agreed to, and finally adopted without dissent.

To understand fully the reasons for so modifying the original creative power, as to require the concurrence of three fourths to make an amendment, it will be necessary to advert to another portion of the proceedings of the convention, intimately connected with the present question. I refer to that which contains a history of its action in regard to the number of States required to ratify the constitution, before it should become binding between those so ratifying it. It is material to state, that although the article in respect to ratifications, which grew out of these proceedings, stands last in the constitution, it was finally agreed on and adopted before the article in regard to amendments;—and had, doubtless, no inconsiderable influence in determining the number of States required for that purpose.

There was, in reference to both, great diversity of opinion as to the requisite number of States. With the exception of one State, all agreed that entire unanimity should not be required; but the majority divided as to the number which should be required. One of the most prominent leaders of the party, originally in favor of a national government, was in favor of requiring only a bare majority of the States. Another, not less distinguished, was in favor of the same proposition; but so modified as to require such majority to contain, also, a majority of the entire population of all the States; and, in default of this, as many additional States as would be necessary to supply the deficiency. On the other hand, the more prominent members of the party in favor of a federal government, inclined to a larger number. One of the most influential of these, moved to require ten States; on which motion the convention was nearly equally divided. Finally, the number nine was agreed on;—constituting *three fourths* of all the States represented in the convention,—and, as nearly as might be, of all the States at that time in the Union.

Why the first propositions were rejected, and the last finally agreed on, requires explanation. The first proposition, requiring the ratification of all the States, before the constitution should become binding between those so ratifying the same, was rejected, doubtless, because it was deemed unreasonable that the fate of the others should be made dependent on the will of a single State. The convention acted under the pressure of very trying exigencies. The confederacy had failed; and it was absolutely necessary that something should be done to save the credit of the Union, and to guard against confusion and anarchy. The plan of the constitution and government adopted, was the only one that could be agreed on; and the fate of the country apparently rested on its ratification by the States. In such a state of things, it seemed to be too hazardous to put it in the power of a single State to defeat it. Nothing short of so great a pressure could justify an act which made so great a change in the articles of confederation;—which expressly provided that no alteration should be made in any of them, "unless such alteration be agreed to in a Congress of the United States, and be afterwards confirmed by the legislatures of every State."

The rejection of the other proposition, which required a mere majority of the States to make it binding as between the States so ratifying it, will scarcely require explanation. It exposed the States to the hazard of forming, not one, but two Unions; or, if this should be avoided,—by forcing the other States to come in reluctantly, under the force of circumstances, it endangered the harmony and duration of the Union, and the proposed constitution and government. It would, besides, have evinced too great an indifference to the stipulation contained in the articles of the confederation just cited.

It remains now to be explained why the particular number, between these two extremes, was finally agreed on. Among other reasons, one, doubtless, is to be found in the fact, that the articles of the then existing confederation, required the consent of nine States to give validity to many of the acts of their Congress;—among which, were the acts declaring war,—granting letters of marque and reprisal in time of peace, and emitting bills, or borrowing money on the credit of the United States. The object of requiring so great a number was, to guard against the abuses of these and the other great and delicate powers contained in the provision. A mere majority of the States, was too few to be intrusted with such powers; and, to make the trust more safe, the consent of nine States was required; which was within a small fraction of *three fourths* of the whole number at the time. The precedent,—and the same consideration which induced the legislatures of all the States to assent to it, in adopting the articles of confederation, must have had, undoubtedly, much weight in determining what number of States should ratify the constitution, before it should become binding between them. If the legislatures of all the States should have unanimously deemed it not unreasonable, that the highest and most delicate acts of the old Congress, when agreed to by nine or more States, should be acquiesced in by the others, it was very natural that the members of the convention should think it not unreasonable to require an equal number to give validity to the constitution, as between them;—leaving it to the others to say whether they would ratify or not. Nine, or *three fourths* of the whole, were, unquestionably, regarded as a safe and sufficient guaranty against oppression and abuse, both in the highest acts of the confederacy, and in establishing the constitution between the States ratifying it. And it is equally certain that a smaller number was not regarded either as safe, or sufficient.

The force of these precedents, combined with the reasons for adopting them, must have had great weight in determining the proportional number which should be required to amend the constitution. Indeed, after determining the proportion in the provision for the ratification of the constitution, it would seem to follow, as a matter of course, that the same proportion should be required in the provision for amending it. It would be difficult to assign a reason, why the proportion should be different in the two cases; and why, if *three fourths* should be required in the one, it should not also be required in the other. If it would have been unreasonable and improper in the one, that a few States in proportion should, by their obstinacy, prevent the others from forming a constitution,—it would have been equally so, and for the same reason, that the like proportion should have the power to prevent amendments, however necessary they might be to the well working and safety of the system. So, again, if it would have been dangerous and improper, to permit a bare majority of the

States, or any proportion less than that required to make the constitution binding as between the States ratifying,—it would have been no less so to permit
such number or proportion to amend it. The two are, indeed, nearly allied, and
involve, throughout, the same principle;—and hence, the same diversity of
opinion between the two parties in the convention, in reference to both, and
the adoption of the same proportion of States in each. I say the same proportion,—for although nine States were rather less than *three fourths* of the whole
number when the constitution was ratified,—this proportion of the States was
required in order to amend it, (without regard to an inconsiderable fraction,)
because of the facility of its application.

But independently of these considerations, there were strong reasons for
adopting that proportion in providing a power to amend. It was, at least, as necessary to guard against too much facility as too much difficulty, in amending it.
If, to require the consent of all the States for that purpose would be, in effect, to
prevent amendments which time should disclose to be,—or change of circumstances make necessary;—so, on the other hand, to require a bare majority only,
or but a small number in proportion to the whole, would expose the constitution to hasty, inconsiderate, and even sinister amendments, on the part of the
party dominant for the time. If the one would give it too much fixedness, the
other would deprive it of all stability. Of the two, the latter would be more dangerous than the former. It would defeat the very ends of a constitution, regarded
as a fundamental law. Indeed, it would involve a glaring absurdity to require the
separate ratification of nine States to make the constitution binding as between
them,—and to provide that a mere majority of States, or even a small one, when
compared with the whole number, should have the power, as soon as it went
into operation, to amend it as they pleased. It would be difficult to find any other
proportion better calculated to avoid this absurdity, and, at the same time, the
difficulties attending the other extreme, than that adopted by the convention.
While it affords sufficient facility, it guards against too much, in amending the
constitution,—and thereby unites stability with the capacity of adjusting itself to
all such changes as may become necessary; and thus combines all the requisites
that are necessary in the amending power. It hardly admits of a doubt, that these
combined reasons,—the conviction that it possessed all the requisites for such a
power, in a higher degree than any other proportion,—with the force of the
two precedents above explained, induced the convention to adopt it.

Possessing these, it possesses all the requisites, of course, to render the power
at once safe in itself, and sufficient to effect the objects for which it was intended.
It is safe; because the proportion is sufficiently large to prevent a dominant por-

tion of the Union, or combination of the States, from using the amending power as an instrument to make changes in the constitution, adverse to the interests and rights of the weaker portion of the Union, or a minority of the States. It may not, in this respect, be as perfectly safe as it would be in the unmodified state in which it ordained and established the constitution; but, for all practical purposes, it is believed to be safe as an *amending* power. It is difficult to conceive a case, where so large a portion as *three fourths* of the States would undertake to insert a power, by way of amendment, which, instead of improving and perfecting the constitution, would deprive the remaining *fourth* of any right, essentially belonging to them as members of the Union, or clearly intended to oppress them. There are many powers, which a dominant combination of States would assume by *construction,* and use for the purpose of aggrandizement, which they would not dare to propose to insert as amendments. But should an attempt be successfully made to engraft an amendment for such a purpose, the case would not be without remedy, as will be shown in the proper place.

I say, as large a proportion as *three fourths;*—for the larger the proportion required to do an act, the less is the danger of the power being used for the purpose of oppression and aggrandizement. The reason is plain. With the increase of the proportion, the difficulty of so using it, is increased;—while the inducement is diminished in the same proportion. The former is increased;—because the difficulty of forming combinations for such purpose is increased with the increase of the number required to combine; and the latter decreased, because the greater the number to be aggrandized, and the less the number, by whose oppression this can be effected, the less the inducement to oppression. And hence, by increasing the proportion, the number to be aggrandized may be made so large, and the number to be oppressed so small, as to make the effort bootless;—when the motive to oppress, as well as to abuse power will, of course, cease.

But, while *three fourths* furnish a safe proportion against making changes in the constitution, under the color of amendments, by the dominant portion of the Union, with a view to oppress the weaker for its aggrandizement, the proportion is equally safe, in view of the opposite danger;—as it furnishes a sufficient protection against the combination of a few States to prevent the rest from making such amendments as may become necessary to preserve or perfect it. It thus guards against the dangers, to which a less, or greater proportion might expose the system.

It is not less sufficient than safe to effect the object intended. As a modification of the power which ordained and established the system, its authority is above all others, except itself in its simple and absolute form. Within its appropriate sphere,—that of *amending* the constitution,—all others are subject to its control, and may be modified, changed and altered at its pleasure. Within that sphere it truly represents the intention of the power, of which it is a modification, when it ordained and established the constitution,—as to the limits to which the system might be safely and properly extended, and beyond which it could not. The same wisdom, which saw the necessity of having as much harmony as possible, in ratifying the constitution, saw, also, the necessity of preserving it, after it went into operation; and therefore required the same proportion of States to make an amendment, as to ratify the instrument, before it could become binding between the States ratifying. It saw, that, if there was danger from *too little,* there was also danger from *too much* union (if I may be allowed so to express myself);—and that, while one led to weakness, the other led to discord and alienation. To guard against each, it so modified the amending power as to avoid both extremes,—and thus to preserve the equilibrium of the powers of the system as originally established, so far as human contrivance could.

Thus the power which, in its simple and absolute form, was the creator, becomes, in its modified form, the preserver of the system. By no other device, nor in any other form, could the high functions appertaining to this character, be safely and efficiently discharged;—and by none other could the system be preserved. It is, when properly understood, the *vis medicatrix* of the system;—its great repairing, healing, and conservative power;—intended to remedy its disorders, in whatever cause or causes originating; whether in the original errors or defects of the constitution itself,—or the operation of time and change of circumstances, or in conflicts between its parts,—including those between the coordinate governments. By it alone, can the equilibrium of the various powers and divisions of the system be preserved; as by it alone, can the stronger be prevented from encroaching on, and finally absorbing the weaker. For this purpose, it is, as has been shown, entirely safe and all-sufficient. In performing its high functions, it acts, not as a judicial power, but in the far more elevated and authoritative character of an *amending* power;—the only one in which it can be called into action at all. In this character, it can amend the constitution, by modifying its existing provisions;—or, in case of a disputed power, whether it be between the federal government and one of its co-ordinates,—or between the former and an interposing State,—by declaring, authoritatively, what is the constitution.

Having now explained the nature and object of the amending power, and shown its safety and sufficiency, in respect to the object for which it was provided;—I shall next proceed to show, that it is the duty of the federal government to invoke its aid, should any dangerous derangement or disorder result from the mutual negative of the two co-ordinate governments, or from the interposition of a State, in its sovereign character, to arrest one of its acts,—in case all other remedies should fail to adjust the difficulty.

In order to form a clear conception of the true ground and reason of this duty, it is necessary to premise, that it is difficult to conceive of a case, where a conflict of power could take place between the government of a State, or the State itself in its sovereign character, and the federal government, in which the former would not be in a minority of the States and of their population, esti-mated in federal numbers; and, of course, the latter in a majority of both. The reason is obvious. If it were otherwise, the remedy would at once be applied through the federal government,—by a repeal of the act asserting the power,—and the question settled by yielding it to the State. Such being the case, the conflict, whenever it takes place, must be between the reserved and delegated powers; the latter, supported by a majority both of the States and of their pop-ulation, claiming the right to exercise the power,—and the former, by a State constituting one of the minority,—(at least as far as it relates to the power in controversy,)—denying the claim.

Now it is a clear and well established principle, that the party who claims the right to exercise a power, is bound to make it good, against the party denying the right; and that, if there should be an authority higher than either provided, by which the question between them can be adjusted, he, in such case, has no right to assert his claim on his own authority,—but is bound to appeal to the tribunal appointed, according to the forms prescribed, and to establish and assert his right through its authority.

If a principle, so clear and well established, should, in a case like the one sup-posed, require confirmation,—it may be found in the fact, that the powers of the federal government are all enumerated and specified in the constitution;—while those belonging to the States embrace the whole residuary mass of pow-ers, not enumerated and specified. Hence, in a conflict of power between the two, the presumption is in favor of the latter, and against the former; and, there-fore, it is doubly bound to establish the power in controversy, through the appointed authority, before it can rightfully undertake to exercise it.

But as conclusive as these reasons are, there are others not less so. Among these, it may be stated, that the federal government, being of the party of the majority in such conflicts, may, at pleasure, make the appeal to the amending power; while the State, being of the party of the minority, cannot possibly do so. The reason is plain. To make it, requires, on the part of the State, more than a bare majority. It would then be absurd, to transfer the duty from the party of the majority, which has the power, to that of the minority, which has it not:— and this, too, when, with such a majority, the question of power could be settled in its favor, more easily and promptly, through the federal government itself.

There is also another reason,—if not more conclusive, yet of deeper import. The federal government never will make an appeal to the amending power, in a case of conflict, unless compelled;—nor, indeed, willingly in any case, except with a view to enlarge the powers it has usurped by construction. The only means, by which it can be compelled to make an appeal, are the negative powers of the constitution;—and especially, so far as the reserved powers are concerned,—by that of its co-ordinates,—and State interposition. But to transfer the duty from itself to the States, would, necessarily, have the effect, so far as they are concerned, of leaving it in the full and quiet exercise of the contested power, until the appeal was made and finally acted on;—instead of suspending the exercise of the power, until the decision was pronounced;—as would be the case, if the duty were not transferred. In the latter case, it would have every motive to exert itself to make the appeal, and to obtain a speedy and final action in its favor, if possible; but in the former, it would be the reverse. The motive would be to use every effort to prevent a successful appeal, and to defeat action on it; as, in the mean time, it would be left in full possession of the power in question. Nor would it have any difficulty in effecting what it desired; as it would be impossible for the State, even without opposition, to succeed in making an appeal, for the reason already assigned.

Its effect would be a revolution in the character of the system. It would virtually destroy the relation of co-ordinates between the federal government and those of the several States, by rendering the negative of the latter, in case of conflict with it, of no effect. It would supersede and render substantially obsolete, not only the amending power, but the original sovereign power of the several States, as parties to the constitutional compact,—by making them, also, of no effect; and, thereby, elevate the federal government to the absolute and supreme authority of the system, with liberty to assume, by construction, whatever power the cupidity or ambition of a dominant party or section might crave.

It would, in a word, practically transform the federal, into a consolidated national government, against the avowed intention of its framers,—the plain meaning of the constitution itself,—and the understanding of the people of the States, when they ratified and adopted it. Such a result is, itself, the strongest, the most conclusive argument against the position. If there were none other, this, of itself, would be ample to prove, that it is the duty of the federal government to invoke the action of the amending power, by proposing a declaratory amendment affirming the power it claims, according to the forms prescribed in the constitution; and, if it fail, to abandon the power.

On the other hand, should it succeed in obtaining the amendment, the act of the government of the separate State which caused the conflict, and operated as a negative on the act of the federal government, would, in all cases, be overruled; and the latter become operative within its limits. But the result is, in some respects, different,—where a State, acting in her sovereign character, and as a party to the constitutional compact, has interposed, and declared an act of the federal government to be unauthorized by the constitution,—and, therefore, null and void. In this case, if the act of the latter be predicated on a power consistent with the character of the constitution, the ends for which it was established, and the nature of our system of government;—or, more briefly, if it come fairly within the scope of the amending power, the State is bound to acquiesce, by the solemn obligation which it contracted, in ratifying the constitution. But if it transcends the limits of the amending power,—be inconsistent with the character of the constitution and the ends for which it was established,—or with the nature of the system,—the result is different. In such case, the State is not bound to acquiesce. It may choose whether it will, or whether it will not secede from the Union. One or the other course it must take. To refuse acquiescence, would be tantamount to secession; and place it as entirely in the relation of a foreign State to the other States, as would a positive act of secession. That a State, as a party to the constitutional compact, has the right to secede,—acting in the same capacity in which it ratified the constitution,—cannot, with any show of reason, be denied by any one who regards the constitution as a compact,—if a power should be inserted by the amending power, which would radically change the character of the constitution, or the nature of the system; or if the former should fail to fulfil the ends for which it was established. This results, necessarily, from the nature of a compact,—where the parties to it are sovereign; and, of course, have no higher authority to which to appeal. That the effect of secession would be to place her in the relation of a foreign State to the others, is equally clear. Nor is it less so, that it would make her, (not her citizens *individually*,) responsible to them, in that character. All this results, necessarily, from the nature of a compact between sovereign parties.

In case the State acquiesces, whether it be where the power claimed is within or beyond the scope of the amending power, it must be done, by rescinding the act, by which, she interposed her authority and declared the act of the federal government to be unauthorized by the constitution,—and, therefore, null and void; and this too by the same authority which passed it. The reason is, that, until this is done, the act making the declaration continues binding on her citizens. As far as they are concerned, the State, as a party to the constitutional compact, has the right to decide, in the last resort,—and, acting in the same character in which it ratified the constitution, to determine to what limits its powers extend, and how far they are bound to respect and obey it, and the acts made under its authority. They are bound to obey them, only, because the State, to which they owe allegiance, by ratifying, ordained and established it as its own constitution and government; just in the same way, in which it ordained and established its own separate constitution and government,—and by precisely the same authority. They owe *obedience* to both; because their State commanded them to obey; but they owe *allegiance* to neither; since sovereignty, by a fundamental principle of our system, resides in the *people,* and not in the *government.* The same authority which commanded *obedience,* has the right, in both cases, to determine, as far as they are concerned, the extent to which they were bound to obey; and this determination remains binding until rescinded by the authority which pronounced and declared it.

I have now finished the discussion of the question,—What means does the constitution, or the system itself furnish, to preserve the division between the delegated and reserved powers? In its progress, I have shown, that the federal government contains, within itself, or in its organization, no provisions, by which, the powers delegated could be prevented from encroaching on the powers reserved to the several States; and that, the only means furnished by the system itself, to resist encroachments, are, the mutual negative between the two co-ordinate governments, where their acts come into conflict as to the extent of their respective powers; and the interposition of a State in its sovereign character, as a party to the constitutional compact, against an unconstitutional act of the federal government. It has also been shown, that these are sufficient to restrict the action of the federal government to its appropriate sphere; and that, if they should lead to any dangerous derangements or disorders, the amending power makes ample and safe provision for their correction. It now remains to be considered, what must be the result, if the federal government is left to operate without these exterior means of restraint.

That the federal government, as the representative of the delegated powers, supported, as it must habitually be, by a majority of the States and of their population, estimated in federal numbers, is vastly stronger than the opposing States and their population, has been shown. But the fact of its greater strength is not more certain than the consequence,—that it will encroach, if left to decide in

the last resort, on the extent of its own powers, and to enforce its own decisions, without some adequate means to restrict it to its allotted sphere. It would
encroach; because the dominant combination of States and population, which,
for the time, may control it, would have every inducement to do so; since it
would increase their power and the means of aggrandizement. Nor would their
encroachments cease until all the reserved powers,—those reserved to the people of the several States in their sovereign character, as well as those delegated
to their respective separate governments, should be absorbed: because, the same
powerful motives which induced the first step towards it, would continue, until
the whole was concentrated in the federal government. The written restrictions
and limitations of the constitution, would oppose no effectual resistance. They
would all be gradually undermined by the slow and certain process of construction; which would be continued until the instrument itself, would be of no
more force or validity than an ordinary act of Congress;—nor would it be more
respected. The opposing construction of the minority would become the subject of ridicule and scorn,—as mere abstractions;—until all encroachments
would cease to be opposed. Nor would the effects end with the absorption of
the reserved powers.

While the process was going on, it would react on the division of the powers of the federal government itself, and disturb its own equilibrium. The legislative department would be the first to feel its influence, and to cumulate
authority, by encroachments; since Congress, as the organ of the delegated powers, possesses, by an express provision of the constitution, all the discretionary
powers of the government. Neither of the other two can constitutionally exercise any power, which is not either expressly delegated by the constitution, or
provided for by law. So long, then, as Congress remained faithful to its trust,
neither of the others could encroach; since the officers of both are responsible
to it, through the impeaching power; and hence the work of aggression must
commence with it, or by its permission. But whatever encroachments it might
make, the benefit, in the end, would accrue, not to itself, but to the President,—
as the head of the executive department. Every enlargement of the powers of
the government which may be made, every measure which may be adopted to
aggrandize the dominant combination which may control the government for
the time, must necessarily enlarge, in a greater or less degree, his patronage and
influence. With their enlargement, his power to control the other departments
of the government, and the organs of public opinion, and through them, the
community at large, must increase, and in the same degree. With their increase,
the motive to obtain possession of the control of the government, in order to

enjoy its honors and emoluments, regardless of all considerations of principle or policy, would become stronger and stronger, until it would stand alone, the paramount and all-absorbing motive. And,—to trace further the fatal progress,— just in proportion as this motive should become stronger, the election of the President would be, more and more, the all-important question,—until every other would be regarded as subordinate to it. But as this became more and more paramount to all others, party combinations, and party organization and discipline, would become more concentrated and stringent;—their control over individual opinion and action more and more decisive; and, with it, the control of the President, as the head of the dominant party. When this should be increased to such a degree, that he, as its head, could, through party organs and party machinery, wield sufficient influence over the constituents of the members of Congress, belonging to his party, as to make their election dependent, not on their fidelity to the constitution or to the country, but on their devotion and submission to party and party interest,—his power would become absolute. They then would cease, virtually, to represent the people. Their responsibility would be, not to them, but to him; or to those who might control and use him as an instrument. The Executive, at this stage, would become absolute, so far as the party in power was concerned. It would control the action of the dominant party as effectually as would an hereditary chief-magistrate, if in possession of its powers,—if not more so; and the time would not be distant, when the President would cease to be elective; when a contested election, or the paid corruption and violence attending an election, would be made a pretext, by the occupant, or his party, for holding over after the expiration of his term.

Such must be the result, if the process of absorption should be permitted to progress regularly, through all its stages. The causes which would control the event, are as fixed and certain as any in the physical world. But it is not probable that they would be permitted to take their regular course, undisturbed. In a country of such vast extent and diversity of interests as ours, parties, in all their stages, must partake, as I have already shown, more or less of a sectional character. The laws which control their formation, necessarily lead to this. Distance, as has been stated, always weakens, and proximity—where there is no counteracting cause—always strengthens the social and sympathetic feelings. Sameness of interests and similarity of habits and character, make it more easy for those who are contiguous, to associate together and form a party than for those who are remote. In the early stages of the government, when principles bore a stronger sway, the effects of these causes were not so perceptible, or their influence so great. But as party violence increases, and party efforts sink down into a mere struggle to obtain the honors and emoluments of government, the tendency to appeal to local feelings, local interests, and local prejudices will become stronger and stronger,—until, ultimately, parties must assume a decidedly sectional character. When it comes to this,—and when the two majorities which control the federal government, come to centre in the same section, and all the powers of the entire system, virtually to unite in the executive department, the dominant section will become the governing, and the other the subordinate section; as much so as if it were a dependent province, without any real participation in the government. Its condition will be even worse; for its nominal participation in the acts of government would afford it no means of protecting itself, where the interests of the dominant and governing section should come into conflict with its own,—whilst it would serve as a covering to disguise its subjection, and, thereby, induce it to bear wrongs, which it would not otherwise tolerate. In this state of things, discontent, alienation, and hostility of feelings would be engendered between the sections; to be followed by discord, disorder, convulsions, and, not improbably, a disruption of the system.

In one or the other of these results, it must terminate, if the federal government be left to decide, definitively and in the last resort, as to the extent of its powers. Having no sufficient counteraction, exterior to itself, it must necessarily move in the direction marked out by the inherent tendency belonging to its character and position. As a constitutional, popular government, its tendency will be, in the first place, to an absolute form, under the control of the numerical majority; and, finally, to the most simple of these forms, that of a single, irresponsible individual. As a federal government, extending over a vast territory, the tendency will be, in the first place, to the formation of sectional parties, and the concentration of all power in the stronger section; and, in the next, to conflict between the sections, and disrupture of the whole system. One or the other must be the end, in the case supposed. The laws that would govern are fixed and certain. The only question would be, as to *which end,* and at *what time.* All the rest is as certain as the future, if not disturbed by causes exterior to the system.

So strong indeed is the tendency of the government in the direction assigned,—if left to itself,—that nothing short of the most powerful negatives, exterior to itself, can effectually counteract and arrest it. These, from the nature of the system, can only be found in the mutual negative of the two co-ordinate governments, and the interposition of a State, as has been explained;—the one to protect the powers which the people of the several States delegated to their respective separate State governments;—and the other, to protect the powers which the people of the several States, in delegating powers to both of their co-ordinate governments, expressly reserved to themselves respectively. The object of the negative power is, to protect the several portions or interests of the community against each other. Ours is a federal community, of which States form the constituent parts. They reserved the powers not delegated to the federal or common government to themselves individually;—but in a twofold character, as embracing separate governments, and as a several people in their sovereign capacity. But where the powers of government are divided, nothing short of a negative,—either positive, or in effect,—can protect those alotted to the weaker, against the stronger;—or the parts of the community against each other. The party to whom the power belongs, is the only party interested in protecting it; and to such party only, can its defence be safely trusted. To intrust it, in this case, to the party interested in absorbing it, and possessed of ample power to do so, is, as has been shown, to trust the lamb to the custody of the wolf.

Nor can any other, so appropriate, so safe or efficient, be devised, as the twofold negative provided by the system. They are appropriate to the twofold character of the State, to which, the powers not delegated, are reserved. That they are safe and sufficient, if called into action, has been shown. All other provisions, without them, would be of little avail:—such as the right of suffrage,—written constitutions,—the division of the powers of the government into three separate and independent departments,—the formation of the people into individual and independent States, and the freedom of the press and of speech. These all have their value. They may retard the progress of the government towards its final termination,—but without the two negative powers, cannot arrest it;—nor can any thing, short of these, preserve the equilibrium of the system. Without them, every other power would be gradually absorbed by the federal government, or be superseded or rendered obsolete. It would remain the only vital power, and the sole organ of a consolidated community.

If we turn now from this to the other aspect of the subject, where these negative powers are brought into full action in order to counteract the tendency of the federal government to supersede and absorb the powers of the system, the contrast will be striking. Instead of weakening the government by counteracting its tendencies, and restricting it to its proper sphere, they would render it far more powerful. A strong government, instead of being weakened, is greatly strengthened, by a correspondingly strong negative. It may lose something in promptitude of action, in calling out the physical force of the country, but would gain vastly in moral power. The security it would afford to all the different parts and interests of the country,—the assurance that the powers confided to it, would not be abused,—and the harmony and unanimity resulting from the conviction that no one section or interest could oppress another, would, in an emergency, put the whole resources of the Union, moral and physical, at the disposal of the government,—and give it a strength which never could be acquired by the enlargement of its powers beyond the limits assigned to it. It is, indeed, only by such confidence and unanimity, that a government can, with certainty, breast the billows and ride through the storms which the vessel of State must often encounter in its progress. The stronger the pressure of the steam, if the boiler be but proportionally strong, the more securely the bark buffets the wave, and defies the tempest.

Nor is there any just ground to apprehend that the federal government would lose any power which properly belongs to it, or which it should desire to retain, by being compelled to resort to the amending power, when this becomes necessary in consequence of a conflict between itself and one of its co-ordinates; or, in case of the interposition of a State. There can certainly be no danger of this, so long as the same feelings and motives which induced them voluntarily to ratify and adopt the constitution unanimously, shall continue to actuate them. While these remain, there can be no hazard in placing what all freely and unanimously adopted, in the charge of three fourths of the States to protect and preserve. Nor can there be any just ground to apprehend that these feelings and motives will undergo any change, so long as the constitution shall fulfil the ends for which it was ordained and established; to wit: that each and all might enjoy, more perfectly and securely, liberty, peace, tranquillity, security from danger, both internal and external, and all other blessings connected with their respective rights and advantages. It was a great mistake to suppose that the States would naturally stand in antagonistic relations to the federal government; or that there would be any disposition, on their part, to diminish its power or to weaken its influence. They naturally stand in a reverse relation,—pledged to cherish, uphold, and support it. They freely and voluntarily created it, for the common good of each and of all,—and will cherish and defend it so long as it fulfils these objects. If its safe-keeping cannot be intrusted to its creators, it can be safely placed in the custody of no other hands.

But it cannot be confined to its proper sphere, and its various powers kept in a state of equilibrium, as originally established, but by the counteracting resistance of the States, acting in their twofold character, as has been explained and established. Nor can it fulfil its end without confining it to its proper sphere, and preserving the equilibrium of its various powers. Without this, the federal government would concentrate all the powers of the system in itself, and become an instrument in the hands of the dominant portion of the States, to aggrandize itself at the expense of the rest;—as has also been fully explained and established. With the defeat of the ends for which it was established, the feelings and motives which induced the States to establish it, would gradually change; and, finally, give place to others of a very different character. The weaker and oppressed portion would regard it with distrust, jealousy, and, in the end, aversion and hostility; while the stronger and more favored, would look upon it, not as the means of promoting the common good and safety of each and all, but as an instrument to control the weaker, and to aggrandize itself at its expense.

As nothing but the counteracting resistance of the States can prevent this result, so nothing short of a full recognition of this, the only means, by which they can make such resistance, and call it freely into action,—can correct the disorders, and avert the dangers which must ensue from an opposite and false conception of the system; and thus restore the feelings and motives which led to the free and unanimous adoption of the federal constitution and government. With their restoration, the amending power may be safely trusted, as the preserving, repairing, and protecting power. There would be no danger whatever, that the government, under its action, would lose any power which properly belonged to it, and which it ought to retain; for there would be no motive or interest, on any side, to divest it of any power necessary to enable it to fulfil the ends for which it was established; or to impair, unduly, the strength of the Union. Indeed, it is so modified as to afford an ample guaranty that the Union would be safe in its custody;—since it was designedly so constructed as to represent, at all times, the extent to which it might be safely carried, and beyond which it ought not to go. It may, indeed, in case of conflict between it and one of its co-ordinate governments, or an interposing state, modify and restrict the power in contest, in strict conformity with the design and the spirit of the constitution. For it may be laid down as a principle, that the power and action of the Union, instead of being increased, ought to be diminished, with the increase of its extent and population. The reason is, that the greater its extent, and the more numerous and populous the members composing it, the greater will be the diversity of interests, the less the sympathy between the remote parts, the less the knowledge and regard of each, for the interests of the others, and, of course, the less *closeness of union,* (so to speak,) consistently with its safety. The same principle, according to which it was provided that there should not be more closeness of union than three fourths should agree to, equally applies in all stages of the growth and progress of the country; to wit: that there should not be, at any time, more than the same proportion would agree to. It ought ever to be borne in mind that the

Union may have too much power, and be too intimate and close; as well as too little power, intimacy, and closeness. Either is dangerous. If the latter, from weakness, exposes it to dissolution, the former, from exuberance of strength, and from the parts being too closely compressed together, exposes it, at least equally, either to consolidation and despotism, on the one hand,—or to rupture and destruction, by the repulsion of its parts, on the other. The amending power, if duly called into action, would protect the Union against either extreme; and thereby guard against the dangers to which it is on either hand exposed.

It is by thus bringing all the powers of the system into active operation,— and only by this means, that its equilibrium can be preserved, and adjusted to the changes, which the enlargement of the Union, and its increase of population, or other causes, may require. Thus only, can the Union be preserved; the government made permanent; the limits of the country be enlarged; the anticipations of the founders of the system, as to its future prosperity and greatness,— be realized; and the revolutions and calamities, necessarily incident to the theory which would make the federal government the sole and exclusive judge of its powers, be averted.

I have now finished the portion of this discourse which relates to the character and structure of the government of the United States;—its various divisions of power, as well as those of the system of which it is a part,—and the means which they furnish to protect each division against the encroachment of the others. The government has now been in operation for more than sixty years; and it remains to be considered, whether it has conformed, in practice, with its true theory; and, if not, what has caused its departure; and what must be the consequence, should its aberrations remain uncorrected. I propose to consider these in the order stated.

There are few who will not admit, that the government has, in practice, departed, more or less, from its original character and structure;—however great may be the diversity of opinion, as to what constitutes a departure;—a diversity caused by the different views entertained in reference to its character and structure. They who believe that the government of the United States is a national, and not a federal government,—or who believe that it is partly national and partly federal,—will, of course, on the question,—whether it has conformed to, or departed from its true theory,—form very different opinions from those who believe that it is federal throughout. They who believe that it is exclusively national, very logically conclude, according to their theory, that the government has the exclusive right, in the last resort, to decide as to the extent of its powers, and to enforce its decisions against all opposition, through some one or all of its departments:—while they who believe it to be exclusively federal, cannot consistently come to any other conclusion, than that the two governments,—federal and State,—are coequal and co-ordinate governments; and, as such, neither can possess the right to decide as to the extent of its own powers, or to enforce its own decision against that of the other. The case is different with those who believe it to be partly national, and partly federal. They seem incapable of forming any definite or distinct opinion on the subject,—vital and important as it is. Indeed, it is difficult to conceive how, with their views, any rational and fixed opinion can be formed on the subject: for, according to their theory, as far as it is national, it must possess the right contended for by those who believe it to be altogether national; and, on the other hand, as far as it is federal, it must possess the right, which those who believe it to be wholly federal contend for. But how the two can coexist, so that the government shall have the final right to decide on the extent of its powers, and to enforce its decisions as to one portion of its powers, and not as to the other, it is difficult to imagine. Indeed, the difficulty of realizing their views extends to the whole theory. Entertaining these different opinions, as to the true theory of the government, it follows, of course, that there must be an equal diversity of opinion, as to what constitutes a departure from it; and, that, what one considers a departure, the other must, almost necessarily, consider a conformity,—and, *vice versa*. When compared with these different views, the course of the government will be found to have conformed, much more closely, to the *national,* than to the *federal* theory.

At its outset, during the first Congress, it received an impulse in that direction, from which it has never yet recovered. Congress, among its earliest measures, adopted one, which, in effect, destroyed the relation of coequals and co-ordinates between the federal government and the governments of the individual States; without which, it is impossible to preserve its federal character. Indeed, I might go further, and assert with truth, that without it, the former would, in effect, cease to be federal, and become national. It would be superior,—and the individual governments of the several States, would become subordinate to it,—a relation inconsistent with the federal, but in strict conformity to the national theory of the government.

I refer to the 25th section of the Judiciary Act, approved the 24th Sept., 1789. It provides for an appeal from, and revisal of a "final judgment or decree in any suit, in the highest courts of law or equity of a State, in which a decision in the suit could be had, where is drawn in question the validity of a treaty or statute of, or an authority exercised under, the United States, and the decision is against their validity; or where is drawn in question the validity of a statute of, or an authority exercised under, any State, on the ground of their being repugnant to the constitution, treaties, or laws of the United States,—and the decision is in favor of their validity; or where is drawn in question the construction of any clause of the constitution, or of a treaty,—or statute of, or commission held under, the United States, and the decision is against such title, &c., specially set up by either, &c." The effect, so far as these cases extend, is to place the highest tribunal of the States, both of law and equity, in the same relation to the Supreme Court of the United States, which the circuit and inferior courts of the United States bear to it. To this extent, they are made equally subordinate and subject to its control; and, of course, the judicial departments of the separate governments of the several States, to the same extent, cease to stand, under these provisions, in the relation of coequal and co-ordinate departments with the federal judiciary. Nor does the effect stop here. Their other departments, the legislative and executive,—to the same extent, through their respective State judiciaries, no longer continue to stand in the relation of coequals and co-ordinates with the corresponding departments of the federal government. The reason is obvious. As the laws and the acts of the government and its departments, can, if opposed, reach the people individually only through the courts,—to whatever extent the judiciary of the United States is made paramount to that of the individual States, to the same extent will the legislative and executive departments of the federal government,—and, thus, the entire government itself, be made paramount to the legislative and executive departments—and the entire governments of the individual States. It results, of course, that if the right of appeal from the State courts to those of the United States, should be extended as far as the government of the United States may claim that its powers and authority extend, the government of the several States would cease, in effect, to be its coequals and co-ordinates; and become, in fact, dependent upon, and subordinate to it. Such being the case, the important question presents itself for consideration,—does the constitution vest Congress with the power to pass an act authorizing such appeals?

It is certain, that no such power is expressly delegated to it: and equally so, that there is none vested in it which would make such a power, as an incident, necessary and proper to carry it into execution. It would be vain to attempt to find either in the constitution. If, then, it be vested in Congress at all, it must be as a power necessary and proper to carry into execution some power vested in one of the two other departments,—or in the government of the United States, or some officer thereof: for Congress, by an express provision of the constitution, is limited, in the exercise of implied powers, to the passage of such laws only, as are necessary and proper to carry into effect, the powers vested in itself, or in some other department, or in the government of the United States, or some officer thereof. But it would be vain to look for a power, either in the executive department, or in the government of the United States or any of its officers, which would make a law, containing the provisions of the section in question, necessary and proper to carry it into execution. No one has ever pretended to find, or can find any such power in either, all, or any one of them. If, then, it exist at all, it must be among the powers of the department of the judiciary itself. But there is only one of its powers which has ever been claimed, or can be claimed, as affording even a pretext for making a law, containing such provisions, necessary and proper to carry it into effect. I refer to the second and third clauses of the third article of the constitution, heretofore cited. The second extends the judicial power "to all cases in law and equity, arising under this constitution, the laws of the United States, and treaties made, or which shall be made under their authority;"—and to all cases between parties therein enumerated, without reference to the nature of the question in litigation. The third enumerates certain cases, in which the Supreme Court shall have original jurisdiction, and then provides, that "in all others before mentioned, it shall have appellate jurisdiction, both as to law and fact, with such exceptions and under such regulations as the Congress shall make."

The question is thus narrowed down to a single point;—Has Congress the authority, in carrying this power into execution, to make a law providing for an appeal from the courts of the several States, to the Supreme Court of the United States?

There is, on the face of the two clauses, nothing whatever to authorize the making of such a law. Neither of them names or refers, in the slightest manner to the States, or to the courts of the States; or gives the least authority, apparently, to legislate over or concerning either. The object of the former of these two clauses, is simply to extend the judicial power, so as to make it commensurate with the other powers of the government; and to confer jurisdiction over certain cases, not arising under the constitution, and laws of the United States, or treaties made under their authority. While the latter simply provides, in what cases the Supreme Court of the United States shall have original, and in what, appellate jurisdiction. Appellate stands in contradistinction to original jurisdiction, and as the latter implies that the case must commence in the Supreme Court, so the former implies that the case must commence in an inferior court, not having final jurisdiction; and, therefore, liable to be carried up to a higher, for final decision. Now, as the constitution vests the judicial power of the

United States, "in one Supreme Court, and such inferior courts, as Congress may, from time to time ordain," the natural and plain meaning of the clause is, that, in the cases enumerated, the Supreme Court should have original jurisdiction; and in all others, originating in the inferior courts of the United States, it should have jurisdiction only on an appeal from their decisions.

Such being the plain meaning and intent of these clauses,—the question is;—How can Congress derive from them, authority to make a law providing for an appeal from the highest courts of the several States, in the cases specified in the 25th sect. of the Judiciary Act, to the Supreme Court of the United States?

To this question no answer can be given, without assuming that the State courts,—even the highest,—stand in the relation of the inferior courts to the Supreme Court of the United States, wherever a question touching their authority comes before them. Without such an assumption, there is not, and cannot be, a shadow of authority to warrant an appeal from the former to the latter. But does the fact sustain the assumption? Do the courts of the States stand, as to such questions, in the relation of the inferior to the Supreme Court of the United States? If so, it must, be by some provision of the constitution of the United States. It cannot be a matter of course. How can it be reconciled with the admitted principle, that the federal government and those of the several States, are each supreme in their respective spheres? Each, it is admitted, is supreme, as it regards the other, in its proper sphere; and, of course, as has been shown, coequal, and co-ordinate.*

---

*Note. Reference is here made to various pencil notes in the margin of the manuscript, which, from the contractions used, and the illegible manner in which they are written, I have not been able satisfactorily to decipher; and have, therefore, not incorporated with the text. They indicate that the author designed to have elaborated, more fully, this part of the subject;—and, as far as I can gather the meaning, to have shown that the State courts, in taking cognizance of cases, in which the constitution, treaties and laws of the United States are drawn in question, act, not in virtue of any provision of the constitution or laws of the United States, but by an authority independent of both. That this authority, is the constitution-making power—the people of the States respectively. That, according to a principle of jurisprudence, universally admitted, courts of justice must look to the *whole* law, by which their decisions are to be guided and governed.—That this principle is eminently applicable in the cases mentioned.—That, as the constitution and laws of the United States, are the constitution and laws of each State, the State courts must have the right,—and are in duty bound to decide on the validity of such laws as may be drawn in question, in all cases rightfully before them. And that the principle which would authorize an appeal from the decision of the highest judicial tribunal of a State, to the Supreme Court of the United States, in cases where the constitution, treaties and laws of the United States are drawn in question, would equally authorize an appeal from the latter to the former, in cases where the constitution and laws of the State have been drawn in question, and the decision has been adverse to them.—*Editor* [Crallé].

If this be true, then the respective departments of each must be necessarily and equally so;—as the whole includes the parts. The State courts are the representatives of the reserved rights, vested in the governments of the several States, as far as it relates to the judicial power. Now as these are reserved *against* the federal government,—as the very object and intent of the reservation, was to place them beyond the reach of its control,—how can the courts of the States be inferior to the Supreme Court of the United States; and, of course, subject to have their decisions re-examined and reversed by it, without, at the same time, subjecting the portion of the reserved rights of the governments of the several States, vested in it, to the control of the federal government? Still higher ground may be taken. If the State courts stand in the relation of inferiors to the Supreme Court of the United States,—what reason can possibly be assigned, why the other departments of the State governments,—the legislative and executive, should not stand in the same relation to the corresponding departments of the federal government? Where is there to be found any provision of the constitution which makes, in this respect, any distinction between the judiciary and the other departments? Or, on what principle can such a distinction be made? There is no such distinction; and, it must follow, that if the judicial department, or the courts of the governments of the individual States, stand in the relation of inferior courts to the Supreme Court of the United States, the other departments must stand in the same relation to the corresponding departments of the federal government. It must also follow, that the governments of the several States, instead of being coequal and co-ordinate with the federal government, are inferior and subordinate. All these are necessary consequences.

But it may be alleged that the section in question does not assume the broad principle, that the State courts stand, in all cases, in the relation of the inferior courts to the Supreme Court of the United States; that it is restricted to appeals from the final judgments of the highest courts of the several States; to suits in law and equity, (excluding criminal cases,) and, in such cases, to those only, where the validity of a treaty, statute of, or an authority exercised under the United States; or the construction of the constitution, or of a treaty, or law of, or commission held under the United States, are drawn in question, and the decision is adverse to the right claimed under the United States; or, where the validity of any law of, or authority exercised under a State are involved, on the ground that they are repugnant to the constitution, treaties or laws of the United States,—and the decision is in favor of the law or the authority of the State. It may, also, be alleged that, to this extent, it was necessary to regard the courts of the States as inferior courts; and, as such, to provide for an appeal from them to the Supreme Court of the United States, in order to preserve uniformity in decisions; and to avoid collision and conflict between the federal government and those of the several States.

If uniformity of decision be one of the objects of the section, its provisions are very illy calculated to accomplish it. They are far better suited to enlarge the powers of the government of the United States, and to contract, to the same degree, those of the governments of the individual States, than to secure uniformity of decision. They provide for appeals only in cases where the decision is *adverse* to the power claimed for the former, or in *favor* of that of the latter. They assume that the courts of the States are always *right* when they decide in *favor* of the government of the United States, and always *wrong,* when they decide in *favor* of the power of their respective States; and, hence, they provide for an appeal in the latter case, but for none in the former. The result is, that if the courts of a State should commit an error, in deciding *against* the State, or in favor of the United States, and the Supreme Court of the latter should, in like cases, make the reverse decisions, the want of uniformity would remain uncorrected. Uniformity, then, would seem to be of no importance, when the decision was calculated to impair the reserved powers; and only so, when calculated to impair the delegated.

But it might have been thought, that, so strong would be the leaning of the State courts towards their respective States, there would be no danger of a decision against them, and in favor of the United States; except in cases, so clear as not to admit of a doubt. This might be the case, if all the State governments stood in antagonistic relations to the federal government. But it has been established that such is not the case; and that, on the contrary, a majority of them must be, habitually, arrayed on its side; and their courts as much inclined to sustain its powers as its own courts. But if the State courts should have a strong leaning in favor of the powers of their respective States, what reason can be assigned, why the Supreme Court of the United States should not have a leaning, equally strong, in favor of the federal government? If one, in consequence, cannot be trusted in making a decision adverse to the delegated powers, on what principle can the other be trusted in making a decision adverse to the reserved powers? Is it to be supposed, that the judges of the courts of the States, who *are sworn to support the constitution of the United States,* are less to be trusted, in cases where the *delegated* powers are involved, than the federal judges, who *are not bound by oath to support the constitutions of the States,* are, in cases, where the *reserved* powers are concerned? Are not the two powers equally independent of each other? And is it not as important to protect the reserved against the encroachments of the delegated, as the delegated against those of the reserved powers?

And are not the latter, being much the weaker, more in need of protection than the former? Why, then, not leave the courts of each, without the right of appeal, on either side, to guard and protect the powers confided to them respectively?

As far as uniformity of decision is concerned,—the appeal was little needed; and well might the author of the section in question be so indifferent about securing it. The extension of the judicial power of the United States, so as to make it commensurate with the government itself, is sufficient, without the aid of an appeal from the courts of the States, to secure all the uniformity consistent with a federal government like ours. It gives choice to the plaintiff to institute his suit, either in the federal or State courts, at his option. If he select the latter, and its decision be adverse to him, he has no right to complain; nor has he a right to a new trial in the former court, as it would, in reality be, under the cover of an appeal. He selected his tribunal, and ought to abide the consequences. But his fate would be a warning to all other plaintiffs in similar cases. It would show that the State courts were adverse;—and admonish them to commence their suits in the federal courts; and, thereby, uniformity of decision, in such cases, would be secured. Nor would the defendant, in such cases, have a right to complain, and have a new trial in the courts of the United States, if the decision of the State courts should be adverse to him. If he be a citizen of the State, he would have no right to do either, if the courts of his own State should decide against him; nor could a resident of the State or sojourner in it,—since both, by voluntarily putting themselves under the protection of its laws, are bound to acquiesce in the decisions of its tribunals.

But there is another object which the appeal is well calculated to effect,—and for the accomplishment of which, its provisions are aptly drawn up, as far as they go;—that is,—to decide all conflicts between the delegated and reserved powers, as to the extent of their respective limits, in favor of the former. For this purpose, it was necessary to provide for an appeal from the State courts, whenever their decisions were *in favor* of the power of the States, or *adverse* to the power of the United States. In no other cases was it necessary; and, hence, probably, the reason why it was limited to these, notwithstanding the alleged object. Uniformity of decision required it to embrace, not only these, but the reverse cases. As it stands, it enables the Supreme Court of the United States, in all cases of conflict between the two powers, coming within the provisions of the section, to overrule the decisions of the courts of the States, and to decide, exclusively, and in the last resort, as to the extent of the delegated powers.

The object of the section was, doubtless, to prevent collision between the federal and State governments,—the delegated and reserved powers,—by giving to the former, (and by far the stronger) through the Supreme Court,—the right, under the color of an appeal, to decide as to the extent of the former,—and to enforce its decisions against the resistance of a State. The expedient may, for a time, be effectual; but must, in the end, lead to collisions of the most dangerous character. It should ever be borne in mind, that collisions are incident to a division of power;—but that without division of power, there can be no organization; and without organization, no constitution; and without this no liberty. To prevent collision, then, by destroying the division of power, is, in effect, to substitute an absolute for a constitutional government, and despotism in the place of liberty,—evils far greater than those intended to be remedied. It is the part of wisdom and patriotism, then, not to destroy the divisions of power in order to prevent collisions, but devise means, by which they may be prevented from leading to an appeal to force. This, as has been shown, the constitution, in a manner most safe and expedient, has provided through the amending power,—a power, so constituted as to preserve in all time, and under all circumstances, an equilibrium between the various divisions of power of which the system is composed.

It is true, as has been alleged, that the provisions of the section are restricted,—that they are limited to civil cases, and to appeals from the highest State courts to the Supreme Court of the United States. Thus restricted, they would not be sufficient to subject the reserved powers completely to the delegated, and to lead, at least,—speedily,—to all the consequences stated. But what assurance can there be, that the right, if admitted, will not be carried much further? The right of appeal itself, can only be maintained, as has been shown, on the assumption that the courts of the States stand in the relation of inferior courts to the Supreme Court of the United States. Resting on this broad assumption; no definite limits can be assigned to the right, if it exists at all. It may be extended to criminal as well as civil cases;—to the circuit courts of the United States as well as to the Supreme Court; to the transfer of a case, civil or criminal, at any stage, before as well as after final decision, from the State courts to either the circuit or Supreme Court of the United States; to the exemption of all the employés and officers of the United States, when acting under the color of their authority, from civil and criminal proceedings in the courts of the State, and subjecting those of the States, acting under their respective laws, to the civil and criminal process of the United States; to authorize the judges of the United States court to grant writs of habeas corpus to persons confined under the authority of the States, on the allegation that the acts for which they were confined, were done under color of the authority of the United States; and, finally, to authorize the President to use the entire force of the Union—the militia, the army and navy—to enforce, in all such cases, the claim of power on the part of the United States. If the courts of the States, be, indeed, inferior courts,—if an appeal from them to the Supreme Court of the United States can be rightfully authorized by Congress, all this may be done. May! It has already been done. All that has been stated as possible, is but a transcript of the provisions of the act approved 3d March, 1833, entitled, "An act to provide for the collection of duties on imports;"—as far as it relates to the matter in question.

But if such powers can be rightfully vested in the courts of the United States by Congress, for the collection of the revenue, no reason can be assigned why it may not vest like powers in them to carry into execution any power which it may choose to claim, or exercise. Take, for illustration, what is called the "guaranty section" of the constitution, which, among other things, provides that, "the United States shall guarantee to each State in this Union a republican form of government; and protect each of them, on application of the legislature, or of the executive (when the legislature cannot be convened,) against domestic violence." Congress, of course, as the representative of the United States, in their legislative capacity, has the right to make laws to carry these guaranties into execution. This involves the right, in reference to the first, to determine what form of government is republican. To decide this important question, the government of the United States and the several State governments, at the time the constitution of the United States was adopted and the States became members of the federal Union, furnished a plain and safe standard, as they were, of course, all deemed republican. But suppose Congress, instead of being regulated by it, should undertake to fix a standard, without regard to that fixed by those who framed, or those who adopted the constitution of the United States; and suppose it should adopt, what now, it is to be feared, is the sentiment of the dominant portion of the Union, that no government is republican where universal suffrage does not prevail,—where the numerical majority of the whole population is not recognized as the supreme governing power: And, suppose, acting on this false standard, that Congress should declare that the governments of certain States of the Union, a large portion of whose population are not permitted to exercise the right of suffrage, were not republican; and should undertake, in execution of its declaration, to make laws to compel all such States to adopt governments conforming to its views, by extending the right of suffrage to every description of its population, and placing the power in the hands of the mere numerical majority. What, in such case, would there be to prevent Congress from adopting the provisions of the act of 3d March, 1833, to carry such laws into execution? If it had the right to adopt them, in that case, it would have an equal right to adopt them in the case supposed, or in any other that might be. No distinction can possibly be made between them, or between it and any other case, where Congress may claim to exercise a power. If it has the right to regard the courts of the States as standing in the relation of inferiors to the courts of the United States, *in any case,* it has a right to consider them so *in every case;* and, as such, subject to the authority of the latter, whenever, and to whatever extent it may think proper. What, then, would be the effect of extending the provisions of the act to the case supposed? The officers of the State, and all in authority under her, and all her citizens, who might stand up in defence of her government and institutions, would be regarded as insurgents, for resisting the act of Congress; and, as such, liable to be arrested, tried and punished by the courts of the United States; while those who might desert the State, and join in overthrowing her government and institutions, would be protected by them against her laws and her courts. To be true to the State, would come to be regarded as treason to the United States, and punishable as the highest crime; whilst to be false to her, would come to be regarded as fidelity to them, and be a passport to the honors of the Union. More briefly, fidelity to her, would be treason to the United States, and treason to her, fidelity to them.

But the clause in question embraces the protection of the government of each State against domestic violence, as well as the guaranty of a republican form of government to each. Suppose, then, a party should be formed in any State to overthrow its government, on the ground that it was not republican,—because its constitution restricted the right of suffrage, and did not recognize the right of the numerical majority to govern absolutely. Suppose that this party should apply to Congress to enforce the pledge of the United States to guarantee a republican form of government,—and the State should apply to enforce the guaranty of protection against domestic violence,—and Congress should side with the former and pass laws to aid them: what reason can be assigned, why the provisions of the act of the 3d March, 1833, could not be extended to such a case,—and the government of the State, with all its functionaries, and all their aiders and abettors, be arrested, tried, convicted and punished as traitors, by the courts of the United States? And all, who combined to overthrow the government of the State, protected against the laws and courts of the State?

It may be objected that the supposition, in both cases, is imaginary and never can occur;—that it is not even to be supposed that Congress ever will so far forget its duty, as to pervert guaranties, solemnly entered into by the States, in forming a federal Union to protect each other in their republican forms of government,—and the separate government of each against domestic violence,—

into means of effecting ends the very opposite of those intended. The objection, if it should ever be made, would indicate very little knowledge of the barriers which constitutions and plighted faith oppose to governments, when they can be transcended with impunity. They may not be openly assailed at first. They are usually sapped and undermined by construction, preparatory to their entire demolition. But what construction may fail to accomplish, the open assaults of fanaticism, or the lust of power, or the violence of party, will, in the end, prostrate. Of the truth of this, history, both political and religious, affords abundant proofs. Already our own furnishes many examples, of which, not a few, much to the point, might be cited. The very act, which the statute of the 3d March, 1833, was intended to enforce, was a gross and palpable perversion of the taxing power; and the movement to subvert the government of Rhode Island, a few years since, threatened, at one time, to furnish, by a like perversion of the guarantee to protect its government against domestic violence, the means of subverting it.

But it may be alleged that, if Congress should so far forget its duty as to make the gross and dangerous perversion supposed, the State would find security in the independent tenure, by which the judges of the United States courts hold their office. As highly important as this tenure is to protect the judiciary against the encroachments of the other departments of the government, and to insure an upright administration of the laws, as between individuals, it would be greatly to over-estimate its importance to suppose, that it secures an efficient resistance against Congress, in the case supposed; or, more generally, against the encroachment of the federal government on the reserved powers. There are many and strong reasons why it cannot.

In the first place, all cases like those supposed, where the power is perverted from the object intended to be effected by it, and made the means of effecting another of an entirely different character,—are beyond the cognizance of the courts. The reason is plain. If the act be constitutional on its face; if its title be such as to indicate that the power exercised, is one which Congress is authorized by the constitution to exercise;—and there be nothing on the face of the act calculated, beyond dispute, to show it did not correspond with the purpose professed,—the courts cannot look beyond to ascertain the real object intended, however different it may be. It has (to illustrate by the case in question) the right to make laws to carry into execution the guaranty of a republican form of government to the several States of the Union; and, for this purpose, to determine whether the form of the government of a certain State be republican or not. But if, under the pretext of exercising this power, it should use it for the purpose of subjecting to its control any obnoxious member, or members of the Union,—be it from the impulse of fanaticism, lust of power, party resentment, or any other motive, it would not be within the competency of the courts to inquire into the objects intended.

But, if it were otherwise,—if the judiciary could take cognizance of this, and any other description of perversion or infraction by the other departments, it could oppose no permanent resistance to them. The reason is to be found in the fact, that, like the others, it emanates from, and is under the control of the two combined majorities;—that of the States, and that of their populations, estimated in federal numbers. The independent tenure, by which the judges hold their office, may render the judiciary less easily and readily acted on by these united majorities; but as they become permanently concentrated in one of the sections of the Union, and as that section becomes permanently the dominant one, the judiciary must yield, ultimately, to its control. It would possess all the means of acting on the hopes and fears of the judges. As high as their office,—or independent as their tenure of office is, it does not place them above the influences which control the other members of government. They may aspire higher. The other judges of the Supreme Court, may, will, and honorably aspire to the place of the Chief Justice;—and he and all of his associates, to the highest post under the government. As far as these influences extend, they must give a leaning to the side which can control the elections, and, through them, the department which has at its disposal the patronage of the government. Nor does their office place them beyond the reach of fear. As independent as it is, they are, like all the other officers of government, liable to be impeached: and the powers of impeaching and of trying impeachments, are vested, respectively, in the House of Representatives and the Senate,—both of which emanate directly from the combined majorities which control the government. But, if both hope and fear should be insufficient to overcome the independence of the judges, the appointing power, which emanates from the same source, would, in time, fill the bench with those only whose opinions and principles accord with the other departments. And hence, all reliance on the judiciary for protection, under the most favorable view that can be taken, must, in the end, prove vain and illusory.

I have now shown that the 25th section of the judiciary act is unauthorized by the constitution; and that it rests on an assumption which would give to Congress the right to enforce, through the judiciary department, whatever measures it might think proper to adopt; and to put down all resistance by force. The effect of this is to make the government of the United States the sole judge, in the last resort, as to the extent of its powers, and to place the States and their separate governments and institutions at its mercy. It would be a waste of time to undertake to show that an assumption, which would destroy the relation of co-ordinates between the government of the United States and those of the several States,—which would enable the former, at pleasure, to absorb the reserved powers and to destroy the institutions, social and political, which the constitution was ordained and established to protect, is wholly inconsistent with the federal theory of the government, though in perfect accordance with the national theory. Indeed, I might go further, and assert, that it is, of itself, all sufficient to convert it into a national, consolidated government;—and thus to consummate, what many of the most prominent members of the convention so long, and so perseveringly contended for. Admit the right of Congress to regard the courts of the States as inferior to those of the United States, and every other act of assumption is made easy. It is the great enforcing power to compel a State to submit to all acts, however unconstitutional, oppressive or outrageous,—or to oppose them at its peril. This one departure, of which the 25th section of the judiciary act was the entering wedge, and the act of the 3rd March, 1833, the consummation, may be fairly regarded as the salient point of all others;—for without it, they either would not have occurred, or if they had, might have been readily remedied. Or, rather, without it, the whole course of the government would have been different,—the conflict between the co-ordinate governments, in reference to the extent of their respective powers, would have been subject to the action of the amending power; and thereby the equilibrium of the system been preserved, and the practice of the government made to conform to its federal character.

It remains to be explained how, at its very outset, the government received a direction so false and dangerous. For this purpose it will be necessary to recur to the history of the formation and adoption of the constitution.

The convention which framed it, was divided, as has been stated, into two parties;—one in favor of a *national,* and the other of a *federal* government. The former, consisting, for the most part, of the younger and more talented members of the body,—but of the less experienced,—prevailed in the early stages of its proceedings. A negative on the action of the governments of the several States, in some form or other, without a corresponding one, on their part, on the acts of the government about to be formed, was indispensable to the consummation of their plan. They, accordingly, as has been shown, attempted, at every stage of the proceedings of the convention, and in all possible forms, to insert some provision in the constitution, which would, in effect, vest it with a negative;—but failed in all. The party in favor of a *federal* form, subsequently gained the ascendency;—the national party acquiesced, but without surrendering their preference for their own favorite plan;—or yielding, entirely, their confidence in the plan adopted,—or the necessity of a negative on the action of the separate governments of the States. They regarded the plan as but an experiment; and determined, as honest men and good patriots, to give it a fair trial. They even assumed the name of federalists; and two of their most talented leaders, Mr. Hamilton and Mr. Madison, after the adjournment of the convention, and while the ratification of the constitution was pending, wrote the major part of that celebrated work, "The Federalist;" the object of which was to secure its adoption. It did much to explain and define it, and to secure the object intended; but it shows, at the same time, that its authors had not abandoned their predilection in favor of the national plan.

When the government went into operation, they both filled prominent places under it: Mr. Hamilton, that of secretary of the treasury—then, by far the most influential post belonging to the executive department,—if we except its head; and Mr. Madison, that of a member of the House of Representatives;— at the time, a much more influential body than the Senate, which sat with closed doors, on legislative, as well as executive business. No position could be assigned, better calculated to give them control over the action of the government, or to facilitate their efforts to carry out their predilections in favor of a national form of government, as far as, in their opinion, fidelity to the constitution would permit. How far this was, may be inferred from the fact, that their joint work, THE FEDERALIST, maintained that the government was partly federal and partly national, notwithstanding it calls itself "the government of the United States;"— and notwithstanding the convention repudiated the word *"national,"* and designated it by the name of *"federal,"* in their letter laying the plan before the old Congress, as has been shown. When to this it is added, that the party, originally in favor of a national plan of government, was strongly represented, and that the President and Vice-President had, as was supposed, a leaning that way, it is not surprising that it should receive from the first, an impulse in that direction much stronger than was consistent with its federal character; and that some measure should be adopted calculated to have the effect of giving it, what was universally desired by that party in the convention, a negative on the action of the separate governments of the several States. Indeed, believing as they did, that they would prove too strong for the government of the United States, and that such a negative was indispensable to secure harmony, and to avoid conflict between them, it was their duty to use their best efforts to adopt some such measure;— provided that, in their opinion, there should be no constitutional objection in the way. Nor would it be difficult, under such impressions, to be satisfied with reasons in favor of the constitutionality of some such measure which, under a different, or neutral state of mind, would be rejected as having little or no weight. But there was none other, except that embraced in the 25th section of the judiciary act, which had the least show, even of plausibility in its favor;— and it is even probable that it was adopted without a clear conception of the principle on which it rested, or the extent to which it might be carried.

Many are disposed to attribute a higher authority to the early acts of the government, than they are justly entitled to;—not only because factions and selfish feelings had less influence at the time, but because many, who had been members of the convention, and engaged in forming the constitution, were members of Congress, or engaged in administering the government;—circumstances, which were supposed to exempt them from improper influence, and to give them better means of understanding the instrument, than could be possessed by those who had not the same advantages. The purity of their motives is admitted to be above suspicion; but it is a great error to suppose that they could better understand the system they had constructed, and the dangers incident to its operation, than those who came after them. It required time and experience to make them fully known,—as is admitted by Mr. Madison himself. After stating the difficulties to be encountered in forming a constitution, he asks; "Is it unreasonable to conjecture, that the errors which may be contained in the plan of the convention, are such as have resulted, rather from defect of antecedent experience on this complicated and difficult subject, than from the want of accuracy or care in the investigation of it, and, consequently, that they are such as will not be ascertained, until an actual trial will point them out? This conjecture is rendered probable, not only by many considerations of a general nature, but by the particular case of the articles of confederation. It is observable, that, among the numerous objections and amendments suggested by the several States, when these articles were under consideration, not one is found which alludes to the great and radical error, which, on trial, has discovered itself!"* If this was true in reference to the confederacy,—an old and well known form of government,—how much more was actual trial necessary to point out the dangers to which the present system was exposed;—a system, so novel in its character, and so vastly more complicated than the confederacy? The very opinion, so confidently entertained by Mr. Madison, Gen. Hamilton, and the national party generally, (and which, in all probability led to the insertion of the 25th section of

---

*38th No. of the Federalist.

the judiciary bill,) that the federal government would prove too weak to resist the State governments,—strongly illustrates the truth of Mr. Madison's remarks. No one can now doubt, that the danger is on the other side. Indeed, the public man, who has had much experience of the working of the system, and does not more clearly perceive where the danger lies, than the ablest and most sagacious member of the convention, must be a dull observer.

But this is not the only instance of a great departure, during the same session, from the principles of the constitution. Among others, a question was decided in discussing the bill to organize the treasury department, which strikingly illustrates how imperfectly, even the framers of so complex a system as ours, understood it; and how necessary time and experience were to a full knowledge of it. During the pendency of the bill, a question arose, whether the President, without the sanction of an act of Congress, had the power to remove an officer of the government, the tenure of whose office was not fixed by the constitution? It was elaborately discussed. Most of the prominent members took part in the debate. Mr. Madison, and others who agreed with him, insisted that he had the power. They rested their argument mainly on the ground, that it belonged to the class of executive powers; and that it was indispensable to the performance of the duty, "to take care that the laws be faithfully executed." Both parties agreed that the power was not expressly vested in him. It was, finally, decided that he had the power;—both sides overlooking a portion of the constitution which expressly provides for the case. I refer to a clause, already cited, and more than once alluded to, which empowers Congress to make all laws necessary and proper to carry its own powers into execution; and, also, whatever power is vested in the government, or any of its departments, or officers. And what makes the fact more striking, the very argument used by those, who contended that he had the power, independently of Congress, conclusively showed that it could not be exercised without its authority, and that the latter department had the right to determine the mode and manner in which it should be executed. For, if it be not expressly vested in the President, and only results as necessary and proper to carry into execution a power vested in him, it irresistibly follows, under the provisions of the clause referred to, that it cannot be exercised without the authority of Congress. But while it effected this important object, the constitution provided means to secure the independence of the other departments; that of the executive, by requiring the approval of the President of all the acts of Congress;—and that of the judiciary, by its right to decide definitively, as far as the other departments are concerned, the constitutionality of all laws involved in cases brought before it.

No decision ever made, or measure ever adopted, except the 25th section of the judiciary act, has produced so great a change in the practical operation of the government, as this. It remains, in the face of this express and important provision of the constitution, unreversed. One of its effects has been, to change, entirely, the intent of the clause, in a most important particular. Its main object, doubtless, was, to prevent collision in the action of the government, without impairing the independence of the departments, by vesting *all discretionary power* in the Legislature. Without this, each department would have had equal right to determine what powers were necessary and proper to carry into execution the powers vested in it; which could not fail to bring them into dangerous conflicts, and to increase the hazard of multiplying unconstitutional acts. Indeed, instead of a government, it would have been little less than the *regime* of three separate and conflicting departments,—ultimately to be controlled by the executive; in consequence of its having the command of the patronage and forces of the Union. This is avoided, and unity of object and action is secured by vesting all its discretionary power in Congress; so that no department or officer of the government, can exercise any power not expressly authorized by the constitution or the laws. It is thus made a legal, as well as a constitutional government; and if there be any departure from the former, it must be either with the sanction or the permission of Congress. Such was the intent of the constitution; but it has been defeated, in practice, by the decision in question.

Another of its effects has been to engender the most corrupting, loathsome and dangerous disease, that can infect a popular government;—I mean that, known by the name of "*the Spoils.*" It is a disease easily contracted under all forms of government;—hard to prevent, and most difficult to cure, when contracted; but of all the forms of governments, it is, by far, the most fatal in those of a popular character. The decision, which left the President free to exercise this mighty power, according to his will and pleasure,—uncontrolled and unregulated by Congress, scattered, broadcast, the seeds of this dangerous disease, throughout the whole system. It might be long before they would germinate;—but that they would spring up in time; and, if not eradicated, that they would spread over the whole body politic a corrupting and loathsome distemper, was just as certain as any thing in the future. To expect, with its growing influence and patronage, that the honors and emoluments of the governmen if left to the free and unchecked will of the Executive, would not be brought, in time, to bear on the presidential election, implies profound ignorance of that constitution of our nature, which renders governments necessary, to preserve society, and constitutions, to prevent the abuses of governments.

There was another departure during the same Congress, which was followed by important consequences; and which strikingly illustrates how dangerous it is for it to permit either of the other departments to exercise any power not expressly vested in it by the constitution, or authorized by law. I refer to the order issued by the, then, Secretary of the Treasury, Gen. Hamilton, authorizing, under certain restrictions, bank-notes to be received in payment of the dues of the government.

To understand the full extent of the evils consequent on this measure, it is necessary to premise, that, during the revolution, the country had been inundated by an issue of paper, on the part of the confederacy and the governments of the several States; and at the time the constitution was adopted, was suffering severely under its effects. To put an end to the evil, and to guard against its recurrence, the constitution vested Congress with the power, "to coin money, regulate the value thereof, and of foreign coins," and prohibited the States from "coining money, emitting bills of credit, and making any thing but gold and silver coin a tender in payment of debts." With the intent of carrying out the object of these provisions, Congress provided, in the act laying duties upon imports, that they should be received in gold and silver coin only. And yet, the Secretary, in the face of this provision, issued an order, authorizing the collectors to receive banknotes; and thus identified them, as far as the fiscal action of the government was concerned, with gold and silver coin, against the express provision of the act, and the intent of the constitution.

This departure led, almost necessarily, to another, which followed shortly after;—the incorporation of, what was called, in the report of the Secretary recommending its establishment, A NATIONAL BANK;—a report strongly indicating the continuance of his predilections in favor of a national government. I say, *almost necessarily;* for if the government has the right to receive, and actually receives and treats bank-notes as money, in its receipts and payments, it would seem to follow that it had the right, and was in duty bound, to adopt all means necessary and proper to give them uniformity and stability of value, as far as practicable. Thus the one departure led to the other, and the two combined, to great and important changes in the character and the course of the government.

During the same Congress, a foundation was laid for other and great departures; the results of which, although not immediately developed, have since led to the most serious evils. I refer to the report of the Secretary of the Treasury on the subject of manufactures. He contended, not only that duties might be imposed to encourage manufactures, but that it belonged (to use his own language) "to the discretion of the national Legislature to pronounce upon the objects which concern the general welfare, and for which, under that description, an appropriation of money is requisite and proper. And there seems to be no doubt, that whatever concerns the general interests of agriculture, of manufactures and of commerce, is within the sphere of the national councils, as far as regards an application of money." It is a bold and an unauthorized assumption, that Congress has the power to pronounce what objects belong, and what do not belong to the general welfare; and to appropriate money, at its discretion, to such as it may deem to belong to it. No such power is delegated to it;—nor is any such necessary and proper to carry into execution those which are delegated. On the contrary, to pronounce on the general welfare of the States is a high constitutional power, appertaining not to Congress, but to the people of the several States, acting in their sovereign capacity. That duty they performed in ordaining and establishing the constitution. This pronounced to what limits the general welfare extended, and beyond which it did not extend. All within them, appertained to the general welfare, and all without them, to the particular welfare of the respective States. The money power, including both the taxing and appropriating powers, and all other powers of the federal government are restricted to these limits. To prove, then, that any particular object belongs to the *general* welfare of the States of the Union, it is necessary to show that it is included in some one of the delegated powers, or is necessary and proper to carry some one of them into effect,—before a tax can be laid or money appropriated to effect it. For Congress, then, to undertake to pronounce what does, or what does not belong to the general welfare,—without regard to the extent of the delegated powers,—is to usurp the highest authority;—one belonging exclusively to the people of the several States in their sovereign capacity. And yet, on this assumption, thus boldly put forth, in defiance of a fundamental principle of a federal system of government, most onerous duties have been laid on imports,—and vast amounts of money appropriated to objects not named among the delegated powers, and not necessary or proper to carry any one of them into execution; to the great impoverishment of one portion of the country, and the corresponding aggrandizement of the other.

Such are some of the leading measures, which were adopted, or had their origin during the first Congress that assembled under the constitution. They all evince a strong predilection for a national government; so strong, indeed, that very feeble arguments were sufficient to satisfy those, who had the control of affairs at the time; provided the measure tended to give the government an impulse in that direction. Not that it was intended to change its character from a *federal* to a *national* government (for that would involve a want of good faith),—but that it was thought to be necessary to strengthen it on, what was sincerely believed to be, its weak side. But, be this as it may, the government then received an impulse adverse to its federal, and in favor of a national, consolidated character, from which it has never recovered;—and which, with slight interruption and resistance, has been constantly on the increase. Indeed, to the measures then adopted and projected, almost all subsequent departures from the federal character of the government, and all encroachments on the reserved powers may be fairly traced, numerous and great as they have been.

So many measures, following in rapid succession, and strongly tending to concentrate all power in the government of the United States, could not fail to excite much alarm among those who were in favor of preserving the reserved rights; and, with them, the federal character of the government. They, accordingly, soon began to rally in opposition to the Secretary of the Treasury and his policy, under Mr. Jefferson,—then Secretary of State,—and in favor of the reserved powers,—or, as they were called, "reserved rights," of the States. They assumed the name of the Republican party. Its great object was to protect the reserved, against the encroachments of the delegated powers; and, with this view, to give a direction to the government of the United States, favorable to the preservation of the one, and calculated to prevent the encroachment of the other. And hence they were often called, "the State Rights party."

Things remained in this state during the administration of General Washington;—but shortly after the accession of his successor—the elder Adams, the advocates of the reserved powers, became a regularly organized party in opposition to his administration. The introduction of, what are well known as, the Alien and Sedition laws, was the immediate cause of systematic and determined resistance. The former was fiercely assailed, as wholly unauthorized by the constitution; and as vesting arbitrary and despotic power in the President, over alien friends as well as alien enemies;—and the latter, not only as unauthorized, but in direct violation of the provision of the constitution, which prohibits Congress from making any law "abridging the freedom of speech or of the press." The passage of these acts, especially the latter,—caused deep and general excitement and opposition throughout the Union; being intended, as was supposed, to protect the government in its encroachment on the reserved powers.

Virginia, seconded by Kentucky, took the lead in opposition to these measures. At the meeting of her legislature, ensuing their passage, a series of resolutions were introduced and passed, early in the session, declaratory of the principles of State rights, and condemnatory of the Alien and Sedition acts, and other measures of the government having a tendency to change its character from a federal to a national government. Among other things, these resolutions affirm that, "it (the General Assembly) views the powers of the federal government, as resulting from the compact, to which the States are parties, as limited by the plain sense and intention of the instrument constituting that compact; as no further valid than they are authorized by the grants enumerated in that compact;—and that in case of a deliberate, palpable, and dangerous exercise of other powers, not granted by said compact, the States who are parties thereto, have the right and are in duty bound to interpose for arresting the progress of the evil, and for maintaining within their respective limits the authorities, rights and liberties appertaining to them. That the general assembly doth also express its deep regret, that a spirit has, in sundry instances, been manifested by the federal government to enlarge its powers by a forced construction of the constitutional charter, which defines them; and that indications have appeared of a design to expound certain general phrases—(which having been copied from the very limited grant of powers, in the former articles of confederation, were the less liable to be misconstrued)—so as to destroy the meaning and effect of the particular enumeration, which, necessarily, explains and limits the general phrases; so as to consolidate the States by degrees into one sovereignty, the obvious tendency and inevitable result of which would be, to transform the present republican system of the United States into an absolute, or, at least, mixed monarchy."

The Kentucky resolutions, which are now known to have emanated from the pen of Mr. Jefferson,—then the Vice-President, and the acknowledged head of the party,—are similar in objects and substance with those of Virginia; but as they are differently expressed, and, in some respects, fuller than the latter, it is proper to give the two corresponding resolutions. The former is in the following words: "That the several States, composing the United States of America, are not united on the principle of unlimited submission to the general government; but that, by a compact under the style and title of a constitution of the United States, and of amendments thereto, they constituted a general government for special purposes;—delegated to that government, certain definite powers; reserving, each State to itself, the residuary mass of right to their own self-government; that whensoever the general government assumes undelegated powers, its acts are unauthoritative, void, and of no force; that to this compact each State acceded as a State, and is an integral party,—its co-States forming, as to itself, the other party; that the government created by this compact, was not made the exclusive or final judge of the extent of the powers delegated to it— since that would have made its discretion, and not the constitution, the measure of its powers; but that, as in all other cases of compact among parties, having no common judge, each party has an equal right to judge for itself, as well of infractions as of the mode and measure of redress." The other is in the following words: "That the construction applied by the general government, (as evinced by sundry of their proceedings,) to those parts of the constitution of the United States, which delegate to Congress a power to lay and collect taxes, duties, imposts and excises; to pay the debts, and provide for the common defence and general welfare of the United States; and to make all laws necessary and proper for carrying into execution the powers vested by the constitution in the government of the United States, or any department thereof, goes to the destruction of all the limits prescribed to their power by the constitution. That words, meant by that instrument to be subsidiary only to the execution of the limited powers, ought not to be so construed, as themselves to give unlimited powers, nor a part so to be taken, as to destroy the whole residue of the instrument."

The resolutions adopted by both States were sent, by the governor of each, at the request of the general assembly of each, to the governors of the other States, to be laid before their respective legislatures.

In the mean time, Mr. Madison had retired from Congress and was elected a member of the legislature of his own State. As thoroughly in favor of a national government, as he had been in the convention; and as strong as his predilections in its favor continued to be, after the adoption of the federal plan of government, he could not, with the views he entertained of the present government, as being partly national and partly federal, go the whole length of the policy recommended and supported by General Hamilton;—and, accordingly, had separated from him and allied himself with Mr. Jefferson.

All the legislatures of the New England States, and that of New-York, responded unfavorably to the principles and views set forth in the Virginia and Kentucky resolutions, and in approbation of the course of the federal government. At the next session of the General Assembly of Virginia, these resolutions were referred to a committee, of which Mr. Madison was the chairman. The result was a report from his pen, which triumphantly vindicated and established the positions taken in the resolutions. It successfully maintained, among other things, that the people of the States—acting in their sovereign capacity, have the right "to decide, in the last resort, whether the compact made by them be violated;" and shows, conclusively, that, without it, and the right of the States to interfere to protect themselves and the constitution, "there would be an end to all relief from usurped powers, and a direct subversion of the rights specified or recognized under all the State constitutions, as well as a plain denial of the fundamental principle, on which our independence itself was declared." It also successfully maintained "that the ultimate right of the parties to the constitution, to judge whether the compact has been dangerously violated, must extend to the violation by one delegated authority as well as another, by the judiciary, as well as by the executive or the legislative." And that, "however true, therefore, it may be, that the judicial department is, in all questions submitted to it by the forms of the constitution, to decide, in the last resort, this resort must necessarily be deemed the last in relation to the authority of the other departments of the government; not in relation to the rights of the parties to the constitutional compact, from which the judicial as well as the other departments hold their delegated trust." It conclusively refutes the position, taken by Gen. Hamilton, that it belongs to the discretion of the national legislature to pronounce upon objects, which concern the general welfare, as far as it regards the application of money, already quoted; denies the right of Congress to use the fiscal power, either in imposing taxes, or appropriating money, to promote any objects but those specified in the constitution;—shows that the effect of the right, for which he contends, would necessarily be consolidation,—by superseding the sovereignty of the States, and extending the power of the federal government to all cases whatsoever; and that, the effect of consolidation would be to transform our federal system into a monarchy.

The unfavorable responses of the other States were, by the House of Representatives of the Kentucky legislature, referred to the committee of the whole,—which reported a resolution containing a summary of their former resolutions, which was unanimously adopted. Among other things, it asserts, "that the several States, which formed that instrument (the constitution), being sovereign and independent, have the unquestionable right to judge of its infraction; and that a nullification, by those sovereignties, of all unconstitutional acts, done under color of that instrument, is the rightful remedy."

The report of Mr. Madison, and the Virginia and Kentucky resolutions, constituted the political creed of the State rights republican party. They were understood as being in full accord with Mr. Jefferson's opinion, who was its acknowledged head. They made a plain and direct issue with the principles and policy maintained by Gen. Hamilton,—who, although not nominally the head of the federal party, as they called themselves, was its soul and spirit. The ensuing presidential election was contested on this issue, and terminated in the defeat of Mr. Adams, the election of Mr. Jefferson as President, and the elevation of the republican party into power. To the principles and doctrines, so plainly and ably set forth in their creed, they owed their elevation, and the long retention of power under many and severe trials. They secured the confidence of the people, because they were in accord with what they believed to be the true character of the constitution, and of our federal system of government.

Mr. Jefferson came into power with an earnest desire to reform the government. He certainly did a good deal in undoing what had been done; and in arresting the progress of the government towards consolidation. His election caused the repeal, in effect, of the alien and sedition laws, and a permanent acquiescence in their unconstitutionality. They constituted the prominent questions in the issue between the parties in the contest. He did much to reduce the expenses of the government, and made ample provisions for the payment of the public debt. He took strong positions against the bank of the United States, and laid the foundation for its final overthrow. Amidst great difficulties, he preserved the peace of the country during the period of his administration. But he did nothing to arrest many great and radical evils;—nothing towards elevating the judicial departments of the governments of the several States, from a state of subordination to the judicial department of the government of the United States, to their rightful, constitutional position, as co-ordinates; nothing towards maintaining the rights of the States as parties to the constitutional compact, to judge, in the last resort, as to the extent of the delegated powers; nothing towards restoring to Congress the exclusive right to adopt measures necessary and proper to carry into execution, its own, as well as all other powers vested in the government, or in any of its departments; nothing towards reversing the order of Gen. Hamilton which united the government with the banks; and nothing effectual towards restricting the money power to objects specifically enumerated and delegated by the constitution.

Why Mr. Jefferson should have failed to undo, effectually, the consolidating, national policy of Gen. Hamilton, and to restore the government to its federal character, many reasons may be assigned. In the first place, the struggle which brought him into power, was too short to make any deep and lasting impression on the great body of the community. It lasted but two or three years, and the principal excitement, as far as constitutional questions were concerned, turned on the two laws which were the immediate cause of opposition. In the next, the state of the world was such as to turn the attention of the government, mainly, to what concerned the foreign relations of the Union, and to party contests growing out of them. To these it may be added, that Gen. Hamilton had laid the foundation of his policy so deep, and with so much skill, that it was difficult, if not impossible, to reverse it; at least, until time and experience should prove it to be destructive to the federal character of the government,—inconsistent with the harmony and union of the States, and fatal to the liberty of the people. It is, indeed, even possible that, not even he,—much less his cabinet and party generally,—had a just and full conception of the danger, and the utter impracticability of some of the leading measures of his policy.

Not long after the expiration of his term, his successor in the presidency, Mr. Madison, was forced into a war with Great Britain, after making every effort to avoid it. This, of course, absorbed the attention of the government and the country for the time, and arrested all efforts to carry out the doctrines and policy which brought the party into power. It did more; for the war, however just and necessary, gave a strong impulse adverse to the federal, and favorable to the national line of policy. This is, indeed, one of the unavoidable consequences of war; and can be counteracted, only by bringing into full action the negatives necessary to the protection of the reserved powers. These would, of themselves, have the effect of preventing wars, so long as they could be honorably and safely avoided;—and, when necessary, of arresting, to a great extent, the tendency of the government to transcend the limits of the constitution, during its prosecution; and of correcting all departures, after its termination. It was by force of the tribunitial power, that the plebeians retained, for so long a period, their liberty, in the midst of so many wars.

How strong this impulse was, was not fully realized until after its termination. It left the country nearly without any currency, except irredeemable bank notes,—greatly depreciated, and of very different value in the different sections of the Union,—which forced on the government the establishment of another national bank;—the charter of the first having expired without a renewal. This, and the embargo, with the other restrictive measures, which preceded it, had diverted a large portion of the capital of the country from commerce and other pursuits to manufactures; which, in time, produced a strong pressure in favor of a protective tariff. The great increase, too, of the public expenditures of the government—in consequence of the war—required a corresponding increase of income; and this, of course, increased, in the same proportion, its patronage and influence. All these causes combined, could not fail to give a direction to the course of government, adverse to the federal and favorable to the national policy,—or, in other words, adverse to the principles and policy which brought Mr. Jefferson and the republican party into power, and favorable to those for which Mr. Adams and the federal party had contended.

In the mean time, the latter party was steadily undergoing the process of dissolution. It never recovered from the false step it took and the unwise course it pursued, during the war. It gradually lost its party organization; and even its name became extinct. But while this process was going on, the republican party, also, was undergoing a great change. It was gradually resolving itself into two parties; one of which was gradually departing from the State rights creed, and adopting the national. It rose into power, by electing the younger Adams, as the successor of Mr. Monroe, and took the name of the *"National Republican party."* It differed little, in doctrine or policy, from the old federal party; but, in tone and character, was much more popular,—and much more disposed to court the favor of the people.

At the same time, the other portion of the party was undergoing a mutation, not less remarkable;—and which finally led to a change of name. It took the title of the *"Democratic party;"* or,—more emphatically— *"the Democracy."* The causes, which led to this change of name, began to operate before Mr. Monroe's administration expired. Indeed, with the end of his administration,—the last of the line of Virginia Presidents,—the old State rights party, ceased to exist as a party, after having held power for twenty-four years. The Democracy, certainly had much more affinity with it in feelings—but, as a party—especially its northern wing— had much less devotion to the reserved powers; and was much more inclined to regard mere numbers as the sole political element,—and the numerical majority as entitled to the absolute right to govern. It was, also, much more inclined to adopt the national than the republican creed,—as far as the money power of the government was concerned; and, to this extent, much more disposed to act with the advocates of the former, than the latter.

No state of things could be more adverse to carrying out the principles and policy which brought the old republican party into power, or to restoring those of the party, which they expelled from power,—as events have proved. One of its first fruits was the passage of the act of 19th May, 1828, entitled, "An act in alteration of the several acts imposing duties on imports,"—called, at the time, the "Bill of Abominations,"—as it truly proved to be. It was passed by the joint support and vote of both parties—National Republicans, and those who, afterwards, assumed the name of "the Democracy,"—the southern wing of each excepted. The latter, indeed, took the lead both in its introduction and support.

All preceding acts imposing duties, which this purported to alter, had some reference to, and regard for revenue; however much the rate of duties might have been controlled by the desire to afford protection. But such was not the case with this. It was passed under such circumstances as conclusively proved that it was intended, wholly and exclusively for protection; without any view, whatever, to revenue. The public debt, including the remnant of that contracted in the war of the Revolution, and the whole of that incurred in the war of 1812, was on the eve of being finally discharged, under the operation of the effective sinking fund, established at the close of the latter. And so ample was the revenue, at the time, that fully one half of the whole, was annually applied to the discharge of the principal and interest of the public debt;—leaving an ample surplus, to meet the current expenses of the government on a liberal scale. It was clear, that under such circumstances, no increase of duties was required for revenue;—so clear, indeed, that the advocates of the bill openly avowed that its object was protection, not revenue; although they refused to adopt an amendment, which proposed to declare its real object, in order that its constitutionality might be decided by the judicial department.

It was under such circumstances that this act was passed; which, instead of reducing the duties one half, (to take effect after the final discharge of the public debt,) as, on every principle of revenue and justice,—of fairness and of good faith, it ought to have done, doubled them. I say of justice, fairness, and good faith,—because the duties were originally raised to meet the expenses of the war, and to discharge the public debt;—with the understanding, that when these objects were effected, they would be reduced,—and the burden they imposed on the tax-payers be lightened. Without this understanding they could not have been raised.

As, then, the duties imposed by the act, were not intended for revenue;— and as there is no power, specifically delegated to Congress, to lay duties except for revenue; it is obvious that it had no right to pass the bill, unless upon the principle contended for by General Hamilton,—of applying the money power to accomplish whatever it might pronounce to be for the general welfare;—not only by the direct appropriation of money, but by the imposition of duties and taxes. Indeed, there is no substantial difference between the two; for if Congress have the right to appropriate money, in the shape of bounties, to encourage manufactures,—it may, for the same purpose, lay protective duties, to give the manufacturer a monopoly of the home market, and *vice versa;*—and such, accordingly, was the opinion of General Hamilton.

But, although the authors of this act aimed at transferring the bounty it conferred, directly into the pockets of the manufacturers, without passing through the treasury, yet they contemplated, and were prepared to meet the contingency of its bringing into the treasury a sum beyond the wants of the government, when the public debt should be extinguished. Their scheme was, to distribute the surplus among the States;—that is, to appropriate to the government of each State, a sum proportioned to its representation in Congress, as an addition to its annual revenue. They thus assumed, not only, that Congress had a right to impose duties to provide, for what it might deem the *general welfare,*—but also, and at the same time, to appropriate the receipts derived from them to the States, respectively,—to be applied to their *individual* and *local welfare*. This last measure was urged, again and again, on Congress, and would, in all probability have been adopted, had not the act, of which it was intended to have been a supplement, been arrested. A more extravagant and gross abuse of the money power can scarcely be conceived. Its consequences were as fatal as its violation of the constitution was outrageous and palpable. The vast surplus revenue, which it threw into the treasury notwithstanding its arrest, did much to corrupt both government and people; and was the principal cause of the explosion of the banking system in 1837; and the overthrow of the party in 1840, which took the lead in introducing and supporting it.

But these were not its only evil consequences. It led to another, and, if possible, a deeper and more dangerous inroad on the principles and policy which brought Mr. Jefferson and the old State rights party into power. The act of the 3rd March, 1833, already referred to,—thoroughly subjecting the judicial departments of the governments of the several States to the federal judiciary, was introduced, expressly, to enforce this grossly unconstitutional and outrageous act. It received the support and votes—as did the original act,—both of the national and the democratic parties, (a few excepted, who still adhered to the creed of the old State rights party,) the latter taking the lead and direction in both instances.

It was thus, from the identity of doctrine and of policy which distinguished both parties, in reference to the money power, that two of the most prominent articles in the creed of the republican party, by force of which Mr. Jefferson, as its leader, came into power, were set aside; and their dangerous opposites, on account of which, Mr. Adams, as the head of the federal party, was expelled, were brought into full and active operation;—namely,—the right claimed by the latter for Congress, to pronounce upon what appertains to the general welfare,—and which is so forcibly condemned in the Virginia and Kentucky resolutions, and the report of Mr. Madison;—and the right of the federal judiciary to decide, in the last resort, as to the extent of the reserved as well as of the delegated powers. The one authorizes Congress to do as it pleases,—and the other endows the court with the power to enforce whatever it may do,—if its authority should be adequate,—and if not, to call in the aid of the Executive with the entire force of the country. Their joint effect is to give unlimited control to the government of the United States, not only over those of the several States, but over the States themselves; in utter subversion of the relation of co-ordinates, and in total disregard of the rights of the several States, as parties to the constitutional compact, to judge, in the last resort, as to the extent of the powers delegated;—a right so conclusively established by Mr. Madison, in his report.

These measures greatly increased the power and patronage of the federal government; and with them, the desire to obtain its control; especially of the executive department,—which is invested mainly with the power of disposing of its honors and emoluments. As a necessary consequence of this, the presidential election became of more absorbing interest,—the struggle between the two parties more and more intense;—and every means which promised success was readily resorted to, without the least regard to their bearing, morally or politically. To secure the desired object, the concentration of party action and the stringency of party discipline were deemed indispensable. And hence, contemporaneously with these measures, party conventions were, for the first time, called to nominate the candidates for the presidency and vice-presidency,—and party organization established all over the Union. And hence, also, for the first time, the power of removing from office, at the discretion of the President, so unconstitutionally conceded to him by the first Congress, was brought into active and systematic operation, as the means of rewarding partisan services, and of punishing party opposition or party delinquencies. In these measures the democratic party took the lead;—but were soon followed by their opponents. There is, at present, no distinction between them in this respect. The effects of the whole have been, to supersede the provision of the constitution, as far as it relates to the election of President and Vice-President, as has been shown; to give a decided control over these elections to those who hold or seek office; to stake all the powers and emoluments of the government as prizes, to be won or lost by victory or defeat; and to make success in the election paramount to every other consideration.

But there is another cause that has greatly contributed to place the control of the presidential elections in the hands of those who hold or seek office. I allude, to what is called, the general ticket system; which has become, with the exception of a single State, the universal mode of appointing electors to choose the President and Vice-President. It was adopted to prevent a division of the vote of the several States, in the choice of their highest officers; and to make the election more popular, by giving it, as was professed to be its object, to the people. The former of these ends it has effected, but it has utterly failed as to the latter. It professes to give the people, individually, a right which it was impossible to exercise, except in the very smallest class of States, and even in these, very imperfectly. To call on a hundred thousand voters, scattered over fifty or sixty thousand square miles, to make out a ticket of a dozen or more electors,

is to ask them to do that which, individually, they cannot properly or successfully do. Very few would have the information necessary to make a proper
selection; and even if every voter had such information, the diversity of opinion and the want of concentration on the same persons, would be so great, that
it would be a matter of mere accident, who would have the majority. To avoid
this, a ticket must be formed by each party. But the few of each, who form the
ticket, actually make the appointment of the electors; for the people individually, have no choice, but to vote for the one or the other ticket,—or otherwise,
virtually, to throw away their vote;—for there would be no chance of success
against the concentrated votes of the two parties. Never was there a scheme better contrived to transfer power from the body of the community, to those
whose occupation is to get or hold offices, and to merge the contests of party
into a mere struggle for the spoils.

It is due to the Democratic party to state that, while they took the lead, and
are principally responsible for bringing about this state of things, they are entitled to the credit of putting down the Bank of the United States; of checking
extravagant expenditures on internal improvements; of separating the government from the banks; and, more recently, of opposing protective tariffs; and of
adopting the ad valorem principle in imposing duties on imports. These are all
important measures; and indicate a disposition to take a stand against the perversion of the money power. But, until the measures which led to these mis-
chiefs,—and in the adoption of which they bore so prominent a part,—are
entirely reversed, nothing permanent will be gained.

In the meanwhile the sectional tendency of parties has been increasing with
the central tendency of the government. They are, indeed, intimately connected. The more the powers of the system are centralized in the federal government, the greater will be its power and patronage; proportionate with these,
and increasing with their increase, will be the desire to possess the control over
them, for the purpose of aggrandizement; and the stronger this desire, the less
will be the regard for principles, and the greater the tendency to unite for sectional objects;—the stronger section with a view to power and aggrandizement,—the weaker, for defence and safety. Any strongly marked diversity will
be sufficient to draw the line; be it diversity of pursuit, of origin, of character,
of habits, or of local institutions. The latter, being more deeply and distinctly
marked than any other existing in the several States composing the Union, has,
at all times, been considered by the wise and patriotic, as a delicate point,—and
to be, with great caution, touched. The dangers connected with this, began to
exhibit themselves in the old Congress of the confederation, in respect to the

North-Western Territory; and continued down to the time of the formation of the present constitution. They constituted the principal difficulty in forming it; but it was fortunately overcome, and adjusted to the satisfaction of both parties.

For a long period, nothing occurred to disturb this happy state of things. But in the session of 1819–20, a question arose that exposed the latent danger. The admission of the territory of Missouri, as a State of the Union, was resisted on the ground that its constitution did not prohibit slavery. The contest, after a long and angry discussion, was finally adjusted by a compromise, which admitted her as a slaveholding State, on condition that slavery should be prohibited in all the territories belonging then to the United States, lying north of 36∞ 30'. This compromise was acquiesced in by the people of the South; and the danger, apparently, and, as every one supposed, permanently removed. Experience, however, has proved how erroneous were their calculations. The disease lay deep. It touched a fanatical as well as a political cord. There were not a few in the northern portion of the Union, who believed that slavery was a sin, as well as a great political evil; and who remained quiet in reference to it, only because they believed that it was beyond their control;—and that they were in no way responsible for it. So long as the government was regarded as a federal government with limited powers, this belief of the sinfulness of slavery remained in a dormant state,—as it still does in reference to the institution in foreign countries; but when it was openly proclaimed, as it was by the passage of the act of 1833, that the government had the right to judge, in the last resort, of the extent of its powers; and to use the military and naval forces of the Union to carry its decisions into execution; and when its passage by the joint votes of both parties furnished a practical assertion of the right claimed in an outrageous case, the cord was touched which roused it into action. The effects were soon made visible. In two years thereafter, in 1835, a systematic movement was, for the first time, commenced to agitate the question of abolition, by flooding the southern States with documents calculated to produce discontent among the slaves;—and Congress, with petitions to abolish slavery in the District of Columbia.

The agitation was, however, at first, confined comparatively to a few; and they obscure individuals without influence. The great mass of the people viewed it with aversion. But here again, the same measure which roused it into action, mainly contributed to keep alive the agitation, and ultimately to raise a party (consisting, at first, of a few fanatics) sufficiently numerous and powerful to exercise a controlling influence over the entire northern section of the Union. By the great increase of power and patronage which it conferred on the government, it contributed vastly to increase the concentration and intensity of party struggles, and to make the election of President the all absorbing question. The effect of this was, to induce both parties to seek the votes of every faction or combination by whose aid they might hope to succeed;—flattering them in return, with the prospect of establishing the doctrines they professed, or of accomplishing the objects they desired. This state of things could not fail to give importance to any fanatical party, however small, which cared more for the object that united them, than for the success of either party; especially if it should be of a character to accord, in the abstract, with the feeling of that portion of the community generally. Each of the great parties, in order to secure their support, would, in turn, endeavor to conciliate them, by professing a great respect for them, and a disposition to aid in accomplishing the objects they wished to effect. This dangerous system of electioneering could not fail to increase the party, and to give it great additional strength; to be followed, of course, by an increased anxiety on the part of those who desired its aid, to conciliate its favor; thus keeping up the action and reaction of those fatal elements, from day to day,—the one, rising in importance, as its influence extended over the section—the other sinking in subserviency to its principles and purposes.

In the meantime, the same causes must needs contribute, in the other section, to a state of things well calculated to aid this process. In proportion to the power and patronage of the government, would be the importance, to party success, of concentration and intensity in party struggles: and in proportion to these, the attachment and devotion to party, where the spoils are the paramount object. In the same proportion also, would be the unwillingness of the two wings of the respective parties, in the different sections, to separate, and their desire to hold together; and, of course, the disposition on the part of that in the weaker, to excuse and palliate the steps taken by their political associates in the stronger section, to conciliate the abolition party, in order to obtain its votes. Thus the section assaulted would be prevented from taking any decided stand to arrest the danger, while it might be safely and easily done;—and seduced to postpone it, until it shall have acquired,—as it already has done,—a magnitude, almost, if not altogether, beyond the reach of means within the constitution. The difficulty and danger have been greatly increased, since the Missouri compromise; and the other sectional measures, in reference to the recently acquired territories, now in contemplation (should they succeed), will centralize the two majorities that constitute the elements of which the government of the United States is composed, permanently in the northern section; and thereby subject the southern, on this, and on all other questions, in which their feelings or interest may come in conflict, to its control.

Such has been the practical operation of the government, and such its effects. It remains to be considered, what will be the consequence? to what will the government of the numerical majority probably lead?

On this point, we are not without some experience. The present disturbed and dangerous state of things are its first fruits. It is the legitimate result of that long series of measures, (of which the acts of the 19th of May, 1828, and the 3rd of March, 1833, are the most prominent,) by which the powers of the whole system have been concentrated, virtually, in the government of the United States; and thereby transformed it from its original federal character, into the government of the numerical majority. To these fatal measures are to be attributed the violence of party struggles;—the total disregard of the provisions of the constitution in respect to the election of the President; the predominance of the honors and emoluments of the government over every other consideration; the rise and growth of the abolition agitation; the formation of geographical parties; and the alienation and hostile feelings between the two great sections of the Union. These are all the unavoidable consequences of the government of the numerical majority, in a country of such great extent, and with such diversity of institutions and interests as distinguish ours. They will continue, with increased and increasing aggregation, until the end comes. In a country of moderate extent, and with an executive department less powerfully constituted than in ours, this termination would be in an appeal to force, to decide the contest between the two hostile parties; and in a monarchy, by the commander of the successful party becoming master of both, and of the whole community, as has been stated. But there is more uncertainty in a country of such extent as ours, and where the executive department is so powerfully constituted. The only thing that is certain is, that it cannot last. But whether it will end in a monarchy, or in disunion, is uncertain. In the one or the other it will, in all probability, terminate if not prevented; but in which, time alone can decide. There are powerful influences in operation;—a part impelling it towards the one, and a part towards the other.

Among those impelling it towards monarchy, the two most prominent are, the national tendency of the numerical majority to terminate in that form of government; and the structure of the executive department of the government of the United States. The former has been fully explained in the preliminary discourse, and will be passed over with the single remark,—that it will add great force to the impulse of the latter in the same direction. To understand the extent of this force will require some explanation.

The vast power and patronage of the department are vested in a single officer, the President of the United States. Among these powers, the most prominent, as far as it relates to the present subject, are those which appertain to the administration of the government; to the office of commander in chief of the army and navy of the United States; to the appointment of the officers of the government, with few exceptions; and to the removal of them at his pleasure,—as his authority has been interpreted by Congress. These, and especially the latter, have made his election the great and absorbing object of party struggles; and on this the appeal to force will be made, whenever the violence of the struggle and the corruption of parties will no longer submit to the decision of the ballot-box. To this end it must come, if the force impelling it in the other direction should not previously prevail. If it comes to this, it will be, in all probability, in a contested election; when the question will be, Which is the President? The incumbent,—if he should be one of the candidates,—or, if not, the candidate of the party in possession of power? or of the party endeavoring to obtain possession? On such an issue, the appeal to force would make the *candidate* of the successful party, master of the whole,—and not the *commander,* as would be the case under different circumstances.

The contest would put an end, virtually, to the elective character of the department. The form of election might, for a time, be preserved; but the ballot-box would be much less relied on for the decision, than the sword and bayonet. In time, even the form would cease, and the successor be appointed by the incumbent:—and thus the absolute form of a popular, would end in the absolute form of a monarchical government. Scarcely a possibility would exist of forming a constitutional monarchy. There would be no material out of which it could be formed; and if formed, it would be too feeble, with such material as would constitute it, to hold in subjection a country of such great extent and population as ours must be.

Such will be the end to which the government, as it is now operating, must, in all probability, come, should the other alternative not occur, and nothing, in the meantime, be done to prevent it. It is idle to suppose that, operating as the system now does—with the increase of the country in extent, population and wealth, and the consequent increase of the power and patronage of the government, the head of the executive department can remain elective. The future is indeed, for the most part, uncertain; but there are causes in the political world as steady and fixed in their operation, as any in the physical; and among them are those, which, *subject to the above conditions,* will lead to the result stated.

Those impelling the government towards disunion are, also, very powerful. They consist chiefly of two; the one, arising from the great extent of the country:—the other, from its division into separate States, having local institutions and interests. The former, under the operation of the numerical majority, has necessarily given to the two great parties, in their contest for the honors and emoluments of the government, a geographical character; for reasons which have been fully stated. This contest must finally settle down in a struggle on the part of the stronger section to obtain the permanent control; and on the part of the weaker to preserve its independence and equality as members of the Union. The conflict will thus become one between the States, occupying the different sections;—that is, between organized bodies on both sides; each, in the event of separation, having the means of avoiding the confusion and anarchy, to which the parts would be subject without such organization. This would contribute much to increase the power of resistance on the part of the weaker section against the stronger, in possession of the government. With these great advantages and resources, it is hardly possible that the parties occupying the weaker section, would consent, quietly, under any circumstances, to sink down from independent and equal sovereignties, into a dependent and colonial condition;—and still less so, under circumstances that would revolutionize them *internally,* and put their very existence, as a people, at stake. Never was there an issue between independent States that involved greater calamity to the conquered, than is involved in that between the States which compose the two sections of this Union. The condition of the weaker, should it sink from a state of independence and equality to one of dependence and subjection, would be more calamitous than ever before befell a civilized people. It is vain to think that, with such consequences before them, they will not resist; especially when resistance *may* save them, and cannot render their condition worse. That this will take place, unless the stronger section desists from its course, may be assumed as certain: and that—if forced to resist, the weaker section would prove successful, and the system end in disunion, is, to say the least, highly probable. But if it should fail, the great increase of power and patronage which must, in consequence, accrue to the government of the United States, would but render certain, and hasten the termination in the other alternative. So that, at all events, to the one, or to the other,—to monarchy, or disunion it must come, if not prevented by strenuous and timely efforts. And this brings up the question,—How is it to be prevented? How can these sad alternatives be averted?

For this purpose, it is indispensable that the government of the United States should be restored to its federal character. Nothing short of a perfect restoration, as it came from the hands of its framers, can avert them. It is folly to suppose that any popular government, except one strictly federal, in *practice,* as well as in *theory,* can last, over a country of such vast extent and diversity of interests and institutions. It would not be more irrational to suppose, that it could last, without the responsibility of the rulers to the ruled. The tendency of the former to oppress the latter, is not stronger than is the tendency of the more powerful section, to oppress the weaker. Nor is the right of suffrage more indispensable to enforce the responsibility of the rulers to the ruled, than a *federal organization,* to compel the parts to respect the rights of each other. It requires the united action of both to prevent the abuse of power and oppression; and to constitute, really and truly, a constitutional government. To supersede either, is to convert it *in fact,* whatever may be its *theory,* into an absolute government.

But it cannot be restored to its federal character, without restoring the separate governments of the several States, and the States themselves, to their true position. From the latter the whole system emanated. They ordained and established all the parts; first, by their separate action, their respective State governments; and next, by their concurrent action, with the indispensable co-operation of their respective governments, they ordained and established a common government, as a supplement to their separate governments. The object was, to do that, by a *common agent,* which could not be as well done, or done at all, by their separate agencies. The relation, then, in which the States stand to the system, is that of the creator to the creature; and that, in which the two governments stand to each other, is of coequals and co-ordinates—as has been fully established:— with the important difference, in this last respect, that the separate governments of the States were the first in the order of time, and that they exercised an active and indispensable agency in the creation of the common government of all the States; or, as it is styled, the government of the United States.

Such is their true position;—a position, not only essential in *theory,* in the *formation* of a federal government—but to its *preservation* in *practice.* Without it, the system could not have been formed,—and without it, it cannot be preserved. The supervision of the creating power is indispensable to the preservation of the created. But they no longer retain their true position. In the practical operation of the system, they have both been superseded and reduced to subordinaate and dependent positions: and this, too, by the power last in the order of formation, and which was brought into existence, as auxiliary to the first,— and through the aid of its active co-operation. It has assumed control over the whole;—and thus a thorough revolution has been effected, the creature taking the place of the creator. This must be reversed, and each restored to its true position, before the federal character of the government can be perfectly restored.

For this purpose the first and indispensable step is to repeal the 25th sect. of the judiciary act,—the whole of the act of the 3rd of March, 1833, and all other acts containing like provisions. These, by subjecting the judiciary of the States to the control of the federal judiciary, have subjected the separate governments of the several States, including all their departments and functionaries,—and, thereby, the States themselves, to a subordinate and dependent condition. It is only by their repeal, that the former can be raised to their true relation as co-equals and co-ordinates,—and the latter can retain their high sovereign power of deciding, in the last resort, on the extent of the delegated powers, or of interposing to prevent their encroachment on the reserved powers. It is only by restoring these to their true position, that the government of the United States can be reduced to its true position, as the coequal and co-ordinate of the separate governments of the several States, and restricted to the discharge of those auxiliary functions assigned to it by the constitution.

But this indispensable and important step will have to be followed by several others, before the work of restoration will have been completed. One of the most important will be, the repeal of all acts by which the money power is carried beyond its constitutional limits, either in laying duties, or in making appropriations. The federal character of the government may be as effectually destroyed by encroaching on, and absorbing all the reserved powers, as by subjecting the governments of the several States themselves directly to its control. Either would make it, in fact, the sole and absolute power, and virtually, the government of the numerical majority. But of all the powers ever claimed for the government of the United States, that which invests Congress with the right to determine what objects belong to the general welfare,—to use the money power in the form of laying duties and taxes, and to make appropriations for the purpose of promoting such as it may deem to be of this character, is the most encroaching and comprehensive. In civilized communities, money may be said to be the universal means, by which all the operations of governments are carried on. If, then, it be admitted, that the government of the United States has the right to decide, at its discretion, what is, and what is not for the common good of the country, and to lay duties and taxes, and to appropriate their proceeds to effect whatever it may determine to be for the common good, it would be difficult to assign any limits to its authority, or to prevent it from absorbing, finally, all the reserved powers, and thereby, destroying its federal character.

But still more must be done to complete the work of restoration. The executive department must be rigidly restricted within its assigned limits, by divesting the President of all discretionary powers, and confining him strictly to those expressly conferred on him by the constitution and the acts of Congress. According to the express provisions of the former, he cannot rightfully exercise any other. Nor can he be permitted to go beyond, and to assume the exercise of whatever power he may deem necessary to carry those vested in him into execution, without finally absorbing all the powers vested in the other departments and making himself absolute. Having the disposal of the patronage of the government, and the command of all its forces, and standing at the head of the dominant party for the time, he will be able, in the event of a contest between him and either of the other departments, as to the extent of their respective powers, to make good his own, against its construction.

There is still another step, connected with this, which will be necessary to complete the work of restoration. The provisions of the constitution in reference to the election of the President and Vice-President, which has been superseded in *practice,* must be restored. The virtual repeal of this provision, as already stated, has resulted in placing the control of their election in the hands of the leaders of the office-seekers and office-holders; and this, with the unrestricted power of removal from office, and the vast patronage of the government, has made their election the all absorbing question; and the possession of the honors and emoluments of the government, the paramount objects in the Presidential contest. The effect has been, to increase vastly the authority of the President, and to enable him to extend his powers with impunity, under color of the right conceded him, against the express provision of the constitution, of deciding what means are necessary to carry into execution the powers vested in him. The first step in the enlargement of his authority, was to pervert the power of removal, (the intent of which was, to enable him to supply the place of an incompetent or an unworthy officer, with the view of better administering the laws,) into an instrument for punishing opponents and rewarding partisans. This has been followed up by other acts, which have greatly changed the relative powers of the departments, by increasing those of the executive. Even the power of making war,—and the unlimited control over all conquests, during its continuance, have, it is to be apprehended, passed from Congress into the hands of the President. His powers, in consequence of all this, have accumulated to a degree little consistent with those of a chief magistrate of a federal republic; and hence, the necessity for reducing them within their strict constitutional limits, and restoring the provisions of the constitution in reference to his election, in order to restore the government completely to its federal character. Experience may, perhaps, prove, that the provisions of the constitution in this respect are imperfect,—that they are too complicated and refined for practice; and that a radical change is necessary in the organization of the executive department. If such should prove to be the case, the proper remedy would be, not to supersede them in practice, as has been done, but to apply to the power which has been provided to correct all its defects and disorders.

But the restoration of the government to its federal character, however entire and perfect it may be,—will not, of itself, be sufficient to avert the evil alternatives,—to the one or the other of which it must tend, as it is now operating. Had its federal character been rigidly maintained in practice from the first, it would have been all sufficient, in itself, to have secured the country against the dangerous condition in which it is now placed, in consequence of a departure from it. But the means which may be sufficient to *prevent* diseases, are not usually sufficient to *remedy* them. In slight cases of recent date, they may be;—but additional means are necessary to restore health, when the system has been long and deeply disordered. Such, at present, is the condition of our political system. The very causes which have occasioned its disorders, have, at the same time, led to consequences, not to be removed by the means which would have prevented them. They have destroyed the equilibrium between the two great sections, and alienated that mutual attachment between them, which led to the formation of the Union, and the establishment of a common government for the promotion of the welfare of all.

When the government of the United States was established, the two sections were nearly equal in respect to the two elements of which it is composed; a fact which, doubtless, had much influence, in determining the convention to select them as the basis of its construction. Since then, their equality in reference to both, has been destroyed, mainly through the action of the government established for their mutual benefit. The first step towards it occurred under the old Congress of the confederation. It was among its last acts. It took place while the convention, which formed the present constitution and government, was in session, and may be regarded as contemporaneous with it. I refer to the ordinance of 1787; which, among other things, contained a provision excluding slavery from the North-Western Territory; that is, from the whole region lying between the Ohio and Mississippi rivers. The effect of this was, to restrict the Southern States, in that quarter, to the country lying south of it; and to extend the Northern over the whole of that great and fertile region. It was literally to restrict the one and extend the other; for the whole territory belonged to Virginia, the leading State of the former section. She, with a disinterested patriotism rarely equalled, ceded the whole, gratuitously, to the Union,—with the exception of a very limited portion, reserved for the payment of her officers and soldiers, for services rendered in the war of the revolution. The South received no equivalent for this magnificent cession, except a pledge inserted in the ordinance, similar to that contained in the constitution of the United States, to deliver up fugitive slaves. It is probable that there was an understanding among the parties, that it should be inserted in both instruments;—as the old Congress and the convention were then in session in the same place; and that it contributed much to induce the southern members of the former to agree to the ordinance. But be this as it may, both, in practice, have turned out equally worthless. Neither have, for many years, been respected. Indeed, the act itself was unauthorized. The articles of confederation conferred not a shadow of authority on Congress to pass the ordinance,—as is admitted by Mr. Madison; and yet this unauthorized, one-sided act (as it has turned out to be), passed in the last moments of the old confederacy, was relied on, as a precedent, for excluding the South from two thirds of the territory acquired from France by the Louisiana treaty, and the whole of the Oregon territory; and is now relied on to justify her exclusion from all the territory acquired by the Mexican war,—and all that may be acquired,—in any manner, hereafter. The territory from which she has already been excluded, has had the effect to destroy the equilibrium between the sections as it originally stood; and to concentrate, permanently, in the northern section the two majorities of which the government of the United States is composed. Should she be excluded from the territory acquired from Mexico, it will give to the Northern States an overwhelming preponderance in the government.

In the meantime the spirit of fanaticism, which had been long lying dormant, was roused into action by the course of the government,—as has been explained. It aims, openly and directly, at destroying the existing relations between the races in the southern section; on which depend its peace, prosperity and safety. To effect this, exclusion from the territories is an important step; and, hence, the union between the abolitionists and the advocates of exclusion, to effect objects so intimately connected.

All this has brought about a state of things hostile to the continuance of the Union, and the duration of the government. Alienation is succeeding to attachment, and hostile feelings to alienation; and these, in turn, will be followed by revolution, or a disruption of the Union, unless timely prevented. But this cannot be done by restoring the government to its federal character;—however necessary that may be as a first step. What has been done cannot be undone. The equilibrium between the two sections has been permanently destroyed by the measures above stated. The northern section, in consequence, will ever concentrate within itself the two majorities of which the government is composed; and should the southern be excluded from all territories, now acquired, or to be hereafter acquired, it will soon have so decided a preponderance in the government and the Union, as to be able to mould the constitution to its pleasure. Against this, the restoration of the federal character of the government can furnish no remedy. So long as it continues, there can be no safety for the weaker section. It places in the hands of the stronger and hostile section, the power to crush her and her institutions; and leaves her no alternative, but to resist, or sink down into a colonial condition. This must be the consequence, if some effectual and appropriate remedy be not applied.

The nature of the disease is such, that nothing can reach it, short of some organic change,—a change which shall so modify the constitution, as to give to the weaker section, in some one form or another, a negative on the action of the government. Nothing short of this can protect the weaker, and restore harmony and tranquillity to the Union, by arresting, effectually, the tendency of the dominant and stronger section to oppress the weaker. When the constitution was formed, the impression was strong, that the tendency to conflict would be between the larger and smaller States; and effectual provisions were, accordingly, made to guard against it. But experience has proved this to have been a mistake; and that, instead of being, as was then supposed, the conflict is between the two great sections, which are so strongly distinguished by their institutions, geographical character, productions and pursuits. Had this been then as clearly perceived as it now is, the same jealousy which so vigilantly watched and guarded against the danger of the larger States oppressing the smaller, would have taken equal precaution to guard against the same danger between the two sections. It is for us, who see and feel it, to do, what the framers of the constitution would have done, had they possessed the knowledge, in this respect, which experience has given to us;—that is,—provide against the dangers which the system has practically developed; and which, had they been foreseen at the time, and left without guard, would undoubtedly have prevented the States, forming the southern section of the confederacy, from ever agreeing to the constitution; and which, under like circumstances, were they now out of, would for ever prevent them from entering into, the Union.

How the constitution could best be modified, so as to effect the object, can only be authoritatively determined by the amending power. It may be done in various ways. Among others, it might be effected through a reorganization of the executive department; so that its powers, instead of being vested, as they now are, in a single officer, should be vested in two;—to be so elected, as that the two should be constituted the special organs and representatives of the respective sections, in the executive department of the government; and requiring each to approve all the acts of Congress before they shall become laws. One might be charged with the administration of matters connected with the foreign relations of the country;—and the other, of such as were connected with its domestic institutions; the selection to be decided by lot. It would thus effect, more simply, what was intended by the original provisions of the constitution, in giving to one of the majorities composing the government, a decided preponderance in the electoral college,—and to the other majority a still more decided influence in the eventual choice,—in case the college failed to elect a President. It was intended to effect an equilibrium between the larger and smaller States in this department,—but which, in practice, has entirely failed; and, by its failure, done much to disturb the whole system, and to bring about the present dangerous state of things.

Indeed, it may be doubted, whether the framers of the constitution did not commit a great mistake, in constituting a single, instead of a plural executive. Nay, it may even be doubted whether a single chief magistrate,—invested with all the powers properly appertaining to the executive department of the government, as is the President,—is compatible with the permanence of a popular government; especially in a wealthy and populous community, with a large revenue and a numerous body of officers and employées. Certain it is, that there is no instance of a popular government so constituted, which has long endured. Even ours, thus far, furnishes no evidence in its favor, and not a little against it; for, to it, the present disturbed and dangerous state of things, which threatens the country with monarchy, or disunion, may be justly attributed. On the other hand, the two most distinguished constitutional governments of antiquity, both in respect to permanence and power, had a dual executive. I refer to those of Sparta and of Rome. The former had two hereditary, and the latter two elective chief magistrates. It is true, that England, from which ours, in this respect, is copied, has a single hereditary head of the executive department of her government;—but it is not less true, that she has had many and arduous struggles, to prevent her chief magistrate from becoming absolute; and that, to guard against it effectually, she was finally compelled to divest him, substantially, of the power of administering the government, by transferring it, practically, to a cabinet of responsible ministers, who, by established custom, cannot hold office, unless supported by a majority of the two houses of Parliament. She has thus avoided the danger of the chief magistrate becoming absolute; and contrived to unite, substantially, a single with a plural executive, in constituting that department of her government. We have no such guard, and can have none such, without an entire change in the character of our government; and her example, of course, furnishes no evidence in favor of a single chief magistrate in a popular form of government like ours,—while the examples of former times, and our own thus far, furnish strong evidence against it.

But it is objected that a plural executive necessarily leads to intrigue and discord among its members; and that it is inconsistent with prompt and efficient action. This may be true, when they are all elected by the same constituency; and may be a good reason, where this is the case, for preferring a single executive, with all its objections, to a plural executive. But the case is very different where they are elected by different constituencies,—having conflicting and hostile interests; as would be the fact in the case under consideration. Here the two would have to act, concurringly, in approving the acts of Congress,—and, separately, in the sphere of their respective departments. The effect, in the latter case, would be, to retain all the advantages of a single executive, as far as the administration of the laws were concerned; and, in the former, to insure harmony and concord between the two sections, and, through them, in the government. For as no act of Congress could become a law without the assent of the chief magistrates representing both sections, each, in the elections, would choose the candidate, who, in addition to being faithful to its interests, would best command the esteem and confidence of the other section. And thus, the presidential election, instead of dividing the Union into hostile geographical parties, the stronger struggling to enlarge its powers, and the weaker to defend its rights,—as is now the case,—would become the means of restoring harmony and concord to the country and the government. It would make the Union a union in truth,—a bond of mutual affection and brotherhood;—and not a mere connection used by the stronger as the instrument of dominion and aggrandizement,—and submitted to by the weaker only from the lingering remains of former attachment, and the fading hope of being able to restore the government to what it was originally intended to be, a blessing to all.

Such is the disease,—and such the character of the only remedy which can reach it. In conclusion, there remains to be considered, the practical question,—Shall it be applied? Shall the only power which can apply it be invoked for the purpose?

The responsibility of answering this solemn question, rests on the States composing the stronger section. Those of the weaker are in a minority, both of the States and of population; and, of consequence, in every department of the government. They, then, cannot be responsible for an act which requires the concurrence of two thirds of both houses of Congress, or two thirds of the States to originate, and three fourths of the latter to consummate. With such difficulties in their way, the States of the weaker section can do nothing, however disposed, to save the Union and the government, without the aid and co-operation of the States composing the stronger section: but with their aid and co-operation both may be saved. On the latter, therefore, rests the responsibility of invoking the high power, which alone can apply the remedy;—and, if they fail to do so, of all the consequences which may follow.

Having now finished what I proposed to say on the constitution and government of the United States, I shall conclude with a few remarks relative to the constitutions and governments of the individual States. Standing, as they do, in the relation of co-ordinates with the constitution and government of the United States, whatever may contribute to derange and disorder the one, must, necessarily contribute, more or less, to derange and disorder the other; and, thus, the whole system. And hence the importance,—viewed simply in reference to the government of the United States, without taking into consideration those of the several States,—that the individual governments of each, as well as the united government of all, should assume and preserve the constitutional, instead of the absolute form of popular government,—that of the concurrent, instead of the numerical majority.

It is much more difficult to give to the governments of the States, this constitutional form, than to the government of the United States; for the same reason that it is more easy to form a constitutional government for a community divided into classes or orders, than for one purely popular. Artificial distinctions of every description, be they of States or Estates, are more simple and strongly marked than the numerous and blended natural distinctions of a community purely popular. But difficult as it is to form such constitutional governments for the separate States, it may be effected by making the several departments, as far as it may be necessary, the organs of the more strongly marked interests of the State, from whatever causes they may have been produced;—and by such other devices, whereby the sense of the State may be taken by its parts, and not as a whole—by the concurrent, and not by the numerical majority. It is only by the former that it can be truly taken. Indeed, the numerical majority often fails to accomplish that at which it professes to aim,—to take truly the sense of the majority. It assumes, that by assigning to every part of the State a representative in every department of its government, in proportion to its population, it secures to each a weight in the government, in exact proportion to its population, under all circumstances. But such is not the fact. The relative weight of population depends as much on circumstances, as on numbers. The concentrated population of cities, for example, would ever have, under such a distribution, far more weight in the government, than the same number in the scattered and sparse population of the country. One hundred thousand individuals concentrated in a city two miles square, would have much more influence than the same number scattered over two hundred miles square. Concert of action and combination of means would be easy in the one, and almost impossible in the other; not to take into the estimate, the great control that cities have over the press, the great organ of public opinion. To distribute power, then, in proportion to population, would be, in fact, to give the control of the government, in the end, to the cities; and to subject the rural and agricultural population to that description of population which usually congregate in them,—and ultimately, to the dregs of their population. This can only be counteracted by such a distribution of power as would give to the rural and agricultural population, in some one of the two legislative bodies or departments of the government a decided preponderance. And this may be done in most cases, by allotting an equal number of members in one of the legislative bodies to each election district; as a majority of the counties or election districts will usually have a decided majority of its population engaged in agricultural or other rural pursuits. If this should not be sufficient, in itself, to establish an equilibrium,—a maximum of representation might be established, beyond which the number allotted to each election district or city should never extend.

Other means of a similar character might be adopted, by which, the different and strongly marked interests of the States,—especially those resulting from geographical features, or the diversity of pursuits, might be prevented from coming into conflict, and the one secured against the control of the other. By these, and other contrivances suited to the peculiar condition of a State, its government might be made to assume the character of that of a concurrent majority, and have all the tranquillity and stability belonging to such a form of government; and thereby avoid the disorder and anarchy in which the government of the numerical majority must ever end. While the government of the United States continues, it will, indeed, require a much less perfect government on the part of a State, to protect it from the evils to which an imperfectly organized government would expose it, than if it formed a separate and independent community. The reason is, that the States, as members of a Union, bound to defend each other against all external dangers and domestic violence, are relieved from the necessity of collecting and disbursing large amounts of revenue, which otherwise would be required; and are, thereby, relieved from that increased tendency to conflict and disorder which ever accompanies an increase of revenue and expenditures. In order to give a practical illustration of the mode in which a State government may be organized, on the principle of the con-current majority, I shall, in concluding this discourse, give a brief account of the constitution and government of the State of South Carolina.

Its government, like that of all the other States, is divided into three depart-ments,—the Legislative, Executive, and Judicial. Its executive powers, as in all the others, are vested in a single chief magistrate. He is elected by the legisla-ture, holds his office for two years, and is not again eligible for two years after the expiration of the term for which he was elected. His powers and patronage are very limited. The judges are, also, appointed by the legislature. They hold their office during good behavior. The legislative department is, like that of all the other States, divided into two bodies, the Senate and the House of Repre-sentatives. The members of the former are divided into two classes, of which the term of one expires every other year. The members of the House are elected for two years. The two are called, when convened, the General Assembly. In addition to the usual and appropriate power of legislative bodies, it appoints all the important officers of the State. The local officers are elected by the people of the respective districts (counties) to which they belong. The right of suffrage, with few and inconsiderable exceptions, is universal. No convention of the peo-ple can be called, but by the concurrence of two thirds of both houses;—that is,—two thirds, respectively, of the entire representative body. Nor can the con-stitution be amended, except by an act of the General Assembly, passed by two thirds of both bodies of the whole representation; and passed again, in like man-ner, at the first session of the assembly immediately following the next election of the members of the House of Representatives. But that which is peculiar to its constitution, and which distinguishes it from those of all the other States, is, the principle on which power is distributed among the different portions of the State. It is this, indeed, which makes the constitution, in contradistinction to the government. The elements, according to which power is distributed, are taxation, property, and election districts. In order to understand why they were adopted, and how the distribution has affected the operations of government, it will be necessary to give a brief sketch of the political history of the State.

The State was first settled, on the coast, by emigrants from England and France. Charleston became the principal town; and to it the whole political power of the colony, was exclusively confined, during the government of the Lords Proprietors,—although its population was spread over the whole length of its coast, and to a considerable distance inland, and the region occupied by the settlements, organized into parishes. The government of these was over-thrown by the people, and the colony became a dependent on the Crown. The right of electing members to the popular branch of the legislature, was extended to the parishes. Under the more powerful protection of the Crown, the colony greatly increased, and extended still further inland, towards the falls of the great rivers;—carrying with them the same organization.

About the middle of the last century, a current of population flowed in from New Jersey, Pennsylvania, Maryland, Virginia, and North Carolina, to the region extending from the falls of the rivers to the mountains,—now known as the upper country, in contradistinction to the section lying below. Between the two settlements there was a wide unsettled space; and for a considerable length of time no political connection, and little intercourse existed between them. The upper country had no representation in the government, and no political existence as a constituent portion of the State, until a period near the commencement of the revolution. Indeed during the revolution, and until the formation of the present constitution, in 1790, its political weight was scarcely felt in the government. Even then, although it had become the most populous section, power was so distributed under the new constitution, as to leave it in a minority in every department of the government.

Such a state of things could not long continue without leading to discontent. Accordingly, a spirited movement or agitation commenced openly in 1794, the object of which was to secure a weight in the government, proportional to its population. Once commenced, it continued to increase with the growing population of that section, until its violence, and the distraction and disorder which it occasioned, convinced the reflecting portion of both sections, that the time had arrived when a vigorous effort should be made to bring it to a close. For this purpose, a successful attempt was made in the session of 1807. The lower section was wise and patriotic enough to propose an adjustment of the controversy, by giving to each an equal participation in the government; and the upper section, as wisely and patriotically, waived its claims, and accepted the compromise. To carry it into execution, an act was passed during the session to amend the constitution, according to the form it prescribes; and again passed, in like manner, during the ensuing session,—an intervening election of the members of the House of Representatives having taken place,—and, thereby, became a part of the constitution as it now stands. The object intended to be effected will explain the provisions of the amendment; and why it was necessary to incorporate in the constitution the three elements above stated.

To effect this, the Senate, which consists of one member from each election district, except Charleston, which has two (one for each of its two parishes), remained unchanged. This, in consequence of the organization of the lower district into parishes, and these again into election districts, gave the lower section a decided preponderance in that branch of the legislature. To give the upper section a like preponderance in the House of Representatives, it became necessary to remodel it. For this purpose, there were assigned to this branch of the legislature, one hundred and twenty-four members;—of which sixty-two were allotted to white population, and sixty-two to taxation; to be distributed according to the election districts,—giving to each the number it would be entitled to under the combined ratios of the two elements. To ascertain this proportion, from time to time, a census of the population was ordered to be taken every ten years, and a calculation made, at the same time, of the amount of the tax paid by each election district during the last ten years; in order to furnish the data on which to make the distribution. These gave to the upper section a preponderance, equally decisive, in the House of Representatives. And thus an equilibrium was established between the two sections in the legislative department of the government; and, as the governor, judges, and all the important officers under the government are appointed by the legislature,—an equilibrium in every department of the government. By making the election districts the element of which one branch of the legislature is constituted, it protects the agricultural and rural interests against the preponderance, which, in time, the concentrated city population might otherwise acquire;—and by making taxation one of the elements of which the other branch is composed, it guards effectually against the abuse of the taxing power. The effect of such abuse would be, to give to the portion of the State which might be overtaxed, an increased weight in the government proportional to the excess;—and to diminish, in the same proportion, the weight of the section which might exempt itself from an equal share of the burden of taxation.

The results which followed the introduction of these elements into the constitution, in the manner stated, were most happy. The government,—instead of being, as it was under the constitution of 1790, the government of the lower section,—or becoming, subsequently, as it must have become, the government of the upper section, had numbers constituted the only element,—was converted into that of the concurrent majority, and made, emphatically, the government of the entire population,—of the whole people of South Carolina;—and not of one portion of its people over another portion. The consequence was, the almost instantaneous restoration of harmony and concord between the two sections. Party division and party violence, with the distraction and disorder attendant upon them, soon disappeared. Kind feelings, and mutual attachment between the two sections, took their place,—and have continued uninterrupted for more than forty years. The State, as far as its internal affairs are concerned, may be literally said to have been, during the whole period, without a party. Party organization, party discipline, party proscription,—and their offspring, *the spoils principle,* have been unknown to the State. Nothing of the kind is necessary to produce concentration; as our happy constitution makes an united people,—with the exception of occasional, but short local dissensions, in reference to the action of the federal government;—and even the most violent of these ceased, almost instantly, with the occasion which produced it.

Such are the happy fruits of a wisely constituted Republic;—and such are some of the means by which it may be organized and established. Ours, like all other well constituted constitutional governments, is the offspring of a conflict, timely and wisely compromised. May its success, as an example, lead to its imitation by others;—until our whole system,—the united government of all the States, as well as the individual governments of each,—shall settle down in like concord and harmony.

CHAPTER III.

*In defending American political life against the "disorganizing effects of French prin-
ciples" and English failings, Calhoun affirmed the need to defend one's country against
potential threats. But true statecraft could not be limited to self-protection, Calhoun
thought—it must cultivate the country's moral, political, and economic potential as well.*

[Note.—The Committee on Foreign Relations, on the 29th of November,
1811, submitted a report, which, after an able examination of the causes of war
with Great Britain, concluded by recommending to the House the adoption of
a series of resolutions, among which was the following:

"2. *Resolved,* That an additional force of ten thousand regular troops ought
to be immediately raised to serve for three years; and that a bounty in lands
ought to be given to encourage enlistments."

This resolution having been amended in committee of the Whole, by striking out the word *"ten,"* was reported to the House, where an animated debate
ensued. A majority of the committee avowed their object to be a preparation
for war; and the discussion took the widest range, embracing almost every topic
of foreign and domestic policy. The principal speaker, on the part of the opposition, was Mr. Randolph of Virginia, to whose remarks Mr. Calhoun seems to
have confined his reply. The resolution was finally adopted—Yeas, 109; Nays,
22 (Crallé).]

Mr. Speaker:—I understood the opinion of the Committee on Foreign
Relations, differently from what the gentleman from Virginia (Mr. Randolph)

has stated to be his impression. I certainly understood that the committee recommended the measures now before the House, as a preparation for war; and such, in fact, was its express resolve, agreed to, I believe, by every member, except that gentleman. I do not attribute any wilful misstatement to him, but consider it the effect of inadvertency or mistake. Indeed, the Report could mean nothing but war or empty menace. I hope no member of this House is in favor of the latter. A bullying, menacing system, has every thing to condemn and nothing to recommend it. In expense, it almost rivals war. It excites contempt abroad, and destroys confidence at home. Menaces are serious things; and ought to be resorted to with as much caution and seriousness, as war itself; and should, if not successful, be invariably followed by it. It was not the gentleman from Tennessee (Mr. Grundy) who made this a war question. The resolve contemplates an additional regular force; a measure confessedly improper but as a preparation for war, but undoubtedly necessary in that event.

Sir, I am not insensible to the weighty importance of the proposition, for the first time submitted to this House, to compel a redress of our long list of complaints against one of the belligerents. According to my mode of thinking, the more serious the question, the stronger and more unalterable ought to be our convictions before we give it our support. War, in our country, ought never to be resorted to but when it is clearly justifiable and necessary; so much so, as not to require the aid of logic to convince our understandings, nor the ardor of eloquence to inflame our passions. There are many reasons why this country should never resort to war but for causes the most urgent and necessary. It is sufficient that, under a government like ours, none but such will justify it in the eyes of the people; and were I not satisfied that such is the present case, I certainly would be no advocate of the proposition now before the House.

Sir, I might prove the war, should it ensure, justifiable, by the express admission of the gentleman from Virginia;—and necessary, by facts undoubted, and universally admitted; such as he did not pretend to controvert. The extent, duration, and character of the injuries received; the failure of those peaceful means heretofore resorted to for the redress of our wrongs, are my proofs that it is necessary. Why should I mention the impressment of our seamen; depredations on every branch of our commerce, including the direct export trade, continued for years, and made under laws which professedly undertake to regulate our trade with other nations; negotiation resorted to, again and again, till it is become hopeless; the restrictive system persisted in to avoid war, and in the vain expectation of returning justice? The evil still grows, and, in each succeeding year, swells in extent and pretension beyond the preceding. The question, even in the opinion and by the admission of our opponents is reduced to this single point—Which shall we do, abandon or defend our own commercial and maritime rights, and the personal liberties of our citizens employed in exercising them? These rights are vitally attacked, and war is the only means of redress. The gentleman from Virginia has suggested none, unless we consider the whole of his speech as recommending patient and resigned submission as the best remedy. Sir, which alternative this House will embrace, it is not for me to say. I hope the decision is made already, by a higher authority than the voice of any man. It is not for the human tongue to instil the sense of independence and honor. This is the work of nature; a generous nature that disdains tame submission to wrongs.

This part of the subject is so imposing as to enforce silence even on the gentleman from Virginia. He dared not deny his country's wrongs, or vindicate the conduct of her enemy. Only one part of his argument had any, the most remote relation to this point. He would not say, we had not a good cause for war; but insisted, that it was our duty to define that cause. If he means that this House ought, at this stage of its proceedings, or any other, to specify any particular violation of our rights to the exclusion of all others, he prescribes a course, which neither good sense nor the usage of nations warrants. When we contend, let us contend for all our rights; the doubtful and the certain; the unimportant and essential. It is as easy to struggle, or even more so, for the whole as for a part. At the termination of the contest, secure all that our wisdom and valor and the fortune of the war will permit. This is the dictate of common sense; such also is the usage of nations. The single instance alluded to, the endeavor of Mr. Fox to compel Mr. Pitt to define the object of the war against France, will not support the gentleman from Virginia in his position. That was an extraordinary war for an extraordinary purpose, and was not governed by the usual rules. It was not for conquest, or for redress of injury, but to impose a government on France, which she refused to receive; an object so detestable that an avowal dared not be made.

Sir, I might here rest the question. The affirmative of the proposition is established. I cannot but advert, however, to the complaint of the gentleman from Virginia when he was first up on this question. He said he found himself reduced to the necessity of supporting the negative side of the question, before the affirmative was established. Let me tell the gentleman, that there is no hardship in his case. It is not every affirmative that ought to be proved. Were I to affirm, that the House is now in session, would it be reasonable to ask for proof? He who would deny its truth, on him would be the proof of so extraordinary a negative. How then could the gentleman, after his admissions, with the facts before him and the country, complain? The causes are such as to warrant, or rather make it indispensable, in any nation not absolutely dependent, to defend its rights by force. Let him, then, show the reasons why we ought not so to defend ourselves. On him lies the burden of proof. This he has attempted; he has endeavored to support his negative. Before I proceed to answer him particularly, let me call the attention of the House to one circumstance; that is,—that almost the whole of his arguments consisted of an enumeration of evils always incident to war, however just and necessary; and which, if they have any force, are calculated to produce unqualified submission to every species of insult and injury. I do not feel myself bound to answer arguments of this description; and if I should touch on them, it will be only incidentally, and not for the purpose of serious refutation.

The first argument of the gentleman which I shall notice, is the unprepared state of the country. Whatever weight this argument might have in a question of immediate war, it surely has little in that of preparation for it. If our country is unprepared, let us remedy the evil as soon as possible. Let the gentleman submit his plan; and if a reasonable one, I doubt not it will be supported by the House. But, Sir, let us admit the fact and the whole force of the argument. I ask whose is the fault? Who has been a member, for many years past, and seen the defenceless state of his country even near home, under his own eyes, without a single endeavor to remedy so serious an evil? Let him not say, "I have acted in a minority." It is no less the duty of the minority than a majority to endeavor to defend the country. For that purpose we are sent here, and not for that of opposition.

We are next told of the expenses of the war; and that the people will not pay taxes. Why not? Is it from want of means? What, with 1,000,000, tons of shipping; a commerce of $100,000,000 annually; manufactures yielding a yearly product of $150,000,000; and agriculture of thrice that amount, shall we be told the country wants capacity to raise and support ten thousand or fifteen thousand additional regulars? No; it has the ability; that is admitted; and will it not have the disposition? Is not the cause a just and necessary one? Shall we then utter this libel on the people? Where will proof be found of a fact so disgraceful? It is answered;—in the history of the country twelve or fifteen years ago. The case is not parallel. The ability of the country is greatly increased since. The whiskey-tax was unpopular. But on this, as well as my memory serves me,— the objection was not to the tax or its amount, but the mode of collection. The people were startled by the number of officers; their love of liberty shocked with the multiplicity of regulations. We, in the spirit of imitation, copied from the most oppressive part of European laws on the subject of taxes, and imposed on a young and virtuous people all the severe provisions made necessary by corruption and long-practised evasions. If taxes should become necessary, I do not hesitate to say the people will pay cheerfully. It is for their government and their cause, and it would be their interest and their duty to pay. But it may be, and I believe was said, that the people will not pay taxes, because the rights violated are not worth defending; or that the defence will cost more than the gain. Sir, I here enter my solemn protest against this low and "calculating avarice" entering this hall of legislation. It is only fit for shops and counting-houses; and ought not to disgrace the seat of power by its squalid aspect. Whenever it touches sovereign power, the nation is ruined. It is too short-sighted to defend itself. It is a compromising spirit, always ready to yield a part to save the residue. It is too timid to have in itself the laws of self-preservation. It is never safe but under the shield of honor. There is, Sir, one principle necessary to make us a great people,—to produce not the form, but real spirit of union;—and that is, to protect every citizen in the lawful pursuit of his business. He will then feel that he is backed by the government;—that its arm is his arm; and will rejoice in its increased strength and prosperity. Protection and patriotism are reciprocal. This is the way which has led nations to greatness. Sir, I am not versed in this calculating policy; and will not, therefore, pretend to estimate in dollars and cents the value of national independence. I cannot measure in shillings and pence the misery, the stripes, and the slavery of our impressed seamen; nor even the value of our shipping, commercial and agricultural losses, under the orders in council, and the British system of blockade. In thus expressing myself, I do not intend to condemn any prudent estimate of the means of a country, before it enters on a war. This is wisdom,—the other folly. The gentleman from Virginia has not failed to touch on the calamity of war, that fruitful source of declamation by which humanity is made the advocate of submission. If he desires to repress the gallant ardor of our countrymen by such topics, let me inform him, that true courage regards only the cause, that it is just and necessary; and that it contemns the sufferings and dangers of war. If he really wishes to promote the cause of humanity, let his eloquence be addressed to Lord Wellesley or Mr. Percival, and not the American Congress. Tell them if they persist in such daring insult and injury to a neutral nation, that, however inclined to peace, it will be bound in honor and safety to resist; that their patience and endurance, however great, will be exhausted; that the calamity of war will ensue, and that they, in the opinion of the world, will be answerable for all its devastation and misery. Let a regard to the interests of humanity stay the hand of injustice, and my life on it, the gentleman will not find it difficult to dissuade his country from rushing into the bloody scenes of war.

We are next told of the dangers of war. I believe we are all ready to acknowledge its hazards and misfortunes; but I cannot think we have any extraordinary danger to apprehend, at least none to warrant an acquiescence in the injuries we have received. On the contrary, I believe, no war can be less dangerous to the internal peace, or safety of the country. But we are told of the black population of the Southern States. As far as the gentleman from Virginia speaks of his own personal knowledge, I shall not question the correctness of his statement. I only regret that such is the state of apprehension in his particular part of the country. Of the Southern section, I, too, have some personal knowledge; and can say, that in South Carolina no such fears in any part are felt. But, Sir, admit the gentleman's statement; will a war with Great Britain increase the danger? Will the country be less able to suppress insurrection? Had we any thing to fear from that quarter (which I do not believe), in my opinion, the period of the greatest safety is during a war; unless, indeed, the enemy should make a lodgment in the country. Then the country is most on its guard; our militia the best prepared; and our standing army the greatest. Even in our revolution no attempts at insurrection were made by that portion of our population; and however the gentleman may alarm himself with the disorganizing effects of French principles, I cannot think our ignorant blacks have felt much of their baneful influence. I dare say more than one half of them never heard of the French revolution.

But as great as he regards the danger from our slaves, the gentleman's fears end not there—the standing army is not less terrible to him. Sir, I think a regular force raised for a period of actual hostilities cannot properly be called a standing army. There is a just distinction between such a force, and one raised as a permanent peace establishment. Whatever would be the composition of the latter, I hope the former will consist of some of the best materials of the country. The ardent patriotism of our young men, and the reasonable bounty in land which is proposed to be given, will impel them to join their country's standard and to fight her battles; they will not forget the citizen in the soldier, and in obeying their officers, learn to contemn their government and constitution. In our officers and soldiers we will find patriotism no less pure and ardent than in the private citizen; but if they should be depraved as represented, what have we to fear from twenty-five thousand or thirty thousand regulars? Where will be the boasted militia of the gentleman? Can one million of militia be overpowered by thirty thousand regulars? If so, how can we rely on them against a foe invading our country? Sir, I have no such contemptuous idea of our militia—their untaught bravery is sufficient to crush all foreign and internal attempts on their country's liberties.

But we have not yet come to the end of the chapter of dangers. The gentleman's imagination, so fruitful on this subject, conceives that our constitution is not calculated for war, and that it cannot stand its rude shock. This is rather extraordinary. If true, we must then depend upon the commiseration or contempt of other nations for our existence. The constitution, then, it seems, has failed in an essential object, "to provide for the common defence." No, says the gentleman from Virginia, it is competent for a defensive, but not for an offensive war. It is not necessary for me to expose the error of this opinion. Why make the distinction in this instance? Will he pretend to say that this is an offensive war; a war of conquest? Yes, the gentleman has dared to make this assertion; and for reasons no less extraordinary than the assertion itself. He says our rights are violated on the ocean, and that these violations affect our shipping, and commercial rights, to which the Canadas have no relation. The doctrine of retaliation has been much abused of late by an unreasonable extension; we have now to witness a new abuse. The gentleman from Virginia has limited it down to a point. By his rule if you receive a blow on the breast, you dare not return it on the head; you are obliged to measure and return it on the precise point on which it was received. If you do not proceed with this mathematical accuracy, it ceases to be just self-defence; it becomes an unprovoked attack.

In speaking of Canada the gentleman from Virginia introduced the name of Montgomery with much feeling and interest. Sir, there is danger in that name to the gentleman's argument. It is sacred to heroism. It is indignant of submission! It calls our memory back to the time of our revolution, to the Congress of '74 and '75. Suppose a member of that day had risen and urged all the arguments which we have heard on this subject; had told that Congress,—your contest is about the right of laying a tax; and that the attempt on Canada had nothing to do with it; that the war would be expensive; that danger and devastation would overspread our country, and that the power of Great Britain was irresistible. With what sentiment, think you, would such doctrines have been then received? Happy for us, they had no force at that period of our country's glory. Had such been then acted on, this hall would never have witnessed a great people convened to deliberate for the general good; a mighty empire, with prouder prospects than any nation the sun ever shone on, would not have risen in the west. No; we would have been base subjected colonies; governed by that imperious rod which Britain holds over her distant provinces.

The gentleman from Virginia attributes the preparation for war to every thing but its true cause. He endeavored to find it in the probable rise in the price of hemp. He represents the people of the Western States as willing to plunge our country into war from such interested and base motives. I will not reason on this point. I see the cause of their ardor, not in such unworthy motives, but in their known patriotism and disinterestedness.

No less mercenary is the reason which he attributes to the Southern States. He says that the Non-Importation Act has reduced cotton to nothing, which has produced a feverish impatience. Sir, I acknowledge the cotton of our plantations is worth but little; but not for the cause assigned by the gentleman from Virginia. The people of that section do not reason as he does; they do not attribute it to the efforts of their government to maintain the peace and independence of their country. They see, in the low price of their produce, the hand of foreign injustice; they know well without the market to the continent, the deep and steady current of supply will glut that of Great Britain; they are not prepared for the colonial state to which again that power is endeavoring to reduce us, and the manly spirit of that section of our country will not submit to be regulated by any foreign power.

The love of France and the hatred of England have also been assigned as the cause of the present measures. France has not done us justice, says the gentleman from Virginia, and how can we, without partiality, resist the aggressions of England. I know, Sir, we have still causes of complaint against France; but they are of a different character from those against England. She professes now to respect our rights, and there cannot be a reasonable doubt but that the most objectionable parts of her decrees, as far as they respect us, are repealed. We have already formally acknowledged this to be a fact. But I protest against the principle from which his conclusion is drawn. It is a novel doctrine, and nowhere avowed out of this House, that you cannot select your antagonist without being guilty of partiality. Sir, when two invade your rights, you may resist both or either at your pleasure. It is regulated by prudence and not by right. The stale imputation of partiality for France is better calculated for the columns of a newspaper, than for the walls of this House.

The gentleman from Virginia is at a loss to account for what he calls our hatred to England. He asks how can we hate the country of Locke, of Newton, Hampden, and Chatham; a country having the same language and customs with ourselves, and descending from a common ancestry. Sir, the laws of human affections are steady and uniform. If we have so much to attach us to that country, potent indeed must be the cause which has overpowered it. Yes, there is a cause strong enough; not in that occult courtly affection which he has supposed to be entertained for France; but it is to be found in continued and unprovoked insult and injury—a cause so manifest, that the gentleman from Virginia had to exert much ingenuity to overlook it. But, the gentleman, in his eager admiration of that country, has not been sufficiently guarded in his argument. Has he reflected on the cause of that admiration? Has he examined the reasons of our high regard for her Chatham? It is his ardent patriotism, the heroic courage of his mind, that could not brook the least insult or injury offered to his country, but thought that her interest and honor ought to be vindicated at every hazard and expense. I hope, when we are called upon to admire, we shall also be asked to imitate. I hope the gentleman does not wish a monopoly of those great virtues for England.

The balance of power has also been introduced, as an argument for submission. England is said to be a barrier against the military despotism of France. There is, Sir, one great error in our legislation. We are ready, it would seem from this argument, to watch over the interests of foreign nations, while we grossly neglect our own immediate concerns. This argument of the balance of power is well calculated for the British Parliament, but not at all suited to the American Congress. Tell the former that they have to contend with a mighty power, and that if they persist in insult and injury to the American people, they will compel them to throw their whole weight into the scale of their enemy. Paint the danger to them, and if they will desist from injuring us, we, I answer for it, will not disturb the balance of power. But it is absurd for us to talk about the balance of power, while they, by their conduct, smile with contempt at what they regard our simple, good-natured vanity. If, however, in the contest, it should be found that they underrate us—which I hope and believe—and that we can affect the balance of power, it will not be difficult for us to obtain such terms as our rights demand.

I, Sir, will now conclude by adverting to an argument of the gentleman from Virginia, used in debate on a preceding day. He asked, why not declare war immediately? The answer is obvious: because we are not yet prepared. But, says the gentleman, such language as is here held, will provoke Great Britain to commence hostilities. I have no such fears. She knows well that such a course would unite all parties here—a thing which, above all others, she most dreads. Besides, such has been our past conduct, that she will still calculate on our patience and submission, until war is actually commenced.

CHAPTER IV.

"SPEECH ON COMMERCIAL TREATY WITH GREAT BRITAIN,"
9 JANUARY 1816

Accepting the Constitution as the fundamental guide for the scope and function of the government, Calhoun explained the difference between the lawmaking power of the House of Representatives and the treaty power of the Senate, which is quite different. In defending the original design of the Constitution, he argued that the American political system rested upon "reason and equity" rather than the "fraud, violence or accident" upon which other political systems were based.

[NOTE.—The Message of the President, of the 26th of December, 1815, communicating to Congress the Commercial Convention with Great Britain, and recommending such legislative provisions as might be deemed necessary to carry it into effect, having been referred to the Committee on Foreign Relations, Mr. Forsyth, its chairman, on December 29th, reported a Bill for the purpose, which was, on the same day, referred to the Committee of the Whole, where it was discussed with much animation and ability until the 9th of January, 1816. Involving, as in the case of Jay's Treaty, questions of moment, as to the constitutional distribution of powers, between the two Houses, the debate was resumed in the House—all the leading men of both parties participating in it. On no question, perhaps, during the period, was there an equal display of eloquence and ability.

On the 10th January, 1816, the Senate, in anticipation of the action of the House, passed a Bill "enacting and declaring so much of any act or acts as is contrary to the provisions" of the Treaty, "to be of no force or effect." This was received by the House on the same day; when it was denounced as an "attempt to evade the question before the House"—and subsequently laid on the table. On the 13th, the House passed its Bill by a vote of 86 to 71, and sent it to the Senate, where, on the 19th it was *rejected* by a vote of 21 to 10. The House, February 6th, amended the Senate's Bill by striking out all after the enacting clause, and inserting its own Bill; on the ground that it "interfered with the judicial power" and, at the same time, "deprived the House of its just powers in respect to provisions affecting the public revenues." Thus amended the Bill was passed and sent to the Senate; where, on February 12, it was, after full debate, again *rejected*. The two Houses being thus at issue, a Committee of Conference was subsequently agreed to; and, by compromise, the Senate's Bill, with some modifications, was finally (February 24) adopted. Yeas, 100; Nays, 15 (Crallé).]

MR. SPEAKER:—The votes on this bill have been ordered to be recorded; and the House will see, in my peculiar situation, a sufficient apology for offering my reasons for the rejection of the bill. I had no disposition to speak on this bill; as I was content to let it take that course, which, in the opinion of the majority, it ought, till the members were called on by the order of the House to record their votes.

The question presented for consideration is perfectly simple, and easily understood:—Is this bill necessary to give validity to the late treaty with Great Britain? It appears to me that this question is susceptible of a decision, without considering whether a treaty can in any case set aside a law; or, to be more particular, whether the treaty which this bill proposes to carry into effect, does repeal the discriminating duties. The House will remember, that a law was passed at the close of last session, conditionally repealing those duties. That act proposed to repeal them in relation to any nation, which would on its part agree to repeal similar duties as to this country. On the contingency happening, the law became positive. It has happened, and it has been announced to the country, that England has agreed to repeal. The President, in proclaiming the treaty, has notified the fact to the House and to the country. Why, then, propose to do that by this bill, which has already been done by a previous act? I know it has been said in conversation, that the provisions of the act are not as broad as the treaty. It does not strike me so. They appear to me to be commensurate. I also infer from the appearance of this House, that it is not very deeply impressed with the necessity of this bill. I have never, on any important occasion, seen it so indifferent. Whence does this arise? From its want of importance? If, indeed, the existence of the treaty depended on the passage of this bill, nothing scarcely could be more interesting. It would be calculated to excite strong feelings. We all know how the country was agitated when Jay's Treaty was before the House. The question then was on an appropriation to carry it into effect; a power acknowledged by all to belong to the House; and on the exercise of which, the existence of the treaty was felt to depend. The feelings manifested corresponded with this conviction. Not so on this occasion. Further, the treaty has already assumed the form of law. It is so proclaimed to the community; the words of the proclamation are not material; it speaks of itself; and if it means any thing, it announces the treaty as a rule of public conduct, as a law exacting the obedience of the people. Were I of the opposite side, if I, indeed, believed this treaty to be a dead letter till it received the sanction of Congress, I would lay the bill on the table and move an inquiry into the fact, why the treaty has been proclaimed as a law before it received the proper sanction. It is true, the Executive has transmitted a copy of the treaty to the House; but has he sent the negotiation? Has he given any light to show why it should receive the sanction of this body? Do gentlemen mean to say that information is not needed; that though we have the right to pass laws, to give validity to treaties, yet we are bound by a moral obligation to pass such laws? To talk of the right of this House to sanction treaties, and at the same time to assert that it is under a moral obligation not to withhold that sanction, is a solecism. No sound mind that understands the terms, can possibly assent to it. I would caution the House, while it is extending its powers to cases which, I believe, do not belong to it, to take care lest it lose its substantial and undoubted power. I would put it on its guard against the dangerous doctrine, that it can in any case become a mere registering body. Another fact in regard to this treaty. It does not stipulate that a law shall pass to repeal the duties proposed to be repealed by this bill, which would be its proper form, if in the opinion of the negotiators a law was necessary; but it stipulates in positive terms for their repeal without consulting or regarding us.

I here conclude this part of the discussion, by stating that it appears to me from the whole complexion of the case, that the bill before the House is a mere form, and cannot be supposed to be necessary to the validity of the treaty. It will be proper, however, to reply to the arguments which have been urged on the general nature of the treaty-making power, and as it is a subject of great importance, I solicit the attentive hearing of the House.

It is not denied, I believe, that the President, with the concurrence of two-thirds of the Senate, has a right to make commercial treaties; it is not asserted that this treaty is couched in such general terms as to require a law to carry the details into execution. Why, then, is this bill necessary? Because, say gentlemen, the treaty of itself, without the aid of this bill, cannot exempt British tonnage, and goods imported in their bottoms, from the operation of the law laying additional duties on foreign tonnage and goods imported in foreign vessels; or, giving the question a more general form, because a treaty cannot annul a law.

The gentleman from Virginia (Mr. Barbour), who argued this point very distinctly, though not satisfactorily, took as his general position, that to repeal a law is a legislative act, and can only be done by law; that in the distribution of the legislative and treaty-making power, the right to repeal a law fell exclusively under the former. How does this comport with the admission immediately made by him, that the treaty of peace repealed the act declaring war? If he admits the fact in a single case, what becomes of his exclusive legislative right? He indeed felt that this rule failed him, and in explanation assumed a position entirely new; for he admitted, that when the treaty did that which was not authorized to be done by law, it did not require the sanction of Congress, and might in its operation repeal a law inconsistent with it. He said, Congress is not authorized to make peace; and for this reason, a treaty of peace repeals the act declaring war. In this position, I understood his colleague substantially to concur. I hope to make it appear, that in taking this ground, they have both yielded the point in discussion. I shall establish, I trust, to the satisfaction of the House, that the treaty-making power, when it is legitimately exercised, always does that which cannot be done by law; and, that the reasons advanced to prove that the treaty of peace repealed the act declaring war, so far from being peculiar to that case, apply to all treaties. They do not form an exception, but in fact constitute the rule. Why then, I ask, cannot Congress make peace? They have the power to declare war. All acknowledge this power. Peace and war are opposites. They are the positive and negative terms of the same proposition; and what rule of construction more clear than that when a power is given to do an act, the power is also given to repeal it? By what right do you repeal taxes, reduce your army, lay up your navy, or repeal any law, but by the force of this plain rule of construction? Why cannot Congress then repeal the act declaring war? I acknowledge, with the gentleman, that they cannot, consistently with reason. The solution of this question explains the whole difficulty. The reason is plain; one power may make war; it requires two to make peace. It is a state of mutual amity succeeding one of mutual hostility;—a state that cannot be created, but with the consent of both parties. It requires a contract or a treaty between the nations at war. Is this peculiar to a treaty of peace? No, it is common to all treaties. It arises out of their nature, and not from any accidental circumstance, attaching to a particular class. It is no more nor less than that Congress cannot make a contract with a foreign nation. Let us apply it to a treaty of commerce, to this very case.

Can Congress do what this treaty has done? It has repealed the discriminating duties between this country and England. Either country could by law repeal its own. But, by law, they could go no farther; and for the reason, that peace cannot be made by law. Whenever, then an ordinary subject of legislation can only be regulated by contract, it passes from the sphere of the ordinary power of making laws, and attaches itself to that of making treaties, wherever it is lodged. All acknowledge the truth of this conclusion, where the subject, on which the treaty operates, is not expressly given to Congress: but in other cases, they consider the two powers as concurrent; and conclude from the nature of such powers, that such treaties must be confirmed by law. Will they acknowledge the opposite—that laws on such subjects must be confirmed by treaties? And if, as they state, a law can repeal a treaty when concurrent, why not a treaty a law? Into such absurdities do false doctrines lead. The truth is, the legislative and treaty-making powers are never, in the strict sense, concurrent. They both may have the same subject, as in this case, viz., commerce; but they discharge functions entirely different in their nature in relation to it. When we speak of concurrent powers, we mean when both can do the same thing; but I contend that when the two powers under discussion are confined to their proper sphere, not only the law cannot do what could be done by treaty, but the reverse is true; that is, they never are nor can be concurrent powers. It is only when we reason on this subject that we mistake; in all other cases the common sense of the House and country decide correctly. It is proposed to establish some regulation of commerce;—we immediately inquire, does it depend on our will? can we make the desired regulation without the concurrence of any foreign power? If so, it belongs to Congress, and any one would feel it to be absurd to attempt to effect it by treaty. On the contrary, does it require the consent of a foreign power? is it proposed to grant a favor for a favor—to repeal discriminating duties on both sides? It is equally felt to belong to the treaty-making power; and he would be thought insane who should propose to abolish the discriminating duties in any case, by an act of the American Congress. It is calculated, I feel, almost to insult the good sense of the House, to dwell on a point evidently so clear. What then do I infer from what has been advanced? That, according to the argument of gentlemen, treaties, producing a state of things inconsistent with the provisions of an existing law, annul such provisions. But as I do not agree with them in the view which they have taken, I will here present my own for consideration.

Why, then, has a treaty the force which I attribute to it? Because it is an act, in its own nature, paramount to laws made by the common legislative powers of the country. It is in fact a law, and something more; a law established by contract between independent nations. By analogy to private life, law has the same relations to treaty, as the resolution taken by an individual to his contract. An individual may make the most deliberate promise; he may swear it in the most solemn form, that he will not sell his house, or any other property he may have; yet, if he should afterward sell, the sale would be valid in law; he would not be admitted in a court of justice to plead his oath against his contract. Take the case of a government in its most simple form, where it is purely despotic; that is, where all power is lodged in the hands of a single individual. Would not his treaties repeal inconsistent edicts? Let us now ascend from the instances cited to illustrate the nature of the two powers, to the principle on which the paramount character of a treaty rests. A treaty always affects the interests of two; a law only that of a single nation. It is an established principle of politics and morality, that the interest of the many is paramount to that of the few. In fact, it is a principle so radical, that without it no system of morality, no rational scheme of government, could exist. It is for this reason that contracts, or that treaties which are only the contracts of independent nations, or, to express both in two words, that plighted faith has in all ages and nations been considered so solemn. But it is said, in opposition to this position, that a subsequent law can repeal a treaty; and to this proposition, I understand that the member from North Carolina (Mr. Gaston) assents. Strictly speaking, I deny the fact. I know that a law may assume the appearance of repealing a treaty; but, I insist, it is only in appearance, and that, in point of fact, it is not a repeal. Whenever a law is proposed, declaring a treaty void, I consider that the House acts not as a legislative body, but judicially. To illustrate my idea: If the House is a moral body,—that is, if it is governed by reason and virtue, which must always be presumed,—the only question that ever can occupy its attention, whenever a treaty is to be declared void, is whether, under all the circumstances of the case, the treaty is not already destroyed, by being violated by the nation with whom it is made, or by the existence of some other circumstance, if other there can be. The House determines this question: Is the country any longer bound by the treaty? Has it not ceased to exist? The nation passes judgment on its own contract; and this from the necessity of the case, as it admits no supreme power to which it can refer for decision. If any other consideration move the House to repeal a treaty, it can be considered only in the light of a violation of a contract acknowledged to be binding on the country. A nation may, it is true, violate its contract; it may even do this under the form of law; but I am not considering what may be done, but what may be rightfully done. It is not a question of power, but of right. Why are not these positions, in themselves so clear, universally assented to? Gentlemen are alarmed at imaginary consequences. They argue not as if seeking for the meaning of the constitution, but as if deliberating on the subject of making one; not as members of the legislature, and acting under a constitution already established, but as those of a convention about to frame one. For my part, I have always regarded the constitution as a work of great wisdom; and, being the instrument under which we exist as a body, it is our duty to bow to its enactments, whatever they may be, with submission. We ought scarcely to indulge a wish that its provisions should be different from what they in fact are. The consequences, however, which appear to work with so much terror on the minds of the gentlemen, I consider to be without any just foundation. The treaty-making power has many and powerful limits; and it will be found, when I come to discuss what those limits are, that it cannot destroy the constitution, or our personal liberty, or involve us, without the assent of this House, in war, or grant away our money. The limits I propose to this power are not the same, it is true; but they appear to me much more rational and powerful than those which were supposed to present effectual guards against its abuse. Let us now consider what they are.

The grant of the power to make treaties is couched in the most general terms. The words of the constitution are, that the President shall have power, by and with the advice and consent of the Senate, to make treaties, provided two-thirds of the Senators present concur. In a subsequent part of the constitution, treaties are declared to be the supreme law of the land. Whatever limits are imposed by these general terms ought to be the result of a sound construction of the instrument. There are, apparently, but two restrictions on its exercise; the one derived from the nature of our government, and the other from that of the power itself. Most certainly all grants of power under the constitution must be construed by that instrument; for, having their existence from it, they must of necessity assume that form which the constitution has imposed. This is acknowledged to be true of the legislative power, and it is doubtless equally so of the power to make treaties. The limits of the former are exactly marked; it was necessary, to prevent collision with similar co-existing State powers. This country is divided into many distinct sovereignties. Exact enumeration on this head is necessary, to prevent the most dangerous consequences. The enumeration of legislative powers in the constitution has relation, then, not to the treaty-making power, but to the powers of the States. In our relation to the rest of the world the case is reversed. Here the States disappear. Divided within, we present the exterior of undivided sovereignty. The wisdom of the constitution, in this, appears conspicuous. Where enumeration was needed, there we find the powers enumerated and exactly defined; where not, we do not find what would be only vain and pernicious. Whatever, then, concerns our foreign relations; whatever requires the consent of another nation, belongs to the treaty-making power, and can only be regulated by it; and it is competent to regulate all such subjects, provided and here are its true limits such regulations are not inconsistent with the constitution. If so, they are void. No treaty can alter the fabric of our government, nor can it do that which the constitution has expressly forbidden to be done; nor can it do that differently which is directed to be done in a given mode,—all other modes being prohibited. For instance, the constitution says, no money "shall be drawn out of the treasury but by an appropriation made by law." Of course no subsidy can be granted without an act of law; and a treaty of alliance could not involve the country in war without the consent of this House. With this limitation, it is easy to explain the case put by my colleague, who said, that according to one limitation, a treaty might have prohibited the introduction of a certain description of persons before the year 1808, notwithstanding the clause in the constitution to the contrary. I will speak plainly on this point:—it was the intention of the constitution that the slave trade should be tolerated till the time mentioned. It covers me with confusion to name it here; I feel ashamed of such a tolerance, and take a large part of the disgrace, as I represent a part of the Union by whose influence it might be supposed to have been introduced. Though Congress alone is prohibited, by the words of the clause, from suppressing that odious traffic, yet my colleague will admit that it was intended to be a general prohibition on the Government of the Union. I perceive my colleague indicates his dissent. It will be necessary to be more explicit.

[Here Mr. C. read that part of the constitution, and showed that the word "Congress" might be left out, in conformity with other parts of the constitution, without injury to the sense of the clause; and he insisted that the plain meaning of the parties to the constitution was, that the trade should continue till 1808, and that a prohibition by treaty would be equally against the spirit of the instrument (Crallé).]

Besides these constitutional limits, the treaty-making power, like all powers, has others derived from its nature and objects. It has for its object, contracts with foreign nations; as the powers of Congress have for their object, whatever may be done in relation to the powers delegated to it, without the consent of foreign nations. Each, in its proper sphere, operates with general influence; but when they become erratic, then they are portentous and dangerous. A treaty never can legitimately do that which can be done by law; and the converse is also true. Suppose the discriminating duties repealed on both sides by law,— still what is effected by this treaty would not even then be done; for the plighted faith of both would be wanting. Either side might repeal its law without breach of contract. It appears to me, that gentlemen are too much influenced on this subject by the example of Great Britain. Instead of looking to the nature of our own, they have been swayed in their opinions by the practice of that government, to which we are but too much in the habit of looking for precedents. Much anxiety has recently been evinced, to be independent of English broadcloths and muslins; I hope it indicates the approach of a period when we shall also throw off the thraldom of thought. The truth is, but little analogy exists between this and any other government. It is the pride of ours, to be founded in reason and equity; all others have originated, more or less, in fraud, violence, or accident. The right to make treaties, in England, can only be determined by the practice of the government; as she has no written constitution. Her practice may be wise in regard to her government, when it would be very imprudent here. Admitting the fact to be, that the king refers all commercial treaties affecting the municipal regulations of the country, to parliament, for its sanction; the argument drawn from this would be very feeble to prove that this, also, was the intention of our constitution. Strong differences exist between the forms of the two governments. The king is hereditary;—he alone, without the participation of either house of parliament, negotiates and makes treaties. England has no constitution emanating from the people, alike superior to the legislature and the king. Not so here. The President is elected for a short period; he is amenable to the public opinion; he is liable to be impeached for corruption; he cannot make treaties without the concurrence of two-thirds of the Senate—a fact very material to be remembered—which body is in like manner responsible to the people at periods not very remote. Above all,—as the laws and constitution are here perfectly distinct, and the latter is alike superior to laws and treaties,—the treaty-making power cannot change the form of government, or encroach on the liberties of the country, without encroaching on that instrument, which, so long as the people are free, will be watched with vigilance.

CHAPTER V.

" 'ONSLOW' 's [CALHOUN] SECOND LETTER TO 'PATRICK HENRY'
[J. Q. ADAMS OR DISCIPLE]," 27 JUNE 1826

The "Patrick Henry"/"Onslow" exchange should be understood as a battle for the essence of American republicanism. The debate began on rather innocuous terms when Vice-President Calhoun refused to preserve "order" and interrupt Senator John Randolph's speech against President John Q. Adams and Secretary of State Henry Clay, with whom Randolph had recently dueled. Responding to Calhoun's failure to stifle Randolph, an essay appeared in the "party press" paper, the National Journal, *under the pseudonym "Patrick Henry," criticizing the vice-president. Some mystery persists over "Patrick Henry"'s authorship, although the attachment of the author to Adams's neo-Federalism cannot be questioned. For our purposes, we contend that the author was either Adams or a confidant acting under the president's direct tutelage.[1] It is unlikely Calhoun would have participated in such a debate if he thought "Patrick Henry" was a surrogate, and public attention to these issues and personages would also have been greatly diminished if some other individual besides President Adams was the acknowledged author of "Patrick Henry." Influenced by the reputation of Sir Arthur Onslow, a noted Speaker of the House of Commons whose expertise in parliamentary procedure influenced Jefferson's* A Manual of Parliamentary Practice, *Calhoun took the nom de plume "Onslow."*

Calhoun argued that the Senate president held "appellate power" as the beneficiary of the Senate's trust; such responsibility did not primarily dictate that the Senate President preside over legislative sessions. In fact, Calhoun cited Senate rules six and seven that allowed the president to "call for the sense of Senate" when order was disputed, and

1. Charles Catlett, New York, to Philip B. Fendall, Washington, D.C., October 17, 1826. Letter in the hand of Charles Catlett, Special Collections, File 21-I, letter 24, Duke University, Durham, North Carolina.

for the recording of "exceptionable" speech before rendering a judgment about a member's comments. The approach Calhoun defended as vice-president was identical to the posture he encouraged the general government to take during forty years in public office: "assume no power in the least degree doubtful." Preserving liberty required diligence in dividing authority and protecting the legitimate agencies of political power.

In this response to "Patrick Henry," Calhoun argued that the theory of power and ultimately of popular rule espoused by "Patrick Henry" tended to support the "uncontrolled and unlimited power" of the executive. To claim that inherent powers were intrinsic to a particular office jeopardized the sources and primary agency genuine authority required. The people, acting through state legislatures, delegated only a modicum of power to the Senate. A symbiotic relationship developed between the recipient of power and its original sources, encouraging deliberation and mutual respect. The Senate had evolved into an institution that was responsive to state preferences, but also sensitive to national needs. With the vice-president, the Senate had crafted certain boundaries of authority through established legislative and procedural habits. In a fashion, the Senate entrusted the vice-president as Senate president with certain delegated powers, while retaining most of its authority, including the power to maintain order "in the body, and not in the presiding officer." Unlike the office of Speaker in the House of Representatives, Senators reserved for themselves the power to preserve and enforce order as a body. In this way, the Senate enjoyed more liberty than the House, but this situation required Senators to exercise self-discipline. Calhoun believed the Senate's position illustrated an important rule for American federalism: without self-restraint, "uncontrolled and unlimited power" will take over and disrupt the constitutional order.

[NOTE.—The following correspondence grew out of the failure of Mr. Calhoun, as President of the Senate, to call Mr. Randolph, of Va., to order, during the delivery of his celebrated Retrenchment Speech, in which he indulged in certain remarks highly offensive to the Administration, and especially to Mr. J. Q. Adams (the President,) and Mr. Clay, his Secretary of State. The former resorted to the newspapers, under the signature of "PATRICK HENRY"—and arraigned the Vice-President (Mr. Calhoun) for neglect of duty; while the latter appealed to the *duello,* and called Mr. Randolph to the field. The letters of "Onslow" (Mr. Calhoun) contain, in a brief space, a clear and forcible exposition of the power of the President of the Senate in questions of order.—EDITOR (Crallé).]

No. I.

IF rumor may be credited, I may be proud in having you as an antagonist [Mr. A., the President of the United States]; and if I were actuated by a sentiment of vanity, much of my reply would be devoted to tracing the strong, but, perhaps, accidental analogy between the style of your numbers and some of our public documents. But truth, and not the gratification of vanity, is my object; and though the pride of victory would be swelled in proportion to the high standing of an opponent, I shall, without stopping to inquire into the question of authorship, proceed directly to the point at issue.

If you have failed in your argument, you have at least succeeded in giving the question a new and interesting aspect. You have abandoned the rules and usages of the Senate, as the source of the Vice-President's authority as the presiding officer of the Senate. You contend that the disputed right is derived directly from the Constitution, and that the Vice-President's authority is wholly independent of the *will* of the Senate, which can neither give nor take it away. It is not my wish to misstate your arguments in the slightest degree, and, to avoid the possibility of misrepresentation, you shall speak for yourself. Spurning the authority of the Senate, your scornfully observe:—

"With the easy assurance of a man stating a conceded postulate, he (Onslow) says, 'After all, the power of the Vice-President must depend upon the rules and usages of the Senate:' a postulate not only false in its principle, but which, if true, would not sustain the cause to whose aid it is invoked. Unless the Constitution of the United States was subjected to some military construction, the power of the Vice-President, in presiding over the Senate, rests on deeper, holier foundations than any rules or usages which that body may adopt. What says the Constitution? 'The Vice-President of the United States shall be President of the Senate, but shall have no vote unless they be equally divided.' 'The Senate shall choose their own officers, and also a President pro tempore, in the absence of the Vice-President, or when he shall exercise the office of President of the United States.'—(Const. U. S. Art. 1. Sec. 3.) It is here made the duty of the Vice-President to preside over the Senate, under the sole restriction of having no vote except in a given case; the right of the Senate to choose their President is confined to two contingencies; his powers, after being so chosen, are identical with those of the President set over them by the Constitution, and any abridgment of those powers by the Senate would be a palpable infraction of that Constitution. Now, sir, what is the import of the term 'to preside,' in relation to a deliberative assembly? Can any sophistry devise a plausible definition of it, which would exclude the power of preserving order? In appointing an officer to preside over the Senate, the people surely intended not to erect an empty pageant, but to accomplish some useful object: and when in another part of the Constitution, they authorize each house 'to determine the rules of its proceedings,' they do not authorize it to adopt rules depriving any office created by the Constitution of powers belonging, *ex vi termini*, to that office. If the plainest or most profound man in the community were asked what powers he supposed to be inherent in the presiding officer of either House of Congress, he would instantly enumerate—First, the power of preserving order in its deliberations; next, that of collecting the sense of its members on any question submitted to their decision; and, thirdly, that of authenticating, by his signature, their legislative acts. I have before said, and I regret that I am obliged to repeat a truism, that 'the right to call to order is a necessary consequence of the power of preserving order;' and that, 'unless a deliberative body, acting within the sphere of its competence, expressly restrict this power and this right, no restriction on them can then be supposed.' In divesting the President set over them by the people, of any power which he had received, either expressly or impliedly from the people, the Senate, instead of 'acting within the sphere of their competence,' would act usurpingly and unconstitutionally—they would nullify the connection which the people had established between themselves and their President; they would reduce themselves to the monstrous spectacle of a body without a head, and their President to the equally monstrous spectacle of a head without a body; and their violent act, while it would be disobeyed as illegal, would be contemned as ridiculous. But, in truth, the Senate have never thus forgotten their allegiance to the Constitution."

There can be no mistake as to the source or the nature of the power, according to your conception. You tell us plainly that it rests "on a deeper, holier foundation" than the rules of the Senate—that it is "inherent in the Vice-President, and that, as presiding officer, he possesses it *ex vi termini;* that an attempt to divest, and, of course, to modify the power 'by the Senate, would be to act' usurpingly and unconstitutionally," and that "such violent act would be disobeyed as illegal, and contemned as ridiculous."

These are, at least, lofty grounds, and if they can be maintained, there is an end of the controversy. It would be absurd to go farther. An inquiry into the rules and usages of the Senate, after much grounds are occupied, becomes ridiculous, and much more so an inquiry into those of the houses of Parliament:

for surely, if it is beyond the power of the Senate to give or withhold the right, it must stand on an elevation far above parliamentary rules or usages; and I was, therefore, not a little surprised to find that, after so bold an assertion, more than four fifths of your long and elaborate essay were devoted to a learned and critical inquiry into these very rules and usages. There can be but one explanation of so strange an inconsistency, but that a very satisfactory one. You lack confidence in your own position; and well might you, for, surely, power so despotic and dangerous, so inconsistent with the first principles of liberty, and every sound view of the Constitution, was never attempted to be established on arguments so imbecile and absurd; to which no intellect, however badly organized, could yield assent, unless associated with feelings leaning strongly to the side of power. That such are your feelings, no one who reads your essay can doubt. None of your sympathies are on the Democratic side of our institutions. If a question be made, as to where power is lodged, it requires but little sagacity to perceive, that you will be found on the side which will place it in the fewest and least responsible hands. You perceive perfection only in the political arrangement, which, with simplicity and energy, gives power to a single will. It is not, then, at all surprising, that you should seize on that portion of the Constitution which appoints the Vice-President to be President of the Senate; and that you should quote it at large, and dwell on it at length, as the source of high and uncontrollable power in that officer; while you have but slightly and casually adverted to another section in the same article, which clothes the Senate with the power "of determining the rules of their proceedings, punishing its members for disorderly conduct, and, with the concurrence of two thirds, of expelling a member."—(See Art. 1, Sec. 5.) Had your predilections for the unity and irresponsibility of power been less strong, you could not have failed to see, that the point of view in which you have thought proper to place the question, made it one of relative power between the Senate and its presiding officer. You place the Vice-President on one side, and the Senate on the other; and the more you augment the constitutional power of the former, as the presiding officer, just in the same proportion you diminish the power of the latter. What is gained to the one is lost to the other; and in this competition of power you were bound to present fully and fairly both sides. This you have not done; and, consequently, you have fallen, not only into gross, but dangerous errors. You set out by asserting that the very object of the appointment of the Vice-President as President of the Senate was, to preserve order; and that he has all the powers, *ex vi termini,* necessary to the attainment of the end for which he was appointed. Having gained this point, you make your next step,—that the right of enforcing order involves that of calling to order; and this again involves the very power in question, which the Vice-President declined to exercise. You then draw two corollaries:—that the power held by the Vice-President, being derived direct from the Constitution, is held independently of the Senate, and is, consequently, beyond their control or participation; and that, as the Vice-President alone possesses it, he, and he alone, is responsible for order and decorum. Such is the summary logic, which you accompany with so much abuse of Mr. Calhoun for not calling the power, which you have, as you suppose, clearly proven he possesses by the Constitution, into active energy, by correcting and controlling, at his sole will and pleasure, the licentious and impertinent debates of Senators.

Let us now turn the same mode of reasoning on the side of the Senate, and you will perceive that it applies with infinitely more force, though you have not thought it deserving of notice.

The Constitution has vested the Senate with the right of determining the rules of its proceedings, and of punishing members for disorderly conduct, which may extend even to expulsion. The great object of giving the power to establish rules is to preserve order. The only effectual means of preserving order is, to prescribe by rules, what shall be a violation of order; and to enforce the same by adequate punishment. The Senate alone has these powers by the Constitution: consequently, the Senate alone has the right of enforcing order, and, consequently, whatever right the Vice-President possesses over order, must be derived from the Senate; and, therefore, he can exercise no power in adopting rules or enforcing them, but what has been delegated to him by the Senate, and only to the extent, both in manner and matter, to which the power has been delegated. The particular power in question, not having been delegated, cannot be exercised by the Vice-President; and, consequently, he is not responsible. Do you not perceive the irresistible force with which your own mode of reasoning applies to the substantial constitutional powers of the Senate, and how partial and absurd your arguments in favor of the inferred constitutional power of its presiding officer, must appear in contrast with it? As absurd as it now appears, it shall be, if possible, infinitely more so, before I have closed this part of the investigation.

With the same predilection, your assumptions are all on the side of uncontrolled and unlimited power. Without proof, or even an attempt at it, you assume, that the power in controversy is *inherent* in the Vice-President; and that he possesses it *ex vi termini* as presiding officer of the Senate. Now I, who have certainly as much right to assume as yourself, deny that he possesses any such power; and what may, perhaps, startle a mind organized like yours, I affirm that, as presiding officer, he has no inherent power whatever, unless that of doing what the Senate may prescribe by its rules, be such a power. There are, indeed, inherent powers; but they are in the *body,* and not in the *officer.* He is a mere agent to execute the will of the former. He can exercise no power which he does not hold by delegation, either express or implied. He stands in the same relation to the body, or assembly over which he presides, that a magistrate, in a republic, does to the state; and it would be as absurd to attribute to the latter inherent powers as to the former. This, in fact, was once a fashionable doctrine. There was a time, when minions of power thought it monstrous, that all the powers of rulers should be derived from so low and filthy a source as the people whom they governed. "A deeper and holier foundation" of power was sought; and that was proclaimed to be in the "inherent," divine "right of rulers;" and, as their powers were thus shown to be independent of the will of the people, it followed that any attempt on their part to divest rulers of power, would be an act of "such violence, as would be disobeyed as illegal, and contemned as ridiculous." I might trace the analogy between your language and principles and those of the advocates of despotic power in all ages and countries, much farther; but I deem it not necessary, either to weaken or refute your argument. A more direct and decisive reply may be given.

An inherent power is one that belongs essentially to the office, and is, in its nature, inseparable from it. To divest the office of it would be to change its nature. It would be no longer the same office. It is, then, a power wholly independent of the circumstances how the office may be created or filled, or in what particular manner its functions may be exercised. If, then, the power belongs to the Vice-President inherently, as presiding officer of the Senate, it is because it is essentially attached to the mere function of presiding in a deliberative assembly, and, consequently, belongs to all presiding officers over such assemblies; for it would be absurd to assert that it is inherent in him as President of the Senate, and then make it depend on the circumstance that he holds his appointment to preside in the Senate by the *Constitution.* The high power, then, which you attribute to the Vice-President, must belong, if your argument be correct, to the Speaker of the House of Commons, to the Lord-Chancellor, as presiding officer of the House of Lords, to the Speaker of the House of Representatives, and those of our State Legislatures. They must not only possess the power, but must hold it independently of the will of the bodies over which they preside; which can neither give nor take it away, nor modify the mode of exercising it, nor control its operation. These consequences, absurd as they appear to be, are legitimately drawn from your premises.

Now, "out of thine own mouth I will condemn thee;"—by your own authorities you shall be refuted. To prove that the Vice-President possesses this power, you have labored to establish the fact that the Speaker of the House of Commons holds and exercises it, and in proof of which you have cited many cases from Jefferson's Manual.

It is true that he has, at least to a certain extent, but how has he acquired it? This is the important inquiry in the point of view in which we are now considering the question. Is it inherent, or is it delegated? If the former, I acknowledge that your argument from analogy, in favor of the inherent power of the Vice-President, would have much force; but, if the latter, it must utterly fail; for, if delegated, it clearly establishes the fact that the power is in the *body,* and not in the *presiding officer,* and, consequently, not inherent in the Vice-President, as you affirm. The instances you have cited shall decide the point. What say the cases? "On the 14th of April, 1604, rule conceived, that if any man speak impertinently, or beside the question in hand, it stands with the *orders of the House* for the Speaker to interrupt him, and to show the *pleasure of the House,* whether they will farther hear him." "On the 17th of April, 1604, agreed for a general rule, if any superfluous motion or tedious speech be offered in the House, the party is to be directed and ordered by Mr. Speaker." "On the 19th of May, 1604, Sir William Paddy entering into a long speech, *a rule agreed,* that, if any man speak not to the matter in question, the Speaker is to moderate." So it is said on the 2d of May, 1610, when a member made what seemed an impertinent speech, and there was much hissing and spitting, "that it was *conceived for a rule,* that Mr. Speaker may stay impertinent speeches." "On the 10th of November, 1640, it was declared that, when a business is begun and in debate, if any man rise to speak to a new business, any member may, but Mr. Speaker ought to, interrupt him."—*See Hatsell's Precedents,* vol. ii., 3d edition.

Do you not notice, that in every case the power was delegated by the House; that the language is, "rule conceived," "it was agreed to as a general rule," "rule agreed," &c., &c.; and this, too, in relation to *the very power in question, according to your own showing?* Thus it is established, beyond controversy, that in the House of Commons the power is really in the body, and not in the presiding officer.

If, to this decisive proof that the power has been delegated to the Speaker of the House of Commons, and is, consequently, not inherent, we add that it is conferred on the Speaker of the House of Representatives (see 19th rule) by an express rule of the House, and that the Lord Chancellor, as presiding officer in the House of Lords, possesses it not, either ex officio or by delegation, as shall be shown hereafter, your monstrous and slavish doctrine, that it is an inherent power, will be completely overthrown, and you are left without the possibility of escape.

Should you attempt to extricate yourself by endeavoring to show that, under our Constitution, the relative powers of the Vice-President and the Senate are different from those of the Speaker and the House of Commons; and that, though the latter may hold the power by delegation from the body, that the Vice-President may possess it by a different and higher tenure, it would, at least, prove that you cede the point that it is not inherent, and, also, that it cannot be deduced from analogy between the *powers* of the two presiding officers, which you have so much relied on in another part of your essay. But this shall not avail you. The door is already closed in that direction. It has been, I trust, conclusively proved that the Constitution, so far from countenancing the idea of the power being inherent in the Vice-President, gives it to the Senate, by the strongest implication, in conferring the express right of establishing its own rules, and punishing for disorderly conduct. If you are not yet convinced, additional arguments are not wanting, which, though they may not extort an acknowledgment of your error, will thoroughly convince you of it.

You have overlooked the most obvious and best-established rules of construction. What are the facts? The Constitution has designated the Vice-President as President of the Senate, and has also clothed that body with the right of determining the rules of its proceedings. It is obvious that the simple intention of the framers of that instrument was to annex to the office of Vice-President that of President of the Senate, without intending to define the extent or the limit of his power in that character; and, in like manner, it was the intention to confer on the Senate simply the power of enacting its own rules of proceeding, without reference to the powers, such as they may be, that had been conferred on their presiding officer. The extent of power as between the two becomes a question of construction. Now the first rule of construction, in such cases, is the known usage and practice of parliamentary bodies; and, as those of the British Parliament were the best known to the framers of the Constitution, it cannot be doubted that, in determining what are the relative powers of the Vice-President and the Senate, they ought to prevail. Under this view, as between the Vice-President and Senate, the latter possesses the same power in determining its rules that is possessed by the Houses of Parliament, without being restricted in the slightest degree by the fact that the Vice-President, under the Constitution, is president of the body, saving only the right of adopting such rules as apply to the appointment or election of a presiding officer, which the Senate would have possessed, if the Constitution had not provided a president of the body; and, as I have proved, from your own cases, that the particular power in question incontrovertibly belongs to the House, it follows necessarily, according to established rules of construction, that the Senate also possesses it.

You have overlooked these obvious truths by affixing too high an idea to the powers of the presiding officer in preserving order. According to your conception, the House is nothing, and the officer every thing on points of order. Nothing can be more erroneous. The power you attribute to him has never been possessed by the president, or speaker, in any deliberative assembly; no, not even by delegation from the body itself.

The right of preserving order must depend on the power of enforcing it, or of punishing for a breach of order—a right *inherent* in the *House alone,* and never, in any instance, delegated to the chair. Our Constitution confines this right to each House of Congress, by providing "that they may punish for disorderly conduct,"—a power which they neither have delegated, nor can delegate, to the presiding officer. What, then, is the right of preserving order, belonging to the Vice-President, which you have so pompously announced, and for not enforcing which, according to your conception, you and your associates have denounced Mr. Calhoun almost as a traitor to his country?

It is simply the right of *calling* to order, *in the strict, literal meaning;* and, so far from being derived from the right of preserving order, as you absurdly suppose, it is not even connected with it. The right of *preserving order depends on the right of enforcing it,* or the *right of punishment for breaches of order,* always possessed by the body, but never, either by delegation or otherwise, by the chair. It is notorious that the chair cannot enforce its calls to order. The body alone can, and that only on its decisions, and not on that of the presiding officer. It is thus manifest, the high right of preserving order, to which you make the right of calling to order incidental, belongs especially to the Senate, and not to the Vice-President; and, if your argument be correct, the incident must follow the right; and, consequently, it is the right and duty of a Senator to call to order for disorderly conduct. So clear is the proposition, that, if the member called to order by the chair for disorderly conduct chooses to persist, the presiding officer has no other remedy but to *repeat his call, or throw himself, for the enforcement of it, on the Senate.* This feebleness of the chair, in questions of order, explains why there has always been such indisposition to call to order, even when it is made the express duty by rule, as in the House of Representatives, and the House of Commons in England. Thousands of instances might be cited to establish the truth of this remark, both there and here: instances in which all that has been said and uttered by Mr. Randolph is nothing, but in which the Speaker waited for the interference of some of the members, in order to preserve order. Such was the case in the recent occurrence in the House of Commons, when Mr. Hume made an attack on the Bishop of London and the Lord Chancellor, both of whom, as members of the House of Lords, were under the protection of positive rules; yet no one, even there, had the assurance to throw the responsibility on the presiding officer. The partisans of power in our country have the honor of leading in these new and dangerous attacks on the freedom of debate.

Some men, of honest intention, have fallen into the error about the right of the Vice-President to preserve order independently of the Senate, because the judges, or, as they express it, the presiding officers in the courts of justice possess the right. A moment's reflection will show the fallacy. There is not the least analogy between the rights and duties of a judge and those of a presiding officer in a deliberative assembly. The analogy is altogether the other way. It is between the court and the House. In fact, the latter is often called a court, and there is a very strict resemblance, in the point under consideration, between what may be called a parliamentary court and a court of justice. They both have the right of causing their decision to be respected, and order and decorum to be observed in their presence, by punishing those who offend. But who ever heard of the Speaker or Vice-President punishing for disorderly conduct? The utmost power they can exercise over disorderly conduct, even in the lobby or gallery, is to cause it to be suppressed, for the time, by the sergeant-at-arms.

Enough has been said, though the subject is far from being exhausted, to demonstrate that your views of the relative powers and duties of the Vice-President and the Senate, in relation to the point in question, are wholly erroneous. It remains to be shown that your opinions (for arguments they cannot be called) are dangerous to our liberty, and that they are in conflict with the first principles of our Government. I do not attribute to you, or those with whom you are associated, any deep laid design against public liberty. Such an attempt, as flagitious as it may be, requires a sagacity and boldness quite beyond what we have now to apprehend from those in power. But that there exists, at the present time, a selfish and greedy appetite to get and to hold office, and that, to effect these grovelling objects, doctrines slavish and dangerous are daily propagated, cannot be doubted by even careless observers. The freedom of debate is instinctively dreaded by the whole corps, high and low, of those who make a speculation of politics; and well they may: for it is the great and only effectual means of detecting and holding up to public scorn every machination against the liberty of the country. It ranks first, even before the liberty of the press, the trial by jury, the rights of conscience, and the writ of habeas corpus, in the estimation of those who are capable of forming a correct estimate of the value of freedom, and the best means of preserving it. Against this palladium of liberty your blows are aimed; and, to do you justice, it must be acknowledged, if the energy be not great, the direction is not destitute of skill. If you could succeed in establishing the points which you labor, that the Vice-President holds a power over the freedom of debate, under the right of preserving order, beyond the will or control of the Senate; and that, consequently, he alone is responsible for what might be considered an undue exercise of the freedom of speech in debate, a solid foundation would be laid, from which, in time, this great barrier against despotic power would be battered down. It is easy to see that the scheme takes the power of protecting this, the first of its rights, wholly out of the hands of the Senate, and places its custody in the hands of a single individual, and he in no degree responsible to the body over which this high power is to be exercised: thus effectually destroying the keystone of freedom—responsibility—and introducing into a vital part of our system uncontrolled, or, what is the same thing, despotic power; which, being derived, by your theory, from the Constitution, and being applicable to all points of order, necessarily would vest in the Vice-President alone an independent and absolute power, that would draw into the vortex of his authority an unlimited control over the freedom of debate.

Mark the consequences! If the Vice-President should belong to the same party or interest which brought the President into power, or if he be dependent on him for his political standing or advancement, *you will virtually place the control over the freedom of debate in the hands of the Executive.*

You thus introduce the *President,* as it were, into the *chamber of the Senate, and place him virtually over the deliberation of the body, with powers to restrain discussion, and shield his conduct from investigation.* Let us, for instance, suppose that the present chief magistrate should be re-elected, and that the party which supports him should succeed, as, in all probability, they would in that event, in electing also their Vice-President, can it be doubted that the rules for the restraint of the freedom of debate in the Senate, which have been insisted on openly by the party during the last winter, would be reduced to practice, through a subservient Vice-President? And what are those rules? One of the leading ones, to advert to no other, is, that the conduct of the Executive, as a co-ordinate branch of that Government, cannot be called in question by a Senator in debate, at least so far as it relates to impeachable offences; and, of course, *an attempt to discuss the conduct of the President, in such cases, would be disorderly, and render the Senator liable to be punished, even to expulsion.* What would be the consequence? The Senate would speedily sink into a body to register the decrees of the President and sing hosannas in his praise, and be as degraded as the Roman Senate under Nero.

But let us suppose the opposite state of things, in which the Vice-President chooses to pursue a course independent of the will of the Executive, and, instead of assuming so dangerous an exercise of power, he should indulge (for indulgence it must be called, if allowed by his courtesy) that freedom of debate which exists in other deliberative assemblies. What will then follow? Precisely that which occurred last winter. Most exaggerated and false accounts would every where be propagated, by hirelings of power, of the slightest occurrence in the Senate. The public indignation would be roused at the supposed disorder and indecorum, and the whole would be artfully directed against the Vice-President, in order to prostrate his reputation; and thus an officer, without patronage or power, or *even the right of defending himself,* would be the target against which the whole force and patronage of the Government would be directed. Few men would have the firmness to ecounter danger so tremendous; and the practical result in the long run, must be a subservient yielding to the Executive will.

ONSLOW.

CHAPTER VI.

For Calhoun, to remove or obstruct the critical nexus between source and agency within a theory of power threatened to destabilize the political order, which would endanger liberties and damage a constitutional democracy's most important feature: popular rule.

HAVING NOW established, I may venture to say beyond the possibility of reasonable controversy, that the idea of an inherent right in the Vice-President, independent of, and beyond the will of the Senate, to control the freedom of debate, is neither sanctioned by the Constitution, nor justified by the relation between the body and its presiding officer, and that it is subversive of the right of free discussion, and, consequently, dangerous to liberty, I might here fairly rest the question. To you, at least, who treat with scorn the rules and usages of the Senate, as the source of the power of the Vice-President, all further inquiry is fairly closed. But as many, who may agree with you in the conclusion, may treat with contempt your high-strained conception of the origin of the power under investigation, it will not be improper to ascertain whether it has been conferred on the Vice-President by any act of the Senate, express or implied, the only source whence the power can be fairly derived. In this view of the subject, the simple inquiry is, Has the Senate conferred the power? It has been fully established that they alone possess it, and, consequently, from the Senate only can it be derived. We, then, affirm that the Senate has not conferred the power. The assertion of the negative, in such cases, is sufficient to throw the burden of proof on those who hold the affirmative. I call on you, then, or any of your associates, to point out the rule or the usage of the Senate by which the power has been conferred. None such has, or can be designated.

If a similar question be asked as to the power of the Speaker of the House of Representatives, how easy would be the reply? The 19th rule, which expressly gives the power to him, would be immediately quoted; and, if that were supposed to be doubtful, the journal of the House would be held up as containing innumerable instances of the actual exercise of the power. No such answer can be given when we turn to the power of the Vice-President. The rules are mute, and the journals of the Senate silent. What means this striking difference, but that, on this point, there is a difference, in fact, between the power of the Speaker and of the Vice-President? a difference which has been always understood and acted on; and when to this we add, that the rules of the two Houses in regard to the power are strikingly different; that, while those of the Representatives expressly delegate the power to the Speaker, those of the Senate, by strong implication, withhold it from the Vice-President, little room can be left for doubt. Compare, in this view, the 19th rule of the House and the 7th of the Senate. The former says, "If any member, by speaking or otherwise, transgress the rules of the House, the Speaker shall, or any member may, call to order: in which case the member so called to order shall immediately sit down, unless permitted to explain; and the House shall, if appealed to, decide on the case without debate; if there be no appeal, the decision of the chair shall be submitted to. If the decision be in favor of the member called to order, he shall be at liberty to proceed; if otherwise, he will not be permitted to proceed without leave of the House; and if the case require it, he shall be liable to the censure of the House." The rule of the Senate, on the contrary, provides, "If the member shall be called to order for words spoken, the exceptionable words shall immediately be taken down in writing, that the President may be better enabled to judge of the matter." These are the corresponding rules of the two Houses: and can any impartial mind contend that similar powers are intended to be conferred by them on the Speaker and Vice-President? Or will it be insisted on that the difference in the phraseology is accidental, when it is known that they have often been revised on the reports of committees, who would not fail to compare the rules of the two Houses on corresponding subjects? Under such circumstances, it is impossible that it could be intended to confer the same power by such difference of phraseology, or that the withholding of the power in question from the Vice-President was unintentional. This rational construction is greatly strengthened, when we advert to the different relations which the two officers bear to their respective Houses. The Speaker is chosen by the House of

Representatives, and is, consequently, directly responsible to the body; and his decision, by the rules, may be appealed from to the House. The Vice-President, on the contrary, is placed in the chair by the Constitution, is not responsible to the Senate, and his decision is without appeal. Need we look farther for the reason of so essential a variation in the rules conferring power on their respective presiding officers? It is a remarkable fact, that the same difference exists in the relation between the presiding officers of the two Houses of the British Parliament, and the bodies over which they respectively preside. In the Commons, the Speaker is chosen as in our House of Representatives, and is, consequently, in like manner responsible; on the contrary, in the House of Lords, the Chancellor presides *ex-officio,* in like manner as the Vice-President in the Senate, and is, in like manner, irresponsible to the body. Now it is no less remarkable that the Speaker possesses the power in question, while it is perfectly certain that the Lord Chancellor does not. Like cause, like effect; dissimilar cause, dissimilar effect. You, sir, have, it is true, made a puny effort to draw a distinction between the mode in which the Vice-President and the Lord Chancellor are appointed, and have also feebly denied that the latter has not the power of calling to order. Both of these efforts show the desperation of your cause. What does it signify by whom an *ex officio* officer is appointed, if not by the body? There can be but one material point, and that without reference to the mode of appointment— is he, or is he not, responsible to the House? If the former, there is good cause for the delegation of the power; for power exercised by responsible agents is substantially exercised by the principal; while by irresponsible agents it is the power of him by whom it is exercised. Nor is your effort to show that the Chancellor has the power less unhappy. You have cited but one instance, and that really renders you ridiculous. The Lord Chancellor, as is well known, has the right of speaking; and you most absurdly cite the commencement of a speech of one of the Chancellors, in which he states that he would call back the attention of the Lords to the question at issue, as an instance of exercising the power of calling to order as presiding officer, for departure from the question! Though you have signally failed to prove your position, you have not less completely established the fact, that your integrity is not above a resort to trick, where argument fails. Nor is this the only instance of subterfuge. You made a similar effort to do away the authority of the venerable Jefferson. He has left on record, that he considered his power as presiding officer of the Senate as the *power of umpirage,* or, what is the same thing, an appellate power. In order to break the force of this authority, you have denied the plain and invariable meaning of the word, and attempted to affix one to it which it never bears. You say that its usual meaning is synonymous with "office," "authority," or "the act of determining," and that it is only in its technical sense that it conveys the idea of an appellate power! Can it be unknown to you that no word in the language more invariably has attached to it the idea of decision by appeal, and that there is not an instance of its being used by any respectable authority in the sense which you state to be its usual meaning?

It only remains to consider the cases that you have cited from the Manual, to prove that the Speaker of the House of Commons possesses the power in question; by which you would infer that it belongs also to the Vice-President. A very strange deduction by one who believes that the power originates in the Constitution, and that it neither can be given nor taken away by the authority of the Senate itself. After asserting that it has "deeper and holier foundations than the rules and usages of the Senate," there is something more than ridiculous, that you at last seek for the power in the rules and usages of the House of Commons! But let such inconsistency pass. You have, indeed, established the fact that the Speaker has the power, but you have overlooked the material circumstance, as I have shown from your own cases, that he possesses it by *positive rules of the House*. You might as well have shown that the Speaker of the House of Representatives possesses it, and then inferred that the Vice-President does also; for he, too, holds the power by positive rules of the body, which makes the analogy as strong in the one case as the other.

But you would have it understood that the rules of Parliament have been adopted by the Senate. No such thing. I challenge you to cite a single rule or act of the Senate that gives countenance to it. Finally, you tell us that Mr. Jefferson has cited these rules as being part of the rules and usages of the Senate. Admitting, for a moment, that Mr. Jefferson had cited them as such, still a very important question would arise, how came they to be the rules of the Senate? The Constitution provides that the Senate shall determine the rules of its proceedings; now, if that body has not, by any rule, adopted the rules of the British Parliament, by what process of reasoning could they be construed to be the rules of the Senate? That the Senate has not adopted the rules of Parliament, is certain; and I confess I am not a little curious to see the process of reasoning by which they are made the rules of the Senate, *without adoption*. Is there not a striking analogy between this and the question, whether the common law is a part of the laws of the Union? We know that they have been decided by the highest judicial authority not to be; and, it seems to me, the arguments which would be applicable to, the one would be equally so to the other question. That the rules and usages of Parliament may be referred to to illustrate the rules of either House of Congress, is quite a distinct proposition, and may be readily admitted. Arguments may be drawn from any source calculated to illustrate, but that is wholly different from giving to the rules of another body a binding force on the Senate, without ever having been recognized as its rules. This is a subject of deep and grave importance; but as it is not necessary to my purpose, I decline entering on it. It is sufficient, at present, to deny that Mr. Jefferson has cited the rules of the Parliament, referred to by you, as those of the Senate. On the contrary, they are expressly cited as the rules of the British House of Commons, without stating them to be obligatory on the Senate. He has notoriously cited many of the rules of that body which are wholly dissimilar from the usages of the Senate. But you cite Mr. Jefferson's opinion, in which he says, "The Senate have, accordingly, formed some rules for its government" (they have been much enlarged since); "but these going only to a few cases, they have referred to the decision of the President, without debate or appeal, all questions of order arising under their own rules, or where there is none. This places under the discretion of the President a very extensive field of decision." If your object in quoting the above passage was to show that, where the Senate has adopted no rules of its own, the rules of Parliament are those of the Senate, it completely fails. Not the slightest countenance is given to such an idea. Mr. Jefferson, on the contrary, says that, in cases of omission, the sound discretion of the President is the rule;* and such has been the practice, and from which it has followed that usages of the Senate are very different from the Parliament, which could not be, if the latter were adopted, where there were no positive rules by the Senate.

If this view of the subject be correct, which is certainly Mr. Jefferson's, the Vice-President had the right to make the rule by exercising a sound discretion; and the only question that could arise in this view is, whether he has acted on correct principles in referring the power to the House, instead of exercising it by the chair. So long as doubtful and irresponsible power ought not to be assumed—so long as the freedom of debate is essential to liberty—and so long as it is an axiom in politics that no power can be safe but what is in the final control and custody of the body over which it is exercised—so long the rule (to view it in that light) adopted by the Vice-President will be considered in

---

*This opinion of Mr. Jefferson's is probably founded on the latter part of the 6th rule, which strongly supports it. The rule is as follows: "When a member shall be called to order, he shall sit down until the President shall have determined whether he is in order or not; and every question of order shall be decided by the President, without debate; but if there be a doubt in his mind, be may call for the sense of the Senate."

conformity with sound political principles. But suppose it to be conceived that the rules of Parliament are those of the Senate, when not overruled by its own positive acts, still, two questions would remain: first, whether the 7th rule of the Senate, by a sound construction, does not restrain the Vice-President from exercising the power, by limiting it to the members of the Senate? and, secondly, whether the practice of the House of Lords, or that of the Commons ought, in this particular, to prevail? Both of these points have already been incidentally considered, and a single remark will now suffice. Whether we regard the nature of the power, or the principles of our system of government, there can be no doubt that the decision ought to be against the practice of the House of Commons, and in favor of that of the House of Lords.

It may not be improper to notice an opinion which, if I mistake not, has, in no small degree, contributed to the error which exists as to the decision of the Vice-President. There are many who are far from agreeing with your absurd and dangerous positions as to the inherent powers of the Vice-President over the freedom of debate, but who have, I think, a vague conception that he has the right in dispute, as presiding officer, but a right subordinate to, and dependent on, the Senate. They concede to the Senate the right of determining their rules, and that this right comprehends that of determining what is, or what is not, disorderly conduct, and how the same shall be noticed or inhibited; but they have an idea that the *ex officio* duty of the Vice-President to regulate the proceedings of the Senate according to their own rules, extends to cases of the freedom of debate. The amount of the argument, as far as I can understand it, is, that, where there is a rule of the Senate, the Vice-President has, *ex officio,* the power of regulating the proceedings of the Senate by it, without any express authority in the rule to that effect. All this may be fairly conceded, but it decides nothing. It brings back the question to the inquiry, Is there, or is there not, such a rule? which has been fully considered, and, I trust, satisfactorily determined in the negative. I will not again repeat the arguments on this point: I do not deem it necessary. It is sufficient to remark, if there be a rule, let it be shown, and the question is at an end. There is none.

As connected with this part of the subject, I do not think it necessary to meet the ridiculous charge of inconsistency which you make against the Vice-President in the exercise of his power, and which you endeavor to support by reference to the stale and false accounts of his conduct in the case of Mr. Dickerson. It is sufficient that Mr. D. has repelled the charge of injustice, and you exhibit but a sorry and factious appearance in defending a Senator from oppression, who is not conscious of any injustice having been inflicted.

Having demonstrated that the powers which you claim for the Vice-President do not belong to him as presiding officer of the Senate, and that they are not conferred on him by the rules or usage of the Senate, or those of Parliament, I may safely affirm that it does not exist, and that, so far from censure, Mr. Calhoun deserves praise for declining to exercise it. He has acted in the spirit that ought to actuate every virtuous public functionary—not to assume doubtful powers—a spirit, under our systems of delegated authority, essential to the preservation of liberty, and for being guided by which he will receive the thanks of the country when the excitement of the day has passed away.

I have now completed what may be considered the investigation of the subject; but there are still several of your remarks that require notice. You have not only attacked the decision of Mr. Calhoun, but you have impugned his motives with licentious severity. The corrupt are the most disposed to attribute corruption, and your unprovoked and unjustifiable attack on Mr. C.'s motives speak as little in favor of your heart as your arguments do of your head. Fortunately for the Vice-President, his general character for virtue and patriotism shields him from the imputation of such gross abuse of power, from such impure motives as you attribute to him. He could not decide differently from what he did without being at war with the principles which have ever governed him. It is well known to all acquainted with him, publicly or privately, that the maxim which he holds in the highest veneration, and which he regards as the foundation of our whole system of government, is, that power should be controlled by the body over which it is exercised, and that, without such responsibility, all delegated power would speedily become corrupt. Whether he is wrong in giving too high an estimate to this favorite maxim is immaterial. It is, and long has been, his, and could not fail in having great influence in the decision which you have so seriously assaulted. Had his principles been like yours, as illustrated in your essay, it is possible he might have taken a different view of the subject; but, as he has decided in conformity with principles long fixed in his mind, there is something malignant in the extreme to attribute his decision to motives of personal enmity. You not only attack Mr. C.'s motives for this decision, but also his motive for the constitution of the Committee of Foreign Relations. You think it a crime in him that the venerable and patriotic Macon should be placed at the head of the committee. I will neither defend him nor the other members of the committee. They need no defence; but I cannot but remark, that the election of Mr. Macon President pro tem. of the Senate is a singular comment on your malignant attack on the Vice-President.

It would have been impossible that you should steer clear of the cant of your party, and we accordingly have a profusion of vague charges about Mr. Calhoun's ambition. The lowest and most mercenary hireling can easily coin such charges; and while they deal in the general, without a single specification, it is utterly impossible to meet or refute them; but, fortunately, they go for nothing with the wise and virtuous, saving only that, on the part of those who make them, they evince an envious, morbid mind, which, having no real ground of attack, indulges in vague, unmeaning abuse. It is highly honorable to Mr. C. that, in the midst of so much political enmity, his personal and public character stands free from all but one specific charge—which is, that he has inclined, in his present station, *too much against his own power, and too much in favor of the inestimable right of the freedom of debate.* That he has been indefatigable in the discharge of his duty; that he has been courteous to the members, and prompt and intelligent, all acknowledge. Not a moment was he absent from his post during a long and laborious session, and often remained in the chair, without leaving it, from eight to twelve hours. He has, however, committed one unpardonable sin which blots out all. He did not stop Mr. Randolph. This is the head and front of his offending. And who is Mr. Randolph? Is he or his manners a stranger in our national councils? For more than a quarter of a century he has been a member of Congress, and during the whole time his character has remained unchanged. Highly talented, eloquent, severe, and eccentric; not unfrequently wandering from the question, but often uttering wisdom worthy of a Bacon, and wit that would not discredit a Sheridan, every Speaker had freely indulged him in his peculiar manner, and that without responsibility or censure; and none more freely than the present Secretary of State, while he presided in the House of Representatives. He is elected, with a knowledge of all this, by the ancient and renowned commonwealth of Virginia, and takes his seat in the Senate. An immediate outcry is made against the Vice-President for permitting him, who has been so long permitted by so many Speakers, to exercise his usual freedom of discussion, though, in no respect, were his attacks on this administration freer than what they had been on those of Mr. Jefferson, Mr. Madison, and Mr. Monroe. Who can doubt, if Mr. Calhoun had yielded to this clamor, that the whole current would have turned; and that he would then have been more severely denounced for, what would have been called, his tyranny and usurpation, than he has been for refusing to interfere with the freedom of debate? His authority would have been denied, and properly denied. The fact that Mr. R. had been permitted, by all other presiding officers, for so long a time, to speak without restraint, would have been dwelt upon; and the injustice done to the Senator, and the insult offered to the State that sent him, would have been painted in the most lively colors.

These considerations, we are satisfied, had no weight with the Vice-President. Those who know him, know that no man is more regardless of consequences in the discharge of his duty; but that the attack on him is personal, in order to shake his political standing and prostrate his character, is clearly evinced by every circumstance; and, with this object, that he would have been assaulted, act as he might, is most certain. It is for the American people to determine, whether this conspiracy against a public servant, whose only fault is, that he has chosen the side of liberty, rather than that of power; and whose highest crime consists, in a reverential regard for the freedom of debate, shall succeed.

ONSLOW.

Chapter VII.

The "Exposition and Protest" is in reality two different documents, but both demonstrate the importance of defending liberty against consolidation. Calhoun drafted the "Exposition," but his role in the composition of "The Protest" is less clear. The essay defends limiting government to a proper realm in order to preserve liberty and to protect society from the capricious will of the majority. At the heart of this protection, lay state governments, which were part of a system of "two distinct and independent" forms of government. As a last resort, it was the state government that was closer to the citizenry and by necessity would need to interpose on the citizen's behalf against the federal government.

THE COMMITTEE of the Whole, to whom were referred the Governor's Message and various memorials on the subject of the Tariff, having reported, and the House having adopted the following resolution, viz.:

"*Resolved,* That it is expedient to protest against the unconstitutionality and oppressive operation of the system of protecting duties, and to have such protest entered on the Journals of the Senate of the United States—Also, to make a public exposition of our wrongs and of the remedies within our power, to be communicated to our sister States, with a request that they will co-operate with this State in procuring a repeal of the Tariff for protection, and an abandonment of the principle; and if the repeal be not procured, that they will co-operate in such measures as may be necessary for arresting the evil.

"*Resolved,* That a committee of seven be raised to carry the foregoing resolution into effect:" which was decided in the affirmative, and the following gentlemen appointed on the committee, viz.: JAMES GREGG, D. L. WARDLAW,

HUGH S. LEGARE, ARTHUR P. HAYNE, WM. C. PRESTON, WILLIAM ELLIOTT, and
R. BARNWELL SMITH.

*The Special Committee to whom the above Resolution was referred, beg leave to
Report the following Exposition and Protest—*

The committee have bestowed on the subjects referred to them the deliberate attention which their importance demands; and the result, on full investigation, is a unanimous opinion that the act of Congress of the last session, with the whole system of legislation imposing duties on imports,—not for revenue, but the protection of one branch of industry at the expense of others,—is unconstitutional, unequal, and oppressive, and calculated to corrupt the public virtue and destroy the liberty of the country; which propositions they propose to consider in the order stated, and then to conclude their report with the consideration of the important question of the remedy.

The committee do not propose to enter into an elaborate or refined argument on the question of the constitutionality of the Tariff system. The General Government is one of specific powers, and it can rightfully exercise only the powers expressly granted, and those that may be necessary and proper to carry them into effect, all others being reserved expressly to the States or the people. It results, necessarily, that those who claim to exercise power under the Constitution, are bound to show that it is expressly granted, or that it is necessary and proper as a means to some of the granted powers. The advocates of the Tariff have offered no such proof. It is true that the third section of the first article of the Constitution authorizes Congress to lay and collect an impost duty, but it is granted as a tax power for the sole purpose of revenue,—a power in its nature essentially different from that of imposing protective or prohibitory duties. Their objects are incompatible. The prohibitory system must end in destroying the revenue from imports. It has been said that the system is a violation of the spirit, and not the letter of the Constitution. The distinction is not material. The Constitution may be as grossly violated by acting against its meaning as against its letter; but it may be proper to dwell a moment on the point in order to understand more fully the real character of the acts under which the interest of this, and other States similarly situated, has been sacrificed. The facts are few and simple. The Constitution grants to Congress the power of imposing a duty on imports for revenue, which power is abused by being converted into an instrument of rearing up the industry of one section of the country on the ruins of another. The violation, then, consists in using a power granted for one object to advance another, and that by the sacrifice of the original object. It is, in a word, a violation by perversion,—

the most dangerous of all because the most insidious and difficult to resist. Others cannot be perpetrated without the aid of the judiciary;—this may be by the Executive and Legislative departments alone. The courts cannot look into the motives of legislators. They are obliged to take acts by their titles and professed objects, and if these be constitutional, they cannot interpose their power, however grossly the acts may, in reality, violate the Constitution. The proceedings of the last session sufficiently prove that the House of Representatives are aware of the distinction, and determined to avail themselves of its advantage.

In the absence of arguments, drawn from the Constitution itself, the advocates of the power have attempted to call in the aid of precedent. The committee will not waste their time in examining the instances quoted. If they were strictly in point, they would be entitled to little weight. Ours is not a Government of precedents, nor can they be admitted, except to a very limited extent, and with great caution, in the interpretation of the Constitution, without changing, in time, the entire character of the instrument. The only safe rule is the Constitution itself,—or, if that be doubtful, the history of the times. In this case, if doubts existed, the journals of the Convention itself would remove them. It was moved in that body to confer on Congress the very power in question to encourage manufactures, but it was deliberately withheld, except to the extent of granting patent rights for new and useful inventions. Instead of granting the power, permission was given to the States to impose duties, with the consent of Congress, to encourage their own manufactures; and thus, in the true spirit of justice, imposing the burden on those who were to be benefited. But, giving the precedents every weight that may be claimed for them, the committee feel confident that, in this case, there are none in point previous to the adoption of the present Tariff system. Every instance which has been quoted, may fairly be referred to the legitimate power of Congress, to impose duties on imports for revenue. It is a necessary incident of such duties to act as an encouragement to manufactures, whenever imposed on articles which may be manufactured in our country. In this incidental manner, Congress has the power of encouraging manufactures; and the committee readily concede that, in the passage of an impost bill, that body may, in modifying the details, so arrange the provisions of the bill, as far as it may be done consistently with its proper object, as to aid manufactures. To this extent Congress may constitutionally go, and has gone from the commencement of the Government, which will fully explain the precedents cited from the early stages of its operation. Beyond this they never proceeded till the commencement of the present system, the inequality and oppression of which they will next proceed to consider.

On entering on this branch of the subject, the committee feel the painful character of the duty which they must perform. They would desire never to speak of our country, as far as the action of the General Government is concerned, but as one great whole, having a common interest, which all the parts ought zealously to promote. Previously to the adoption of the Tariff system, such was the unanimous feeling of this State; but in speaking of its operation, it will be impossible to avoid the discussion of sectional interest, and the use of sectional language. On its authors, and not on us, who are compelled to adopt this course in self-defence, by injustice and oppression, be the censure.

So partial are the effects of the system, that its burdens are exclusively on one side and its benefits on the other. It imposes on the agricultural interest of the South, including the South-west, and that portion of the country particularly engaged in commerce and navigation, the burden not only of sustaining the system itself, but that also of the Government. In stating the case thus strongly, it is not the intention of the committee to exaggerate. If exaggeration were not unworthy of the gravity of the subject, the reality is such as to make it unnecessary.

That the manufacturing States, even in their own opinion, bear no share of the burden of the Tariff in reality, we may infer with the greatest certainty from their conduct. The fact that they urgently demand an increase, and consider every addition as a blessing, and a failure to obtain one as a curse, is the strongest confession that, whatever burden it imposes, in reality falls, not on them, but on others. Men ask not for burdens, but benefits. The tax paid by the duties on imports, by which, with the exception of the receipts from the sale of the public lands, and a few incidental items, the Government is wholly supported, and which, in its gross amount, annually equals about $23,000,000, is then, in truth, no tax on them. Whatever portion of it they advance as consumers of the articles on which it is imposed, returns to them with usurious interest through an artfully contrived system. That such are the facts, the committee will proceed to demonstrate by other arguments besides the confession of the parties interested in these acts, as conclusive as that ought to be considered. If the duties were imposed on the exports instead of the imports, no one would doubt their partial operation, or that the duties, in that form, would fall on those engaged in producing articles for the foreign market; and as rice, tobacco, and cotton, constitute the great mass of our exports, such duties would, of necessity, mainly fall on the Southern States, where they are exclusively cultivated. To prove, then, that the burden of the Tariff falls also on them almost exclusively, it is only necessary to show that, as far as their interest is concerned, there is little or no difference between an export and an import duty. We export to import. The object is an exchange of the fruits of our labor for those of other countries. We have, from soil and climate, a facility in rearing certain great agricultural staples, while other and older countries, with dense population and capital greatly accumulated, have equal facility in manufacturing various articles suited to our use; and thus a foundation is laid for an exchange of the products of labor mutually advantageous. A duty, whether it be on the imports or exports, must fall on this exchange; and, however laid, must, in reality, be paid by the producer of the articles exchanged. Such must be the operation of all taxes on sales or exchanges. The producer, in reality, pays it, whether laid on the vendor or purchaser. It matters not in the sale of a tract of land, or any other article, if a tax be imposed, whether it be paid by him who sells or him who buys. The amount must, in both cases, be deducted from the price. Nor can it alter, in this particular, the operation of such a tax, by being imposed on the exchanges of different countries. Such exchanges are but the aggregate of sales of the individuals of the respective countries; and must, if taxed, be governed by the same rules. Nor is it material whether the exchange be barter or sale, direct or circuitous. In any case it must fall on the producer. To the growers of cotton, rice, and tobacco, it is the same, whether the Government takes one third of what they raise, for the liberty of sending the other two thirds abroad, or one third of the iron, salt, sugar, coffee, cloth, and other articles they may need in exchange, for the liberty of bringing them home. In both cases he gets a third less than he ought. A third of his labor is taken; yet the one is an import duty, and the other an export. It is true that a tax on the imports, by raising the price of the articles imported, may in time produce the supply at home, and thus give a new direction to the exchanges of the country; but it is also true that a tax on the exports, by diminishing at home the price of the same material, may have the same effect, and with no greater burden to the grower. Whether the situation of the South will be materially benefited by this new direction given to its exchanges, will be considered hereafter; but whatever portion of her foreign exchanges may, in fact, remain, in any stage of this process of changing her market, must be governed by the rule laid down. Whatever duty may be imposed to bring it about, must fall on the foreign trade which remains, and be paid by the South almost exclusively,—as much so, as an equal amount of duty on their exports. Let us now trace the operation of the system in some of its prominent details, in order to understand, with greater precision, the extent of the burden it imposes on us, and the benefits which it confers, at our expense, on the manufacturing States. The committee, in the discussion of this point, will not aim at minute accuracy.

They have neither the means nor the time requisite for that purpose, nor do they deem it necessary, if they had, to estimate the fractions of loss or gain on either side on subjects of such great magnitude. The exports of domestic produce, in round numbers, may be estimated as averaging $53,000,000 annually; of which the States growing cotton, rice, and tobacco, produce about $37,000,000. In the last four years the average amount of the export of cotton, rice, and tobacco, exceeded $35,500,000; to which, if we add flour, corn, lumber, and other articles exported from the States producing the former, their exports cannot be estimated at a less sum than that stated. Taking it at that sum, the exports of the Southern or staple States, and other States, will stand as $37,000,000 to $16,000,000,—or considerably more than the proportion of two to one; while their population, estimated in federal numbers, is the reverse; the former sending to the House of Representatives but 76 members, and the latter 137. It follows that about one third of the Union exports more than two thirds of the domestic products. Such, then, is the amount of labor which our country annually exchanges with the rest of the world,—and such our proportion. The Government is supported almost exclusively by a tax on this exchange, in the shape of an impost duty, and which amounts annually to about $23,000,000, as has already been stated. Previous to the passage of the act of the last session, this tax averaged about 37 ;1/2 per cent. on the value of imports. What addition that has made, it is difficult, with the present data, to estimate with precision; but it may be assumed, on a very moderate calculation, to be 7 ;1/2 per cent.,—thus making the present duty to average at least 45 per cent, which, on $37,000,000, the amount of our share of the exports, will give the sum of $16,650,000, as our share of the contribution to the general Treasury.

Let us take another, and perhaps more simple and striking view of this important point. Exports and imports, allowing for the profit and loss of trade, must be equal in a series of years. This is a principle universally conceded. Let it then be supposed, for the purpose of illustration, that the United States were organized into two separate and distinct custom-house establishments,—one for the staple States, and the other for the rest of the Union; and that all commercial intercourse between the two sections were taxed in the same manner and to the same extent with the commerce of the rest of the world. The foreign commerce, under such circumstances, would be carried on from each section, direct with the rest of the world; and the imports of the Southern Custom-House, on the principle that exports and imports must be equal, would amount annually to $37,000,000; on which 45 per cent., the average amount of the impost duty, would give an annual revenue of $16,650,000, without increasing the burden already imposed on the people of those States one cent. This would be the amount of revenue on the exchanges of that portion of their products which go abroad; but if we take into the estimate the duty which would accrue on the exchange of their products with the manufacturing States,—which now, in reality, is paid by the Southern States in the shape of increased prices, as a bounty to manufactures, but which, on the supposition, would constitute a part of their revenue, many millions more would have to be added.

But, it is contended, that the consumers really pay the impost,—and that, as the manufacturing States consume a full share, in proportion to their population, of the articles imported, they must also contribute their full share to the Treasury of the Union. The committee will not deny the position that their consumption is in proportion to their population,—nor that the consumers pay, provided they be mere consumers, without the means, through the Tariff, of indemnifying themselves in some other character. Without the qualification, no proposition can be more fallacious than that the consumers pay. That the manufacturing States do, in fact, indemnify themselves, and more than indemnify themselves for the increased price they pay on the articles they consume, we have, as has already been stated, their confession in a form which cannot deceive,—we mean their own acts. Nor is it difficult to trace the operation by which this is effected. The very acts of Congress, imposing the burdens on them, as consumers, give them the means, through the monopoly which it affords their manufactures in the home market, not only of indemnifying themselves for the increased price on the imported articles which they may consume, but, in a great measure, to command the industry of the rest of the Union. The argument urged by them for the adoption of the system (and with so much success), that the price of property and products in those States must be thereby increased,—clearly proves that the facts are as stated by your committee. It is by this very increased price, which must be paid by their fellow-citizens of the South, that their industry is affected, and the fruits of our toil and labor, which, on any principle of justice, ought to belong to ourselves, are transferred from us to them. The maxim, that the consumers pay, strictly applies to us. We are mere consumers, and destitute of all means of transferring the burden from ours to the shoulders of others. We may be assured that the large amount paid into the Treasury under the duties on imports, is really derived from the labor of some portion of our citizens. The Government has no mines. Some one must bear the burden of its support. This unequal lot is ours. We are the serfs of the system,—out of whose labor is raised, not only the money paid into the Treasury, but the funds out of which are drawn the rich rewards of the manufacturer and his associates in interest. Their encouragement is our discouragement. The duty on imports, which is mainly paid out of our labor, gives them the means of selling to us at a higher price; while we cannot, to compensate the loss, dispose of our products at the least advance. It is then, indeed, not a subject of wonder, when understood, that our section of the country, though helped by a kind Providence with a genial sun and prolific soil, from which spring the richest products, should languish in poverty and sink into decay, while the rest of the Union, though less fortunate in natural advantages, are flourishing in unexampled prosperity. The assertion, that the encouragement of the industry of the manufacturing States is, in fact, discouragement to ours, was not made without due deliberation. It is susceptible of the clearest proof. We cultivate certain great staples for the supply of the general market of the world:—They manufacture almost exclusively for the home market. Their object in the Tariff is to keep down foreign competition, in order to obtain a monopoly of the domestic market. The effect on us is, to compel us to purchase at a higher price, both what we obtain from them and from others, without receiving a correspondent increase in the price of what we sell. The price at which we can afford to cultivate must depend on the price at which we receive our supplies. The lower the latter, the lower we may dispose of our products with profit,—and in the same degree our capacity of meeting competition is increased; and, on the contrary, the higher the price of our supplies, the less the profit, and the less, consequently, the capacity for meeting competition. If, for instance, cotton can be cultivated at 10 cents the pound, under an increase price of forty-five per cent on what we purchase, in return, it is clear, if the prices of what we consume were reduced forty-five per cent. (the amount of the duty), we could, under such reduced prices, afford to raise the article at 5 ;1/2 cents per pound, with a profit, as great as what we now obtain at 10 cents; and that our capacity of meeting the competition of foreigners in the general market of the world, would be increased in the same proportion. If we can now, with the increased price from the Tariff, contend with success, under a reduction of 45 per cent. in the prices of our products, we could drive out all competition; and thus add annually to the consumption of our cotton, three or four hundred thousand bales, with a corresponding increase of profit. The case, then, fairly stated between us and the manufacturing States is, that the Tariff gives them a protection against foreign competition in our own market, by diminishing, in the same proportion, our capacity to compete with our rivals, in the general market of the world. They who say that they cannot compete with foreigners at their own doors, without an advantage of 45 per cent., expect us to meet them abroad under disadvantage equal to their encouragement. But this oppression, as great as it is, will not stop at this point. The trade between us and Europe has, heretofore, been a mutual exchange of products. Under the existing duties, the consumption of European fabrics must, in a great measure, cease in our country; and the trade must become, on their part, a cash transaction. He must be ignorant of the principles of commerce, and the policy of Europe, particularly England, who does not see that it is impossible to carry on a trade of such vast extent on any other basis than barter; and that, if it were not so carried on, it would not long be tolerated. We already see indications of the commencement of a commercial warfare, the termination of which no one can conjecture,—though our fate may easily be. The last remains of our great and once flourishing agriculture must be annihilated in the conflict. In the first instance, we will be thrown on the home market, which cannot consume a fourth of our products; and instead of supplying the world, as we would with a free trade, we would be compelled to abandon the cultivation of three fourths of what we now raise, and receive for the residue, whatever the manufacturers, who would then have their policy consummated by the entire possession of our market, might choose to give. Forced to abandon our ancient and favorite pursuit, to which our soil, climate, habits, and peculiar labor are adapted, at an immense sacrifice of property, we would be compelled, without capital, experience, or skill, and with a population untried in such pursuits, to attempt to become the rivals instead of the customers of the manufacturing States. The result is not doubtful. If they, by superior capital and skill, should keep down successful competition on our part, we would be doomed to toil at our unprofitable agriculture,—selling at the prices which a single and very limited market might give. But, on the contrary, if our necessity should triumph over their capital and skill,—if, instead of raw cotton, we should ship to the manufacturing States cotton yarn and cotton goods, the thoughtful must see that it would inevitably bring about a state of things which could not long continue. Those who now make war on our gains, would then make it on our labor. They would not tolerate, that those, who now cultivate our plantations, and furnish them with the material, and the market for the products of their arts, should, by becoming their rivals, take bread out of the mouths of their wives and children. The committee will not pursue this painful subject; but, as they clearly see that the system, if not arrested, must bring the country to this hazardous extremity, neither prudence nor patriotism would permit them to pass it by without raising a warning voice against a danger of such menacing character.

It was conceded, in the course of the discussion, that the consumption of the manufacturing States, in proportion to population, was as great as ours. How they, with their limited means of payment, if estimated by the exports of their own products, could consume as much as we do with our ample exports, has been partially explained; but it demands a fuller consideration. Their population, in round numbers, may be estimated at about eight, and ours at four millions; while the value of their products exported, compared with ours, is as sixteen to thirty-seven millions of dollars. If to the aggregate of these sums be added the profits of our foreign trade and navigation, it will give the amount of the fund out of which is annually paid the price of foreign articles consumed in our country. This profit, at least so far as it constitutes a portion of the fund out of which the price of the foreign articles is paid, is represented by the difference between the value of the exports and imports,—that of both being estimated at our own ports,—and which, taking the average of the last five years, amount to about $4,000,000,—and which, as the foreign trade of the country is principally in the hands of the manufacturing States, we will add to their means of consumption; which will raise theirs to $20,000,000, and will place the relative means of the consumption of the two sections, as twenty to thirty-seven millions of dollars; while, on the supposition of equal consumption in proportion to population, their consumption would amount to thirty-eight millions of dollars, and ours to nineteen millions. Their consumption would thus exceed their capacity to consume, if judged by the value of their exports, and the profits of their foreign commerce, by eighteen millions; while ours, judged the same way, would fall short by the same sum. The inquiry which naturally presents itself is, how is this great change in the relative condition of the parties, to our disadvantage, affected?—which the committee will now proceed to explain.

It obviously grows out of our connections. If we were entirely separated, without political or commercial connection, it is manifest that the consumption of the manufacturing States, of foreign articles, could not exceed twenty-two millions,—the sum at which the value of their exports and profit of their foreign trade is estimated. It would, in fact, be much less; as the profits of foreign navigation and trade, which have been added to their means, depend almost exclusively on the great staples of the South, and would have to be deducted, if no connection existed, as supposed. On the contrary, it is equally manifest, that the means of the South to consume the products of other countries, would not be so materially affected in the state supposed. Let us, then, examine what are the causes growing out of this connection, by which so great a change is effected. They may be comprehended under three heads;—the Custom-House,—the appropriations,—and the monopoly of the manufacturers; all of which are so intimately blended as to constitute one system, which its advocates, by a perversion of all that is associated with the name, call the "AMERICAN SYSTEM." The Tariff is the soul of this system.

It has already been proved that our contribution, through the Custom-House, to the Treasury of the Union, amounts annually to $16,650,000, which leads to the inquiry,—What becomes of so large an amount of the products of our labor, placed, by the operation of the system, at the disposal of Congress? One point is certain,—a very small share returns to us, out of whose labor it is extracted. It would require much investigation to state, with precision, the proportion of the public revenue disbursed annually in the Southern, and other States respectively; but the committee feel a thorough conviction, on examination of the annual appropriation acts, that a sum much less than two millions of dollars falls to our share of the disbursements; and that it would be a moderate estimate to place our contribution, above what we receive back, through all of the appropriations, at $15,000,000; constituting, to that great amount, an annual, continued, and uncompensated draft on the industry of the Southern States, through the Custom-House alone. This sum, deducted from the $37,000,000,—the amount of our products annually exported, and added to the $20,000,000, the amount of the exports of the other States, with the profits of foreign trade and navigation, would reduce our means of consumption to $22,000,000, and raise theirs to $35,000,000;—still leaving $3,000,000 to be accounted for; and which may be readily explained, through the operation of the remaining branch of the system,—the monopoly which it affords the manufacturers in our market; and which empowers them to force their goods on us at a price equal to the foreign article of the same description, with the addition of the duty;—thus receiving, in exchange, our products, to be shipped, on their account,—and thereby increasing their means, and diminishing ours in the same proportion. But this constitutes a part only of our loss under this branch. In addition to the thirty-five millions of our products which are shipped to foreign countries, a very large amount is annually sent to the other States, for their own use and consumption. The article of cotton alone, is estimated at 150,000 bales,—which, valued at thirty dollars the bale, would amount to $4,500,000, and constitutes a part of this forced exchange.

Such is the process, and the amount, in part, of the transfer of our property annually to other sections of the country, estimated on the supposition that each section consumes of imported articles, an amount equal in proportion to its population. But the committee are aware that they have rated our share of the consumption far higher than the advocates of the system place it. Some of them rate it as low as five millions of dollars annually; not perceiving that, by thus reducing ours, and raising that of the manufacturing States, in the same proportion, they demonstratively prove how oppressive the system is to us, and how gainful to them; instead of showing, as they suppose, how little we are affected by its operation. Our complaint is, that we are not permitted to consume the fruits of our labor; but that, through an artful and complex system, in violation of every principle of justice, they are transferred from us to others. It is, indeed, wonderful that those who profit by our loss, blinded as they are by self-interest, when reducing our consumption as low as they have, never thought to inquire what became of the immense amount of the products of our industry, which are annually sent out in exchange with the rest of the world; and if we did not consume its proceeds, who did,—and by what means. If, in the ardent pursuit of gain, such a thought had occurred, it would seem impossible, that all the sophistry of self-interest, deceiving as it is, could have disguised from their view our deep oppression, under the operation of the system. Your committee do not intend to represent, that the commercial connection between us and the manufacturing States is wholly sustained by the Tariff system. A great, natural, and profitable commercial communication would exist between us, without the aid of monopoly on their part; which, with mutual advantage, would transfer a large amount of their products to us, and an equal amount of ours to them, as the means of carrying on their commercial operations with other countries. But even this legitimate commerce is greatly affected, to our disadvantage, through the Tariff system; the very object of which is, to raise the price of labor, and the profits of capital, in the manufacturing States,—which, from the nature of things, cannot be done, without raising, correspondingly, the price of all products, in the same quarter, as well those protected, as those not protected. That such would be the effect, we know has been urged in argument mainly to reconcile all classes in those States to the system; and with such success, as to leave us no room to doubt its correctness; and yet, such are the strange contradictions, in which the advocates of an unjust cause must ever involve themselves, when they attempt to sustain it, that the very persons, who urge the adoption of the system in one quarter, by holding out the temptation of high prices for all they make, turn round and gravely inform us, that its tendency is to depress, and not to advance prices. The capitalist, the farmer, the wool-grower, the merchant and laborer, in the manufacturing States, are all to receive higher rates of wages and profits,—while we, who consume, are to pay less for the products of their labor and capital. As contradictory and absurd as are their arguments, they, at least, conclusively establish the important fact, that those who advance them are conscious that the proof of the partial and oppressive operation of the system, is unanswerable if it be conceded that we, in consequence, pay higher prices for what we consume. Were it possible to meet this conclusion on other grounds, it could not be, that men of sense would venture to encounter such palpable contradictions. So long as the wages of labor, and the profits of capital, constitute the principal elements of price, as they ever must, the one or the other argument—that addressed to us, or that to the manufacturing States—must be false. But, in order to have a clear conception of this important point, the committee propose to consider more fully the assertion, that it is the tendency of high duties, by affording protection, to reduce, instead of to increase prices; and if they are not greatly mistaken, it will prove, on examination, to be utterly erroneous.

Before entering on the discussion, and in order to avoid misapprehension, the committee will admit, that there is a single exception. When a country is fully prepared to manufacture, that is, when wages and interest are as low, and natural advantages as great, as in the countries from which it draws its supplies, it may happen, that high duties, by starting manufactories, under such circumstances, may be followed by a permanent reduction in prices; and which, if the Government had the power, and the people possessed sufficient guarantees against abuse, might render it wise and just, in reference to the general interest, in many instances to afford protection to infant manufacturing establishments. But, where permanent support is required,—which must ever be the case when a country is not ripe,—such duties must ever be followed by increased prices. The temporary effect may be different, from various causes. Against this position, it is urged, that the price depends on the proportion between the supply and demand,—that protection, by converting mere consumers into rival manufacturers, must increase the supply without raising the demand,—and, consequently, must tend to reduce prices. If it were necessary, it might be conclusively shown, that this tendency must be more than countervailed, by subtracting, as must ever be the case when the system is forced, capital and labor from more profitable, and turning them to less profitable pursuit, by an expensive bounty, paid out of the labor of the country. But, admitting the argument to be true, the reduction of price must be in proportion to the addition made to the general supply of the commercial world, which is so great that, if we were to suppose our share of the demand to be wholly withdrawn, its tendency to reduce the general price would be small compared to the tendency to high prices, in consequence of the high duties. But the argument rests on an assumption wholly false. It proceeds on the supposition that, without the Tariff, the manufacturing States would not have become such,—than which nothing can be more erroneous. They had no alternative, but to emigrate, or to manufacture. How could they otherwise obtain clothing or other articles necessary for their supply? How could they pay for them? To Europe they could ship almost nothing. Their agricultural products are nearly the same with those of that portion of the globe; and the only two articles, grain and lumber, in the production of which they have advantages, are, in that quarter, either prohibited, or subject to high duties. From us, who are purely an agricultural people, they could draw nothing but the products of the soil. The question, then, is not, whether those States should or should not manufacture,—for necessity, and the policy of other nations had decided that question,—but whether they should, with or without a bounty. It was our interest that they should without. It would compel them to contend with the rest of the world in our market, in free and open competition; the effects of which would have been, a reduction of prices to the lowest point; thereby enabling us to exchange the products of our labor most advantageously,—giving little, and receiving much; while, on the other hand, in order to meet European competition, they would have been compelled to work at the lowest wages and profits. To avoid this, it was their interest to manufacture with a bounty; by which our situation was completely reversed. They were relieved by our depression. Thus, through our political connection, by a perversion of the powers of the Constitution, which was intended to protect the States of the Union in the enjoyment of their natural advantages, they have stripped us of the blessings bestowed by nature, and converted them to their own advantage. Restore our advantages, by giving us free trade with the world, and we would become, what they now are by our means, the most flourishing people on the globe. But these are withheld from us under the fear that, with their restoration, they would become, what we are by their loss, among the most depressed.

Having answered the argument in the abstract, the committee will not swell their report by considering the various instances which have been quoted, to show that prices have not advanced since the commencement of the system. We know that they would instantly fall nearly fifty per cent., if its burdens were removed; and that is sufficient for us to know. Many and conclusive reasons might be urged, to show why, from other causes, prices have declined since that period. The fall in the price of raw materials,—the effects of the return of peace,—the immense reduction in the amount of the circulating medium of the world, by the withdrawal from circulation of a vast amount of paper, both in this country and in Europe,—the important improvements in the mechanical and chemical arts,—and, finally, the still progressive depression arising from the great improvements which preceded that period a short time, particularly in the use of steam and the art of spinning and weaving,—have all contributed to this result. The final reduction of prices, which must take place in the articles whose production is affected by such improvements, cannot be suddenly realized. Another generation will probably pass away, before they will reach that point of depression which must follow their universal introduction.

We are told, by those who pretend to understand our interest better than we do, that the excess of production, and not the Tariff, is the evil which afflicts us; and that our true remedy is, a reduction of the quantity of cotton, rice, and tobacco, which we raise, and not a repeal of the Tariff. They assert, that low prices are the necessary consequence of excess of supply, and that the only proper correction is in diminishing the quantity. We would feel more disposed to respect the spirit in which the advice is offered, if those from whom it comes accompanied it with the weight of their example. *They* also, occasionally, complain of low prices; but instead of diminishing the supply, as a remedy for the evil, demand an enlargement of the market, by the exclusion of all competition. *Our market is the world;* and as we cannot imitate their example by enlarging it for our products, through the exclusion of others, we must decline their advice,—which, instead of alleviating, would increase our embarrassments. We have no monopoly in the supply of our products; one half of the globe may produce them. Should we reduce our production, others stand ready, by increasing theirs, to take our place; and, instead of raising prices, we would only diminish our share of the supply. We are thus compelled to produce, on the penalty of losing our hold on the general market. Once lost, it may be lost for ever;—and lose it we must, if we continue to be constrained, as we now are, on the one hand, by the general competition of the world, to sell *low;* and, on the other, by the Tariff to buy *high.* We cannot withstand this double action. Our ruin must follow. In fact, our only permanent and safe remedy is, not from the rise in the price of what we *sell,* in which we can receive but little aid from our Government, but a reduction in the price of what we *buy;* which is prevented by the interference of the Government. Give us a free and open competition in our own market, and we fear not to encounter like competition in the general market of the world. If, under all our discouragement by the acts of our Government, we are still able to contend there against the world, can it be doubted, if this impediment were removed, we would force out all competition; and thus, also enlarge our market,—not by the oppression of our fellow-citizens of other States, but by our industry, enterprise, and natural advantages.

But while the system prevents this great enlargement of our foreign market, and endangers what remains to us, its advocates attempt to console us by the growth of the home market for our products, which, according to their calculation, is to compensate us amply for all our losses; though, in the leading article of our products, cotton, the home market now consumes but a sixth; and if the prohibitory system as to cotton goods were perfected by the exclusion of all importations, the entire consumption of cotton goods would not raise the home consumption of cotton above a fifth of what we raise.

In the other articles, rice and tobacco, it is much less. But brilliant prospects are held out, of our immense export trade in cotton goods, which is to consume an immense amount of the raw material,—without reflecting to what countries they are to be shipped. Not to Europe, for there we will meet prohibition for prohibition;—not to the Southern portions of this continent, for already they have been taught to imitate our prohibitory policy. The most sanguine will not expect extensive or profitable markets in the other portions of the globe. But, admitting that no other impediment existed, the system itself is an effectual barrier against extensive exports. The very means which secures the domestic market must lose the foreign. High wages and profits are an effectual stimulus when enforced by monopoly, as in our market, but they must be fatal to competition in the open and free market of the world. Besides, when manufactured articles are exported, they must follow the same law to which the products of the soil are subject when exported. They will be sent out in order to be exchanged for the products of other countries; and if these products be taxed, on their introduction as a back return, it has been demonstrated that, like all other taxes on exchange, it must be paid by the producer of the articles. The nature of the operation will be seen, if it be supposed, in their exchange with us, instead of receiving our products free of duty, the manufacturer had to pay forty-five per cent, in the back return, on the cotton and other products which they may receive from us in exchange. If to these insuperable impediments to a large export trade it be added, that our country rears the products of almost every soil and climate, and that scarcely an article can be imported, but what may come in competition with some of the products of our arts or our soil, and consequently ought to be excluded on the principles of the system, it must be apparent, when perfected, the system itself must essentially exclude exports; unless we should charitably export for the supply of the wants of others, without expecting a return trade. The loss of the exports, and with it the imports also, must, in truth, be the end of the system. If we export, we must import; and if we exclude all imported products which come in competition with ours, unless we can invent new articles of exchange, or enlarge, tenfold, the consumption of the few which we cannot produce, with the ceasing of importation, exportation must also cease. If it did not, then neither would importation cease; and the continuance of imports must be followed, as stated, by that of exports;—and this again would require—in order to complete the system by excluding competition in our own markets—new duties; and thus, an incessant and unlimited increase of duties would be the result of the competition, of which the manufacturing States complain. The evil is in the exports,—and the most simple and efficient system to secure the home market, would, in fact, be, to prohibit exports; and as the Constitution only prohibits duties on exports, and as duties are not *prohibition,* we may yet witness this addition to the system;—the same construction of the instrument which justifies the system itself, would equally justify this, as a necessary means to perfect it.

The committee deemed it more satisfactory to present the operation of the system on the staple States generally, than its peculiar operation on this. In fact, they had not the data, had they felt the inclination, to distinguish the oppression under which this State labors, from that of the other staple States. The fate of the one must be that of the others. It may, however, be truly said, that we are among the greatest sufferers. No portion of the world, in proportion to population and wealth, ever exchanged with other countries a greater amount of its products. With the proceeds of the sales of a few great staples we purchase almost all our supplies; and that system must, indeed, act with the desolation of a famine on such a people, where the Government exacts a tax of nearly fifty per cent, on so large a proportion of their exchanges, in order that a portion of their fellow-citizens might, in effect, lay one as high on the residue.

The committee have, thus far, considered the question in its relative effects on the staple and manufacturing States,—comprehending, under the latter, all those that support the Tariff system. It is not for them to determine whether all those States have an equal interest in its continuance. It is manifest that their situation, in respect to its operation, is very different. While, in some, the manufacturing interest wholly prevails,—in others, the commercial and navigating interests,—and in a third, the agricultural interest greatly predominates,—as is the case in all the Western States. It is difficult to conceive what real interest the last can have in the system. They manufacture but little, and must consequently draw their supplies, principally, either from abroad, or from the real manufacturing States; and, in either case, must pay the increased price in consequence of the high duties, which, at the same time, must diminish their means with ours, from whom they are principally derived, through an extensive interior commercial intercourse. From the nature of our commercial connections, our loss must precede theirs; but theirs will with certainty follow, unless compensation for the loss of our trade can be found somewhere in the system. Its authors have informed us that it consists of two parts,—of which *protection* is the essence of one, and *appropriation* of the other. In both capacities it impoverishes us,—and in both it enriches the real manufacturing States. The agricultural States of the West are differently affected. As a *protective* system, they lose in common with us,—and it will remain with them to determine, whether an adequate compensation can be found, in appropriations for internal improvements, or any other purpose, for the steady and rich returns which a free exchange of the produce of their fertile soil with the staple States must give, provided the latter be left in full possession of their natural advantages.

The question, in what manner the loss and gain of the system distribute themselves among the several classes of society, is intimately connected with that of their distribution among the several sections. Few subjects present more important points for consideration; but as it is not possible for the committee to enter fully into the discussion of them, without swelling their report beyond all reasonable bounds, they will pass them over with a few brief and general remarks.

The system has not been sufficiently long in operation with us, to display its real character in reference to the point now under discussion. To understand its ultimate tendency, in distributing the wealth of society among the several classes, we must turn our eyes to Europe, where it has been in action for centuries,—and operated as one among the efficient causes of that great inequality of property which prevails in most European countries. No system can be more efficient to rear up a moneyed aristocracy. Its tendency is, to make the poor poorer, and the rich richer. Heretofore, in our country, this tendency has displayed itself principally in its effects, as regards the different sections,—but the time will come when it will produce the same results between the several classes in the manufacturing States. After we are exhausted, the contest will be between the capitalists and operatives; for into these two classes it must, ultimately, divide society. The issue of the struggle here must be the same as it has been in Europe. Under the operation of the system, wages must sink more rapidly than the prices of the necessaries of life, till the operatives will be reduced to the lowest point,—when the portion of the products of their labor left to them, will be barely sufficient to preserve existence. For the present, the pressure of the system is on our section. Its effects on the staple States produce almost universal suffering. In the mean time, an opposite state of things exists in the manufacturing States. For the present, every interest among them,—except that of foreign trade and navigation, flourishes. Such must be the effect of a monopoly of so rich and extensive a market as that of the Southern States, till it is impoverished,—as ours rapidly must be, by the operation of the system, when its natural tendencies, and effects on the several classes of the community, will unfold themselves, as has been described by the committee.

It remains to be considered, in tracing the effects of the system, whether the gain of one section of the country be equal to the loss of the other. If such were the fact,—if all we lose be gained by the citizens of the other sections, we would, at least, have the satisfaction of thinking that, however unjust and oppressive, it was but a transfer of property, without diminishing the wealth of the community. Such, however, is not the fact; and to its other mischievous consequences we must add, that it destroys much more than it transfers. Industry cannot be forced out of its natural channel without loss; and this, with the injustice, constitutes the objection to the improper intermeddling of the Government with the private pursuits of individuals, who must understand their own interests better than the Government. The exact loss from such intermeddling, it may be difficult to ascertain, but it is not, therefore, the less certain. The committee will not undertake to estimate the millions, which are annually lost to our country, under the existing system; but some idea may be formed of its magnitude, by stating, that it is, at least, equal to the difference between the profits of our manufacturers, and the duties imposed for their protection, where these are not prohibitory. The lower the profit, and the higher the duty (if not, as stated, prohibitory),—the greater the loss. If, with these certain data, the evidence reported by the Committee on Manufactures at the last session of Congress, be examined, a pretty correct opinion may be formed of the extent of the loss of the country,—provided the manufacturers have fairly stated their case. With a duty of about forty per cent, on the leading articles of consumption (if we are to credit the testimony reported), the manufacturers did not realize, generally, a profit equal to the legal rate of interest; which would give a loss of largely upwards of thirty per cent to the country on its products. It is different with the foreign articles of the same description. On them, the country, at least, loses nothing. There, the duty passes into the Treasury,—lost, indeed, to the Southern States, out of whose labor, directly or indirectly, it must, for the most part, be paid,—but transferred, through appropriations in a hundred forms, to the rockets of others. It is thus the system is cherished by appropriations; and well may its advocates affirm, that *they* constitute an essential portion of the American System. Let this conduit, through which it is so profusely supplied, be closed, and we feel confident that scarcely a State, except a real manufacturing one, would tolerate its burden. A total prohibition of importations, by cutting off the revenue, and thereby the means of making appropriations, would, in a short period, destroy it. But the excess of its loss over its gains leads to the consoling reflection, that its abolition would relieve us much more than it would embarrass the manufacturing States. We have suffered too much to desire to see others afflicted, even for our relief, when it can be possibly avoided. We would rejoice to see our manufactures flourish on any constitutional principle, consistent with justice and the public liberty. It is not against them, but the means by which they have been forced, to our ruin, that we object. As far as a moderate system, founded on imposts for revenue, goes, we are willing to afford protection, though we clearly see that, even under such a system, the national revenue would be based on our labor, and be paid by our industry. With such constitutional and moderate protection, the manufacturer ought to be satisfied. His loss would not be so great as might be supposed. If low duties would be followed by low prices, they would also diminish the costs of manufacturing; and thus the reduction of profit would be less in proportion than the reduction of the prices of the manufactured article. Be this, however, as it may, the General Government cannot proceed beyond this point of protection, consistently with its powers, and justice to the whole. If the manufacturing States deem further protection necessary, it is in their power to afford it to their citizens, within their own limits, against foreign competition, to any extent they may judge expedient. The Constitution authorizes them to lay an impost duty, with the assent of Congress, which, doubtless, would be given; and if that be not sufficient, they have the additional and efficient power of giving a direct bounty for their encouragement,—which the ablest writers on the subject concede to be the least burdensome and most effectual mode of encouragement. Thus, they who are to be benefited, will bear the burden, as they ought; and those who believe it is wise and just to protect manufactures, may have the satisfaction of doing it at their expense, and not at that of their fellow-citizens of the other States, who entertain precisely the opposite opinion.

The committee having presented its views on the partial and oppressive operation of the system, will proceed to discuss the next position which they proposed,—its tendency to corrupt the Government, and to destroy the liberty of the country.

If there be a political proposition universally true,—one which springs directly from the nature of man, and is independent of circumstances,—it is, that irresponsible power is inconsistent with liberty, and must corrupt those who exercise it. On this great principle our political system rests. We consider all powers as delegated by the people, and to be controlled by them, who are interested in their just and proper exercise; and our Governments, both State and General, are but a system of judicious contrivances to bring this fundamental principle into fair, practical operation. Among the most prominent of these is, the responsibility of representatives to their constituents, through frequent periodical elections, in order to enforce a faithful performance of their delegated trust. Without such a check on their powers, however clearly they may be defined and distinctly prescribed, our liberty would be but a mockery. The Government, instead of being directed to the general good, would speedily become but the instrument to aggrandize those who might be intrusted with its administration. On the other hand, if laws were uniform in their operation,—if that which imposed a burden on one, imposed it likewise on all—or that which acted beneficially for one, acted also, in the same manner, for all—the responsibility of representatives to their constituents would alone be sufficient to guard against abuse and tyranny—provided the people be sufficiently intelligent to understand their interest, and the motives and conduct of their public agents. But, if it be supposed that, from diversity of interests in the several classes and sections of the country, the laws act differently, so that the same law, though couched in general terms and apparently fair, shall, in reality, transfer the power and property of one class or section to another,—in such case, responsibility to constituents, which is but the means of enforcing fidelity of representatives to them, must prove wholly insufficient to preserve the purity of public agents, or the liberty of the country. It would, in fact, fall short of the evil. The disease would be in the community itself,—in the constituents, and not their representatives. The opposing interests of the community would engender, necessarily opposing, hostile parties,—organized on this very diversity of interests,—the stronger of which, if the Government provided no efficient check, would exercise unlimited and unrestrained power over the weaker. The relation of equality between the parts of the community, established by the Constitution, would be destroyed, and in its place there would be substituted the relation of sovereign and subject, between the stronger and weaker interests, in its most odious and oppressive form. That this is a possible state of society, even where the representative system prevails, we have high authority. Mr. Hamilton, in the 51st number of the Federalist, says,—"It is of the greatest importance in a republic, not only to guard society against the oppression of its rulers, but to guard one part of society against the injustice of the other part. Different interests necessarily exist in different classes of citizens. If a majority be united by a common interest, the rights of the minority will be insecure." Again—"In a society, under the forms of which the stronger faction can readily unite and oppress the weaker, anarchy may be said as truly to reign, as in a state of nature, where the weaker individual is not secured against the violence of the stronger." We have still higher authority,—the unhappy existing example, of which we are the victims. The committee has labored to little purpose, if they have not demonstrated that the very case, which Mr Hamilton so forcibly describes, does not now exist in our country, under the name of the AMERICAN SYSTEM,—and which, if not timely arrested, must be followed by all the consequences which never fail to spring from the exercise of irresponsible power. On the great and vital point—the industry of the country—which comprehends almost every interest—the interest of the two great sections is opposed. We want free trade,—they restrictions; we want moderate taxes, frugality in the Government, economy, accountability, and a rigid application of the public money to the payment of the debt, and to the objects authorized by the Constitution. In all these particulars, if we may judge by experience, their views of their interest are precisely the opposite. They feel and act, on all questions connected with the American System, as sovereigns,—as men invariably do who impose burdens on others for their own benefit; and we, on the other hand, like those on whom such burdens are imposed. In a word, to the extent stated, the country is divided and organized into two great parties—the one sovereign and the other subject—bearing towards each other all the attributes which must ever accompany that relation, under whatever form it may exist. That our industry is controlled by many, instead of one,—by a majority in Congress, *elected* by a majority in the community having an opposing interest, instead of by *hereditary* rulers,—forms not the slightest mitigation of the evil. In fact, instead of mitigating, it aggravates. In our case, one opposing branch of industry cannot prevail without associating others; and thus, instead of a single act of oppression, we must bear many. The history of the Woollen's Bill will illustrate the truth of this position. The woollen manufacturers found they were too feeble to enforce their exactions alone, and, of necessity, resorted to the expedient, which will ever be adopted in such cases, of associating other interests, till a majority be formed,—and the result of which, in this case, was, that instead of increased duties on woollens alone—which would have been the fact if that interest alone governed, we have to bear equally increased duties on more than a dozen other of the leading articles of consumption. It would be weakness to attempt to disguise the fact,—on a full knowledge of which, and of the danger it threatens, the hope of devising some means of security depends,—that different and opposing interests do, and must ever exist in all societies, against the evils of which representation opposes not the slightest resistance. Laws, so far from being uniform in their operation, are scarcely ever so. It requires the greatest wisdom and moderation to extend over any country a system of equal laws; and it is this very diversity of interests, which is found in all associations of men for a common purpose, be they private or public, that constitutes the main difficulty in forming and administering free and just governments. It is the door through which despotic power has, heretofore, ever entered, and must ever continue to enter, till some effectual barrier be provided. Without some such, it would be folly to hope for the duration of liberty;—as much so as to expect it without representation itself,—and for the same reason. The essence of liberty comprehends the idea of responsible power,—that those who make and execute the laws should be controlled by those on whom they operate,—that the *governed* should *govern*. To prevent rulers from abusing their trusts, constituents must control them through elections; and to prevent the major from oppressing the minor interests of society, the Constitution must provide (as the committee hope to prove it does) a check, founded on the same principle and equally efficacious. In fact, the abuse of delegated power, and the tyranny of the stronger over the weaker interests, are the two dangers, and the only two to be guarded against; and if this be done effectually, liberty must be eternal. Of the two, the latter is the greater and most difficult to resist. It is less perceptible. Every circumstance of life teaches us the liability of delegated power to abuse. We cannot appoint an agent without being admonished of the fact; and, therefore, it has become well understood, and is effectually guarded against in our political institutions. Not so as to the latter. Though it in fact exists in all associations, yet the law, the courts, and the Government itself, act as a check to its extreme abuse in most cases of private and subordinate companies, which prevents the full display of its real tendency. But let it be supposed that there was no paramount authority,—no court, no government to control, what sober individual, who expected himself to act honestly, would place his property in joint-stock with any number of individuals, however respectable, to be disposed of by the unchecked will of the majority, whether acting in a body as stockholders, or through representation, by a direction? Who does not see that a major and a minor interest would, sooner or later, spring up, and that the result would be that, after the stronger had divested the feebler of all interest in the concern, they would, in turn, divide until the whole would centre in a single interest? It is the principle which must ever govern such associations; and what is government itself, but a great joint-stock company, which comprehends every interest, and which, as there can be no higher power to restrain its natural operation, must, if not checked within itself, follow the same law? The actual condition of our race in every country, at this and all preceding periods, attests the truth of the remark. No government, based on the naked principle that the majority ought to govern, however true the maxim in its proper sense, and under proper restrictions, can preserve its liberty even for a single generation. The history of all has been the same;—violence, injustice, and anarchy,—succeeded by the government of one, or a few, under which the people seek refuge from the more oppressive despotism of the many. Those governments only which provide checks,—which limit and restrain within proper bounds the power of the majority, have had a prolonged existence, and been distinguished for virtue, patriotism, power, and happiness; and, what is strikingly true, they have been thus distinguished almost in exact proportion to the number and efficacy of their checks. If arranged in relation to these, we would place them in the order of the Roman, English, Spartan, the United Provinces, the Athenian, and several of the small confederacies of antiquity; and if arranged according to the higher attributes which have been enumerated, they would stand almost precisely in the same order. That this coincidence is not accidental, we may be fully assured. The latest and most profound investigator of the Roman History and Constitution (Niebuhr), has conclusively shown that, after the expulsion of the kings, this great commonwealth continued to decline in power, and was the victim of the most violent domestic struggles, which tainted both public and private morals, till the passage of the Licinian law, which gave to the people an efficient veto through their tribunes, as a check on the predominant power of the Patricians. From that period she began to rise superior to all other States in virtue, patriotism, and power. May we profit by the example, and restore the almost lost virtue and patriotism of the Republic, by giving due efficiency, in practice, to the check which our Constitution has provided against a danger so threatening,—and which constitutes the only efficient remedy against that unconstitutional and dangerous system which the committee have been considering,—as they will now proceed to show.

The committee has demonstrated that the present disordered state of our political system originated in the diversity of interests which exists in the country;—a diversity recognized by the Constitution itself, and to which it owes one of its most distinguished and peculiar features,—the division of the delegated powers between the State and General Governments. Our short experience, before the formation of the present Government, had conclusively shown that, while there were powers which in their nature were local and peculiar, and which could not be exercised by all, without oppression to some of the parts,—so, also, there were those which, in their operation, necessarily affected the whole, and could not, therefore, be exercised by any of the parts, without affecting injuriously the others. On this different character, by which powers are distinguished in their geographical operation, our political system was constructed. Viewed in relation to them, to a certain extent we have a community of interests, which can only be justly and fairly supervised by concentrating the will and authority of the several States in the General Government; while, at the same time, the States have distinct and separate interests, over which no supervision can be exercised by the general power without injustice and oppression. Hence the division in the exercise of sovereign powers. In drawing the line between the powers of the two—the General and State Governments—the great difficulty consisted in determining correctly to which of the two the various political powers ought to belong. This difficult task was, however, performed with so much success that, to this day, there is an almost entire acquiescence in the correctness with which the line was drawn. It would be extraordinary if a system, thus resting with such profound wisdom on the diversity of geographical interests among the States, should make no provision against the dangers to which its very basis might be exposed. The framers of our Constitution have not exposed themselves to the imputation of such weakness. When their work is fairly examined, it will be found that they have provided, with admirable skill, the most effective remedy; and that, if it has not prevented the danger with which the system is now threatened, the fault is not theirs, but ours, in neglecting to make its proper application. In the primary division of the sovereign powers, and in their exact and just classification, as stated, are to be found the first provisions or checks against the abuse of authority on the part of the absolute majority. The powers of the General Government are particularly enumerated and specifically delegated; and all powers not expressly delegated, or which are not necessary and proper to carry into effect those that are so granted, are reserved expressly to the States or the people. The Government is thus positively restricted to the exercise of those general powers that were supposed to act uniformly on all the parts,—leaving the residue to the people of the States, by whom alone, from the very nature of these powers, they can be justly and fairly exercised, as has been stated.

Our system, then, consists of two distinct and independent Governments. The general powers, expressly delegated to the General Government, are subject to its sole and separate control; and the States cannot, without violating the constitutional compact, interpose their authority to check, or in any manner to counteract its movements, so long as they are confined to the proper sphere. So, also, the peculiar and local powers reserved to the States are subject to their exclusive control; nor can the General Government interfere, in any manner, with them, without violating the Constitution.

In order to have a full and clear conception of our institutions, it will be proper to remark that there is, in our system, a striking distinction between *Government* and *Sovereignty*. The separate governments of the several States are vested in their Legislative, Executive, and Judicial Departments; while the sovereignty resides in the people of the States respectively. The powers of the General Government are also vested in its Legislative, Executive, and Judicial Departments, while the sovereignty resides in the people of the several States who created it. But, by an express provision of the Constitution, it may be amended or changed by three fourths of the States; and thus each State, by assenting to the Constitution with this provision, has modified its original right as a sovereign, of making its individual consent necessary to any change in its political condition; and, by becoming a member of the Union, has placed this important power in the hands of three fourths of the States,—in whom the highest power known to the Constitution actually resides. Not the least portion of this high sovereign authority resides in Congress, or any of the departments of the General Government. They are but the creatures of the Constitution, and are appointed but to execute its provisions; and, therefore, any attempt by all, or any of these departments, to exercise any power which, in its consequences, may alter the nature of the instrument, or change the condition of the parties to it, would be an act of usurpation.

It is thus that our political system, resting on the great principle involved in the recognized diversity of geographical interests in the community, has, in theory, with admirable sagacity, provided the most efficient check against their dangers. Looking to facts, the Constitution has formed the States into a community only to the extent of their common interests; leaving them distinct and independent communities as to all other interests, and drawing the line of separation with consummate skill, as before stated. It is manifest that, so long as this beautiful theory is adhered to in practice, the system, like the atmosphere, will press equally on all the parts. But reason and experience teach us that theory of itself, however excellent, is nugatory, unless there be means of efficiently enforcing it in practice;—which brings under consideration the highly important question.—What means are provided by the system for enforcing this fundamental provision?

If we look to the history and practical operation of the system, we shall find, on the side of the States, no means resorted to in order to protect their reserved rights against the encroachments of the General Government; while the latter has, from the beginning, adopted the most efficient to prevent the States from encroaching on those delegated to them. The 25th section of the Judiciary Act, passed in 1789,—immediately after the Constitution went into operation,—provides for an appeal from the State courts to the Supreme Court of the United States in all cases, in the decision of which, the construction of the Constitution,—the laws of Congress, or treaties of the United States may be involved; thus giving to that high tribunal the right of final interpretation, and the power, in reality, of nullifying the acts of the State Legislatures whenever, in their opinion, they may conflict with the powers delegated to the General Government. A more ample and complete protection against the encroachments of the governments of the several States cannot be imagined; and to this extent the power may be considered as indispensable and constitutional. But, by a strange misconception of the nature of our system,—and, in fact, of the nature of government,—it has been regarded as the ultimate power, not only of protecting the General Government against the encroachments of the governments of the States, but also of the encroachments of the former on the latter;—and as being, in fact, the only means provided by the Constitution of confining all the powers of the system to their proper constitutional spheres; and, consequently, of determining the limits assigned to each. Such a construction of its powers would, in fact, raise one of the departments of the General Government above the parties who created the constitutional compact, and virtually invest it with the authority to alter, at its pleasure, the relative powers of the General and State Governments, on the distribution of which, as established by the Constitution, our whole system rests;—and which, by an express provision of the instrument, can only be altered by three fourths of the States, as has already been shown. It would go farther. Fairly considered, it would, in effect, divest the people of the States of the sovereign authority, and clothe that department with the robe of supreme power. A position more false and fatal cannot be conceived. Fortunately, it has been so ably refuted by Mr. Madison, in his Report to the Virginia Legislature in 1800, on the Alien and Sedition Acts, as to supersede the necessity of further comments on the part of the committee. Speaking of the right of the State to interpret the Constitution for itself, in the last resort, he remarks:— "It has been objected that the Judicial Authority is to be regarded as the sole expositor of the Constitution. On this objection, it might be observed,—*first*— that there may be instances of usurped power" (the case of the Tariff is a striking illustration of the truth), "which the forms of the Constitution could never draw within the control of the Judicial Department;—*secondly,*—that if the decision of the Judiciary be raised above the authority of the sovereign parties to the Constitution, the decision of the other departments, not carried by the forms of the Constitution before the Judiciary, must be equally authoritative and final with the decision of that department. But the proper answer to the objection is, that the resolution of the General Assembly relates to those great and extraordinary cases in which the forms of the Constitution may prove ineffectual against infractions dangerous to the essential rights of the parties to it. The resolution supposes that dangerous powers not delegated, may not only be usurped and exercised by the other departments, but that the Judicial Department also may exercise or sanction dangerous powers beyond the grant of the Constitution; and consequently, that the ultimate right of the parties to the Constitution to judge whether the compact has been dangerously violated, must extend to violations by one delegated authority as well as by another; by the Judiciary as well as by the Executive or the Legislative. However true, therefore, it may be that the Judicial Department is, in all questions submitted to it by the forms of the Constitution, to decide in the last resort, this resort must necessarily be considered the last in relation to the authorities of the other departments of the Government; not in relation to the rights of the parties to the constitutional compact, from which the Judicial and all other departments hold their delegated trusts. On any other hypothesis the delegation of judicial power would annul the authority delegating it; and the concurrence of this department with others in usurped powers might subvert for ever, and beyond the possible reach of any rightful remedy, the very Constitution which all were instituted to preserve."

As a substitute for the rightful remedy, in the last resort, against the encroachments of the General Government on the reserved powers, resort has been had to a rigid construction of the Constitution. A system like ours, of divided powers, must necessarily give great importance to a proper system of construction; but it is perfectly clear that no rule of construction, however perfect, can, in fact, prescribe bounds to the operation of power. All such rules constitute, in fact, but an appeal from the minority to the justice and reason of the majority; and if such appeals were sufficient of themselves to restrain the avarice or ambition of those vested with power, then may a system of technical construction be sufficient to protect against the encroachment of power; but, on such supposition, reason and justice might alone be relied on, without the aid of any constitutional or artificial restraint whatever. Universal experience, in all ages and countries, however, teaches that power can only be restrained by power, and not by reason and justice; and that all restrictions on authority, unsustained by an equal antagonist power, must for ever prove wholly inefficient in practice. Such, also, has been the decisive proof of our own short experience. From the beginning, a great and powerful minority gave every force of which it was susceptible to construction, as a means of restraining the majority of Congress to the exercise of its proper powers; and though that original minority, through the force of circumstances, has had the advantage of becoming a majority, and to possess, in consequence, the administration of the General Government during the greater portion of its existence, yet we this day witness, under these most favorable circumstances, such an extension of its powers as to leave to the States scarcely a right worth the possessing. In fact, the power of construction, on which its advocates relied to preserve the rights of the States, has been wielded, as it ever must be, if not checked, to destroy those rights. If the minority has a right to prescribe its rule of construction, a majority, on its part, will exercise a similar right; but with this striking difference,— that the right of the former will be a mere nullity against that of the latter. But that protection, which the minor interests must ever fail to find in any technical system of construction, may be found in the reserved rights of the States themselves, if they be properly called into action; and there only will they ever be found of sufficient efficacy. The right of protecting their powers results, necessarily, by the most simple and demonstrative arguments, from the very nature of the relation subsisting between the States and General Government.

If it be conceded, as it must be by every one who is the least conversant with our institutions, that the sovereign powers delegated are divided between the General and State Governments, and that the latter hold their portion by the same tenure as the former, it would seem impossible to deny to the States the right of deciding on the infractions of their powers, and the proper remedy to be applied for their correction. The right of judging, in such cases, is an essential attribute of sovereignty,—of which the States cannot be divested without losing their sovereignty itself,—and being reduced to a subordinate corporate condition. In fact, to divide power, and to give to one of the parties the exclusive right of judging of the portion allotted to each, is, in reality, not to divide it at all; and to reserve such exclusive right to the General Government (it matters not by what department to be exercised), is to convert it, in fact, into a great consolidated government, with unlimited powers, and to divest the States, in reality, of all their rights. It is impossible to understand the force of terms, and to deny so plain a conclusion. The opposite opinion can be embraced only on hasty and imperfect views of the relation existing between the States and the General Government. But the existence of the right of judging of their powers, so clearly established from the sovereignty of States, as clearly implies a veto or control, within its limits, on the action of the General Government, on contested points of authority; and this very control is the remedy which the Constitution has provided to prevent the encroachments of the General Government on the reserved rights of the States; and by which the distribution of power, between the General and State Governments, may be preserved for ever inviolable, on the basis established by the Constitution. It is thus effectual protection is afforded to the minority, against the oppression of the majority. Nor does this important conclusion stand on the deduction of reason alone. It is sustained by the highest contemporary authority. Mr. Hamilton, in the number of the Federalist already cited, remarks that,—"in a single republic, all the power surrendered by the people is submitted to the administration of a single government; and usurpations are guarded against, by a division of the government into distinct and separate departments. In the compound republic of America, the power surrendered by the people is first divided between two distinct governments, and then the portion allotted to each subdivided among distinct and separate departments. Hence a double security arises to the rights of the people. The different governments will control each other; at the same time that each will be controlled by itself." He thus clearly affirms the control of the States over the General Government, which he traces to the division in the exercise of the sovereign powers under our political system; and by comparing this control to the veto, which the departments in most of our constitutions respectively exercise over the acts of each other, clearly indicates it as his opinion, that the control between the General and State Governments is of the same character. Mr. Madison is still more explicit. In his report, already alluded to, in speaking on this subject, he remarks;—"The resolutions, having taken this view of the Federal compact, proceed to infer that, in cases of a deliberate, palpable, and dangerous exercise of other powers, not granted by the said compact, the States, who are parties thereto, have the right, and are in duty bound to interpose to arrest the evil, and for maintaining, within their respective limits, the authorities, rights, and liberties appertaining to them. It appears to your committee to be a plain principle, founded in common sense, illustrated by common practice, and essential to the nature of compacts, that where resort can be had to no tribunal superior to the rights of the parties, the parties themselves must be the rightful judges, in the last resort, whether the bargain made has been pursued or violated. The Constitution of the United States was formed by the sanction of the States, given by each in its sovereign capacity. It adds to the stability and dignity, as well as to the authority of the Constitution, that it rests on this solid foundation. The States, then, being parties to the constitutional compact, and in their sovereign capacity, it follows of necessity that there can be no tribunal above their authority to decide, in the last resort, whether the compact made by them be violated; and, consequently, as parties to it, they must themselves decide, in the last resort, such questions as may be of sufficient magnitude to require their interposition." To these the no less explicit opinions of Mr. Jefferson may be added; who, in the Kentucky resolutions on the same subject, which have always been attributed to him,* states that—"The Government, created by this compact, was not made the exclusive or final judge of the extent of the powers delegated to itself; since that would have made its discretion, and not the Constitution, the measure of its powers;—but, as in all other cases of compact between parties having no common judge, each party has an equal right to judge for itself, as well of infractions as of the mode and measure of redress."

To these authorities, which so explicitly affirm the right of the States, in their sovereign capacity, to decide, in the last resort, on the infraction of their rights and the remedy, there may be added the solemn decisions of the Legislatures of two leading States—Virginia and Kentucky—that the power in question rightfully belongs to the States,—and the implied sanction which a majority of the States gave, in the important political revolution which shortly followed, and brought Mr. Jefferson into power. It is scarcely possible to add to the weight of authority by which this fundamental principle in our system is sustained.

The committee have thus arrived, by what they deem conclusive reasoning, and the highest authority, at the constitutional and appropriate remedy against the unconstitutional oppression under which this, in common with the other staple States, labors,—and the menacing danger which now hangs over the liberty and happiness of our country;—and this brings them to the inquiry,—How is the remedy to be applied by the States? In this inquiry a question may be made,—whether a State can interpose its sovereignty through the ordinary Legislature, but which the committee do not deem it necessary to investigate. It is sufficient that plausible reasons may be assigned against this mode of action, if there be one (and there is one) free from all objections. Whatever doubts may be raised as to the question,—whether the respective Legislatures fully represent the sovereignty of the States for this high purpose, there can be none as to the fact that a Convention fully represents them for all purposes whatever. Its authority, therefore, must remove every objection as to form, and leave the question on the single point of the right of the States to interpose at all. When convened, it will belong to the Convention itself to determine, authoritatively, whether the acts of which we complain be unconstitutional; and, if so, whether they constitute a violation so deliberate, palpable, and dangerous, as to justify

---

*Not now a matter of doubt. The manuscript, in his own handwriting, has since been published.—*Editor* [Crallé].

the interposition of the State to protect its rights. If this question be decided in the affirmative, the Convention will then determine in what manner they ought to be declared null and void within the limits of the State; which solemn declaration, based on her rights as a member of the Union, would be obligatory, not only on her own citizens, but on the General Government itself; and thus place the violated rights of the State under the shield of the Constitution.

The committee, having thus established the constitutional right of the States to interpose, in order to protect their reserved powers, it cannot be necessary to bestow much time or attention, in order to meet possible objections;—particularly as they must be raised, not against the soundness of the arguments, by which the position is sustained, and which they deem unanswerable—but against apprehended consequences, which, even if well founded, would be an objection, not so much to the conclusions of the committee, as to the Constitution itself. They are persuaded that, whatever objection may be suggested, it will be found, on investigation, to be destitute of solidity. Under these impressions, the committee propose to discuss such as they suppose may be urged, with all possible brevity.

It may be objected, then,—in the first place, that the right of the States to interpose rests on mere inference, without any express provision in the Constitution; and that it is not to be supposed—if the Constitution contemplated the exercise of powers of such high importance—that it would have been left to inference alone. In answer, the committee would ask, whether the power of the Supreme Court to declare a law unconstitutional is not among the very highest and most important that can be exercised by any department of the Government,—and if any express provision can be found to justify its exercise? Like the power in question, it also rests on mere inference;—but an inference so clear, that no express provision could render it more certain. The simple fact, that the Judges must decide according to law, and that the Constitution is paramount to the acts of Congress, imposes a necessity on the court to declare the latter void whenever, in its opinion, they come in conflict, in any particular case, with the former. So, also, in the question under consideration. The right of the States,—even supposing it to rest on inference, stands on clearer and stronger grounds than that of the Court. In the distribution of powers between the General and State Governments, the Constitution professes to *enumerate* those assigned to the former, in whatever department they may be vested; while the powers of the latter are reserved in general terms, without attempt at enumeration. It may, therefore, constitute a presumption against the former,—that the Court has no right to declare a law unconstitutional, because the power is not enumerated among those belonging to the Judiciary;—while the omission to enumerate the power of the States to interpose in order to protect their rights,—being strictly in accord with the principles on which its framers formed the Constitution, raises not the slightest presumption against its existence. Like all other *reserved* rights, it is to be inferred from the simple fact that it is *not delegated,*—as is clearly the case in this instance.

Again—it may be objected to the power, that it is inconsistent with the necessary authority of the General Government,—and, in its consequences, must lead to feebleness, anarchy, and finally disunion.

It is impossible to propose any limitation on the authority of governments, without encountering, from the supporters of power, this very objection of feebleness and anarchy: and we accordingly find, that the history of every country which has attempted to establish free institutions, proves that, on this point, the opposing parties—the advocates of power and of freedom—have ever separated. It constituted the essence of the controversy between the Patricians and Plebeians in the Roman Republic,—the Tories and Whigs in England,—the Ultras and Liberals in France,—and, finally, the Federalists and Republicans in our own country,—as illustrated by Mr. Madison's Report;—and if it were proposed to give to Russia or Austria a representation of the people, it would form the point of controversy between the Imperial and Popular parties. It is, in fact, not at all surprising that, to a people unacquainted with the nature of liberty, and inexperienced in its blessings, all limitations on supreme power should appear incompatible with its nature, and as tending to feebleness and anarchy. Nature has not permitted us to doubt the necessity of a paramount power in all institutions. All see and feel it; but it requires some effort of reason to perceive that, if not controlled, such power must necessarily lead to abuse;—and still higher efforts to understand that it may be checked without destroying its efficiency. With us, however, who know from our own experience, and that of other free nations, the truth of these positions, and that power can only be rendered useful and secure by being properly checked,—it is, indeed, strange that any intelligent citizen should consider limitations on the authority of government incompatible with its nature;—or should fear danger from any check properly lodged, which may be necessary to guard against usurpation or abuse, and protect the great and distinct interests of the country. That there are such interests represented by the States, and that the States are the only competent powers to protect them, has been sufficiently established; and it only remains, in order to meet the objection, to prove that, for this purpose, the States may be safely vested with the right of interposition.

If the committee do not greatly mistake, the checking or veto power never has, in any country, or under any institutions, been lodged where it was less liable to abuse. The great number, by whom it must be exercised, of the people of a State,—the solemnity of the mode,—a Convention specially called for the purpose, and representing the State in her highest capacity,—the delay,—the deliberation,—are all calculated to allay excitement,—to impress on the people a deep and solemn tone, highly favorable to calm investigation and decision. Under such circumstances, it would be impossible for a mere party to maintain itself in the State, unless the violation of its rights be palpable, deliberate, and dangerous. The attitude in which the State would be placed in relation to the other States,—the force of public opinion which would be brought to bear on her,—the deep reverence for the General Government,—the strong influence of all public men who aspire to office or distinction in the Union,—and, above all, the local parties which must ever exist in the State, and which, in this case, must ever throw the powerful influence of the minority on the side of the General Government,—constitute impediments to the exercise of this high protective right of the State, which must render it safe. So powerful, in fact, are these difficulties, that nothing but truth and a deep sense of oppression on the part of the people of the State, will ever sustain the exercise of the power;—and if it should be attempted under other circumstances, it must speedily terminate in the expulsion of those in power, to be replaced by others who would make a merit of closing the controversy, by yielding the point in dispute.

But, in order to understand more fully what its operation really would be in practice, we must take into the estimate the effect which a recognition of the power would have on the tone of feeling, both of the General and State Governments. On the part of the former, it would necessarily produce, in the exercise of doubtful powers, the most marked moderation. In the discussion of measures involving such powers, the argument would be felt with decisive weight, that the State, also, had the right of judging of the constitutionality of the power; which would cause an abandonment of the measure,—or, at least, lead to such modifications as would make it acceptable. On the part of the State, a feeling of conscious security, depending on herself,—with the effect of moderation and kindness on the part of the General Government, would effectually put down jealousy, hatred, and animosity,—and thus give scope to the natural attachment to our institutions, to expand and grow into the full maturity of patriotism. But withhold this protective power from the State, and the reverse of all these happy consequences must follow;—which the committee will not undertake to describe, as the living example of discord, hatred, and jealousy,—

threatening anarchy and dissolution, must impress on every beholder a more vivid picture than any they could possibly draw. The continuance of this unhappy state must lead to the loss of all affection;—when the Government must be sustained by *force* instead of *patriotism*. In fact, to him who will duly reflect, it must be apparent that, where there are important separate interests, there is no alternative but a veto to protect them, or the military to enforce the claims of the majority interests.

If these deductions be correct,—as can scarcely be doubted,—under that state of moderation and security, followed by mutual kindness, which must accompany the acknowledgment of the right, the necessity of exercising the veto would rarely exist, and the possibility of its abuse, on the part of the State, would be almost wholly removed. Its acknowledged existence would thus supersede its exercise. But suppose in this the committee should be mistaken,—still there exists a sufficient security. As high as this right of interposition on the part of a State may be regarded in relation to the General Government, the constitutional compact provides a remedy against its abuse. There is a higher power,—placed above all by the consent of all,—the creating and preserving power of the system,—to be exercised by three fourths of the States,—and which, under the character of the amending power, can modify the whole system at pleasure,—and to the acts of which none can object. Admit, then, the power in question to belong to the States,—and admit its liability to abuse,—and what are the utmost consequences, but to create a presumption against the constitutionality of the power exercised by the General Government,—which, if it be well founded, must compel them to abandon it;—or, if not, to remove the difficulty by obtaining the contested power in the form of an amendment to the Constitution. If, on an appeal for this purpose, the decision be favorable to the General Government, a disputed power will be converted into an expressly granted power;—but, on the other hand, if it be adverse, the refusal to grant will be tantamount to an inhibition of its exercise: and thus, in either case, the controversy will be determined. And ought not a sovereign State, as a party to the constitutional compact, and as the guardian of her citizens and her peculiar interests, to have the power in question? Without it, the amending power must become obsolete, and the Constitution, through the exercise of construction, in the end utterly subverted. Let us examine the case. The disease is, that a majority of the States, through the General Government, by construction, usurp powers not delegated, and by their exercise, increase their wealth and authority at the expense of the minority. How absurd, then, to expect the injured States to attempt a remedy by proposing an amendment to be ratified by three fourths of the States, when, by supposition, there is a majority opposed to them? Nor would it be less absurd to expect the General Government to propose amendments, unless compelled to that course by the acts of a State. The Government can have no inducement. It has a more summary mode,—the assumption of power by construction. The consequence is clear;—neither would resort to the amending power;—the one, because it would be useless,—and the other, because it could effect its purpose without it;—and thus the highest power known to the Constitution,—on the salutary influence of which, on the operations of our political institutions, so much was calculated, would become, in practice, obsolete, as stated; and in lieu of it, the will of the majority, under the agency of construction, would be substituted, with unlimited and supreme power. On the contrary, giving the right to a State to compel the General Government to abandon its pretensions to a constructive power, or to obtain a positive grant of it, by an amendment to the Constitution, would call efficiently into action, on all important disputed questions, this highest power of the system,—to whose controlling authority no one can object, and under whose operation all controversies between the States and General Government would be adjusted, and the Constitution gradually acquire all the perfection of which it is susceptible. It is thus that the *creating* becomes the *preserving* power; and we may rest assured it is no less true in politics than in theology, that the power which creates can alone preserve,—and that preservation is perpetual creation. Such will be the operation and effect of State interposition.

But it may be objected, that the exercise of the power would have the effect of placing the majority under the control of the minority. If the objection were well founded, it would be fatal. If the majority cannot be trusted, neither can the minority: and to transfer power from the former to the latter, would be but the repetition of the old error, in taking shelter under monarchy or aristocracy, against the more oppressive tyranny of an illy constructed republic. But it is not the consequence of proper checks to change places between the majority and minority. It leaves the power controlled still independent; as is exemplified in our political institutions, by the operation of acknowledged checks. The power of the Judiciary to declare an act of Congress, or of a State Legislature, unconstitutional, is, for its appropriate purpose, a most efficient check; but who that is acquainted with the nature of our Government ever supposed that it ever really vested (when confined to its proper object) a supreme power in the Court over Congress or the State Legislatures? Such was neither the intention, nor is it the effect.

The Constitution has provided another check, which will still further illustrate the nature of their operation. Among the various interests which exist under our complex system, that of large and small States is, perhaps, the most prominent, and among the most carefully guarded in the organization of our Government. To settle the relative weight of the States in the system, and to secure to each the means of maintaining its proper political consequence in its operation, formed one of the most difficult duties in framing the Constitution. No one subject occupied greater space in the proceedings of the Convention. In its final adjustment, the large States had assigned to them a preponderating influence in the House of Representatives, by having therein a weight proportioned to their numbers; but to compensate which, and to secure their political rights against this preponderance, the small States had an equality assigned them in the Senate; while, in the constitution of the Executive branch, the two were blended. To secure the consequence allotted to each, as well as to insure due deliberation in legislating, a veto is allowed to each in the passage of bills; but it would be absurd to suppose that this veto placed either above the other; or was incompatible with the portion of the sovereign power intrusted to the House, the Senate, or the President.

It is thus that our system has provided appropriate checks between the Departments,—a veto to guard the supremacy of the Constitution over the laws, and to preserve the due importance of the States, considered in reference to large and small, without creating discord or weakening the beneficent energy of the Government. And so, also, in the division of the sovereign authority between the General and State Governments,—by leaving to the States an efficient power to protect, by a veto, the minor against the major interests of the community, the framers of the Constitution acted in strict conformity with the principle which invariably prevails throughout the whole system, where separate interests exist. They were, in truth, no ordinary men. They were wise and practical statesmen, enlightened by history and their own enlarged experience, acquired in conducting our country through a most important revolution;—and understood profoundly the nature of man and of government. They saw and felt that there existed in our nature the necessity of government, and government of adequate powers;—that the selfish predominate over the social feelings; and that, without a government of such powers, universal conflict and anarchy must prevail among the component parts of society; but they also clearly saw that, our nature remaining unchanged by change of condition, unchecked power, from this very predominance of the selfish over the social feelings, which rendered government necessary, would, of necessity, lead to corruption and oppression on the part of those vested with its exercise. Thus the necessity of government and of checks originates in the same great principle of our nature; and thus the very selfishness which impels those who have power to desire more, will also, with equal force, impel those on whom power operates to resist aggression; and on the balance of these opposing tendencies, liberty and happiness must for ever depend. This great principle guided in the formation of every part of our political system. There is not one opposing interest throughout the whole that is not counterpoised. Have the rulers a separate interest from the people? To check its abuse, the relation of representative and constituent is created between them, through periodical elections, by which the fidelity of the representative to the constituent is secured. Have the States, as members of the Union, distinct political interests in reference to their magnitude? Their relative weight is carefully settled, and each has its appropriate agent, with a veto on each other, to protect its political consequence. May there be a conflict between the Constitution and the laws, whereby the rights of citizens may be affected? A remedy may be found in the power of the courts to declare the law unconstitutional in such cases as may be brought before them. Are there, among the several States, separate and peculiar geographical interests? To meet this, a particular organization is provided in the division of the sovereign powers between the State and General Governments. Is there danger, growing out of this division, that the State Legislatures may encroach on the powers of the General Government? The authority of the Supreme Court is adequate to check such encroachments. May the General Government, on the other hand, encroach on the rights reserved to the States respectively? To the States respectively—each in its sovereign capacity—is reserved the power, by its veto, or right of interposition, to arrest the encroachment. And, finally, may this power be abused by a State, so as to interfere improperly with the powers delegated to the General Government? There is provided a power, even over the Constitution itself, vested in three fourths of the States, which Congress has the authority to invoke, and may terminate all controversies in reference to the subject, by granting or withholding the right in contest. Its authority is acknowledged by all; and to deny or resist it, would be, on the part of the State, a violation of the constitutional compact, and a dissolution of the political association, as far as it is concerned. This is the ultimate and highest power,—and the basis on which the whole system rests.

That there exists a case which would justify the interposition of this State, in order to compel the General Government to abandon an unconstitutional power, or to appeal to this high authority to confer it by express grant, the committee do not in the least doubt; and they are equally clear in the necessity of its exercise, if the General Government should continue to persist in its improper assumption of powers belonging to the State;—which brings them to the last point they propose to consider,—viz.: When would it be proper to exercise this high power?

If the committee were to judge only by the magnitude of the interests at stake, they would, without hesitation, recommend the call of a Convention without delay. But they deeply feel the obligation of respect for the other members of the confederacy, and the necessity of great moderation and forbearance in the exercise even of the most unquestionable right, between parties who stand connected by the closest and most sacred political compact. With these sentiments, they deem it advisable, after presenting the views of the Legislature in this solemn manner (if the body concur with the committee), to allow time for further consideration and reflection, in the hope that a returning sense of justice on the part of the majority, when they come to reflect on the wrongs which this and the other staple States have suffered, and are suffering, may repeal the obnoxious and unconstitutional acts,—and thereby prevent the necessity of interposing the veto of the State.

The committee are further induced, at this time, to recommend this course, under the hope that the great political revolution, which will displace from power, on the 4th of March next, those who have acquired authority by setting the will of the people at defiance,—and which will bring in an eminent citizen, distinguished for his services to his country, and his justice and patriotism, may be followed up, under his influence, with a complete restoration of the pure principles of our Government. But, in thus recommending delay, the committee wish it to be distinctly understood, that neither doubts of the rightful power of the State, nor apprehension of consequences, constitute the smallest part of their motives. They would be unworthy of the name of freemen,—of Americans,—of Carolinians, if danger, however great, could cause them to shrink from the maintenance of their constitutional rights. But they deem it preposterous to anticipate danger under a system of laws, where a sovereign party to the compact, which formed the Government, exercises a power which, after the fullest investigation, she conscientiously believes to belong to her under the guarantee of the Constitution itself,—and which is essential to the preservation of her sovereignty. The committee deem it not only the right of the State, but her duty, under the solemn sanction of an oath, to interpose, if no other remedy be applied. They interpret the oath to defend the Constitution, not simply as imposing an obligation to abstain from violation, but to prevent it on the part of others. In their opinion, he is as guilty of violating that sacred instrument, who permits an infraction, when it is in his power to prevent it, as he who actually perpetrates the violation. The one may be bolder, and the other more timid,—but the sense of duty must be weak in both.

With these views the committee are solemnly of the impression,—if the present usurpations and the professed doctrines of the existing system be persevered in,—after due forbearance on the part of the State,—that it will be her sacred duty to interpose;—a duty to herself,—to the Union,—to the present, and to future generations,—and to the cause of liberty over the world, to arrest the progress of a usurpation which, if not arrested, must, in its consequences, corrupt the public morals and destroy the liberty of the country.

[NOTE.—The above is indorsed, in the handwriting of the author,— *"Rough draft of what is called the* SOUTH CAROLINA EXPOSITION." On the concluding page is written in the same hand:

"Concluded by a few remarks on the proposition for the State to impose an excise duty on protected articles, and on her consumption of the same. The first disapproved, and the last approved.

"And, finally, with sundry resolutions."

These "remarks" are not preserved; nor the resolutions which accompanied the report. The committee, to whom the subject was referred, reported a series of resolutions, which the reader will find below. Whether they be identical with those referred to, is a matter of conjecture. Those reported and adopted are in the following words (Crallé)]:—

PROTEST.

The Senate and House of Representatives of South Carolina, now met and sitting in General Assembly, through the Hon. William Smith and the Hon. Robert Y. Hayne, their Representatives in the Senate of the United States, do in the name and on behalf of the good people of the said Commonwealth, solemnly protest against the system of protecting duties, lately adopted by the Federal Government, for the following reasons:—

1st. Because the good people of this commonwealth believe, that the powers of Congress were delegated to it, in trust for the accomplishment of certain specified objects which limit and control them, and that every exercise of them, for any other purposes, is a violation of the Constitution as unwarrantable as the undisguised assumption of substantive, independent powers not granted, or expressly withheld.

2d. Because the power to lay duties on imports is, and in its very nature can be, only a means of effecting objects specified by the Constitution; since no free government, and least of all a government of enumerated powers, can, of right, impose any tax, any more than a penalty, which is not at once justified by public necessity and clearly within the scope and purview of the social compact; and since the right of confining appropriations of the public money to such legitimate and constitutional objects is as essential to the liberties of the people, as their unquestionable privilege to be taxed only by their own consent.

3d. Because they believe that the Tariff Law passed by Congress at its last session, and all other acts of which the principal object is the protection of manufacturers, or any other branch of domestic industry, if they be considered as the exercise of a supposed power in Congress to tax the people at its own good will and pleasure, and to apply the money raised to objects not specified in the Constitution, is a violation of these fundamental principles, a breach of a well-defined trust, and a perversion of the high powers vested in the Federal Government for federal purposes only.

4th. Because such acts, considered in the light of a regulation of commerce, are equally liable to objection—since, although the power to regulate commerce, may like other powers be exercised so as to protect domestic manufactures, yet it is clearly distinguishable from a power to do so, *eo nomine,* both in the nature of the thing and in the common acceptation of the terms; and because the confounding of them would lead to the most extravagant results, since the encouragement of domestic industry implies an absolute control over all the interests, resources, and pursuits of a people, and is inconsistent with the idea of any other than a simple, consolidated government.

5th. Because, from the contemporaneous exposition of the Constitution in the numbers of the Federalist (which is cited only because the Supreme Court has recognized its authority), it is clear that the power to regulate commerce was considered by the Convention as only incidentally connected with the encouragement of agriculture and manufactures; and because the power of laying imposts and duties on imports, was not understood to justify, in any case, a prohibition of foreign commodities, except as a means of extending commerce, by coercing foreign nations to a fair reciprocity in their intercourse with us, or for some other bona fide commercial purpose.

6th. Because, whilst the power to protect manufactures is nowhere expressly granted to Congress, nor can be considered as necessary and proper to carry into effect any specified power, it seems to be expressly reserved to the States, by the tenth section of the first article of the Constitution.

7th. Because, even admitting Congress to have a constitutional right to protect manufactures by the imposition of duties or by regulations of commerce, designed principally for that purpose, yet a Tariff, of which the operation is grossly unequal and oppressive, is such an abuse of power, as is incompatible with the principles of a free government and the great ends of civil society,—justice, and equality of rights and protection.

8th. Finally, because South Carolina, from her climate, situation, and peculiar institutions, is, and must ever continue to be, wholly dependent upon agriculture and commerce, not only for her prosperity, but for her very existence as a State—because the valuable products of her soil—the blessings by which Divine Providence seems to have designed to compensate for the great disadvantages under which she suffers in other respects—are among the very few that can be cultivated with any profit by slave labor—and if, by the loss of her foreign commerce, these products should be confined to an inadequate market, the fate of this fertile State would be poverty and utter desolation; her citizens, in despair, would emigrate to more fortunate regions, and the whole frame and constitution of her civil polity, be impaired and deranged, if not dissolved entirely.

Deeply impressed with these considerations, the representatives of the good people of this commonwealth, anxiously desiring to live in peace with their fellow-citizens, and to do all that in them lies to preserve and perpetuate the union of the States and the liberties of which it is the surest pledge,—but feeling it to be their bounden duty to expose and resist all encroachments upon the true spirit of the Constitution, lest an apparent acquiescence in the system of protecting duties should be drawn into precedent,—do, in the name of the commonwealth of South Carolina, claim to enter upon the journals of the Senate, their protest against it as unconstitutional, oppressive, and unjust.

Which Exposition and Protest are respectfully submitted.

J. GREGG, *Chairman.*

Chapter VIII.

"Letter to Samuel D. Ingham, Secretary of the Treasury,"
30 October 1830

In this letter to a close friend and political advisor, Calhoun defended some of the fundamental protective qualities of the Constitution. He explained the "constitutional right" of a state to "interpose" itself between the federal government and its citizens—when the basic freedoms of citizens of the state were threatened. Calhoun also explained that without the recovery of the constitutional protections of minorities, a political majority could become tyrannical.

To Samuel D. Ingham, Secretary of the Treasury

I have not acknowledged your letter of the 29th August at an earlier period, simply because I was much occupied in my domestick concerns, and its contents were of that general nature tho deeply important, which did not require an immediate answer.

You need not, I assure you, give me any assurance of the friendly motives of any thing that comes from you. The experience of more than fifteen years, has afforded me ample proof of your sincere disinterested friendship, which would render it very painful to me, as I am sure it would be to you, to take different sides on any great political question. Few have acted so long and closely together, through so many scenes, and I pray heaven, that nothing may ever place us politically in hostile attitude. In none other can we ever be placed. I do not in the least doubt, that every effort will be made to render the movements in this State as odious as possible, and that ultimately it will be attempted to bring the whole to bear against me. As far as the advocating the great truth, that the States have the constitutional right to interpose and are in duty bound to do so, to protect their citizens against the unconstitutional acts of the General Government, when no other redress can be had, is calculated to identify me with these moves, I am fully so. It is this great constitutional power, which involves the right of veto, or nullification as it has been called, which alone makes our system a federal, instead, of a consolidated Government, and gives it the capacity of extending over so large an extent of country, and to act on so great a diversity of interest, without the most oppressive Tyranny. The assertion of this doctrine, I do most religiously believe, is essential to the union & liberty of the country, and even to almost the existence of the South, placed, as she is, in a minority and distinguished, as she is, from the other sections, by a peculiar population and industry. If entertaining these opinions is to proscribe me from the honors of the country be it so. Believing in them, as I do, I would be traitor to the Constitution and my conscience to abandon them for the paltry consideration of office, or honor. Beyond the maintenance of this great truth, I am no farther responsible for the movements in this State. They were made in opposition to my opinion. I thought the true policy of the State was to hold the executive responsible, for that construction of the Mays Ville Message most favourable to the South, and to wait for a great and successful effort for relief, the period of the payment of the publick debt. A different course was taken; but knowing the patriotism of those, who advocated it, and the purity and disinterestedness of their views I could not but wish them success, tho' I deemed their efforts injudicious.

I entirely concur with you in the opinion, that Pennsylvania will not abandon the principle of the protective system, and, I will add, that she will be supported by the non exporting States, or rather those which have a greater interest in the protective system, than in foreign commerce, and this is the universal conviction of those who are called the State right party in this State, in opposition to what is called the Submission party, who believe in the oppression of the system, but hope, that Pennsylvania and the other States of the majority will finally yield. I must say, however that you are in a great error in supposing, that the movements in the State originate, in any degree, in a system of menace. It is far otherwise. An utter dispair of redress through the General Government is the approximate cause of the movements. You have been deceived by the occasional loose expressions, which will always be thrown out in such political struggles, and which always lead into error, if we fix on them, as the cause of the excitement, or the motive of action.

I would not be doing justice to our intimate and ancient friendship, were I not to state in a case so momentious, and where for the want of coincident of views, we, who have acted so long together may be separated, (tho' it is painful to think of it) were I not to state my conception of the grievance and excitement of the South; not that I hope to bring you to my conception of our case, for I have long seen how the strongest heads and purest hearts are controlled by the positions that they occupy, and the circumstances under which they act; but that, if we must differ, we may respect at least the patriotism of the motives, if not the soundness of the principles, on which we may respectively act. I will be as brief as possible.

To commence with the protective system, we believe that there is a deep diversity of interest between our section and the others, which that system brings into immediate conflict. The object of all our toil and industry is to obtain a supply of the necessaries, the conveniences or luxuries of life. To obtain many of the leading and most essential of these such as iron, woollens, cottons and a thousand others, the North and the South have two different modes, (I may call it,) of fabricating them; the former by the direct manufacture of the articles themselves, and the latter by the exchange of certain great staples, for these supplies. We as essentially make the iron, woollens & other articles we consume by raising cotton, rice & tobacco, as you who make them by your forges, looms, & factories. Turn it as you please the effect of the protective system is to tax our manufacturing process, and to give a bounty to yours. This must be the necessary effect of any tax on the exchange of the products of ours with foreign industry, as much so, as if the North & South both raised the same staples, & if you were, in that case, to levy a tax on the rice, cotton and tobacco raised South of the Potomac, and give the proceeds, as a bounty on that raised North of that river, or rather the Deleware. It is really at bottom a struggle for the home market. Were you to leave us free, we would send our staples abroad, bring home foreign articles in return, and after supplying ourselves, would exchange the balance with you for all of the products of farming, as distinguished from planting, and those articles of manufacture, which you would have such an advantage over the foreign as to enable you to manufacture without protection; but by the protective system you reverse all this. You compel an exchange with you by taxing our exchanges with the rest of the world, thereby obtain possession of our staples, ship them and obtain those foreign supplies, which you need, duty free in point of fact, having previously obtained from us, in the compelled exchange, a profit equal to the duty, which you pay at the custom house for what you consume. It is obvious, if this view be correct, which I think is certain, that we can no more shift from us the burden of an impost, than we could an export duty, and that they are substantially the same in effect, as far as we are

concerned. I say substantially, because I acknowledge, there is a slight difference, but which is not worth the discussion. To illustrate this position, so essential to the just understanding of this great conflict between this and the other
sections, suppose the staple States did their own export and import business, and
suppose, to simplyfy the process of reason in order to show, what is the actual
operation on them as producing States, that the profits on the shipments simply covered all charges of shipment. They ship say $32,000,000 annually, tho it
is probable, that it is nearer $35,000,000 and that the duty is on an average 40
percent, tho I think it nearer 50. If they consumed all of the return cargo all
acknowledge, that they would pay the duty exclusively, that is that they would
pay into the treasury annually $12,800,000. But let us suppose they consumed
but half of their imports, or any other proportion, and disposed of the residue
to the rest of the Union. Now, if the tariff really does not raise the prices of the
articles, on which it is laid, as is contended for by most of its supporters, it is
clear, that the staple States could not in that case add the duty to the price of the
imported article and consequently must bear it themselves, & of course pay the
whole duty of $12,800,000, as if they were the sole consumers. But let us see,
in case the price of the foreign article should rise, if that would vary the result.
The duty in that event could be added to the foreign prices, and there would
be a *monied* remuneration to the South for the surplus that she did not consume
herself, but the monied remuneration would prove to be a *nominal* remuneration. With the foreign, the domestick article of the same kind and quality would
take an equal rise; for it would be absurd to suppose that there could be two
prices for articles of the same quality at the same time, & place. In the purchase
of these, to protect which is the object of the Tariff, the South would lose, as
much as she would gain in the money price in the sale of the foreign articles, to
the non exporting States. These protected articles furnish the great mass of her
exchanges with those States. The case I acknowledge is some what different, as
to the unprotected articles, or rather those which need none, and this difference
constitutes the only difference between the effect of an export & import duty
on the South. I acknowledge, that the 40 per cent on the foreign imports will
not raise the prices of these articles that need no protection? forty per cent, but
it must at the same time be conceded, that by the diversion of labour and capital in the North from the production of these in which they have a natural
advantage in our market, to that of the protected articles, they come much
higher to the staple States, and to that extent constitute a real tax on them. The
difference between this rise, and the forty percent, which all have assumed to
be the average import duty is really the only part of the import duty, which the

South can shift of what she consumes in exchange with the other sections, and the rest of the world; and surely this difference is much more than covered by the export of the products of our labour, which go direct to those sections, without appearing in the foreign exports of the staple States. It thus appears, that the tax paid by those States to the protective system, and to the revenue of the Government is at least equal to a duty of 40 percent on their foreign exports, and, if we add, that this enormous amount on their industry is spent almost exclusively in the other States, we will have a true conception of the unequal operation of the system. If this conclusion be correct, and I think it cannot be contested, it follows, that this Union is divided, as far as the monied action of the Government is concerned into two sections, one paying and the other receiving, that is they have in this great operation of the Government, which is of so preëminent a nature, that Edmund Burke, the greatest of political philosophers, calls the state itself, directly opposing relations; the very opposing relations in fact which exist between King and subject, and which by the concession of all, is despotism itself, if unchecked by constitutional guards. The necessity of these guards does not spring from the fact that one may be called King and the other subject, but from the relation to which I refer, and which, I think, I have established to exist between the two great sections of our country, and against which, if our Constitution does not guard, it places us in the same despotick relation to the Government, as a subject stands to an absolute monarch. To protect the subject against the Government is in fact the only object & value of a Constitution. The government needs no constitution. It is the governed, that needs its protection. The great question then is, does our Government afford this protection under its practical operation, or can it in fact do so, under any other construction, than that for which we contend? To determine this question, so deeply important to our feeble section, it will be necessary to determine who constitutes the governing power in our country, as the system now operates. It is clear that the President, the majority of the two houses of Congress and of the Judges for the time being exercise the powers of government, but it is equally clear that they are but agents subject to be controlled by a higher power, which power is really the government. Whose agents then are they and to whom responsible? Certainly the majority who elected them; the majority of the members of the Senate to the majority of the States, of that of the House of Representatives to the majority of the people of the States, the President, to the majority of the two in a compound ratio, and the Judges of a joint action of both. If then a majority of the States & the people of the States in any of the sections should come to settle down on any common point of interest, however oppressive the promotion of it might be to the other portion of the country, the weaker portion to the extent, at least, would in fact be excluded from all control over the operation of the Government, as much so as if they were unrepresented; and if such majority has the sole and exclusive right of interpreting the Constitution, whether by their Executive, Legislative or Judicial Department it matters not, the subject minority, on whom the Government really acts, and for whose protection it was really intended, (for the governing majority really needs no constitutional protection,) would be without protection. For surely there is not the least practical difference between a government of unlimitted powers, and one of limited powers on paper, but with unlimitted right of construction. That there is such a fixed majority settled down on the *common interest* of the *protective system,* your letter & all we see proclaim, and that common interest can only be promoted by the sacrifice of the other portion, I think, I have demonstrated, and that the condition of the latter is hopeless, unless the States, as we contend, have the right of interposition, is so clear, as not to admit of farther proof. What must be the ruinous consequences of this state of things to us in the South, and its final destructive effect on our system of government I have not time to trace.

I have written you a very long letter, far longer than what I intended, but you must attribute the intrusion on your patience, my dear friend, to the value, which I place on your friendship, and the deep solicitude, which I feel for liberty and happiness of our country. Do examine with care, as I am sure you will do with candor, what I have written, and if there be error point it out to me. I would be deeply gratified to be convinced that I am mistaken. It would relieve me from much solicitude, and prevent the possibility of my seperation politically from you, & many other friends, whose good opinion I value, as I do my life. Till I am convinced of error, I must act under the high & solemn responsibility of duty, tho I know it must place me under the ban of the Republick, as much so, as any unhappy subject, who is forced to contest the power of his sovereign, and for the same reason. This, however, I consider the least of evils, and would willingly bear that, and, I might say with truth, martyrdom itself, if I could thereby place the liberty and union of these States on a desirable basis.

I write to you in the confidence of long established friendship. You are permitted to show it to our mutual friend Virgil Maxcy, as an answer to two letters to which I am indebted to him, and no one else. I put unlimitted confidence in you both.

As to the State, it is said, there is a majority for convention in both houses, but not 2/3 as is required so that there is no probability of a call at present.

I do not think I will be on to Washington till after the holidays, before which time, I suppose the impeachment trial of James H. Peck will not be closed. Mrs. Floride Colhoun Calhoun will not accompany me.

CHAPTER IX.

"FORT HILL ADDRESS," 26 JULY 1831

While serving as vice-president, Calhoun was forced to respond to the Nullification Crisis that had pitted his home state of South Carolina against President Andrew Jackson. The federal Constitution, Calhoun argued, was designed to limit the power of the federal government. The only reliable means of preserving the Constitution was to return to the "compact" that formed the republic, where the state and federal governments are "each in its sphere sovereign and independent, each perfectly adapted to their respective objects." In affirming a state veto as a calm and temporary remedy to the abuses of the federal government, Calhoun articulated an insight he learned from Thomas Jefferson: the protection of states and the basic liberty of the citizenry required vigilance against a centralized, national government.

THE QUESTION of the relation which the States and General Government bear to each other is not one of recent origin. From the commencement of our system, it has divided public sentiment. Even in the Convention, while the Constitution was struggling into existence, there were two parties as to what this relation should be, whose different sentiments constituted no small impediment in forming that instrument. After the General Government went into operation, experience soon proved that the question had not terminated with the labors of the Convention. The great struggle that preceded the political revolution of 1801, which brought Mr. Jefferson into power, turned essentially on it, and the doctrines and arguments on both sides were embodied and ably sustained;—on the one, in the Virginia and Kentucky Resolutions, and the Report to the Virginia Legislature;—and on the other, in the replies of the Legislature of Massachusetts and some of the other States. These Resolutions and this

Report, with the decision of the Supreme Court of Pennsylvania about the same time (particularly in the case of Cobbett, delivered by Chief Justice M'Kean, and concurred in by the whole bench), contain what I believe to be the true doctrine on this important subject. I refer to them in order to avoid the necessity of presenting my views, with the reasons in support of them, in detail.

As my object is simply to state my opinions, I might pause with this reference to documents that so fully and ably state all the points immediately connected with this deeply-important subject; but as there are many who may not have the opportunity or leisure to refer to them, and as it is possible, however clear they may be, that different persons may place different interpretations on their meaning, I will, in order that my sentiments may be fully known, and to avoid all ambiguity, proceed to state, summarily, the doctrines which I conceive they embrace.

The great and leading principle is, that the General Government emanated from the people of the several States, forming distinct political communities, and acting in their separate and sovereign capacity, and not from all of the people forming one aggregate political community; that the Constitution of the United States is, in fact, a compact, to which each State is a party, in the character already described; and that the several States, or parties, have a right to judge of its infractions; and in case of a deliberate, palpable, and dangerous exercise of power not delegated, they have the right, in the last resort, to use the language of the Virginia Resolutions, *"to interpose for arresting the progress of the evil, and for maintaining, within their respective limits, the authorities, rights, and liberties appertaining to them."* This right of interposition, thus solemnly asserted by the State of Virginia, be it called what it may,—State-right, veto, nullification, or by any other name,—I conceive to be the fundamental principle of our system, resting on facts historically as certain as our revolution itself, and deductions as simple and demonstrative as that of any political or moral truth whatever; and I firmly believe that on its recognition depend the stability and safety of our political institutions.

I am not ignorant that those opposed to the doctrine have always, now and formerly, regarded it in a very different light, as anarchical and revolutionary. Could I believe such, in fact, to be its tendency, to me it would be no recommendation. I yield to none, I trust, in a deep and sincere attachment to our political institutions and the union of these States. I never breathed an opposite sentiment; but, on the contrary, I have ever considered them the great instruments of preserving our liberty, and promoting the happiness of ourselves and our posterity; and next to these I have ever held them most dear. Nearly half my life has been passed in the service of the Union, and whatever public reputation I have acquired is indissolubly identified with it. To be too national has, indeed, been considered by many, even of my friends, my greatest political fault. With these strong feelings of attachment, I have examined, with the utmost care, the bearing of the doctrine in question; and, so far from anarchical or revolutionary, I solemnly believe it to be the only solid foundation of our system, and of the Union itself; and that the opposite doctrine, which denies to the States the right of protecting their reserved powers, and which would vest in the General Government (it matters not through what department) the right of determining, exclusively and finally, the powers delegated to it, is incompatible with the sovereignty of the States, and of the Constitution itself, considered as the basis of a Federal Union. As strong as this language is, it is not stronger than that used by the illustrious Jefferson, who said, to give to the General Government the final and exclusive right to judge of its powers, is to make *"its discretion, and not the Constitution, the measure of its powers;"* and that, *"in all cases of compact between parties having no common judge, each party has an equal right to judge for itself, as well of the infraction as of the mode and measure of redress."* Language cannot be more explicit, nor can higher authority be adduced.

That different opinions are entertained on this subject, I consider but as an additional evidence of the great diversity of the human intellect. Had not able, experienced, and patriotic individuals, for whom I have the highest respect, taken different views, I would have thought the right too clear to admit of doubt; but I am taught by this, as well as by many similar instances, to treat with deference opinions differing from my own. The error may, possibly, be with me; but if so, I can only say that, after the most mature and conscientious examination, I have not been able to detect it. But, with all proper deference, I must think that theirs is the error who deny what seems to be an essential attribute of the conceded sovereignty of the States, and who attribute to the General Government a right utterly incompatible with what all acknowledge to be its limited and restricted character: an error originating principally, as I must think, in not duly reflecting on the nature of our institutions, and on what constitutes the only rational object of all political constitutions.

It has been well said by one of the most sagacious men of antiquity, that the object of a constitution is, to *restrain the government, as that of laws* is to restrain *individuals.* The remark is correct; nor is it less true where the government is vested in a majority, than where it is in a single or a few individuals—in a republic, than a monarchy or aristocracy. No one can have a higher respect for the maxim that the majority ought to govern than I have, taken in its proper sense, subject to the restrictions imposed by the Constitution, and confined to objects in which every portion of the community have similar interests; but it is a great error to suppose, as many do, that the right of a majority to govern is a natural and not a conventional right, and therefore absolute and unlimited. By nature, every individual has the right to govern himself; and governments, whether founded on majorities or minorities, must derive their right from the assent, expressed or implied, of the governed, and be subject to such limitations as they may impose. Where the interests are the same, that is, where the laws that may benefit one will benefit all, or the reverse, it is just and proper to place them under the control of the majority; but where they are dissimilar, so that the law that may benefit one portion may be ruinous to another, it would be, on the contrary, unjust and absurd to subject them to its will; and such I conceive to be the theory on which our Constitution rests.

That such dissimilarity of interests may exist, it is impossible to doubt. They are to be found in every community, in a greater or less degree, however small or homogeneous; and they constitute every where the great difficulty of forming and preserving free institutions. To guard against the unequal action of the laws, when applied to dissimilar and opposing interests, is, in fact, what mainly renders a constitution indispensable; to overlook which, in reasoning on our Constitution, would be to omit the principal element by which to determine its character. Were there no contrariety of interests, nothing would be more simple and easy than to form and preserve free institutions. The right of suffrage alone would be a sufficient guarantee. It is the conflict of opposing interests which renders it the most difficult work of man.

Where the diversity of interests exists in separate and distinct classes of the community, as is the case in England, and was formerly the case in Sparta, Rome, and most of the free States of antiquity, the rational constitutional provision is, that each should be represented in the government, as a separate estate, with a distinct voice, and a negative on the acts of its co-estates, in order to check their encroachments. In England, the Constitution has assumed expressly this form, while in the governments of Sparta and Rome, the same thing was effected under different, but not much less efficacious forms. The perfection of their organization, in this particular, was that which gave to the constitutions of these renowned States all their celebrity, which secured their liberty for so many centuries, and raised them to so great a height of power and prosperity. Indeed, a constitutional provision giving to the great and separate interests of the community the right of self-protection, must appear, to those who will duly reflect on the subject, not less essential to the preservation of liberty than the right of suffrage itself. They, in fact, have a common object, to effect which the one is as necessary as the other to secure *responsibility; that is, that those who make and execute the laws should be account-*

able to those on whom the laws in reality operate—the only solid and durable foundation of liberty. If, without the right of suffrage, our rulers would oppress us, so, without the right of self-protection, the major would equally oppress the minor interests of the community. The absence of the former would make the governed the slaves of the rulers; and of the latter, the feebler interests, the victim of the stronger.

Happily for us, we have no artificial and separate classes of society. We have wisely exploded all such distinctions; but we are not, on that account, exempt from all contrariety of interests, as the present distracted and dangerous condition of our country, unfortunately, but too clearly proves. With us they are almost exclusively geographical, resulting mainly from difference of climate, soil, situation, industry, and production; but are not, therefore, less necessary to be protected by an adequate constitutional provision, than where the distinct interests exist in separate classes. The necessity is, in truth, greater, as such separate and dissimilar geographical interests are more liable to come into conflict, and more dangerous, when in that state, than those of any other description: so much so, that *ours is the first instance on record where they have not formed, in an extensive territory, separate and independent* communities, *or subjected the whole to despotic sway.* That such may not be our unhappy fate also, must be the sincere prayer of every lover of his country.

So numerous and diversified are the interests of our country, that they could not be fairly represented in a single government, organized so as to give to each great and leading interest a separate and distinct voice, as in governments to which I have referred. A plan was adopted better suited to our situation, but perfectly novel in its character. The powers of government were divided, not, as heretofore, in reference to classes, but geographically. One General Government was formed for the whole, to which were delegated all the powers supposed to be necessary to regulate the interests common to all the States, leaving others subject to the separate control of the States, being, from their local and peculiar character, such that they could not be subject to the will of a majority of the whole Union, without the certain hazard of injustice and oppression. It was thus that the interests of the whole were subjected, as they ought to be, to the will of the whole, while the peculiar and local interests were left under the control of the States separately, to whose custody only they could be safely confided. This distribution of power, settled solemnly by a constitutional compact, to which all the States are parties, constitutes the peculiar character and excellence of our political system. It is truly and emphatically *American, without example or parallel.*

To realize its perfection, we must view the General Government and those of the States as a whole, each in its proper sphere independent; each perfectly adapted to its respective objects; the States acting separately, representing and protecting the local and peculiar interests; and acting jointly through one General Government, with the weight respectively assigned to each by the Constitution, representing and protecting the interest of the whole; and thus perfecting, by an admirable but simple arrangement, the great principle of representation and responsibility, without which no government can be free or just. To preserve this sacred distribution as originally settled, by coercing each to move in its prescribed orbit, is the great and difficult problem, on the solution of which the duration of our Constitution, of our Union, and, in all probability, our liberty depends. How is this to be effected?

The question is new, when applied to our peculiar political organization, where the separate and conflicting interests of society are represented by distinct but connected governments; but it is, in reality, an old question under a new form, long since perfectly solved. Whenever separate and dissimilar interests have been separately represented in any government; whenever the sovereign power has been divided in its exercise, the experience and wisdom of ages have devised but one mode by which such political organization can be preserved,—the mode adopted in England, and by all governments, ancient and modern, blessed with constitutions deserving to be called free,—to give to each co-estate the right to judge of its powers, with a negative or veto on the acts of the others, in order to protect against encroachments the interests it particularly represents: a principle which all of our constitutions recognize in the distribution of power among their respective departments, as essential to maintain the independence of each; but which, to all who will duly reflect on the subject, must appear far more essential, for the same object, in that great and fundamental distribution of powers between the General and State Governments. So essential is the principle, that, to withhold the right from either, where the sovereign power is divided, is, in fact, *to annul the division* itself, and to *consolidate,* in the one left in the exclusive possession of the right, *all* powers of government; for it is not possible to distinguish, practically, between a government having all power, and one having the right to take what powers it pleases. Nor does it in the least vary the principle, whether the distribution of power be between co-estates, as in England, or between distinctly organized but connected governments, as with us. The reason is the same in both cases, while the necessity is greater in our case, as the danger of conflict is greater where the interests of a society are divided geographically than in any other, as has already been shown.

These truths do seem to me to be incontrovertible; and I am at a loss to understand how any one, who has maturely reflected on the nature of our institutions, or who has read history or studied the principles of free government to any purpose, can call them in question. The explanation must, it appears to me, be sought in the fact that, in every free State there are those who look more to the necessity of maintaining power than guarding against its abuses. I do not intend reproach, but simply to state a fact apparently necessary to explain the contrariety of opinions among the intelligent, where the abstract consideration of the subject would seem scarcely to admit of doubt. If such be the true cause, I must think the fear of weakening the government too much, in this case, to be in a great measure unfounded, or, at least, that the danger is much less from that than the opposite side. I do not deny that a power of so high a nature may be abused by a State; but when I reflect that the States unanimously called the General Government into existence with all its powers, which they freely delegated on their part, under the conviction that their common peace, safety, and prosperity required it; that they are bound together by a common origin, and the recollection of common suffering and common triumph in the great and splendid achievement of their independence; and that the strongest feelings of our nature, and among them the love of national power and distinction, are on the side of the Union, it does seem to me that the fear which would strip the States of their sovereignty, and degrade them, in fact, to mere dependent corporations, lest they should abuse a right indispensable to the peaceable protection of those interests which they reserved under their own peculiar guardianship when they created the General Government, is unnatural and unreasonable. If those who voluntarily created the system cannot be trusted to preserve it, who can?

So far from extreme danger, I hold that there never was a free State in which this great conservative principle, indispensable to all, was ever so safely lodged. In others, when the co-estates representing the dissimilar and conflicting interests of the community came into contact, the only alternative was compromise, submission, or force. Not so in ours. Should the General Government and a State come into conflict, we have a higher remedy: the power which called the General Government into existence, which gave it all its authority, and can enlarge, contract, or abolish its powers at its pleasure, may be invoked. The States themselves may be appealed to,—three fourths of which, in fact, form a power, whose decrees are the Constitution itself, and whose voice can silence all discontent. The utmost extent, then, of the power is, that a State, acting in its sovereign capacity as one of the parties to the constitutional compact, may compel the Government, created by that compact, to submit a question touching its infraction, to the parties who created it; to avoid the supposed dangers of which, it is proposed to resort to the novel, the hazardous, and, I must add, fatal project of giving to the General Government the sole and final right of interpreting the Constitution;—thereby reversing the whole system, making that instrument the creature of its will, instead of a rule of action impressed on it at its creation, and annihilating, in fact, the authority which imposed it, and from which the Government itself derives its existence.

That such would be the result, were the right in question vested in the Legislative or Executive branch of the Government, is conceded by all. No one has been so hardy as to assert that Congress or the President ought to have the right, or deny that, if vested finally and exclusively in either, the consequences which I have stated would necessarily follow; but its advocates have been reconciled to the doctrine, on the supposition that there is one department of the General Government which, from its peculiar organization, affords an independent tribunal, through which the Government may exercise the high authority which is the subject of consideration, with perfect safety to all.

I yield, I trust, to few in my attachment to the Judiciary Department. I am fully sensible of its importance, and would maintain it, to the fullest extent, in its constitutional powers and independence; but it is impossible for me to believe it was ever intended by the Constitution that it should exercise the power in question, or that it is competent to do so; and, if it were, that it would be a safe depository of the power.

Its powers are judicial, and not political; and are expressly confined by the Constitution "to all *cases* in law and equity arising under this Constitution, the laws of the United States, and the treaties made, or which shall be made, under its authority;" and which I have high authority in asserting excludes political questions, and comprehends those only where there are parties amenable to the process of the court.* Nor is its incompetency less clear than its want of consti-

---

*I refer to the authority of Chief Justice Marshall, in the case of Jonathan Robbins. I have not been able to refer to the speech, and speak from memory.

[The following are the remarks referred to by Mr. Calhoun:—

"By extending the judicial power to all cases in law and equity, the Constitution *had never been understood* to confer on that department any *political power whatever*. To come within this description, a question must assume a *legal* form, for forensic litigation and judicial decision. There must be parties to come into court, who can be reached by its process, and bound by its power; whose rights admit of ultimate decision by a tribunal, to which they are bound to submit. A 'case in Law and Equity,' proper for judicial decision, may arise under a treaty, where the *rights of individuals,* acquired or secured by a treaty, are to be asserted or defended in court;—as under the fourth and sixth articles of the treaty of peace with Great Britain; or under those articles of our late treaties with France, Prussia, and other nations, which secure to *the subjects* of these nations *their property* within the United States; but the *judicial power cannot extend to political compacts.*" Speech in the House of Representatives, in the case of Thomas Nash, *alias* Jonathan Robbins, Sept. 1797.—*Editor* (Crallé)].

tutional authority. There may be many, and the most dangerous infractions on the part of Congress, of which, it is conceded by all, the court, as a judicial tribunal, cannot, from its nature, take cognizance. The Tariff itself is a strong case in point; and the reason applies equally *to all others where Congress perverts a power from an object intended, to one not intended, the most insidious and dangerous of all infractions; and which may be extended to all of its powers, more especially to the taxing and appropriating.* But, supposing it competent to take cognizance of all infractions of every description, the insuperable objection still remains, that it would not be a safe tribunal to exercise the power in question.

It is a universal and fundamental political principle, that the power to protect can safely be confided only to those interested in protecting, or their responsible agents,—a maxim not less true in private than in public affairs. The danger in our system is, that the General Government, which represents the interests of the whole, may encroach on the States, which represent the peculiar and local interests, or that the latter may encroach on the former.

In examining this point, we ought not to forget that the Government, through all its departments, judicial as well as others, is administered by delegated and responsible agents; and that the *power which really controls, ultimately, all the movements, is not in the agents, but those who elect or appoint them.* To understand, then, its real character, and what would be the action of the system in any supposable case, we must raise our view from the mere agents to this high controlling power, which finally impels every movement of the machine. By doing so, we shall find all under the control of the will of a majority, compounded of the majority of the States, taken as political bodies, and the majority of the people of the States, estimated in federal numbers. These, united, constitute the real and final power which impels and directs the movements of the General Government. The majority of the States elect the majority of the Senate; of the people of the States, that of the House of Representatives; the two united, the President; and the President and a majority of the Senate appoint the judges: a majority of whom, and a majority of the Senate and House, with the President, really exercise all the powers of the Government, with the exception of the cases where the Constitution requires a greater number than a majority. The judges are, in fact, as truly the judicial representatives of this united majority, as the majority of Congress itself, or the President, is its legislative or executive representative; and to confide the power to the Judiciary to determine finally and conclusively what powers are delegated and what reserved, would be, in reality, to confide it to the majority, whose agents they are, and by whom they can be controlled in various ways; and, of course, to subject (against the fundamental principle of our system and all sound political reasoning) the reserved powers of the States, with all the local and peculiar interests they were intended to protect, to the will of the very majority against which the protection was intended. Nor will the tenure by which the judges hold their office, however valuable the provision in many other respects, materially vary the case. Its highest possible effect would be to *retard,* and not *finally* to *resist,* the will of a dominant majority.

But it is useless to multiply arguments. Were it possible that reason could settle a question where the passions and interests of men are concerned, this point would have been long since settled for ever by the State of Virginia. The report of her Legislature, to which I have already referred, has really, in my opinion, placed it beyond controversy. Speaking in reference to this subject, it says: "It has been objected" (to the right of a State to interpose for the protection of her reserved rights) "that the judicial authority is to be regarded as the sole expositor of the Constitution. On this objection it might be observed, first, that there may be instances of usurped powers which the forms of the Constitution could never draw within the control of the Judicial Department; secondly, that, if the decision of the judiciary be raised above the sovereign parties to the Constitution, the decisions of the other departments, not carried by the forms of the Constitution before the Judiciary, must be equally authoritative and final with the decision of that department. But the proper answer to the objection is, that the resolution of the General Assembly relates to those great and extraordinary cases, in which all the forms of the Constitution may prove ineffectual against infractions dangerous to the essential rights of the parties to it. The resolution supposes that dangerous powers, not delegated, may not only be usurped and executed by the other departments, but that the Judicial Department may also exercise or sanction dangerous powers, beyond the grant of the Constitution, and, consequently, that the ultimate right of the parties to the Constitution to judge whether the compact has been dangerously violated, must extend to violations by one delegated authority, as well as by another,—by the judiciary, as well as by the executive or legislative."

Against these conclusive arguments, as they seem to me, it is objected that, if one of the parties has the right to judge of infractions of the Constitution, so has the other; and that, consequently, in cases of contested powers between a State and the General Government, each would have a right to maintain its opinion, as is the case when sovereign powers differ in the construction of treaties or compacts; and that, of course, it would come to be a mere question of force. The error is in the assumption that the General Government is a party to the constitutional compact. The States, as has been shown, formed the compact, acting as sovereign and independent communities. The General Government is but its creature; and though, in reality, a government, with all the rights and authority which belong to any other government, within the orbit of its powers, it is, nevertheless, a government emanating from a compact between sovereigns, and partaking, in its nature and object, of the character of a joint commission, appointed to superintend and administer the interests in which all are jointly concerned; but having, beyond its proper sphere, no more power than if it did not exist. To deny this would be to deny the most incontestable facts and the clearest conclusions; while to acknowledge its truth is, to destroy utterly the objection that the appeal would be to force, in the case supposed. For, if each party has a right to judge, then, under our system of government, the final cognizance of a question of contested power would be in the States, and not in the General Government. It would be the duty of the latter, as in all similar cases of a contest between one or more of the principals and a joint commission or agency, to refer the contest to the principals themselves. Such are the plain dictates of both reason and analogy. On no sound principle can the agents have a right to final cognizance, as against the principals, much less to use force against them to maintain their construction of their powers. Such a right would be monstrous, and has never, heretofore, been claimed in similar cases.

That the doctrine is applicable to the case of a contested power between the States and the General Government, we have the authority, not only of reason and analogy, but of the distinguished statesman already referred to. Mr. Jefferson, at a late period of his life, after long experience and mature reflection, says, "With respect to our State and Federal Governments, I do not think their relations are correctly understood by foreigners. They suppose the former are subordinate to the latter. This is not the case. They are co-ordinate departments of one simple and integral whole. But you may ask, If the two departments should claim each the same subject of power, where is the umpire to decide between them? In cases of little urgency or importance, the prudence of both parties will keep them aloof from the questionable ground; but, if it can neither be avoided nor compromised, a convention of the States must be called to ascribe the doubtful power to that department which they may think best."

It is thus that our Constitution, by authorizing amendments, and by prescribing the authority and mode of making them, has, by a simple contrivance, with its characteristic wisdom, provided a power which, in the last resort, supersedes effectually the necessity, and even the pretext for force: a power to which none can fairly object; with which the interests of all are safe; which can definitively close all controversies in the only effectual mode, by freeing the compact of every defect and uncertainty, by an amendment of the instrument itself. It is impossible for human wisdom, in a system like ours, to devise another mode which shall be safe and effectual, and, at the same time, consistent with what are the relations and acknowledged powers of the two great departments of our Government. It gives a beauty and security peculiar to our system, which, if duly appreciated, will transmit its blessings to the remotest generations; but, if not, our splendid anticipations of the future will prove but an empty dream. Stripped of all its covering, the naked question is, whether ours is a federal or a consolidated government; a constitutional or absolute one; a government resting ultimately on the solid basis of the sovereignty of the States or on the unrestrained will of a majority; a form of government, as in all other unlimited ones, in which injustice, and violence, and force must finally prevail. *Let it never be forgotten that, where the majority rules without restriction, the minority is the subject;* and that, if we should absurdly attribute to the former the exclusive right of construing the Constitution, there would be, in fact, between the sovereign and subject, under such a government, no Constitution, or, at least, nothing deserving the name, or serving the legitimate object of so sacred an instrument.

How the States are to exercise this high power of interposition, which constitutes so essential a portion of their reserved rights that it *cannot be delegated without an entire surrender of their sovereignty,* and converting our system from a *federal* into a *consolidated* Government, is a question that the States only are competent to determine. The arguments which prove that they possess the power, equally prove that they are, in the language of Jefferson, "*the rightful judges of the mode and measure of redress.*" But the spirit of forbearance, as well as the nature of the right itself, forbids a recourse to it, except in cases of dangerous infractions of the Constitution; and then only in the last resort, when all reasonable hope of relief from the ordinary action of the Government has failed; when, if the right to interpose did not exist, the alternative would be submission and oppression on one side, or resistance by force on the other. That our system should afford, in such extreme cases, an intermediate point between these dire alternatives, by which the Government may be brought to a pause, and thereby an interval obtained to compromise differences, or, if impracticable, be compelled to submit the question to a constitutional adjustment, through an appeal to the States themselves, is an evidence of its high wisdom: an element not, as is supposed by some, of weakness, but of strength; not of anarchy or revolution, but of peace and safety. *Its general recognition would of itself, in a great measure, if not altogether, supersede the necessity of its exercise, by impressing on the movements of the Government that moderation and justice so essential to harmony and peace, in a country of such vast extent and diversity of interests as ours;* and would, if controversy should come, turn the resentment of the aggrieved from the system to those who had abused its powers (a point all-important), and cause them to seek redress, *not in revolution or overthrow, but in reformation.* It is, in fact, properly understood, *a substitute,— where the alternative would be force,—tending to prevent, and, if that fails, to correct peaceably the aberrations to which all systems are liable, and which, if permitted to accumulate without correction, must finally end in a general catastrophe.*

I have now said what I intended in reference to the abstract question of the relation of the States to the General Government, and would here conclude, did I not believe that a mere general statement on an abstract question, without including that which may have caused its agitation, would be considered by many imperfect and unsatisfactory. Feeling that such would be justly the case, I am compelled, reluctantly, to touch on the Tariff, so far, at least, as may be necessary to illustrate the opinions which I have already advanced. Anxious, however, to intrude as little as possible on the public attention, I will be as brief as possible; and with that view will, as far as may be consistent with my object, avoid all debatable topics.

Whatever diversity of opinion may exist in relation to the principle, or the effect on the productive industry of the country, of the present, or any other Tariff of protection, there are certain political consequences flowing from the present which none can doubt, and all must deplore. It would be in vain to attempt to conceal, that it has divided the country into two great geographical divisions, and arrayed them against each other, in opinion at least, if not interests also, on some of the most vital of political subjects,—on its finance, its commerce, and its industry,—subjects calculated, above all others, in time of peace, to produce excitement, and in relation to which the Tariff has placed the sections in question in deep and dangerous conflict. If there be any point on which the (I was going to say, southern section, but to avoid, as far as possible, the painful feelings such discussions are calculated to excite, I shall say) weaker of the two sections is unanimous, it is, that its prosperity depends, in a great measure, on free trade, light taxes, economical, and, as far as possible, equal disbursements of the public revenue, and unshackled industry;—leaving them to pursue whatever may appear most advantageous to their interests. From the Potomac to the Mississippi, there are few, indeed, however divided on other points, who would not, if dependent on their volition, and if they regarded the interest of their particular section only, remove from commerce and industry every shackle, reduce the revenue to the lowest point that the wants of the Government fairly required, and restrict the appropriations to the most moderate scale consistent with the peace, the security, and the engagements of the public; and who do not believe that the opposite system is calculated to throw on them an unequal burden, to repress their prosperity, and to encroach on their enjoyment.

On all these deeply-important measures, the opposite opinion prevails, if not with equal unanimity, with at least a greatly preponderating majority, in the other and stronger section; so much so, that no two distinct nations ever entertained more opposite views of policy than these two sections do, on all the important points to which I have referred. Nor is it less certain that this unhappy conflict, flowing directly from the Tariff, has extended itself to the halls of legislation, and has converted the deliberations of Congress into an annual struggle between the two sections; the stronger to maintain and increase the superiority it has already acquired, and the other to throw off or diminish its burdens: a struggle in which all the noble and generous feelings of patriotism are gradually subsiding into sectional and selfish attachments.* Nor has the effect of this dangerous conflict ended here. It has not only divided the two sections on the important point already stated, but on the deeper and more dangerous questions, the constitutionality of a protective Tariff, and the general principles and theory of the Constitution itself: the stronger, in order to maintain their superiority, giving a construction to the instrument which the other believes would convert the General Government into a consolidated, irresponsible government, with the total destruction of liberty; and the weaker, seeing no hope of relief with such assumption of powers, turning its eye to the reserved sovereignty of the States, as the only refuge from oppression. I shall not extend these remarks, as I might, by showing that, while the effect of the system of protection was rapidly alienating one section, it was not less rapidly, by its necessary operation, distracting and corrupting the other; and, between the two, subjecting the administration to violent and sudden changes, totally inconsistent with all stability and wisdom in the management of the affairs of the nation, of which we already see fearful symptoms. Nor do I deem it necessary to inquire whether this unhappy conflict grows out of true or mistaken views of interest on either or both sides. Regarded in either light, it ought to admonish us of the extreme danger to which our system is exposed, and the great moderation and wisdom necessary to preserve it. If it comes from mistaken views,—if the interests of the

---

*The system, if continued, must end, not only in subjecting the industry and property of the weaker section to the control of the stronger, but in proscription and political disfranchisement. It must finally control elections and appointments to offices, as well as acts of legislation, to the great increase of the feelings of animosity, and of the fatal tendency to a complete alienation between the sections.

two sections, as affected by the Tariff, be really the same, and the system, instead of acting unequally, in reality diffuses equal blessings, and imposes equal burdens on every part,—it ought to teach us how liable those who are differently situated, and who view their interests under different aspects, are to come to different conclusions, even when their interests are strictly the same; and, consequently, with what extreme caution any system of policy ought to be adopted, and with what a spirit of moderation pursued, in a country of such great extent and diversity as ours. But if, on the contrary, the conflict springs really from contrariety of interests,—if the burden be on one side and the benefit on the other,—then are we taught a lesson not less important, how little regard we have for the interests of others while in pursuit of our own; or, at least, how apt we are to consider our own interest the interest of all others; and, of course, how great the danger, in a country of such acknowledged diversity of interests, of the oppression of the feebler by the stronger interest, and, in consequence of it, of the most fatal sectional conflicts. But whichever may be the cause, the real or supposed diversity of interest, it cannot be doubted that the political consequences of the prohibitory system, be its effects in other respects beneficial or otherwise, are really such as I have stated; nor can it be doubted that a conflict between the great sections, on questions so vitally important, indicates a condition of the country so distempered and dangerous, as to demand the most serious and prompt attention. It is only when we come to the consider of the remedy, that, under the aspect I am viewing the subject, there can be, among the informed and considerate, any diversity of opinion.

Those who have not duly reflected on its dangerous and inveterate character, suppose that the disease will cure itself; that events ought to be left to take their own course; and that experience, in a short time, will prove that the interest of the whole community is the same in reference to the Tariff, or, at least, whatever diversity there may now be, time will assimilate. Such has been their language from the beginning, but, unfortunately, the progress of events has been the reverse. The country is now more divided than in 1824, and then more than in 1816. The majority may have increased, but the opposite sides are, beyond dispute, more determined and excited than at any preceding period. Formerly, the system was resisted mainly as inexpedient; but now, as unconstitutional, unequal, unjust, and oppressive. Then, relief was sought exclusively from the General Government; but now, many, driven to despair, are raising their eyes to the reserved sovereignty of the States as the only refuge. If we turn from the past and present to the future, we shall find nothing to lessen, but much to aggravate the danger. The increasing embarrassment and distress of the staple

States, the growing conviction, from experience, that they are caused by the prohibitory system principally, and that, under its continued operation, their present pursuits must become profitless, and with a conviction that their great and peculiar agricultural capital cannot be diverted from its ancient and hereditary channels without ruinous losses,—all concur to increase, instead of dispelling, the gloom that hangs over the future. In fact, to those who will duly reflect on the subject, the hope that the disease will cure itself must appear perfectly illusory. The question is, in reality, one between the exporting and non-exporting interests of the country. *Were there no exports, there would be no tariff.* It would be perfectly useless. On the contrary, so long as there are States which raise the great agricultural staples with the view of obtaining their supplies, and which must depend on the general market of the world for their sales, the conflict must remain if the system should continue, and the disease become more and more inveterate. Their interest, and that of those who, by high duties, would confine the purchase of their supplies to the home market, must, from the nature of things, in reference to the Tariff, be in conflict. Till, then, we cease to raise the great staples, cotton, rice, and tobacco, for the general market, and till we can find some other profitable investment for the immense amount of capital and labor now employed in their production, the present unhappy and dangerous conflict cannot terminate, unless with the prohibitory system itself.

In the mean time, while idly waiting for its termination through its own action, the progress of events in another quarter is rapidly bringing the contest to an immediate and decisive issue. We are fast approaching a period very novel in the history of nations, and bearing directly and powerfully on the point under consideration—the final payment of a long-standing funded debt—a period that cannot be greatly retarded, or its natural consequences eluded, without proving disastrous to those who attempt either, if not to the country itself. When it arrives, the Government will find itself in possession of a surplus revenue of $10,000,000 or $12,000,000, if not previously disposed of,—which presents the important question, What previous disposition ought to be made? a question which must press urgently for decision at the very next session of Congress. It cannot be delayed longer without the most distracting and dangerous consequences.

The honest and obvious course is, to prevent the accumulation of the surplus in the Treasury by a timely and judicious reduction of the imposts; and thereby to leave the money in the pockets of those who made it, and from whom it cannot be honestly nor constitutionally taken, unless required by the fair and legitimate wants of the Government. If, neglecting a disposition so obvious and just, the Government should attempt to keep up the present high

duties, when the money is no longer wanted, or to dispose of this immense surplus by enlarging the old, or devising new schemes of appropriations; or, finding that to be impossible, it should adopt the most dangerous, unconstitutional,
and absurd project ever devised by any government, of dividing the surplus
among the States,—a project which, if carried into execution, would not fail to
create an antagonist interest between the States and General Government on all
questions of appropriations, which would certainly end in reducing the latter to
a mere office of collection and distribution,—either of these modes would be
considered, by the section suffering under the present high duties, as a fixed
determination to perpetuate for ever what it considers the present unequal,
unconstitutional, and oppressive burden; and from that moment it would cease
to look to the General Government for relief. This deeply-interesting period,
which must prove so disastrous should a wrong direction be given, but so fortunate and glorious, should a right one, is just at hand. The work must commence at the next session, as I have stated, or be left undone, or, at least, be
badly done. The succeeding session would be too short, and too much agitated
by the presidential contest, to afford the requisite leisure and calmness; and the
one succeeding would find the country in the midst of the crisis, when it would
be too late to prevent an accumulation of the surplus; which I hazard nothing
in saying, judging from the nature of men and government, if once permitted
to accumulate, would create an interest strong enough to perpetuate itself; supported, as it would be, by others so numerous and powerful; and thus would
pass away a moment, never to be quietly recalled, so precious, if properly used,
to lighten the public burden; to equalize the action of the Government; to
restore harmony and peace; and to present to the world the illustrious example,
which could not fail to prove most favorable to the great cause of liberty every
where, of a nation the freest, and, at the same time, the best and most cheaply
governed; of the highest earthly blessing at the least possible sacrifice.

As the disease will not, then, heal itself, we are brought to the question, Can
a remedy be applied? and if so, what ought it to be?

To answer in the negative would be to assert that our Union has utterly
failed; and that the opinion, so common before the adoption of our Constitution, that a free government could not be practically extended over a large country, was correct; and that ours had been destroyed by giving it limits so great as
to comprehend, not only dissimilar, but irreconcilable interests. I am not prepared to admit a conclusion that would cast so deep a shade on the future; and
that would falsify all the glorious anticipations of our ancestors, while it would
so greatly lessen their high reputation for wisdom. Nothing but the clearest

demonstration founded on actual experience, will ever force me to a conclusion so abhorrent to all my feelings. As strongly as I am impressed with the great dissimilarity, and, as I must add, as truth compels me to do, contrariety of interests in our country, resulting from the causes already indicated, and which are so great that they cannot be subjected to the unchecked will of a majority of the whole without defeating the great end of government, and without which it is a curse—justice—yet I see in the Union, as ordained by the Constitution, the means, if wisely used, not only of reconciling all diversities, but also the means, and the only effectual one, of securing to us justice, peace, and security, at home and abroad, and with them that national power and renown, the love of which Providence has implanted, for wise purposes, so deeply in the human heart: in all of which great objects every portion of our country, widely extended and diversified as it is, has a common and identical interest. If we have the wisdom to place a proper relative estimate on these more elevated and durable blessings, the present and every other conflict of like character may be readily terminated; but if, reversing the scale, each section should put a higher estimate on its immediate and peculiar gains, and, acting in that spirit, should push favorite measures of mere policy, without some regard to peace, harmony, or justice, our sectional conflicts would then, indeed, without some constitutional check, become interminable, except by the dissolution of the Union itself. That we have, in fact, so reversed the estimate, is too certain to be doubted, and the result is our present distempered and dangerous condition. The cure must commence in the correction of the error; and not to admit that we have erred would be the worst possible symptom. It would prove the disease to be incurable, through the regular and ordinary process of legislation; and would compel, finally, a resort to extraordinary, but I still trust, not only constitutional, but safe remedies.

No one would more sincerely rejoice than myself to see the remedy applied from the quarter where it could be most easily and regularly done. It is the only way by which those, who think that it is the only quarter from which it may constitutionally come, can possibly sustain their opinion. To omit the application by the General Government, would compel even them to admit the truth of the opposite opinion, or force them to abandon our political system in despair; while, on the other hand, all their enlightened and patriotic opponents would rejoice at such evidence of moderation and wisdom, on the part of the General Government, as would supersede a resort to what they believe to be the higher powers of our political system, as indicating a sounder state of public sentiment than has ever heretofore existed in any country; and thus affording the highest possible assurance of the perpetuation of our glorious institutions to the latest generation.

For, as a people advance in knowledge, in the same degree they may dispense with mere artificial restrictions in their government; and we may imagine (but dare not expect to see) a state of intelligence so universal and high, that all the guards of liberty may be dispensed with, except an enlightened public opinion, acting through the right of suffrage; but it presupposes a state where every class and every section of the community are capable of estimating the effects of every measure, not only as it may affect itself, but every other class and section; and of fully realizing the sublime truth that the highest and wisest policy consists in maintaining justice, and promoting peace and harmony; and that, compared to these, schemes of mere gain are but trash and dross. I fear experience has already proved that we are far removed from such a state; and that we must, consequently, rely on the old and clumsy, but approved mode of checking power, in order to prevent or correct abuses; but I do trust that, though far from perfect, we are, at least, so much so as to be capable of remedying the present disorder in the ordinary way; and thus to prove that, with us, public opinion is so enlightened, and our political machine so perfect, as rarely to require for its preservation the intervention of the power that created it. How is this to be effected?

The application may be painful, but the remedy, I conceive, is certain and simple. There is but one effectual cure—an honest reduction of the duties to a fair system of revenue, adapted to the just and constitutional wants of the Government. Nothing short of this will restore the country to peace, harmony, and mutual affection. There is already a deep and growing conviction in a large section of the country, that the impost, even as a revenue system, is extremely unequal, and that it is mainly paid by those who furnish the means of paying the foreign exchanges of the country on which it is laid; and that the case would not be varied, taking into the estimate the entire action of the system, whether the producer or consumer pays in the first instance.

I do not propose to enter formally into the discussion of a point so complex and contested; but, as it has necessarily a strong practical bearing on the subject under consideration in all its relations, I cannot pass it without a few general and brief remarks.

If the producer, in reality, pays, none will doubt but the burden would mainly fall on the section it is supposed to do. The theory that the consumer pays, in the first instance, renders the proposition more complex, and will require, in order to understand where the burden, in reality, ultimately falls, on that supposition, to consider the protective, or, as its friends call it, the American System, under its threefold aspect of taxation, of protection, and of distribution,—or as performing, at the same time, the several functions of giving a revenue to the Government, of affording protection to certain branches of domestic industry, and furnishing means to Congress of distributing large sums through its appropriations: all of which are so blended in their effects, that it is impossible to understand its true operation without taking the whole into the estimate.

Admitting, then, as supposed, that he who consumes the article pays the tax in the increased price, and that the burden falls wholly on the consumers, without affecting the producers as a class (which, by the by, is far from being true, except in the single case, if there be such a one, where the producers have a monopoly of an article so indispensable to life that the quantity consumed cannot be affected by any increase of price), and that, considered in the light of a tax merely, the impost duties fall equally on every section in proportion to its population, still, when combined with its other effects, the burden it imposes as a tax may be so transferred from one section to the other as to take it from one and place it wholly on the other. Let us apply the remark first to its operation as a system of protection:

The tendency of the tax or duty on the imported article is not only to raise its price, but also, in the same proportion, that of the domestic article of the same kind, for which purpose, when intended for protection, it is, in fact, laid; and, of course, in determining where the system ultimately places the burden in reality, this effect, also, must be taken into the estimate. If one of the sections exclusively produces such domestic articles and the other purchases them from it, then it is clear that, to the amount of such increased prices, the tax or duty on the consumption of foreign articles would be transferred from the section producing the domestic articles to the one that purchased and consumed them;—unless the latter, in turn, be indemnified by the increased price of the objects of its industry, which none will venture to assert to be the case with the great staples of the country, which form the basis of our exports, the price of which is regulated by the foreign, and not the domestic market. To those who grow them, the increased price of the foreign and domestic articles both, in consequence of the duty on the former, is in reality, and in the strictest sense, a tax, while it is clear that the increased price of the latter acts as a bounty to the section producing them; and that, as the amount of such increased prices on what it sells to the other section is greater or less than the duty it pays on the imported articles, the system will, in fact, operate as a bounty or tax; if greater, the difference would be a bounty; if less, a tax.

Again, the operation may be equal in every other respect, and yet the pressure of the system, relatively, on the two sections, be rendered very unequal by the appropriations or distribution. If each section receives back what it paid into the treasury, the equality, if it previously existed, will continue; but if one receives back less, and the other proportionably more than is paid, then the difference in relation to the sections will be to the former a loss, and to the latter a gain; and the system, in this aspect, would operate to the amount of the difference, as a contribution from the one receiving less than it paid to the other that receives more. Such would be incontestably its general effects, taken in all its different aspects, even on the theory supposed to be most favorable to prove the equal action of the system, that the consumer pays, in the first instance, the whole amount of the tax.

To show how, on this supposition, the burden and advantages of the system would actually distribute themselves between the sections, would carry me too far into details; but I feel assured, after full and careful examination, that they are such as to explain, what otherwise would seem inexplicable, that one section should consider its repeal a calamity, and the other a blessing; and that such opposite views should be taken by them as to place them in a state of determined conflict in relation to the great fiscal and commercial interest of the country. Indeed, were there no satisfactory explanation, the opposite views that prevail in the two sections, as to the effects of the system, ought to satisfy all of its unequal action. There can be no safer, or more certain rule, than to suppose each portion of the country equally capable of understanding their respective interests, and that each is a much better judge of the effects of any system or measures on its peculiar interests than the other can possibly be.

But, whether the opinion of its unequal action be correct or erroneous, nothing can be more certain than that the impression is widely extending itself, that the system, under all its modifications, is essentially unequal; and if to this be added a conviction still deeper and more universal, that every duty imposed *for the purpose of protection is not only unequal, but also unconstitutional,* it would be a fatal error to suppose that any remedy, short of that which I have stated, can heal our political disorders.

In order to understand more fully the difficulty of adjusting this unhappy contest on any other ground, it may not be improper to present a general view of the constitutional objection, that it may be clearly seen how hopeless it is to expect that it can be yielded by those who have embraced it.

They believe that all the powers vested by the Constitution in Congress are, not only restricted by the limitations expressly imposed, but also by the nature and object of the powers themselves. Thus, though the power to impose duties on imports be granted in general terms, without any other express limitations but that they shall be equal, and no preference shall be given to the ports of one

State over those of another, yet, as being a portion of the taxing power given with the view of raising revenue, it is, from its nature, restricted to that object, as much so as if the Convention had expressly so limited it; and that to use it to effect any other purpose not specified in the Constitution, is an infraction of the instrument in its most dangerous form—an infraction by perversion, more easily made, and more difficult to resist, than any other. The same view is believed to be applicable to the power of regulating commerce, as well as all the other powers. To surrender this important principle, it is conceived, would be to surrender all power, and to render the Government unlimited and despotic; and to yield it up, in relation to the particular power in question, would be, in fact, to surrender the control of the whole industry and capital of the country to the General Government, and would end in placing the weaker section in a colonial relation towards the stronger. For nothing are more dissimilar in their nature, or may be more unequally affected by the same laws, than different descriptions of labor and property; and if taxes, by increasing the amount and changing the intent only, may be perverted, in fact, into a system of penalties and rewards, it would give all the power that could be desired to subject the labor and property of the minority to the will of the majority, to be regulated without regarding the interest of the former in subserviency to the will of the latter. Thus thinking, it would seem unreasonable to expect, that any adjustment, based on the recognition of the correctness of a construction of the Constitution which would admit the exercise of such a power, would satisfy the weaker of two sections, particularly with its peculiar industry and property, which experience has shown may be so injuriously affected by its exercise. Thus much for one side.

The just claim of the other ought to be equally respected. Whatever excitement the system has justly caused in certain portions of our country, I hope and believe all will conceive that the change should be made with the least possible detriment to the interests of those who may be liable to be affected by it; consistently, with what is justly due to others, and the principles of the Constitution. To effect this will require the kindest spirit of conciliation and the utmost skill; but, even with these, it will be impossible to make the transition without a shock, greater or less, though I trust, if judiciously effected, it will not be without many compensating advantages. That there will be some such cannot be doubted. It will, at least, be followed by greater stability, and will tend to harmonize the manufacturing with all the other great interests of the country, and bind the whole in mutual affection. But these are not all. Another advantage of essential importance to the ultimate prosperity of our manufacturing industry will follow. *It will cheapen production;* and, in that view, the loss of any one branch will be nothing like in proportion to the reduction of duty on that particular branch. Every reduction will, in fact, operate as a bounty to every other branch except the one reduced; and thus the effect of a general reduction will be to cheapen, universally, the price of production, by cheapening living, wages, and material, so as to give, if not equal profits after the reduction—profits by no means reduced proportionally to the duties—an effect which, as it regards the foreign markets, is of the utmost importance. It must be apparent, on reflection, that the means adopted to secure the home market for our manufactures are precisely the opposite of those necessary to obtain the foreign. In the former, the increased expense of production, in consequence of a system of protection, may be more than compensated by the increased price at home of the article protected; but in the latter, this advantage is lost; and, as there is no other corresponding compensation, the increased cost of production must be a dead loss in the foreign market. But whether these advantages, and many others that might be mentioned, will ultimately compensate to the full extent or not the loss to the manufacturers, on the reduction of the duties, certain it is, that we have approached a point at which a great change cannot be much longer delayed; and that the more promptly it may be met, the less excitement there will be, and the greater leisure and calmness for a cautious and skilful operation in making the transition; and which it becomes those more immediately interested duly to consider. Nor ought they to overlook, in considering the question, the different character of the claims of the two sides. The one asks from Government no advantage, but simply to be let alone in the undisturbed possession of their natural advantages, and to secure which, as far as was consistent with the other objects of the Constitution, was one of their leading motives in entering into the Union; while the other side claims, for the advancement of their prosperity, the positive interference of the Government. In such cases, on every principle of fairness and justice, such interference ought to be restrained within limits strictly compatible with the natural advantages of the other. He who looks to all the causes in operation—the near approach of the final payment of the public debt—the growing disaffection and resistance to the system in so large a section of the country—the deeper principles on which opposition to it is gradually turning—must be, indeed, infatuated not to see a great change is unavoidable; and that the attempt to elude or much longer delay it must, finally, but increase the shock and disastrous consequences which may follow.

In forming the opinions I have expressed, I have not been actuated by an unkind feeling towards our manufacturing interest. I now am, and ever have been, decidedly friendly to them, though I cannot concur in all of the measures which have been adopted to advance them. I believe considerations higher than any question of mere pecuniary interest forbade their use. But subordinate to these higher views of policy, I regard the advancement of mechanical and chemical improvements in the arts with feelings little short of enthusiasm; not only as the prolific source of national and individual wealth, but as the great means of enlarging the domain of man over the material world, and thereby of laying the solid foundation of a highly-improved condition of society, morally and politically. I fear not that we shall extend our power too far over the great agents of nature; but, on the contrary, I consider such enlargement of our power as tending more certainly and powerfully to better the condition of our race, than any one of the many powerful causes now operating to that result. With these impressions, I not only rejoice at the general progress of the arts in the world, but in their advancement in our own country; and as far as protection may be incidentally afforded, in the fair and honest exercise of our constitutional powers, I think now, as I have always thought, that sound policy, connected with the security, independence, and peace of the country, requires it should be done; but that we cannot go a single step beyond without jeopardizing our peace, our harmony and our liberty—considerations of infinitely more importance to us than any measure of mere policy can possibly be.

In thus placing my opinions before the public, I have not been actuated by the expectation of changing the public sentiment. Such a motive, on a question so long agitated, and so beset with feelings of prejudice and interest, would argue, on my part, an insufferable vanity, and a profound ignorance of the human heart. To avoid, as far as possible, the imputation of either, I have confined my statement, on the many and important points on which I have been compelled to touch, to a simple declaration of my opinion, without advancing any other reasons to sustain them than what appeared to me to be indispensable to the full understanding of my views; and if they should, on any point, be thought to be not clearly and explicitly developed, it will, I trust, be attributed to my solicitude to avoid the imputations to which I have alluded, and not from any desire to disguise my sentiments, nor the want of arguments and illustrations to maintain positions, which so abound in both, that it would require a volume to do them any thing like justice. I can only hope the truths which, I feel assured, are essentially connected with all that we ought to hold most dear, may not be weakened in the public estimation by the imperfect manner in which I have been, by the object in view, compelled to present them.

With every caution on my part, I dare not hope, in taking the step I have, to escape the imputation of improper motives; though I have, without reserve, freely expressed my opinions, not regarding whether they might or might not be popular. I have no reason to believe that they are such as will conciliate public favor, but the opposite, which I greatly regret, as I have ever placed a high estimate on the good opinion of my fellow-citizens. But, be that as it may, I shall, at least, be sustained by feelings of conscious rectitude. I have formed my opinions after the most careful and deliberate examination, with all the aids which my reason and experience could furnish; I have expressed them honestly and fearlessly, regardless of their effects personally, which, however interesting to me individually, are of too little importance to be taken into the estimate, where the liberty and happiness of our country are so vitally involved.

JOHN C. CALHOUN.

FORT HILL, *July 26th,* 1831.

CHAPTER X.

"Draft Report on Federal Relations," 20 November 1831

Like the "Exposition," the "Report" was probably written at the request of members of the South Carolina state legislature. It extends the arguments of the "Exposition," obviously answering some criticisms that had arisen in the intervening three years. In the "Report," Calhoun showed how the "right of [state] interposition" was in agreement with the American political tradition and "the principles of reason, and analogy."

The committee, to whom was referred so much of the Governor's message as refers to the relation between the States and General Government, and the subjects immediately connected therewith,—have had the same under consideration, with that anxious solicitude to arrive at the truth, which their deep importance, and the existing relations growing out of them, so seriously demand. The result has been a deeper conviction, if possible, of the truth of the doctrines for which this State contends, and the necessity of maintaining them at every sacrifice, in order to preserve the Constitution,—the Union,—and the liberty of the country.

In presenting the result of their deliberations, your committee propose to touch on a few prominent points only, which the present state of this long protracted struggle on the part of the State to maintain its rights, seems to render necessary,—passing by in silence all of minor importance, including those which they deem already sufficiently established.

The relations existing between this State and the General Government, grew, as is well known to all, out of the Tariff. But, as deeply interesting as your committee consider the questions involved in a protective Tariff, to this and the other Southern States, particularly when connected with its unconstitutionality,—they deem it of vastly inferior importance to the great question to which it has given rise, and which is now at issue in the controversy; the right of a State to interpose, in the last resort, in order to arrest an unconstitutional act of the General Government, within its limits. This they conceive to be by far the most important question which can be presented under our system;—as on its determination depends the fact, whether ours be, in reality, a federated or consolidated government;—a government with a constitution imposing checks and restrictions on the governing power, or one with the form of a constitution, but, in reality, without any practical check or restriction whatever. Such is its magnitude; such the great question which has become so prominent in the present controversy, and which so long divided the two great political parties of our country.

Whether the Constitution be a compact between the people of the several States, forming separate and distinct political communities, or an act of the American people, forming one aggregate community, derives its importance wholly from the bearing which it has on the question of the right of a State to interpose. Without such bearing,—however curious the question might be, as involving a mere historical fact, it would have very little more interest than any other connected with our constitutional history,—being destitute of all practical consequence, and having no greater power to agitate the feelings and passions of the community. It is only when viewed in connection with the question of interposition that it swells into importance;—an importance which must continue to increase just in proportion as the intimate relation between the two is perceived and appreciated. That the relation between them is, in fact, of the most intimate character,—so intimate that, if it be conceded, that the Constitution is a compact between the States in the manner stated, it follows as a necessary consequence, that the States have the right to interpose,—your committee deem susceptible of the most demonstrative proofs; and that, consequently, the only issue is, in reality, between those who maintain the doctrine above stated, and those who contend that the Constitution is the act of the American people, taken collectively. In making this assertion, your committee are aware that there is a very respectable class, which, while it admits the Constitution to be a compact between the States, denies the right of a State to interpose; but, if they do not greatly misapprehend the views of those to whom they refer, they feel confident it will appear, on examination, that, while they deny the right of interposition, they are compelled, in order to distinguish their doctrines from those who deny the Constitution to be a compact between the States, to assume grounds which necessarily involve the right of interposition. Perceiving that, to deny to the States all right of resistance to an unconstitutional act, would, in fact, be to divest them of all rights in virtue of their being parties to the Constitution,—and that the denial of the right to interpose, would practically confound their doctrines with those who deny the instrument to be a compact between the States, they are compelled to contend for the right of secession, as distinct from that of rebellion, or resistance by mere force,—which all admit belong to the oppressed, be the form of government what it may. But to maintain the distinction, it is not only necessary to assume that the Constitution is a compact between the States, but that they have, in virtue of being parties to it, a right to judge, in their political and sovereign capacity as States, whether the instrument has been violated or not; and to determine, if violated, that the act is null and void;—all of which are absolutely necessary to distinguish secession from the forcible resistance of mere individuals against an unjust and oppressive government: but it is no less clear that secession, thus distinguished, is not only an act of interposition on the part of the State, but the very highest possible act of the kind,—and that it assumes principles which cover the whole ground of the State-rights doctrines. Concede that the State is a party to the constitutional compact,—that, in virtue thereof, she has a right, as a State, to judge of its infractions, and to determine whether it be, or be not obligatory,—and all will be conceded for which this State has ever contended. The State would, accordingly, in all cases of infraction, necessarily become the rightful judge of the "mode and measure of redress;" and no mode would be interdicted to her, unless it could be shown that there was something in its nature incompatible with the right. This has been attempted, as to the one proposed by this State; but, in the opinion of your committee, with such complete failure of success, as to confirm, rather than weaken the position which they have taken. With this view, it has been objected that the exercise of the right of interposition, by arresting within the limits of the State an unconstitutional act of the General Government, would be absurd,— because it would involve the supposed contradiction, that a State might be both *in* and *out* of the Union at the same time. Your committee find some difficulty in treating an argument, at once so false in its assumptions and so scholastic in its character, with the gravity which becomes a public document, discussing subjects of such dignity and deep importance. In fact, they would have deemed it utterly unworthy, both of their notice and the occasion, were they not satisfied that, destitute of weight as it is, it has been the leading cause of error, on the part of a large portion of those whose views they are at present considering. It is only under this impression that they feel justified in giving it a passing notice.

It is certainly not a little remarkable, that what has been so often asserted to be impossible,—for a State to be both *in* and *out* of the Union at the same time,—so far from being true, is the very reverse,—the only true and constitutional position of a State being precisely that which the argument supposes to be impossible. A State is at all times, so long as its proper position is maintained, both *in* and *out* of the Union;—*in*, for all constitutional purposes,—and *out*, for all others;—*in*, to the extent of the delegated powers, and *out*, to that of the reserved. Any other position would be either consolidation on the one side, or disunion on the other; and the argument, if it be good for any thing, would prove that our *federated system*, which is justly our pride and boast, is but a political paradox. Nor would it be much short of an equal paradox, if the States, in truth, possessed no right—as those who maintain the argument contend—to resist an attempt to force them from their true federative, constitutional position,—of being *in* and *out*, into that of being *entirely in*, or *entirely out*,—either of which (the disease—and the only admitted remedy, according to this view without withdrawing from the Union), would be equally destructive of the system. And yet, by a strange confusion of ideas, this very right of resisting an attempt to force a State from its constitutional position, and which is indispensable to the preservation of the system, is considered as incompatible with its existence!

With the same view, it is also objected, from the same quarter, that it is a principle in the laws regulating contracts, that a party has no right to consider a contract as violated and null in part, and not violated and null in the whole,—a principle which your committee consider, at least, of doubtful authority; but which they do not deem it necessary at this time to investigate. This State, in asserting the right of interposition, has never gone on the assumption, that the Constitution was null and void, either in whole or in part, in consequence of the infractions of which she so justly complains. She is not ignorant that, when an instrument is violated, it belongs to the aggrieved party to determine, whether it shall be obligatory or not; but she places too high an estimate on the great value of our Constitutional compact, to raise a question as to its obligation, notwithstanding it has been so long and grossly violated to her very great injury. She has been contending for a very different, and, it may be added, far less revolutionary right; the right, not of setting aside the provisions of the Constitution, either in whole, or in part, but the right to maintain or preserve them in their full force, by arresting all attempts on the part of the General Government to violate them. Her object is not to *destroy*, but to *preserve*; and she acts on the broad and radical distinction, between the right to prevent, and arrest infractions, and the right to set aside the instrument in consequence of such infractions. If, indeed, as contended, the system contains no provision, by which the parties might effectually prevent or arrest a violation of the constitutional compact, but by the destruction of the instrument itself, this, according to her opinion,—however admirable the government might be in other respects, would, of itself be a defect, so radical, and fatal, as to doom it, inevitably, to a short and inglorious career. But your committee feel assured, the builders of our noble political fabric have constructed it on far more durable and imperishable principles. Nor do they feel less confidence, that the more thoroughly the subject is investigated, and the more perfectly it is understood, the more clearly it will be seen, that the true conservative principle—that which will enable the fabric to resist the action of time, force, and fraud—will be found in the doctrines on which this State has taken so high and so honorable a stand.

It is likewise objected that, if a State interfere to arrest an unconstitutional act of the General Government, she must necessarily interfere with some of its regular functions; and that it is, therefore, a power inhibited to the State. Your committee readily admit, that a State, in exercising a power to preserve the Constitution,—which is the object of interposition,—has no right to adopt measures incompatible with it,—and that all such measures are necessarily inhibited: but to assert that such must be the necessary consequence of the exercise of the right, is plainly to beg the question. It is the very point at issue;—to be proved, and not to be assumed. The real question is,—Has a State, acting in its sovereign capacity, a right to judge of the infractions of the compact?—and what, according to the true theory of our Government, would be the effect, if, acting in such capacity, as a party to the compact, a State should declare an act of Congress to be a violation of the Constitution, and, therefore, null and void?— Whether such an act on the part of a State is not, in its nature, paramount on its citizens,—binding them through their allegiance to the State, as fully and absolutely, as an Act of Secession, founded on a similar declaration, and asserting that, in consequence of such infraction, the Constitution itself is null and void,—which those who urge the objection, maintain the State has a right to make? If the latter be obligatory on its citizens, it is clear the former would be also. They both stand on the same ground,—the sovereignty of the State,—and the consequent allegiance of its citizens. But it is obvious that, if a State have this right,—which those, at least, who admit of secession, cannot deny,—the effect of such declaration,—so binding its citizens, judges, juries, and all others—must necessarily be to arrest the unconstitutional act of the General Government within its limits,—which, thanks to the Constitution,—can only be executed, like all other acts of that Government, through courts and juries; thus affording a new and powerful illustration of the admirable privilege of jury-trial, and the

essential importance to the preservation of liberty, that the people should be represented, as well in the Judicial, as in the Legislative or Executive Departments
of the Government. But, if the exercise of such power on the part of a State be
rightful,—which those who hold the Constitution to be a compact between the
people of the several States cannot deny,—such a declaration on the part of a
State, would not only have an obligatory force on its own citizens, but on the
General Government itself, through all of its departments. It would be, in truth,
an act of a distinct department of our complex political system,—exercised
within the limits of its peculiar sphere (as the reserved powers are clearly within
the proper and exclusive sphere of the States), and would be as binding on the
other department, as an act of one of the departments of the General Government itself, within its assigned and peculiar sphere would be on the other co-
departments. In all complex and free governments, where the powers of
government are divided, it is an essential attribute of such division, that each,
within its own assigned sphere, should be paramount to the other; a principle
which necessarily extends to the great and fundamental division of power
between the States and General Government, as well as to the divisions of power
within their respective organizations. The reason is the same in both,—while
the necessity is even greater, if possible, in the former than the latter.

Such being the fact, it is manifest, that the General Government would be
as much bound to respect the declaration of a State, acting within its peculiar
sphere, on powers belonging exclusively to itself, and the maintenance of which
would be indispensable to her proper attitude in the system, as either of its
departments would be to respect the other,—the Legislative or Executive to
respect the Judiciary, or *vice versa;*—and that it would be just as reasonable to
apply force to compel the Supreme Court to reverse its decision on a question
within its jurisdiction, as to compel a State to abandon its declaration on a question appertaining to her reserved rights. They both stand on the same ground,—
and the remedy is the same in both cases:—the co-departments must yield the
power in contest, or obtain it by a positive grant from three fourths of the
States,—the legitimate and peculiar remedy, provided by our admirable system,
by which every jar in its highly complicated machinery, may be quietly, peacefully, and permanently removed.

But it is objected, from the same quarter,—by those who assert, with us, that
the Constitution is a compact to which the States are parties,—and who affirm
the right of secession, but deny the right of interposition *in any other form,*—that
the right for which the State contends, though it might be inferred on general
principles, from the character of the Government,—has been actually surren-

dered by the Constitution itself, and cannot, therefore, be exercised constitutionally by the States. They assert that the Supreme Court is the tribunal
expressly ordained by the Constitution itself, to decide all controversies between
the States and the General Government,—which necessarily divests the State of
the right in question.

It is not the intention of your committee to enter into a minute examination
of the assumption on which this objection rests,—that the Supreme Court is
vested with the power to determine all disputes between the General and State
Governments. They do not deem it necessary in replying to those, who concur
with the State,—that the Constitution is a compact between the States ratifying
it,—as they are prepared to prove that the assumption, if true, would be as fatal
to those who maintain the right of secession, as to those who contend for the
right of arresting the operation of an unconstitutional act. But they deem it their
duty to say, that never was there an assumption more perfectly gratuitous than
that the Supreme Court is vested, by the Constitution, with power to decide all
controversies between the States and the General Government. So far from the
Constitution containing any such express grant,—as has been often asserted,—it
contains none from which it can be inferred by any argument entitled to be called
even plausible. The right of the court to exercise so high a power was, at first,
placed on the provision of the Constitution, extending its jurisdiction to "all cases
in law and equity, arising under the Constitution,—the laws of the United States,
and treaties made, or which shall be made under their authority." Never was a
conclusion of such deep import, drawn from feebler premises. We have the highest authority for asserting that the expression, *"cases in law and equity,"* is technical, and limited to questions of a *judicial* character, between parties amenable to
the process of the court: and that it does not extend to questions of a *political* character, we have the decision of the court itself in the recent Cherokee case.

But finding that the high power in question could not be inferred from this
provision of the Constitution, it has been attempted, with no greater success, to
draw it from another, which extends the jurisdiction of the court to,—"Controversies to which the United States are parties."—It is true that the term,
"Controversies," is broader and less technical than, *"Cases in Law and Equity,"*
and might, when considered in the abstract, be extended to all controversies
whatever, in which the United States were *concerned*. But it is an axiom that a
Government cannot be sued but with its own consent; and, of course, the term,
"controversies," as used in this case, must, of necessity, be limited to the cases
where the United States are plaintiff,—or where they have voluntarily permitted themselves to be sued; and, of course, excludes the idea that a State can bring

a controversy between itself and the General Government, before the court. The term, taken in its broad sense, would lead to the most absurd consequences; and among others, that a foreign nation might bring its controversy before the Supreme Court;—and, instead of enforcing the observance of treaties by arms, enforce them by the decree of the court. Its powers are strictly *judicial,*—and under our peculiar system, so far from being appointed by the Constitution as the special guardian of that instrument, even the right to decide an act of Congress unconstitutional, is a mere matter of inference, growing out of the nature of the system itself,—and is limited strictly to the necessity of the case. When a "case in law or equity" is brought before the court regularly, it must decide according to law;—and as the Constitution is of higher authority than an act of Congress, it follows, as a necessary consequence, that the decision must conform to the Constitution;—but so strictly is it a mere resulting power, and the creature of necessity, that the court can take no cognizance of an unconstitutional act, unless it be apparent on its face;—and thus, as an incidental check on the Legislative and Executive Departments of the Government, can exert no salutary influence, where a constitutional power has been perverted to an unconstitutional purpose,—the most insidious and dangerous of all infractions. But be these views sound or not, it belongs not to those to object, who claim for a State the right to secede from the Union.

Considered in reference to those who urge them, your committee are at a loss to explain, how doctrines so manifestly contradictory as the right of secession, on the part of a State, and the right of the Supreme Court to decide in all controversies between the States and General Government, can possibly be entertained by the same individuals. The two rights obviously rest on opposite assumptions; the former, as has been shown, necessarily presupposing that the State, as a party to the constitutional compact, has the right to judge of its infractions, and to determine whether it be any longer obligatory;—the latter expressly negativing these assumptions, by affirming that the very power in question has been surrendered, in the Constitution itself, to the court,—and, therefore, cannot be exercised by the parties to it;—and assertion which, if correct, would manifestly be as fatal to the right of secession, as to that of arresting an unconstitutional act of the General Government within the limits of the State;—thus leaving, if well founded, no other mode of resistance than that of force.

These are believed to be the only objections of any weight, which have been urged against the right of interposition, by those who concur in the opinion that the Constitution is a compact,—but who, at the same time, deny to the State the right to interpose;—and, unless your committee be under a great mistake, they are so utterly destitute of all solidity, as to authorize them to conclude, that there is no intermediate position that can be maintained, between that assumed by the State, and that sustained by those who deny that the States, as distinct political communities, had any agency in its formation, or any right, in any form, to judge of its infractions;—and, consequently, any right, either to interpose, or to secede or resist in any other mode. If this conclusion be correct,—of which your committee has the firmest conviction,—it will be impossible that those, who, from a hasty view of the subject, or from any other cause, have attempted to take an intermediate position, can maintain a ground so utterly untenable; and they must be ultimately compelled to occupy, either that assumed by the State-Rights, or that by the Consolidation Party;—a term they use without any desire to attach odium to its members, but simply to avoid circumlocution;—and believing, at the same time, that they do no injustice;—for it is impossible for them to form a conception of a consolidated, as opposed to a federative system, that is not embraced by the doctrines which this party supports.

The question of interposition, turning, then, simply on the great historical fact,—whether our Constitution be, in truth, a compact between the people of the States, as distinct political communities, or the act of the American people, taken collectively,—your committee propose, in the next place, to offer a few remarks on the question, viewed in this aspect:—and surely a more momentous one, regarded in all its connections, was never offered for the consideration of a free people. It is impossible to bestow on it too much reflection, or to regard it with too deep, or too serious a consideration.

Were it possible to establish the fact, that the Constitution was the act of the American people, considered in the aggregate, consequences would inevitably follow which would radically affect the entire character of the Government;—and which could not fail to lead to the most disastrous results. Admit its truth, and the States at once sink into mere geographical divisions,—bearing the same relation to the whole, as counties do to the States,—possessed of no right, and exercising no power, but such as may be derived from the concession of the majority of the people of the whole Union,—from whom all power would be derived, and to whom, only, allegiance would be due. Viewed in this light, it would be a mere concession from the majority, that the assent of the States was necessary to give validity to the Constitution;—that three fourths of them are necessary to alter or amend the instrument;—that they have an equal representation in the Senate;—or that they possess reserved rights at all;—concessions which could, at any time, be resumed, whenever the majority should deem fit, by a call of a Convention of the whole,—which, according to the theory in question, would have the right to strip the States of all their powers,—and even to substitute another Constitution in the place of the present,—moulded as the majority might think proper. But the exercise of this high power on the part of the majority, would be, under this view of the subject, an act of supererogation. Let it be conceded that the States, as separate and distinct communities, had no agency in the formation of the Constitution,—that the instrument, instead of being a compact between *them,* is the act of the *American people in the aggregate,*— and that the States have no right to interpose, in order to resist encroachments on their reserved powers, and the unlimited and unquestioned right of the majority to construe it at its will,—which would be a necessary consequence;— and it would inevitably, in time, mould the Constitution to its pleasure, without the trouble or hazard of substituting, formally, a new one in place of the old. When we look at the progress which this system of construction has already made in substituting the old, and rearing a new edifice in its place, contested as the right has been,—it is manifest, that, it would be impossible to assign any limits to its power, if it be once conceded that the majority have the right of placing what construction they please on the Constitution;—or, what is the same thing, that there is no right on the part of the States to resist their construction.

If such dangerous and heretical doctrines as these should gain the ascendency, it would be impossible for any situation to be more exposed than ours;— but, fortunately for us, they rest on an assumption utterly destitute of truth. If there be any historical fact certain, it is, that the Constitution is the act of the States, as distinct and separate bodies politic, and not that of the American People as a single community. Your committee do not propose to enter into an examination of the question, historically; for they do not deem it necessary after the full and conclusive evidence which has been so frequently adduced in support of the assertion. The truth is, that the very idea of an *American People,* as constituting a single community, is a mere chimera. Such a community never, for a single moment, existed,—neither before nor since the Declaration of Independence. While under the authority of Great Britain, these States existed as separate and distinct colonies,—having no common union, except through the mother country; and on the termination of their colonial state, the very act declaring that condition at an end, declared them at the same time to be *free and independent States.* Were it possible to raise a doubt as to the meaning intended to be conveyed by the use of these terms, it would be removed by the fact, that, contemporaneous with this declaration, there was pending before the body which declared their independence, the project of a government for them, based on federal principles, and which resulted in establishing, what is called, the Old Confederation,—under which, it is conceded, each State was left in possession of its freedom and independence:—thus confirming, beyond the possibility of doubt, the meaning for which your committee contend.

If it were possible to add strength to a position of itself so clear, it would be furnished by the feebleness of the arguments by which the opposite views are attempted to be sustained. Those who maintain them assert that the Union preceded even the Declaration of Independence,—and, of course, the formation of the Government,—and that the Government is derived from the Union, and not the Union from the Government,—forgetting that the real question relates to the *character* of the Union, and not to the *time* of its commencement:— whether it was formed of pre-existing political communities, which still retained under it their separate and independent existence, or of the entire people as one body politic;—a Union, in other words, of *communities,* or of *individuals.* That it was the former, it is just as impossible to doubt, as it is the existence of the War of the Revolution itself. The members of the old Congress, which preceded the Declaration of Independence, met as representatives of colonies, forming separate communities,—voted by colonies,—and finally declared, when that state was terminated, that "these united *Colonies* are, and of right ought to be, free and independent *States;*—thus placing it beyond all doubt, that the informal union, which preceded the Declaration of Independence, and which grew out of the common danger, was, in fact, the Union of *Colonies,* as *political communities,* and not of *individuals,* as forming a *single community.*

But it is contended, that the expression in the preamble of the Constitution,— "We, the People of the United States," is properly descriptive of the people in the aggregate, and not of the people of the States separately;—and that it proves the Constitution to have been the act of the former, and not of the latter.

It is no feeble proof of the strength of the side this State supports, and the weakness of the opposite, that the advocates of the latter are compelled to resort to mere verbal criticism,—and that, too, of the most equivocal character,—in the discussion of a question of deepest import, and involving the fundamental principles of our political system. It is perfectly gratuitous to assume, that the expression,—"We the People of the United States," applies more properly to the people, in the sense for which the Consolidation Party contends, than in that for which the State Rights Party contends.—If there be a difference, it is more strictly applicable to the people of the several States, than to the whole, as one people. It may, in fact, be fairly considered as a concise mode of expressing the same idea that a formal enumeration of the States, by name, would have conveyed, and used to avoid prolixity. That the expression was not intended to indicate the people of the United States, taken collectively, we have conclusive proof in the seventh and last article of the Constitution, which provides that "the ratification of nine States shall be sufficient to establish this Constitution between the States so ratifying the same;"—clearly indicating that "People," as used in the Preamble, meant the people of the several States, considered as separate communities.

Such, and so feeble are the arguments by which it is attempted to subvert the very foundations of our system;—that the Constitution is a compact between the several States;—that, as parties to it, the States have a right to interpose, in the last resort, in order to preserve the Constitution, and to arrest encroachments on their reserved rights;—a doctrine, without which, our Government would be without check or balance, subject to the control of an interested and unrestricted majority. That arguments so slight and unconclusive,—leading to consequences so fatal to our liberty,—should ever have gained the assent of a large portion of the community, is but additional proof of the ascendency, which interest holds over the human judgment,—and of which history abounds with so many, and such melancholy examples. With these before us, we ought not to be surprised, that those who are profiting by our erroneous construction, should be deluded into a belief of its truth; but we, who are its victims, ought to see in it additional reasons for the most zealous and strenuous resistance.

It is, indeed, high time for the people of the South to be roused to a sense of impending calamities,—on an early and full knowledge of which their safety depends. It is time that they should see and feel that in regard to climate, property and production, their situation in the Union is peculiar, and that they are in a permanent and hopeless minority on the great and vital connected questions,—with a powerful, adverse and monopolizing interest opposed,—supported by a strong, united and preponderating majority. Thus situated, there is, to us, no hope in the administration of the powers of the General Government,—over every department of which,—Legislative, Executive, and Judicial,—the will of the majority prevails. Our only safety is in the Constitution itself,—on maintaining which inviolate, is involved the liberty and happiness of ourselves and our posterity. Fortunately for us, our relative power and security are very different, as it relates to the Constitution, and to the administration of the powers granted under it,—a difference which we ought never, for a moment, to forget. It is one that is fundamental in our system, and, to us, all-important. While in the latter,—the execution of the powers granted,—the will of the majority predominates on every subject, with a few special exceptions—

in the former,—determining the grants of power,—the consent of three fourths of all the States is required. This great and primary distinction between the *grant-ing* and the *executing,*—the *constitution-making,* and the *law-making* power, is the rock of our political salvation. It is the refuge—and the only refuge—of the minority States, against the encroachments of an interested majority, wielding the administration of the powers of the Government through all its departments, at its will, and according to the dictates of avarice or ambition. We make no complaint that the majority should control the administration. It is correct that the granted powers,—in the exercise of which all are supposed to have a com-mon interest,—should be under the control of the majority;—but this ought not, in the smallest degree, to weaken our determination to maintain, with the utmost vigor, and at every hazard, the higher and more essential right that belongs to us, as a distinct portion of the *constitution-making power,*—to arrest infractions, and to see that no power shall be exercised by the General Govern-ment, which has not, in fact, been granted by three fourths of all the States. And it is because we feel the deepest conviction that this fundamental and, to us, vital right can only be enforced and made effectual by that of interposition, that we are so strongly impressed with the solemn and sacred obligation of maintaining it at every sacrifice. There is no mystery in this subject. The right of interposi-tion which this State claims, is not only deducible, by the clearest demonstra-tion, from the principles and character of our political institutions, but is, also, strictly consonant to those of reason and analogy. The General Government, properly considered, is but a great political association, in which the States, as parties to the contract that formed it, are *partners,* and the Government the *direc-tion.** Among the leading and essential provisions of the contract are,—that no power should be granted to the *association,* or exercised by the *direction,* except such as have been assented to by three fourths of all the *partners,* and that the *compact,* forming the association, shall not be changed or altered but by a pro-portional number of the partners; but that the powers granted, with a few speci-fied exceptions, should be exercised by a majority of the direction, appointed by a majority of the partners; thus subjecting the two to a very different con-trol; in the former, the will of the majority prevails,—while in the latter, the consent of three fourths of the partners is required.

Thus organized, it is impossible not to see, that the interest which controls in the direction, must come into conflict with that which prevails with the partners

---

*The verbal critic may read *director,* and thus save the labor of a philological disquisition.—*Editor* [Crallé].

or stockholders; and that, unless there be, on the part of the latter, a right to compel the former to submit all questions touching the compact of association, to the stockholders themselves, according to the provision of the contract, the interests of the direction would absorb those of the stockholders,—the *By-Laws* would prevail over the *Charter;*—and we accordingly find, in all private associations, such a right universally recognized, as essential to protect the rights and interests of the stockholders, against those of the direction. But as essential as this is in all such associations, it is far more so in our great Political Joint-Stock Association,—comprehending, as it does, powers that may touch the labor and capital of the whole community; and when, of course, the motives to encroachment are infinitely stronger than they can be in any case of private association.

But, on the question,—whether the States have a right to interpose, depends the fact, whether they are, or are not possessed of this power, so clearly indispensable to protect the higher and more sacred rights that belong to them as a portion of the constitution-making power, against the mere law-making or administrative power;—or, in other words,—whether the Constitution or the laws shall be paramount; as it must be perfectly clear that, unless the States, in their high and sovereign character, as parties to the constitutional compact, can interpose to arrest, within their respective limits, the unconstitutional acts of the Government, and thereby compel it to abandon the exercise of an unconstitutional power, or to submit the question to the decision of the States themselves, to be determined according to the provisions of the Constitution,—the will of the majority, acting through the Government, must become, in practice, stronger than the will of three fourths of the States, acting through the Constitution. Yet it is this very power, so absolutely necessary to maintain the ascendency of the Constitution over the laws, which, under the name of nullification, is denounced as anarchy, treason, and rebellion; and those who advocate it threatened with the vengeance of the laws; as if it were possible to commit treason under a constitutional system, by maintaining the practical supremacy of the Constitution over the laws,—of the constitution-making power over the law-making power, and of the act of a State touching a question relating to its reserved rights, and acting in her high character, as a party to the constitutional compact,—over the acts of the Government appointed to administer the delegated rights, and whose acts, beyond the granted powers, are absolutely null and void! But conscious of the truth and justice of our cause, and feeling thoroughly convinced, that nothing short of the practical assertion of the supremacy of the Constitution over the laws,—of the *stockholding,* over the *direction* interest,—can possibly avert from us and our posterity (standing, as the South does, in a permanent minority), the most overwhelming calamity—or preserve the liberty of the country,—neither denunciations nor threats can drive us from maintaining the ground, which the State has assumed, and of the triumph of which, finally, your committee feel the most perfect assurance.

Having devoted so much time to the all-important question of the right of interposition on the part of a State to arrest an unconstitutional act of the General Government, within its limits, your committee feel compelled to pass over, with a few brief remarks only, that of the character and operation of the present Tariff. Nor, had they leisure, would they deem, at this time,—after so many and such able discussions,—a minute or full examination necessary.

Whatever may be the difference in opinion, as to the degree of oppression, there are few, indeed, who do not believe the Tariff to be oppressive, unjust, and unconstitutional. Without deeming it a matter of importance to ascertain the precise extent of the burden it imposes on us, your committee consider it essential that the general character of its operation, in respect to this and other States similarly situated, should be clearly understood; and to this point their remarks will be principally confined.

They, who are most disposed to deny its unjust operation, base their opinion on the principle or assumption, that the duty is a tax on *consumption,*—that every part of the community pays in proportion to the amount of its consumption,—and that, as consumption is, probably, nearly in proportion to population and wealth, all the sections of the country pay in nearly equal proportions. The foundation of the argument is, that the consumer pays the tax, and that all consumers bear the burden in proportion to the amount consumed. The rule is laid down without exception or limitation, and, as it is believed, contains the creed of those who are inclined to question the unequal action of the protective system. Were there no other, there is one conclusive argument against the position, that all consumers bear a burden equal to their consumption. It confounds all distinctions between the *tax-payers* and the *tax-consumers;*—those who pay for the liberty of consuming, and those who consume the proceeds of the tax;—two classes that are clearly affected in a directly opposite manner by the tax; and who bear a relation to it as antagonistic as that of payer and receiver. The effect of the tax is to diminish the consumption of the one, while it increases that of the other; the higher the tax, the less is left to the former to consume, while the more is given to the latter. It seems to be overlooked by those who maintain the burden to be equal, that taxation and appropriation are necessarily connected; that the fiscal system consists, not only in taking *from,* but in giving *to;*—and, that these two operations are equal; that as much as is taken from the tax-payers, just so much goes, through appropriations, to the tax-consumers;—and, so far from the two classes of consumers bearing an equal portion of the burden, the benefits of the system to the tax-consumers, is just equal to the pressure on the tax-payers. To illustrate the position:—Let it be supposed that a planter ships one hundred bales of cotton to Liverpool,—that he sells or exchanges them for one hundred pieces of goods;—and, to simplify the case,—let it be supposed that the duty is paid *in kind,* which we will assume to be forty per cent., though the average greatly exceeds this amount. The goods arrive at Charleston, and forty pieces are deposited in the Custom-House, for the liberty of introducing sixty. The consumption of the planter is thus clearly reduced from one hundred pieces, which he would have a right to consume, were there no duty, to sixty pieces.

But the forty, taken from him by the Tariff, are not lost. They have become the property of the Government; or, what with us is the same thing, of the majority, which passes them away through its appropriations, and they are consumed by those who receive them. Repeal the duty, and the planter would have forty pieces more to consume, and those who received them through the appropriations, forty less. Double the duty,—make it eighty, instead of forty per cent., and the consumption of the planter would be reduced from sixty to twenty pieces, while that of those who receive, would be raised from forty to eighty pieces;—thus showing, beyond the possibility of doubt, that, so far from bearing equal burdens as *consumers,* the consumption, on the one side, is increased in exact proportion as the other is diminished. What is true in a single instance, is true in every other;—and we may be perfectly assured that the $24,000,000 collected annually from the imports, are, in reality, taken from one class and go to another; and that, while it diminishes the consumption of the former by the whole amount, it increases that of the latter by the same. To confound the two,—to suppose they bear equal burdens, is clearly and manifestly to overlook a most important distinction, and to confound things of the most opposite character, because they happen all to be classed under the name of consumers.

But there is another circumstance, not much less important, which is also overlooked in estimating the relative burdens of the system. In affirming that the burden is in proportion to the consumption, it is meant,—the consumption of imported articles paying duties;—omitting, entirely, the effects of the system in increasing the price of the domestic articles of the same description;—as well as of all other, produced in the manufacturing section, and which must necessarily be raised in price, by the great subtraction of labor and capital from their production to that of manufactures. It is clear, that the consumers of these domestic articles must be taken into the estimate, as well as the consumers of the foreign articles, in order to determine where the burden of the system falls; and it is no less clear that, to the producing section, the increased prices act as a bounty instead of a tax, while to the other, the reverse is the fact. Thus far admits of no doubt, and proves, beyond all controversy, that the position, that all pay in proportion to their consumption, must, at least, be taken with very important qualifications.

But your committee are of opinion, that objections still more decisive may be taken to the position. They cannot doubt, after the most mature investigation, that the impost is a tax on the foreign exchanges of the country, and must, from its nature, fall on the section or interest which furnishes the means of payment, without reference to consumption.

It is an unquestionable fact, that the imports are, at least, equal to the exports: in fact, they exceed them by several millions of dollars annually; which, however, is accounted for by adding the profits of our navigation and commerce to the value of the articles of export, estimated at the ports of shipment. Assuming them to be equal, it follows, as a necessary consequence, that our foreign exchanges are, in effect, barter transactions;—that though we may buy and sell for *cash,* in the intermediate stages, yet the final result is an exchange, *in kind,* of all we export, for all we import. The Custom-House books settle this point beyond controversy; and fully authorize your committee to consider the foreign trade of the country, in the simple form of barter, without the intervention of cash or specie;—which only facilitates the intermediate stages, without affecting the final result, or, consequently, the principle, in determining how a tax or duty on the exchange acts. Supposing, then, specie to be banished, and the foreign trade carried on by direct barter throughout, and that the duties were paid at the Custom-House *in kind* instead of *cash,*—and it would be impossible to doubt on whom the tax or duty would fall. It would, beyond all controversy, fall on the section or interest which would furnish the exports. Assuming, as they have, the duty to be forty per cent., nothing can be more certain than that, if a planter should ship an amount of tobacco, rice or cotton, which would exchange for one hundred pieces of manufactured goods in Liverpool, or any other foreign port,—after leaving forty pieces at the Custom-House to pay the duty, he would have but sixty left;—without any reference whatever to the fact, whether he consumed them or not: nor is it less certain that, if instead of exporting the produce himself, he exchanges it with a merchant at home for goods, he must receive less than sixty pieces, as the latter must deduct his profit,—the cost of buying, insurance, and other charges, whatever they might be. And it is equally certain, that what would be true of a part of the exports of the country, and as a barter transaction, would be true of all. Considered in this simple form, as a mere barter, without the intervention of specie,—and it is as clear a proposition as any possibly can be, that the rate of duty or tax on the imports, is neither more nor less than the ratio of division, between the producer of the articles exported in exchange for foreign products, and the Government. If it be forty per cent., then forty of the whole will be the Government's, and sixty the producer's. If raised to sixty per cent., then the Government's share will be sixty, and the producer's forty;—and so for any higher or lower rate, without the least reference to the consumption of the producer. These conclusions are perfectly simple and incontrovertible;—so much so, that there never could have been the least doubt as to the operation, had it not been for the complexity, which the introduction of specie, in the intermediate stages, to facilitate the process of exchange, has given to the calculation; and it only remains to be shown that this circumstance cannot possibly vary the result.

It is true, that specie is duty free;—it is, however, equally true, that it is not an article of consumption, but a part of the machinery of commerce,—imported to be exported,—as the equilibrium between the two demonstratively proves,— except of course, that inconsiderable portion, which is necessary to be added annually to the metallic currency of the country, or that may be converted into jewelry, or other articles of consumption. It is also equally clear, that, considered as an article of export for the purpose of importing goods (and it is only with this view, finally, that it is exported), it must, in fact, be worth less by the amount of the duties on the articles to be imported. For example,—if a sum be exported sufficient to buy one hundred pieces of goods in Liverpool, or any other foreign port, and the duty at the Custom-House be forty pieces of the hundred imported, the specie would only exchange for sixty pieces at home, and hence it follows that it would be impossible to elude the duty which, as has been shown, would inevitably fall on the exporting or staple interests, either on the supposition that the foreign trade was carried on wholly by barter or by importing specie in the first instance instead of goods. Had it been possible for the great producing interest of the country to elude the tax by such a device, it is clear it would have been discovered long since, and that trade would have taken universally that shape; which is known not to be the fact,—the amount of specie imported annually, bearing but a small proportion to the whole amount of the imports. The result is clear. The effect of the duty on imports is, to lessen the value of specie at home proportionally. It will bring less of what we want for our supplies, in consequence, because we must receive less for it, in our foreign exchanges, in consequence of the duties. If a particular portion of the specie of the country had the exclusive privilege of being exchanged for the goods of foreign countries, duty free, it is clear that it would rise in value in proportion to the amount of the duty;—leaving no doubt that the effect of the duty is such as has been stated. But this opens a most important question,—How does this depreciation affect, relatively, the great interests of the country? the examination of which will but confirm the position which has been laid down,—that the duty falls on the great exporting or producing interests of the country; and that, without reference to the question of consumption, specie itself being an article of import. But very little gold or silver is purchased in our country; and all that is imported must be paid for by what we export. The great interests, producing the articles of export, may be considered the purchasers and first receivers of the specie imported; which is only introduced in exchange for their export labor,—and on these interests, of course, must fall whatever depreciation in value the specie suffers in the home market, in consequence of the duties. In speaking of the export labor, your committee do not intend only the labor which is *directly* applied in producing the articles of export, but all others in the same portion of the country and immediately connected therewith. All such, as appendages of the great interests in question, must sink or rise with it. In its character, it is an associated, not an opposing interest; and suffers, instead of gaining by the depreciation of the main interest.

They have noticed this distinction, because the principle for which they contend,—that the duty falls on the exporting interests, has been supposed to place the whole burden on the immediate producers of the staples exported; and, under this erroneous view, has been considered as absurd. Viewed in this light, it has been pronounced impossible that the repeal of the Tariff could by any possibility, raise the profits of the planter forty per cent.;—which may be readily admitted, without affecting the principle for which your committee contend,— that the duty on imports necessarily falls on the exporting interests. That interest consists, not only of the planters, but of a large circle of interests, of which it is the centre, and which must suffer in common with it. It includes all locally connected with it,—professional men of every description,—teachers, public servants, merchants, artisans, overseers, and a long list of others;—the receipts of all of whom are diminished in value, not only by receiving less money from the planters,—the ultimate payers,—and to which interest it is owing that their suffering under the system is mitigated,—but doubly from the diminution in the value of the money in their hands,—the means of obtaining their supplies,—in consequence of the system. The forty per cent. on the imports,—assuming it to be that,—diffuses itself over the whole of these great interests, by their immediate sympathy with the planting or exporting interests;—and when it is asserted that the State pays, in consequence of the duty, forty per cent. on her exports, it is not meant that the whole of that sum falls on the planters, who raise the eight millions of produce, by means of which the same amount of imports are paid for. The eight millions are in fact but a small portion of the annual labor of the State. It is but the surplus, intended for the supplies of the whole,—the annual product of whose labor,—estimating provisions, and putting a fair valuation on the services of the classes alluded to, and of others omitted, cannot, it is believed, be estimated at less than forty millions of dollars. Taken at this sum, which your committee present conjecturally, without any regular estimate or inquiry,—a duty of forty per cent. on the export labor, estimated at eight millions of dollars, would be but eight per cent. on the whole,—a sum, they believe, much less than the real burden imposed by the protective system.

But there is another great interest, very differently affected by the system, and which, in consequence of the depreciation of specie from the duties, is enabled to exchange the products of its labor more advantageously with the exporting interest; and which, of course, profits by the depreciation. This is true of all who are engaged in supplying the articles which, were it not for the duties, would be obtained more cheaply abroad,—and the interests immediately connected with them.

It has been already shown, that a sum in specie, which would exchange for one hundred pieces of goods in Liverpool, or any other foreign port, would,—estimating the duty at forty per cent., only exchange at home for sixty pieces, in consequence of the duty;—and it is perfectly clear, that those in our own country, engaged in manufacturing goods of the same description, and who, but for the duty, would have to give one hundred pieces for the specie in question, may now get it for sixty pieces. The duty, which would exact forty per cent. on the foreign exchange, does, in point of fact, give to the interest in question, forty per cent. on the domestic; and it is thus, two great antagonist interests are created by the system;—the *exporting,* and all others immediately connected with it;—and that, which has been falsely called, the *home interest,* or *domestic industry,* with all of its immediate connections;—interests, as it relates to the Tariff, directly opposed on all questions;—on that of repealing or retaining;—of diminishing or increasing,—and on all others connected therewith; and which involve, in their consequences, the entire system of policy—extending from questions of economy and frugality of expenditure, up to those on which turn those great constitutional principles, on the observance of which, depends that,—the most important of all,—whether ours is a federation or consolidate system,—restricted or unrestricted,—despotic or free. On all these points, your committee again repeat,—what cannot be too deeply impressed,—that the South—the seat of the great exporting interests of the country—is in a fixed and hopeless minority; and we may rest perfectly assured, that the great, antagonist majority-interest of the country, which controls the power of the General Government, through all its departments, according to the instinct of profit, will resist every limitation on those powers;—because it would be, in fact, a limitation on its own;—and that, unless we can find refuge in the Constitution itself, where our rights are held, not at the mercy of an interested majority, but under the safeguard of three fourths of the States, as our associates and equals,—there is no safety for us. The period is now rapidly approaching, when this great issue must be finally determined. The payment of the public debt is now just at hand, when there will be no pretext to continue the present burden on us; and when it must be finally removed, or fixed in some more permanent, and more odious form. We have made every effort to enlighten our brethren, as to the character and amount of our burden. For years we have petitioned, remonstrated, and resolved. Our representatives have faithfully performed their duty. They have ably portrayed our suffering—the unjust, the unequal, and unconstitutional burden which we bear;—and, finally, we have joined the other States and interests, suffering with us, in a representation of our grievance, as a last effort at redress through the General Government. We wait the result. Should it fail, it will only remain for us, to sink down in hopeless submission, or to place this State on its sovereignty, and interpose its veto to arrest, within its limits, the encroachments on our constitutional rights; as the only peaceful means left, by which a great question, touching the construction of our constitutional compact, can be submitted to the august and conclusive jurisdiction of the States themselves, in their original and sovereign capacity, as parties to our great political *Association*;—a jurisdiction peculiar to our admirable political system;—which constitutes its great conservative principle;—but which, without the high right of interposition, on the part of the States, would be perfectly nugatory.

Chapter XI.

"Letter to Governor James Hamilton, Jr.,"
28 August 1832

In this piece of published correspondence, Calhoun continued his explication of the concept of interposition, arguing in favor of the states' unique role in protecting the citizenry from the abuses of the federal government. Ultimate authority, for Calhoun, resided "in the people, not in the Government; and with us, the people mean the people of the several States originally formed into thirteen distinct and independent communities . . ."

My Dear Sir—I have received your note of the 31st July, requesting me to give you a fuller development of my views than that contained in my address last summer, on the right of a State to defend her reserved powers against the encroachments of the General Government.

As fully occupied as my time is, were it doubly so, the quarter from which the request comes, with my deep conviction of the vital importance of the subject, would exact a compliance.

No one can be more sensible than I am that the address of last summer fell far short of exhausting the subject. It was, in fact, intended as a simple statement of my views. I felt that the independence and candor which ought to distinguish one occupying a high public station, imposed a duty on me to meet the call for my opinion by a frank and full avowal of my sentiments, regardless of consequences. To fulfil this duty, and not to discuss the subject, was the object of the address. But, in making these preliminary remarks, I do not intend to prepare you to expect a full discussion on the present occasion. What I propose is, to touch some of the more prominent points that have received less of the public attention than their importance seems to me to demand.

Strange as the assertion may appear, it is, nevertheless, true, that the great difficulty in determining whether a State has the right to defend her reserved powers against the General Government, or, in fact, any right at all beyond those of a mere corporation, is to bring the public mind to realize plain historical facts connected with the origin and formation of the Government. Till they are fully understood it is impossible that a correct and just view can be taken of the subject. In this connection, the first and most important point is to ascertain who are the real authors of the Constitution of the United States—whose powers created it—whose voice clothed it with authority; and whose agent the Government it formed in reality is. At this point, I commence the execution of the task which your request has imposed.

The formation and adoption of the Constitution are events so recent, and all the connected facts so fully attested, that it would seem impossible that there should be the least uncertainty in relation to them; and yet, judging by what is constantly heard and seen, there are few subjects on which the public opinion is more confused. The most indefinite expressions are habitually used in speaking of them. Sometimes it is said that the Constitution was made by the States, and at others, as if in contradistinction, by the people, without distinguishing between the two very different meanings which may be attached to those general expressions; and this not in ordinary conversation, but in grave discussions before deliberative bodies, and in judicial investigations, where the greatest accuracy on so important a point might be expected; particularly as one or the other meaning is intended, conclusions the most opposite must follow, not only in reference to the subject of this communication, but as to the nature and character of our political system. By a State may be meant either the Government of a State or the people, as forming a separate and independent community; and by the people, either the American people taken collectively, as forming one great community, or as the people of the several States, forming, as above stated, separate and independent communities. These distinctions are essential in the inquiry. If by the people be meant the people collectively, and not the people of the several States taken separately; and if it be true, indeed, that the Constitution is the work of the American people collectively; if it originated with them, and derives its authority from their will, then there is an end of the argument. The right claimed for a State of defending her reserved powers against the General Government, would be an absurdity. Viewing the American people collectively as a source of political power, the rights of the States would be mere concessions—concessions from the common majority, and to be revoked by them with the same facility that they were granted. The States would, on this supposition, bear to the Union the same relation that counties do to the States; and it would, in that case, be just as preposterous to discuss the right of interposition, on the part of a State, against the General Government, as that of the counties against the States themselves. That a large portion of the people of the United States thus regard the relation between the States and the General Government, including many who call themselves the friends of State-Rights and opponents of consolidation, can scarcely be doubted, as it is only on that supposition it can be explained that so many of that description should denounce the doctrine for which the State contends as so absurd. But, fortunately, the supposition is entirely destitute of truth. So far from the Constitution being the work of the American people collectively, no such political body either now or ever did exist. In that character the people of this country never performed a single political act, nor, indeed, can, without an entire revolution in all our political relations.

I challenge an instance. From the beginning, and in all the changes of political existence through which we have passed, the people of the United States have been united as forming political communities, and not as individuals. Even in the first stage of existence, they formed distinct colonies, independent of each other, and politically united only through the British crown. In their first imperfect union, for the purpose of resisting the encroachments of the mother country, they united as distinct political communities; and passing from their colonial condition, in the act announcing their independence to the world, they declared themselves, by name and enumeration, free and independent States. In that character, they formed the old confederation; and, when it was proposed to supersede the articles of the confederation by the present Constitution, they met in convention as States, acted and voted as States; and the Constitution, when formed, was submitted for ratification to the people of the several States; it was ratified by them as States, each State for itself; each by its ratification binding its own citizens: the parts thus separately binding themselves, and not the whole the parts; to which, if it be added, that it is declared in the preamble of the Constitution to be ordained by the people of the *United States,* and in the article of ratification, when ratified, it is declared *"to be binding between the States so ratifying,"* the conclusion is inevitable, that the Constitution is the work of the people of the States, considered as separate and independent political communities; that they are its authors—their power created it, their voice clothed it with authority; that the government formed is, in reality, their agent; and that the Union, of which the Constitution is the bond, is a union of States, and not of individuals. No one, who regards his character for intelligence and truth, has ever ventured directly to deny facts so certain; but while they are too certain for denial, they are also too conclusive in favor of the rights of the States for admission. The usual course has been adopted—to elude what can neither be denied nor admitted; and never has the device been more successfully practised. By confounding States with State governments, and the people of the States with the American people *collectively*—things, as it regards the subject of this communication, totally dissimilar, as much so as a triangle and a square—facts of themselves perfectly certain and plain, and which, when well understood, must lead to a correct conception of the subject, have been involved in obscurity and mystery.

I will next proceed to state some of the results which necessarily follow from the facts which have been established.

The first, and, in reference to the subject of this communication, the most important, is, that there is *no direct* and *immediate* connection between the individual citizens of a State and the General Government. The relation between them is through the State. The Union is a union of States as communities, and not a union of individuals. As members of a State, her citizens were originally subject to no control but that of the State, and could be subject to no other, except by the act of the State itself. The Constitution was, accordingly, submitted to the States for their separate ratification; and it was only by the ratification of the State that its citizens became subject to the control of the General Government. The ratification of any other, or all the other States, without its own, could create no connection between them and the General Government, nor impose on them the slightest obligation. Without the ratification of their own State, they would stand in the same relation to the General Government as do the citizens or subjects of any foreign state; and we find the citizens of North Carolina and Rhode Island actually bearing that relation to the Government for some time after it went into operation; these States having, in the first instance, declined to ratify. Nor had the act of any individual the least influence in subjecting him to the control of the General Government, except as it might influence the ratification of the Constitution by his own State. Whether subject to its control or not, depended wholly on the act of the State. His dissent had not the least weight against the assent of the State, nor his assent against its dissent. It follows, as a necessary consequence, that the act of ratification bound the State as a community, as is expressly declared in the article of the Constitution above quoted, and not the citizens of the State as individuals; the latter being bound through their State, and in consequence of the ratification of the former. Another, and a highly important consequence, as it regards the subject under investigation, follows with equal certainty; that, on a question whether a particular power exercised by the General Government be granted by the Constitution, it belongs to the State as a member of the Union, in her sovereign capacity in convention, to determine definitively, as far as her citizens are concerned, the extent of the obligation which she contracted; and if, in her opinion, the act exercising the power be unconstitutional, to declare it null and void, *which declaration would be obligatory on her citizens.* In coming to this conclusion, it may be proper to remark, to prevent misrepresentation, that I do not claim for a State the right to abrogate an act of the General Government. It is the Constitution that annuls an unconstitutional act. Such an act is of itself void and of no effect. What I claim is, the right of the State, *as far as its citizens are concerned, to declare the extent of the obligation, and that such declaration is binding on them*—a right, when limited to its citizens, flowing directly from the relation of the State to the General Government on the one side, and its citizens on the other, as already explained, and resting on the most plain and solid reasons.

Passing over, what of itself might be considered conclusive, the obvious principle, that it belongs to the authority which imposed the obligation to declare its extent, as far as those are concerned on whom the obligation is placed, I shall present a single argument, which of itself is decisive. I have already shown that there is no immediate connection between the citizens of a State and the General Government, and that the relation between them is through the State. I have also shown that whatever obligations were imposed on the citizens, were imposed by the act of the State ratifying the Constitution. A similar act by the same authority, made with equal solemnity, declaring the extent of the obligation, must, as far as they are concerned, be of equal authority. I speak, of course, on the supposition that the right has not been transferred, as it will hereafter be shown that it has not. A citizen would have no more right to question the one than he would have the other declaration. They rest on the same authority; and as he was bound by the declaration of his State assenting to the Constitution, whether he assented or dissented, so would he be equally bound by a declaration declaring the extent of that assent, whether opposed to, or in favor of, such declaration. In this conclusion I am supported by analogy. The case of a treaty between sovereigns is strictly analogous. There, as in this, case, the State contracts for the citizen or subject; there, as in this, the obligation is imposed by the State, and is independent of his will; and there, as in this, the declaration of the State, determining the extent of the obligation contracted *is obligatory on him,*—as much so as the treaty itself.

Having now, I trust, established the very important point, that the declaration of a State, as to the extent of the power granted, is obligatory on its citizens,

I shall next proceed to consider the effects of such declarations in reference to the General Government;—a question which necessarily involves the consideration of the relation between it and the States. It has been shown that the people of the States, acting as distinct and independent communities, are the authors of the Constitution, and that the General Government was organized and ordained by them to execute its powers. The Government, then, with all of its departments, is, in fact, the agent of the States, constituted to execute their joint will, as expressed in the Constitution.

In using the term agent, I do not intend to derogate in any degree from its character as a government. It is as truly and properly a government as are the State governments themselves. I have applied it simply because it strictly belongs to the relation between the General Government and the States, as, in fact, it does also to that between a State and its own government. Indeed, according to our theory, governments are in their nature but trusts, and those appointed to administer them, trustees or agents to execute the trust powers. The sovereignty resides elsewhere—in the people, not in the government; and with us, *the people* mean *the people of the several States* originally formed into thirteen distinct and independent communities, and now into twenty-four. Politically speaking, in reference to our own system, there are *no other people*. The General Government, as well as those of the States, is but the organ of their power: the latter, that of their respective States, through which are exercised separately that portion of power not delegated by the Constitution, and in the exercise of which each State has a local and peculiar interest; the former, the joint organ of all the States confederated into one general community, and through which they jointly and concurringly exercise the delegated powers, in which all have a common interest. Thus viewed, the Constitution of the United States, with the government it created, is truly and strictly the Constitution of each State,—as much so as its own particular Constitution and Government, ratified by the same authority,—in the same mode, and having, as far as its citizens are concerned, its powers and obligations from the same source,—differing only in the aspect under which I am considering the subject,—in the *plighted faith* of the State to its co-States, and of which, as far as its citizens are considered, the State, in the last resort, is the exclusive judge.

Such, then, is the relation between the State and General Government, in whatever light we may consider the Constitution, whether as a compact between the States, or of the nature of the legislative enactment by the joint and concurring authority of the States in their high sovereignty. In whatever light it may be viewed, I hold it as necessarily resulting, that, in the case of a power disputed between them, the Government, as the agent, has no right to enforce its construction against the construction of the State as one of the sovereign parties to the Constitution, any more than the State government would have against the people of the States in their sovereign capacity,—the relation being the same between them. That such would be the case between agent and principal in the ordinary transactions of life, no one will doubt; nor will it be possible to assign a reason why it is not as applicable to the case of governments as to that of individuals. The principle, in fact, springs from the *relation itself,* and *is applicable to it in all its forms and characters.* It may, however, be proper to notice a distinction between the case of a single principal and his agent, and that of several principals and their joint agent, which might otherwise cause some confusion. In both cases, as between the agent and a principal, the construction of the principal, whether he be a single principal or one of several, is equally conclusive; but, in the latter case, both the principal and the agent bear relation to the other principals, which must be taken into the estimate, in order to understand fully all the results which may grow out of the contest for power between them. Though the construction of the principal is conclusive against the joint agent, as between them, such is not the case between him and his associates. They both have an equal right of construction, and it would be the duty of the agent to bring the subject before the principal to be adjusted, according to the terms of the instrument of association, and of the principal to submit to such adjustment. In such cases the contract itself is the law which must determine the relative rights and powers of the parties to it. The General Government is a case of joint agency—the joint agent of the twenty-four sovereign States. It would be its duty, according to the principles established in such cases, instead of attempting to enforce its construction of its powers against that of the States, to bring the subject before the States themselves, in the only form which, according to the provision of the Constitution, it can be—by a proposition to amend, in the manner prescribed in the instrument, to be acted on by them in the only mode they can, by expressly granting or withholding the contested power. Against this conclusion there can be raised but one objection, that the States have surrendered or transferred the right in question. If such be the fact, there ought to be no difficulty in establishing it. The grant of the powers delegated is contained in a written instrument, drawn up with great care, and adopted with the utmost deliberation. It provides that the powers not granted are reserved to the States or the people. If it be surrendered, let the grant be shown, and the controversy will be terminated; and, surely, it ought to be shown, plainly and clearly shown, before the States are asked to admit what, if true, would not only divest them of a right which, under all its forms, belongs to the principal over his agent, unless surrendered, but which cannot be surrendered without in effect, and for all practical purposes, reversing the relation between them; putting the agent in the place of the principal, and the principal in that of the agent; and which would degrade the States from the high and sovereign condition which they have ever held, under every form of their existence, to be mere subordinate and dependent corporations of the Government of its own creation. But, instead of showing any such grant, not a provision can be found in the Constitution *authorizing the General Government to exercise any control whatever over a State* by force, by veto, by judicial process, or in any other form—*a most important omission, designed, and not accidental,* and as will be shown in the course of these remarks,— omitted by the dictates of the profoundest wisdom.

The journal and proceedings of the Convention which formed the Constitution afford abundant proof that there was in the body a powerful party, distinguished for talents and influence, intent on obtaining for the General Government a grant of the very power in question, and that they attempted to effect this object in all possible ways, but, fortunately, without success. The first project of a Constitution submitted to the Convention (Governor Randolph's) embraced a proposition to grant power "to negative all laws contrary, in the opinion of the National Legislature, to the articles of the Union, or any treaty subsisting under the authority of the Union; and to call forth the force of the Union against any member of the Union failing to fulfil its duty under the articles thereof." The next project submitted (Charles Pinckney's) contained a similar provision. It proposed, that "the Legislature of the United States should have the power to revise the laws of the several States that may be supposed to infringe the powers exclusively delegated by this Constitution to Congress, and to negative and annul such as do." The next was submitted by Mr. Patterson, of New Jersey, which provided, "if any State, or body of men in any State shall oppose or prevent the carrying into execution such acts or treaties" (of the Union), the Federal Executive shall be authorized to call forth the powers of the confederated States, or so much thereof as shall be necessary to enforce, or compel the obedience to such acts, or observance of such treaties." General Hamilton's next succeeded, which declared "all laws of the particular States contrary to the Constitution or laws of the United States, to be utterly void; and, the better to prevent such laws being passed, the Governor or President of each State shall be appointed by the General Government, and shall have a negative on the laws about to be passed in the State of which he is Governor or President."

At a subsequent period, a proposition was moved and referred to a committee, to provide that "the jurisdiction of the Supreme Court shall extend to all controversies between the United States and any individual State;" and, at a still later period, it was moved to grant power "to negative all laws passed by the several States interfering, in the opinion of the Legislature, with the general harmony and interest of the Union, provided that two thirds of the members of each House assent to the same," which, after an ineffectual attempt to commit, was withdrawn.

I do not deem it necessary to trace through the journals of the Convention the fate of these various propositions. It is sufficient that they were moved and failed, to prove conclusively, in a manner never to be reversed, that the Convention which framed the Constitution, was opposed to granting the power to the General Government in any form, through any of its departments, legislative, executive, or, judicial, to coerce or control a State, though proposed in all conceivable modes, and sustained by the most talented and influential members of the body. This, one would suppose, ought to settle for ever the question of the surrender or transfer of the power under consideration; and such, in fact, would be the case, were the opinion of a large portion of the community not biased, as, in fact, it is, by interest. A majority have almost always a direct interest in enlarging the power of the Government, and the interested adhere to power with a pertinacity which bids defiance to truth, though sustained by evidence as conclusive as mathematical demonstration; and, accordingly, the advocates of the powers of the General Government, notwithstanding the impregnable strength of the proof to the contrary, have boldly claimed, on construction, a power, the grant of which was so perseveringly sought and so sternly resisted by the Convention. They rest the claim on the provisions in the Constitution, which declare "that this Constitution, and the laws made in pursuance thereof, shall be the supreme law of the land," and that "the judicial power shall extend to all cases in law and equity arising under this Constitution, the laws of the United States, and treaties made, or which shall be made under their authority."

I do not propose to go into a minute examination of these provisions. They have been so frequently and so ably investigated, and it has been so clearly shown that they do not warrant the assumption of the power claimed for the Government, that I do not deem it necessary. I shall, therefore, confine myself to a few detached remarks.

I have already stated that a distinct proposition was made to confer the very power in controversy on the Supreme Court, which failed; and which, of itself, ought to overrule the assumption of the power by construction, unless sustained by the most conclusive arguments; but when it is added that this proposition was moved (20th August) subsequent to the period of adopting the provisions, above cited, vesting the Court with its present powers (18th July), and that an effort was made, at a still later period (23rd August), to invest Congress with a negative on all State laws which, in its opinion, might interfere with the general interest and harmony of the Union, the argument would seem too conclusive against the powers of the Court to be overruled by construction, however strong.

Passing, however, by this, and also the objection that the terms *"cases in law and equity"* are technical, embracing only questions between parties *amenable* to the process of the Court, and, of course, excluding questions between the States and the General Government—an argument which has never been answered—there remains another objection perfectly conclusive.

The construction which would confer on the Supreme Court the power in question, rests on the ground that the Constitution has conferred on that tribunal the high and important right of deciding on the *constitutionality of laws.* That it possesses this power I do not deny;—but I do utterly that it is conferred by the Constitution either in the provisions above cited, or any other. It is a power derived from the necessity of the case; and, so far from being possessed by the Supreme Court exclusively or peculiarly, it not only belongs to every Court of the country, high or low, civil or criminal, but to all foreign Courts, before which a case may be brought involving the construction of a law which may conflict with the provisions of the Constitution. The reason is plain. Where there are two sets of rules prescribed in reference to the same subject, one by a higher and the other by an inferior authority, the judicial tribunal called in to decide on the case, must unavoidably determine, should they conflict, which is the law; and that necessity compels it to decide that the rule prescribed by the inferior power, if in its opinion inconsistent with that of the higher, is void,—be it a conflict between the Constitution and a law, or between a charter and the by-laws of a corporation, or any other higher and inferior authority. The principle and source of authority are the same in all such cases. Being derived from necessity, it is restricted within its limits, and cannot pass an inch beyond the narrow confines of deciding, in a case before the Court, and, of course, between parties amenable to its process,—excluding thereby political questions,—which of the two is, in reality, the law, the act of Congress or the Constitution, when on their face they are inconsistent; and yet, from this resulting limited power,—derived from necessity, and held in common with every Court in the world which, by possibility, may take cognizance of a case involving the interpretation of our Constitution and laws,—it is attempted to confer on the

Supreme Court a power which would work a thorough and radical change in our system, and which, moreover, was positively refused by the Convention.

The opinion that the General Government has the right to enforce its construction of its powers against a State in any mode whatever, is, in truth, founded on a fundamental misconception of our system. At the bottom of this, and, in fact, almost every other misconception as to the relation between the States and the General Government, lurks the radical error, that the latter is a national, and not, as in reality it is, a confederated Government; and that it derives its powers from a higher source than the States. There are thousands influenced by these impressions without being conscious of it, and who, while they believe themselves to be opposed to consolidation, have infused into their conception of our Constitution almost all the ingredients which enter into that form of government. The striking difference between the present government and that under the old confederation (I speak of governments as distinct from constitutions) has mainly contributed to this dangerous impression. But however dissimilar their governments, the present *Constitution is as far removed from consolidation, and is as strictly and as purely a confederation, as the one which it superseded.*

Like the old confederation, it was formed and ratified by State authority. The only difference in this particular is, that one was ratified by the people of the States, and the other by the State Governments; one forming strictly a union of the State Governments,—the other of the States themselves; one, of the agents exercising the powers of sovereignty, and the other, of the sovereigns themselves; but both were unions of political bodies, as distinct from a union of the people individually. They are, indeed, *both confederations,* but the present in a higher and purer sense than that which it succeeded,—just as the act of a sovereign is higher and more perfect than that of his agent; and it was, doubtless, in reference to this difference that the preamble of the Constitution, and the address of the Convention laying the Constitution before Congress, speak of consolidating and perfecting the Union; yet this difference, which, while it elevated the General Government in relation to the State Governments, placed it more immediately in the relation of the *creature and agent* of the States themselves, by a natural misconception, has been the principal cause of the impression so prevalent of the inferiority of the States to the General Government, and of the consequent right of the latter to coerce the former. Raised from below to the same level with the State Governments, it was conceived to be placed above the States themselves.

I have now, I trust, conclusively shown that a State has a right, in her sovereign capacity, in convention, to declare an unconstitutional act of Congress to be null and void, and that such declarations would be obligatory on her cit-izens,—as highly so as the Constitution itself,—and conclusive against the Gen-eral Government, which would have no right to enforce its construction of its powers against that of the State.

I next propose to consider the practical effect of the exercise of this high and important right—which, as the great conservative principle of our system, is known under the various names of nullification, interposition, and State veto—in reference to its operation viewed under different aspects: nullification,—as declaring null an unconstitutional act of the General Government, as far as the State is concerned; interposition,—as throwing the shield of protection between the citizens of a State and the encroachments of the Government; and veto,—as arresting or inhibiting its unauthorized acts within the limits of the State.

The practical effect, if the right was fully recognized, would be plain and simple, and has already, in a great measure, been anticipated. If the State has a right, there must, of necessity, be a corresponding obligation on the part of the General Government to acquiesce in its exercise; and, of course, it would be its duty to abandon the power, at least as far as the State is concerned,—to com-promise the difficulty,—or apply to the States themselves, according to the form prescribed in the Constitution, to obtain the power by a grant. If granted, acquiescence, then, would be a duty on the part of the State; and, in that event, the contest would terminate in converting a doubtful constructive power into one positively granted; but should it not be granted, no alternative would remain for the General Government but a compromise or its permanent aban-donment. In either event, the controversy would be closed and the Constitu-tion fixed: a result of the utmost importance to the steady operation of the Government and the stability of the system, and which can never be attained, under its present operation, without the recognition of the right, as experience has shown.

From the adoption of the Constitution, we have had but one continued agi-tation of constitutional questions embracing some of the most important pow-ers exercised by the Government; and yet, in spite of all the ability and force of argument displayed in the various discussions, backed by the high authority claimed for the Supreme Court to adjust such controversies, not a single con-stitutional question, of a political character, which has ever been agitated dur-ing this long period, has been settled in the public opinion, except that of the unconstitutionality of the Alien and Sedition Law; and, what is remarkable, that was settled *against the decision of the Supreme Court.* The tendency is to increase, and not diminish, this conflict for power. New questions are yearly added without diminishing the old; while the contest becomes more obstinate as the list increases, and, what is highly ominous, more sectional. It is impossible that the Government can last under this increasing diversity of opinion, and growing uncertainty as to its power in relation to the most important subjects of legislation; and equally so, that this dangerous state can terminate without a power somewhere to compel, in effect, the Government to abandon doubtful constructive powers, or to convert them into positive grants by an amendment of the Constitution; in a word, to substitute the positive grants of the parties themselves for the constructive powers interpolated by the agents. Nothing short of this, in a system constructed as ours is, with a double set of agents,—one for local, and the other for general purposes,—can ever terminate the conflict for power, or give uniformity and stability to its action.

Such would be the practical and happy operation were *the right recognized;* but the case is far otherwise; and as the right is not only denied, but violently opposed, the General Government, so far from acquiescing in its exercise, and abandoning the power, as it ought, may endeavor, by all the means within its command, to enforce its construction against that of the State. It is under this aspect of the question that I now propose to consider the practical effect of the exercise of the right, with the view to determine which of the two, the State or the General Government, must prevail in the conflict; which compels me to revert to some of the grounds already established.

I have already shown that the declaration of nullification would be obligatory on the citizens of the State;—as much so, in fact, as its declaration ratifying the Constitution, resting, as it does, on the same basis. It would *to them* be the highest possible evidence that the power contested was not granted, and, of course, that the act of the General Government was unconstitutional. They would be bound, in all the relations of life, private and political, to respect and obey it; and, when called upon as jurymen, to render their verdict accordingly,—or as judges, to pronounce judgment in conformity with it. The right of jury trial is secured by the Constitution (thanks to the jealous spirit of liberty, doubly secured and fortified); and, with this inestimable right—inestimable, not only as an essential portion of the judicial tribunals of the country, but infinitely more so, considered as a popular, and still more, a local representation, in that department of the Government which, without it, would be the farthest removed from the control of the people, and a fit instrument to sap the foundation of the system—with, I repeat, this inestimable right, it would be impossible for the General Government, within the limits of the State, to execute, *legally,* the act nullified, or any other passed with a view to enforce it; while, on the other hand, the State would be able to enforce, *legally and peaceably,* its declaration of nullification. Sustained by its courts and juries, it would calmly and quietly, but successfully, meet every effort of the General Government to enforce its claim of power. The result would be inevitable. Before the judicial tribunals of the country, the State must prevail, unless, indeed, jury trial could be eluded by the refinement of the Court, or by some other device; which, however, guarded as it is by the ramparts of the Constitution, would, I hold, be impossible. The attempt to elude, should it be made, would itself be unconstitutional; and, in turn, would be annulled by the sovereign voice of the State. Nor would the right of appeal to the Supreme Court, under the judiciary act, avail the General Government. If taken, it would but end in a new trial, and that in another verdict against the Government; but whether it may be taken, would be optional with the State. The Court itself has decided that a copy of the record is requisite to review a judgment of a State court, and, if necessary, the State would take the precaution to prevent, by proper enactments, any means of obtaining a copy. But if obtained, what would it avail against the execution of the penal enactments of the State, intended to enforce the declaration of nullification? The judgment of the State court would be pronounced and executed before the possibility of a reversal,—and executed, too, without responsibility incurred by any one.

Beaten before the courts, the General Government would be compelled to abandon its unconstitutional pretensions, or resort to force; a resort, the difficulty (I was about to say, the impossibility) of which would very soon fully manifest itself, should folly or madness ever make the attempt.

In considering this aspect of the controversy, I pass over the fact that the General Government has no right to resort to force against a State—to coerce a sovereign member of the Union—which, I trust, I have established beyond all possible doubt. Let it, however, be determined to use force, and the difficulty would be insurmountable, unless, indeed, it be also determined to set aside the Constitution, and to subvert the system to its foundations.

Against whom would it be applied? Congress has, it is true, the right to call forth the militia "to execute the laws and suppress insurrection;" but there would be no law resisted, unless, indeed, it be called resistance for the juries to refuse to find, and the courts to render judgment, in conformity with the wishes of the General Government; no insurrection to suppress; no armed force to reduce; not a sword unsheathed; not a bayonet raised; none, absolutely none, on whom force could be used, except it be on the unarmed citizens engaged peaceably and quietly in their daily occupations.

No one would be guilty of treason ("levying war against the United States, adhering to their enemies, giving them aid and comfort"), or any other crime made penal by the Constitution or the laws of the United States.

To suppose that force could be called in, implies, indeed, a great mistake both as to the nature of our Government and that of the controversy. It would be a legal and constitutional contest—a conflict of moral, and not physical force—a trial of constitutional, and not military power,—to be decided before the judicial tribunals of the country, and not on the field of battle. In such contest, there would be no object for force, but those peaceful tribunals—nothing on which it could be employed, but in putting down courts and juries, and preventing the execution of judicial process. Leave these untouched, and all the militia that could be called forth, backed by a regular force of ten times the number of our small, but gallant and patriotic army, could have not the slightest effect on the result of the controversy; but subvert these by an armed body, and you subvert the very foundation of this our free, constitutional, and legal system of government, and rear in its place a military despotism.

Feeling the force of these difficulties, it is proposed, with the view, I suppose, of disembarrassing the operation, as much as possible, of the troublesome interference of courts and juries, to change the scene of coercion from land to water; as if the Government could have one particle more right to coerce a State by water than by land; but, unless I am greatly deceived, the difficulty on that element will not be much less than on the other. The jury trial, at least the local jury trial (the trial by the vicinage), may, indeed, be evaded there, but in its place other, and not much less formidable, obstacles must be encountered.

There can be but two modes of coercion resorted to by water—blockade and abolition of the ports of entry of the State, accompanied by penal enactments, authorizing seizures for entering the waters of the State. If the former be attempted, there will be other parties besides the General Government and the State. Blockade is a belligerent right; it presupposes a state of war, and, unless there be war (war in due form, as prescribed by the Constitution), the order for blockade would not be respected by other nations or their subjects. Their vessels would proceed directly for the blockaded port, with certain prospects of gain; if seized under the order of blockade, through the claim of indemnity against the General Government; and, if not, by a profitable market, without the exaction of duties.

The other mode, the abolition of the ports of entry of the State, would also have its difficulties. The Constitution provides that "no preference shall be given by any regulation of commerce or revenue to the ports of one State over those of another; nor shall vessels bound to or from one State be obliged to enter, clear, or pay duties in another;" provisions too clear to be eluded even by the force of construction. There will be another difficulty. If seizures be made in port, or within the distance assigned by the laws of nations as the limits of a State, the trial must be in the State, with all the embarrassments of its courts and juries; while beyond the ports and the distance to which I have referred, it would be difficult to point out any principle by which a foreign vessel, at least, could be seized, except as an incident to the right of blockade, and, of course, with all the difficulties belonging to that mode of coercion.

But there yet remains another, and, I doubt not, insuperable barrier, to be found in the judicial tribunals of the Union, against all the schemes of introducing force, whether by land or water. Though I cannot concur in the opinion of those who regard the Supreme Court as the mediator appointed by the Constitution between the States and the General Government; and though I cannot doubt there is a natural bias on its part towards the powers of the latter, yet I must greatly lower my opinion of that high and important tribunal for intelligence, justice, and attachment to the Constitution,—and particularly of that pure and upright magistrate who has so long, and with such distinguished honor to himself and the Union, presided over its deliberations, with all the weight that belongs to an intellect of the first order, united with the most spotless integrity,—to believe, for a moment, that an attempt so plainly and manifestly unconstitutional as a resort to force would be in such a contest, could be sustained by the sanction of its authority. In whatever form force may be used, it must present questions for legal adjudication. If in the shape of blockade, the vessels seized under it must be condemned, and thus would be presented the question of prize or no prize, and, with it, the legality of the blockade; if in that of a repeal of the acts establishing ports of entries in the State, the legality of the seizure must be determined, and that would bring up the question of the constitutionality of giving a preference to the ports of one State over those of another; and so, if we pass from water to land, we will find every attempt there to substitute force for law must, in like manner, come under the review of the courts of the Union; and the unconstitutionality would be so glaring, that the Executive and Legislative Departments, in their attempt to coerce, should either make an attempt so lawless and desperate, would be without the support of the Judicial Department. I will not pursue the question farther, as I hold it perfectly clear that, so long as a State retains its federal relations; so long, in a word, as it continues a member of the Union, the contest between it and the General Government must be before the courts and juries; and every attempt, in whatever form, whether by land or water, to substitute force as the arbiter in their place, must fail. The unconstitutionality of the attempt would be so open and palpable, that it would be impossible to sustain it.

There is, indeed, one view, and one only, of the contest, in which force could be employed; but that view, as between the parties, would supersede the Constitution itself:—that nullification is secession,—and would, consequently, place the State, as to the others, in the relation of a foreign state. Such, clearly, would be the effect of secession; but it is equally clear that it would place the State beyond the pale of all her federal relations, and, thereby, all control on the part of the other States over her. She would stand to them simply in the relation of a foreign state, divested of all federal connection, and having none other between them but those belonging to the laws of nations. Standing thus towards one another, force might, indeed, be employed against a State, but it must be a belligerent force, preceded by a declaration of war, and carried on with all its formalities. Such would be the certain effect of secession; and if nullification be secession—if it be but a different name for the same thing—such, too, must be its effect; which presents the highly important question, Are they, in fact, the same? on the decision of which depends the question whether it be a *peaceable* and *constitutional* remedy that may be exercised without *terminating* the *federal* relations of the State *or not*.

I am aware that there is a considerable and respectable portion of our State, with a very large portion of the Union, constituting, in fact, a great majority, who are of the opinion that they are the same thing, differing only in name, and who, under that impression, denounce it as the most dangerous of all doctrines; and yet, so far from being the same, they are, unless, indeed, I am greatly deceived, not only perfectly distinguishable, but totally dissimilar in their nature, their object, and effect; and that, so far from deserving the denunciation, so properly belonging to the act with which it is confounded, it is, in truth, the highest and most precious of all the rights of the States, and essential to preserve that very Union, for the supposed effect of destroying which it is so bitterly anathematized.

I shall now proceed to make good my assertion of their *total dissimilarity*.

First, they are wholly dissimilar in their nature. *One has reference to the parties themselves, and the other to their agents.* Secession is a *withdrawal from the Union;* a separation from *partners,* and, as far as depends on the member withdrawing, a *dissolution* of the partnership. It presupposes an association; a union of several States or individuals for a common object. Wherever these exist, secession may; and where they do not, it cannot. Nullification, on the contrary, *presupposes the relation of principal and agent:* the one granting a power to be executed,—the other, appointed by him with authority to execute it; *and is simply a declaration on the part of the principal, made in due form, that an act of the agent transcending his power is null and void.* It is a right belonging exclusively to the relation between principal and agent, to be found *wherever it exists, and in all its forms,* between several, or an association of principals, and their joint agents, as well as between a single principal and his agent.

The difference in their object is no less striking than in their nature. The object of secession is to *free* the withdrawing member from the *obligation* of the association or union, and is applicable to cases where the object of the association or union *has failed,* either by an abuse of power on the part of *its members,* or other causes. Its *direct and immediate object, as it concerns the withdrawing member, is the dissolution of the association or union,* as far as it is concerned. On the contrary, the object of nullification is to confine the agent within the limits of his powers, by arresting his acts transcending them, *not with the view of destroying the delegated or trust power, but to preserve it, by compelling the agent to fulfil the object for which the agency or trust was created; and is applicable only to cases where the trust or delegated powers are transcended on the part of the agent.* Without the power of secession, an association or union, formed for the common good *of all* the members, might prove ruinous to some, by the abuse of power on the part of the others; and without nullification the agent might, under color of construction, assume a power never intended to be delegated, or to convert those delegated to objects never intended to be comprehended in the trust, to the ruin of the principal, or, in case of a joint agency, to the ruin of some of the principals. Each has, thus, its appropriate object, but objects in their nature very dissimilar; so much so, that, in case of an association or union, where the powers are delegated to be executed by an agent, the abuse of power, on the part of the *agent,* to the injury of one or more of the members, would not justify secession on their part. The rightful remedy in that case would be nullification. There would be neither right nor pretext to secede: not right, because secession is applicable only to the acts of the members of the association or union, and not to the act of the agent; nor pretext, because there is another, and equally efficient remedy, short of the dissolution of the association or union, which can only be justified by necessity. Nullification may, indeed, be succeeded by secession. In the case stated, should the other members undertake to grant the power nullified, and should the nature of the power be such as to *defeat the object of the association or union,* at least as far as the member nullifying is concerned, it would then become an abuse of power on the part of the principals, and thus present a case where secession would apply; but in no other could it be justified, except it be for a failure of the association or union to effect the object for which it was created, independent of any abuse of power.

It now remains to show that their effect is as dissimilar as their nature or object.

Nullification leaves the members of the association or union in the condition it found them—subject to all its burdens, and entitled to all its advantages, comprehending the member nullifying as well as the others—its object being, not to destroy, but to preserve, as has been stated. It simply arrests the act of the agent, as far as the principal is concerned, leaving in every other respect the operation of the joint concern as before; secession, on the contrary, destroys, as far as the withdrawing member is concerned, the association or union, and restores him to the relation he occupied towards the other members before the existence of the association or union. He loses the benefit, but is released from the burden and control, and can no longer be dealt with, by his former associates, as one of its members.

Such are clearly the differences between them—differences so marked, that, instead of being identical, as supposed, they form a contrast in all the aspects in which they can be regarded. The application of these remarks to the political association or Union of these twenty-four States and the General Government, their joint agent, is too obvious, after what has been already said, to require any additional illustration, and I will dismiss this part of the subject with a single additional remark.

There are many who acknowledge the right of a State to secede, but deny its right to nullify; and yet, it seems impossible to admit the one without admitting the other. They both presuppose the same structure of the Government,—that it is a Union of the States, as forming political communities,—the same right on the part of the States, as members of the Union, to determine for their citizens the extent of the powers delegated and those reserved,—and, of course, to decide whether the Constitution has or has not been violated. The simple difference, then, between those who admit secession and deny nullification, and those who admit both, is, that one acknowledges that the declaration of a State pronouncing that the Constitution has been violated, and is, therefore, null and void, would be obligatory on her citizens, and would arrest all the acts of the Government within the limits of the State; while they deny that a similar declaration, made by the same authority, and in the same manner, that an act of the Government has transcended its powers, and that it is, therefore, null and void, would have any obligation; while the other acknowledges the obligation in both cases. The one admits that the declaration of a State assenting to the Constitution bound her citizens, and that her declaration can unbind them; but denies that a similar declaration, as to the extent she has, in fact, bound them, has any obligatory force on them; while the other gives equal force to the declaration in the several cases. The one denies the obligation, where the object is to *preserve the Union in the only way it can be,* by confining the Government, formed to execute the trust powers, strictly within their limits, and to the objects for which they were delegated, though they give *full* force where the object is *to destroy the Union itself;* while the other, in giving equal weight to both, *prefers the one because it preserves,* and *rejects the other because it destroys;* and yet the former is the *Union,* and the latter the *disunion party!* And all this strange distinction originates, as far as I can judge, in attributing to nullification what belongs exclusively to secession. The difficulty as to the former, it seems, is, that a State cannot be in and out of the Union at the same time.

This is, indeed, true, if applied to secession—the throwing off *the authority of the Union itself.* To nullify the Constitution, if I may be pardoned the solecism, would, indeed, be tantamount to disunion; and, as applied to such an act it would be true that a State could not be in and out of the Union at the same time; but the act would be secession.

But to apply it to nullification, properly understood, the object of which, instead of resisting or diminishing the powers of the Union, is to preserve them as they are, neither increased nor diminished, and thereby the Union itself (for the Union may be as effectually destroyed by increasing as by diminishing its powers—by consolidation, as by disunion itself), would be, I would say,—had I not great respect for many who do thus apply it,—egregious trifling with a grave and deeply-important constitutional subject.

I might here finish the task which your request imposed,—having, I trust, demonstrated, beyond the power of refutation, that a State has the right to defend her reserved powers against the encroachments of the General Government; and I may add that the right is, in its nature, peaceable, consistent with the federal relations of the State, and perfectly efficient, whether contested before the Courts, or attempted to be resisted by force. But there is another aspect of the subject not yet touched, without adverting to which, it is impossible to understand the full effects of nullification, or the real character of our political institutions: I allude to the power which the States, as a confederated body, have acquired directly over each other, and on which I will now proceed to make some remarks, though, I fear, at the hazard of fatiguing you.

Previous to the adoption of the present Constitution, no power could be exercised over any State by any other, or all of the States, without its own consent; and we accordingly find that the old Confederation and the present Constitution were both submitted for ratification to each of the States, and that each ratified for itself, and was bound only in consequence of its own particular ratification, as has been already stated. The present Constitution has made, in this particular, a most important modification in their condition. I allude to the provision which gives validity to amendments of the Constitution when ratified by three fourths of the States—a provision which has not attracted as much attention as its importance deserves. Without it, no change could have been made in the Constitution, unless with the unanimous consent of all the States, in like manner as it was adopted. This provision, then, contains a highly-important concession by each to all of the States, of a portion of the original and inherent right of self-government, possessed previously by each separately, in favor of their general confederated powers,—giving thereby increased energy to the States in their united capacity, and weakening them in the same degree in their separate. Its object was to facilitate and strengthen the action of the amending, or (to speak a little more appropriately, as it regards the point under consideration) *the repairing power*. It was foreseen that experience would, probably, disclose errors in the Constitution itself; that time would make great changes in the condition of the country, which would require corresponding changes in the Constitution; that the irregular and conflicting movements of the bodies composing so complex a system might cause derangements requiring correction; and that, to require the unanimous consent of all the States to meet these various contingencies, would be placing the whole too much under the control of the parts: to remedy which, this great additional power was given to the amending or repairing power—this *vis medicatrix* of the system.

To understand correctly the nature of this concession, we must not confound it with the delegated powers conferred on the General Government, and to be exercised by it as the joint agent of the States. They are essentially different. The former is, in fact, but a modification of the original sovereign power residing in the people of the several States—of *the creating or constitution-making power itself, intended, as stated, to facilitate and strengthen its action, and not change its character. Though modified, it is not delegated. It still resides in the States, and is still to be exercised by them, and not by the Government.*

I propose next to consider this important modification of the sovereign powers of the States, in connection with the right of nullification.

It is acknowledged on all sides that the duration and stability of our system depend on maintaining *the equilibrium* between the States and the General Government—the reserved and delegated powers. We know that the Convention which formed the Constitution, and the various State conventions which adopted it, as far as we are informed of their proceedings, felt the deepest solicitude on this point. They saw and felt there would be an incessant conflict between them, which would menace the existence of the system itself, unless properly guarded. The contest between the States and General Government— the reserved and delegated rights—will, in truth, be a conflict between the great predominant interests of the Union on one side,—controlling and directing the movements of the Government, and seeking to enlarge the delegated powers, and thereby advance their influence and prosperity; and, on the other, the minor interests rallying on the reserved powers, as the only means of protecting themselves against the encroachment and oppression of the other. In such a contest, without the most effectual check, the stronger will absorb the weaker interest; while, on the other hand, without an adequate provision of some description or other, the efforts of the weaker to guard against the encroachments and oppression of the stronger might permanently derange the system.

On the side of the reserved powers, no check more effectual can be found or desired than nullification, or the right of arresting, within the limits of a State, the exercise, by the General Government, of any powers but the delegated—a right which, if the States be true to themselves and faithful to the Constitution, will ever prove, on the side of the reserved powers, an effectual protection to both.

Nor is the check on the side of the delegated less perfect. Though less strong, it is ample to guard against encroachments; and is as strong as the nature of the system would bear, as will appear in the sequel. It is to be found in the amending power. Without the modification which it contains of the rights of self-government on the part of the States, as already explained, the consent of each State would have been requisite to any additional grant of power, or other amendment of the Constitution. While, then, nullification would enable a State to arrest the exercise of a power not delegated, the right of self-government, if unmodified, would enable her to prevent the grant of a power not delegated; and thus her conception of what power ought to be granted would be as conclusive against the co-States, as her construction of the powers granted is against the General Government. In that case, the danger would be on the side of the States or reserved powers. The amending power, *in effect,* prevents this danger. In virtue of the provisions which it contains, the resistance of a State to a power cannot finally prevail, unless she be sustained by one fourth of the co-States; and in the same degree that her resistance is weakened, the power of the General Government, or the side of the delegated powers, is *strengthened.* It is true that the right of a State to arrest an unconstitutional act is of itself complete against the Government; but it is equally so that the controversy may, *in effect,* be terminated against her by a grant of the contested powers by three fourths of the States. It is thus by this simple, and apparently incidental contrivance, that the right of a State to nullify an unconstitutional act, so essential to the protection of the reserved rights, but which, unchecked, might too much debilitate the Government, is counterpoised: not by weakening the energy of a State in her direct resistance to the encroachment of the Government, or by giving to the latter a direct control over the States, as proposed in the Convention, but in a manner infinitely more safe, and, if I may be permitted so to express myself, scientific, by strengthening the amending or repairing power—the power of correcting all abuses or derangements, by whatever cause, or from whatever quarter.

To sum all in a few words. The General Government has the right, in the first instance, of construing its own powers, which, if final and conclusive, as is supposed by many, would have placed the reserved powers at the mercy of the delegated, and thus destroy the equilibrium of the system. Against this, a State has the right of nullification. This right, on the part of the State, if not counterpoised, might tend too strongly to weaken the General Government and derange the system. To correct this, the amending or repairing power is strengthened. The former cannot be made too strong if the latter be proportionably so. The increase of the latter is, in effect, the decrease of the former. Give to a majority of the States the right of amendment, and the arresting power, on the part of the State, would, in fact, be annulled. The amending power and the powers of the Government would, in that case, be, in reality, in the same hands. The same majority that controlled the one would the other,— and the power arrested, as not granted, would be immediately restored in the shape of a grant. This modification of the right of self-government, on the part of the States, is, in fact, the pivot of the system. By shifting its position as the preponderance is on the one side or the other, or, to drop the simile, by increasing or diminishing the energy of the repairing power, effected by diminishing or increasing the number of States necessary to amend the Constitution, the equilibrium between the reserved and the delegated rights may be preserved or destroyed at pleasure.

I am aware it is objected that, according to this view, one fourth of the States may, in reality, change the Constitution, and thus take away powers which have been unanimously granted by all the States. The objection is more specious than solid. The *right* of a State is not to *resume* delegated powers, but to *prevent* the reserved from being *assumed* by the Government. It is, however, certain the right may be abused, and, thereby, powers be resumed which were, in fact, delegated; and it is also true, if sustained by one fourth of the co-States, such resumption may be successfully and permanently made by the State. This is the danger, and the utmost extent of the danger from the side of the reserved powers. It would, I acknowledge, be desirable to avoid or lessen it; but neither can be effected without increasing a greater and opposing danger.

If the right be denied to the State to defend her reserved powers, for fear she might resume the delegated, that denial would, in effect, yield to the General Government the power, under the color of construction, to assume at pleasure all the reserved powers. It is, in fact, a question between the danger of the States resuming the delegated powers on one side, and the General Government assuming the reserved on the other. Passing over the far greater probability of the latter than the former, which I endeavored to illustrate in the address of last summer, I shall confine my remarks to the striking difference between them, viewed in connection with the genius and theory of our Government.

The right of a State originally to complete self-government is a fundamental principle in our system, in virtue of which *the grant of power required the consent of all the States, while to withhold power the dissent of a single State was sufficient.* It is true, that this original and absolute power of self-government has been modified by the Constitution, as already stated, so that three fourths of the States may now grant power; and, consequently, it requires more than one fourth to withhold. The boundary between the reserved and the delegated powers marks the limits of the Union. The States are united to the extent of the latter, and separated beyond that limit. It is then clear that it was not intended that the States should be more united than the will of one fourth of them, or, rather, one more than a fourth, would permit. It is worthy of remark, that it was proposed in the Convention to increase the confederative power, as it may be called, by vesting two thirds of the States with the right of amendment, so as to require more than a third, instead of a fourth, to withhold power. The proposition was rejected, and three fourths unanimously adopted. It is, then, *more hostile to the nature and genius of our system to assume powers not delegated, than to resume those that are; and less hostile that a State, sustained by one fourth of her co-States, should prevent the exercise of power really intended to be granted, than that the General Government should assume the exercise of powers not intended to be delegated.* In the latter case, the usurpation of power would be against the fundamental principle of our system—the original right of the States to self-government; while in the former, if it be usurpation at all, it would be, if so bold an expression may be used, a usurpation in the spirit of the Constitution itself—the spirit ordaining that the utmost extent of our Union should be limited by the will of any number of

States exceeding a fourth, and that most wisely. In a country having so great a diversity of geographical and political interest, with so vast a territory, to be filled, in a short time, with almost countless millions—a country of which the parts will equal empires—a union more intimate than that ordained in the Constitution, and so intimate, of course, that it might be permanently hostile to the feelings of more than a fourth of the States, instead of strengthening, would have exposed the system to certain destruction. There is a deep and profound philosophy—which he who best knows our nature will the most highly appreciate—that would make the intensity of the Union, if I may so express myself, inversely to the extent of territory and the population of a country, and the diversity of its interests, geographical and political—and would hold in deeper dread the assumption of reserved rights by the agent appointed to execute the delegated, than the resumption of the delegated by the authority which granted the powers and ordained the agent to administer them. There appears, indeed, to be a great and prevailing principle that tends to place the delegated power in opposition to the delegating—the created to the creating power—reaching far beyond man and his works, up to the universal source of all power. The earliest pages of Sacred History record the rebellion of the archangels against the high authority of Heaven itself—and in ancient mythology, the war of the Titans against Jupiter, which, according to its narrative, menaced the universe with destruction. This all-pervading principle is at work in our system—the created warring against the creating power; and unless the Government be bolted and chained down with links of adamant by the hand of the States which created it, the creature will usurp the place of the creator, and universal political idolatry overspread the land.

If the views presented be correct, it follows that, on the interposition of a State in favor of the reserved rights, it would be the duty of the General Government to abandon the contested power, or to apply to the States themselves, the source of all political authority, for the power, in one of the two modes prescribed in the Constitution. If the case be a simple one, embracing a single power, and that in its nature easily adjusted, the more ready and appropriate mode would be an amendment in the ordinary form, on a proposition of two thirds of both Houses of Congress, to be ratified by three fourths of the States; but, on the contrary, should the derangement of the system be great, embracing many points difficult to adjust, the States ought to be convened in a general Convention—the most august of all assemblies—representing the united sovereignty of the confederated States, and having power and authority to correct every error, and to repair every dilapidation or injury, whether caused by time or accident, or the conflicting movements of the bodies which compose the system. With institutions every way so fortunate, possessed of means so well calculated to prevent disorders, and so admirable to correct them when they cannot be prevented, *he* who would prescribe for our political disease *disunion* on the one side, or *coercion* of *a State* in the assertion of its rights on the other, *would deserve, and will receive, the execrations of this and all future generations.*

I have now finished what I had to say on the subject of this communication, in its immediate connection with the Constitution. In the discussion, I have advanced nothing but on the authority of the Constitution itself, or that of recorded and unquestionable facts connected with the history of its origin and formation; and have made no deduction but such as rested on principles which I believe to be unquestionable; but it would be idle to expect, in the present state of the public mind, a favorable reception of the conclusions to which I have been carried. There are too many misconceptions to encounter—too many prejudices to combat—and, above all, too great a weight of interest to resist. I do not propose to investigate these great impediments to the reception of the truth, though it would be an interesting subject of inquiry to trace them to their cause, and to measure the force of their impeding power; but there is one among them of so marked a character, and which operates so extensively, that I cannot conclude without making it the subject of a few remarks, particularly as they will be calculated to throw much light on what has already been said.

Of all the impediments opposed to a just conception of the nature of our political system, the impression that the right of a State to arrest an unconstitutional act of the General Government is inconsistent with the great and fundamental principle of all free states—that a majority has the right to govern—is the greatest. Thus regarded, nullification is, without farther reflection, denounced as the most dangerous and monstrous of all political heresies, as, in truth, it would be, were the objection as well-founded as, in fact, it is destitute of all foundation, as I shall now proceed to show.

Those who make the objection seem to suppose that the right of a majority to govern is a principle too simple to admit of any distinction; and yet, if I do not mistake, it is susceptible of the most important distinction—entering deeply into the construction of our system, and, I may add, into that of all free States in proportion to the perfection of their institutions—and is essential to the very existence of liberty.

When, then, it is said that a majority has the right to govern, there are two modes of estimating the majority, to either of which the expression is applicable. The one, in which the whole community is regarded in the aggregate, and the majority is estimated in reference to the entire mass. This may be called the majority of the whole, or the absolute majority. The other, in which it is regarded in reference to its different political interests, whether composed of different classes, of different communities, formed into one general confederated community, and in which the majority is estimated, not in reference to the whole, but to each class or community of which it is composed,—the assent of each taken separately,—and the concurrence of all constituting the majority. A majority thus estimated may be called the concurring majority.

When it is objected to nullification, that it is opposed to the principle that a majority ought to govern, he who makes the objection must mean the absolute, as distinguished from the concurring. It is only in the sense of the former the objection can be applied. In that of the concurring, it would be absurd, as the concurring assent of all the parts (with us, all the States) is of the very essence of such majority. Again, it is manifest, that in the sense in which it would be good against nullification, it would be equally so against the Constitution itself; for, in whatever light that instrument may be regarded, it is clearly not the work of the absolute, but of the concurring majority. It was formed and ratified by the concurring assent of all the States, and not by the majority of the whole taken in the aggregate, as has been already stated. Thus, the acknowledged right of each State, *in reference to the Constitution,* is unquestionably the same right which nullification attributes to each *in reference to the unconstitutional acts of the Government;* and, if the latter be opposed to the right of a majority to govern, the former is equally so. I go farther. The objection might, with equal truth, be applied to all free States that have ever existed: I mean States deserving the name,— excluding, of course, those which, after a factious and anarchical existence of a few years, have sunk under the yoke of tyranny or the dominion of some foreign power. There is not, with this exception, a single free State whose institutions were not based on the principle of the concurring majority: not one in which the community was not regarded in reference to its different political interests, and which did not, in some form or other, take the assent of each in the operation of the Government.

In support of this assertion, I might begin with our own Government and go back to that of Sparta, and show conclusively that there is not one on the list whose institutions were not organized on the principle of the concurring majority, and in the operation of which the sense of each great interest was not separately consulted. The various devices which have been contrived for this purpose, with the peculiar operation of each, would be a curious and highly important subject of investigation. I can only allude to some of the most prominent.

The principle of the concurring majority has sometimes been incorporated in the regular and ordinary operation of the Government—each interest having a distinct organization—and a combination of the whole forming the Government; but still requiring the consent of each, within its proper sphere, to give validity to the measures of Government. Of this modification the British and Spartan Governments are by far the most memorable and perfect examples. In others, the right of acting—of making and executing the laws—was vested in one interest, and the right of arresting or nullifying in another. Of this description, the Roman Government is much the most striking instance. In others, the right of originating or introducing projects of laws was in one, and of enacting them in another: as at Athens before its Government degenerated—where the Senate proposed, and the General Assembly of the people enacted, laws.

These devices were all resorted to with the intention of consulting the separate interests of which the several communities were composed, and against all of which the objection to nullification, that it is opposed to the will of a majority, could be raised with equal force—as strongly, and I may say much more so, against the unlimited, unqualified, and uncontrollable veto of a single tribune out of ten at Rome on all laws and the execution of laws, as against the same right of a sovereign State (one of the twenty-four tribunes of this Union), limited, as the right is, to the unconstitutional acts of the General Government, and liable, as in effect it is, to be controlled by three fourths of the co-States; and yet the Roman Republic, and the other States to which I have referred, are the renowned among free States, whose examples have diffused the spirit of liberty over the world, and which, if struck from the list, would leave behind but little to be admired or imitated. There, indeed, would remain one class deserving from us particular notice, as ours belongs to it—I mean confederacies; but, as a class, heretofore far less distinguished for power and prosperity than those already alluded to; though I trust, with the improvements we have made, destined to be placed at the very head of the illustrious list of States which have blessed the world with examples of well-regulated liberty; and which stand as so many oases in the midst of the desert of oppression and despotism, which occupies so vast a space in the chart of governments. That such will be the great and glorious destiny of our system, I feel assured, provided we do not permit our Government to degenerate into the worst of all possible forms—a consolidated Government—swayed by the will of an absolute majority. But to proceed.

Viewing a confederated community as composed of as many distinct political interests as there are States, and as requiring the consent of each to its measures, no government can be conceived in which the sense of the whole community can be more perfectly taken, and all its interests be more fully represented and protected. But, with this great advantage—united with the means of the most just and perfect local administration through the agency of the States, and combined with the capacity of embracing within its limits the greatest extent of territory and variety of interests—it is liable to one almost fatal objection, the tardiness and feebleness of its movements—a defect difficult to be remedied, and when not, so great as to render a form of government—in other respects so admirable—almost worthless. To overcome this difficulty was the great desideratum in political science, and the most difficult problem within its circle. To us belongs the glory of its solution, if, indeed, our experiment (for such it must yet be called) shall prove that we have overcome it, as I sincerely believe and hope it will, on account of our own, as well as the liberty and happiness of our race.

Our first experiment in government was on the old form of a simple confederacy—unmodified, and extending the principle of the concurring majority alike to the Constitution (the articles of union) and to the Government which it constituted. It failed—and the present structure was reared in its place, combining, for the first time in a confederation, the absolute with the concurring majority; and thus uniting the justice of the one with the energy of the other.

The new Government was reared on the foundation of the old, strengthened, but not changed. It stands on the same solid basis of the concurring majority, perfected by the sanction of the people of the States directly given, and not indirectly through the State governments, as their representatives, as in the old confederation. With this difference, the authority which made the two Constitutions—which granted their powers, and ordained and organized their respective Governments to execute them—is the same. But, in passing from the Constitution to the Government (the law-making and the law-administering powers), the difference between the two becomes radical and essential. There, in the present, the concurring majority is dropped, and the absolute substituted. In determining, then, what powers ought to be granted, and how the Government appointed for their execution ought to be organized, the separate and concurring voice of the States was required—the union being regarded, for this purpose, in reference to its various and distinct interests; but in the execution of these powers (delegated only because all the States had a common interest in their exercise), the Union is no longer regarded in reference to its parts, but as forming, to the extent of its delegated powers, one great community—to be governed by a common will—just as the States are in reference to their separate interests, and by a Government organized on principles similar to theirs. By this simple but fortunate arrangement, we have ingrafted the absolute on the concurring majority, thereby giving to the administration of the powers of the Government, where they were required, all the energy and promptness belonging to the former—while we have retained in the power granting and organizing authority (if I may so express myself), the principle of the concurring majority, and with it that justice, moderation, and full and perfect representation of all the interests of the community which belong exclusively to it.

Such is the solidity and beauty of our admirable system—but which, it is perfectly obvious, can only be preserved by maintaining the ascendency of the CONSTITUTION-MAKING AUTHORITY OVER THE LAW-MAKING—THE CONCURRING OVER THE ABSOLUTE MAJORITY. Nor is it less clear that this can only be effected by the right of a State to annul the unconstitutional acts of the Government—a right confounded with the idea of a minority governing a majority, but which, so far from being the case, is indispensable to prevent the more energetic but imperfect majority which controls the movements of the Government from usurping the place of that more perfect and just majority which formed the Constitution and ordained government to execute its powers.

Nor need we apprehend that this check, as powerful as it is, will prove excessive. The distinction between the constitution and the law making powers, so strongly marked in our institutions, may yet be considered as a new and untried experiment. It can scarcely be said to have existed at all before our system of government. We have yet much to learn as to its practical operation; and, among other things, if I do not mistake, we are far from realizing the many and great difficulties of holding the latter subordinate to the former, and without which, it is obvious, the entire scheme of constitutional government, at least in our sense, must prove abortive. Short as has been our experience, some of these, of a very formidable character, have begun to disclose themselves, particularly between the Constitution and the Government of the Union. The two powers there represent very different interests: the one, that of all the States taken separately; and the other, that of a majority of the States as forming a confederated community. Each acting under the impulse of these respective and very different interests, must necessarily strongly, tend to come into collision, and, in the conflict, the advantage will be found almost exclusively on the side of the Government or law-making power. A few remarks will be sufficient to illustrate these positions.

The Constitution, while it grants powers to the Government, at the same time imposes restrictions on its action, with the intention of confining it within a limited range of powers, and of the means of executing them. The object of the powers is to protect the rights and promote the interests of all; and of the restrictions, to prevent the majority, or the dominant interests of the Government, from perverting powers intended for the common good into the means of oppressing the minor interests of the community. Thus circumstanced, the dominant interest in possession of the powers of the Government, and the minor interest on whom they are exercised, must regard these restrictions in a very different light; the latter as a protection, and the former as a restraint—and of course, accompanied with all the impatient feelings with which restrictions on cupidity and ambition are ever regarded by those unruly passions. Under their influence, the Constitution will be viewed by the majority, not as the source of their authority, as it should be, but as shackles on their power. To them it will have no value as the means of protection. As a majority they require none. Their number and strength, and not the Constitution, are their protection; and, of course, if I may so speak, their instinct will be to weaken and destroy the restrictions, in order to enlarge the powers. He must have a very imperfect knowledge of the human heart who does not see, in this state of things, an incessant conflict between the Government or the law-making power and the constitution-making power. Nor is it less certain that, in the contest, the advantage will be exclusively with the former.

The law-making power is organized and in constant action,—having the control of the honors and emoluments of the country, and armed with the power to punish and reward: the other, on the contrary, is unorganized, lying dormant in the great inert mass of the community, till called into action on extraordinary occasions and at distant intervals; and then bestowing no honors, exercising no patronage, having neither the faculty to reward nor to punish, but endowed simply with the attribute to grant powers and ordain the authority to execute them. The result is inevitable. With so strong an instinct on the part of the Government to throw off the restrictions of the Constitution and to enlarge its powers, and with such powerful faculties to gratify this instinctive impulse, the law-making must necessarily encroach on the constitution-making power, unless restrained by the most efficient check—at least as strong as that for which we contend. It is worthy of remark, that, all other circumstances being equal, the more dissimilar the interests represented by the two, the more powerful will be this tendency to encroach; and it is from this, among other causes, that it is so much stronger between the Government and the constitution-making powers of the Union, where the interests are so very dissimilar, than between the two in the several States.

That the framers of the Constitution were aware of the danger which I have described, we have conclusive proof in the provision to which I have so frequently alluded—I mean that which provides for amendments to the Constitution.

I have already remarked on that portion of this provision which, with the view of strengthening the confederated power, conceded to three fourths of the States a right to amend, which otherwise could only have been exercised by the unanimous consent of all. It is remarkable, that, while this provision thus strengthened the amending power as it regards the States, it imposed impediments on it as far as the Government was concerned. The power of acting, as a general rule, is invested in the majority of Congress; but, instead of permitting a majority to propose amendments, the provision requires for that purpose two thirds of both Houses—clearly with a view of interposing a barrier against this strong instinctive appetite of the Government for the acquisition of power. But it would have been folly in the extreme thus carefully to guard the passage to the direct acquisition, had the wide door of construction been left open to its indirect; and hence, in the same spirit in which two thirds of both Houses were required to propose amendments, the Convention that framed the Constitution rejected the many propositions which were moved in the body with the intention of divesting the States of the right of interposing, and, thereby, of the only effectual means of preventing the enlargement of the powers of the Government by construction.

It is thus that the constitution-making power has fortified itself against the law-making,—and so effectually, that, however strong the disposition and capacity of the latter to encroach, the means of resistance on the part of the former are not less powerful. If, indeed, encroachments have been made, the fault is not in the system, but in the inattention and neglect of those whose interest and duty it was to interpose the ample means of protection afforded by the Constitution.

To sum up in few words, in conclusion, what appears to me to be the entire philosophy of government, in reference to the subject of this communication.

Two powers are necessary to the existence and preservation of free States: a power on the part of the ruled to prevent rulers from abusing their authority, by compelling them to be faithful to their constituents, and which is effected through the right of suffrage; and a power TO COMPEL THE PARTS OF SOCIETY TO BE JUST TO ONE ANOTHER, BY COMPELLING THEM TO CONSULT THE INTEREST OF EACH OTHER—which can only be effected, whatever may be the device for the purpose, by requiring the concurring assent of all the great and distinct interests of the community to the measures of the Government. This result is the sum-total of all the contrivances adopted by free States to preserve their liberty, by preventing the conflicts between the several classes or parts of the community. Both powers are indispensable. The one as much so as the other. The rulers are not more disposed to encroach on the ruled than the different interests of the community on one another; nor would they more certainly convert their power from the just and legitimate objects for which governments are instituted into an instrument of aggrandizement, at the expense of the ruled,—unless made responsible to their constituents,—than would the stronger interests theirs, at the expense of the weaker, unless compelled to consult them in the measures of the Government by taking their separate and concurring assent. The same cause operates in both cases. The constitution of our nature, which would impel the rulers to oppress the ruled, unless prevented, would in like manner, and with equal force, impel the stronger to oppress the weaker interest. To vest the right of government in the absolute majority, would be, in fact—BUT TO EMBODY THE WILL OF THE STRONGER INTEREST IN THE OPERATIONS OF THE GOVERNMENT AND NOT THE WILL OF THE WHOLE COMMUNITY—AND TO LEAVE THE OTHERS UNPROTECTED, A PREY TO ITS AMBITION AND CUPIDITY—just as would be the case between rulers and ruled, if the right to govern was vested exclusively in the hands of the former. They would both be, in reality, absolute and despotic governments: the one as much so as the other.

They would both become mere instruments of cupidity and ambition in the hands of those who wielded them. No one doubts that such would be the case were the government placed under the control of irresponsible rulers, but, unfortunately for the cause of liberty, it is not seen with equal clearness that it must as necessarily be so when controlled by an absolute majority; and yet, the former is not more certain than the latter. To this we may attribute the mistake so often and so fatally repeated, that to expel a despot is to establish liberty—a mistake to which we may trace the failure of many noble and generous efforts in favor of liberty. The error consists in considering communities as formed of interests strictly identical throughout, instead of being composed, as they in reality are, of as many distinct interests as there are individuals. The interests of no two persons are the same, regarded in reference to each other, though they may be, viewed in relation to the rest of the community. It is this diversity which the several portions of the community bear to each other, in reference to the whole, that renders the principle of the concurring majority necessary to preserve liberty. Place the power in the hands of the absolute majority, and the strongest of these would certainly pervert the government from the object for which it was instituted—the equal protection of the rights of all—into an instrument of advancing itself at the expense of the rest of the community. Against this abuse of power no remedy can be devised but that of the concurring majority. Neither the right of suffrage nor public opinion can possibly check it. They, in fact, but tend to aggravate the disease. It seems really surprising that truths so obvious should be so imperfectly understood. There would appear, indeed, a feebleness in our intellectual powers on political subjects when directed to large masses. We readily see why a single individual, as a ruler, would, if not prevented, oppress the rest of the community; but are at a loss to understand why seven millions would, if not also prevented, oppress six millions, as if the relative numbers on either side could in the least degree vary the principle.

In stating what I have, I have but repeated the experience of ages, comprehending all free governments preceding ours, and ours as far as it has progressed. The PRACTICAL operation of ours has been substantially on the principle of *the absolute* majority. We have acted, with some exceptions, as if the General Government had the right to interpret its own powers, without limitation or check; and though many circumstances have favored us, and greatly impeded the natural progress of events, under such an operation of the system, yet we already see, in whatever direction we turn our eyes, the growing symptoms of disorder and decay—the growth of faction, cupidity, and corruption; and the decay of patriotism, integrity, and disinterestedness. In the midst of youth, we see the flushed check, and the short and feverish breath, that mark the approach of the fatal hour; and come it will, unless there be a speedy and radical change—a return to the great conservative principles which brought the Republican party into authority, but which, with the possession of power and prosperity, it has long ceased to remember.

I have now finished the task which your request imposed. If I have been so fortunate as to add to your fund a single new illustration of this great conservative principle of our Government, or to furnish an additional argument calculated to sustain the State in her noble and patriotic struggle to revive and maintain it, and in which you have acted a part long to be remembered by the friends of freedom, I shall feel amply compensated for the time occupied in so long a communication. I believe the cause to be the cause of truth and justice, of union, liberty, and the Constitution, before which the ordinary party struggles of the day sink into perfect insignificance; and that it will be so regarded by the most distant posterity, I have not the slightest doubt.

With great and sincere regard,

I am yours, &c., &c.,

JOHN C. CALHOUN.

His Excellency JAMES HAMILTON, Jr., Governor of South Carolina.

CHAPTER XII.

"ADDRESS TO THE PEOPLE OF THE UNITED STATES,"
NOVEMBER 1832

*As the draft document for one of four texts approved by the South Carolina Nullifi-
cation Convention (1832), Calhoun's "Address" is a profound statement of political
principle and self-restraint in the midst of great national political turmoil. The "Address"
stressed the constitutionality of South Carolina's position. The state had interposed herself between the state's citizenry and the national government, while also affirming the
nonviolent and temporary nature of the response. It encouraged other states to respectfully
consider South Carolina's stance and presented them with a statement of the principles
that had prompted such a decision.*

To *the People of Maine, New Hampshire, Massachusetts, Rhode Island, Connecticut, Vermont, New York, New Jersey, Pennsylvania, Delaware, Maryland, Virginia, North Carolina, Georgia, Kentucky, Tennessee, Ohio, Louisiana, Indiana,
Mississippi, Illinois, Alabama and Missouri:*

WE, the people of South Carolina assembled in Convention in our sovereign capacity, as one of the parties to the compact, which formed the Constitution of the United States, have declared the act of Congress, approved the 14th
of July, 1832, to alter and amend the several acts imposing duties on imports,
and the acts, which it alters and amends,—to be unconstitutional, and therefore
null and void; and have invested the Legislature of the State with power to adopt
such measures, not repugnant to the Constitution of the United States, nor of
this State,—as it may deem proper, to carry the same into effect. In taking this
step, we feel it to be due to the intimate political relations existing between the
States of the Union, to make known to them, distinctly, the principles on which

we have acted, with the cause and motive by which we have been influenced;—to fulfil which is the object of the present communication.

For this purpose, it will be necessary to state, summarily, what we conceive to be the nature and character of the Constitution of the United States, with the rights and duties of the States,—so far as they relate to the subject,—in reference both to the Union and to their own citizens;—and also the character and effect, in a political point of view, of the system of protective duties, contained in the acts which we have declared to be unconstitutional, as far as it may be necessary, in reference to the same subject.

We, then, hold it as unquestionable, that, on the separation from the Crown of Great Britain, the people of the several colonies became free and independent States, possessed of the full right of self-government;—and that no power can be rightfully exercised over them, but by the consent and authority of their respective States, expressed or implied. We also hold it as equally unquestionable, that the Constitution of the United States is a compact between the people of the several States, constituting free, independent, and sovereign communities;—that the Government it created was formed and appointed to execute, according to the provisions of the instrument, the powers therein granted, as the joint agent of the several States; that all its acts, transcending these powers, are simply and of themselves, null and void, and that in case of such infractions, it is the right of the States, in their sovereign capacity, each acting for itself and its citizens, in like manner as they adopted the Constitution, to judge thereof in the last resort, and to adopt such measures—not inconsistent with the compact—as may be deemed fit, to arrest the execution of the act within their respective limits. Such we hold to be the right of the States, in reference to an unconstitutional act of the Government; nor do we deem their duty to exercise it on proper occasions, less certain and imperative, than the right itself is clear.

We hold it to be a very imperfect conception of the obligation, which each State contracted in ratifying the Constitution, and thereby becoming a member of the Union, to suppose that it would be fully and faithfully discharged, simply by abstaining, on its part, from exercising the powers delegated to the Government of the Union, or by sustaining it in the due execution of those powers. These are, undoubtedly, important federal duties, but there is another not less important,—to resist the Government, should it, under color of exercising the delegated, encroach on the reserved powers. The duty of the States is no less clear in the one case than in the other; and the obligation as binding in the one as in the other; and in like manner, the solemn obligation of an oath, imposed by the States through the Constitution, on all public functionaries, federal and

State, to support that instrument, comprehends the one as well as the other duty;—as well that of maintaining the Government in the due exercise of its powers, as that of resisting it when it transcends them.

But the obligation of a State to resist the encroachments of the Government on the reserved powers, is not limited simply to the discharge of its federal duties. We hold that it embraces another, if possible, more sacred;—that of protecting its citizens, derived from their original sovereign character, viewed in their separate relations. There are none of the duties of a State of higher obligation. It is, indeed, the primitive duty,—preceding all others, and in its nature paramount to them all; and so essential to the existence of a State, that she cannot neglect or abandon it, without forfeiting all just claims to the allegiance of her citizens, and with it, her sovereignty itself. In entering into the Union, the States by no means exempted themselves from the obligation of this, the first and most sacred of their duties; nor, indeed, can they without sinking into subordinate and dependent corporations. It is true, that in ratifying the Constitution, they placed a large and important portion of the rights of their citizens, under the joint protection of all the States, with a view to their more effectual security; but it is not less so, that they reserved, at the same time, a portion still larger, and not less important, under their own immediate guardianship; and in relation to which, the original obligation, to protect the rights of their citizens, from whatever quarter assailed, remained unchanged and unimpaired. Nor is it less true, that the General Government, created in order to preserve the rights placed under the joint protection of the States, and which, when restricted to its proper sphere, is calculated to afford them the most perfect security, may become, when not so restricted, the most dangerous enemy to the rights of their citizens, including those reserved under the immediate guardianship of the States respectively, as well as those under their joint protection; and thus, the original and inherent obligation of the States to protect their citizens, is united with that which they have contracted to support the Constitution; thereby rendering it the most sacred of all their duties to watch over and resist the encroachments of the Government;—and on the faithful performance of which, we solemnly believe the duration of the Constitution and the liberty and happiness of the country depend.

But, while we hold the rights and duties of the States to be such as we have stated, we are deeply impressed with the conviction, that it is due to the relation existing between them, as members of a common Union, and the respect which they ought ever to entertain towards the Government ordained to carry into effect the important objects for which the Constitution was formed, that the occasion to justify a State in interposing its authority, ought to be one of necessity; where all other peaceful remedies have been unsuccessfully tried; and where the only alternative is, interposition on one side, or oppression of its citizens, and imminent danger to the Constitution and liberty of the country on the other; and such we hold to be the present.

That the prohibitory, or protective system, which, as has been stated, is embraced in the acts which we have declared to be unconstitutional, and therefore null and void, is, in fact, unconstitutional, unequal, and oppressive in its operation on this, and the other staple and exporting States, and dangerous to the Constitution and liberty of the country,—and that (all other peaceful remedies having been tried without success) an occasion has occurred, where it becomes the right and duty of the State to interpose its authority to arrest the evil within its limits, we hold to be certain; and it is under this deep and solemn conviction, that we have acted.

For more than ten years, the system has been the object of continued, united, and strenuous opposition on the part both of the Government of the State and its representatives in Congress; and, we may add, of the other staple and exporting States. During this long period, all the ordinary means of opposition—discussion, resolution, petition, remonstrance, and protest—have been tried and exhausted, without effect. We have, during the whole time, waited with patience under the unequal and oppressive action of the system, hoping that the final payment of the public debt, when there would be no longer a pretext for its continuance, would bring it to a termination. That period, for all practical purposes, is now passed. The small remnant of debt which now remains, is amply provided for by the revenue already accrued; but the system remains in full force;—its restrictive character established and openly avowed; the inequality of its action, between this and other sections, greatly increased; and the amount of its exertions vastly exceeding,—probably doubling, the just and constitutional wants of the Government. The event, which, it was hoped, would put an end to its duration, has thus but served to give it increased strength; and, instead of mitigating, has aggravated its most obnoxious features. Having stood this shock, it seems almost impossible that any other within the ordinary scope of events, can shake it. It now stands for the first time, exclusively on its own basis, as an independent system; having a self-existing power, with an unlimited capacity of increasing,—which, left unopposed, must continue to expand, till it controls the entire labor and capital of the staple and exporting States;—subjecting them completely, as tributaries, to the great dominant and sectional interest, which has grown up at their expense. With this prospect of the indefinite extent and duration of the system, we had thus presented the alternative of silently acquiescing in its oppression and danger, or of interposing, as the last peaceful measure of redress, the authority of the State to arrest the evil within its limits. We did not hesitate.

When we reflect on the principle on which the system rests, and from which the Government claims the power to control the labor and capital of the country, and the bitter fruits it has already produced,—the decay and impoverishment of an entire section of the country;—and the wide spread of discord and corruption,—we cannot doubt, that there is involved in the issue, not only the prosperity of this and the other staple and exporting States, but also the Constitution and liberty of the country. In rearing up the system it was not pretended, nor is it now, that there is in the Constitution any positive grant of power to protect manufactures; nor can it be denied that frequent attempts were made in the Convention to obtain the power, and that they all failed: and yet, without any grant, and notwithstanding the failure to obtain one, it has become one of the leading powers of the Government,—influencing more extensively its movements, and affecting more deeply and permanently the relative interests and condition of the States, and the probable fate of the Government itself, than any, or all of the enumerated powers united.

From whatever source its advocates may derive this power,—whether from the right, "to lay and collect taxes, duties, imposts, and excises," or from that, "to regulate commerce," it plainly rests on the broad assumption, that the power to impose duties may be applied, not only to effect the original objects,—to raise revenue, or regulate commerce, but also to protect manufactures; and this, not as an incidental, but as a substantive and independent power,—without reference to revenue or commerce; and, in this character, it has been used in building up the present system.

That such a power, resting on such a principle, is unauthorized by the Constitution;—that it has become an instrument in the hands of the great dominant interests of the country, to oppress the weaker;—that it must, ultimately, concentrate the whole power of the community in the General Government, and abolish the sovereignty of the States;—and that discord, corruption, and, eventually, despotism must follow, if the system be not resisted,—we hold to be certain. Already we see the commencement of this disastrous train of consequences;—the oppression of the weaker;—the assumption by Government of the right to determine, finally and conclusively, the extent of its own powers;—the denial and denunciation of the right of the States to judge of their reserved powers, and to defend them against the encroachments of the Government;—followed by discord, corruption, and the steady advance of despotic power.

That something is wrong, all admit; and that the assumption, by Government, of a power so extensive and dangerous,—and the control which it has thereby acquired, through its fiscal operations, over the wealth and labor of the country,—exacting, in the shape of high duties, a large portion of the annual income of our section, and bestowing it in the form of monopolies and appropriations on the other,—is the true cause of the existing disorder,—and the only adequate one that can be assigned,—we cannot entertain a doubt. To this unequal and excessive fiscal action of the Government, may be immediately and clearly traced the growing discontent and alienation on the part of the oppressed portion of the community, and the greedy pursuit of office;—and with it, the increasing spirit of servility subserviency and corruption on the other;—which all must see and acknowledge, and which every lover of the country, and its institutions must deplore. Nor is it less clear, that this dangerous assumption, by which the reserved powers of the States have been transferred to the General Government, is rapidly concentrating, by a necessary operation, the whole power of the Government, in the hands of the Executive. We must be blind to the lessons of reason and experience not to see, that, the more a government interferes with the labor and wealth of a community,—the more it exacts from one portion, and bestows on another,—just in the same proportion must the power of that department, which is vested with its patronage, be increased. It ought not, then, to be a subject of surprise, that, with this vast increase of the power and revenues of the Federal Government, and its unequal fiscal action, both in the collection and distribution of the latter, the power of the Executive, on whose will the disposition of the patronage of the Government mainly depends, and on which, in turn, depends that powerful, active and mercenary corps of expectants, created by the morbid moneyed action of the Government,—should be, of late, so greatly and dangerously increased. It is indeed not difficult to see that the present state of things, if continued, must end,—and that speedily,—in raising this department of the Government into an irresponsible and despotic power, with the capacity of perpetuating itself through its own influence;—first, virtually appointing its successor, or, by controlling the Presidential election, through the patronage of the Government; and, finally,—as the virtue and patriotism of the people decay, by the introduction and open establishment of the hereditary principle.

The Federal Government has, indeed, already passed through the first and most difficult part of this process,—which, if permitted to proceed, must terminate, as it ever has, in the absolute and unlimited power of a single despot.

We hold it as certain, that, wherever the majority of a people becomes the advocate of high taxes, and profuse appropriations and expenditures, there the despotic power is already, in fact, established, and liberty virtually lost,—be the form of government what it may; and experience has proved that the transition from this stage to the absolute power of a single individual, is certain and rapid;—and that it can only be arrested by the interposition of some high power out of the ordinary course. Our Government has already clearly reached the first stage; and will inevitably—unless the process be arrested by some such power—speedily terminate its career in the last. In the mean time, while this train of events is consummating itself in the loss of the liberty of all, the oppression and impoverishment of this and the other staple and exporting States will necessarily advance with equal steps. The very root of the system,—that from which it derives its existence and sprouts forth all its evils, is its unjust and unequal action;—giving to one portion what it takes from another,—and thus creating that powerful and irresistible interest in favor of high taxes and profuse expenditures, which are fast sweeping away, at the same time, the foundation of our liberty, and exhausting and reducing to poverty a large portion of the community. That such is, in truth, the real state of things, the extraordinary spectacle, which our Government now exhibits to the world, affords the most conclusive proof. On what other principle can it be explained, that a popular government, with all the forms of freedom, after having discharged a long standing and heavy public debt, should resist every effort to make a corresponding reduction of the public burden? What other cause can be assigned for a fact so remarkable, as that of a free community refusing to repeal this tax, when the proceeds are, confessedly, no longer wanted,—and when the embarrassment of the Government is,—not to find the revenue, but the objects on which to expend it?

Such is the nature of the disorder which the system has engendered. Of all the diseases which can afflict the body politic, we hold it to be the most inveterate and difficult to remedy. Others, originating in ignorance, delusion, or some sudden popular impulse,—yield to the influence of time and reflection; and we may, accordingly, look in such cases, with confidence, for relief, to the returning good sense and feelings of the community. Not so in this. Having its source in the most powerful passions of the human heart,—the love of gain and power,—neither time, reflection, reason, discussion, entreaty, nor remonstrance can arrest or impede its course: nor, if left to itself, will it stop while there is a cent to be exacted, or a particle of power to be acquired. With us, the disease must assume the most aggravated character. There is no country in which so many and such powerful causes exist to give to the unequal fiscal action of the government, in which it originates, so powerful an impetus, and an operation so oppressive and dangerous. When we reflect on the extent of our country, and the diversity of its interests;—on the peculiar nature of the labor and production of this, and the other suffering States;—with how much facility they may be made subservient to the power and wealth of the other sections,—as experience has shown,—and how deep, radical, and disastrous must be the change in the social and political condition of this and the other States similarly situated in reference to pursuits and population, when the increasing pressure shall reach the point at which the exactions of the Government shall not leave a sufficient amount of the proceeds of labor to remunerate the expense of maintenance and supervision;—we cannot but foresee, if the system be not arrested, calamity awaiting us and our posterity, greater than ever befell a free and enlightened people. Already we perceive indications of its approach, that cannot be mistaken. It appears in that quarter, to which, from the nature of the disease, we would naturally look for it; that quarter where labor is the least productive, and is least capable of bearing the pressure of the system.

Such, we hold to be the general character of the system, viewed in its political connections, and its certain effects, if left to its natural operations;—to arrest the evils of which, within our limits, we have interposed the authority of the State as the only peaceful remedy that remains of defending the Constitution against its encroachments,—the citizens of the State against its oppression,—and the liberty of the country against its corrupting influence and danger.

In performing this high and sacred duty, our anxious desire has been to embarrass the action of the Government in the smallest degree possible, consistent with the object we have in view; and had it been possible to separate the portion of duties necessary for revenue, from that imposed for the purpose of protection, the action of the State would have been limited exclusively to the latter. But we could have no right to discriminate when the Government had made no discrimination; and if we had, it would have been impossible; as revenue and protection are so blended throughout,—and the duties, as well those included in the act of July last, as those contained in the acts it alters and amends, comprehending the unprotected and the protected articles,—are adjusted so obviously with the design to form one entire system of protection,—as much so, as if the whole had been incorporated in a single act, passed expressly with that intention, and without regard to revenue, except as a mere incident. The whole, thus forming one system, equally contaminated throughout by the same unconstitutional principle,—no alternative was left, but to declare the entire system unconstitutional; and as such, null and void. Anxious however, while thus compelled to arrest an unconstitutional act, to continue in the discharge of all our constitutional obligations, and to bear our just and full share of the public burdens, we have, with a view to effect these objects, pledged the State to make good her proportional part of the revenue that would have accrued on the imports into the State, which may be exempted from duties, by the interposition of the State;—calculated according to the rate per centum on the general imports which may, on a fair estimate, be considered requisite to meet the just and constitutional wants of the Government; and have, accordingly, authorized the Government of the State, to adopt the necessary measures on its part to adjust the same, on the termination of the present unhappy controversy.

That so desirable an event may be speedily brought about to the satisfaction of all, is our sincere desire. In taking the stand which she has, the State has been solely influenced by a conscientious sense of duty to her citizens, and to the Constitution, without the slightest feeling of hostility towards the interests of any section of the country, or the remotest view to revolution,—or wish to terminate her connection with the Union;—to which she is now, as she ever has been, devotedly attached. Her object is, not to destroy, but to restore and preserve: and, in asserting her right to defend her reserved powers, she disclaims all pretension to control or interfere with the action of the Government within its proper sphere,—or to resume any powers that she has delegated to the Government, or conceded to the confederated States. She simply claims the right of exercising the powers which, in adopting the Constitution, she reserved to herself;—and among them,—the most important and essential of all,—the right to judge, in the last resort, of the extent of her reserved powers,—a right never delegated nor surrendered,—nor, indeed, could be, while the State retains her sovereignty. That it has not been, we appeal with confidence to the Constitution itself, which contains not a single grant that, on a fair construction, can be held to comprehend the power. If to this we add the fact, which the Journals of the Convention abundantly establish, that reiterated, but unsuccessful attempts were made, in every stage of its proceedings, to divest the States of the power in question, by conferring on the General Government the right to annul such acts of the States, as it might deem to be repugnant to the Constitution, and the corresponding right to coerce their obedience,—we have the highest proof of which the subject is susceptible, that the power in question was not delegated, but reserved to the States. To suppose that a State, in exercising a power so unquestionable, resists the Union, would be a fundamental and dangerous error,—originating in a radical misconception of the nature of our political institutions. The Government is neither the Union, nor its representative, except as an agent to execute its powers. The States themselves, in their confederated character, represent the authority of the Union; and, acting in the manner prescribed by the Constitution, through the concurring voice of three fourths of their number, have the right to enlarge or diminish, at pleasure, the powers of the Government,—and to amend, alter, or even abolish the Constitution, and, with it, the Government itself. Correctly understood, it is not the State that interposes to arrest an unconstitutional act,—but the Government that passed it, which resists the authority of the Union. The Government has not the right to add a particle to its powers; and to assume, on its part, the exercise of a power, not granted, is plainly to oppose the confederated authority of the States, to which the right of granting powers exclusively belongs;—and, in so doing, the Union itself, which they represent. On the contrary, a State, as a member of the body in which the authority of the Union resides,—in arresting an unconstitutional act of the Government, within its limits,—so far from opposing, in reality supports the Union, and that in the only effectual mode in which it can be done in such cases. To divest the States of this right, would be, in effect, to give to the Government that authority over the Constitution, which belongs to them exclusively; and which can only be preserved to them, by leaving to each State,—as the Constitution has done,—to watch over and defend its reserved powers against the encroachments of the Government,—and in performing which, it acts, at the same time, as a faithful and vigilant sentinel over the confederate powers of the States. It was doubtless with these views, that the Convention which framed the Constitution, steadily resisted, as has been observed, the many attempts which were made, under the specious but fallacious argument of preserving the peace and harmony of the Union, to divest the States of this important right,—which is not less essential to the defence of their joint confederate powers, than to the preservation of their separate sovereignty, and the protection of their citizens.

With these views,—views on which the Convention acted in refusing to divest the States of this right,—has this State acted, in asserting it on the present occasion;—and this with a full understanding of all the responsibilities attached to the position she has assumed, and with a determination as fixed as her conception of her right and duty is clear, to maintain it under every circumstance, and at every hazard. She has weighed all the consequences, and can see, in no possible result, greater disasters than those which must certainly follow a surrender of the right, and an abandonment of her duty.

Having thus taken, immovably, her stand, there remain,—to bring the controversy to a happy termination, but two possible courses. It may be effected, by the Government ceasing to exercise the unconstitutional power, through which, under the name of duties, it has assumed the control over the labor and wealth of the country, and substituting, for the present high rates, an average ad valorem duty,—or some other system of revenue equally just and fair;—or by obtaining a positive grant of the power, in the manner prescribed by the Constitution.

But, when we consider the great interests at stake, and the number and magnitude of the questions involved in the issue, directly and indirectly; and the necessity of a full understanding on all the points, in order to a satisfactory and permanent adjustment of the controversy; we hold it difficult, if not impracticable, to bring it to a final and satisfactory close, short of convening again, the body, to whose authority and wisdom we are indebted for the Constitution: and under this conviction we have made it the duty of the Legislature of the State to apply, in the manner prescribed by the Constitution, for a general convention of the States, as the most certain, prompt, and effectual, if not the only practicable mode of terminating the conflict, and restoring harmony and confidence to the country. If the other States of the Union be actuated by the same feelings which govern us;—if their desire to maintain the Constitution,—to preserve the Union,—and to transmit to posterity the blessings of liberty,—be as strong as ours (and we doubt not that it is), this most august of all assemblies,—provided by the Constitution to meet this and similar emergencies,—as a great moral substitute for revolution and force,—may be convened in a few months; when the present, and every other constitutional question, endangering the peace and harmony of the Union,—may be satisfactorily adjusted.

If there be any conceivable occasion that can justify the call of a Convention of the States, we hold the present to be that occasion; and surely the framers of the Constitution, in providing a mode for calling one, contemplated that great emergencies would arise in the course of events, in which it ought to be convened. They were not so vain as to suppose that their work was so perfect, as to be too clear to admit of diversity of opinion,—or too strong for passion or interest to derange. They accordingly, in their wisdom, provided a double remedy to meet the contingencies, which, if not provided for, might endanger our political system;—one, to meet ordinary and less pressing occurrences,—by vesting in two thirds of Congress the power to propose amendments to the Constitution, to be ratified by three fourths of the States;—the other, for those of a more urgent character, when some deep derangement of the system,—or some great and dangerous conflict of interests or opinion, might threaten, with a catastrophe, the institutions of the country. That such a remedy is provided, is proof of the profound wisdom of the great men who formed our Constitution; and entitles them to the lasting gratitude of the country. But it will be in vain that their wisdom devised a remedy so admirable,—a substitute so infinitely superior to the old and irrational mode of terminating such controversies as are of too high a nature to be adjusted by the force of reason, or through the ordinary tribunals,—if their descendants be so blind as not to perceive its efficacy,—or so intently bent on schemes of ambition and avarice, as to prefer to this constitutional, peaceful, and safe remedy, the wanton, hazardous, and, we may add, immoral arbitrament of force. We hold that our country has arrived at the very point of difficulty and danger, contemplated by the framers of the Constitution, in providing for a General Convention of the States of the Union; and that, of course, the question now remaining to be tested, is,—whether there be sufficient moral elevation, patriotism, and intelligence in the country, to adjust, through the interposition of this highest of tribunals, whose right none can question, the conflicts which now threaten the very existence of our institutions, and liberty itself,—and which, as experience has proved, there is no other body belonging to the system, having sufficient weight of authority to terminate.

Such, at least, is our conviction; and we have acted accordingly. It now rests with the other States to determine whether a General Convention shall be called or not;—and on that determination hangs, we solemnly believe, the future fate of the country. If it should be in favor of a call, we may, with almost perfect certainty, entertain the prospect of a speedy and happy termination of all our difficulties,—followed by peace, prosperity, and lengthened political existence: but if not, we shall, by rejecting the remedy provided by the wisdom of our ancestors, prove that we deserve the fate, which, in that event, will, in all probability, await the country.

CHAPTER XIII.

"Speech on the Force Bill," 15 and 16 February 1833

After resigning the vice-presidency in December 1832, Calhoun assumed a seat in the U. S. Senate. While working to mediate nullification tensions, Calhoun was obliged to respond to a proposed "Force Bill." The problem with the proposed legislation was that it granted the president special authority for the enforcement of duties and allowed him to use the "irresistible energy" of the national government. It was a struggle between "power and liberty" for Calhoun, and he was determined to defend liberty against the potentially tyrannical and coercive power of the president.

Mr. President:—I know not which is most objectionable, the provisions of the bill, or the temper in which its adoption has been urged. If the extraordinary powers with which the bill proposes to clothe the Executive, to the utter prostration of the constitution and the rights of the States, be calculated to impress our minds with alarm at the rapid progress of despotism in our country; the zeal with which every circumstance calculated to misrepresent or exaggerate the conduct of Carolina in the controversy, is seized on with a view to excite hostility against her, but too plainly indicates the deep decay of that brotherly feeling which once existed between these States, and to which we are indebted for our beautiful federal system, and by the continuance of which alone it can be preserved. It is not my intention to advert to all these misrepresentations; but there are some so well calculated to mislead the mind as to the real character of the controversy, and to hold up the State in a light so odious, that I do not feel myself justified in permitting them to pass unnoticed.

Among them, one of the most prominent is, the false statement that the object of South Carolina is to exempt herself from her share of the public burdens, while she participates in the advantages of the Government. If the charge were true—if the State were capable of being actuated by such low and unworthy motives, mother as I consider her, I would not stand up on this floor to vindicate her conduct. Among her faults,—and faults I will not deny she has,—no one has ever yet charged her with that low and most sordid of vices—avarice. Her conduct, on all occasions, has been marked with the very opposite quality. From the commencement of the Revolution—from its first breaking out at Boston till this hour, no State has been more profuse of its blood in the cause of the country; nor has any contributed so largely to the common treasury in proportion to wealth and population. She has, in that proportion, contributed more to the exports of the Union,—on the exchange of which with the rest of the world the greater portion of the public burden has been levied,—than any other State. No: the controversy is not such as has been stated; the State does not seek to participate in the advantages of the Government without contributing her full share to the public treasury. Her object is far different. A deep constitutional question lies at the bottom of the controversy. The real question at issue is: Has this Government a right to impose burdens on the capital and industry of one portion of the country, not with a view to revenue, but to benefit another? And I must be permitted to say that, after the long and deep agitation of this controversy, it is with surprise that I perceive so strong a disposition to misrepresent its real character. To correct the impression which those misrepresentations are calculated to make, I will dwell on the point under consideration for a few moments longer.

The Federal Government has, by an express provision of the constitution, the right to lay on imports. The State has never denied or resisted this right, nor even thought of so doing. The Government has, however, not been contented with exercising this power as she had a right to do, but has gone a step beyond it, by laying imposts, not for revenue, but protection. This the State considers as an unconstitutional exercise of power—highly injurious and oppressive to her and the other staple States, and has, accordingly, met it with the most determined resistance. I do not intend to enter, at this time, into the argument as to the unconstitutionality of the protective system. It is not necessary. It is sufficient that the power is nowhere granted; and that, from the journals of the Convention which formed the constitution, it would seem that it was refused. In support of the journals, I might cite the statement of Luther Martin, which has already been referred to, to show that the Convention, so far from conferring the power on the Federal Government, left to the State the right to impose duties on imports, with the express view of enabling the several States to protect their own manufactures. Notwithstanding this, Congress has assumed, without any warrant from the constitution, the right of exercising this most important power; and has so exercised it as to impose a ruinous burden on the labor and capital of the State, by which her resources are exhausted—the enjoyments of her citizens curtailed—the means of education contracted—and all her interests essentially and injuriously affected. We have been sneeringly told that she is a small State; that her population does not much exceed half a million of souls; and that more than one-half are not of the European race. The facts are so. I know she never can be a great State, and that the only distinction to which she can aspire must be based on the moral and intellectual acquirements of her sons. To the development of these much of her attention has been directed; but this restrictive system, which has so unjustly exacted the proceeds of her labor, to be bestowed on other sections, has so impaired her resources, that, if not speedily arrested, it will dry up the means of education, and with it, deprive her of the only source through which she can aspire to distinction.

There is another misstatement, as to the nature of the controversy, so frequently made in debate, and so well calculated to mislead, that I feel bound to notice it. It has been said that South Carolina claims the right to annul the constitution and laws of the United States; and to rebut this supposed claim, the gentleman from Virginia (Mr. Rives) has gravely quoted the constitution, to prove that the constitution, and the laws made in pursuance thereof, are the supreme laws of the land—as if the State claimed the right to act contrary to this provision of the constitution. Nothing can be more erroneous: her object is not to resist laws made in pursuance of the constitution, but those made without its authority, and which encroached on her reserved powers. She claims not even the right of judging of the delegated powers, but of those that are reserved; and to resist the former, when they encroach upon the latter. I will pause to illustrate this important point.

All must admit that there are delegated and reserved powers, and that the powers reserved are reserved to the States respectively. The powers, then, of the system are divided between the General and the State Governments; and the point immediately under consideration is, whether a State has any right to judge as to the extent of its reserved powers, and to defend them against the encroachments of the General Government. Without going deeply into this point at this stage of the argument, or looking into the nature and origin of the Government, there is a simple view of the subject which I consider as conclusive. The very idea of a divided power implies the right on the part of the State for which I contend. The expression is metaphorical when applied to power. Every one readily understands that the division of matter consists in the separation of the parts. But in this sense it is not applicable to power. What, then, is meant by a division of power? I cannot conceive of a division, without giving an equal right to each to judge of the extent of the power allotted to each. Such right I hold to be essential to the existence of a division; and that, to give to either party the conclusive right of judging, not only of the share allotted to it, but of that allotted to the other, is to annul the division, and to confer the whole power on the party vested with such right.

But it is contended that the constitution has conferred on the Supreme Court the right of judging between the States and the General Government. Those who make this objection, overlook, I conceive, an important provision of the constitution. By turning to the 10th amended article, it will be seen that the reservation of power to the States is not only against the powers, delegated to Congress, but against the United States themselves; and extends, of course, as well to the judiciary as to the other departments of the Government. The article provides, that all powers not delegated to the United States, or prohibited by it to the States, are reserved to the States respectively, or to the people. This presents the inquiry, What powers are delegated to the United States? They may be classed under four divisions: first, those that are delegated by the States to each other, by virtue of which the constitution may be altered or amended by three-fourths of the States, when, without which, it would have required the unanimous vote of all; next, the powers conferred on Congress; then those on the President; and finally, those on the judicial department—all of which are particularly enumerated in the parts of the constitution which organize the respective departments. The reservation of powers to the States is, as I have said, against the whole; and is as full against the judicial as it is against the executive and legislative departments of the Government. It cannot be claimed for the one without claiming it for the whole, and without, in fact, annulling this important provision of the constitution.

Against this, as it appears to me, conclusive view of the subject, it has been urged that this power is expressly conferred on the Supreme Court by that portion of the constitution which provides that the judicial power shall extend to all cases in law and equity arising under the constitution, the laws of the United States, and treaties made under their authority. I believe the assertion to be utterly destitute of any foundation. It obviously is the intention of the constitution simply to make the judicial power commensurate with the law-making and treaty-making powers; and to vest it with the right of applying the constitution, the laws, and the treaties, to the cases which might arise under them; and not to make it the judge of the constitution, the laws, and the treaties themselves. In fact, the power of applying the laws to the facts of the case, and deciding upon such application, constitutes, in truth, the judicial power. The distinction between such power, and that of judging of the laws, will be perfectly apparent when we advert to what is the acknowledged power of the court in reference to treaties or compacts between sovereigns. It is perfectly established, that the courts have no right to judge of the violation of treaties; and that, in reference to them, their power is limited to the right of judging simply of the violation of rights under them; and that the right of judging of infractions belongs exclusively to the parties themselves, and not to the courts: of which we have an example in the French treaty, which was declared by Congress null and void, in consequence of its violation by the Government of France. Without such declaration, had a French citizen sued a citizen of this country under the treaty, the court could have taken no cognizance of its infraction; nor, after such a declaration, would it have heard any argument or proof going to show that the treaty had not been violated.

The declaration, of itself, is conclusive on the court. But it will be asked how the court obtained the power to pronounce a law or treaty unconstitutional, when it comes in conflict with that instrument. I do not deny that it possesses the right; but I can by no means concede that it was derived from the constitution. It had its origin in the necessity of the case. Where there are two or more rules established, one from a higher, the other from a lower authority, which may come into conflict in applying them to a particular case, the judge cannot avoid pronouncing in favor of the superior against the inferior. It is from this necessity, and this alone, that the power which is now set up to over-rule the rights of the States against an express provision of the constitution was derived. It had no other origin. That I have traced it to its true source, will be manifest from the fact that it is a power which, so far from being conferred exclusively on the Supreme Court, as is insisted, belongs to every court—inferior and superior—State and General—and even to foreign courts.

But the senator from Delaware (Mr. Clayton) relies on the journals of the Convention to prove that it was the intention of that body to confer on the Supreme Court the right of deciding, in the last resort, between a State and the General Government. I will not follow him through the journals, as I do not deem that to be necessary to refute his argument. It is sufficient for this purpose to state, that Mr. Rutledge reported a resolution, providing expressly that the United States and the States might be parties before the Supreme Court. If this proposition had been adopted, I would ask the senator whether this very controversy between the United States and South Carolina might not have been brought before the court? I would also ask him whether it can be brought before the court as the constitution now stands? If he answers the former in the affirmative, and the latter in the negative, as he must, then it is clear, his elaborate argument to the contrary notwithstanding, that the report of Mr. Rutledge was not, in substance, adopted as he contended; and that the journals, so far from supporting, are in direct opposition to the position which he attempts to maintain. I might push the argument much farther against the power of the court, but I do not deem it necessary, at least in this stage of the discussion. If the views which have already been presented be correct, and I do not see how they can be resisted, the conclusion is inevitable, that the reserved powers were reserved equally against every department of the Government, and as strongly against the judicial as against the other departments, and, of course, were left under the exclusive will of the States.

There still remains another misrepresentation of the conduct of the State, which has been made with the view of exciting odium. I allude to the charge, that South Carolina supported the tariff of 1816, and is, therefore, responsible for the protective system. To determine the truth of this charge, it becomes necessary to ascertain the real character of that law—whether it was a tariff for revenue or for protection—and, as involved in this, to inquire, What was the condition of the country at the period? The late war with Great Britain had just terminated, which, with the restrictive system that preceded it, had diverted a large amount of capital and industry from commerce to manufacturers, particularly to the cotton and woollen branches. There was a debt, at the same time, of one hundred and thirty millions of dollars hanging over the country, and the heavy war duties were still in existence. Under these circumstances, the question was presented, as to what point the duties ought to be reduced? This question involved another—at what time the debt ought to be paid? which was a question of policy, involving in its consideration all the circumstances connected with the then condition of the country. Among the most prominent arguments in favor of an early discharge of the debt was, that the high duties which it would require to effect it would have, at the same time, the effect of sustaining the infant manufactures, which had been forced up under the circumstances to which I have adverted. This view of the subject had a decided influence in determining in favor of an early payment of the debt. The sinking fund was, accordingly, raised from seven to ten millions of dollars, with the provision to apply the surplus which might remain in the treasury as a contingent appropriation to that fund; and the duties were graduated to meet this increased expenditure. It was thus that the policy and justice of protecting the large amount of capital and industry which had been diverted by the measures of the Government into new channels, as I have stated, was combined with the fiscal action of the Government, and which, while it secured a prompt payment of the debt, prevented the immense losses to the manufacturers which would have followed a sudden and great reduction. Still, revenue was the main object, and protection but the incidental. The bill to reduce the duties was reported by the Committee of Ways and Means, and not of Manufactures, and it proposed a heavy reduction on the then existing rate of duties. But what of itself, without other evidence, is decisive as to the character of the bill, is the fact that it fixed a much higher rate of duties on the unprotected than on the protected articles. I will enumerate a few leading articles only. Woollen and cotton above the value of 25 cents on the square yard, though they were the leading objects of protection, were subject to a permanent duty of only 20 per cent. Iron, another leading article among the protected, had a protection of not more than 9 per cent. as fixed by the act, and of but fifteen as reported in the bill. These rates were all below the average duties as fixed in the act, including the protected, the unprotected, and even the free articles. I have entered into some calculation, in order to ascertain the average rate of duties under the act. There is some uncertainty in the data, but I feel assured that it is not less than thirty per cent. *ad valorem:* showing an excess of the average duties above that imposed on the protected articles enumerated of more than 10 per cent., and thus clearly establishing the character of the measure—that it was for revenue, and not protection.

Looking back, even at this distant period, with all our experience, I perceive but two errors in the act: the one in reference to iron, and the other the minimum duty on coarse cottons. As to the former, I conceive that the bill, as reported, proposed a duty relatively too low, which was still farther reduced in its passage through Congress. The duty, at first, was fixed at seventy-five cents the hundredweight; but, in the last stage of its passage, it was reduced, by a sort of caprice, occasioned by an unfortunate motion, to forty-five cents. This injustice was severely felt in Pennsylvania, the State, above all others, most productive of iron; and was the principal cause of that great reaction which has since thrown her so decidedly on the side of the protective policy. The other error was that as to coarse cottons, on which the duty was as much too high as that on iron was too low. It introduced, besides, the obnoxious minimum principle, which has since been so mischievously extended; and to that extent, I am constrained in candor to acknowledge, as I wish to disguise nothing, the protective principle was recognized by the act of 1816. How this was overlooked at the time, it is not in my power to say. It escaped my observation, which I can account for only on the ground that the principle was then new, and that my attention was engaged by another important subject—the question of the currency, then so urgent, and with which, as chairman of the committee, I was particularly charged. With these exceptions, I again repeat, I see nothing in the bill to condemn; yet it is on the ground that the members from the State voted for the bill, that the attempt is now made to hold up Carolina as responsible for the whole system of protection which has since followed, though she has resisted its progress in every stage. Was there ever greater injustice? And how is it to be accounted for, but as forming a part of that systematic misrepresentation and calumny which has been directed for so many years, without interruption, against that gallant and generous State? And why has she thus been assailed? Merely because she abstained from taking any part in the Presidential canvass— believing that it had degenerated into a mere system of imposition on the people—controlled, almost exclusively, by those whose object it is to obtain the patronage of the Government, and that without regard to principle or policy. Standing apart from what she considered a contest in which the public had no interest, she has been assailed by both parties with a fury altogether unparalleled; but which, pursuing the course which she believed liberty and duty required, she has met with a firmness equal to the fierceness of the assault. In the midst of this attack, I have not escaped. With a view of inflicting a wound on the State through me, I have been held up as the author of the protective system, and one of its most strenuous advocates. It is with pain that I allude to myself on so deep and grave a subject as that now under discussion, and which, I sincerely believe, involves the liberty of the country. I now regret that, under the sense of injustice which the remarks of a senator from Pennsylvania (Mr. Wilkins) excited for the moment, I hastily gave my pledge to defend myself against the charge which has been made in reference to my course in 1816: not that there will be any difficulty in repelling the charge, but because I feel a deep reluctance in turning the discussion, in any degree, from a subject of so much magnitude to one of so little importance as the consistency or inconsistency of myself, or any other individual, particularly in connection with an event so long since passed. But for this hasty pledge, I would have remained silent as to my own course on this occasion, and would have borne with patience and calmness this, with the many other misrepresentations with which I have been so incessantly assailed for so many years.

The charge that I was the author of the protective system has no other foundation but that I, in common with the almost entire South, gave my support to the tariff of 1816. It is true that I advocated that measure, for which I may rest my defence, without taking any other, on the ground that it was a tariff for revenue, and not for protection, which I have established beyond the power of controversy. But my speech on the occasion has been brought in judgment against me by the senator from Pennsylvania. I have since cast my eyes over the speech; and I will surprise, I have no doubt, the senator, by telling him that, with the exception of some hasty and unguarded expressions. I retract nothing I uttered on that occasion. I only ask that I may be judged, in reference to it, in that spirit of fairness and justice which is due to the occasion: taking into consideration the circumstances under which it was delivered, and bearing in mind that the subject was a tariff for revenue, and not for protection; for reducing, and not raising the duties. But, before I explain the then condition of the country, from which my main arguments in favor of the measure were drawn, it is nothing but an act of justice to myself that I should state a fact in connection with my speech, that is necessary to explain what I have called hasty and unguarded expressions. My speech was an *impromptu;* and, as such, I apologized to the House, as appears from the speech as printed, for offering my sentiments on the question without having duly reflected on the subject. It was delivered at the request of a friend, when I had not previously the least intention of addressing the House. I allude to Samuel D. Ingham, then and now, as I am proud to say, a personal and political friend—a man of talents and integrity—with a clear head, and firm and patriotic heart; then among the leading members of the House; in the palmy state of his political glory, though now for a moment depressed;—depressed, did I say? no! it is his State which is depressed—Pennsylvania, and not Samuel D. Ingham! Pennsylvania, which has deserted him under circumstances which, instead of depressing, ought to have elevated him in her estimation. He came to me, when sitting at my desk writing, and said that the House was falling into some confusion, accompanying it with a remark, that I knew how difficult it was to rally so large a body when once broken on a tax bill, as had been experienced during the late war. Having a higher opinion of my influence than it deserved, he requested me to say something to prevent the confusion. I replied that I was at a loss what to say; that I had been busily engaged on the currency, which was then in great confusion, and which, as I have stated, had been placed particularly under my charge, as the chairman of the committee on that subject. He repeated his request, and the speech which the senator from Pennsylvania has complimented so highly was the result.

I will ask whether the facts stated ought not, in justice, to be borne in mind by those who would hold me accountable, not only for the general scope of the speech, but for every word and sentence which it contains? But, in asking this question, it is not my intention to repudiate the speech. All I ask is, that I may be judged by the rules which, in justice, belong to the case. Let it be recollected that the bill was a revenue bill, and, of course, that it was constitutional. I need not remind the Senate that, when the measure is constitutional, all arguments calculated to show its beneficial operation may be legitimately pressed into service, without taking into consideration whether the subject to which the arguments refer be within the sphere of the constitution or not. If, for instance, a question were before this body to lay a duty on Bibles, and a motion were made to reduce the duty, or admit Bibles duty free, who could doubt that the argument in favor of the motion—that the increased circulation of the Bible would be in favor of the morality and religion of the country, would be strictly proper? But who would suppose that he who adduced it had committed himself on the constitutionality of taking the religion or morals of the country under the charge of the Federal Government? Again: suppose the question to be, to raise the duty on silk, or any other article of luxury; and that it should be supported on the ground that it was an article mainly consumed by the rich and extravagant— could it be fairly inferred that in the opinion of the speaker, Congress had a right to pass sumptuary laws? I only ask that these plain rules may be applied to my argument on the tariff of 1816. They turn almost entirely on the benefits which manufactures conferred on the country in time of war, and which no one could doubt. The country had recently passed through such a state. The world was at that time deeply agitated by the effects of the great conflict which had so long raged in Europe, and which no one could tell how soon again might return. Bonaparte had but recently been overthrown; the whole southern part of this continent was in a state of revolution, and threatened with the interference of the Holy Alliance, which, had it occurred, must almost necessarily have involved this country in a most dangerous conflict. It was under these circumstances that I delivered the speech, in which I urged the House that, in the adjustment of the tariff, reference ought to be had to a state of war as well as peace, and that its provisions ought to be fixed on the compound views of the two periods—making some sacrifice in peace, in order that less might be made in war. Was this principle false? and, in urging it, did I commit myself to that system of oppression since grown up, and which has for its object the enriching of one portion of the country at the expense of the other?

The plain rule in all such cases is, that when a measure is proposed, the first thing is to ascertain its constitutionality; and, that being ascertained, the next is its expediency; which last opens the whole field of argument for and against. Every topic may be urged calculated to prove it wise or unwise: so in a bill to raise imposts. It must first be ascertained that the bill is based on the principles of revenue, and that the money raised is necessary for the wants of the country. These being ascertained, every argument, direct and indirect, may be fairly offered, which may go to show that, under all the circumstances, the provisions of the bill are proper or improper. Had this plain and simple rule been adhered to, we should never have heard of the complaint of Carolina. Her objection is not against the improper modification of a bill acknowledged to be for revenue, but that, under the name of imposts, a power essentially different from the taxing power is exercised—partaking much more of the character of a penalty than a tax. Nothing is more common than that things closely resembling in appearance should widely and essentially differ in their character. Arsenic, for instance, resembles flour, yet one is a deadly poison, and the other that which constitutes the staff of life. So duties imposed, whether for revenue or protection, may be called imposts; though nominally and apparently the same, yet they differ essentially in their real character.

I shall now return to my speech on the tariff of 1816. To determine what my opinions really were on the subject of protection at that time, it will be proper to advert to my sentiments before and after that period. My sentiments preceding 1816, on this subject, are a matter of record. I came into Congress in 1812, a devoted friend and supporter of the then administration; yet one of my first efforts was to brave the administration, by opposing its favorite measure, the restrictive system—embargo, non-intercourse, and all—and that upon the principle of free trade. The system remained in fashion for a time; but, after the overthrow of Bonaparte, I reported a bill from the Committee on Foreign Relations, to repeal the whole system of restrictive measures. While the bill was under consideration, a worthy man, then a member of the House (Mr. M'Kim of Baltimore), moved to except the Non-Importation Act, which he supported on the ground of encouragement to manufactures. I resisted the motion on the very grounds on which Mr. M'Kim supported it. I maintained that the manufacturers were then receiving too much protection, and warned its friends that the withdrawal of the protection which the war and the high duties then afforded would cause great embarrassment; and that the true policy, in the mean time, was to admit foreign goods as freely as possible, in order to diminish the anticipated embarrassment on the return of peace; intimating, at the same time, my desire to see the tariff revised, with a view of affording a moderate and permanent protection.

Such was my conduct before 1816. Shortly after that period I left Congress, and had no opportunity of making known my sentiments in reference to the protective system, which shortly after began to be agitated. But I have the most conclusive evidence that I considered the arrangement of the revenue, in 1816, as growing out of the necessity of the case, and due to the consideration of justice. But, even at that early period, I was not without my fears that even that arrangement would lead to abuse and future difficulties. I regret that I have been compelled to dwell so long on myself; but trust that, whatever censure may be incurred, will not be directed against me, but against those who have drawn my conduct into the controversy; and who may hope, by assailing my motives, to wound the cause with which I am proud to be identified.

I may add, that all the Southern States voted with South Carolina in support of the bill: not that they had any interest in manufactures, but on the ground that they had supported the war, and, of course, felt a corresponding obligation to sustain those establishments which had grown up under the encouragement it had incidentally afforded; whilst most of the New England members were opposed to the measure principally, as I believe, on opposite principles.

I have now, I trust, satisfactorily repelled the charge against the State, and myself personally, in reference to the tariff of 1816. Whatever support the State has given the bill, originated in the most disinterested motives. There was not within the limits of the State, so far as my memory serves me, a single cotton or woollen establishment. Her whole dependence was on agriculture, and the cultivation of two great staples, rice and cotton. Her obvious policy was to keep open the market of the world unchecked and unrestricted;—to buy cheap, and to sell high: but from a feeling of kindness, combined with a sense of justice, she added her support to the bill. We had been told by the agents of the manufacturers that the protection which the measure afforded would be sufficient; to which we the more readily conceded, as it was considered a final adjustment of the question.

Let us now turn our eyes forward, and see what has been the conduct of the parties to this arrangement. Have Carolina and the South disturbed this adjustment? No; they have never raised their voice in a single instance against it, even though this measure, moderate, comparatively, as it is, was felt with no inconsiderable pressure on their interests. Was this example imitated on the opposite side? Far otherwise. Scarcely had the President signed his name, before application was made for an increase of duties, which was repeated, with demands continually growing, till the passage of the act of 1828. What course now, I would ask, did it become Carolina to pursue in reference to these demands? Instead of acquiescing in them, because she had acted generously in adjusting the tariff of 1816, she saw, in her generosity on that occasion, additional motives for that firm and decided resistance which she has since made against the system of protection. She accordingly commenced a systematic opposition to all further encroachments, which continued from 1818 till 1828; by discussions and by resolutions, by remonstrances and by protests through her legislature. These all proved insufficient to stem the current of encroachment: but, notwithstanding the heavy pressure on her industry, she never despaired of relief till the passage of the act of 1828—that bill of abominations—engendered by avarice and political intrigue. Its adoption opened the eyes of the State, and gave a new character to the controversy. Till then, the question had been, whether the protective system was constitutional and expedient; but, after that, she no longer considered the question whether the right of regulating the industry of the States was a reserved or delegated power, but what right a State possesses to defend her reserved powers against the encroachments of the Federal Government: a question on the decision of which the value of all the reserved powers depends. The passage of the act of 1828, with all its objectionable features, and under the circumstances connected with it, almost, if not entirely, closed the door of hope through the General Government. It afforded conclusive evidence that no reasonable prospect of relief from Congress could be entertained; yet, the near approach of the period of the payment of the public debt, and the elevation of General Jackson to the Presidency, still afforded a ray of hope—not so strong, however, as to prevent the State from turning her eyes for final relief to her reserved powers.

Under these circumstances commenced that inquiry into the nature and extent of the reserved powers of a State, and the means which they afford of resistance against the encroachments of the General Government, which has been pursued with so much zeal and energy, and, I may add, intelligence. Never was there a political discussion carried on with greater activity, and which appealed more directly to the intelligence of a community. Throughout the whole, no address has been made to the low and vulgar passions; but, on the contrary, the discussion has turned upon the higher principles of political economy, connected with the operations of the tariff system, calculated to show its real bearing on the interests of the State, and on the structure of our political system; and to show the true character of the relations between the State and the General Government, and the means which the States possess of defending those powers which they reserved in forming the Federal Government.

In this great canvass, men of the most commanding talents and acquirements have engaged with the greatest ardor; and the people have been addressed through every channel—by essays in the public press, and by speeches in their public assemblies—until they have become thoroughly instructed on the nature of the oppression, and on the rights which they possess, under the constitution, to throw it off.

If gentlemen suppose that the stand taken by the people of Carolina rests on passion and delusion, they are wholly mistaken. The case is far otherwise. No community, from the legislator to the ploughman, were ever better instructed in their rights; and the resistance on which the State has resolved, is the result of mature reflection, accompanied with a deep conviction that their rights have been violated, and that the means of redress which they have adopted are consistent with the principles of the constitution.

But while this active canvass was carried on, which looked to the reserved powers as the final means of redress if all others failed, the State at the same time cherished a hope, as I have already stated, that the election of General Jackson to the presidency would prevent the necessity of a resort to extremities. He was identified with the interests of the staple States; and, having the same interest, it was believed that his great popularity—a popularity of the strongest character, as it rested on military services—would enable him, as they hoped, gradually to bring down the system of protection, without shock or injury to any interest. Under these views, the canvass in favor of General Jackson's election to the Presidency was carried on with great zeal, in conjunction with that active inquiry into the reserved powers of the States on which final reliance was placed. But little did the people of Carolina dream that the man whom they were thus striving to elevate to the highest seat of power would prove so utterly false to all their hopes. Man is, indeed, ignorant of the future; nor was there ever a stronger illustration of the observation than is afforded by the result of that election! The very event on which they had built their hopes has been turned against them; and the very individual to whom they looked as a deliverer, and whom, under that impression, they strove for so many years to elevate to power, is now the most powerful instrument in the hands of his and their bitterest opponents to put down them and their cause!

Scarcely had he been elected, when it became apparent, from the organization of his cabinet and other indications, that all their hopes of relief through him were blasted. The admission of a single individual into the cabinet, under the circumstances which accompanied that admission, threw all into confusion. The mischievous influence over the President, through which this individual was admitted into the cabinet, soon became apparent. Instead of turning his eyes forward to the period of the payment of the public debt, which was then near at hand, and to the present dangerous political crisis, which was inevitable unless averted by a timely and wise system of measures, the attention of the President was absorbed by mere party arrangements, and circumstances too disreputable to be mentioned here, except by the most distant allusion.

Here I must pause for a moment to repel a charge which has been so often made, and which even the President has reiterated in his proclamation—the charge that I have been actuated, in the part which I have taken, by feelings of disappointed ambition. I again repeat, that I deeply regret the necessity of noticing myself in so important a discussion; and that nothing can induce me to advert to my own course but the conviction that it is due to the cause, at which a blow is aimed through me. It is only in this view that I notice it.

It illy became the chief magistrate to make this charge. The course which the State took, and which led to the present controversy between her and the General Government, was taken as far back as 1828—in the very midst of that severe canvass which placed him in power—and in that very canvass Carolina openly avowed and zealously maintained those very principles which he, the chief magistrate, now officially pronounces to be treason and rebellion. That was the period at which he ought to have spoken. Having remained silent then, and having, under his approval, implied by that silence, received the support and the vote of the State, I, if a sense of decorum did not prevent it, might recriminate with the double charge of deception and ingratitude. My object, however, is not to assail the President, but to defend myself against a most unfounded charge. The time alone when that course was taken, on which this charge of *disappointed ambition* is founded, will of itself repel it, in the eye of every unprejudiced and honest man. The doctrine which I now sustain, under the present difficulties, I openly avowed and maintained immediately after the act of 1828, that "bill of abominations," as it has been so often and properly termed. Was I, at that period, disappointed in any views of ambition which I might be supposed to entertain? I was Vice-President of the United States, elected by an overwhelming majority. I was a candidate for re-election on the ticket with General Jackson himself, with a certain prospect of the triumphant success of that ticket, and with a fair prospect of the highest office to which an American citizen can aspire. What was my course under these prospects? Did I look to my own advancement, or to an honest and faithful discharge of my duty? Let facts speak for themselves. When the bill to which I have referred came from the other House to the Senate, the almost universal impression was, that its fate would depend upon my casting vote. It was known that, as the bill then stood, the Senate was nearly equally divided; and as it was a combined measure, originating with the politicians and manufacturers, and intended as much to bear upon the Presidential election as to protect manufactures, it was believed that, as a stroke of political policy, its fate would be made to depend on my vote, in order to defeat General Jackson's election, as well as my own. The friends of General Jackson were alarmed, and I was earnestly entreated to leave the chair in order to avoid the responsibility, under the plausible argument that, if the Senate should be equally divided, the bill would be lost without the aid of my casting vote. The reply to this entreaty was, that no consideration personal to myself could induce me to take such a course; that I considered the measure as of the most dangerous character, and calculated to produce the most fearful crisis; that the payment of the public debt was just at hand; and that the great increase of revenue which it would pour into the treasury would accelerate the approach of that period, and that the country would be placed in the most trying of situations—with an immense revenue without the means of absorption upon any legitimate or constitutional object of appropriation, and compelled to submit to all the corrupting consequences of a large surplus, or to make a sudden reduction of the rates of duties, which would prove ruinous to the very interests which were then forcing the passage of the bill. Under these views I determined to remain in the chair, and if the bill came to me, to give my casting vote against it, and in doing so, to give my reasons at large; but at the same time I informed my friends that I would retire from the ticket, so that the election of General Jackson might not be embarrassed by any act of mine. Sir, I was amazed at the folly and infatuation of that period. So completely absorbed was Congress in the game of ambition and avarice—from the double impulse of the manufacturers and politicians—that none but a few appeared to anticipate the present crisis, at which all are now alarmed, but which is the inevitable result of what was then done. As to myself, I clearly foresaw what has since followed. The road of ambition lay open before me—I had but to follow the corrupt tendency of the times—but I chose to tread the rugged path of duty.

It was thus that the reasonable hope of relief through the election of General Jackson was blasted; but still one other hope remained, that the final discharge of the public debt—an event near at hand—would remove our burden. That event would leave in the treasury a large surplus: a surplus that could not be expended under the most extravagant schemes of appropriation, having the least color of decency or constitutionality. That event at last arrived. At the last session of Congress, it was avowed on all sides that the public debt, as to all practical purposes, was in fact paid, the small surplus remaining being nearly covered by the money in the treasury and the bonds for duties which had already accrued; but with the arrival of this event our last hope was doomed to be disappointed.

After a long session of many months, and the most earnest effort on the part of South Carolina and the other Southern States to obtain relief, all that could be effected was a small reduction in the amount of the duties; but a reduction of such a character, that, while it diminished the amount of burden, distributed that burden more unequally than even the obnoxious act of 1828: reversing the principle adopted by the bill of 1816, of laying higher duties on the unprotected than the protected articles, by repealing almost entirely the duties laid upon the former, and imposing the burden almost entirely on the latter. It was thus that, instead of relief—instead of an equal distribution of the burdens and benefits of the Government, on the payment of the debt, as had been fondly anticipated—the duties were so arranged as to be, in fact, bounties on one side and taxation on the other; thus placing the two great sections of the country in direct conflict in reference to its fiscal action, and thereby letting in that flood of political corruption which threatens to sweep away our constitution and our liberty.

This unequal and unjust arrangement was pronounced, both by the administration, through its proper organ, the Secretary of the Treasury, and by the opposition, to be a *permanent* adjustment; and it was thus that all hope of relief through the action of the General Government terminated; and the crisis so long apprehended at length arrived, at which the State was compelled to choose between absolute acquiescence in a ruinous system of oppression, or a resort to her reserved powers—powers of which she alone was the rightful judge, and which only, in this momentous juncture, could save her. She determined on the latter.

The consent of two-thirds of her legislature was necessary for the call of a convention, which was considered the only legitimate organ through which the people, in their sovereignty, could speak. After an arduous struggle the State Rights party succeeded: more than two-thirds of both branches of the legislature favorable to a convention were elected; a convention was called—the ordinance adopted. The convention was succeeded by a meeting of the legislature, when the laws to carry the ordinance into execution were enacted: all of which have been communicated by the President, have been referred to the Committee on the Judiciary, and this bill is the result of their labor.

Having now corrected some of the prominent misrepresentations as to the nature of this controversy, and given a rapid sketch of the movement of the State in reference to it, I will next proceed to notice some objections connected with the ordinance and the proceedings under it.

The first and most prominent of these is directed against what is called the test oath, which an effort has been made to render odious. So far from deserving the

denunciation which has been levelled against it, I view this provision of the
ordinance as but the natural result of the doctrines entertained by the State, and
the position which she occupies. The people of Carolina believe that the Union
is a union of States, and not of individuals; that it was formed by the States, and
that the citizens of the several States were bound to it through the acts of their
several States; that each State ratified the constitution for itself, and that it was
only by such ratification of a State that any obligation was imposed upon its citizens. Thus believing, it is the opinion of the people of Carolina that it belongs
to the State which has imposed the obligation to declare, in the last resort, the
extent of this obligation, as far as her citizens are concerned; and this upon the
plain principles which exist in all analogous cases of compact between sovereign bodies. On this principle, the people of the State, acting in their sovereign
capacity in convention, precisely as they did in the adoption of their own and
the federal constitution, have declared, by the ordinance, that the acts of Congress which imposed duties under the authority to lay imposts, are acts, not for
revenue, as intended by the constitution, but for protection, and therefore null
and void. The ordinance thus enacted by the people of the State themselves,
acting as a sovereign community, is as obligatory on the citizens of the State as
any portion of the constitution. In prescribing, then, the oath to obey the ordinance, no more was done than to prescribe an oath to obey the constitution. It
is, in fact, but a particular oath of allegiance, and in every respect similar to that
which is prescribed, under the constitution of the United States, to be administered to all the officers of the State and Federal Governments; and is no more
deserving the harsh and bitter epithets which have been heaped upon it, than
that, or any similar oath. It ought to be borne in mind, that, according to the
opinion which prevails in Carolina, the right of resistance to the unconstitutional acts of Congress belongs to the State, and not to her individual citizens;
and that, though the latter may, in a mere question of *meum* and *tuum,* resist,
through the courts, an unconstitutional encroachment upon their rights, yet the
final stand against usurpation rests not with them, but with the State of which
they are members; and such act of resistance by a State binds the conscience and
allegiance of the citizen. But there appears to be a general misapprehension as
to the extent to which the State has acted under this part of the ordinance.
Instead of sweeping every officer by a general proscription of the minority, as
has been represented in debate, as far as my knowledge extends, not a single
individual has been removed. The State has, in fact, acted with the greatest ten-
derness, all circumstances considered, towards citizens who differed from the
majority; and, in that spirit, has directed the oath to be administered only in case

of some official act directed to be performed, in which obedience to the ordinance is involved.

It has been further objected, that the State has acted precipitately. What! precipitately! after making a strenuous resistance for twelve years—by discussion here and in the other House of Congress—by essays in all forms—by resolutions, remonstrances, and protests on the part of her legislature—and, finally, by attempting an appeal to the judicial power of the United States? I say attempting, for they have been prevented from bringing the question fairly before the court, and that by an act of that very majority in Congress who now upbraid them for not making that appeal; of that majority who, on a motion of one of the members in the other House from South Carolina, refused to give to the act of 1828 its true title—that it was a *protective,* and not a *revenue* act. The State has never, it is true, relied upon that tribunal, the Supreme Court, to vindicate its reserved rights; yet they have always considered it as an auxiliary means of defence, of which they would gladly have availed themselves to test the constitutionality of protection, had they not been deprived of the means of doing so by the act of the majority.

Notwithstanding this long delay of more than ten years, under this continued encroachment of the Government, we now hear it on all sides, by friends and foes, gravely pronounced that the State has acted precipitately—that her conduct has been rash! That such should be the language of an interested majority, who, by means of this unconstitutional and oppressive system, are annually extorting millions from the South, to be bestowed upon other sections, is not at all surprising. Whatever impedes the course of avarice and ambition, will ever be denounced as rash and precipitate; and had South Carolina delayed her resistance fifty instead of twelve years, she would have heard from the same quarter the same language; but it is really surprising, that those who are suffering in common with herself, and who have complained equally loud of their grievances; who have pronounced the very acts which she has asserted within *her* limits to be oppressive, unconstitutional, and ruinous, after so long a struggle—a struggle longer than that which preceded the separation of these States from the mother-country—longer than the period of the Trojan war—should now complain of precipitancy! No, it is not Carolina which has acted precipitately; but her sister States, who have suffered in common with her, have acted tardily. Had they acted as she has done; had they performed their duty with equal energy and promptness, our situation this day would be very different from what we now find it. Delays are said to be dangerous; and never was the maxim more true than in the present case, a case of monopoly. It is the very nature of monopolies to grow. If we take from one side a large portion of the proceeds of its labor, and give it to the other, the side from which we take must constantly decay, and that to which we give must prosper and increase. Such is the action of the protective system. It exacts from the South a large portion of the proceeds of its industry, which it bestows upon the other sections, in the shape of bounties to manufactures, and appropriations in a thousand forms; pensions, improvement of rivers and harbors, roads and canals, and in every shape that wit or ingenuity can devise. Can we, then, be surprised that the principle of monopoly grows, when it is so amply remunerated at the expense of those who support it? And this is the real reason of the fact which we witness, that all acts for protection pass with small minorities, but soon come to be sustained by great and overwhelming majorities. Those who seek the monopoly endeavor to obtain it in the most exclusive shape; and they take care, accordingly, to associate only a sufficient number of interests barely to pass it through the two Houses of Congress, on the plain principle, that the greater the number from whom the monopoly takes, and the fewer on whom it bestows, the greater is the advantage to the monopolists. Acting in this spirit, we have often seen with what exact precision they count: adding wool to woollens, associating lead and iron, feeling their way, until a bare majority is obtained, when the bill passes, connecting just as many interests as are sufficient to ensure its success, and no more. In a short time, however, we have invariably found that this *lean* becomes a decided majority, under the certain operation which compels individuals to desert the pursuits which the monopoly has rendered unprofitable, that they may participate in those which it has rendered profitable. It is against this dangerous and growing disease that South Carolina has acted—a disease, whose cancerous action would soon have spread to every part of the system, if not arrested.

There is another powerful reason why the action of the State could not have been safely delayed. The public debt, as I have already stated, for all practical purposes, has already been paid; and, under the existing duties, a large annual surplus of many millions must come into the treasury. It is impossible to look at this state of things without seeing the most mischievous consequences; and, among others, if not speedily corrected, it would interpose powerful and almost insuperable obstacles to throwing off the burden under which the South has been so long laboring. The disposition of the surplus would become a subject of violent and corrupt struggle, and could not fail to rear up new and powerful interests in support of the existing system, not only in those sections which have been heretofore benefited by it, but even in the South itself. I cannot but trace to the anticipation of this state of the treasury the sudden and extraordinary movements which took place at the last session in the Virginia Legislature, in which the whole South is vitally interested.* It is impossible for any rational man to believe that that State could seriously have thought of effecting the scheme to which I allude by her own resources, without powerful aid from the General Government.

It is next objected, that the enforcing acts have legislated the United States out of South Carolina. I have already replied to this objection on another occasion, and will now but repeat what I then said: that they have been legislated out only to the extent that they had no right to enter. The constitution has admitted the jurisdiction of the United States within the limits of the several States only so far as the delegated powers authorize; beyond that they are intruders, and may rightfully be expelled; and that they have been efficiently expelled by the legislation of the State through her civil process, as has been acknowledged on all sides in the debate, is only a confirmation of the truth of the doctrine for which the majority in Carolina have contended.

The very point at issue between the two parties there is, whether nullification is a peaceable and an efficient remedy against an unconstitutional act of the General Government, and may be asserted, as such, through the State tribunals. Both parties agree that the acts against which it is directed are unconstitutional and oppressive. The controversy is only as to the means by which our citizens may be protected against the acknowledged encroachments on their rights. This being the point at issue between the parties, and the very object of the majority being an efficient protection of the citizens through the State tribunals, the measures adopted to enforce the ordinance, of course received the most decisive character. We were not children, to act by halves. Yet for acting thus efficiently the State is denounced, and this bill reported, to overrule, by military force, the civil tribunals and civil process of the State! Sir, I consider this bill, and the arguments which have been urged on this floor in its support, as the most triumphant acknowledgment that nullification is peaceful and efficient, and so deeply intrenched in the principles of our system, that it cannot be assailed but by prostrating the constitution, and substituting the supremacy of military force in lieu of the supremacy of the laws. In fact, the advocates of this bill refute their own argument. They tell us that the ordinance is unconstitutional; that it infracts the constitution of South Carolina, although, to me, the objection appears absurd, as it was adopted by the very authority which adopted the constitution itself. They also tell us that the Supreme Court is the appointed

*Having for their object the emancipation and colonization of slaves.

arbiter of all controversies between a State and the General Government. Why, then, do they not leave this controversy to that tribunal? Why do they not confide to them the abrogation of the ordinance, and the laws made in pursuance of it, and the assertion of that supremacy which they claim for the laws of Congress? The State stands pledged to resist no process of the court. Why, then, confer on the President the extensive and unlimited powers provided in this bill? Why authorize him to use military force to arrest the civil process of the State? But one answer can be given: That, in a contest between the State and the General Government, if the resistance be limited on both sides to the civil process, the State, by its inherent sovereignty, standing upon its reserved powers, will prove too powerful in such a controversy, and must triumph over the Federal Government, sustained by its delegated and limited authority; and in this answer we have an acknowledgment of the truth of those great principles for which the State has so firmly and nobly contended.

Having made these remarks, the great question is now presented, Has Congress the right to pass this bill? Which I will next proceed to consider. The decision of this question involves an inquiry into the provisions of the bill. What are they? It puts at the disposal of the President the army and navy, and the entire militia of the country; it enables him, at his pleasure, to subject every man in the United States, not exempt from militia duty, to martial law; to call him from his ordinary occupation to the field, and under the penalty of fine and imprisonment, inflicted by a court martial, to imbrue his hand in his brother's blood. There is no limitation on the power of the sword;—and that over the purse is equally without restraint; for among the extraordinary features of the bill, it contains no appropriation, which, under existing circumstances, is tantamount to an unlimited appropriation. The President may, under its authority, incur any expenditure, and pledge the national faith to meet it. He may create a new national debt, at the very moment of the termination of the former—a debt of millions, to be paid out of the proceeds of the labor of that section of the country whose dearest constitutional rights this bill prostrates! Thus exhibiting the extraordinary spectacle, that the very section of the country which is urging this measure, and carrying the sword of devastation against us, is, at the same time, incurring a new debt, to be paid by those whose rights are violated; while those who violate them are to receive the benefits, in the shape of bounties and expenditures.

And for what purpose is the unlimited control of the purse and of the sword thus placed at the disposition of the Executive? To make war against one of the free and sovereign members of this confederation, which the bill proposes to deal with, not as a State, but as a collection of banditti or outlaws. Thus exhibiting the impious spectacle of this Government, the creature of the States, making war against the power to which it owes its existence.

The bill violates the constitution, plainly and palpably, in many of its provisions, by authorizing the President at his pleasure, to place the different ports of this Union on an unequal footing, contrary to that provision of the constitution which declares that no preference shall be given to one port over another. It also violates the constitution by authorizing him, at his discretion, to impose cash duties on one port, while credit is allowed in others; by enabling the President to regulate commerce, a power vested in Congress alone; and by drawing within the jurisdiction of the United States Courts, powers never intended to be conferred on them. As great as these objections are, they become insignificant in the provisions of a bill which, by a single blow—by treating the States as a mere lawless mass of individuals—prostrates all the barriers of the constitution. I will pass over the minor considerations, and proceed directly to the great point. This bill proceeds on the ground that the entire sovereignty of this country belongs to the American people, as forming one great community, and regards the States as mere fractions or counties, and not as integral parts of the Union; having no more right to resist the encroachments of the Government than a county has to resist the authority of a State; and treating such resistance as the lawless acts of so many individuals, without possessing sovereignty or political rights. It has been said that the bill declares war against South Carolina. No. It decrees a massacre of her citizens! War has something ennobling about it, and, with all its horrors, brings into action the highest qualities, intellectual and moral. It was, perhaps, in the order of Providence that it should be permitted for that very purpose. But this bill declares no war, except, indeed, it be that which savages wage—a war, not against the community, but the citizens of whom that community is composed. But I regard it as worse than *savage* warfare—as an attempt to take away life under the color of law, without the trial by jury, or any other safeguard which the constitution has thrown around the life of the citizen! It authorizes the President, or even his deputies, when they may suppose the law to be violated, without the intervention of a court or jury, to kill without mercy or discrimination!

It has been said by the senator from Tennessee (Mr. Grundy) to be a measure of peace! Yes, such peace as the wolf gives to the lamb—the kite to the dove! Such peace as Russia gives to Poland, or death to its victim! A peace, by extinguishing the political existence of the State, by awing her into an abandonment of the exercise of every power which constitutes her a sovereign community. It is to South Carolina a question of self-preservation; and I proclaim it, that, should this bill pass, and an attempt be made to enforce it, it will be resisted, at every hazard—even that of death itself. Death is not the greatest calamity: there are others still more terrible to the free and brave, and among them may be placed the loss of liberty and honor. There are thousands of her brave sons who, if need be, are prepared cheerfully to lay down their lives in defence of the State, and the great principles of constitutional liberty for which she is contending. God forbid that this should become necessary! It never can be, unless this Government is resolved to bring the question to extremity, when her gallant sons will stand prepared to perform the last duty— to die nobly.

I go on the ground that this constitution was made by the States; that it is a federal union of the States, in which the several States still retain their sovereignty. If these views be correct, I have not characterized the bill too strongly; and the question is, whether they be or be not. I will not enter into the discussion of this question now. I will rest it, for the present, on what I have said on the introduction of the resolutions now on the table, under a hope that another opportunity will be afforded for more ample discussion. I will, for the present, confine my remarks to the objections which have been raised to the views which I presented when I introduced them. The authority of Luther Martin has been adduced by the Senator from Delaware, to prove that the citizens of a State, acting under the authority of a State, are liable to be punished as traitors by this government. Eminent as Mr. Martin was as a lawyer, and high as his authority may be considered on a legal point, I cannot accept it in determining the point at issue. The attitude which he occupied, if taken into view, would lessen, if not destroy, the weight of his authority. He had been violently opposed in convention to the constitution, and the very letter from which the Senator has quoted was intended to dissuade Maryland from its adoption. With this view, it was to be expected that every consideration calculated to effect that object should be urged; that real objections should be exaggerated; and that those having no foundation, except mere plausible deductions, should be presented. It is to this spirit that I attribute the opinion of Mr. Martin in reference to the point under consideration. But if his authority be good on one point, it must be admitted to be equally so on another. If his opinion be sufficient to prove that a citizen of a State may be punished as a traitor when acting under allegiance to the State, it is also sufficient to show that no authority was intended to be given in the constitution for the protection of manufactures by the General Government, and that the provision in the constitution permitting a State to lay an impost duty, with the consent of Congress, was intended to reserve the right of protection to the States themselves, and that each State should protect its own industry. Assuming his opinion to be of equal authority on both points, how embarrassing would be the attitude in which it would place the Senator from Delaware, and those with whom he is acting—that of using the sword and bayonet to enforce the execution of an unconstitutional act of Congress. I must express my surprise that the slightest authority in favor of *power* should be received as the most conclusive evidence, while that which is, at least, equally strong in favor of right and *liberty,* is wholly overlooked or rejected.

Notwithstanding all that has been said, I may say that neither the Senator from Delaware (Mr. Clayton), nor any other who has spoken on the same side, has directly and fairly met the great question at issue: Is this a federal union? a union of States, as distinct from that of individuals? Is the sovereignty in the several States, or in the American people in the aggregate? The very language which we are compelled to use when speaking of our political institutions, affords proof conclusive as to its real character. The terms union, federal, united, all imply a combination of sovereignties, a confederation of States. They are never applied to an association of individuals. Who ever heard of the United State of New-York, of Massachusetts, or of Virginia? Who ever heard the term federal or union applied to the aggregation of individuals into one community? Nor is the other point less clear—that the sovereignty is in the several States, and that our system is a union of twenty-four sovereign powers, under a constitutional compact, and not of a divided sovereignty between the States severally and the United States. In spite of all that has been said, I maintain that sovereignty is in its nature indivisible. It is the supreme power in a State, and we might just as well speak of half a square, or half of a triangle, as of half a sovereignty. It is a gross error to confound the *exercise* of sovereign powers with *sovereignty* itself, or the *delegation* of such powers with the *surrender* of them. A sovereign may delegate his powers to be exercised by as many agents as he may think proper, under such conditions and with such limitations as he may impose; but to surrender any portion of his sovereignty to another is to annihilate the whole. The Senator from Delaware (Mr. Clayton) calls this metaphysical reasoning, which he says he cannot comprehend. If by metaphysics he means that scholastic refinement which makes distinctions without difference, no one can hold it in more utter contempt than I do; but if, on the contrary, he means the power of analysis and combination—that power which reduces the most complex idea into its elements, which traces causes to their first principle, and, by the power of generalization and combination, unites the whole in one harmonious system—then, so far from deserving contempt, it is the highest attribute of the human mind. It is the power which raises man above the brute—which distinguishes his faculties from mere sagacity, which he holds in common with inferior animals. It is this power which has raised the astronomer from being a mere gazer at the stars to the high intellectual eminence of a Newton or a Laplace, and astronomy itself from a mere observation of insulated facts into that noble science which displays to our admiration the system of the universe. And shall this high power of the mind, which has effected such wonders when directed to the laws which control the material world, be for ever prohibited, under a senseless cry of metaphysics, from being applied to the high purpose of political science and legislation? I hold them to be subject to laws as fixed as matter itself, and to be as fit a subject for the application of the highest intellectual power. Denunciation may, indeed, fall upon the philosophical inquirer into these first principles, as it did upon Galileo and Bacon when they first unfolded the great discoveries which have immortalized their names; but the time will come when truth will prevail in spite of prejudice and denunciation, and when politics and legislation will be considered as much a science as astronomy and chemistry.

In connection with this part of the subject, I understood the Senator from Virginia (Mr. Rives) to say that sovereignty was divided, and that a portion remained with the States severally, and that the residue was vested in the Union. By Union, I suppose the Senator meant the United States. If such be his meaning—if he intended to affirm that the sovereignty was in the twenty-four States, in whatever light he may view them, our opinions will not disagree; but according to my conception, the whole sovereignty is in the several States, while the exercise of sovereign powers is divided—a part being exercised under compact, through this General Government, and the residue through the separate State Governments. But if the Senator from Virginia (Mr. Rives) means to assert that the twenty-four States form but one community, with a single sovereign power as to the objects of the Union, it will be but the revival of the old question, of whether the Union is a union between States, as distinct communities, or a mere aggregate of the American people, as a mass of individuals; and in this light his opinions would lead directly to consolidation.

But to return to the bill. It is said that the bill ought to pass, because the law must be enforced. The law must be enforced! The imperial edict must be executed! It is under such sophistry, couched in general terms, without looking to the limitations which must ever exist in the practical exercise of power, that the most cruel and despotic acts ever have been covered. It was such sophistry as this that cast Daniel into the lion's den, and the three Innocents into the fiery furnace. Under the same sophistry the bloody edicts of Nero and Caligula were executed. The law must be enforced. Yes, the act imposing the "tea-tax must be executed." This was the very argument which impelled Lord North and his administration to that mad career which for ever separated us from the British crown. Under a similar sophistry, "that religion must be protected," how many massacres have been perpetrated? and how many martyrs have been tied to the stake? What! acting on this vague abstraction, are you prepared to enforce a law without considering whether it be just or unjust, constitutional or unconstitutional? Will you collect money when it is acknowledged that it is not wanted? He who earns the money, who digs it from the earth with the sweat of his brow, has a just title to it against the universe. No one has a right to touch it without his consent except his government, and this only to the extent of its legitimate wants; to take more is robbery, and you propose by this bill to enforce robbery by murder. Yes: to this result you must come, by this miserable sophistry, this vague abstraction of enforcing the law, without a regard to the fact whether the law be just or unjust, constitutional or unconstitutional.

In the same spirit, we are told that the Union must be preserved, without regard to the means. And how is it proposed to preserve the Union? By force! Does any man in his senses believe that this beautiful structure—this harmonious aggregate of States, produced by the joint consent of all—can be preserved by force? Its very introduction will be certain destruction to this Federal Union. No, no. You cannot keep the States united in their constitutional and federal bonds by force. Force may, indeed, hold the parts together, but such union would be the bond between master and slave—a union of exaction on one side and of unqualified *obedience* on the other. That *obedience* which, we are told by the Senator from Pennsylvania (Mr. Wilkins), is the Union! Yes, exaction on the side of the master; for this very bill is intended to collect what can be no longer called taxes—the voluntary contribution of a free people—but tribute—tribute to be collected under the mouths of the cannon! Your custom-house is already transferred to a garrison, and that garrison with its batteries turned, not against the enemy of your country, but on subjects (I will not say citizens), on whom you propose to levy contributions. Has reason fled from our borders? Have we ceased to reflect? It is madness to suppose that the Union can be preserved by force. I tell you plainly, that the bill, should it pass, cannot be enforced. It will prove only a blot upon your statute-book, a reproach to the year, and a disgrace to the American Senate. I repeat, it will not be executed; it will rouse the dormant spirit of the people, and open their eyes to the approach of despotism. The country has sunk into avarice and political corruption, from which nothing can arouse it but some measure, on the part of the Government, of folly and madness, such as that now under consideration.

Disguise it as you may, the controversy is one between power and liberty; and I tell the gentlemen who are opposed to me, that, as strong as may be the love of power on their side, the love of liberty is still stronger on ours. History furnishes many instances of similar struggles, where the love of liberty has prevailed against power under every disadvantage, and among them few more striking than that of our own Revolution; where, as strong as was the parent country, and feeble as were the colonies, yet, under the impulse of liberty, and the blessing of God, they gloriously triumphed in the contest. There are, indeed, many and striking analogies between that and the present controversy. They both originated substantially in the same cause—with this difference—in the present case, the power of taxation is converted into that of regulating industry; in the other, the power of regulating industry, by the regulation of commerce, was attempted to be converted into the power of taxation. Were I to trace the analogy further, we should find that the perversion of the taxing power, in the one case, has given precisely the same control to the Northern section over the industry of the Southern section of the Union, which the power to regulate commerce gave to Great Britain over the industry of the colonies in the other; and that the very articles in which the colonies were permitted to have a free trade, and those in which the mother-country had a monopoly, are almost identically the same as those in which the Southern States are permitted to have a free trade by the act of 1832, and in which the Northern States have, by the same act, secured a monopoly. The only difference is in the means. In the former, the colonies were permitted to have a free trade with all countries south of Cape Finisterre, a cape in the northern part of Spain; while north of that, the trade of the colonies was prohibited, except through the mother-country, by means of her commercial regulations. If we compare the products of the country north and south of Cape Finisterre, we shall find them almost identical with the list of the protected and unprotected articles contained in the act of last year. Nor does the analogy terminate here. The very arguments resorted to at the commencement of the American Revolution, and the measures adopted, and the motives assigned to bring on that contest (to enforce the law), are almost identically the same.

But to return from this digression to the consideration of the bill. Whatever difference of opinion may exist upon other points, there is one on which I should suppose there can be none: that this bill rests on principles which, if carried out, will ride over State sovereignties, and that it will be idle for any of its advocates hereafter to talk of State rights. The Senator from Virginia (Mr. Rives) says that he is the advocate of State rights; but he must permit me to tell him that, although he may differ in premises from the other gentlemen with whom he acts on this occasion, yet, in supporting this bill, he obliterates every vestige of distinction between him and them, saving only that, professing the principles of '98, his example will be more pernicious than that of the most open and bitter opponents of the rights of the States. I will also add, what I am compelled to say, that I must consider him (Mr. Rives) as less consistent than our old opponents, whose conclusions were fairly drawn from their premises, while his premises ought to have led him to opposite conclusions. The gentleman has told us that the new-fangled doctrines, as he chooses to call them, have brought State rights into disrepute. I must tell him, in reply, that what he calls new-fangled are but the doctrines of '98; and that it is he (Mr. Rives), and others with him, who, professing these doctrines, have degraded them by explaining away their meaning and efficacy. He (Mr. R.) has disclaimed, in behalf of Virginia, the authorship of nullification. I will not dispute that point. If Virginia chooses to throw away one of her brightest ornaments, she must not hereafter complain that it has become the property of another. But while I have, as a representative of Carolina, no right to complain of the disavowal of the Senator from Virginia, I must believe that he (Mr. R.) has done his native State great injustice by declaring on this floor, that when she gravely resolved, in '98, that "in cases of deliberate and dangerous infractions of the constitution, the States, as parties to the compact, have the right, and are in duty bound, to interpose to arrest the progress of the evil, and to maintain within their respective limits the authorities, rights, and liberties, appertaining to them," she meant no more than to proclaim the right to protest and to remonstrate. To suppose that, in putting forth so solemn a declaration, which she afterwards sustained by so able and elaborate an argument, she meant no more than to assert what no one had ever denied, would be to suppose that the State had been guilty of the most egregious trifling that ever was exhibited on so solemn an occasion.

In reviewing the ground over which I have passed, it will be apparent that the question in controversy involves that most deeply important of all political questions, whether ours is a federal or a consolidated government;—a question, on the decision of which depend, as I solemnly believe, the liberty of the people, their happiness, and the place which we are destined to hold in the moral and intellectual scale of nations. Never was there a controversy in which more important consequences were involved; not excepting that between Persia and Greece, decided by the battles of Marathon, Platea, and Salamis—which gave ascendency to the genius of Europe over that of Asia—and which, in its consequences, has continued to affect the destiny of so large a portion of the world even to this day. There are often close analogies between events apparently very remote, which are strikingly illustrated in this case. In the great contest between Greece and Persia, between European and Asiatic polity and civilization, the very question between the federal and consolidated form of government was involved. The Asiatic governments, from the remotest time, with some exceptions on the eastern shore of the Mediterranean, have been based on the principle of consolidation, which considers the whole community as but a unit, and consolidates its powers in a central point. The opposite principle has prevailed in Europe—Greece, throughout all her states, was based on a federal system. All were united in one common but loose bond, and the governments of the several States partook, for the most part, of a complex organization, which distributed political power among different members of the community. The same principles prevailed in ancient Italy; and, if we turn to the Teutonic race, our great ancestors—the race which occupies the first place in power, civilization, and science, and which possesses the largest and the fairest part of Europe— we shall find that their governments were based on federal organization, as has been clearly illustrated by a recent and able writer on the British Constitution (Mr. Palgrave), from whose works I take the following extract:

"In this manner the first establishment of the Teutonic States was effected. They were assemblages of septs, clans, and tribes; they were confederated hosts and armies, led on by princes, magistrates, and chieftains; each of whom was originally independent, and each of whom lost a portion of his pristine independence in proportion as he and his compeers became united under the supremacy of a sovereign, who was superinduced upon the state, first as a military commander and afterward as a king. Yet, notwithstanding this political connection, each member of the state continued to retain a considerable portion of the rights of sovereignty. Every ancient Teutonic monarchy must be considered as a federation; it is not a unit, of which the smaller bodies politic therein contained are the fractions, but they are the integers, and the state is the multiple which results from them. Dukedoms and counties, burghs and baronies, towns and townships, and shires, form the kingdom; all, in a certain degree, strangers to each other, and separate in jurisdiction, though all obedient to the supreme executive authority. This general description, though not always strictly applicable in terms, is always so substantially and in effect; and hence it becomes necessary to discard the language which has been very generally employed in treating on the English Constitution. It has been supposed that the kingdom was reduced into a regular and gradual subordination of government, and that the various legal districts of which it is composed, arose from the divisions and subdivisions of the country. But this hypothesis, which tends greatly to perplex our history, cannot be supported by fact; and, instead of viewing the constitution as a whole, and then proceeding to its parts, we must examine it synthetically, and assume that the supreme authorities of the state were created by the concentration of the powers originally belonging to the members and corporations of which it is composed."

[Here Mr. C. gave way for a motion to adjourn (Crallé).]

On the next day Mr. Calhoun said: I have omitted at the proper place, in the course of my observations yesterday, two or three points, to which I will now advert, before I resume the discussion where I left off. I have stated that the ordinance and acts of South Carolina were directed, not against the revenue, but against the system of protection. But it may be asked, if such was her object, how happens it that she has declared the whole system void—revenue as well as protection, without discrimination? It is this question which I propose to answer. Her justification will be found in the necessity of the case; and if there be any blame, it cannot attach to her. The two are so blended, throughout the whole, as to make the entire revenue system subordinate to the protective, so as to constitute a complete system of protection, in which it is impossible to discriminate the two elements of which it is composed. South Carolina, at least, could not make the discrimination; and she was reduced to the alternative of acquiescing in a system which she believed to be unconstitutional, and which she felt to be oppressive and ruinous, or to consider the whole as one, equally contaminated through all its parts, by the unconstitutionality of the protective portion, and as such, to be resisted by the act of the State. I maintain that the State has a right to regard it in the latter character, and that, if a loss of revenue follow, the fault is not hers, but of this Government, which has improperly blended together, in a manner not to be separated by the State, two systems wholly dissimilar. If the sincerity of the State be doubted; if it be supposed that her action is against revenue as well as protection, let the two be separated—let so much of the duties as are intended for revenue be put in one bill, and the residue intended for protection be put in another, and I pledge myself that the ordinance and the acts of the State will cease as to the former, and be directed exclusively against the latter.

I also stated, in the course of my remarks yesterday, and I trust that I have conclusively shown, that the act of 1816, with the exception of a single item, to which I have alluded, was, in reality, a revenue measure; and that Carolina and the other States, in supporting it, have not incurred the slightest responsibility in relation to the system of protection which has since grown up, and which now so deeply distracts the country. Sir, I am willing, as one of the representatives of Carolina, and I believe I speak the sentiment of the State, to take that act as the basis of a permanent adjustment of the tariff, simply reducing the duties, in an average proportion, on all the items to the revenue point. I make that offer now to the advocates of the protective system; but I must, in candor, inform them that such an adjustment would distribute the revenue between the protected and unprotected articles more favorably to the State, and to the South, and less to the manufacturing interest, than an average uniform *ad valorem,* and accordingly, more so than that now proposed by Carolina through her convention. After such an offer, no man who values his candor will dare accuse the State, or those who have represented her here, with inconsistency in reference to the point under consideration.

I omitted, also, on yesterday, to notice a remark of the Senator from Virginia (Mr. Rives), that the only difficulty in adjusting the tariff grew out of the ordinance and the acts of South Carolina. I must attribute an assertion, so inconsistent with the facts, to an ignorance of the occurrences of the last few years in reference to this subject, occasioned by the absence of the gentleman from the United States, to which he himself has alluded in his remarks. If the Senator will take pains to inform himself, he will find that this protective system advanced with a continued and rapid step, in spite of petitions, remonstrances, and protests, of not only Carolina, but also of Virginia and of all the Southern States, until 1828, when Carolina, for the first time, changed the character of her resistance, by holding up her reserved rights as the shield of her defence against further encroachment. This attitude alone, unaided by a single State, arrested the further progress of the system, so that the question from that period to this, on the part of the manufacturers, has been, not how to acquire more, but to retain that which they have acquired. I will inform the gentleman that, if this attitude had not been taken on the part of the State, the question would not now be how duties ought to be repealed, but a question, as to the protected articles, between prohibition on one side and the duties established by the act of 1828 on the other. But a single remark will be sufficient in reply to, what I must consider, the invidious remark of the Senator from Virginia (Mr. Rives). The act of 1832, which has not yet gone into operation, and which was passed but a few months since, was declared by the supporters of the system to be a *permanent* adjustment, and the bill proposed by the Treasury Department, not essentially different from the act itself, was in like manner declared to be intended by the administration as a permanent arrangement. What has occurred since, except this ordinance, and these abused acts of the calumniated State, to produce this mighty revolution in reference to this odious system? Unless the Senator from Virginia can assign some other cause, he is bound, upon every principle of fairness, to retract this unjust aspersion upon the acts of South Carolina.

The Senator from Delaware (Mr. Clayton), as well as others, has relied with great emphasis on the fact that we are citizens of the United States. I do not object to the expression, nor shall I detract from the proud and elevated feelings with which it is associated; but I trust that I may be permitted to raise the inquiry, In what manner are we citizens of the United States? without weakening the patriotic feeling with which, I trust, it will ever be uttered. If by citizen of the United States he means a citizen at large, one whose citizenship extends to the entire geographical limits of the country, without having a local citizenship in some State or territory, a sort of citizen of the world, all I have to say is, that such a citizen would be a perfect nondescript; that not a single individual of this description can be found in the entire mass of our population. Notwithstanding all the pomp and display of eloquence on the occasion, every citizen is a citizen of some State or territory, and, as such, under an express provision of the constitution, is entitled to all privileges and immunities of citizens in the several States; and it is in this, and in no other sense, that we are citizens of the United States. The Senator from Pennsylvania (Mr. Dallas), indeed, relies upon that provision in the constitution which gives Congress the power to establish an uniform rule of naturalization; and the operation of the rule actually established under this authority, to prove that naturalized citizens are citizens at large, without being citizens of any of the States. I do not deem it necessary to examine the law of Congress upon this subject, or to reply to the argument of the Senator, though I cannot doubt that he (Mr. D.) has taken an entirely erroneous view of the subject. It is sufficient that the power of Congress extends simply to the establishment of a uniform rule by which foreigners may be naturalized in the several States or territories, without infringing, in any other respect, in reference to naturalization, the rights of the States as they existed before the adoption of the constitution.

Having supplied the omissions of yesterday, I now resume the subject at the point where my remarks then terminated. The Senate will remember that I stated, at their close, that the great question at issue is, whether ours is a federal or a consolidated system of government; a system in which the parts, to use the emphatic language of Mr. Palgrave, are the integers, and the whole the multiple, or in which the whole is an unit and the parts the fractions. I stated, that on the decision of this question, I believed, depended not only the liberty and prosperity of this country, but the place which we are destined to hold in the intellectual and moral scale of nations. I stated, also, in my remarks on this point, that there is a striking analogy between this and the great struggle between Persia and Greece, which was decided by the battles of Marathon, Platea, and Salamis, and which immortalized the names of Miltiades and Themistocles. I illustrated this analogy by showing that centralism or consolidation, with the exception of a few nations along the eastern borders of the Mediterranean, has been the pervading principle in the Asiatic governments, while the federal system, or, what is the same in principle, that system which organizes a community in reference to its parts, has prevailed in Europe.

Among the few exceptions in the Asiatic nations, the government of the twelve tribes of Israel, in its early period, is the most striking. Their government, at first, was a mere confederation without any central power, till a military chieftain, with the title of king, was placed at its head, without, however, merging the original organization of the twelve distinct tribes. This was the commencement of that central action among that peculiar people which, in three generations, terminated in a permanent division of their tribes. It is impossible even for a careless reader to peruse the history of that event without being forcibly struck with the analogy in the causes which led to their separation, and those which now threaten us with a similar calamity. With the establishment of the central power in the king commenced a system of taxation, which, under King Solomon, was greatly increased, to defray the expenses of rearing the temple, of enlarging and embellishing Jerusalem, the seat of the central government, and the other profuse expenditures of his magnificent reign. Increased taxation was followed by its natural consequences—discontent and complaint, which, before his death, began to excite resistance. On the succession of his son, Rehoboam, the ten tribes, headed by Jeroboam, demanded a reduction of the taxes; the temple being finished, and the embellishment of Jerusalem completed, and the money which had been raised for that purpose being no longer required, or, in other words, the debt being paid, they demanded a reduction of the duties—a repeal of the tariff. The demand was taken under consideration, and after consulting the old men, the counsellors of '98, who advised a reduction, he then took the opinion of the younger politicians, who had since grown up, and knew not the doctrines of their fathers; he hearkened unto their counsel, and refused to make the reduction, and the secession of the ten tribes under Jeroboam followed. The tribes of Judah and Benjamin, which had received the disbursements, alone remained to the house of David.

But to return to the point immediately under consideration. I know that it is not only the opinion of a large majority of our country, but it may be said to be the opinion of the age, that the very beau ideal of a perfect government is the government of a majority, acting through a representative body, without check or limitation on its power; yet, if we may test this theory by experience and reason, we shall find that, so far from being perfect, the necessary tendency of all governments, based upon the will of an absolute majority, without constitutional check or limitation of power, is to faction, corruption, anarchy, and despotism; and this, whether the will of the majority be expressed directly through an assembly of the people themselves, or by their representatives. I know that, in venturing this assertion, I utter what is unpopular both within and without these walls; but where truth and liberty are concerned, such considerations should not be regarded. I will place the decision of this point on the fact that no government of the kind, among the many attempts which have been made, has ever endured for a single generation, but, on the contrary has invariably experienced the fate which I have assigned to it. Let a single instance be pointed out, and I will surrender my opinion. But, if we had not the aid of experience to direct our judgment, reason itself would be a certain guide. The view which considers the community as an unit, and all its parts as having a similar interest, is radically erroneous. However small the community may be, and however homogeneous its interests, the moment that government is put into operation—as soon as it begins to collect taxes and to make appropriations, the different portions of the community must, of necessity, bear different and opposing relations in reference to the action of the government. There must inevitably spring up two interests—a direction and a stock-holder interest—an interest profiting by the action of the government, and interested in increasing its powers and action; and another, at whose expense the political machine is kept in motion. I know how difficult it is to communicate distinct ideas on such a subject, through the medium of general propositions, without particular illustration; and in order that I may be distinctly understood, though at the hazard of being tedious, I will illustrate the important principle which I have ventured to advance, by examples.

Let us, then, suppose a small community of five persons, separated from the rest of the world; and, to make the example strong, let us suppose them all to be engaged in the same pursuit, and to be of equal wealth. Let us further suppose that they determine to govern the community by the will of a majority; and, to make the case as strong as possible, let us suppose that the majority, in order to meet the expenses of the government, lay an equal tax, say of one hundred dollars on each individual of this little community. Their treasury would contain five hundred dollars. Three are a majority; and they, by supposition, have contributed three hundred as their portion, and the other two (the minority), two hundred. The three have the right to make the appropriations as they may think proper. The question is, How would the principle of the absolute and unchecked majority operate, under these circumstances, in this little community? If the three be governed by a sense of justice—if they should appropriate the money to the objects for which it was raised, the common and equal benefit of the five, then the object of the association would be fairly and honestly effected, and each would have a common interest in the government. But, should the majority pursue an opposite course—should they appropriate the money in a manner to benefit their own particular interest, without regard to the interest of the two (and that they will so act, unless there be some efficient check, he who best knows human nature will least doubt), who does not see that the three and the two would have directly opposite interests in reference to the action of the government? The three who contribute to the common treasury but three hundred dollars, could, in fact, by appropriating the five hundred to their own use, convert the action of the government into the means of making money, and, of consequence, would have a direct interest in increasing the taxes. They put in three hundred and take out five; that is, they take back to themselves all that they put in, and, in addition, that which was put in by their associates; or, in other words, taking taxation and appropriation together, they have gained, and their associates have lost, two hundred dollars by the fiscal action of the government. Opposite interests, in reference to the action of the government, are thus created between them: the one having an interest in favor, and the other against the taxes; the one to increase, and the other to decrease the taxes; the one to retain the taxes when the money is no longer wanted, and the other to repeal them when the objects for which they were levied have been secured.

Let us now suppose this community of five to be raised to twenty-four individuals, to be governed, in like manner, by the will of a majority: it is obvious that the same principle would divide them into two interests—into a majority and a minority, thirteen against eleven, or in some other proportion; and that all the consequences which I have shown to be applicable to the small community of five would be applicable to the greater, the cause not depending upon the number, but resulting necessarily from the action of the government itself.

Let us now suppose that, instead of governing themselves directly in an assembly of the whole, without the intervention of agents, they should adopt the representative principle; and that, instead of being governed by a majority of themselves, they should be governed by a majority of their representatives. It is obvious that the operation of the system would not be affected by the change: the representatives being responsible to those who chose them, would conform to the will of their constituents, and would act as they would do were they present and acting for themselves; and the same conflict of interest, which we have shown would exist in one case, would equally exist in the other. In either case, the inevitable result would be a system of hostile legislation on the part of the majority, or the stronger interest, against the minority, or the weaker interest; the object of which, on the part of the former, would be to exact as much as possible from the latter, which would necessarily be resisted by all the means in their power. Warfare, by legislation, would thus be commenced between the parties, with the same object, and not less hostile than that which is carried on between distinct and rival nations—the only distinction would be in the instruments and the mode. Enactments, in the one case, would supply what could only be effected by arms in the other; and the inevitable operation would be to engender the most hostile feelings between the parties, which would merge every feeling of patriotism—that feeling which embraces the whole—and substitute in its place the most violent party attachment; and instead of having one common centre of attachment, around which the affections of the community might rally, there would in fact be two—the interests of the majority, to which those who constitute that majority would be more attached than they would be to the whole,—and that of the minority, to which they, in like manner, would also be more attached than to the interests of the whole. Faction would thus take the place of patriotism; and, with the loss of patriotism, corruption must necessarily follow, and in its train, anarchy, and, finally, despotism, or the establishment of absolute power in a single individual, as a means of arresting the conflict of hostile interests; on the principle that it is better to submit to the will of a single individual, who by being made lord and master of the whole community, would have an equal interest in the protection of all the parts.

Let us next suppose that, in order to avert the calamitous train of consequences, this little community should adopt a written constitution, with limitations restricting the will of the majority, in order to protect the minority against the oppression which I have shown would necessarily result without such restrictions. It is obvious that the case would not be in the slightest degree varied, if the majority be left in possession of the right of judging exclusively of the extent of its powers, without any right on the part of the minority to enforce the restrictions imposed by the constitution on the will of the majority. The point is almost too clear for illustration. Nothing can be more certain than that, when a constitution grants power, and imposes limitations on the exercise of that power, whatever interests may obtain possession of the government, will be in favor of extending the power at the expense of the limitation; and that, unless those in whose behalf the limitations were imposed have, in some form or mode, the right of enforcing them, the power will ultimately supersede the limitation, and the government must operate precisely in the same manner as if the will of the majority governed without constitution or limitation of power.

I have thus presented all possible modes in which a government founded upon the will of an absolute majority will he modified; and have demonstrated that, in all its forms, whether in a majority of the people, as in a mere Democracy, or in a majority of their representatives, without a constitution or with a constitution, to be interpreted as the will of the majority, the result will be the same: two hostile interests will inevitably be created by the action of the government, to be followed by hostile legislation, and that by faction, corruption, anarchy, and despotism.

The great and solemn question here presents itself, Is there any remedy for these evils? on the decision of which depends the question, whether the people can govern themselves, which has been so often asked with so much skepticism and doubt. There is a remedy, and but one,—the effect of which, whatever may be the form, is to organize society in reference to this conflict of interests, which springs out of the action of government; and which can only be done by giving to each part the right of self-protection; which, in a word, instead of considering the community of twenty-four a single community, having a common interest, and to be governed by the single will of an entire majority, shall upon all questions tending to bring the parts into conflict, the thirteen against the eleven, take the will, not of the twenty-four as a unit, but of the thirteen and of the eleven separately,—the majority of each governing the parts, and where they concur, governing the whole,—and where they disagree, arresting the action of the government. This I will call the concurring, as distinct from the absolute majority. In either way the number would be the same, whether taken as the absolute or as the concurring majority. Thus, the majority of the thirteen is seven, and of the eleven six; and the two together make thirteen, which is the majority of twenty-four. But, though the number is the same, the mode of counting is essentially different: the one representing the strongest interest, and the other, the entire interests of the community. The first mistake is, in supposing that the government of the absolute majority is the government of the people—that beau ideal of a perfect government which has been so enthusiastically entertained in every age by the generous and patrotic, where civilization and liberty have made the smallest progress. There can be no greater error: the government of the people is the government of the whole community—of the twenty-four—the self-government of all the parts—too perfect to be reduced to practice in the present, or any past stage of human society. The government of the absolute majority, instead of being the government of the people, is but the government of the strongest interests, and, when not efficiently checked, is the most tyrannical and oppressive that can be devised. Between this ideal perfection on the one side, and despotism on the other, no other system can be devised but that which considers society in reference to its parts, as differently affected by the action of the government, and which takes the sense of each part separately, and thereby the sense of the whole, in the manner already illustrated.

These principles, as I have already stated, are not affected by the number of which the community may be composed, but are just as applicable to one of thirteen millions—the number which composes ours—as of the small community of twenty-four, which I have supposed for the purpose of illustration; and are not less applicable to the twenty-four States united in one community, than to the case of the twenty-four individuals. There is, indeed, a distinction between a large and a small community, not affecting the principle, but the violence of the action. In the former, the similarity of the interests of all the parts will limit the oppression from the hostile action of the parts, in a great degree, to the fiscal action of the government merely; but in the large community, spreading over a country of great extent, and having a great diversity of interests, with different kinds of labor, capital, and production, the conflict and oppression will extend, not only to a monopoly of the appropriations on the part of the stronger interests, but will end in unequal taxes, and a general conflict between the entire interests of conflicting sections, which, if not arrested by the most powerful checks, will terminate in the most oppressive tyranny that can be conceived, or in the destruction of the community itself.

If we turn our attention from these supposed cases, and direct it to our government and its actual operation, we shall find a practical confirmation of the truth of what has been stated, not only of the oppressive operation of the system of an absolute majority, but also a striking and beautiful illustration, in the formation of our system, of the principle of the concurring majority, as distinct from the absolute, which I have asserted to be the only means of efficiently checking the abuse of power, and, of course, the only solid foundation of constitutional liberty. That our government, for many years, has been gradually verging to consolidation; that the constitution has gradually become a dead letter; and that all restrictions upon the power of government have been virtually removed, so as practically to convert the General Government into a government of an absolute majority, without check or limitation, cannot be denied by any one who has impartially observed its operation.

It is not necessary to trace the commencement and gradual progress of the causes which have produced this change in our system; it is sufficient to state that the change has taken place within the last few years. What has been the result? Precisely that which might have been anticipated: the growth of faction, corruption, anarchy, and, if not despotism itself, its near approach, as witnessed in the provisions of this bill. And from what have these consequences sprung? We have been involved in no war. We have been at peace with all the world. We have been visited with no national calamity. Our people have been advancing in general intelligence, and, I will add, as great and alarming as has been the advance of political corruption among the mercenary corps who look to Government for support, the morals and virtue of the community at large have been advancing in improvement. What, I again repeat, is the cause? No other can be assigned but a departure from the fundamental principles of the constitution, which has converted the Government into the will of an absolute and irresponsible majority, and which, by the laws that must inevitably govern in all such majorities, has placed in conflict the great interests of the country, by a system of hostile legislation, by an oppressive and unequal imposition of taxes, by unequal and profuse appropriations, and by rendering the entire labor and capital of the weaker interest subordinate to the stronger.

This is the cause, and these the fruits, which have converted the Government into a mere instrument of taking money from one portion of the community, to be given to another; and which has rallied around it a great, a powerful, and mercenary corps of office-holders, office-seekers, and expectants, destitute of principle and patriotism, and who have no standard of morals or politics but the will of the Executive—the will of him who has the distribution of the loaves and the fishes. I hold it impossible for any one to look at the theoretical illustration of the principle of the absolute majority in the cases which I have supposed, and not be struck with the practical illustration in the actual operation of our Government. Under every circumstance, the absolute majority will ever have its American system (I mean nothing offensive to any Senator); but the real meaning of the American system is, that system of plunder which the strongest interest has ever waged, and will ever wage, against the weaker, where the latter is not armed with some efficient and constitutional check to arrest its action. Nothing but such check on the part of the weaker interest can arrest it: mere constitutional limitations are wholly insufficient. Whatever interest obtains possession of the Government, will, from the nature of things, be in favor of the powers, and against the limitations imposed by the constitution, and will resort to every device that can be imagined to remove those restraints. On the contrary, the opposite interest, that which I have designated as the stockholding interest, the tax-payers, those on whom the system operates, will resist the abuse of powers, and contend for the limitations. And it is on this point, then, that the contest between the delegated and the reserved powers will be waged; but in this contest, as the interests in possession of the Government are organized and armed by all its powers and patronage, the opposite interest, if not in like manner organized and possessed of a power to protect themselves under the provisions of the constitution, will be as inevitably crushed as would be a band of unorganized militia when opposed by a veteran and trained corps of regulars. Let it never be forgotten, that power can only be opposed by power, organization by organization; and on this theory stands our beautiful federal system of Government. No free system was ever further removed from the principle that the absolute majority, without check or limitation, ought to govern. To understand what our Government is, we must look to the constitution, which is the basis of the system. I do not intend to enter into any minute examination of the origin and the source of its powers: it is sufficient for my purpose to state, what I do fearlessly, that it derived its power from the people of the separate States, each ratifying by itself, each binding itself by its own separate majority, through its separate convention,—the concurrence of the majorities of the several States forming the constitution;—thus taking the sense of the whole by that of the several parts, representing the various interests of the entire community. It was this concurring and perfect majority which formed the constitution, and not that majority which would consider the American people as a single community, and which, instead of representing fairly and fully the interests of the whole, would but represent, as has been stated, the interests of the stronger section. No candid man can dispute that I have given a correct description of the constitution-making power: that power which created and organized the Government, which delegated to it, as a common agent, certain powers, in trust for the common good of all the States, and which imposed strict limitations and checks against abuses and usurpations. In administering the delegated powers, the constitution provides, very properly, in order to give promptitude and efficiency, that the Government shall be organized upon the principle of the absolute majority, or, rather, of two absolute majorities combined: a majority of the States considered as bodies politic, which prevails in this body; and a majority of the people of the States, estimated in federal numbers, in the other House of Congress. A combination of the two prevails in the choice of the President, and, of course, in the appointment of Judges, they being nominated by the President and confirmed by the Senate. It is thus that the concurring and the absolute majorities are combined in one complex system: the one in forming the constitution, and the other in making and executing the laws; thus beautifully blending the moderation, justice, and equity of the former, and more perfect majority, with the promptness and energy of the latter, but less perfect.

To maintain the ascendency of the constitution over the law-making majority is the great and essential point, on which the success of the system must depend. Unless that ascendency can be preserved, the necessary consequence must be, that the laws will supersede the constitution; and, finally, the will of the Executive, by the influence of his patronage, will supersede the laws—indications of which are already perceptible. This ascendency can only be preserved through the action of the States as organized bodies, having their own separate governments, and possessed of the right, under the structure of our system, of judging of the extent of their separate powers, and of interposing their authority to arrest the unauthorized enactments of the General Government within their respective limits. I will not enter, at this time, into the discussion of this important point, as it has been ably and fully presented by the Senator from Kentucky (Mr. Bibb), and others who preceded him in this debate on the same side, whose arguments not only remain unanswered, but are unanswerable. It is only by this power of interposition that the reserved rights of the States can be peacefully and efficiently protected against the encroachments of the General Government—that the limitations imposed upon its authority can be enforced, and its movements confined to the orbit allotted to it by the constitution.

It has, indeed, been said in debate, that this can be effected by the organization of the General Government itself, particularly by the action of this body, which represents the States—and that the States themselves must look to the General Government for the perservation of many of the most important of their reserved rights. I do not underrate the value to be attached to the organic arrangement of the General Government, and the wise distribution of its powers between the several departments, and, in particular, the structure and the important functions of this body; but to suppose that the Senate, or any department of this Government, was intended to be the only guardian of the reserved rights, is a great and fundamental mistake. The Government, through all its departments, represents the delegated, and not the reserved powers; and it is a violation of the fundamental principle of free institutions to suppose that any but the responsible representative of any interest can be its guardian. The distribution of the powers of the General Government, and its organization, were arranged to prevent the abuse of power in fulfilling the important trusts confided to it, and not, as preposterously supposed, to protect the reserved powers, which are confided wholly to the guardianship of the several States.

Against the view of our system which I have presented, and the right of the States to interpose, it is objected that it would lead to anarchy and dissolution. I consider the objection as without the slightest foundation; and that, so far from tending to weakness or disunion, it is the source of the highest power and of the strongest cement. Nor is its tendency in this respect difficult of explanation. The government of an absolute majority, unchecked by efficient constitutional restraints, though apparently strong, is, in reality, an exceedingly feeble government. That tendency to conflict between the parts, which I have shown to be inevitable in such governments, wastes the powers of the state in the hostile action of contending factions, which leaves very little more power than the excess of the strength of the majority over the minority. But a government based upon the principle of the concurring majority, where each great interest possesses within itself the means of self-protection, which ultimately requires the mutual consent of all the parts, necessarily causes that unanimity in council, and ardent attachment of all the parts to the whole, which give an irresistible energy to a government so constituted. I might appeal to history for the truth of these remarks, of which the Roman furnishes the most familiar and striking proofs. It is a well-known fact, that, from the expulsion of the Tarquins to the time of the establishment of the tribunitian power, the government fell into a state of the greatest disorder and distraction, and, I may add, corruption. How did this happen? The explanation will throw important light on the subject under consideration. The community was divided into two parts—the Patricians and the Plebeians; with the power of the state principally in the hands of the former, without adequate checks to protect the rights of the latter. The result was as might be expected. The patricians converted the powers of the government into the means of making money, to enrich themselves and their dependants. They, in a word, had their American system, growing out of the peculiar character of the government and condition of the country. This requires explanation. At that period, according to the laws of nations, when one nation conquered another, the lands of the vanquished belonged to the victor; and, according to the

Roman law, the lands thus acquired were divided into two parts—one allotted to the poorer class of the people, and the other assigned to the use of the treasury,—of which the patricians had the distribution and administration. The patricians abused their power by withholding from the plebeians that which ought to have been allotted to them, and by converting to their own use that which ought to have gone to the treasury. In a word, they took to themselves the entire spoils of victory,—and had thus the most powerful motive to keep the state perpetually involved in war, to the utter impoverishment and oppression of the plebeians. After resisting the abuse of power by all peaceable means, and the oppression becoming intolerable, the plebeians, at last, withdrew from the city—they, in a word, seceded; and to induce them to reunite, the patricians conceded to them, as the means of protecting their separate interests, the very power, which I contend is necessary to protect the rights of the States, but which is now represented as necessarily leading to disunion. They granted to them the right of choosing three tribunes from among themselves, whose persons should be sacred, and who should have the right of interposing their veto, not only against the passage of laws, but even against their execution—a power which those, who take a shallow insight into human nature, would pronounce inconsistent with the strength and unity of the state, if not utterly impracticable; yet so far from this being the effect, from that day the genius of Rome became ascendant, and victory followed her steps till she had established an almost universal dominion. How can a result so contrary to all anticipation be explained? The explanation appears to me to be simple. No measure or movement could be adopted without the concurring assent of both the patricians and plebeians, and each thus became dependent on the other; and, of consequence, the desire and objects of neither could be effected without the concurrence of the other. To obtain this concurrence, each was compelled to consult the good-will of the other, and to elevate to office, not those only who might have the confidence of the order to which they belonged, but also that of the other. The result was, that men possessing those qualities which would naturally command confidence—moderation, wisdom, justice, and patriotism—were elevated to office; and the weight of their authority and the prudence of their counsel, combined with that spirit of unanimity necessarily resulting from the concurring assent of the two orders, furnish the real explanation of the power of the Roman State, and of that extraordinary wisdom, moderation, and firmness which in so remarkable a degree characterized her public men. I might illustrate the truth of the position which I have laid down by a reference to the history of all free states ancient and modern, distinguished for their power and patriotism, and

conclusively show, not only that there was not one which had not some contrivance, under some form, by which the concurring assent of the different portions of the community was made necessary in the action of government, but
also that the virtue, patriotism, and strength of the state were in direct proportion to the perfection of the means of securing such assent.

In estimating the operation of this principle in our system, which depends,
as I have stated, on the right of interposition on the part of a State, we must not
omit to take into consideration the amending power, by which new powers may
be granted, or any derangement of the system corrected, by the concurring
assent of three-fourths of the States; and thus, in the same degree, strengthening the power of repairing any derangement occasioned by the eccentric action
of a State. In fact, the power of interposition, fairly understood, may be considered in the light of an appeal against the usurpations of the General Government, the joint agent of all the States, to the States themselves,—to be decided
under the amending power, by the voice of three-fourths of the States, as the
highest power known under the system. I know the difficulty, in our country,
of establishing the truth of the principle for which I contend, though resting
upon the clearest reason, and tested by the universal experience of free nations.
I know that the governments of the several States, which, for the most part, are
constructed on the principle of the absolute majority, will be cited as an argument against the conclusion to which I have arrived; but, in my opinion, the
satisfactory answer can be given,—that the objects of expenditure which fall
within the sphere of a State Government are few and inconsiderable, so that be
their action ever so irregular, it can occasion but little derangement. If, instead
of being members of this great confederacy, they formed distinct communities,
and were compelled to raise armies, and incur other expenses necessary to their
defence, the laws which I have laid down as necessarily controlling the action
of a State where the will of an absolute and unchecked majority prevailed,
would speedily disclose themselves in faction, anarchy, and corruption. Even as
the case is, the operation of the causes to which I have referred is perceptible in
some of the larger and more populous members of the Union, whose governments have a powerful central action, and which already show a strong moneyed tendency, the invariable forerunner of corruption and convulsion.

But, to return to the General Government. We have now sufficient experience to ascertain that the tendency to conflict in its action is between the
southern and other sections. The latter having a decided majority, must habitually be possessed of the powers of the Government, both in this and in the
other House; and, being governed by that instinctive love of power so natural

to the human breast, they must become the advocates of the power of Government, and in the same degree opposed to the limitations; while the other and weaker section is as necessarily thrown on the side of the limitations. One section is the natural guardian of the delegated powers, and the other of the reserved; and the struggle on the side of the former will be to enlarge the powers, while that on the opposite side will be to restrain them within their constitutional limits. The contest will, in fact, be a contest between power and liberty, and such I consider the present—a contest in which the weaker section, with its peculiar labor, productions, and institutions, has at stake all that can be dear to freemen. Should we be able to maintain in their full vigor our reserved rights, liberty and prosperity will be our portion; but if we yield, and permit the stronger interest to concentrate within itself all the powers of the Government, then will our fate be more wretched than that of the aborigines whom we have expelled. In this great struggle between the delegated and reserved powers, so far from repining that my lot, and that of those whom I represent, is cast on the side of the latter, I rejoice that such is the fact; for, though we participate in but few of the advantages of the Government, we are compensated, and more than compensated, in not being so much exposed to its corruptions. Nor do I repine that the duty, so difficult to be discharged, of defending the reserved powers against apparently such fearful odds, has been assigned to us. To discharge it successfully requires the highest qualities, moral and intellectual; and should we perform it with a zeal and ability proportioned to its magnitude, instead of mere planters, our section will become distinguished for its patriots and statesmen. But, on the other hand, if we prove unworthy of the trust—if we yield to the steady encroachments of power, the severest calamity and most debasing corruption will overspread the land. Every Southern man, true to the interests of his section, and faithful to the duties which Providence has allotted him, will be for ever excluded from the honors and emoluments of this Government, which will be reserved for those only who have qualified themselves, by political prostitution, for admission into the *Magdalen* Asylum.

Chapter XIV.

"Letter to M. LaBorde, J. Terry, and J. F. Carroll,
Edgefield District, S.C.," 27 March 1833

*This brief missive was intended for public consumption. Calhoun urged prudence as
a basic quality of statesmanship. In confronting the defenders of secession, Calhoun
responded that such a response was appropriate only as the "last resort of an oppressed
State." In celebrating the American constitutional order, Calhoun interpreted the regime
as predicated upon a compact between the states, with "the reserved powers and the sovereignty of the States" as the only means of protecting popular rule.*

To Maximilian Laborde, J. Terry, and James Parsons Carroll,
Edgefield District, S.C.

Gentlemen—I have been honored by your note of the 18th instant, invit-
ing me, in the behalf of my friends in the vicinity of Edgefield, to partake of a
public dinner to be given at such time, as would suit my convenience.

In declining to accept this testimony of the approval of my public conduct,
in the trying scenes through which I have so lately passed, I am governed by the
course, to which I have adhered throughout the arduous and noble struggle,
which this State has maintained in the cause of liberty and the Constitution for
so many years, and not from any indifference to the honor intended, nor want
of respect for those, who have tendered it, in a manner so kind, and with an
approbation so warm and flattering, as to command my most profound gratitude.

Foreseeing from the commencement of this controversy, that the part,
which a sense of duty compelled me to take, would, from the position I occupied, expose the State, as well as myself, to the imputation of false and unworthy motives, and thereby tend to weaken the sacred cause, for which she

contended, I deemed it my duty, in order to obviate, as far as practicable, such effect, to decline accepting all such testimonials of the public approval of my course, as have been offered me. This originating in a sense of duty, has been in strict accordance with my feelings. Having no personal object in view, I have looked singly to an honest and faithful discharge of what I believe to be my duty, regardless of the effects on my future prospects, or even on the standing I may have acquired by past services with a large portion of my fellow citizens, with whom it has and still continues to be my misfortune to differ, in reference to the public interest, at this important crisis. The reason, which has heretofore governed my conduct, must still continue to influence me. The struggle to preserve the liberty and constitution of the country, and to arrest the corrupt and dangerous tendency of the Government, so far from being over, is not more than fairly commenced. In making this assertion, I do not intend to say, that we have not gained already an important advantage. Commencing the contest, as the State did alone and under so many disadvantages—against a system apparently so immovably established and sustained by so large a majority, and so powerful an interest; opposed and denounced both by the administration and the opposition—to come off not only without defeat, but with decided success, is indeed a triumph. In spite of all these difficulties, we have upheld and successfully asserted our doctrines, and proved by actual experience, that the rejected and reviled right of nullification is not, as its opponents asserted, revolution or disunion, but is that high, peaceable and efficient remedy; that great conservative principle of the system, which we claim it to be, and as it has proved, and that, too, after all the usual remedies had failed, and when without it none other remained, but secession, the last resort of an oppressed State, but which, like some powerful but dangerous medecine, cannot be prescribed, till the disease has become more dangerous, than the remedy, and when the life of the patient with or without it, is almost despaired of. Nor let any one suppose, that I have stated the facts too strongly, in saying, that we have successfully asserted our doctrines. To these assertions must be attributed, the recent adjustment of the tariff, which, whatever objections there may be to some of the details, there can be no division of opinion on the point, that the principle for which the State contended, that the duties ought to be imposed for revenue, and that no more ought to be raised, than the economical wants of the Government may demand, is openly and explicitly acknowledged by the Government. Time, it is true, has been liberally allowed for the gradual termination of the system, in order to avoid the shock and losses to individuals, which necessarily follow all sudden transitions, even from an erroneous to a correct principle of legislation; but, I feel, I hazard little in asserting, that the system will expire, at the appointed time, never more to be revived. For this great result, you owe little to me, or any other individual. It is the work of the State—the truth of the doctrines for which she contended, and the firm and heroic zeal, with which she has been sustained by her sons, in asserting them; and by none more so, than those of Edgefield, a District, which has distinguished itself among the foremost for its union and promptitude in this great contest. It is I repeat, to the noble resolve of her sons, to prefer the constitution and liberty to life itself, to which, under Providence, we are to attribute this success of our righteous cause.

But, let us not deceive ourselves, by supposing, that the danger is past. We have but checked the disease. If one evil has been remedied, another has succeeded—the force act in the place of the protective system—a measure, striking directly at the fundamental principle of the Constitution and deliberately passed to place on the statute book, and thereby to give legal sanction to a theory of the Constitution, utterly hostile to that entertained by us, and, I may add, almost the entire South. I rest not this assertion on inference. What I state, was openly avowed in debate, and among others by its leading advocate, the distinguished Senator from Massachusetts [Daniel Webster], who conceded that if the theory be true, that the Constitution is a compact, formed by the people of the several States, as distinct sovereign communities, and is binding between them as such, then would the bill be, as we have asserted it to be, directly opposed to the fundamental principles of the Constitution, and utterly subversive of that instrument; and that the bill could be vindicated only on the opposite view, which he maintained, and on which he advocated its passage—the view, which regarded the people of these States, as forming one nation, and the Government, as possessing the exclusive right of interpreting, in the last resort, its own powers; and thus practically substituting for the Constitution the will of the majority, with the right of assuming at discretion, whatever powers it might think proper, and to enforce their exercise, however oppressive and unconstitutional, at the point of the bayonet, or even with the noose of a halter. Such now is our Constitution as attempted to be established by an existing law of the land; and such will be the Constitution in fact, should this odious act not be resisted, till it be erased from the statute book. If it be not resisted—if by our acquiescence, the principles, on which it rests, be practically established, then will there be an end to our constitutional and limited Government, and, with it, to liberty and the Constitution, for to expect to preserve either, under such a Government, would be one of the vainest thoughts, that ever entered into the imagination of man.

The theory of our Constitution, which is thus attempted to be established by law—a theory, which denies, that the Constitution is a compact, between the States, and which traces all its powers to a majority of the American people, or, in other words, which denies the federal character of the Government, and asserts that it is a consolidated system, is of recent origin, avowed for the first time, but three years since, and first officially proclaimed and asserted, within the last few months. There was a party, it is said, in the Convention, which framed the Constitution, in favor of consolidation; but it is a fact perfectly established by the journals of its proceedings, that they were defeated in that design; and from the dissolution of that body, till the time stated, all parties, the federal, as well as the Republican, professed, at least, to believe, that ours was a federal system of Government, to use the language of Fisher Ames, one of the most zealous and distinguished of the former party, "a Republic of States, arrayed in a federal Union." The dangerous heresy, of which the odious Force Bill is the first fruit, after having been thus suppressed in the Convention, was revived, under the belief that it was the certain and effectual means of fixing on the country forever the unequal, unjust and unconstitutional system, which so long oppressed the Staple States, and is now placed among the acts of the Government for future use; like fetters forged and fitted to the limbs of the States, and hung up to be used, as occasion may hereafter require. If it be permitted to remain there quietly, the time will come, when it will be certainly employed for the use intended; and we may rest assured that an army of fifty thousand bayonets, encamped in the midst of the Staple States, would not half so certainly subject them to the will of a lawless, unchecked and unrestrained majority, who would not fail to wage a war under the colour of legislation on their property and prosperity, more oppressive and more degrading, than would be a tribute exacted by actual force.

But as formidable, as would be this measure, if acquiesced in, it may be easily overthrown, if promptly and spiritedly opposed, which I may add, would do more to restore the Constitution and reform the Government, than any other conceivable event. I found my belief, as to the facility, with which it may be overthrown, if properly opposed, on the character of the measure itself, its palpable unconstitutionality, in many particulars; its dangerous tendency; its novelty; the daring assumptions on one side and denial of facts on the other as necessary to sustain it, the absence of any direct and powerful pecuniary interest (as in the protective system,) to support it; but above all, on the deep conviction, which the weaker portion of the Union must shortly feel, if it does not already, of a concert of sentiment and action, not only to arrest the measures in question, but to guard against a recurrence of similar danger.

Another, and an important advantage, in this contest, will also result from the character of the measure. It will effectually separate the real, from the pretended friends of State Rights—a class that has done the cause of constitutional liberty more injury, than the most open and bitter opponents. To advocate or support the measure, is to be a consolidationist in the strongest and most odious sense, by whatever profession accompanied, and of course all who advocate and support it, will forfeit all claims to be ranked among the friends of State Rights.

Looking to the effects, which must follow its overthrow, we shall find much to animate us in the contest. The point at issue is not, whether this, or that particular policy of the General Government, be right, or wrong, but whether the General Government be a consolidated Government, of unrestricted powers, or a Federal Republic of States, with limited powers—an issue for the first time presented and on the decision of which depends the liberty and the Constitution of the country; and, I may add, the very existence of the Southern States. Let us not forget in this great contest, that we are acting, in maintaining the rights of the States, in our appropriate sphere of political duties, and that the due performance is not only essential to our security, but to the preservation of our System of Government.

On maintaining the balance between the delegated and reserved powers, as established in the Constitution, the success and duration of our novel and complex, but beautiful and perfect system of Government, obviously depends. Experience has now shown, where the pressure and benefit of that unequal monied action, which necessarily results from the fiscal operations of all governments, in a greater or less degree, falls. We now know, that the pressure must be ours, as the weaker party, at least in the present condition of the country. To those who profit by this unequal monied action, may be safely confided the defence of the delegated powers: and the passage of the Force Bill, as well as the history of the last sixteen years, clearly demonstrates, that there will be no lack of zeal, on their part, in the discharge of that duty. To us belongs the defence of the reserved powers; and if we but perform that high duty with the same zeal, on our part, the balance will be preserved, and the system be safe. In this conflict, between the two powers, the patronage of the General Government will necessarily be on the side of the stronger party, who will be in authority; and let us constantly bear in mind, that this great advantage cannot be countervailed, but by maintaining in full force and authority the reserved powers and the sovereignty of the States. Nor let us forget, that if the General Government and the delegated authority represent our power and majesty, that the sovereignty of the States and the reserved powers constitute the citadel of our liberty.

In this action and reaction of our system, between the two, let us not repine, at the part allotted us. If it has its disadvantages, it has also its advantages. What we lose, in a monied point of view, will be more than compensated in a moral and political point of view, if we but properly discharge our duty to our country and ourselves. To restrict the General Government to its proper sphere; to guard against the approaches of corruption; and to correct that tendency to despotic rule, so natural to Governments of every description; these are the high duties assigned to us, to perform which, the highest qualities, intellectual and moral, are required; but which, if faithfully performed, will certainly be followed by their acquisition—an acquisition in whatever light regarded worth more, than the wealth of the world.

Chapter XV.

Calhoun believed all agents of government should practice self-restraint. As part of a larger republican tradition, he began to see a damaging trend in President Jackson's abuse of the powers of appointment and removal as well as in his increasing disregard for the Senate's duty of advising and consenting to appointments. In arguing for a balance— defending the power of the president to appoint officials and asserting the need for the protection of officeholders against presidential whimsy—Calhoun offered a moderate and insightful critique of presidential power.

Mr. Calhoun said: The question involved in the third section of the bill, whether the power to dismiss an officer of the Government can be controlled and regulated by Congress, or is under the exclusive and unlimited control of the President, is no ordinary question, which may be decided either way, without materially affecting the character and practical operation of the Government. It is, on the contrary, a great and fundamental question, on the decision of which will materially depend the fact, whether this Government shall prove to be what those who framed it supposed it was—a free, popular, and republican Government, or a monarchy in disguise.

This important question, said Mr. C., has been very fully and ably discussed by those who have preceded me on the side I intend to advocate. It is not my intention to repeat their arguments, nor to enforce them by additional illustrations. I propose to confine myself to a single point of view; but that point I hold to be decisive of the question.

If the power to dismiss is possessed by the Executive, he must hold it in one of two modes: either by an express grant of the power in the constitution, or as a power necessary and proper to execute some power expressly granted by that instrument. All the powers under the constitution may be classed under one or the other of these heads; there is no intermediate class. The first question then is, Has the President the power in question by any express grant in the constitution? He who affirms he has, is bound to show it. That instrument is in the hands of every member; the portion containing the delegation of power to the President is short. It is comprised in a few sentences. I ask Senators to open the constitution, to examine it, and to find, if they can, any authority given to the President to dismiss a public officer. None such can be found; the constitution has been carefully examined, and no one pretends to have found such a grant. Well, then, as there is none such, if it exists at all, it must exist as a power necessary and proper to execute some granted power; but if it exists in that character, it belongs to Congress, and not to the Executive. I venture not this assertion hastily; I speak on the authority of the constitution itself—an express and unequivocal authority which cannot be denied nor contradicted. Hear what that sacred instrument says: "Congress shall have power to make all laws which shall be necessary and proper for carrying into execution the foregoing powers (those granted to Congress itself), and all other powers vested by this constitution in the Government of the United States, or in any department or officer thereof." Mark the fulness of the expression. Congress shall have power to make all laws, not only to carry into effect the powers expressly delegated to itself, but those delegated to the Government, or any department or officer thereof; comprehending, of course, the power to pass laws necessary and proper to carry into effect the powers expressly granted to the executive department. It follows that, to whatever express grant of power to the Executive the power of dismissal may be supposed to attach; whether to that of seeing the laws faithfully executed, or to the still more comprehensive grant, as contended for by some, vesting executive powers in the President, the mere fact that it is a power appurtenant to another power, and necessary to carry it into effect, transfers it, by the provisions of the constitution cited, from the Executive to Congress, and places it under its control, to be regulated in the manner which it may judge best. If there be truth in reasoning on political subjects, the conclusion at which I have arrived cannot be resisted. I would entreat gentlemen who are opposed to me, said Mr. C., to pause and reflect; and to point out, if possible, the slightest flaw in the argument, or to find a peg on which to hang a doubt. Can they deny that all powers under the constitution are either powers specifically granted, or powers necessary and proper to carry such into execution? Can it be said that there are inherent powers comprehended in neither of these classes, and existing by a sort of divine right in the Government? The Senator from New-York (Mr. Wright) attempted to establish some such position; but the moment my colleague touched it with the spear of truth, he, Mr. W., shrunk from the deformity of his own conception. Or can it be asserted that there are powers derived from obligations higher than the constitution itself? The very intimation of such a source of power hurled from office the predecessor of the present incumbent. But if it cannot be denied that all the powers under the constitution are comprised under one or the other of these classes, and if it is acknowledged, as it is on all sides, that the power of dismissal is not specifically granted by the constitution, it follows by an irresistible and necessary consequence, that the power belongs not to the Executive, but to Congress, to be regulated and controlled at its pleasure.

I should be gratified, said Mr. C., if any one who entertains an opposite opinion would attempt to refute this argument, and to point out wherein it is defective; for such perfect confidence do I feel in its soundness, that I will yield the floor to any Senator who may rise and say that he is prepared to refute it.

[Here Mr. Talmadge, from New-York, rose, and said that he was not satisfied with the argument, and would attempt to show its error. Mr. C. sat down for the purpose of giving him an opportunity, when Mr. T. began a formal speech on the subject generally, without attempting to meet Mr. C.'s argument, when the latter arose and said, that Mr. T. had mistaken him; that he did not yield the floor for the purpose of enabling Mr. T. to make a speech, but to enable him to refate the argument which Mr. C. had advanced; and that if Mr. T. was not prepared to do so, he, Mr. C., would proceed in the discussion (Crallé).]

Mr. C. proceeded, and said: The argument on which I have relied, has been alluded to by the Senator from Tennessee (Judge White), and my friend from Kentucky, who sits before me (Judge Bibb);—and the Senator from Tennessee (Mr. Grundy), whom I am sorry not to see in his place, attempted a reply. He objected to the argument, on the ground that the construction put upon the clause which has been quoted, would divest the President of a power expressly granted him by the constitution. I must, said Mr. C., express my amazement, that one so clear-sighted, and so capable of appreciating the just force of an argument, should give such an answer. Were the power of dismissal a granted power, the argument would be sound; but as it is not, to contend that the construction would divest him of the power, is an assumption, without the slightest foundation to sustain it. It is his construction, in fact, which divests Congress of an expressly granted power, and not ours which divests the President: by his, he would take from Congress the authority expressly granted, of passing all laws necessary and proper to carry into effect the granted powers, under the pretext that the exercise of such a power on the part of Congress would divest the Executive of a power nowhere granted in the constitution.

I feel, said Mr. C., that I must appear to repeat unnecessarily, what of itself is so clear and simple as to require no illustration; but I know the obstinacy of party feelings and preconceived opinions, and with what difficulty they yield to the clearest demonstration. Nothing can overthrow them but repeated blows.

Such, said Mr. C., are the arguments by which I have been forced to conclude, that the power of dismissing is not lodged in the President, but is subject to be controlled and regulated by Congress. I say forced, because I have been compelled to the conclusion in spite of my previous impressions. Relying upon the early decision of the question, and the long acquiescence in that decision, I had concluded, without examination, that it had not been disturbed, because it rested upon principles too clear and strong to admit of doubt. I remained passively under this impression, until it became necessary, during the last session, to examine the question—when I took up the discussion on it in 1789, with the expectation of having my previous impression confirmed. The result was different. I was struck, on reading the debate, with the force of the arguments of those who contended that the power was not vested by the constitution in the Executive. To me they appeared to be far more statesman-like than the opposite arguments, and to partake much more of the spirit of the constitution. After reading this debate, I turned to the constitution, which I read with care in reference to the subject discussed, when, for the first time, I was struck with the full force of the clause which I have quoted, and which, in my opinion, for ever settles the controversy.

I will now, said Mr. C., proceed to consider what will be the effect on the operation of the system under the construction which I have given. In the first place, it would put down all discretionary power, and convert the Government into what the framers intended it should be—a government of laws and not of discretion. If the construction be established, no officer from the President to the constable, and from the Chief Justice to the lowest judicial officer, could exercise any power but what is expressly granted by the constitution or by some act of Congress: and thus that, which in a free state is the most odious and dangerous of all things—the discretionary power of those who are charged with the execution of the laws—will be effectually suppressed, and the dominion of the laws be fully established.

It would, in the next place, unite, harmonize, and blend into one whole all the powers of the Government, and prevent that perpetual and dangerous conflict which would necessarily exist between its departments, under the opposite construction. Permit each department to judge of the extent of its own powers, and to assume the right to exercise all powers which it may deem necessary and proper to execute the powers granted to it, and who does not see that, in fact the Government would consist of three independent, separate, and conflicting departments, without any common point of union—instead of one united authority controlling the whole? Nor would it be difficult to foresee in what this contest between conflicting departments would terminate. The Executive must prevail over the other departments; for without its concurrence the action of the other departments are impotent. Neither the decrees of the Court nor the acts of Congress can be executed but through the executive authority; and if the President be permitted to assume whatever power he may deem to be appurtenant to his granted powers, and to decide according to his will and pleasure, and on his own responsibility, whether the decision of the Court or the acts of Congress are or are not consistent with the rights which he may arrogate to himself, it is impossible not to see that the authority of the legislative and judicial departments would be under his control. Nor is it difficult to foresee that if he may add the power of dismissal to that of appointment, and thus assert unlimited control over all who hold office, he would find but little difficulty in maintaining himself in the most extravagant assumptions of power. We are not without experience on this subject. To what but to the false and dangerous doctrine against which I am contending, and into which the present Chief Magistrate has fallen, are we to attribute the frequent conflicts between the Executive and the other departments of the Government; and which so strongly illustrate the truth of what I have stated? Under the opposite and true view of our system, all these dangerous jars and conflicts would cease. It unites the whole into one, and the legislative becomes, as it ought to be, the centre of the system,— the stomach, and the brain,—into which all is taken, digested, and assimilated, and by which the action of the whole is regulated by a common intelligence; and this without destroying the distinct and independent functions of the parts. Each is left in possession of the powers expressly granted by the constitution, and which may be executed without the aid of the legislative department, and, in the exercise of which, there is no possibility of coming into conflict with the other departments; while all discretionary powers necessary to execute the granted, and in the exercise of which the separate departments would necessarily come into conflict, are by a wise and beautiful provision of the constitution transferred to Congress, to be exercised solely according to its discretion;—thus avoiding, as far as the departments of the Government are concerned, the possibility of collision between the parts. By a provision no less wise, this union of power in Congress is so regulated as to prevent the legislative from absorbing the other departments of the Government. To guard the Executive against the encroachments of Congress, the President is raised from his mere ministerial functions to a participation in the enactment of laws. By a provision in the constitution, his approval is required to the acts of Congress; and his veto, given him as a shield to protect him against the encroachments of the legislative department, can arrest the acts of Congress, unless passed by two-thirds of both Houses. And here let me say, that I cannot concur in the resolution offered by my friend from Maryland (Mr. Kent), which proposes to divest the Executive of his veto. I hold it to be indispensable; mainly on the ground that the constitution has vested in Congress the high discretionary power under consideration, which, but for the veto, however necessary for the harmony and unity of the Government, might prove destructive to the independence of the President. He must indeed be a most feeble and incompetent Chief Magistrate if, aided by the veto, he would not have sufficient influence to protect his necessary powers against the encroachments of Congress. Nor is the judiciary left without ample protection against the encroachment of Congress. The independent tenure by which the judges hold their office, and the right of the Court to pronounce when a case comes before them upon the constitutionality of the acts of Congress, as far at least as the other departments are concerned, affords to the judiciary an ample protection. Thus all the departments are united in one, so as to constitute a single government, instead of three distinct, separate, and conflicting departments, without impairing their separate and distinct functions, while at the same time the peace and harmony of the whole are preserved.

There remains, said Mr. C., to be noticed another consequence not less important. The construction for which I contend strikes at the root of that dangerous control which the President would have over all who hold office, if the power of appointment and removal without limitation or restriction were united in him. Let us not be deceived by names. The power in question is too great for the Chief Magistrate of a free state. It is in its nature an imperial power, and if he be permitted to exercise it, his authority must become as absolute as that of the autocrat of all the Russias. To give him the power to dismiss at his will and pleasure, without limitation or control, is to give him an absolute and unlimited control over the subsistence of almost all who hold office under Government. Let him have the power, and the sixty thousand who now hold employments under Government would become dependent upon him for the means of existence. Of that vast multitude, I may venture to assert that there are very few whose subsistence does not, more or less, depend upon their public employments. Who does not see that a power so unlimited and despotic over this great and powerful corps must tend to corrupt and debase those who compose it, and to convert them into the supple and willing instruments of him who wields it? And here let me remark, said Mr. C., that I have been unfairly represented in reference to this point. I have been charged with asserting that the whole body of office-holders is corrupt, debased, and subservient: with what views, those who make the charge can best explain. I have made no such assertion, nor could it with truth be made. I know that there are many virtuous and high-minded citizens who hold public office; but it is not, therefore, the less true that the tendency of the power of dismissal is such as I have attributed to it; and that if the power be left unqualified, and the practice be continued as it has of late, the result must be the complete corruption and debasement of those in public employment. What, Mr. C. asked, has been the powerful cause that has wrought the wonderful changes which history teaches us have occurred at different periods in the character of nations? What has bowed down that high, generous, and chivalrous feeling—that independent and proud spirit which characterized all free states in rising from the barbarous to the civilized condition, and which finally converted their citizens into base sycophants and flatterers? Under the operation of what cause did the proud and stubborn conquerors of the world, the haughty Romans, sink down to that low and servile debasement which followed the decay of the republic? What but the mighty cause which I am considering; the power which one man exercised over the fortunes and subsistence, the honor and the standing of all those in office, or who aspire to public employment? Man is naturally proud and independent; and if he loses these noble qualities in the progress of civilization, it is because, by the concentration of power, he who controls the government becomes deified in the eyes of those who live or expect to live by its bounty. Instead of resting their hopes on a kind Providence and their own honest exertions, all who aspire are taught to believe that the most certain road to honor and fortune is servility and flattery. We already experience its corroding operation. With the growth of executive patronage and the control which the Executive has established over those in office by the exercise of this tremendous power, we witness among ourselves the progress of this base and servile spirit, which already presents so striking a contrast between the former and present character of our people.

It is in vain to attempt to deny the charge. I have marked its progress in a thousand instances within the last few years. I have seen the spirit of independent men, holding public office, sink under the dread of this fearful power; too honest and too firm to become the instruments or flatterers of power, yet too prudent, with all the consequences before them, to whisper disapprobation of what, in their hearts, they condemned. Let the present state of things continue—let it be understood that none are to acquire the public honors or to obtain them but by flattery and base compliance, and in a few generations the American character will become utterly corrupt and debased.

Now is the time to arrest this fatal tendency. Much will depend upon the vote on the measure which is now before you. Should it receive the sanction of this body and the other branch of the legislature, and the principle be once established that the power of dismissal is subject to be regulated by the action of Congress, and is not, as is contended, under the sole control of the Executive, the danger which now menaces the destruction of our system may yet be arrested. The discretionary and despotic power which the President has assumed to exercise over all in public employment would be subject to the control of law; and public officers instead of considering themselves as the mere agents of the executive department, and liable to be dismissed at his will and pleasure without regard to conduct, would be placed under the protection of the law.

But it is objected by the Senator from Tennessee (Mr. Grundy), that the construction for which I contend, would destroy the power of the President, and arrest the action of the Government. I must be permitted to express my surprise, said Mr. C., that such an objection should come from that experienced and sagacious Senator. He seems entirely to forget that the President not only possesses executive powers, but also legislative; and that he is not only a Chief Magistrate, but also a part of the law-making power. Does he not recollect that the President has his veto; and that no law can be passed which would improperly diminish the authority which ought to belong to him as Chief Magistrate without his consent, unless passed against his veto by two-thirds of both Houses?—an event which it is believed has not occurred since the commencement of the Government, and the occurrence of which is highly improbable. How then can it be asserted, that the construction for which I contend would destroy the just authority of the President? Let it be established, and what would follow? Every proposition to regulate and control the power of dismissal would become a question of expediency, and would be liable to be assailed by all who might suppose that it would impair improperly the power of the Chief Magistrate. And seconded as they would be by the veto, if necessary, there could be but little danger that restrictions too rigid would be imposed on his authority. The Senator from Tennessee also objects that the measure would be impracticable, and asks with an air of triumph, what would the Senate do if the reasons of the President should be unsatisfactory? I do not, said Mr. C., agree with those who think that the Senate can or ought to continue to reject the nominations of the President in such cases, until the officer who has been dismissed shall be restored. I believe that course to be impracticable; and that, in such a struggle, the resistance of the Senate would be finally overcome. My hope is, that the fact itself that the President must assign reasons for removals, will go far to check the abuses which now exist. I cannot think that any President would assign to the Senate as a reason for removal, that the officer removed was opposed to him on party grounds. Such is the deceptive character of the human heart, that it is reconciled to do many things under plausible covering which it would not openly avow. But suppose there should be a President who would act upon the principle of removing on a mere difference of opinion without any other fault in the officer, and who would be bold enough to avow such a reason, Congress would not be at a less for a remedy, on the principles for which I contend. A law might be passed that would reach the case; it might be declared that the removal of the President, if his reasons should not prove satisfactory, should act merely as a suspension to the termination of the next ensuing session, unless filled by the advice and consent of the Senate.

The Senator from Tennessee has conjured up a state of frightful collision between the Executive and the dismissed officers, and has represented the Senate chamber as the arena where this conflict must be carried on. He says, if the President should be bound to assign his reasons, the party dismissed would of right have a claim to be heard as to the truth and correctness of those reasons, and that the Senate would have its whole time engrossed in listening to the trial. All this is mere imagination, if the President on his part should exercise the power of removal with the discretion and justice which he ought, and with which all the predecessors of the present Chief Magistrate have in fact exercised it. Does he suppose if a measure, such as is now before the Senate, had been in operation at the commencement of the Government, that the Father of his country—a man no less distinguished by his moderation than his wisdom, would have experienced the least embarrassment from its operation? Does he suppose that the dismissal of nine officers in eight years during his presidency, would have given all that annoyance to him and to this body, which the Senator anticipates from the measure? Would there have been any difficulty in the time of the elder Adams, either to himself or to the Senate, from the ten officers whom he dismissed during his presidency? Would any have been experienced during Mr. Jefferson's term of eight years, even with the forty-two whom he dismissed? Or in the presidency of Mr. Madison, that mild and amiable man, who, in eight years of great excitement, of which nearly three was a period of war, dismissed but five officers? Or, during the presidency of Mr. Monroe, who in eight years dismissed but nine officers? Or of the younger Mr. Adams, who in four years dismissed but two officers? I come now, said Mr. C., to the present administration; and here I concede, that with the dismissal of two hundred and thirty officers in the first year, and I know not how many since, the scene of trouble and difficulty both to the President and the Senate, which the Senator from Tennessee (Mr. Grundy) painted in such lively colors, might have occurred, had the measure been in operation. This, however, constitutes no objection to the measure, but to the abuse—the gross and dangerous abuse of the power of dismissal which it is intended to correct. It is a recommendation that it would impede and embarrass the abuse of so dangerous a power. The more numerous and powerful the impediments to such abuses, the better. I apprehend, said Mr. C., that the Senator from Tennessee (Mr. Grundy) entirely misconceives the operation of the measure under a discreet and moderate administration. Under such an one, the charges exhibited against an officer would be transmitted to the accused; would undergo a regular investigation in the presence of the party, and the accused would be heard in his own defence before the charge would be acted on. If sustained, and the officer be discharged, the whole proceedings would accompany the nomination of the successor as showing the grounds on which he was dismissed.

During the time, said Mr. C., that I occupied the place of Secretary of War under Mr. Monroe, two officers of the Government holding civil employments connected with that department, were dismissed for improper conduct; and in both cases the course which I have indicated was adopted. The officers were not dismissed until after a full investigation, and the reasons for dismission reduced to writing and communicated to them.

But the Senator from Tennessee (Mr. Grundy) further objects, that the construction for which we contend would concentrate all the powers of the Government in Congress, and would thus constitute the very essence of despotism, which consists, as he asserts, in uniting the powers of the three departments in one. I could, said Mr. C., hardly have anticipated, that one whose conceptions are so clear on most subjects would venture so bold an assertion. Has not the Senator reflected on the nature of the legislative department in our system? To make a law, it is necessary not only to have the participation of the two Houses, but that also of the Executive; except, indeed, in the case of a veto, when, as has been stated, the measure must be passed by two-thirds of both Houses. Does he not see from this, that to vest Congress, as the constitution has done, with all the discretionary power, is to vest the power not simply in the two Houses, but also in the President, and in fact to require the concurrence of both departments to the exercise of such high and dangerous powers, instead of leaving it to each separately, as would have been the fact without this wise provision! I will tell the Senator, that it is the doctrine for which he, and not that for which we contend, which leads to concentration—a doctrine which would leave to each department to assume whatever power it might choose, and which in its necessary effects, as has been shown, would concentrate all the powers of the Government in the Chief Magistrate. This process has been going on under our eyes rapidly for the last few years; and yet the gentleman who appears now to be so sensitive as to the danger of concentration, looks on with perfect indifference, not to say with approbation. We have, said Mr. C., lost all sensibility; we have become callous and hardened under the operation of those deleterious practices and principles which characterize the times. What a few years since would have shocked and roused the whole community, is now scarcely perceived or felt. Then the dismissal of a few inconsiderable officers, on party grounds as was supposed, was followed by a general burst of indignation; but now the dismissal of thousands, when it is openly avowed that the public officers are the "spoils of the victors," produces scarcely a sensation. It passes as an ordinary event. The present state of the country, said Mr. C., was then anticipated. It was foreseen, as far back as 1826, that the time would come when the income of the Government and the number of those in its employment would be doubled—and that the control of the President, with the power of dismissal, would become irresistible. All of which was urged as an inducement for reform at that early period; and as a reason why the administration then in power should be expelled, and those opposed to them should be elevated to their places. But now when this prophecy has been realized, we seem perfectly insensible of the danger to which the liberty and institutions of the country are exposed. Among the symptoms of the times, said Mr. C., which indicate a deep and growing decay, I would place among the most striking, the difference in the conduct of those who seek public employment before and after their elevation. In the language of the indignant Roman, they solicit offices in one manner and use them in another. And this remark was not more true of that degenerated state of the noblest of all the republics of antiquity, than it is of ours at the present time. It is not only, said Mr. C., a symptom of decay, but it is also a powerful cause.

When it comes to be once understood that politics is a game; that those who are engaged in it but act a part; that they make this or that profession, not from honest conviction or an intent to fulfil them, but as the means of deluding the people, and through that delusion to acquire power;—when such professions are to be entirely forgotten—the people will lose all confidence in public men; all will be regarded as mere jugglers—the honest and the patriotic as well as the cunning and the profligate; and the people will become indifferent and passive to the grossest abuses of power, on the ground that those whom they may elevate under whatever pledges, instead of reforming, will but imitate the example of those whom they have expelled.

I, said Mr. C., rejoice, however, that there are many who are counted in the administration ranks, who have a proper regard for the professions of the party while canvassing for power. I see the commencement of a separation between those who are disposed to go all lengths, to abandon all former principles in the support of power, and those who are not disposed to advance beyond the point where they now stand. Let those who are disposed to sustain the power of the Executive, however extravagant, reflect on what has occurred during the present discussion, and the manly and independent sentiments which have been expressed in the ranks of the administration itself, and they will see cause to halt in their course. They have pushed things as far as they can be pushed with safety—to push them further must end in division and overthrow.

But the Senator from New-York (Mr. Wright) regards all this alarm on account of the vast increase of executive power, as perfectly imaginary. He contends that the view drawn in the report of the committee, as to the extent of patronage, is greatly exaggerated; and for this purpose assails that part of the report which treats of the number of those in the employment of the Government and living on its bounty, as constituting one of the elements of Executive patronage. The Senator is possessed of clear perception and strong powers of discrimination, and I anticipated from the confident manner in which he expressed himself, that he had discovered some flaw or weakness in that portion of the report. He is not usually the man to make bold assertions without his proof; but I must say that, in this case, the Senator has disappointed me. What error or exaggeration has he discovered in the report? Has he shown the number stated to be greater than in reality it is? Has he shown that there is any error in the various heads under which they are classified? Or that there is a single class which does not contribute to swell the power and influence of the Executive? He has not even made an attempt to point out any error of the kind. He drew his number and classification from the report itself, and has not pre-

tended to show that there has been any over estimate on the part of the committee attached to any one of the classes. But though the Senator has not succeeded in showing an over estimate, he has labored strenuously, though I must
say unsuccessfully, to show that the patronage is far less than in reality it is. The
Senator would, for instance, have us lay aside the pensioners, as adding little or
nothing to the patronage of the Government! I had, said Mr. C., supposed that
he was too good a judge of human nature, not to know that the mere fact of
living on the bounty of Government, naturally disposes a man to take sides with
power. If to this we add the fact, that the pensioner is liable to have his pension
questioned, whether he is rightfully entitled to it or not, and that the decision
of this question, so important to him, rests with those in power; that there are
thousands who are seeking pensions who must look in the same direction for
the gratification of their wishes—to say nothing of the host of pension-agents,
in and out of Congress whose importance and influence with the people may
depend upon their success in obtaining pensions—we may realize the vast addition which so large a pension-list as ours is calculated to give to the patronage
of the Executive. I am informed, said Mr. C., that a single member, in one session, obtained upwards of three hundred and fifty pensions; and can the Senator doubt how much he was strengthened in his district by his success, when a
majority of those whom he so successfully served were probably voters? Taking every thing into consideration, so far from considering the pensions as an
inconsiderable source of influence and patronage, as the Senator would have us
believe, I am of the impression that it is among the most fruitful sources of both;
and that to the late extension of the number of pensioners, we may attribute the
strength of the administration in some of the States of the Union. I have great
respect for the Secretary of War and the Chief of the Pension Bureau, and I do
not wish to be considered as making any personal imputations.

The Senator from New-York next tells us that the army contributes very
little to the influence and patronage of the Executive; that it consists principally
of soldiers, and those for the most part located on the frontiers, far removed
from the scenes of political struggles. The Senator would seem to have very
imperfect conceptions of the nature of the influence which an army brings to a
government. Is he ignorant that it is to be fed, and clothed, and housed, and
removed at the expense of millions, wherever employed? and that all this heavy
expenditure must bring a corresponding increase of power and influence? I, for
my part, said Mr. C., consider an army among a spirited people, armed and
accustomed to the use of arms as the Americans are, as far more dangerous on
account of the patronage which it brings to the Government, than on account

of its physical force, and it is mainly under this impression, that I have ever been opposed to its increase beyond the point necessary to preserve proper military organization and skill.

The Senator, taking the same fallacious view, would put the navy out of the list, as contributing but little to the patronage of the Government. What I have said in reference to the army is equally applicable to the navy, and supersedes the necessity of saying more on the subject.

But the final objection of the Senator implies that the power and patronage of the Government would be great, as far as the number of officers who are employed may contribute to it, if they were all custom-house officers, and some other classes of officers, which he estimates at some three or four thousand, and which he admits are calculated to exercise some influence. I acknowledge, said Mr. Calhoun, they are not so powerful as they would be if they consisted of the classes referred to by the Senator; but let me tell him, that if we had a corps of one hundred thousand such, the friends of liberty might surrender in despair—our cause would be hopeless! The people could not resist them for six months.

I have now, said Mr. C., concluded what I intended to say on the question involved in the third section of the bill, and will next proceed to notice some objections to the other portions. The Senator from Tennessee (Mr. Grundy) objects to the first section, which proposes to repeal the Four Years' Law, on the ground that it would diminish the power of the Senate, and increase that of the President. If such was the fact, the last quarter from which I should expect such an objection would be that from which it comes. But the Senator may dismiss his fears. There is not the slightest ground for the apprehension which he professes. It is true that, without that law, the Senate would not have the opportunity of passing on the conduct of the officers who may be renominated under it; but let me bring the Senator to reflect how little influence that fact gives to the Senate, compared to the influence which the President acquires by the law over all those who must depend on him under its provisions, for a renomination. Let him reflect how few of those renominated are rejected by the Senate, compared to those whom the President has refused to nominate; and how little influence the Senate acquires, or the President loses, by the rejection of the former. Should the Senate reject on party grounds, it has no power to fill the place of the person rejected—that depends upon the President. What, then, is the fact? The Senate makes an enemy without acquiring a friend, while the President is sure to acquire two friends without making an enemy—the rejected and the one who fills his place. If to this we add, that the present President has made it an invariable practice to reward, in some shape or other, every man rejected by the Senate, however good the cause for rejection, it must be obvious that the apprehension of the Senator from Tennessee, that the repeal of the Four Years' Law would weaken the Senate and strengthen the Executive, is without foundation. He may dismiss all anxiety on that head.

But it is further objected that the repeal of the Four Years' Law would destroy the principle of rotation in office, which the Senator from Maine (Mr. Shepley), and some others on the same side, represent as the very basis of republican institutions. We often, said Mr. C., confound things that are entirely dissimilar, by not making the proper distinction. I will not undertake to inquire now whether the principle of rotation, as applied to the ordinary ministerial officers of a government, may not be favorable to popular and free institutions, when such officers are chosen by the people themselves. It certainly would have a tendency to cause those who desire office, when the choice is in the people, to seek their favor; but certain it is, that in a Government where the Chief Magistrate has the filling of vacancies instead of the people, there will be an opposite tendency—to court the favor of him who has the disposal of offices—and this for the very reason that when the choice is in the people their favor is courted. If the latter has a popular tendency, it is no less certain that the former must have a contrary one. I, for my part, must say, that, according to my conception, the true principle is, to render those who are charged with mere ministerial offices secure in their places, so long as they continue to discharge their duty with ability and integrity; and I would no more permit the Chief Magistrate of a country to displace them without cause, on party grounds, than I would permit him to divest them of their freeholds: the power to divest them of the one is calculated to make them as servile and dependent as the power to divest them of the other.

I have now, said Mr. C., concluded what I intended to say. I have omitted several subjects which I was desirous of discussing connected with the highly important question which has so deeply occupied the attention of the Senate; but the session is so near a close that I feel the necessity of brevity, and will therefore forego what I would otherwise say.

Chapter XVI.

"Speech on the Bill to Regulate the Deposits of Public Money,"
28 May 1836

*Perhaps the most neglected aspect of Calhoun's thought is his contribution to eco-
nomics. The diligent labors of the Carolinian lead to the enactment of the Deposit Act,
which regulated and standardized the "pet banks" that proliferated in the country at the
end of the Jackson presidency. The act also forced the federal government to return excess
treasury funds to the states. For Calhoun, concentrated economic power threatened liberty
just as much as political consolidation.*

[After some remarks from Mr. Wright, in explanation, Mr. Calhoun said
(Crallé):]

This bill, which the Senator from New-York proposes to strike out, in order
to substitute his amendment, is no stranger to this body. It was reported at the
last session by the Select Committee on Executive Patronage, and passed the
Senate, after a full and deliberate investigation, by a mixed vote of all parties, of
twenty to twelve. As strong as is this presumptive evidence in its favor, I would,
notwithstanding, readily surrender the bill, and adopt the amendment of the
Senator from New-York, if I did not sincerely believe that it is liable to strong
and decisive objections. I seek no lead on this important subject; my sole aim is
to aid in applying a remedy to what I honestly believe to be a deep and dangerous disease of the body politic; and I stand prepared to co-operate with any
one, be he of what party he may, who may propose a remedy, provided it shall
promise to be safe and efficient. I, in particular, am desirous of co-operating
with the Senator from New-York, not only because I desire the aid of his distinguished talents, but, still more, of his decisive influence with the powerful

party of which he is so distinguished a member, and which now, for good or evil, holds the destinies of the country in its hands. It was in this spirit that I examined the amendment proposed by the Senator; and, I regret to say, after a full investigation, I cannot acquiesce in it, as I feel a deep conviction that it will be neither safe nor efficient. So far from being substantially the same as the bill, as stated by the Senator, I cannot but regard it as essentially different, both as to objects and means. The objects of the bill are: first, to secure the public interest as far as it is connected with the deposits; and, next, to protect the banks in which they are made against the influence and control of the executive branch of this Government, with a view both to their and the public interest. Compared with the bill, in respect to both, the proposed amendment will be found to favor the banks against the people, and the Executive against the banks. I do not desire the Senate to form their opinion on my authority. I wish them to examine for themselves; and, in order to aid them in the examination, I shall now proceed to state, and briefly illustrate, the several points of difference between the bill and the proposed amendment, taking them in the order in which they stand in the bill.

The first section of the bill provides that the banks shall pay at the rate of two per cent. per annum on the deposits for the use of the public money. This provision is entirely omitted in the amendment, which proposes to give to the banks the use of the money without interest. That the banks ought to pay something for the use of the public money, all must agree, whatever diversity of opinion there may be as to the amount. According to the last return of the treasury department, there was, on the first of this month, $45,000,000 of public money in the thirty-six depository banks, which they are at liberty to use as their own for discount or business, till drawn out for disbursements—an event that may not happen for years. In a word, this vast amount is so much additional banking capital, giving the same, or nearly the same, profit to those institutions as their permanent chartered capital, without rendering any other service to the public than paying away, from time to time, the portion that may be required for the service of the Government. Assuming that the banks realize a profit of six per cent. on these deposits (it cannot be estimated at less), it would give, on the present amount, nearly three millions of dollars per annum; and on the probable average public deposits of the year, upwards of two millions of dollars; which enormous profit is derived from the public by comparatively few individuals, without any return or charge, except the inconsiderable service of paying out the draughts of the treasury when presented. But it is due to the Senator to acknowledge that his amendment is predicated on the supposition that some disposition must be made of the surplus revenue, which would leave in the banks a sum not greater than would be requisite to meet the current expenditure: a supposition which must necessarily affect, very materially affect, the decision of the question as to the amount of compensation the banks ought to make to the public for the use of its funds. But, let the decision be what it may, the omission in the amendment of any compensation whatever is, in my opinion, wholly indefensible.

The next point of difference relates to transfer warrants. The bill prohibits the use of transfer warrants, except with a view to disbursement—while the amendment leaves them, without regulation, under the sole control of the treasury department. To understand the importance of this difference, it must be borne in mind that the transfer warrants are the lever by which the whole banking operations of the country may be controlled through the deposits. By them the public money may be transferred from one bank to another, or from one State or section of the country to another State or section; and thus one bank may be elevated and another depressed, and a redundant currency created in one State or section, and a deficient in another; and, through such redundancy or deficiency, all the moneyed engagements and business transactions of the whole community may be made dependent on the will of one man. With the present enormous surplus, it is difficult to assign limits to the extent of this power. The Secretary—or the irresponsible agent unknown to the laws, who, rumor says, has the direction of this immense power (we are permitted to have no certain information), may raise and depress stocks and property of all descriptions at his pleasure, by withdrawing from one place and transferring to another, to the unlimited gain of those who are in the secret, and the certain ruin of those who are not. Such a field of speculation has never before been opened in any country; a field so great, that the Rothschilds themselves might be tempted to enter it with their immense funds. Nor is the control which it would give over the politics of the country much less unlimited. To the same extent that it may be used to affect the interests and the fortunes of individuals, to the like extent it may be employed as an instrument of political influence and control. I do not intend to assert that it has or will be so employed; it is not essential at present to inquire how it has been or will be used. It is sufficient for my purpose to show, as I trust I have satisfactorily, that it may be so employed. To guard against the abuse of so dangerous a power, the provision was inserted in the bill to prohibit the use of transfer warrants, except, as stated, for the purpose of disbursement; the omission of which provision in the amendment is a fatal objection to it of itself, were there no other. But it is far from standing alone: the next point of difference will be found to be not less striking and fatal.

The professed object of both the bill and the amendment is, to place the safe-keeping of the public money under the regulation and control of law, instead of being left, as it now is, at the discretion of the Executive. However strange it may seem, the fact is nevertheless so, that the amendment entirely fails to effect the object which it is its professed aim to accomplish. In order that it may be distinctly seen that what I state is the case, it will be necessary to view the provisions of the bill and the amendment in reference to the deposit separately—as they relate to the banks in which the public funds are now deposited—and as to those which may hereafter be selected to receive them.

The bill commences with the former, which it adopts as banks of deposit, and prescribes the regulations and conditions on the observance of which they shall continue such; while, at the same time, it puts them beyond the control and influence of the executive department, by placing them under the protection of law so long as they continue faithfully to perform their duty as fiscal agents of the Government. It next authorizes the Secretary of the Treasury to select, under certain circumstances, additional banks of deposit, as the exigency of the public service may require, on which it imposes like regulations and conditions, and places, in like manner, under the protection of law. In all this, the amendment pursues a very different course. It begins with authorizing the Secretary to select the banks of deposit, and limits the regulations and conditions it imposes on such banks; leaving, by an express provision, the present banks wholly under the control of the treasury or the executive department, as they now are, without prescribing any time for the selection of other banks of deposit, or making it the duty of the Secretary so to do. The consequence is obvious. The Secretary may continue the present banks as long as he pleases; and so long as he may choose to continue them, the provisions of the amendment, so far as relates to the deposits, will be a dead letter; and the banks, of course, instead of being under the control of the law, will be—contrary, as I have said, to the professed object both of the bill and amendment—subject exclusively to his will.

The Senator has attempted to explain this difference, but, I must say, very unsatisfactorily. He said that the bill prohibited the selection of other banks; and, as he deemed others to be necessary, at certain important points, in consequence of the present enormous surplus, he inserted the provision authorizing the selection of other banks. The Senator has not stated the provisions of the bill accurately. So far from not authorizing, it expressly authorizes the selection of other banks where there are now none. But I presume he intended to limit his remarks to places where there are no existing banks of deposit. Thus limited, the fact is as he states; but it by no means explains the extraordinary omission (for such I must consider it) of not extending the regulations to the existing banks, as well as to those hereafter to be selected. If the public service requires additional banks at New-York and other important points, in consequence of the vast sums deposited there (as I readily agree it does); if no disposition is to be made of the surplus, it is certainly a very good reason for enlarging the provisions of the bill, by authorizing the Secretary to select other banks at those points; but it is impossible for me to comprehend how it proves that the regulations which the amendment proposes to impose should be exclusively limited to such newly-selected banks. Nor do I see why the Senator has not observed the same rule, in this case, as that which he adopted in reference to the compensation the banks ought to pay for the use of the public money. He omitted to provide for any compensation, on the ground that his amendment proposed to dispose of all the surplus money, leaving in the possession of the banks a sum barely sufficient to meet the current expenditure, for the use of which he did not consider it right to charge a compensation. On the same principle, it was unnecessary to provide for the selection of additional banks where there are now banks of deposit, as they would be ample if the surplus were disposed of. In this I understood the Senator himself to concur.

But it is not only in the important point of extending the regulations to existing banks of deposit that the bill and the amendment differ. There is a striking difference between them in reference to the authority of Congress over the banks of deposit embraced both in the bill and the amendment. The latter, following the provision in the charter of the late Bank of the United States, authorizes the Secretary to withdraw the public deposits, and to discontinue the use of any one of the banks whenever, in his opinion, such a bank shall have violated the conditions on which it has been employed, or the public funds are not safe in its vaults, with the simple restriction, that he shall report the fact to Congress. We know, from experience, how slight is the check which this restriction imposes. It not only requires the concurrence of both Houses of Congress to overrule the act of the Secretary, where his power may be improperly exercised, but the act of Congress itself, intended to control such exercise of power, may be overruled by the veto of the President, at whose will the Secretary holds his place; so as to leave the control of the banks virtually under the control of the executive department of the Government. To obviate this, the bill vests the Secretary with the power simply of withdrawing the deposits and suspending the use of the bank as a place of deposit; and provides that, if Congress shall not confirm the removal, the deposits shall be returned to the bank after the termination of the next session of Congress.

The next point of difference is of far less importance, and is only mentioned as tending to illustrate the different character of the bill and the amendment. The former provides that the banks of deposit shall perform the duties of commissioners of loans without compensation, in like manner as it was required of the late Bank of the United States and its branches, under its charter. Among these duties is that of paying the pensioners—a very heavy branch of disbursement, and attended with considerable expense, which will be saved to the Government under the bill, but will be lost if the amendment should prevail.

Another difference remains to be pointed out, relating to the security of the deposits. With so large an amount of public money in their vaults, it is important that the banks should always be provided with ample means to meet their engagements. With this view, the bill provides that the specie in the vaults of the several banks, and the aggregate of the balance in their favor with other specie-paying banks, shall be equal to one-fifth of the entire amount of their notes and bills in circulation, and their public and private deposits—a sum believed to be sufficient to keep them in a sound, solvent condition. The amendment, on the contrary, provides that the banks shall keep in their own vaults, or the vaults of other banks, specie equal to one-fourth of its notes and bills in circulation, and the balance of its accounts with other banks payable on demand.

I regret that the Senator has thought proper to change the phraseology, and to use terms less clear and explicit than those in the bill. I am not certain that I comprehend the exact meaning of the provision in the amendment. What is meant by specie in the vaults of other banks? In a general sense, all deposits are considered as specie; but I cannot suppose that to be the meaning in this instance, as it would render the provision in a great measure inoperative. I presume the amendment means special deposits in gold and silver in other banks, placed there for safe-keeping, or to be drawn on, and not to be used by the bank in which it is deposited. Taking this to be the meaning, what is there to prevent the same sum from being twice counted in estimating the means of the several banks of deposit? Take two of them—one having $100,000 in specie in its vaults, and the other the same amount in the vaults of the other bank, which, in addition, has, besides, another $100,000 of its own; what is there to prevent the latter from returning, under the amendment, $200,000 of specie in its vaults, while the former would return $100,000 in its own vaults, and another in the vaults of the other bank, making in the aggregate, between them, $400,000, when, in reality, the amount in both would be but $300,000?

But this is not the only difference between the bill and amendment, in this particular, deserving of notice. The object of the provision is to compel the banks of deposit to have, at all times, ample means to meet their liabilities; so that the Government should have sufficient assurance that the public moneys in their vaults would be forthcoming when demanded. With this view, the bill provides that the available means of the bank shall never be less than one-fifth of its aggregate liabilities, including bills, notes, and deposits, public and private; while the amendment entirely omits the private deposits, and includes only the balance of its deposits with other banks. This omission is the more remarkable, inasmuch as the greater portion of the liabilities of the deposit banks must, with the present large surplus, result from their deposits—as every one who is familiar with banking operations will readily perceive.

I have now presented to the Senate the several points of difference which I deem material between the bill and the amendment, with such remarks as may enable them to form their own opinion in reference to the difference, so that they may decide how far the assertion is true with which I set out, that, wherever they differ, the amendment favors the banks against the interests of the public, and the Executive against the banks.

The Senator, acting on the supposition that there would be a permanent surplus beyond the expenditures of the Government, which neither justice nor regard to the public interest would permit to remain in the banks, has extended the provisions of his amendment, with great propriety, so as to comprehend a plan to withdraw the surplus from the banks. His plan is to vest the commissioners of the sinking fund with authority to estimate, at the beginning of every quarter, the probable receipts and expenditures of the quarter; and if, in their opinion, the receipts, with the money in the treasury, should exceed the estimated expenditure by a certain sum, say $5,000,000, the excess should be vested in State stocks; and if it should fall short of that sum, a sufficient amount of the stocks should be sold to make up the deficit. We have thus presented for consideration the important subject of the surplus revenue, and with it the question so anxiously and universally asked, What shall be done with the surplus? Shall it be expended by the Government, or remain where it is, or be disposed of as proposed by the Senator? or, if not, what other disposition shall be made of it? questions, the investigation of which necessarily embraces the entire circle of our policy, and on the decision of which the future destiny of the country may depend.

But before we enter on the discussion of this important question, it will be proper to ascertain what will be the probable available means of the year, in order that some conception may be formed of the probable surplus which may remain, by comparing it with the appropriations that may be authorized.

According to the late report of the Secretary of the Treasury, there were deposited in the several banks a little upwards of $33,000,000 at the termination of the first quarter of the year, not including the sum of about $3,000,000 deposited by the disbursing agents of the Government. The same report stated the receipts of the quarter at about $11,000,000, of which lands and customs yielded nearly an equal amount. Assuming for the three remaining quarters an equal amount, it would give, for the entire receipts of the year, $44,000,000. I agree with the Senator, that this sum is too large. The customs will probably average an amount throughout the year corresponding with the receipts of the first quarter, but there probably will be a considerable falling off in the receipts from the public lands. Assuming $7,000,000 as the probable amount, which I presume will be ample, the receipts of the year, subtracting that sum from $44,000,000, will be $37,000,000; and subtracting from this, $11,000,000, the receipts of the first quarter, would leave $26,000,000 as the probable receipts of the last three quarters. Add to this sum $33,000,000, the amount in the treasury on the last day of the first quarter, and it gives $59,000,000. To this add the amount of stock in the United States Bank, which, at the market price, is worth at least $7,000,000, and we have $66,000,000, which I consider as the least amount at which the probable available means of the year can be fairly estimated. It will, probably, very considerably exceed this amount. The range may be put down at between $66,000,000 and $73,000,000, which may be considered as the two extremes between which the means of the year may vibrate. But, in order to be safe, I have assumed the least of the two.

The first question which I propose to consider is, Shall this sum be expended by the Government in the course of the year? A sum nearly equal to the entire debt of the war of the Revolution, by which the liberty and independence of these States were established; more than five times greater than the expenditure of the Government at the commencement of the present administration,— deducting the payments on account of the public debt,—and more than four times greater than the average annual expenditure of the present administration, making the same deduction, extravagant as its expenditure has been. The very magnitude of the sum decides the question against expenditure. It may be wasted, thrown away, but it cannot be expended. There are not objects on which to expend it; for proof of which I appeal to the appropriations already made and contemplated. We have passed the navy appropriations, which, as liberal as they are admitted to be on all sides, are raised only about $2,000,000 compared with the appropriations of last year. The appropriations for fortifications, supposing the bills now pending should pass, will amount to about

$3,500,000, and would exceed the ordinary appropriations, assuming them at $1,000,000, which I hold to be ample, by $2,500,000. Add a million for ordance, seven or eight for Indian treaties, and four for Indian wars, and supposing the companies of the regular army to be filled as recommended by the war department, the aggregate amount, including the ordinary expenditures, would be between thirty and thirty-five millions, which would leave a balance of at least $30,000,000 in the treasury at the end of the year.

But suppose objects could be devised on which to expend the whole of the available means of the year, it would still be impossible to make the expenditure without immense waste and confusion. To expend so large an amount, regularly and methodically, would require a vast increase of able and experienced disbursing officers, and a great enlargement of the organization of the Government, in all the branches connected with disbursements. To effect such an enlargement, and to give suitable organization, placed under the control of skilful and efficient officers, must necessarily be a work of time; but, without it, so sudden and great an increase of expenditure would necessarily be followed by inextricable confusion and heavy losses.

But suppose this difficulty overcome, and suitable objects be devised, would it be advisable to make the expenditure? Would it be wise to draw off so vast an amount of productive labor, to be employed in unproductive objects—in building fortifications, dead walls, and in lining the interior frontier with a large military force, neither of which would add a cent to the productive power of the country?

The ordinary expenditure of the Government, under the present administration, may be estimated, say at $18,000,000, a sum exceeding by five or six millions what, in my opinion, is sufficient for a just and efficient administration of the Government. Taking eighteen from sixty-six would leave forty-eight millions as the surplus, if the affairs of the Government had been so administered as to avoid the heavy expenditures of the year, which I firmly believe, by early and prudent management, might have been effected. The expenditure of this sum, estimating labor at $20 a month, would require 200,000 operatives, equal to one-third of the whole number of laborers employed in producing the great staple of our country, which is spreading wealth and prosperity over the land, and controlling, in a great measure, the commerce and manufactures of the world. But take what will be the actual surplus, and estimate that at half the sum which, with prudence and economy, it might have been, and it would require the subtraction of 100,000 operatives from their present useful employment, to be employed in the unproductive service of the Government. Would it, I again repeat, be wise to draw off this immense mass of productive labor, in order to employ it in building fortifications and swelling the military establishment of the country? Would it add to the strength of the Union, or give increased security to its liberty, or accelerate its prosperity? the great objects for which the Government was constituted.

To ascertain how the strength of any country may be best developed, its peculiar state and condition must be taken into consideration. Looking to ours with this view, who can doubt that, next to our free institutions, the main source of our growing greatness and power is to be found in our great and astonishing increase of numbers, wealth, and facility of intercourse? If we desire to see our country powerful, we ought to avoid any measure opposed to their development, and, in particular, to make the smallest possible draught, consistent with our peace and security, on the productive powers of the country. Let these have the freest possible play. Leave the resources of individuals under their own direction, to be employed in advancing their own and their country's wealth and prosperity, with the extraction of the least amount required for the expenditure of the Government; and draw off not a single laborer from his present productive pursuits to the unproductive employment of the Government, excepting such as the public service may render indispensable. Who can doubt that such a policy would add infinitely more to the power and strength of the country than the extravagant schemes of spending millions on fortifications and the increase of the military establishment?

Let us next examine how the liberty of the country may be affected by the scheme of disposing of the surplus by disbursements. And here I would ask, Is the liberty of the country at present in a secure and stable condition? and, if not, by what is it endangered? and will an increase of disbursements augment or diminish the danger.

Whatever may be the diversity of opinion on other points, there is not an intelligent individual of any party, who regards his reputation, that will venture to deny that the liberty of the country is at this time more insecure and unstable than it ever has been. We all know that there is in every portion of the Union, and with every party, a deep feeling that our political institutions are undergoing a great and hazardous change. Nor is the feeling much less strong, that the vast increase of the patronage and influence of the Government is the cause of the great and fearful change which is so extensively affecting the character of our people and institutions. The effect of increasing the expenditures at this time, so as to absorb the surplus, would be to double the number of those who live, or expect to live, by the Government, and, in the same degree, to augment its patronage and influence, and accelerate that downward course which, if not arrested, must speedily terminate in the overthrow of our free institutions.

These views I hold to be decisive against the wild attempt to absorb the immense means of the Government by the expenditures of the year. In fact, with the exception of a few individuals, all seem to regard the scheme either as impracticable or unsafe; but there are others, who, while they condemn the attempt to dispose of the surplus by immediate expenditures, believe it can be safely and expediently expended in a period of four or five years, on what they choose to call the defences of the country.

In order to determine how far this opinion may be correct it will be necessary first to ascertain what will be the available means of the next four or five years; by comparing which with what ought to be the expenditure, we may determine whether the plan would, or would not, be expedient. In making the calculation, I will take the term of five years, including the present, and which will, of course, include 1840, after the termination of which, the duties above twenty per cent are to go off, by the provisions of the Compromise Act, in eighteen months, when the revenue is to be reduced to the economical and just wants of the Government.

The available means of the present year, as I have already shown, will equal at least $66,000,000. That of the next succeeding four years (including 1840) may be assumed to be 21,000,000 annually. The reason for this assumption may be seen in the report of the select committee at the last session, which I have reviewed, and in the correctness of which I feel increased confidence. The amount may fall short of, but will certainly not exceed, the estimate in the report, unless some unforeseen event should occur. Assuming, then, $21,000,000 as the average receipts of the next four years, it will give an aggregate of $84,000,000, which, added to the available means of this year, will give $150,000,000 as the sum that will be at the disposal of the Government for the period assumed. Divide this sum by five, the number of years, and it will give $30,000,000 as the average annual available means of the period.

The next question for consideration is, Will it be expedient to raise the disbursements during the period to an average expenditure of $30,000,000 annually? The first and strong objection to the scheme is, that it would leave in the deposit banks a heavy surplus during the greater part of the time,—beginning with a surplus of upward of thirty millions at the commencement of next year, and decreasing at the rate of eight or nine millions a year till the termination of the period. But, passing this objection by, I meet the question directly. It would be highly inexpedient and dangerous to attempt to keep up the disbursements at so high a rate. I ask, On what shall this money be expended? Shall it be expended by an increase of the military establishment? by an enlargement of the appropriations for fortifications, ordinance, and the navy, far beyond what is proposed for the present year? Have those who advocate the scheme reflected to what extent this enlargement must be carried to absorb so great a sum? Even this year, with the extraordinary expenditure upon Indian treaties and Indian wars, and with profuse expenditures in every other branch of service, the aggregate amount of appropriations will not greatly exceed $30,000,000, and that of disbursements will not, probably, equal that sum.

To what extent, then, must the appropriations for the army, the navy, the fortifications, and the like, be carried, in order to absorb this sum, especially with a declining expenditure in several branches of the service, particularly in the pensions, which, during the period, will fall off more than a million of dollars? But, in order to perceive fully the folly and danger of the scheme, it will be necessary to extend our view beyond 1842, in order to form some opinion of what will be the income of the Government when the tariff shall be so reduced, under the Compromise Act, that no duty shall exceed twenty per cent. ad valorem. I know that any estimate made at this time cannot be considered much more than conjectural; but still, it would be imprudent to adopt a system of expenditure now, without taking into consideration the probable state of the revenue a few years hence.

After bestowing due reflection on the subject, I am of the impression that the income from the imposts, after the period in question, will not exceed $10,000,000. It will probably fall below, rather than rise above, that sum. I assume as the basis of this estimate, that our consumption of foreign articles will not then exceed $150,000,000. We all know that the capacity of the country to consume depends upon the value of its domestic exports, and the profits of its commerce and navigation. Of its domestic exports it would not be safe to assume any considerable increase in any article except cotton. To what extent the production and consumption of this great staple, which puts in motion so vast an amount of the industry and commerce of the world, may be increased between now and 1842, it is difficult to conjecture; but I deem it unsafe to suppose that it can be so increased as to extend the capacity of the country to consume beyond the limits I have assigned. Assuming, then, the amount which I have, and dividing the imports into free and dutiable articles, the latter, according to the existing proportion between the two descriptions, would amount in value to something less than $70,000,000. According to the Compromise Act no duty after the period in question, can exceed twenty per cent, and the rates would range from that down to five or six per cent. Taking fifteen per cent as the average, which would be, probably, full high, and allowing for the expenses of collection, the net income would be something less than $10,000,000.

The income from public lands is still more conjectural than that from customs. There are so many, and such various causes in operation affecting this source of the public income, that it is exceedingly difficult to form even a conjectural estimate as to its amount, beyond the current year. But, in the midst of this uncertainty, one fact may be safely assumed, that the purchasers during the last year, and thus far during this, greatly exceed the steady, progressive demand for public lands, from increased population, and the consequent emigration to the new States and territories. Many of the purchases have been, unquestionably, upon speculation, with a view to resales; and must, of course, come into market hereafter in competition with the lands of the Government, and to that extent reduce the income from their sales. Estimating the demand for public lands even from what it was previous to the recent large sales, and taking into estimate the increased population and wealth of the country, I do not consider it safe to assume more than $5,000,000 annually from this branch of the revenue, which, added to the customs, would give for the annual receipts between fourteen and fifteen millions of dollars after 1842.

I now ask whether it would be prudent to raise the public expenditures to the sum of $30,000,000 annually during the intermediate period, with the prospect that they must be suddenly reduced to half that amount? Who does not see the fierce conflict which must follow between those who may be interested in keeping up the expenditures, and those who have an equal interest against an increase of the duties as the means of keeping them up? I appeal to the Senators from the South, whose constituents have so deep an interest in low duties, to resist a course so impolitic, unwise, and extravagant—and which, if adopted, might again renew the tariff, so recently thrown off by such hazardous and strenuous efforts, with all its oppression and disaster. Let us remember what occurred in the fatal session of 1828. With a folly unparalleled, Congress then raised the duties to a rate so enormous as to average one-half the value of the imports, when on the eve of discharging the debt, and when, of course, there would be no objects on which the immense income from such extravagant duties could be justly and constitutionally expended. It is amazing that there was such blindness then as not to see what has since followed—the sudden discharge of the debt, and an overflowing treasury, without the means of absorbing the surplus; the violent conflict resulting from such a state of things; and the vast increase of the power and patronage of the Government, with all its corrupting consequences.

We are now about to commit an error of a different character: to raise the expenditure far beyond all example, in time of peace, and with a decreasing revenue—which must, with equal certainty, bring on another conflict, not much less dangerous, in which the struggle will not be to find objects to absorb an overflowing treasury, but to devise means to continue an expenditure far beyond the just and legitimate wants of the country. It is easy to foresee that, if we are thus blindly to go on in the management of our affairs, without regard to the future, the frequent and violent concussions which must follow from such folly cannot but end in a catastrophe that will ingulf our political institutions.

With such decided objections to the dangerous and extravagant scheme of absorbing the surplus by disbursements, I proceed to the next question, Shall the public money remain where it now is? Shall the present extraordinary state of things, without example or parallel, continue—of a Government, calling itself free, exacting from the people millions beyond what it can expend, and placing that vast sum in the custody of a few monopolizing corporations, selected at the sole will of the Executive, and continued during his pleasure, to be used as their own from the time it is collected till it is disbursed? To this question there must burst from the lips of every man who loves his country and its institutions, and who is the enemy of monopoly, injustice, and oppression, an indignant *No*. And here let me express the pleasure I feel that the Senator from New-York, in moving his amendment, however objectionable his scheme, has placed himself in opposition to the continuance of the present unheard-of and dangerous state of things; and I add, as a simple act of justice, that the tone and temper of his remarks in support of his amendment, were characterized by a courtesy and liberality which I, on my part, shall endeavor to imitate. But I fear, notwithstanding this favorable indication in so influential a quarter, the very magnitude of the evil (too great to be concealed) will but serve to perpetuate it. So great and various are the interests enlisted in its favor, that I greatly fear all the efforts of the wise and patriotic to arrest it will prove unavailing. At the head of these stand the depository banks themselves, with their numerous stockholders and officers; with their $40,000,000 of capital, and an equal amount of public deposits, associated into one great combination extending over the whole Union, and under the influence and control of the treasury department. The whole weight of this mighty combination, so deeply interested in the continuance of the present state of things, is opposed to any change. To this powerful combination must be added the numerous and influential body who are dependent on banks to meet their engagements, and who, whatever may be their political opinions, must be alarmed at any change which may limit their discounts and accommodations. Then come the stock-jobbers, a growing and formidable class, who live by raising and depressing stocks, and who behold in the present state of things the most favorable opportunity of carrying on their dangerous and corrupting pursuits. With the control which the Secretary of the Treasury has over the banks of deposit, through transfer warrants, with the power of withdrawing the deposits at pleasure, he may, whenever he chooses, raise or depress the stock of any bank; and, if disposed to use this tremendous power for corrupt purposes, may make the fortunes of the initiated, and overwhelm in sudden ruin those not in the secret. To the stock-jobbers must be added speculators of every hue and form; and, in particular, the speculators in public lands, who, by the use of the public funds, are rapidly divesting the people of the noble patrimony left by our ancestors in the public domain, by giving in exchange what may, in the end, prove to be broken credit and worthless rags. To these we must add the artful and crafty politicians, who wield this mighty combination of interests for political purposes. I am anxious to avoid mingling party politics in this discussion; and, that I may not even seem to do so, I shall not attempt to exhibit, in all its details, the fearful, and, I was about to add, the overwhelming power which the present state of things places in the hands of those who have control of the Government, and which, if it be not wielded to overthrow our institutions and destroy all responsibility, must be attributed to their want of inclination, and not to their want of means.

Such is the power and influence interested to continue the public money where it is now deposited. To these there are opposed the honest, virtuous, and patriotic of every party, who behold in the continuance of the present state of things the almost certain convulsion and overthrow of our liberty. There would be found, on the same side, the great mass of the industrious and labouring portion of the community, whose hard earnings are extracted from them without their knowledge, were it not that what is improperly taken from them is successfully used as the means of deceiving and controlling them. If such were not the case—if those who work could see how those who profit are enriched at their expense—the present state of things would not be endured for a moment; but as it is, I fear that, from misconception, and consequent want of union and co-operation, things may continue as they are, till it will be too late to apply a remedy. I trust, however, that such will not be the fact; that the people will be roused from their false security; and that Congress will refuse to adjourn till an efficient remedy is applied. In this hope, I recur to the inquiry, What shall that remedy be? Shall we adopt the measure recommended by the Senator from New-York, which, as has been stated, proposes to authorize the Commissioners of the Sinking Fund to ascertain the probable income of each quarter, and, if there should be a probable excess above $5,000,000, to vest the surplus in the purchase of State stocks; but, if there shall be a deficiency, to sell so much of the stock previously purchased as would make up the difference?

I regret that the Senator has not furnished a statement of facts sufficiently full to enable us to form an opinion of what will be the practical operation of his scheme. He has omitted, for instance, to state what is the aggregate amount of stocks issued by the several States—a fact indispensable in order to ascertain how the price of the stocks would be affected by the application of the surplus to their purchase. All who are in the least familiar with subjects of this kind, must know that the price of stocks rises proportionably with the amount of the sum applied to their purchase. I have already shown that the probable surplus at the end of this year, notwithstanding the extravagance of the appropriations, will be between thirty and thirty-five millions; and, before we can decide understandingly, whether this great sum can with propriety be applied as the Senator proposes, we should know whether the amount of State stocks be sufficient to absorb it, without raising their price extravagantly high.

The Senator should also have informed us, not only as to the amount of the stock, but how it is distributed among the States, in order to enable us to determine whether his scheme would operate equally between them. In the absence of correct information on both of these points, we are compelled to use such as we may possess, however defective and uncertain, in order to make up our mind on his amendment.

We all know, then, that while several of the States have no stocks, and many a very inconsiderable amount, three of the large States (Pennsylvania, Ohio, and New-York) have a very large amount—not less in the aggregate, if I am correctly informed, than thirty-five or forty millions. What amount is held by the rest of the States is uncertain; but I suppose it may be safely assumed that, taking the whole, it is less than that held by those States. With these facts, it cannot be doubted that the application of the surplus, as proposed by the Senator, would be exceedingly unequal among the States, and that the advantage of the application would mainly accrue to these States. To most of these objections, the Senator, while he does not deny that the application of the surplus will greatly raise the price of stocks, insists that the States issuing them will not derive any benefit from the advance, and, consequently, have no interest in the question of the application of the surplus to their purchase.

If by States he means the governments of the States, the view of the Senator may be correct. They may, as he says, have but little interest in the market value of their stocks, as it must be redeemed by the same amount, whether that be high or low. But if we take a more enlarged view, and comprehend the people of the States as well as their government, the argument entirely fails. The Senator will not deny that the holders have a deep interest in the application of so large a sum as the present surplus to the purchase of their stocks. He will not deny that such application must greatly advance the price; and, of course, in determining whether the States having stocks will be benefited by applying the surplus as he proposes, we must first ascertain who are the holders. Where do they reside? Are they foreigners residing abroad? If so, would it be wise to apply the public money so as to advance the interests of foreigners, to whom the States are under no obligation but honestly to pay to them the debts which they have contracted? But if not held by foreigners, are they held by citizens of such States? If such be the fact, will the Senator deny that those States will be deeply interested in the application of the surplus, as proposed in his amendment, when the effects of such application must be, as is conceded on all sides, greatly to enhance the price of the stocks, and, consequently, to increase the wealth of their citizens? Let us suppose that, instead of purchasing the stocks of the States in which his constituents are interested, the Senator's amendment had proposed to apply the present enormous surplus to the purchase of cotton or slaves, in which the constituents of the Southern Senators are interested, would any one doubt that the cotton-growing or slaveholding States would have a deep interest in the question? It will not be denied that, if so applied, their price would be greatly advanced, and the wealth of their citizens proportionably increased. Precisely the same effect would result from the application to the purchase of stocks, with like benefits to the citizens of the States which have issued large amounts of stock. The principle is the same in both cases.

But there is another view of the subject which demands most serious consideration. Assuming, what will not be questioned, that the application of the surplus, as proposed by the amendment, will be very unequal among the States, some having little or none, and others a large amount of stocks, the result would necessarily be to create, in effect, the relation of debtor and creditor between the States. The States whose stocks might be purchased by the commissioners would become the debtors of the Government; and as the Government would, in fact, be but the agent between them and the other States, the latter would, in reality, be their creditors. This relation between them could not fail to be productive of important political consequences, which would influence all the operations of the Government. It would, in particular, have a powerful bearing upon the presidential election; the debtor and creditor States each striving to give such a result to the elections as might be favorable to their respective interests; the one to exact, and the other to exempt themselves from the payment of the debt. Supposing the three great States to which I have referred, whose united influence would have so decided a control, to be the principal debtor States, as would, in all probability, be the fact, it is easy to see that the result would be, finally, the release of the debt, and, consequently, a corresponding loss to the creditor, and gain to the debtor States.

But there is another view of the subject still more deserving, if possible, of attention than either of those which have been presented. It is impossible not to see, after what has been said, that the power proposed to be conferred by the amendment of the Senator, of applying the surplus in buying and selling the stocks of the States, is one of great extent, and calculated to have powerful influence, not only on a large body of the most wealthy and influential citizens of the States which have issued stocks, but on the States themselves. The next question is, In whom is the exercise of this power to be vested? Where shall we find individuals sufficiently detached from the politics of the day, and whose virtue, patriotism, disinterestedness, and firmness can raise them so far above political and sinister motives as to exercise powers so high and influential exclusively for the public good, without any view to personal or political aggrandizement? Who has the amendment selected as standing aloof from politics, and possessing these high qualifications? Who are the present commissioners of the sinking fund, to whom this high and responsible trust is to be confided? At the head stands the Vice-President of the United States, with whom the Chief-Justice of the United States, the Secretary of State, the Secretary of the Treasury, and the Attorney General, are associated; all party men, deeply interested in the maintenance of power in the present hands, and having the strongest motives to apply the vast power which the amendment would confer upon them, should it become a law, to party purposes. I do not say it would be so applied; but I must ask, Would it be prudent, would it be wise, would it be seemly, to vest such great and dangerous powers in those who have so strong a motive to abuse it—and who, if they should have elevation and virtue enough to resist the temptation, would still be suspected of having used the power for sinister and corrupt purposes? I am persuaded, in drawing the amendment, the Senator from New-York has, without due reflection on the impropriety of vesting the power where he proposes, inadvertently inserted the provision which he has; and that, on a review, he will concur with me, that, should his amendment be adopted, the power ought to be vested in others, less exposed to temptation, and, consequently, less exposed to suspicion.

I have now stated the leading objections to the several modes of disposing of the surplus revenue which I proposed to consider; and the question again recurs, What shall be done with the surplus? The Senate is not uninformed of my opinion on this important subject. Foreseeing that there would be a large surplus, and the mischievous consequences that must follow, I moved, during the last session, for a select committee, which, among other measures, reported a resolution so to amend the constitution as to authorize the temporary distribution of the surplus among the States; but so many doubted whether there would be a surplus at the time, that it rendered all prospect of carrying the resolution hopeless. My opinion still remains unchanged, that the measure then proposed was the best; but so rapid has been the accumulation of the surplus, even beyond my calculation, and so pressing the danger, that what would have been then an efficient remedy, would now be too tardy to meet the danger; and, of course, another remedy must be devised, more speedy in its action.

After bestowing on the subject the most deliberate attention, I have come to the conclusion that there is no other so safe, so efficient, and so free from objections as the one I have proposed, of depositing the surplus that may remain at the termination of the year, in the treasuries of the several States, in the manner provided for in the amendment. But the Senator from New-York objects to the measure, that it would, in effect, amount to a distribution—on the ground, as he conceives, that the States would never refund. He does not doubt but that they would refund, if called on by the Government; but he says that Congress will, in fact, never make the call. He rests this conclusion on the supposition that there would be a majority of the States opposed to it. He admits, in case the revenue should become deficient, that the Southern or staple States would prefer to refund their quota rather than to raise the imposts to meet the deficit; but he insists that the contrary would be the case with the manufacturing States, which would prefer to increase the imposts to refunding their quota, on the ground that the increase of the duties would promote the interests of manufactures. I cannot agree with the Senator that those States would assume a position so entirely untenable as to refuse to refund a deposit which their faith would be plighted to return, and rest the refusal on the ground of preferring to lay a tax, because it would be a bounty to them, and would consequently, throw the whole burden of the tax on the other States. But, be this as it may, I can tell the Senator that, if they should take a course so unjust and monstrous, he may rest assured that the other States would most unquestionably resist the increase of the imposts; so that the Government would have to take its choice, either to go without the money, or call on the States to refund the deposits. But I so far agree with the Senator as to believe that Congress would be very reluctant to make the call; that it would not make it till, from the wants of the treasury, it should become absolutely necessary; and that, in order to avoid such necessity, it would resort to a just and proper economy in the public expenditures as the preferable alternative. I see in this, however, much good instead of evil. The Government has long since departed from habits of economy, and fallen into a profusion, a waste, and an extravagance in its disbursements, rarely equalled by any free state, and which threatens the most disastrous consequences.

But I am happy to think that the ground on which the objection of the Senator stands may be removed, without materially impairing the provisions of the bill. It will require but the addition of a few words to remove it, by giving to the deposits all the advantages, without the objections, which he proposes by his plan. It will be easy to provide that the States shall authorize the proper officers to give negotiable certificates of deposit, which shall not bear interest till demanded, when they shall bear the usual rates till paid. Such certificates would be, in fact, State stocks, every way similar to that in which the Senator proposes to vest the surplus, but with this striking superiority—that, instead of being partial, and limited to a few States, they would be fairly and justly apportioned among the several States. They would have another striking advantage over his. They would create among all the members of the confederacy, reciprocally, the relation of debtor and creditor, in proportion to their relative weight in the Union; which, in effect, would leave them in their present relation, and, of course, avoid the danger that would result from his plan, which, as has been shown, would necessarily make a part of the States debtors to the rest, with all the dangers resulting from such relation.

The next objection of the Senator is to the ratio of distribution, proposed in the bill, among the States, which he pronounces to be unequal, if not unconstitutional. He insists that the true principle would be, to distribute the surplus among the States in proportion to the representation in the House of Representatives, without including the Senators, as is proposed in the bill—for which he relies on the fact, that, by the constitution, representation and taxation are to be apportioned in the same manner among the States.

The Senate will see that the effect of adopting the ratio supported by the Senator would be to favor the large States, while that in the bill will be more favorable to the small.

The State I in part represent, occupies a neutral position between the two. She cannot be considered either a large or a small State, forming, as she does, one twenty-fourth part of the Union; and, of course, it is the same to her whichever ratio may be adopted. But I prefer the one contained in my amendment, on the ground that it represents the relative weight of the States in the Government. It is the weight assigned to them in the choice of the President and Vice-President in the electoral college, and, of course, in the administration of the laws. It is also that assigned to them in the making of the laws by the action of the two Houses, and corresponds very nearly to their weight in the judicial department of the Government—the judges being nominated by the President and confirmed by the Senate. In addition, I was influenced, in selecting the ratio, by the belief that it was a wise and magnanimous course, in case of doubt, to favor the weaker members of the confederacy. The larger can always take care of themselves; and, to avoid jealousy and improper feelings, ought to act liberally towards the weaker members of the confederacy. To which may be added, that I am of the impression—even on the principle assumed by the Senator, that the distribution of the surplus ought to be apportioned on the ratio of direct taxation (which may be well doubted)—the ratio which I support would conform, in practice, more nearly to the principle than that which he supports. It is a fact not generally known, that representation in the other House, and direct taxes, should they be laid, would be very far from being equal, although the constitution provides that they shall be. The inequality would result from the mode of apportioning the representatives. Instead of apportioning them among the States, as near as may be, as directed by the constitution, an artificial mode of distribution has been adopted, which, in its effects, gives to the large States a greater, and to the small a less number, than that to which they are entitled. I would refer those who may desire to understand how this inequality is effected, to the discussion in this body on the apportionment bill under the last census. So great is this inequality, that, were a direct tax to be laid, New-York, for instance, would have at least three members more than her apportionment of the tax would require. The ratio which I have proposed would, I admit, produce as great an inequality in favor of some of the small States—particularly the old, whose population is nearly stationary; but among the new and growing members of the confederacy, which constitute the greater portion of the small States, it would not give a larger share of the deposits than what they would be entitled to on the principle of direct taxes. But the objection of the Senator to the ratio of distribution, like his objection to the condition on which the bill proposes to make it, is a matter of small comparative consequence. I am prepared, in the spirit of concession, to adopt either, as one or the other may be more acceptable to the Senate.

It now remains to compare the disposition of the surplus proposed in the bill with the others I have discussed; and unless I am greatly deceived, it possesses great advantages over them. Compared with the scheme of expending the surplus, its advantages are, that it would avoid the extravagance and waste which must result from suddenly more than quadrupling the expenditures, without a corresponding organization in the disbursing department of the Government to enforce economy and responsibility. It would also avoid the diversion of so large a portion of the industry of the country from its present useful direction to unproductive objects, with heavy loss to the wealth and prosperity of the country, as has been shown;—while it would, at the same time, avoid the increase of the patronage and influence of the Government, with all their corruption and danger to the liberty and institutions of the country. But its advantages would not be limited simply to avoiding the evil of extravagant and useless disbursements. It would confer positive benefits, by enabling the States to discharge their debts, and complete a system of internal improvements, by railroads and canals, which would not only greatly strengthen the bonds of the confederacy, but increase its power, by augmenting infinitely our resources and prosperity.

I do not deem it necessary to compare the disposition of the surplus which is proposed in the bill with the dangerous, and, I must say, wicked scheme of leaving the public funds where they are, in the banks of deposit, to be loaned out by those institutions to speculators and partisans, without authority or control of law.

Compared with the plan proposed by the Senator from New-York, it is sufficient, to prove its superiority, to say that, while it avoids all the objections to which his is liable, it at the same time possesses all the advantages, with others peculiar to itself. Among these, one of the most prominent is, that it provides the only efficient remedy for the deep-seated disease which now afflicts the body politic, and which threatens to terminate so fatally, unless it be speedily and effectually arrested.

All who have reflected on the nature of our complex system of government, and the dangers to which it is exposed, have seen that it is susceptible, from its structure, to two dangers of an opposite character—one threatening consolidation, and the other anarchy and dissolution. From the beginning of the Government, we find a difference of opinion among the wise and patriotic as to which the Government was most exposed: one part believing the danger was, that the Government would absorb the reserved powers of the States, and terminate in consolidation, while the other were equally confident that the States would absorb the powers of the Government, and the system end in anarchy and dissolution. It was this diversity of opinion which gave birth to the two great, honest, and patriotic parties which so long divided the community, and to the many political conflicts which so long agitated the country. Time has decided the controversy. We are no longer left to doubt that the danger is on the side of this Government; and that, if not arrested, the system must terminate in an entire absorption of the powers of the States.

Looking back, with the light which experience has furnished, we now clearly see that both of the parties took a false view of the operation of the system. It was admitted by both, that there would be a conflict for power between the Government and the States, arising from a disposition on the part of those who, for the time being, exercised the powers of the Government and the States, to enlarge their respective powers at the expense of each other, and which would induce each to watch the other with incessant vigilance. Had such proved to be the fact, I readily concede that the result would have been the opposite of what has occurred, and the republican, and not the federal party, would have been mistaken as to the tendency of the system. But so far from this jealousy, experience has shown that, in the operation of the system, a majority of the States have acted in concert with the Government at all times, except upon the eve of political revolution, when one party was about to go out, to make room for the other to come in; and we now clearly see that this has not been the result of accident, but that the habitual operation must necessarily be so. The misconception resulted from overlooking the fact, that the Government is but an agent of the States, and that the dominant majority of the Union, which elect and control a majority of the State Legislatures, would elect also those who would control this Government;—whether that majority rested on sectional interests, on patronage and influence, or on whatever other basis, and that they would use the influence both of the General and State Governments jointly, for aggrandizement and the perpetuation of their power. Regarded in this light, it is not at all surprising that the tendency of the system is such as it has proved itself to be,—and which any intelligent observer now sees must necessarily terminate in a central, absolute, irresponsible, and despotic power. It is this fatal tendency that the measure proposed in the bill is calculated to counteract, and which, I believe, would prove effective if now applied. It would place the States in the relation in which it was universally believed they would stand to this Government at the time of its formation; and make them those jealous and vigilant guardians of its action on all measures touching the disbursements and expenditures of the Government, which it was confidently believed they would be; which would arrest the fatal tendency to the concentration of the entire powers of the system in this Government, if any thing on earth can.

But it is objected that the remedy would be too powerful, and would produce an opposite and equally dangerous tendency. I coincide that such would be the danger, if permanently applied; and, under that impression, and believing that the present excess of revenue would not continue longer, I have limited the measure to the duration of the Compromise Act. Thus limited, it will act sufficiently long, I trust, to eradicate the present disease, without superinducing one of an opposite character.

But the plan proposed is supported by its justice, as well as these high considerations of political expediency. The surplus money in the treasury is not ours. It properly belongs to those who made it, and from whom it has been unjustly taken. I hold it an unquestionable principle, that the Government has no right to take a cent from the people beyond what is necessary to meet its legitimate and constitutional wants. To take more intentionally would be robbery; and, if the Government has not incurred the guilt in the present case, its exemption can only be found in its folly—the folly of not seeing and guarding against a vast excess of revenue, which the most ordinary understanding ought to have foreseen and prevented. If it were in our power—if we could ascertain from whom the vast amount now in the treasury was improperly taken, justice would demand that it should be returned to its lawful owners. But, as that is impossible, the measure next best, as approaching nearest to restitution, is that which is proposed, to deposit it in the treasuries of the several States, which will place it under the disposition of the immediate representatives of the people, to be used by them as they may think fit, till the wants of the Government may require its return.

But it is objected that such a disposition would be a bribe to the people. A bribe to the people to return it to those to whom it justly belongs, and from whose pockets it should never have been taken! A bribe to place it in the charge of the immediate representatives of those from whom we derive our authority, and who may employ it so much more usefully than we can! But what is to be done? If not returned to the people, it must go somewhere; and is there no danger of bribing those to whom it may go? If we disburse it, is there no danger of bribing the thousands of agents, contractors, and jobbers, through whose hands it must pass, and in whose pockets, and those of their associates, so large a part would be deposited? If, to avoid this, we leave it where it is, in the banks,—is there no danger of bribing the banks in whose custody it is, with their various dependants, and the numerous swarms of speculators which hover about them in hopes of participating in the spoil? Is there no danger of bribing the political managers, who, through the deposits, have the control of these banks, and, by them, of their dependants, and the hungry and voracious hosts of speculators who have overspread and are devouring the land? Yes, literally devouring the land. Finally, if it should be vested, as proposed by the Senator from New-York, is there no danger of bribing the holders of State stocks, and, through them, the States which have issued them? Are the agents, the jobbers, and contractors; are the directors and stockholders of the banks; are the speculators and stock-jobbers; are the political managers and holders of State securities, the only honest portion of the community? Are they alone incapable of being bribed? And are the people the least honest, and most liable to be bribed? Is this the creed of those now in power? of those who profess to be the friends of the people, and to place implicit confidence in their virtue and patriotism?

I have now, said Mr. Calhoun, stated what, in my opinion, ought to be done with the surplus. Another question still remains: not what shall, but what will be done with the surplus? With a few remarks on this question, I shall conclude what I intended to say.

There was a time, in the better days of the republic, when to show what ought to be done was to insure the adoption of the measure. Those days have passed away, I fear, for ever. A power has risen up in the Government greater than the people themselves, consisting of many, and various, and powerful interests, combined into one mass, and held together by the cohesive power of the vast surplus in the banks. This mighty combination will be opposed to any change; and it is to be feared that, such is its influence, no measure to which it is opposed can become a law, however expedient and necessary; and that the public money will remain in their possession, to be disposed of, not as the public interest, but as theirs may dictate. The time, indeed, seems fast approaching, when no law can pass, nor any honor be conferred, from the Chief Magistrate to the tide-waiter, without the assent of this powerful and interested combination, which is steadily becoming the Government itself, to the utter subversion of the authority of the people. Nay, I fear we are in the midst of it; and I look with anxiety to the fate of this measure as the test whether we are or not.

If nothing should be done—if the money which justly belongs to the people be left where it is, with the many and overwhelming objections to it—the fact will prove that a great and radical change has been effected; that the Government is subverted; that the authority of the people is suppressed by an union of the banks and the Executive—an union a hundred times more dangerous than that of church and state, against which the constitution has so jealously guarded. It would be the announcement of a state of things from which, it is to be feared, there can be no recovery—a state of boundless corruption, and the lowest and basest subserviency. It seems to be the order of Providence that, with the exception of these, a people may recover from any evil. Piracy, robbery, and violence of every description may, as history proves, be followed by virtue, patriotism, and national greatness; but where is the example to be found of a degenerate, corrupt and subservient people, who have ever recovered their virtue and patriotism? Their lot has ever been the lowest state of wretchedness and misery: scorned, trodden down, and obliterated for ever from the list of nations. May Heaven grant that such may never be our doom!

CHAPTER XVII.

"FIRST SPEECH ON THE BILL FOR THE ADMISSION OF MICHIGAN,"
2 JANUARY 1837

The insightful speeches on the admission of Michigan into the Union are two of Calhoun's most important attempts to explain the nature of the republic. If the republic was composed of a "Union of States," and if the "relation of the citizens to this [federal] government is through the States exclusively," than the underlying principles of the country should be taken to heart. Congress had treated the Territory of Michigan as a state in some instances, but as a territory in others. This ambivalent position thwarted the people of Michigan's attempt to establish themselves as a sovereign entity. For Calhoun, the appropriate constitutional path was simple: "a Territory cannot be admitted till she becomes a State; and in this, I stand on the authority of the constitution itself, which expressly limits the power of Congress to admitting new States into the Union."

SEC. 2. *And be it further enacted,* That the Secretary of the Treasury, in carrying into effect the thirteenth and fourteenth sections of the twenty-third of June, eighteen hundred and thirty-six, entitled "An act to regulate the deposits of the public money," shall consider the State of Michigan as being one of the United States.

[Mr. Calhoun then rose and addressed the Senate as follows (Crallé):]

I HAVE bestowed on this subject all the attention that was in my power, and, although actuated by a most anxious desire for the admission of Michigan into the Union, I find it impossible to give my assent to this bill. I am satisfied the Judiciary Committee has not bestowed upon the subject all that attention which its magnitude requires; and I can explain, on no other supposition, why they should place the admission on the grounds they have. One of the committee, the Senator from Ohio on my left (Mr. Morris), has pronounced the grounds dangerous and revolutionary. He might have gone further, and with truth pronounced them utterly repugnant to the principles of the constitution.

I have not ventured this assertion, as strong as it is, without due reflection, and weighing the full force of the terms I have used; and do not fear, with an impartial hearing, to establish its truth beyond the power of controversy.

To understand fully the objection to this bill, it is necessary that we should have a correct conception of the facts. They are few, and may be briefly told.

Some time previous to the last session of Congress, the Territory of Michigan, through its Legislature, authorized the people to meet in convention, for the purpose of forming a State Government. They met accordingly, and agreed upon a constitution, which they forthwith transmitted to Congress. It was fully discussed in this Chamber, and, objectionable as the instrument was, an act was finally passed, which accepted the constitution, and declared Michigan to be a State, and admitted into the Union, on the single condition, that she should, by a convention of the people, assent to the boundaries prescribed by the act. Soon after our adjournment the Legislature of the State of Michigan (for she had been raised by our assent to the dignity of a State) called a convention of the people of the State, in conformity to the act—which met at the time appointed, at Ann Arbor. After full discussion, the convention withheld its assent, and formally transmitted the result to the President of the United States. This is the first part of the story. I will now give the sequel. Since then, during the last month, a self-constituted assembly met,—professedly as a convention of the people of the State,—but without the authority of the State. This unauthorized and lawless assemblage assumed the high function of giving the assent of the State of Michigan to the condition of admission, as prescribed in the act of Congress. They communicated their assent to the Executive of the United States, and he to the Senate. The Senate referred his message to the Committee on the Judiciary, and that committee reported this bill for the admission of the State.

Such are the facts out of which grows the important question. Had this self-constituted assembly the authority to assent for the State? Had they the authority to do what is implied in giving assent to the condition of admission? That assent introduces the State into the Union, and pledges it in the most solemn manner to the constitutional compact which binds these States in one confederated body; imposes on her all its obligations, and confers on her all its benefits. Had this irregular, self-constituted assemblage the authority to perform these high and solemn acts of sovereignty in the name of the State of Michigan? She could only come *in as a State,* and none could act or speak for her without her express authority; and to assume the authority without her sanction is nothing short of treason against the State.

Again: the assent to the conditions prescribed by Congress implies an authority in those who gave it, to supersede in part the constitution of the State of Michigan; for her constitution fixes the boundaries of the State as part of that instrument which the condition of admission entirely alters, and to that extent the assent would supersede the constitution; and thus the question is presented, whether this self-constituted assembly, styling itself a convention, had the authority to do an act which necessarily implies the right to supersede, in part, the constitution.

But further: the State of Michigan, through its legislature, authorized a convention of the people, in order to determine whether the condition of admission should be assented to or not. The convention met; and, after mature deliberation, it dissented from the condition of admission; and thus again the question is presented, whether this self-called, self-constituted assemblage, this caucus—for it is entitled to no higher name—had the authority to annul the dissent of the State, solemnly given by a convention of the people, regularly convoked under the express sanction of the constituted authorities of the State?

If all or any of these questions be answered in the negative—if the self-created assemblage of December had no authority to speak in the name of the State of Michigan—if none to supersede any portion of her constitution—if none to annul her dissent to the condition of admission regularly given by a convention of the people of the State, convoked by the authority of the State—to introduce her on its authority would be, not only revolutionary and dangerous, but utterly repugnant to the principles of our constitution. The question then submitted to the Senate is, Had that assemblage the authority to perform these high and solemn acts?

The chairman of the Committee on the Judiciary holds that this self-constituted assemblage had the authority; and what is his reason? Why, truly, because a greater number of votes were given for those who constituted that assemblage than for those who constituted the convention of the people of the State, convened under its constituted authorities. This argument resolves itself into two questions—the first of fact, and the second of principle. I shall not discuss the first. It is not necessary to do so. But if it were, it would be easy to show that never was so important a fact so loosely testified. There is not one particle of official evidence before us. We had nothing but the private letters of individuals, who do not know even the numbers that voted on either occasion; they know nothing of the qualification of voters, nor how their votes were received, nor by whom counted. Now, none knows better than the honorable chairman himself, that such testimony as is submitted to us to establish a fact of this moment, would not be received in the lowest magistrate's court in the land. But I waive this. I come to the question of the principle involved; and what is it? The argument is, that a greater number of persons voted for the last convention than for the first; and therefore the acts of the last of right abrogated those of the first; in other words, *that mere numbers,* without regard to the forms of law, or the principles of the constitution, give authority. *The authority of numbers, according to this argument, sets aside the authority of the law and the constitution.* Need I show that such a principle goes to the entire overthrow of our constitutional Government, and would subvert all social order? It is the identical principle which prompted the late revolutionary and anarchical movement in Maryland, and which has done more to shake confidence in our system of government than any event since the adoption of our constitution,—but which, happily, has been frowned down by the patriotism and intelligence of the people of the State.

What was the ground of this insurrectionary measure, but that the government of Maryland did not represent the voice of the numerical majority of the people of Maryland, and that the authority of law and constitution was nothing against that of numbers? Here we find, on this floor, and from the head of the Judiciary Committee, the same principle revived, and, if possible, in a worse form; for, in Maryland, the anarchists assumed that they were sustained by the numerical majority of the people of the State in their revolutionary movements; but the utmost the chairman can pretend to have is a mere plurality. The largest number of votes claimed for this self-created assemblage is 8,000; and no man will undertake to say that this constitutes any thing like a majority of the voters of Michigan: and he claims the high authority which he does for it, not because it is a majority of the people of Michigan, but because it is a greater number than voted for the authorized convention of the people that refused to agree to the condition of admission. It may be shown by his own witness, that a majority of the voters of Michigan greatly exceed 8,000. Mr. Williams, the president of the self-created assemblage, states that the population of the State amounted to nearly 200,000 persons. If so, there cannot be less than from 21,000 to 30,000 voters, considering how nearly universal the right of suffrage is under its constitution; and it thus appears that this irregular, self-constituted meeting, did not represent the vote of one-third of the State: and yet, on a mere principle of plurality, we are to supersede the constitution of Michigan, and annul the act of a convention of the people regularly convened under the authority of the government of the State.

But, says the Senator from Pennsylvania (Mr. Buchanan), this assembly was not self-constituted. It met under the authority of an act of Congress; and that act had no reference to the State, but only to the people; and that the assemblage in December was just such a meeting as that act contemplated. It is not my intention to discuss the question, whether the honorable Senator has given a plausible interpretation to the act; but, if he has, I could very easily show his interpretation to be erroneous; for, if such had been the intention of Congress, the act surely would have specified the time when the convention was to be held—who were to be the managers—who the voters—and would not have left it to individuals, who might choose to assume the authority to determine all these important points. I might also readily show that the word "convention" of the people, as used in law or the constitution, always means a meeting of the people regularly convened *by the constituted authority of the States,* in their high sovereign capacity, and never such an assemblage as the one in question. But I waive this; I take higher ground. If the act be, indeed, such as the Senator says it is, then I maintain that it is utterly opposed to the fundamental principles of our Federal Union. Congress has no right whatever to *call a convention in a State.* It can call but one convention, and that is a convention of the United States to amend the federal constitution; nor can it call that, except authorized by two-thirds of the States.

Ours is a Federal Republic—a union of States. Michigan is a State,—a State in the course of admission,—and differing only from the other States in her federal relations. She is declared to be a State in the most solemn manner by your own act. She can come into the Union only as a State; and by her voluntary assent, given by the people of the State in convention, called by the constituted authorities of the State. To admit the State of Michigan on the authority of a self-created meeting, or one called by the direct authority of Congress, passing by the authorities of the State, would be the most monstrous proceeding under our constitution that can be conceived; the most repugnant to its principles, and dangerous in its consequences. It would establish a direct relation between the individual citizens of a State and the General Government, in utter subversion of the federal character of our system. The relation of their citizens to this Government, is through the States exclusively. They are subject to its authority and laws only because the State has assented to it. If *she* dissents, *their* assent is nothing; on the other hand, if *she* assents, *their* dissent is nothing. It is through the State, then, and through the State alone, that the United States Government can have any connection with the people of a State; and does not, then, the Senator from Pennsylvania see, that if Congress can authorize a convention of the people in the State of Michigan, without the authority of the State—it matters not what is the object—it may in like manner authorize conventions in any other State for whatever purpose it may think proper.

Michigan is as much a sovereign State as any other—differing only, as I have said, as to her federal relations. If we give our sanction to the assemblage of December, on the principle laid down by the Senator from Pennsylvania, then we establish the doctrine that Congress has power to call, at pleasure, conventions within the States. Is there a Senator on this floor who will assent to such a doctrine? Is there one especially, who represents the smaller States of this Union, or the weaker section? Admit the power, and every vestige of State Rights would be destroyed. Our system would be subverted; and instead of a *confederacy of free and sovereign States,* we would have all power concentrated here, and this would become the most odious despotism. He, indeed, must be blind, who does not see that such a power would give the Federal Government a complete control of all the States. I call upon Senators now to arrest a doctrine so dangerous. Let it be remembered, that, under our system, bad precedents live for ever; good ones only perish. We may not feel all the evil consequences at once, but this precedent, once set, will surely be revived, and will become the instrument of infinite evil.

It will be asked, what shall be done? Will you refuse to admit Michigan into the Union? I answer, no: I desire to admit her; and if the Senators from Indiana and Ohio will agree, am ready to admit her as she stood at the beginning of the last session, without giving sanction to the unauthorized assemblage of December.

But if this does not meet their wishes, there is still another way, by which she may be admitted. We are told two-thirds of the legislature and people of Michigan are in favor of accepting the conditions of the act of last session. If that be the fact, then all that is necessary is, that the legislature shall call another convention. All difficulty will thus be removed, and there will be still abundant time for her admission at this session. And shall we, for the sake of gaining a few months, give our assent to a bill fraught with principles so monstrous as this?

We have been told that, unless she is admitted immediately, it will be too late for her to receive her proportion of the surplus revenue under the Deposit Bill. I trust that, on so great a question, a difficulty like this will have no weight. Give her at once her full share. I am ready to do so at once, without waiting her admission. I was mortified to hear, on so grave a question, such motives assigned for her admission, contrary to the law and the constitution. Such considerations ought not to be presented when we are settling great constitutional principles.

I trust that we shall pass by all such frivolous motives on this occasion, and take ground on the great and fundamental principle that an informal, irregular, self-constituted assembly—a mere caucus, has no authority to speak for a sovereign State in any case whatever; to supersede its constitution, or to reverse its dissent deliberately given by a convention of the people of the State, regularly convened under its constituted authorities.

XVIII.

VB

ADMISSION OF MICHIGAN,"

nmittee on the Judiciary, having moved
gan into the Union be now read a third

Mr. Calhoun addressed the Senate in opposition to the Bill (Crallé).]

I HAVE, said Mr. C., been connected with this Government more than half the term of its existence, in various capacities; and during that long period I have looked on its action with attention, and have endeavored to make myself acquainted with the principles and character of our political institutions,—and I can truly say that, within that time, no measure has received the sanction of Congress which has appeared to me more unconstitutional and dangerous than the present. It assails our political system in its *weakest point,* and where, *at this time, it most requires defence.*

The great and leading objections to the bill rest mainly on the ground that Michigan is a State. They have been felt by its friends to have so much weight, that its advocates have been compelled to deny the fact, as the only way of meeting the objections. Here, then, is the main point at issue between the friends and the opponents of the bill. It turns on a fact, and that fact presents the question, Is Michigan a State?

If, said Mr. C., there ever was a party committed on a fact—if there ever was one estopped from denying it—that party is the present majority in the Senate,—and that fact is, that Michigan is a State. It is the very party who urged through this body, at the last session, a bill for the admission of the State of

Michigan—which accepted her constitution, and declared in the most explicit and strongest terms that *she was a State*. I will not take up the time of the Senate by reading this solemn declaration. It has frequently been read during this debate, is familiar to all who hear me, and has not been questioned or denied. But it has been said there is a condition annexed to the declaration, with which she must comply, before she can become a State. There is, indeed, a condition; but it has been shown by my colleague and others, from the plain wording of the act, that the condition is not attached to the acceptance of the constitution, nor the declaration that she is a State, but simply to her *admission* into the Union. I will not repeat the argument, but, in order to place the subject beyond controversy, I shall recall to memory the history of the last session, as connected with the admission of Michigan. The facts need but to be referred to, in order to revive their recollection.

There were two points proposed to be effected by the friends of the bill at the last session. The first was to settle the controversy, as to boundary, between Michigan and Ohio; and it was this object alone which imposed the condition that Michigan should assent to the boundary prescribed by the act as the condition of her admission. But there was another object to be accomplished. Two respectable gentlemen, who had been elected by the State as Senators, were then waiting to take their seats on this floor; and the other object of the bill was to provide for their taking their seats as Senators on the admission of the State,— and for this purpose it was necessary to make the positive and unconditional declaration that Michigan was a State,—as a State only could choose Senators, by an express provision of the constitution; and hence the admission was made conditional, and the declaration that she was a State was made absolute, in order to effect both objects. To show that I am correct, I will ask the Secretary to read the third section of the bill.

[The section was read accordingly as follows:—

"SECT. 3. *And be it further enacted,* That, as a compliance with the fundamental condition of admission contained in the last preceding section of this act, the boundaries of the said State of Michigan, as in that section described, declared and established, shall receive the assent of a convention of delegates elected by the people of said State, for the sole purpose of giving the assent herein required; and as soon as the assent herein required shall be given, the President of the United States shall announce the same by proclamation; and thereupon, and without any further proceedings on the part of Congress, the admission of the said State into the Union, as one of the United States of America, on an equal footing with all the original States in every respect whatever, shall be considered as complete, and the Senators and Representatives who have been elected by the said State as its representative in the Congress of the United States, shall be entitled to take their seats in the Senate and House of Representatives respectively, without further delay" (Cralle).]

Mr. Calhoun then asked—Does not every Senator see the two objects—the one to settle the boundary, and the other to admit her Senators to a seat in this body; and that the section is so worded as to effect both, in the manner I have stated? If this needed confirmation, it would be found in the debate on the passage of the bill, when the ground was openly taken by the present majority, that Michigan had a right to form her constitution, under the ordinance of 1787, without our consent; and that she was of right, and in fact, a State, beyond our control.

I will, said Mr. C., explain my own views on this point, in order that the consistency of my course at the last and present session may be clearly seen.

My opinion was, and still is, that the movement of the people of Michigan in forming for themselves a State constitution, without waiting for the assent of Congress, was revolutionary, as it threw off the authority of the United States over the territory; and that we were left at liberty to treat the proceedings as revolutionary, and to remand her to her territorial condition,—or to waive the irregularity, and to recognize what was done as rightfully done,—as our authority alone was concerned.

My impression was, that the former was the proper course; but I also thought that the act remanding her back should contain our assent in the usual manner for her to form a constitution, and thus to leave her free to become a State. This, however, was overruled. The opposite opinion prevailed,—that she had a perfect right to do what she had done, and that she was, as I have stated, a State both in fact and right, and that we had no control over her; and our act accordingly recognized her as a State, from the time she had adopted her constitution, and admitted her into the Union on the condition of her assenting to the prescribed boundaries. Having thus solemnly recognized her as a State, we cannot now undo what was then done. There were, in fact, many irregularities in the proceedings, all of which were urged in vain against its passage; but the Presidential election was then pending, and the vote of Michigan was considered of sufficient weight to overrule all objections, and correct all irregularities. They were all accordingly overruled, and we cannot now go back.

Such was the course, and such the acts of the majority at the last session. A few short months have since passed. Other objects are now to be effected, and all is forgotten as completely as if they had never existed. The very Senators who then forced the act through, on the ground that Michigan was a State, have wheeled completely round, to serve the present purpose, and taken directly the opposite ground! We live in strange and inconsistent times. Opinions are taken up and laid down, as suits the occasion, without hesitation, or the slightest regard to principle or consistency. It indicates an unsound state of the public mind, pregnant with future disasters.

I turn to the position now assumed by the majority to suit the present occasion; and, if I mistake not, it will be found as false in fact, and as erroneous in principle, as it is inconsistent with that maintained at the last session. They now take the ground, that Michigan is not a State, and cannot, in fact, be a State till she is admitted into the Union; and this on the broad principle that a territory cannot become a State till admitted. Such is the position distinctly taken by several of the friends of this bill, and implied in the arguments of nearly all who have spoken in its favor. In fact, its advocates had no choice. As untenable as it is, they were forced on this desperate position. They had no other which they could occupy.

I have shown that it is directly in the face of the law of the last session, and that it denies the recorded acts of those who now maintain it. I now go further, and assert that it is in direct opposition to plain and unquestionable matter of fact. There is no fact more certain than that Michigan is a State. She is in the full exercise of sovereign authority, with a legislature and a chief magistrate. She passes laws; she executes them; she regulates titles; and even takes away life—all on her own authority. Ours has entirely ceased over her; and yet there are those who can deny, with all these facts before them, that she is a State. They might as well deny the existence of this Hall! We have long since assumed unlimited control over the constitution, to twist, and turn, and deny it, as it suited our purpose;—and it would seem that we are presumptuously attempting to assume like supremacy over facts themselves, as if their existence or non-existence depended on our volition. I speak freely. The occasion demands that the truth should be boldly uttered.

But those who may not regard their own recorded acts, nor the plain facts of the case, may possibly feel the awkward condition in which coming events may shortly place them. The admission of Michigan is not the only point involved in the passage of this bill. A question will follow,—which may be presented to the Senate in a very few days,—as to the right of Mr. Norvell and Mr. Lyon, the two respectable gentlemen who have been elected Senators of Michigan, to take their seats in this Hall. The decision of this question will require a more sudden facing about than has been yet witnessed. It required seven or eight months for the majority to wheel about from the position maintained at the last session to that taken at this, but there may not be allowed them now as many days to wheel back to the old position. These gentlemen cannot be refused their seats after the admission of the State by those gentlemen who passed the act of the last session. It provides for the case. I now put it to the friends of this bill, and I ask them to weigh the question deliberately—to bring it home to their bosoms and consciences before they answer—Can a territory elect Senators to Congress? The constitution is express; *States* only can choose Senators. Were not these gentlemen chosen long before the admission of Michigan; before the Ann Arbor meeting, and while Michigan was, according to the doctrines of the friends of this bill, a territory? Will they, in the face of the constitution, which they are sworn to support, admit as Senators on this floor those who, by their own statement, were elected by a territory? These questions may soon be presented for decision. The majority, who are forcing this bill through, are already committed by the act of the last session, and I leave them to reconcile, as they can, the ground they now take with the vote they must give when the question of their right to take their seats is presented for decision.

A total disregard of all principle and consistency has so entangled this subject, that there is but one mode left of extricating ourselves without trampling the constitution in the dust; and that is, to return back to where we stood when the question was first presented; to acquiesce in the right of Michigan to form a constitution, and erect herself into a State, under the ordinance of 1787; and to repeal so much of the act of the last session as prescribed the condition on which she was to be admitted. This was the object of the amendment which I offered last evening, in order to relieve the Senate from its present dilemma. The amendment involved the merits of the whole case. It was too late in the day for discussion, and I asked for indulgence till to-day, that I might have an opportunity of presenting my views. Under the iron rule of the present majority, the indulgence was refused, and the bill ordered to its third reading; and I have been thus compelled to address the Senate when it is too late to amend the bill, and after a majority have committed themselves both as to its principles and details. Now, of such proceedings I complain not. I, as one of the minority, ask no favors. All I ask is, that the constitution be not violated. Hold it sacred, and I shall be the last to complain.

I now return to the assumption, that a territory cannot become a State till admitted into the Union, which is now relied on with so much confidence to prove that Michigan is not a State. I reverse the position. I assert the opposite, that a territory cannot be admitted till she becomes a State; and in this, I stand on the authority of the constitution itself, which expressly limits the power of Congress to admitting new *States* into the Union. But, if the constitution had been silent, he would indeed be ignorant of the character of our political system, who does not see that States, sovereign and independent communities, and not territories, can only be admitted. Ours is *a Union of States, a Federal* Republic. States, and not territories, form its component parts, bound together by a solemn league, in the form of a constitutional compact. In coming into the Union, the State pledges its faith to this sacred compact; an act which none but a sovereign and independent community is competent to perform; and, of course, a territory must first be raised to that condition before she can take her stand among the confederated States of our Union. How can a territory pledge its faith to the constitution? It has no will of its own. You give it all its powers, and you can at pleasure overrule all her actions. If she enters as a territory, the act *is yours, not hers. Her consent is nothing without your authority and sanction.* Can you—can Congress, become a party to the constitutional compact? How absurd.

But I am told, if this be so, if a territory must become a State before it can be admitted, it would follow that she might refuse to enter the Union after she had acquired the right of acting for herself. Certainly she may. A State cannot *be forced* into the Union. She must come in *by her own free assent,* given in her highest sovereign capacity through a convention of the people of the State. Such is the constitutional provision; and those who make the objection must overlook both the constitution and the elementary principles of our Government, of which the right of *self-government is the first;* the right of every people to form their own government, and to determine their political condition. This is the doctrine on which our fathers acted in our glorious Revolution, which has done more for the cause of liberty throughout the world than any event within the records of history,—and on which the Government has acted from the first, as regards all that portion of our extensive territory that lies beyond the limits of the original States. Read the ordinance of 1787, and the various acts for the admission of new States, and you will find the principle invariably recognized and acted on, to the present unhappy instance, without any departure from it, except in the case of Missouri. The admission of Michigan is destined, I fear, to mark a great change in the history of the admission of new States; a total departure from the old usage, and the noble principle of self-government on which that usage was founded. Every thing, thus far, connected with her admission, has been irregular and monstrous. I trust it is not ominous. Surrounded by lakes within her natural limits (which ought not to have been departed from), and possessed of fertile soil and genial climate, with every prospect of wealth, power, and influence, who but must regret that she should be ushered into the Union in a manner so irregular and unworthy of her future destiny.

But I will waive these objections, constitutional and all. I will suppose, with the advocates of the bill, that a territory cannot become a State till admitted into the Union. Assuming all this, I ask them to explain to me *how the mere act of admission can transmute a territory into a State?* By whose authority would she be made a State? By ours? How can we make a State? We can form a territory; we can admit States into the Union; but, I repeat the question, how can we make a State? I had supposed this Government was the creature of the States—formed by their authority, and dependent on their will for its existence. Can the creature form the creator? If not by our authority, then by whose? Not by her own—that would be absurd. The very act of admission makes her a member of the Confederacy, with no other or greater power than is possessed by all the others; all of whom, united, cannot create a State. By what process, then, by what authority, can a territory become a State, if not one before it is admitted? Who can explain? How full of difficulties, compared to the long established, simple, and noble process which has prevailed to the present instant. According to old usage, the General Government first withdraws its authority over a certain portion of its territory, as soon as it has a sufficient population to constitute a State. They are thus left to themselves freely to form a constitution, and to exercise the noble right of self-government. They then present their constitution to Congress, and ask *the privilege* (for one it is of the highest character) to become a member of this glorious confederacy of States. The constitution is examined,—and, if republican, as required by the federal constitution, she is admitted, with no other condition except such as may be necessary to secure the authority of Congress over the public domain within her limits. This is the old, the established form, instituted by our ancestors of the Revolution, who so well understood the great principles of liberty and self-government. How simple! how sublime! What a contrast to the doctrines of the present day, and the precedent which, I fear, we are about to establish! And shall we fear, so long as these sound principles are observed, that a State will reject this high privilege— will refuse to enter this Union? No; she will rush into your embrace, so long as your institutions are worth preserving. When the advantages of the Union shall have become a matter of calculation and doubt; when new States shall pause to determine whether the Union is a curse or blessing, the question which now agitates us will cease to have any importance.

Having now, I trust, established beyond all controversy, that Michigan is a State, I come to the great point at issue—to the decision of which all that has been said is but preparatory—Had the self-created assembly which met at Ann Arbor the authority to speak in the name of the people of Michigan; to assent to the conditions contained in the act of the last session; to supersede a portion of the constitution of the State, and to overrule the dissent of the convention of the people—regularly called by the constituted authorities of the State—to the condition of admission? I shall not repeat what I said when I first addressed the Senate on this bill. We all, by this time, know the character of that assemblage; that it met without the sanction of the authorities of the State; and that it did not pretend to represent one-third of the people. We all know that the State had regularly convened a convention of the people, expressly to take into consideration the condition on which it was proposed to admit her into the Union; and that the convention, after full deliberation, had declined to give its assent by a considerable majority. With a knowledge of all these facts, I put the question—Had the assembly a right to act for the State? Was it a convention of the people of Michigan in the true, legal, and constitutional sense of that term? Is there one within the limits of my voice, that can lay his hand on his breast, and honestly say, it was? Is there one that does not feel that it was neither more nor less than a *mere caucus*—nothing but a *party caucus*—of which we have the strongest evidence in the perfect unanimity of those who assembled? Not a vote was given against admission. Can there be stronger proof that it was a meeting got up by party machinery, for party purpose?

But I go further. It was not only a party caucus, for party purpose, *but a criminal meeting*—a meeting to subvert the authority of the State, and to assume its sovereignty. I know not whether Michigan has yet passed laws to guard her sovereignty. It may be that she has not had time to enact laws for this purpose, which no community is long without; but I do aver, if there be such an act, or if the common law be in force in the State, the actors in that meeting might be indicted, tried, and punished *for the very act on which it is now proposed to admit the State into the Union*. If such a meeting as this were to undertake to speak in the name of South Carolina, we would speedily teach its authors what they owed to the authority and dignity of the State. The act was not only in contempt of the authority of the State of Michigan, but a direct insult to this Government. Here is a self-created meeting, convened for a criminal object, which has dared to present to this Government an act of theirs, and to ask that we receive it as a fulfilment of the condition which we had prescribed for the admission of the State! Yet, I fear, forgetting our own dignity, and the rights of Michigan, that we are about to recognize the validity of the act, and quietly to submit to the insult.

The year 1836, said Mr. C., is destined to mark the most remarkable change in our political institutions, since the adoption of the constitution. The events of the year have made a deeper innovation on the principles of the constitution, and evinced a stronger tendency to revolution, than any which have occurred from its adoption to the present day. Sir, said Mr. C. (addressing the Vice-President), duty compels me to speak of facts intimately connected with yourself. In deference to your feelings as presiding officer of the body, I shall speak of them with all possible reserve—much more reserve than I should otherwise have done if you did not occupy that seat. Among the first of these events, which I shall notice, is the caucus at Baltimore; that too, like the Ann Arbor caucus, has been dignified with the name of a convention of the people. This caucus was got up under the countenance and express authority of the President himself; and its edict, appointing you his successor, has been sustained,—not only by the whole patronage and power of the Government, but by his active personal influence and exertion. Through its instrumentality he has succeeded in controlling the voice of the people, and for the first time the President has appointed his successor; and thus, the first great step—of converting our Government into a monarchy, has been sustained. These are solemn and ominous facts. No one who has examined the result of the last election can doubt their truth. It is now certain that you are not the free and unbiased choice of the people of these United States. If left to your own popularity,—without the active and direct influence of the President, and the power and patronage of the Government, acting through a mock convention of the people,—instead of the highest, you would, in all probability, have been the lowest of the candidates.

During the same year, the State in which this ill-omened caucus convened, has been agitated by revolutionary movements of the most alarming character. Assuming the dangerous doctrine that they were not bound to obey the injunctions of the constitution, because it did not place the powers of the State in the hands of an unchecked numerical majority, the electors belonging to the party of the Baltimore caucus, who had been chosen to appoint the State Senators, refused to perform the functions for which they had been elected, with the deliberate intention of subverting the government of the State, and reducing her to the condition of a territory, till a new government could be formed. And now we have before us a measure, not less revolutionary, but of an opposite character. In the case of Maryland, those who undertook, without the authority of law or constitution, to speak and act in the name of the people of the State, proposed to place her out of the Union by reducing her from a State to a territory; but in this, those who, in like manner, undertook to act for Michigan, have assumed the authority to bring her into the Union without her consent, the very condition which she had rejected by a convention of the people, convened under the authority of the State. If we sanction the authority of the Michigan caucus to force a State into the Union without its consent, why might we not here sanction a similar caucus in Maryland, if one had been called, to place the State out of the Union?

These occurrences, which have distinguished the past year, mark the commencement of no ordinary change in our political system. They announce *the ascendency of the caucus system over the regularly constituted authorities of the country.* I have long anticipated this event. In early life my attention was attracted to the working of the caucus system. It was my fortune to spend five or six years of my youth in the northern portion of the Union, where, unfortunately, the system has so long prevailed. Though young, I was old enough to take interest in public affairs, and to notice the working of this odious party machine; and, after reflection, with the experience then acquired, has long satisfied me that, in the course of time, the edicts of the caucus would eventually supersede the authority of law and constitution. We have at last arrived at the commencement of this great change which is destined to go on till it has consummated itself in the entire overthrow of all legal and constitutional authority, unless speedily and effectually resisted. The reason is obvious: for obedience or disobedience to the edicts of the caucus, where the system is firmly established, is more certainly and effectually rewarded or punished, than obedience to the laws and to the constitution. Disobedience to the former is sure to be followed by complete political disfranchisement. It deprives the unfortunate individual who falls under its vengeance, of all public honors and emoluments, and consigns him, if dependent on the Government, to poverty and obscurity; while he who bows down before its mandates, it matters not how monstrous, secures to himself the honors of the State—becomes rich, and distinguished, and powerful. Offices, jobs, and contracts, flow on him and his connections. But to obey the law and respect the constitution, for the most part brings little except the approbation of conscience—a reward, indeed, high and noble, and prized by the virtuous above all other,—but, unfortunately, little valued by the mass of mankind. It is easy to see what must be the end, unless indeed, an effective remedy be applied. Are we so blind as not to see in this why it is that the advocates of this bill—the friends of the system, are so tenacious on the point that Michigan should be admitted on the authority of the Ann Arbor caucus, and on no other? Do we not see why the amendment proposed by myself to admit her, by rescinding the condition imposed at the last session, should be so strenuously opposed? Why, even the preamble would not be surrendered; though many of our friends were willing to vote for the bill on that slight concession, in their anxiety to admit the State.

And here let me say, that I listened with attention to the speech of the Senator from Kentucky (Mr. Crittenden). I know the clearness of his understanding, and the soundness of his heart; and I am persuaded, in declaring that his objection to the bill was confined to the preamble, that he has not investigated the subject with the attention it deserves. I feel the objections to the preamble are not without some weight; but the true and insuperable objections lie far deeper in the facts of the case, which would still exist were the preamble expunged. It is these which render it impossible to pass this bill without trampling under foot the rights of the States, and subverting the first principles of our Government. It would require but a few steps more to effect a complete revolution,—and the Senator from North Carolina has taken the first. I will explain. If you wish to mark the first indications of a revolution,—the commencement of those profound changes in the character of a people which are working beneath before a ripple appears on the surface,—look to the change of language. You will first notice it in the altered meaning of important words;—which, as it indicates a change in the feelings and principles of the people, becomes, in turn, a powerful instrument in accelerating the change, till an entire revolution is effected. The remarks of the Senator will illustrate what I have said. He told us that the terms "convention of the people" were of very uncertain meaning, and difficult to be defined;—but that their true meaning was, *any meeting* of the people in their individual and primary character for political purposes. I know it is difficult to define complex terms; that is, to enumerate all the ideas that belong to them, and exclude all that do not; but there is always, in the most complex, some prominent idea which marks the meaning of the terms, and in relation to which there is usually no disagreement. Thus, according to the old meaning (and which I had supposed was its legal and constitutional meaning), a convention of the people invariably implied a meeting of the people, either by themselves, or by delegates expressly chosen for the purpose, in *their high sovereign authority,*— in express contradistinction to such assemblies of individuals in their private character, or having only derivative authority. It is, in a word, a meeting of the people in the majesty of their power—in that in which they may rightfully make or abolish constitutions, and put up or put down governments at their pleasure. Such was the august conception which formerly entered the mind of every American, when the terms "convention of the people" were used. But now, according to the ideas of the dominant party, as we are told on the authority of the Senator from North Carolina, it means any meeting of individuals for

political purposes,—and, of course, applies to the meeting at Ann Arbor, or any
other party caucus for party purposes, which the leaders may choose to designate as a convention of the people. It is thus the highest authority known to our
laws and constitution, is gradually sinking to the level of those meetings which
regulate the operation of political parties, and through which, the edicts of their
leaders are announced, and their authority enforced; or, rather, to speak more
correctly, the latter are gradually rising to the authority of the former. When
they come to be completely confounded; when the distinction between a caucus and the convention of the people shall be completely obliterated,—which
the definition of the Senator, and the acts of this body on this bill, would lead
us to believe is not far distant,—this fair political fabric of ours, erected by the
wisdom and patriotism of our ancestors, and once the gaze and admiration of
the world, will topple to the ground in ruins.

It has, perhaps, been too much my habit to look more to the future and less
to the present, than is wise; but such is the constitution of my mind, that, when
I see before me the indications of causes calculated to effect important changes
in our political condition, I am led irresistibly to trace them to their sources, and
follow them out in their consequences. Language has been held in this discussion which is clearly revolutionary in its character and tendency, and which
warns us of the approach of the period when the struggle will be between the
conservatives and the *destructives*. I understood the Senator from Pennsylvania
(Mr. Buchanan) as holding language countenancing the principle, that the will
of a mere numerical majority is paramount to the authority of law and constitution. He did not, indeed, announce distinctly this principle, but it might fairly
be inferred from what he said; for he told us the people of a State, where the
constitution gives the same weight to a smaller as to a greater number, might
take the remedy into their own hands; meaning, as I understood him, that a
mere majority might, at their pleasure, subvert the constitution and government
of a State,—which he seemed to think was the essence of democracy. Our little State has a constitution that could not stand a day against such doctrines, and
yet we glory in it as the best in the Union. It is a constitution which respects all
the great interests of the State—giving to each a separate and distinct voice in
the management of its political affairs,—by means of which the feebler interests
are protected against the preponderance of the stronger. We call our State a
Republic—a Commonwealth not a Democracy; and let me tell the Senator it
is a far more popular government than if it had been based on the simple principle of the numerical majority. It takes more voices to put the machine of government in motion, than in those that the Senator would consider more

popular. It represents all the interests of the State,—and is in fact the government of the people, in the true sense of the term, and not that of the mere majority, or the dominant interests.

I am not familiar with the constitution of Maryland, to which the Senator alluded, and cannot, therefore, speak of its structure with confidence; but I believe it to be somewhat similar in its character to our own. That it is a government not without its excellence, we need no better proof than the fact, that, though within the shadow of Executive influence, it has nobly and successfully resisted all the seductions by which a corrupt and artful Administration, with almost boundless patronage, has attempted to seduce her into its ranks.

Looking, then, to the approaching struggle, I take my stand immovably. *I am a conservative in its broadest and fullest sense, and such I shall ever remain, unless, indeed, the Government shall become so corrupt and disordered, that nothing short of revolution can reform it.* I solemnly believe that our political system is, in its purity, not only the best that ever was formed, but the best possible that can be devised for us. It is the only one by which free States, so populous and wealthy, and occupying so vast an extent of territory, can preserve their liberty. Thus thinking, I cannot hope for a better. Having no hope of a better, I am a conservative; and *because I am a conservative, I am a State Rights man.* I believe that in the rights of the States are to be found the only effectual means of checking the overaction of this Government; to resist its tendency to concentrate all power here, and to prevent a departure from the constitution; or, in case of one, to restore the Government to its original simplicity and purity. State interposition, or, to express it more fully, the right of a State to interpose her sovereign voice as one of the parties to our constitutional compact, against the encroachments of this Government, is the only means of sufficient potency to effect all this; and I am, therefore, its advocate. I rejoiced to hear the Senator from North Carolina (Mr. Brown), and from Pennsylvania (Mr. Buchanan), do us the justice to distinguish between nullification and the anarchical and revolutionary movements in Maryland and Pennsylvania. I know they did not intend it as a compliment; but I regard it as the highest. They are right. Day and night are not more different—more unlike in every thing. They are unlike in their principles, their objects, and their consequences.

I shall not stop to make good this assertion, as I might easily do. The occasion does not call for it. As a conservative, and a State Rights man, or if you will have it, a nullifier, I have resisted, and shall resist all encroachments on the constitution—whether of this Government on the rights of the States, or the opposite:—whether of the Executive on Congress, or Congress on the Executive.

My creed is to hold both governments, and all the departments of each to their proper sphere,—and to maintain the authority of the laws and the constitution against all revolutionary movements. I believe the means which our system furnishes to preserve itself are ample, if fairly understood and applied; and I shall resort to them, however corrupt and disordered the times, so long as there is hope of reforming the Government. The result is in the hands of the Disposer of events. It is my part to do my duty. Yet, while I thus openly avow myself a conservative, God forbid I should ever deny the glorious right of rebellion and revolution. Should corruption and oppression become intolerable, and not otherwise be thrown off—if liberty must perish, or the government be overthrown, I would not hesitate, at the hazard of life, to resort to revolution, and to tear down a corrupt government that could neither be reformed nor borne by freemen. But I trust in God things will never come to that pass. I trust never to see such fearful times; for fearful, indeed, they would be, if they should ever befall us. It is the last remedy, and not to be thought of till common sense and the voice of mankind would justify the resort.

Before I resume my seat, I feel called on to make a few brief remarks on a doctrine of fearful import, which has been broached in the course of this debate—the right to repeal laws granting bank charters, and, of course, of railroads, turnpikes, and joint-stock companies. It is a doctrine of fearful import and calculated to do infinite mischief. There are countless millions vested in such stocks, and it is a description of property of the most delicate character. To touch it is almost to destroy it. But, while I enter my protest against all such doctrines, I have been greatly alarmed with the thoughtless precipitancy (not to use a stronger phrase) with which the most extensive and dangerous privileges have been granted of late. It can end in no good, and, I fear, may be the cause of convulsions hereafter. We already feel the effects on the currency, which no one competent of judging can fail to see, is in an unsound condition. I must say (for truth compels me) I have ever distrusted the banking system, at least in its present form, both in this country and Great Britain. It will not stand the test of time; but I trust that all shocks, or sudden revolutions, may be avoided,—and that it may gradually give way, before some sounder and better regulated system of credit, which the growing intelligence of the age may devise. That a better may be substituted I cannot doubt; but of what it shall consist, and how it shall finally supersede the present uncertain and fluctuating currency, time alone can determine. All that I can see is, that the present must, one day or another, come to an end, or be greatly modified—if that, indeed, can save it from an entire overthrow. It has within itself the seeds of its own destruction.

Chapter XIX.

"Speech on the Bill to Distribute the Proceeds of the Sales of Public Lands to the States," 24 August 1841

According to Calhoun, more federal control over economic matters would eventually mean less freedom for the citizenry. For the federal government to collect revenue and then attempt to redistribute the resources to the states would threaten the federal relationship by making the states more dependent on the federal government. Calhoun argued, "Instead of harmony and tranquility within, there would be discord, distraction, and conflict, followed by the absorption of the attention of the Government, and exhaustion of its means and energy on objects never intended to be placed under its control."

Mr. Calhoun said, if this bill should become a law, it would make a wider breach in the constitution, and be followed by changes more disastrous, than any one measure which has ever been adopted. It would, in its violation of the constitution, go far beyond the general welfare doctrine of former days, which stretched the power of the Government as far as it was then supposed was possible by construction, however bold. But, as wide as were the limits which this doctrine assigned to the powers of the Government, it admitted, by implication, that there were limits: while this bill, as I shall show, rests on principles which, if admitted, would supersede all limits.

According to the general welfare doctrine, Congress had power to raise money, and appropriate it to all objects which it might deem calculated to promote the general welfare,—that is, the prosperity of the States, regarded in their aggregate character as members of the Union; or, to express it more briefly, and in language once so common,—to national objects; thus excluding, by necessary implication, all that were not national, as falling within the spheres of the separate

States. As wide as are these limits, they are too narrow for this bill. It takes in what is excluded under the general welfare doctrine, and assumes for Congress the right to raise money, to give by distribution to the States; that is, to be applied by them to those very local State objects to which that doctrine, by necessary implication, denied that Congress had a right to appropriate money; thus superseding all the limits of the constitution,—as far, at least, as the money-power is concerned. The advocates of this extraordinary doctrine have, indeed, attempted to restrict it, in their argument, to revenue derived from the public lands; but facts speak louder than words. To test the sincerity of their argument, amendments after amendments have been offered to limit the operation of the bill exclusively to the revenue derived from this source, but which, as often as offered, have been steadily voted down by their united voices. But I take higher ground. The aid of these test votes, strong as they are, is not needed to make good the assumption that Congress has the right to lay and collect taxes for the separate use of the States. The circumstances under which it is attempted to force this bill through, speak of themselves a language too distinct to be misunderstood.

The treasury is exhausted; the revenues from the public lands cannot be spared; they are needed for the pressing and necessary wants of the Government. For every dollar withdrawn from the treasury, and given to the States, a dollar must be raised from the customs to supply its place: this is admitted. Now, I put it to the advocates of this bill,—Is there, can there be, any real difference, either in principle or effect, between raising money from customs, to be divided among the States, and raising the same amount from them to supply the place of an equal sum withdrawn from the treasury to be divided among the States? If there be a difference, my faculties are not acute enough to perceive it; and I would thank any one who can point it out. But, if this difficulty could be surmounted, it would avail nothing, unless another, not inferior, can also be got over. The land from which the revenue, proposed to be divided, is derived, was purchased (with the exception of a small portion, comparatively, lying between the Ohio and Mississippi rivers) out of the common funds of the Union, and with money derived, for the most part, from customs. I do not exempt the portion acquired from Georgia, which was purchased at its full value, and cost as much, in proportion, as Florida purchased from Spain, or Louisiana from France.

If money cannot be raised from customs or other sources for distribution, I ask, how can money derived from the sales of land purchased with money raised from the customs or other sources, be distributed among the States? If the money could not be distributed before it was vested in land, on what principle can it be when it is converted back again into money by the sales of the land?

If, prior to the purchase, it was subject, in making appropriations, to the limits prescribed by the constitution, how can it, after having been converted back again into money by the sale of the land, be freed from those limits? By what art, what political alchemy, could the mere passage of the money through the lands free it from the constitutional shackles to which it was previously subject?

But if this difficulty also could be surmounted, there is another, not less formidable and more comprehensive, still to be overcome. If the lands belong to the States at all, they must belong to them in one of two capacities,—either in their federative character, as members of a common union; or in their separate character, as distinct and independent communities. If the former, this Government, which was created as a common agent to carry into effect the objects for which the Union was formed, holds its authority over the lands, as it does all its other delegated powers, as a trustee for the States in their federal character, for those objects only, and for no other purpose whatever; and can, of course, under the grant of the constitution "to dispose of the territory or other property belonging to the United States," dispose of the lands only under its trust powers, and in execution of the objects for which they were granted by the constitution. When, then, the lands, or other property of the United States, are disposed of by sale—that is, converted into money—the trust, with all its limitations, attaches as fully to the money, as it did to the lands or property of which it is the proceeds. Nor would the Government have any more right to divide the land or the money among the States,—that is, to surrender it to them,—than it would have to surrender any other subject of its delegated powers. If it may surrender either to the States, it may also surrender the power of declaring war, laying duties, or coining money. They are all delegated by the same parties, held by the same instrument, and in trust, for the execution of the same objects. The assumption of such a right is neither more nor less than the assumption of a right paramount to the constitution itself—the right on the part of the Government to destroy the instrument, and dissolve the Union from which it derives its existence. To such monstrous results must the principle on which this bill rests lead, on the supposition that the lands (that is, the territory) belong to the United States,—as is expressly declared by the constitution.

But the difficulty would not be less if they should be considered as belonging to the States, in their individual and separate character. So considered, what right can this Government possibly have over them? It is the agent, or trustee of the United States,—the States as members of a common union, and not of the States individually, each of which has a separate government of its own to represent it in that capacity. For this Government to assume to represent them in both capacities, would be to assume all power—to centralize the whole system in itself. But, admitting this bold assumption; on what principle of right or justice, if the lands really belong to the States—or, which is the same thing, if the revenue from the lands belong to them—can this Government impose the various limitations prescribed in the bill? What right has it, on this supposition, to appropriate funds belonging to the States separately, to the use of the Union, in the event of war, or in case the price of the lands should be increased above a dollar and a quarter an acre; or any article of the tariff be raised above 20 per centum ad valorem?

Such, and so overwhelming are the constitutional difficulties which beset this measure. No one who can overcome them—who can bring himself to vote for this bill—need trouble himself about constitutional scruples hereafter. He may swallow, without hesitation, bank, tariff, and every other unconstitutional measure which has been adopted or proposed. Yes; it would be easier to make a plausible argument for the constitutionality of the most monstrous of the measures proposed by the abolitionists—for abolition itself—than for this detestable bill; and yet we find Senators from slave-holding States,—the very safety of whose constituents depends on a strict construction of the constitution,—recording their names in favor of a measure from which they have nothing to hope, and every thing to fear. To what is a course so blind to be attributed, but to that fanaticism of party zeal, openly avowed on this floor, which regards the preservation of the power of the Whig party as the paramount consideration? It has staked its existence on the passage of this and other measures for which this extraordinary session was called; and when it is brought to the alternative of their defeat or success, in the anxiety to avoid the one and secure the other, constituents, constitution, duty, and country,—all are forgotten.

A measure which would make so wide and fatal a breach in the constitution, could not but involve, in its consequences, many and disastrous changes in our political system, too numerous to be traced in a speech. It would require a volume to do them justice. As many as may fall within the scope of my remarks, I shall touch on in their proper place. Suffice it for the present to say, that such and so great would they be, as to disturb and confound the relations of all the constituent parts of our beautiful but complex system—of that between this and co-ordinate governments of the States, and between them and their respective constituencies. Let the principle of the distribution of the revenue, on which this bill rests, be established,—and it would follow, as certainly as it is now before us, that this Government and those of the States would be placed in antagonist relations on all subjects except the collection and distribution of revenue; which would end, in time, by converting this into a mere machine of collection and distribution for those of the States, to the utter neglect of all the functions for which it was created. Then the proper responsibility of each to their respective constituencies would be destroyed; then would succeed a scene of plunder and corruption without parallel, to be followed by dissolution, or an entire change of system. Yes; if any one measure can dissolve this Union, this is that measure. The revenue is the state, said the great British statesman, Burke. With us, to divide the revenue among its members is to divide the Union. This bill proposes to divide that from the lands. Take one step more, to which this will lead if not arrested: divide the revenue from the customs, and what of union would be left? I touched more fully on this, and other important points connected with this detestable measure, during the discussions of the last session, and shall not now repeat what I then said.

What I now propose is, to trace the change it would make in our financial system, with its bearings on what ought to be the policy of the Government. I have selected it, not because it is the most important, but because it is that which has heretofore received the least attention.

This Government has heretofore been supported almost exclusively from two sources of revenue—the lands and the customs; excepting a short period at its commencement, and during the late war, when it drew a great portion of its means from internal taxes. The revenue from lands has been constantly and steadily increasing with the increase of population; and may, for the next ten years, be safely estimated to yield an annual average income of $5,000,000, if properly administered—a sum equal to more than a fourth of what the entire expenditures of the Government ought to be, with due economy, and restricted to the objects for which it was instituted.

This bill proposes to withdraw this large, permanent, and growing source of revenue, from the treasury of the Union, and to distribute it among the several States; and the question is,—Would it be wise to do so, viewed as a financial measure, in reference to what ought to be the policy of the Government? which brings up the previous question,—what that policy ought to be? In the order of things, the question of policy precedes that of finance. The latter has reference to, and is dependent on, the former. It must first be determined what ought to be done, before it can be ascertained how much revenue will be required, and on what subject it ought to be raised.

To the question, then, What ought to be the policy of the Government? the shortest and most comprehensive answer which I can give is,—that it ought to be the very opposite of that for which this extraordinary session was called, and of which this measure forms so prominent a part. The effect of these measures is to divide and distract the country within, and to weaken it without; the very reverse of the objects for which the Government was instituted—which was to give peace, tranquillity, and harmony within, and power, security, and respectability without. We find, accordingly, that without, where strength was required, its powers are undivided. In its exterior relations—abroad,—this Government is the sole and exclusive representative of the united majesty, sovereignty, and power of the States, constituting this great and glorious Union. To the rest of the world, we are one. Neither State nor State government is known beyond our borders. Within, it is different. There we form twenty-six distinct, independent, and sovereign communities, each with its separate government, whose powers are as exclusive within, as that of this Government is without,—with the exception of three classes of powers which are delegated to it. The first is, those that were necessary to the discharge of its exterior functions—such as declaring war, raising armies, providing a navy, and raising revenue. The reason for delegating these requires no explanation. The next class consists of those powers that were necessary to regulate the exterior or international relations of the States among themselves, considered as distinct communities—powers that could not be exercised by the States separately, and the regulation of which was necessary to their peace, tranquillity, and that free intercourse, social and commercial, which ought to exist between confederated States. Such are those of regulating commerce between the States, coining money, and fixing the value thereof, and the standard of weights and measures. The remaining class consists of those powers which, though not belonging to the exterior relations of the States, are of such nature that they could not be exercised by States separately, without one injuring the other—such as imposing duties on imports; in exercising which, the maritime States, having the advantage of good ports, would tax those who would have to draw their supplies through them. In asserting that, with these exceptions, the powers of the States are exclusive within, I speak in general terms. There are, indeed, others not reducible to either of these two classes; but they are too few and inconsiderable to be regarded as exceptions.

On the moderate and prudent exercise of these, its interior powers, the success of the Government, and with it our entire political system, mainly depends. If the Government should be restricted, in their exercise, to the objects for which they were delegated—peace, harmony, and tranquillity would reign within; and the attention of the Government unabsorbed by distracting questions within, and its entire resources unwasted by expenditures on objects foreign to its duties—would be directed with all its energy to guard against danger from without, to give security to our vast commercial and navigating interest, and to acquire that weight and respectability for our name in the family of nations which ought to belong to the freest, most enterprising, and most growing people on the globe. If thus restricted in the exercise of these, the most delicate of its powers, and in the exercise of which only it can come in conflict with the Governments of the States, or interfere with their interior policy and interest, this Government, with our whole political system, would work like a charm, and become the admiration of the world. The States, left undisturbed within their separate spheres, and each in the full possession of its resources, would—with that generous rivalry which always takes place between clusters of free states of the same origin and language, and which gives the greatest possible impulse to improvement—carry excellence in all that is desirable beyond any former example.

But if, instead of restricting these powers to their proper objects, they should be perverted to those never intended; if, for example, that of raising revenue should be perverted into that of protecting one branch of industry at the expense of others;—that of collecting and disbursing the revenue, into that of incorporating a great central bank to be located at some favored point, and placed under local control;—and that of making appropriations for specified objects, into that of expending money on whatever Congress should think proper;—all this would be reversed. Instead of harmony and tranquillity within, there would be discord, distraction, and conflict;—followed by the absorption of the attention of the Government, and exhaustion of its means and energy on objects never intended to be placed under its control, to the utter neglect of the duties belonging to the exterior relations of the Government, and which are exclusively confided to its charge. Such has been, and ever must be, the effect of perverting these powers to objects foreign to the constitution. When thus perverted, they become unequal in their action, operating to the benefit of one part or class to the injury of another part or class,—to the benefit of the manufacturing against the agricultural and commercial portions,—or of the non-productive against the producing class. The more extensive the country, the greater would be the inequality and oppression. In ours, stretching over two thousand square miles, they would become intolerable when pushed beyond moderate limits. It is then conflicts take place, from the struggle on the part of those who are benefited by the operation of an unequal system of legislation to retain their advantage, and on the part of the oppressed to resist it. When this state of things occurs, it is neither more nor less than a state of hostility between the oppressor and oppressed—war waged not by armies, but by laws; acts and sections of acts are sent by the stronger party on a plundering expedition, instead of divisions and brigades, which often return more richly laden with spoils than a plundering expedition after the most successful foray.

That such must be the effect of the system of measures now attempted to be forced on the Government by the perversion of its interior powers, I appeal to the voice of experience in aid of the dictates of reason. I go back to the beginning of the Government, and ask what, at its outset, but this very system of measures, caused the great struggle which continued down to 1828, when the system reached its full growth in the tariff of that year? And what, from that period to the termination of the late election which brought the present party into power, has disturbed the harmony and tranquillity of the country, deranged its currency, interrupted its business, endangered its liberty and institutions, but a struggle on one side to overthrow, and on the other to uphold the system? In that struggle it fell prostrate:—and what now agitates the country?—what causes this extraordinary session, with all its excitement, but the struggle on the part of those in power to restore the system; to incorporate a bank; to re-enact a protective tariff; to distribute the revenue from the lands; to originate another debt, and renew the system of wasteful expenditures; and the resistance on the part of the opposition to prevent it? Gentlemen talk of settling these questions; they deceive themselves. They cry Peace! peace! when there is no peace. There never can be peace till they are abandoned, or till our free and popular institutions are succeeded by the calm of despotism; and that not till the spirit of our patriotic and immortal ancestors, who achieved our independence and established our glorious political system, shall become extinct, and their descendants a base and sordid rabble. Till then, or till our opponents shall be expelled from power, and their hope of restoring and maintaining their system of measures is blasted,—the struggle will be continued,—the tranquillity and harmony of the country be disturbed, and the strength and resources of the Government be wasted within, and its duties neglected without.

But, of all the measures which constitute this pernicious system, there is not one more subversive of the objects for which the Government was instituted,— none more destructive of harmony within, and security without, than that now under consideration. Its direct tendency is to universal discord and distraction; to array the new States against the old, the non-indebted against the indebted, the staple against the manufacturing; one class against another; and, finally, the people against the Government. But I pass these. My object is not to trace political consequences; but to discuss the financial bearings of this measure, regarded in reference to what ought to be the policy of the Government; which I trust I have satisfactorily shown ought to be, to turn its attention, energy, and resources, from within to without,—to its appropriate and exclusive sphere,—that of guarding against danger from abroad; giving free scope and protection to our commerce and navigation, and that elevated standing to the country, to which it is so fairly entitled in the family of nations. It becomes necessary to repeat, preparatory to what I propose, that the object of this measure is to withdraw the revenue from the public lands from the treasury of the Union, to be divided among the States; that the probable annual amount that would be so withdrawn, would average, during the next ten years, not less than $5,000,000; and that, to make up the deficit, an equal sum must be laid on the imports. Such is the measure, regarded as one of finance; and the question is, Would it be just, wise, or expedient, considered in its bearings on what ought to be the policy of the Government?

The measure, on its face, is but a surrender of one of the two sources of revenue to the States,—to be divided among them in proportion to their joint delegation in the two Houses of Congress, and to impose a burden to an equal amount on the imports; that is, on the foreign commerce of the country. In every view I can take, it is preposterous, unequal, and unjust. Regarded in its most favorable aspect—that is, on the supposition that the people of each State would pay back to the treasury of the Union, through the tax on the imports, in order to make up the deficit, a sum equal to that received by the State as its distributive share; and that each individual would receive, of that sum, an amount equal to what he paid of the taxes; what would that be, but the folly of giving with one hand and taking back with the other? It would, in fact, be worse. The labour of giving and taking back must be paid for, which, in this case, would be one not a little expensive and troublesome. The expense of collecting the duties on imports is known to be about 10 per cent.; to which must be added the expense and trouble of distribution, with the loss of the use of the money while the process is going on, which may be fairly estimated at 2 per cent. additional; making in all, 12 per cent. for the cost of the process. It follows that the people of the State, in order to return back to the treasury of the Union an amount equal to the sum received by distribution, would have each to pay, by the supposition, 12 per cent. more of taxes than their share of the sum distributed. This sum (equal to $600,000 on $5,000,000) would go to the collectors of the taxes—the custom-house officers—for their share of the public spoils.

But it is still worse. It is unequal and unjust, as well as foolish and absurd. The case supposed would not be the real state of the facts. It would be scarcely possible so to arrange a system of taxes, under which the people of each State would pay back a sum just equal to that received; much less that the taxes should fall on each individual in the State in the same proportion that he would receive of the sum distributed to the State. But, if this were possible, it is certain that no system of taxes on imports—especially the bill sent from the other House—can make such equalization. So far otherwise, I hazard nothing in asserting that the staple States would pay into the treasury, under its operation, three times as much as they would receive, on an average, by the distribution,—and some of them far more: while to the manufacturing States, if we are to judge from their zeal in favor of the bill, the duties it proposes to impose would be bounties, not taxes. If judged by their acts, both measures—the distribution and the duties—would favor their pockets. They would be gainers, let who might be losers, in this financial game.

But be the inequality greater or less than my estimate, what could be more unjust than to distribute a common fund, in a certain proportion, among the States, and to compel the people of the States to make up the deficit in a different proportion; so that some shall pay more, and others less, than what they respectively received? What is it but a cunningly devised scheme to take from one State, and to give to another—to replenish the treasury of some of the States from the pockets of the people of the others; in reality, to make them support the Governments, and pay the debts of other States as well as their own? Such must be the necessary result, as between the States which may pay more than they receive, and those which may receive more than they pay. The injustice and inequality will increase or decrease, just in proportion to the respective excess or deficit between receipts and payments, under this flagitious contrivance for plunder.

But I have not yet reached the extent of this profligate and wicked scheme. As unequal and unjust as it would be between State and State, it is still more so regarded in its operation between individuals. It is between them its true character and hideous features fully disclose themselves. The money to be distributed would not go to the people, but to the legislatures of the States; while that to be paid in taxes to make up the deficiency, would be taken from them individually. A small portion only of that which would go to the legislatures would ever reach the pockets of the people. It would be under the control and management of the dominant party in the legislature, and they under the control and management of the leaders of the party. That it would be administered to the advantage of themselves, and their friends and partisans, and that they would profit more by their use and management of an irresponsible fund, taken from nobody knows who, than they would lose as payers of the taxes to supply its place, will not be doubted by any one who knows how such things are managed. What would be the result? The whole of the revenue from the immense public domain would, if this wicked measure should become the settled policy, go to the profit and aggrandizement of the leaders, for the time, of the dominant party in the twenty-six State Legislatures, and their partisans and supporters; that is, to the most influential, if not the most wealthy, clique for the time in the respective States; while the deficiency would be supplied from the pockets of the great mass of the community, by taxes on tea, coffee, salt, iron, coarse woollens, and, for the most part, other necessaries of life. And what is this but taking from the many and giving to the few,—taking from those who look to their own means and industry for the support of themselves and families, and giving to those who look to the Government for support?—to increase the profit and influence of political managers and their partisans, and diminish that of the people? When it is added, that the dominant party in each State, for the time, would have a direct interest in keeping up and enlarging this pernicious fund, and that their combined influence must, for the time, be irresistible, it is difficult to see by what means the country can ever extricate itself from this measure, should it be once established,—or what limits can be prescribed to its growth, or the extent of the disasters which must follow. It contains the germ of mighty and fearful changes, if it be once permitted to shoot its roots into our political fabric, unless, indeed, it should be speedily eradicated.

In what manner the share that would fall to the States would, in the first instance, be applied, may, for the most part, be anticipated. The indebted States would probably pledge it to the payment of their debts; the effect of which would be, to enhance their value in the hands of the holders—the Rothschilds, the Barings, the Hopes, on the other side the Atlantic, and wealthy brokers and stock-jobbers on this. Were this done at the expense of the indebted States, none could object. But far different is the case when at the expense of the Union, by the sacrifice of the noble inheritance left by our ancestors; and when the loss of this great and permanent fund must be supplied from the industry and property of a large portion of the community, who had no agency or responsibility in contracting the debts, or benefit from the objects on which the funds were expended. On what principle of justice, honor, or constitution, can this Government interfere, and take from their pockets to increase the profit of the most wealthy individuals in the world.

The portion that might fall to the States not indebted,—or those not so deeply so,—would probably for the most part be pledged as a fund on which to make new loans for new schemes similar to those for which the existing State debts were contracted. It may not be applied so at first; but such would most likely be the application on the first swell of the tide of expansion. Supposing one-half of the whole sum to be derived from the lands should be so applied: estimating the income from that source at five millions, the half would furnish the basis of a new debt of forty or fifty millions. Stock to that amount would be created; would find its way to foreign markets; and would return, as other stocks of like kind have, in swelling the tide of imports in the first instance, but in the end by diminishing them to an amount equal to the interest on the sum borrowed, and cutting off in the same proportion the permanent revenue from the customs;—and this, when the whole support of the Government is about to be thrown exclusively on the foreign commerce of the country. So much for the permanent effects, in a financial view, of this measure.

The swelling of the tide of imports, in the first instance, from the loans, would lead to a corresponding flush of revenue, and that to extravagant expenditures, to be followed by embarrassment of the treasury, and a glut of goods, which would bring on a corresponding pressure on the manufacturers; when my friend from Massachusetts (Mr. Bates), and other Senators from that quarter, would cry out for additional protection, to guard against the necessary consequences of the very measure they are now so urgently pressing through the Senate. Such would be the consequences of this measure, regarded as one of finance, and in reference to its internal operation. It is not possible but that such a measure, so unequal and unjust between State and State, section and section—between those who live by their own means and industry, and those who live or expect to live on the public crib—would add greatly to that discord and strife within and weakness without, which is necessarily consequent on the entire system of measures of which it forms a part.

But its mischievous effects on the exterior relations of the country would not be limited to its indirect consequences. There it would strike a direct and deadly blow, by withdrawing entirely from the defences of the country one of the only two sources of our revenue, and that much the most permanent and growing. It is now in the power of Congress to pledge permanently this great and increasing fund to that important object—to completing the system of fortifications, and building, equipping, and maintaining a gallant navy. It was proposed to strike out the whole bill; to expunge the detestable project of distribution; and to substitute in its place the revenue from the public lands, as a permanent fund, sacred to the defences of the country. And from what quarter did this patriotic and truly statesmanlike proposition come? From the far and gallant West; from a Senator (Mr. Linn) of a State the most remote from the ocean, and secure from danger. And by whom was it voted down? Strange to tell, by Senators from maritime States—States most exposed, and having the deepest interest in the measure defeated by their representatives on this floor! Wonderful as it may seem, Louisiana, Mississippi, Georgia, and South Carolina, each gave a vote against it. North Carolina, Virginia, Maryland, Delaware, and New Jersey, gave each two votes against it. New-York gave one; and every vote from New England, but two from New Hampshire and one from Maine, was cast against it. Be it remembered in all after times, that these votes from States so exposed, and having so deep a stake in the defence of the country, were cast in favor of distribution—of giving gratuitously a large portion of the fund from the public domain to wealthy British capitalists, and against the proposition for applying it permanently to the sacred purpose of defending their own shores from insult and danger. How strange that New-York and New England, with their hundreds of millions of property, and so many thousands of hardy and enterprising sailors annually afloat, should give so large a vote for a measure above all others best calculated to withdraw protection from both, and so small a vote against one best calculated to afford them protection! But, strange as this may be, it is still more strange that the staple States,—the States that will receive so little from distribution, and which must pay so much to make up the deficiency it will cause—States so defenceless on their maritime frontier—should cast so large a vote for their own oppression, and against their own defence! Can folly, can party infatuation—be the cause one or both—go further?

Let me say to the Senators from the commercial and navigating States, in all soberness,—there is now a warm and generous feeling diffused throughout the whole Union in favor of the arm of defence with which your interest and glory are so closely identified. Is it wise, by any act of yours, to weaken or alienate such feelings? And could you do an act more directly calculated to effect it? Remember, it is a deep principle of our nature not to regard the safety of those who do not regard their own. If you are indifferent to your own safety, you must not be surprised if those less interested should become more so.

But, as much as the defences of the country would be weakened directly by the withdrawal of so large a fund, the blow would be by no means so heavy as that which, in its consequences, would fall on them. It would paralyze the right arm of power. To understand fully how it would have this effect, we must look, not only to the amount of the sum to be withdrawn, but also on what the burden would fall to make up the deficiency. It would fall on the commerce of the country, exactly where it would do most to cripple the means of defence. To illustrate the truth of what I state, it will be necessary to inquire,—What would be our best system of defence? And this would involve the prior question,—From what quarter are we most exposed to danger? With this, I shall accordingly begin.

There is but one nation on the globe from which we have any thing serious to apprehend; but that is the most powerful that now exists, or ever did exist. I refer to Great Britain. She is in effect our near neighbor, though the wide Atlantic divides us. Her colonial possessions stretch along the whole extent of our eastern and northern borders, from the Atlantic to the Pacific ocean. Her power and influence extend over the numerous Indian tribes scattered along our western border, from our northern boundary to the infant republic of Texas. But it is on our maritime frontier, extending from the mouth of the Sabine to that of the St. Croix—a distance, with the undulations of the coast, of thousands of miles, deeply indented with bays and navigable rivers, and studded with our great commercial emporiums;—it is there, on that long line of frontier, that she is the most powerful, and we the weakest and most vulnerable. It is there she stands ready, with her powerful navy, sheltered in the commanding positions of Halifax, Bermuda, and the Bahamas, to strike a blow at any point she may select on this long line of coast. Such is the quarter from which only we have danger to apprehend; and the important inquiry which next presents itself is, How can we best defend ourselves against a power so formidable, thus touching us on all points, except the small portion of our boundary along which Texas joins us?

Every portion of our extended frontier demands attention, inland as well as maritime; but with this striking difference:—that, on the former, our power is as much greater than hers, as hers is greater than ours on the latter. There we would be the assailant, and whatever works may be erected there ought to have reference to that fact, and look mainly to protecting important points from sudden seizure and devastation, rather than to guard against any permanent lodgment of a force within our borders.

The difficult problem is the defence of our maritime frontier. This, of course, must consist of fortifications and a navy; but the question is,—which ought to be mainly relied on, and to what extent the one may be considered as superseding the other? On both points I propose to make a few remarks.

Fortifications, as a means of defence, are liable to two formidable objections, either of which is decisive against them as an exclusive system. The first is, that they are purely defensive. Let the system be ever so perfect,—the works located to the greatest advantage, and planned and constructed in the best manner,—

and all they can do is to repel attack. They cannot assail. They are like a shield without a sword. If they should be regarded as sufficient to defend our maritime cities, still they cannot command respect, of give security to our widely spread and important commercial and navigating interests.

But regarded simply as the means of defence, they are defective. Fortifications are nothing without men to garrison them; and if we should have no other means of defence, Great Britain could compel us—with a moderate fleet stationed at the points mentioned, and with but a small portion of her large military establishment—to keep up on our part, to guard our coast, ten times the force, at many times the cost, to garrison our numerous forts. Aided by the swiftness of steam, she could menace, at the same time, every point of our coast; while we, ignorant of the time or point where the blow might fall, would have to stand prepared, at every moment and at every point, to repel her attack. A hundred thousand men constantly under arms would be insufficient for the purpose; and we would be compelled to yield, in the end, ingloriously, without striking a blow, simply from the exhaustion of our means.

Some other mode of defence, then, must be sought. There is none other but a navy. I, of course, include steam as well as sails. If we want to defend our coast and protect our rights abroad, it is absolutely necessary. The only questions are, how far our naval force ought to be carried; and to what extent it would supersede the system of fortification?

Before I enter on the consideration of this important point, I owe it to myself and the subject to premise,—that my policy is peace, and that I look to the navy but as the right arm *of defence,—not as an instrument of conquest or aggrandizement.* Our road to greatness, as I said on a late occasion, lies not over the ruins of others. Providence has bestowed on us a new and vast region, abounding in resources beyond any country of the same extent on the globe. Ours is a peaceful task—to improve this rich inheritance; to level its forests; cultivate its fertile soil; develope its vast mineral resources; give the greatest rapidity and facility of intercourse between its widely-extended parts; stud its wide surface with flourishing cities, towns, and villages; and spread over it richly-cultivated fields. So vast is our country, that generations after generations may pass away in executing this task, during the whole of which time we would be rising more surely and rapidly in numbers, wealth, greatness, and influence, than any other people have ever done by arms. But, to carry out successfully this, our true plan of acquiring greatness and happiness, it is not of itself sufficient to have peace and tranquility within. These are indeed necessary, in order to leave the States and their citizens in the full and undisturbed possession of their resources and energy, by which to work out, in generous rivalry, the high destiny which certainly awaits our country if we should be but true to ourselves. But, as important as they may be, it is not much less so to have safety against external danger, and the influence and respectability abroad necessary to secure our exterior interests and rights (so important to our prosperity) against aggression. I look to a navy for these objects; and it is within the limits they assign I would confine its growth. To what extent, then, with these views, ought our navy to be carried? In my opinion, any navy less than that which would give us the habitual command of our own coast and seas, would be little short of useless. One that could be driven from sea and kept in harbor by the force which Great Britain could safely and constantly allot to our coast, would be of little more service than an auxiliary aid to our fortifications in defending our harbors and maritime cities. It would be almost as passive as they are; and would do nothing to diminish the expense, which I have shown would be so exhausting, to defend the coast exclusively by fortifications.

But the difficult question still remains to be solved—What naval force would be sufficient for that purpose? It will not be expected that I should give more than a conjectural answer to such a question. I have neither the data nor the knowledge of naval warfare to speak with any thing like precision; but I feel assured that the force required would be far less than what would be thought when the question is first propounded. The very idea of defending ourselves on the ocean against the immense power of Great Britain on that element, has something startling at the first blush. But, as greatly as she outnumbers us in ships and naval resources, we have advantages that countervail this, in reference to the subject in hand. If she has many ships, she has also many points to guard, and these as widely separated as are the parts of her widely extended empire. She is forced to keep a home fleet in the channel,—another in the Baltic,—another in the Mediterranean,—one beyond the Cape of Good Hope, to guard her important possessions in the East,—and another in the Pacific. Our situation is the reverse. We have no foreign possessions, and not a point to guard beyond our own maritime frontier. There our whole force may be concentrated, ready to strike whenever a vulnerable point is exposed. If to these advantages be added, that both France and Russia have large naval forces; that between us and them there is no point of conflict; that they both watch the naval supremacy of Great Britain with jealousy; and that nothing is more easy than for us to keep on good terms with both powers, especially with a respectable naval force at our command;—it will be readily perceived that a force far short of that of Great Britain would effect what I contemplate. I would say a force equal to one-third of hers would suffice; but if not, certainly less than half would. And if so, a naval force of that size would enable us to dispense with all fortifications, except at important points, and such as might be necessary in reference to the navy itself, to the great relief of the treasury, and saving of means to be applied to the navy, where it would be far more efficient. The less considerable points might be safely left to the defence of cheap works, sufficient to repel plundering attacks; as no large fleet, such as would be able to meet us, with such a naval force as that proposed, would ever think of disgracing itself by attacking places so inconsiderable.

Assuming, then, that a navy is indispensable to our defence, and that one less than that supposed would be in a great measure useless, we are naturally led to look into the sources of our naval power preparatory to the consideration of the question, how they will be affected by imposing on commerce the additional burden this bill would make necessary.

Two elements are necessary to naval power—sailors and money. A navy is an expensive force, and is only formidable when manned with regularly bred sailors. In our case, both of these depend on commerce. Commerce is indispensable to form a commercial marine, and that to form a naval marine; while commerce is with us, if this bill should pass, the only source of revenue. A flourishing commerce is, then, in every respect, the basis of our naval power; and to cripple commerce is to cripple that power—to paralyze the right arm of our defence. But the imposition of onerous duties on commerce is the most certain way to cripple it. Hence, this detestable and mischievous measure, which surrenders the only other source of revenue, and throws the whole burden of supporting the Government exclusively on commerce, aims a deadly blow at the vitals of our power.

The fatal effect of high duties on commerce is no longer a matter of speculation. The country has passed recently through two periods—one of protective tariffs and high duties, and the other of a reduction of duties; and we have the effects of each in our official tables, both as it regards our tonnage and commerce. They speak a language not to be mistaken, and far stronger than any one could anticipate who has not looked into them, or made himself well acquainted with the powerful operation of low duties in extending navigation and commerce. As much as I had anticipated from the reduction of the duties, the lightening of the burdens of commerce has greatly exceeded my most sanguine expectation.

I shall begin with the tonnage, as more immediately connected with naval power; and, in order to show the relative effects of high duties and low on our navigation, I shall compare the period from 1824, when the first great increase of protective duties took place, to 1830, inclusive, when the first reduction of duties commenced. During these seven years, which include the operation of the two protective tariffs of 1824 and 1828,—that is, the reign of the high protective tariff system,—our foreign tonnage fell off from 639,972 tons to 576,475, equal to 61,497; our coasting tonnage from 719,190 to 615,310, equal to 103,880 tons—making the falling off in both equal to 165,370 tons. Yes; to that extent (103,880) did our coasting tonnage decline—the very tonnage, the increase of which it was confidently predicted by the protective party would make up for every possible loss in our foreign tonnage from their miserable quack system. Instead of that, the falling off in the coasting trade is even greater than in the foreign; proving clearly that high duties are not less injurious to the home than to the foreign trade.

I pass now to the period (I will not say of free trade—it is far short of that) of reduction of high protective duties; and now mark the contrast between the two. I begin with the year 1831, the first after the reduction was made on a few articles (principally coffee and tea), and will take in the entire period down to the last returns—that of 1840—making a period of ten years. This period includes the great reduction under the Compromise Act, which is not yet completed, and which, in its further progress, would add greatly to the increase, if permitted to go through undisturbed. The tonnage in the foreign trade increased during that period from 576,475 tons to 899,764, equal to 323,288 tons—not much less than two-thirds of the whole amount at the commencement of the period; and the coasting, for the same period, increased from 615,310 to 1,280,999, equal to 665,699 tons—more than double; and this, too, when, according to the high tariff doctrine, our coasting trade ought to have fallen off, instead of increasing (in consequence of the reduction of the duties): and thus incontestably proving that low duties are not less favorable to our domestic than to our foreign trade. The aggregate tonnage for the period has increased from 1,191,776 to 2,180,763—nearly doubled. Such and so favorable to low duties, in reference to tonnage, is the result of the comparison between the two periods.

The comparison in reference to commerce will prove not less so. In making the comparison, I shall confine myself to the export trade, not because it gives results more favorable,—for the reverse is the fact,—but because the heavy loans contracted by the States during the latter period (between 1830 and 1841) gave a factitious increase to the imports, which would make the comparison appear more favorable than it ought in reality to be. Their effects were different on the exports. They tended to decrease rather than increase their amount.

Of the exports, I shall select domestic articles only because they only are affected by the rate of the duties, as the duties on foreign articles, paid or secured by bond on their importation, are returned on reshipment. With these explanatory remarks, I shall now proceed to the comparison.

The amount in value of domestic articles exported for 1825 was $66,944,745, and in the year 1830 $59,462,029; making a falling off, under the high tariff system, during that period, of $7,482,718. Divide the period into two equal parts, of three years each, and it will be found that the falling off in the aggregate of the latter part, compared to the former, is $13,090,255; showing an average annual decrease of $4,963,418 during the latter part, compared with the former.

The result will be found very different on turning to the period from 1830, when the reduction of the duties commenced, to 1840, during the whole of which the reduction has been going on. The value of domestic exports for 1831 was $61,277,057, and for 1840 $113,895,634, making a difference of $52,618,577, equal to 83 per cent. (omitting fractions) for the ten years. If the period be divided into two equal parts, of five years each, the increase of the latter, compared to the former, will be found to be $139,089,371; making an average annual increase for the latter period (from 1835 to 1840) of $27,817,654. This rapid increase began with the great reduction under the Compromise Act of 1833. The very next year after it passed, the domestic exports rose from $81,034,162 to $101,189,082—just like the recoil which takes place when the weight is removed from the spring.

But my friends from the manufacturing States will doubtless say that this vast increase of exports from reduction of duties was confined to the great agricultural staples, and that the effects were the reverse as to the export of domestic manufactures. With their notion of protection, they cannot be prepared to believe that low duties are favorable to them. I ask them to give me their attention, while I show how great their error is. So far from not partaking of this mighty impulse from the reduction, they felt it more powerfully than other articles of domestic exports, as I shall now proceed to show from the tables.

The exports of domestic manufactures during the period from 1824 to 1832, inclusive,—that is, the period of the high protective duties under the tariffs of 1824 and 1828,—fell from $5,729,797 to $5,050,633, making a decline of $679,133 during that period. This decline was progressive, and nearly uniform, from year to year, through the whole period. In 1833 the Compromise Act was passed, which reduced the duties at once nearly half, and has since made very considerable progressive reductions. The exports of domestic manufactures suddenly, as if by magic, sprung forward, and have been rapidly and uniformly increasing ever since; having risen, in the eight years from 1832 to 1840, from $505,633 to $12,108,538,—a third more than double in that short period, and that immediately following a great decline in the preceding period of eight years, under high duties.

Such were the blighting effects of high duties on the tonnage and the commerce of the country, and such the invigorating effects of their reduction. There can be no mistake. The documents from which the statements are taken are among the public records, and open to the inspection of all. The results are based on the operations of a series of years, showing them to be the consequence of fixed and steady causes, and not accidental circumstances; while the immediate and progressive decrease and increase of tonnage, both coastwise and foreign, and of exports, including manufactured as well as other articles, with the laying on of high duties, and the commencement and progress of their reduction, point out, beyond all controversy, *high duties to be the cause of one, and reduction—low duties—that of the other.*

It will be in vain for the advocates of high duties to seek for a different explanation of the cause of these striking and convincing facts in the history of the two periods. The first of these, from 1824 to 1832, is the very period when the late Bank of the United States was in the fullest and most successful operation;—when exchanges, according to their own showing, were the lowest and most steady, and the currency the most uniform and sound; and yet, with all these favorable circumstances, which they estimate so highly, and with no hostile cause operating from abroad, our tonnage and commerce, in every branch on which the duties could operate, fell off. On the contrary, during the latter period, when all the hostile causes which they are in the habit of daily denouncing on this floor, and of whose disastrous consequences we have heard so many eloquent lamentations;—yes, in spite of contractions and expansions; in spite of tampering with the currency and the removal of the deposits; in spite of the disordered state of the whole machinery of commerce; the deranged state of the currency, both at home and abroad; in spite of the state of the exchanges, and of what we are constantly told of the agony of the country;—both have increased, rapidly increased,—increased beyond all former example! Such is the overpowering effect of removing weights from the springs of industry, and striking off shackles from the free exchange of products, as to overcome all adverse causes.

Let me add, Mr. President, that of this highly prosperous period to industry (however disastrous to those who have over-speculated, or invested their funds in rotten and swindling institutions), the most prosperous of the whole, as the tables will show, is that during the operation of the Sub-Treasury,—a period when some progress was made towards the restoration of the currency of the constitution. In spite of the many difficulties and embarrassments of that trying period, the progressive reduction of the duties, and the gradual introduction of a sounder currency, gave so vigorous a spring to our industry as to overcome them all; showing clearly, if the country was blessed with the full and steady operation of the two, under favorable circumstances, that it would enjoy a degree of prosperity exceeding what even the friends of that measure anticipated.

Having now shown that the navy is the right arm of our defence; that it depends on commerce for its resources, both as to men and means; and that high duties destroy the growth of our commerce, including navigation and tonnage; I have, I trust, satisfactorily established the position which I laid down,—that this measure, which would place the entire burden of supporting the Government on commerce, would paralyze the right arm of our power. Vote it down, and leave commerce as free as possible; and it will furnish ample resources, skilful and gallant sailors, and an overflowing treasury, to repel danger far from our shores, and maintain our rights and dignity in our external relations. With the aid of the revenue from land, and proper economy, we might soon have ample means to enlarge our navy to that of a third of the British, with duties far below the limits of 20 per cent, prescribed by the Compromise Act. The annual appropriation, or cost of the British navy, is about $30,000,000. Ours, with the addition of the appropriation for the home squadron made this session, is (say) $6,000,000; requiring only the addition of four millions to make it equal to a third of that of Great Britain, provided that we can build, equip, man, and maintain ours as cheaply as she can hers. That we can, with proper management, can scarcely be doubted, when we reflect that our navigation, which involves almost all the elements of expense that a navy does, successfully competes with hers over the world. Nor are we deficient in men—gallant and hardy sailors—to man a navy on as large a scale as is suggested. Already our tonnage is two-thirds of that of Great Britain, and will in a short time approach an equality with hers, if our commerce should be fairly treated. Leave, then, in the treasury, the funds proposed to be withdrawn by this detestable bill; apply it to the navy and defences of the country; and even at its present amount, with small additional aid from the imposts, it will give the means of raising it, with the existing appropriation, to the point suggested; and with the steady increase of the fund from the increased sales of lands, keeping pace with the increase of our population, and the like increase of commerce under a system of light and equal duties, we may, with proper economy in the collection and disbursements of the revenue, raise our navy steadily, without feeling the burden, to half the size of the British,—or more, if more be needed for defence and the maintenance of our rights. Beyond this, we ought never to aim.

I have (said Mr. C.) concluded what I proposed to say. I have passed over many and weighty objections to this measure which I could not bring within the scope of my remarks, without exhausting the patience of the body. And now, Senators, in conclusion, let me entreat you, in the name of all that is good and patriotic—in the name of our common country and the immortal fathers of our Revolution and founders of our Government—to reject this dangerous bill. I implore you to pause and ponder before you give your final vote for a measure which, if it should pass and become a permanent law, would do more to defeat the ends for which this Government was instituted, and to subvert the constitution and destroy the liberty of the country, than any which has ever been proposed.

CHAPTER *XX.*

In responding to Henry Clay's effort to restrict presidential veto power, Calhoun refrained from discussing the partisan issues of the debate and chose instead to focus on the first principles of the American regime. In criticizing a mere numerical majority as the basis for governmental decision making, Calhoun noted that although "simple majorities" played an important role, relying on them was not the only way of resolving conflict.

The combination of the concurrent majority (or voice) and voting majority produced genuine constitutional and popular rule. As the foundation of republican government, popular rule must acknowledge other means of recognizing preferences among the citizenry than voting by simple plebiscite. Appropriately, Calhoun argued that concurrent measures were already present in the American constitutional structure and clearly operative during the Founding. The original American Constitution abounds with examples of measures designed to counterbalance the perversion of republican government into plebiscitarianism, or a government of the "simple majority." In this essay and in the Discourse, *Calhoun explained how concurrent features —such as the Senate, the Electoral College, the Supreme Court, and relevant aspects of the separation of powers contributed to the Founders' design for popular rule. In defending this understanding of American politics, Calhoun insisted that a numerical majority could not represent the full character of the republic. Federal institutions encouraged, nurtured, and protected popular participation only through the implementation of the concurrent majority. Without it, not only would federal institutions overstep their authority and threaten liberty, popular participation would begin to decline as people lost confidence in the government's ability to protect their interests. Recovering the concurrent majority, Calhoun argued, would rejuvenate participation long discouraged by decades of neglect and patronage. For Calhoun, the disadvantages of limiting temporary majorities were outweighed by the benefits that accrued from allowing for thoughtful deliberation and authentic consensus building. Recovering the concurrent majority in union with a disciplined mode of true majoritarian participation offered for Calhoun the possibility of reclaiming popular rule.*

THE Senator from Kentucky (Mr. Clay), in support of his amendment, maintained that the people of these States constitute a nation; that the nation has a will of its own; that the numerical majority of the whole was the appropriate organ of its voice; and that whatever derogated from it, to that extent departed from the genius of the Government, and set up the will of the minority against the majority. We have thus presented, at the very threshold of the discussion, a question of the deepest import,—not only as it regards the subject under consideration, but the nature and character of our Government; and this question is, Are these propositions of the Senator true?

[Mr. Clay here interrupted Mr. Calhoun, and said that he meant a majority according to the forms of the constitution.

Mr. Calhoun, in return, said he had taken down the words of the Senator at the time, and would vouch for the correctness of his statement. The Senator not only laid down the propositions as stated, but he drew conclusions from them against the President's veto, which could only be sustained on the principle of the numerical majority. In fact, his course at the extra session, and the grounds assumed both by him and his colleague in this discussion, had their origin in the doctrines embraced in that proposition (Crallé).]

If they be, then he admitted the argument against the veto would be conclusive; not, however, for the reason assigned by him,—that it would make the voice of a single functionary of the Government (the President) equivalent to that of some six Senators and forty members of the other House,—but, for the far more decisive reason, according to his theory, that the President is not chosen by the voice of numerical majority, and does not, therefore, according to his principle, represent truly the will of the nation.

It is a great mistake to suppose that he is elected simply on the principle of numbers. They constitute, it is true, the principal element in his election; but not the exclusive. Each State is, indeed, entitled to as many votes in his election, as it has representatives in the other House—that is, in proportion to its federal population; but to these, two others are added, having no regard to numbers for their representation in the Senate; which greatly increases the relative influence of the small States compared with the large, in the Presidential election. What effect this latter element may have on the numbers necessary to elect a President, may be made apparent by a very short and simple calculation.

The population of the United States, in federal numbers, by the late census, is 15,908,376. Assuming that 68,000, the number reported by the committee of the other House, will be fixed on for the ratio of representation, it will give, according to the calculation of the committee, 224 members to the other House. Add 52,—the number of the Senators,—and the electoral college will be found to consist of 276, of which 139 is a majority. If nineteen of the smaller States, excluding Maryland, be taken,—beginning with Delaware and ending with Kentucky inclusive,—they will be found to be entitled to 140 votes,—1 more than a majority,—with a federal population of only 7,227,869; while the seven other States, with a population of 8,680,507, would be entitled to but 136 votes,—3 less than a majority,—with a population of almost a million and a half greater than the others. Of the 140 electoral votes of the smaller States, 38 would be on account of the addition of 2 to each State for their representation in this body; while of the larger there would be but 14 on this account;—making a difference of 24 votes,—being 2 more than the entire electoral vote of Ohio, the third State, in point of numbers, in the Union.

The Senator from Kentucky, with these facts, but acts in strict conformity with his theory of government, in proposing the limitation he has on the veto power; but as much cannot be said in favor of the substitute he has offered. The argument is as conclusive against the one as the other, or any other modification of the veto that could possibly be devised. It goes further,—and is conclusive against the Executive Department itself, as elected; for there can be no good reason offered why the will of the nation, if there be one, should not be as fully and perfectly represented in that department as in the legislative.

But it does not stop here. It would be still more conclusive, if possible, against this branch of the Government. In constituting the Senate, numbers are totally disregarded. The smallest State stands on a perfect equality with the largest,—Delaware with her seventy-seven thousand, and New-York with her two millions and a half. Here a majority of States control, without regard to population; and fourteen of the smallest States, with a federal population of but 4,064,457,—little less than a fourth of the whole,—can, if they unite, overrule the twelve others with a population of 11,844,919. Nay, more; they could virtually destroy the Government, and put a veto on the whole system, by refusing to elect Senators; and yet this equality among States, without regard to numbers, including the branch where it prevails, would seem to be the favorite with the constitution. It cannot be altered without the consent of every State; and this branch of the Government where it prevails, is the only one that participates in the powers of all the others. As a part of the legislative department, it has full participation with the other in all matters of legislation, except originating money bills; while it participates with the Executive in two of its highest functions,—those of appointing to office and making treaties; and in that of the Judiciary, in being the high court before which all impeachments are tried.

But we have not yet got to the end of the consequences. The argument would be as conclusive against the Judiciary as against the Senate, or the Executive and his veto. The judges receive their appointments from the Executive and the Senate—the one nominating, and the other consenting to and advising the appointment; neither of which departments, as has been shown, is chosen by the numerical majority. In addition, they hold their office during good behavior, and can only be turned out by impeachment; and yet they have the power, in all cases in law and equity brought before them, in which an act of Congress is involved, to decide on its constitutionality—that is, in effect, to pronounce an absolute veto.

If, then, the Senator's theory be correct, its clear and certain result, if carried out in practice, would be to sweep away, not only the veto, but the Executive, the Senate, and the Judiciary, as now constituted; and to leave nothing standing in the midst of the ruins but the House of Representatives, where only, in the whole range of the Government, numbers exclusively prevail. But, as desolating as would be its sweep, in passing over the Government, it would be far more destructive in its whirl over the constitution. There it would not leave a fragment standing amidst the ruin in its rear.

In approaching this topic, let me premise (what all will readily admit), that if the voice of the people may be sought for any where with confidence, it may be in the constitution, which is conceded by all to be the fundamental and paramount law of the land. If, then, the people of these States do really constitute a nation, as the Senator supposes; if the nation has a will of its own, and if the numerical majority of the whole is the only appropriate and true organ of that will, we may fairly expect to find that will, pronounced through the absolute majority, pervading every part of that instrument, and stamping its authority on the whole. Is such the fact? The very reverse. Throughout the whole—from first to last—from the beginning to the end—in its formation, adoption, and amendment, there is not the slightest evidence, trace, or vestige of the existence of the facts on which the Senator's theory rests; neither of the nation, nor its will, nor of the numerical majority of the whole, as its organ, as I shall next proceed to show.

The convention which formed it was called by a portion of the States; its members were all appointed by the States; received their authority from their separate States; voted by States in forming the constitution; agreed to it, when formed, by States; transmitted it to Congress to be submitted to the States for their ratification; it was ratified by the people of each State in convention, each ratifying by itself, for itself, and bound exclusively by its own ratification; and by express provision it was not to go into operation, unless nine out of the twelve States should ratify, and then to be binding only between the States ratifying. It was thus put in the power of any four States, large or small, without regard to numbers, to defeat its adoption; which might have been done by a very small proportion of the whole, as will appear by reference to the first census. That census was taken very shortly after the adoption of the constitution,— at which time the federal population of the then twelve States was 3,462,279, of which the four smallest, Delaware, Rhode Island, Georgia, and New Hampshire, with a population of only 241,490 (something more than the fourteenth part of the whole), could have defeated the ratification. Such was the total disregard of population in the adoption and formation of the constitution.

It may, however, be said, it is true, that the constitution is the work of the States, and that there was no nation prior to its adoption; but that its adoption fused the people of the States into one, so as to make a nation of what before constituted separate and independent sovereignties. Such an assertion would be directly in the teeth of the constitution, which says that, when ratified, "it should be binding" (not over the States ratifying, for that would imply that it was imposed by some higher authority; nor between the individuals composing the States, for that would imply that they were all merged in one; but) "between the States ratifying the same;" and thus, by the strongest implication, recognizing them as the parties to the instrument, and as maintaining their separate and independent existence as States, after its adoption. But let this pass. I need it not to rebut the Senator's theory—to test the truth of the assertion, that the constitution has formed a nation of the people of these States. I go back to the grounds already taken,—that if such be the fact—if they really form a nation, since the adoption of the constitution, and the nation has a will, and the numerical majority is its only proper organ,—in such case the mode prescribed for the amendments of the constitution would furnish abundant and conclusive evidence of the fact. But here again, as in its formation and adoption, there is not the slightest trace or evidence of the fact; on the contrary, most conclusive to sustain the very opposite opinion.

There are two modes in which amendments to the constitution may be proposed. The one, such as that now proposed, by a resolution to be passed by two-thirds of both Houses; and the other, by a call of a convention, by Congress, to propose amendments, on the application of two-thirds of the States; neither of which gives the least countenance to the theory of the Senator. In both cases, the mode of ratification, which is the material point, is the same,—and requires the concurring assent of three-fourths of the States, regardless of population, to ratify an amendment. Let us now pause for a moment to trace the effects of this provision.

There are now twenty-six States, and the concurring assent, of course, of twenty States, is sufficient to ratify an amendment. It then results that twenty of the smaller States, of which Kentucky would be the largest, are sufficient for this purpose, with a population, in federal numbers, of only 7,652,097,—less by several hundred thousand than the numerical majority of the whole,—against the united voice of the other six, with a population of 8,216,279,—exceeding the former by more than half a million. And yet this minority, under the amending power, may change, alter, modify, or destroy every part of the constitution, except that which provides for an equality of representation of the States in the Senate: while, as if in mockery and derision of the Senator's theory, nineteen of the larger States, with a population, in federal numbers, of 14,526,073, cannot, even if united to a man, alter a letter in the constitution, against the seven others, with a population of only 1,382,303; and this, too, under the existing constitution, which is supposed to form the people of these States into a nation. Finally, Delaware, with a population of little more than 77,000, can put her veto on all the other States, on a proposition to destroy the equality of the States in the Senate. Can facts more clearly illustrate the total disregard of the numerical majority, as well in the process of amending, as in that of forming and adopting the constitution?

All this must appear anomalous, strange, and unaccountable, on the theory of the Senator; but harmonious and easily explained on the opposite; that ours is a union, not of individuals, united by what is called a social compact—for that would make it a nation; nor of governments—for that would have formed a confederacy, like the one superseded by the present constitution; but a union of States, founded on a written, positive compact, forming a Federal Republic, with the same equality of rights among the States composing the Union, as among the citizens composing the States themselves. Instead of a nation, we are in reality an assemblage of nations, or peoples (if the plural noun may be used where the language affords none), united in their sovereign character immediately and directly by their own act, but without losing their separate and independent existence.

It results from all that has been stated, that either the theory of the Senator is wrong, or that our political system is throughout a profound and radical error. If the latter be the case, then that complex system of ours, consisting of so many parts, but blended, as was supposed, into one harmonious and sublime whole, raising its front on high and challenging the admiration of the world, is but a misshapen and disproportionate structure, that ought to be demolished to the ground, with the single exception of the apartment allotted to the House of Representatives. Is the Senator prepared to commence the work of demolition? Does he believe that all other parts of this complex structure are irregular and deformed appendages; and that if they were taken down, and the Government erected exclusively on the will of the numerical majority, it would effect as well, or better, the great objects for which it was instituted: "to establish justice; ensure domestic tranquillity; provide for the common defence; promote the general welfare; and secure the blessings of liberty to ourselves and our posterity?" Will the Senator—will any one—can any one—venture to assert this? And if not, why not? This is the question, on the proper solution of which hangs not only the explanation of the veto, but that of the real nature and character of our complex, but beautiful and harmonious system of governments. To give a full and systematic solution, it would be necessary to descend to the elements of political science, and discuss principles little suited to a discussion in a deliberative assembly. I waive the attempt, and shall content myself with giving a much more matter-of-fact solution.

It is sufficient, for this purpose, to point to the actual operation of the Government, through all the stages of its existence, and the many and important measures which have agitated it from the beginning; the success of which one portion of the people regarded as essential to their prosperity and happiness, while other portions have viewed them as destructive of both. What does this imply, but a deep conflict of interests, real or supposed, between the different portions of the community, on subjects of the first magnitude—the currency, the finances, including taxation and disbursements; the bank, the protective tariff, distribution, and many others; on all of which the most opposite and conflicting views have prevailed? And what would be the effect of placing the powers of the Government under the exclusive control of the numerical majority—of 8,000,000 over 7,900,000, of six States over all the rest—but to give the dominant interest, or combination of interests, an unlimited and despotic control over all others? What, but to vest it with the power to administer the Government for its exclusive benefit, regardless of all others, and indifferent to their oppression and wretchedness? And what, in a country of such vast extent and diversity of condition, institutions, industry, and productions, would this be, but to subject the rest to the most grinding despotism and oppression? But what is the remedy? It would be but to increase the evil, to transfer the power to a minority,—to abolish the House of Representatives, and place the control exclusively in the hands of the Senate—in that of the four millions, instead of the eight. If one must be sacrificed to the other, it is better that the few should be to the many, than the many to the few.

What then is to be done, if neither the majority nor the minority, the greater nor less part, can be safely trusted with exclusive control? What but to vest the powers of the Government in the whole—the entire people; to make it, in truth and reality, the government of the people, instead of the government of a dominant over a subject part, be it the greater or less—of the whole people—self-government; and, if this should prove impossible in practice, then to make the nearest approach to it, by requiring the concurrence in the action of the Government, of the greatest possible number consistent with the great ends for which Government was instituted—justice and security, within and without. But how is this to be effected? Not, certainly, by considering the whole community as one, and taking its sense as a whole by a single process, which, instead of giving the voice of all, can but give that of a part. There is but one way by which it can possibly be accomplished; and that is by a judicious and wise division and organization of the Government and community, with reference to its different and conflicting interests,—and by taking the sense of each part separately, and the concurrence of all as the voice of the whole. Each may be imperfect of itself; but if the construction be good, and all the keys skilfully touched, there will be given out, in one blended and harmonious whole, the true and perfect voice of the people.

But on what principle is such a division and organization to be made to effect this great object, without which it is impossible to preserve free and popular institutions? To this no general answer can be given. It is the work of the wise and experienced,—having full and perfect knowledge of the country and the people, in every particular—for whom the Government is intended. It must be made to fit; and when it does, it will fit no other, and will be incapable of being imitated or borrowed. Without, then, attempting to do what cannot be done, I propose to point out how that which I have stated has been accomplished in our system of governments, and the agency the veto is intended to have in effecting it.

I begin with the House of Representatives. There each State has a representation according to its federal numbers,—and, when met, a majority of the whole number of members controls its proceedings; thus giving to the numerical majority the exclusive control throughout. The effect is to place its proceedings in the power of eight millions of people over all the rest, and six of the largest States, if united, over the other twenty; and the consequence, if the House were the exclusive organ of the voice of the people, would be the domination of the stronger over the weaker interests of the community, and the establishment of an intolerable and oppressive despotism. To find the remedy against what would be so great an evil, we must turn to this body. Here an entirely different process is adopted to take the sense of the community. Population is entirely disregarded, and States, without reference to the number of the people, are made the basis of representation; the effect of which is to place the control here in a majority of the States, which, had they the exclusive power, would exercise it as despotically and oppressively as would the House of Representatives.

Regarded, then, separately, neither truly represents the sense of the community, and each is imperfect of itself; but when united, and the concurring voice of each is made necessary to enact laws, the one corrects the defects of the other; and, instead of the less popular derogating from the more popular, as is supposed by the Senator, the two together give a more full and perfect utterance to the voice of the people than either could separately. Taken separately, six States might control the House; and a little upwards of four millions might control the Senate, by a combination of the fourteen smaller States; but by requiring the concurrent votes of the two, the six largest States must add eight others to have the control in both bodies. Suppose, for illustration, they should unite with the eight smallest (which would give the least number by which an act could pass both Houses), it will be found, by adding the population in federal numbers of the six largest to the eight smallest States, that the least number by which an act can pass both Houses, if the members should be true to those they represent, would be 9,788,570 against a minority of 6,119,797, instead of 8,000,000 against 7,900,000, if the assent of the most popular branch alone were required.

This more full and perfect expression of the voice of the people by the concurrence of the two, compared to either separately, is a great advance towards a full and perfect expression of their voice; but, great as it is, it falls far short, and the framers of the constitution were accordingly not satisfied with it. To render it still more perfect, their next step was to require the assent of the President, before an act of Congress could become a law; and, if he disapproved, to require two-thirds of both Houses to overrule his veto. We are thus brought to the point immediately under discussion, and which, on that account, claims a full and careful examination.

One of the leading motives for vesting the President with this high power, was, undoubtedly, to give him the means of protecting the portion of the powers allotted to him by the constitution, against the encroachment of Congress. To make a division of power effectual, a veto in one form or another is indispensable. The right of each to judge for itself of the extent of the power allotted to its share, and to protect itself in its exercise, is what in reality is meant by a division of power. Without it, the allotment to each department would be a mere partition, and no division at all. Acting under this impression, the framers of the constitution have carefully provided that his approval should be necessary, not only to the acts of Congress, but to every resolution, vote, or order, requiring the consent of the two Houses, so as to render it impossible to elude it by any conceivable device. This of itself, was an adequate motive for the provision, and, were there no other, ought to be a sufficient reason for the rejection of this resolution. Without it, the division of power between the Legislative and Executive Departments would have been merely nominal.

But it is not the only motive. There is another and deeper, to which the division itself of the Government into departments is subordinate;—to enlarge the popular basis, by increasing the number of voices necessary to its action. Numerous as are the voices required to obtain the assent of the people through the Senate and the House to an act, it was not thought by the framers of the constitution sufficient for the action of the Government in all cases. 9,800,000—large as is the number—were regarded as still too few, and 6,100,000 too many, to remove all motives for oppression; the latter being not too few to be plundered, and the former not too large to divide the spoils of plunder among. Till the increase of numbers on one side, and the decrease on the other, reaches that point, there is no security for the weaker against the stronger, especially in so extensive a country as ours. Acting in the spirit of these remarks, the authors of the constitution, although they deemed the concurrence of the Senate and the House as sufficient, with the approval of the President, to the enactment of laws in ordinary cases; yet, when he dissented, they deemed it a sufficient presumption against the measure to require a still greater enlargement of the popular basis for its enactment. With this view, the assent of two-thirds of both Houses was required to overrule his veto; that is, eighteen States in the Senate, and a constituency of 10,600,000 in the other House.

But it may be said that nothing is gained towards enlarging the popular basis of the Government by the veto power; because the number necessary to elect a majority to the two Houses, without which the act could not pass, would be sufficient to elect him. This is true. But he may have been elected by a different portion of the people; or, if not, great changes may take place during his four years, both in the Senate and the House, which may change the majority that brought him into power; and with it the measures and policy to be pursued. In either case, he might find it necessary to interpose his veto to maintain his views of the constitution, or the policy of the party of which he is the head, and which elevated him to power.

But a still stronger consideration for vesting him with the power may be found in the difference in the manner of his election, compared with that of the members of either House. The Senators are elected by the vote of the Legislatures of the respective States; and the members of the House by the people, who, in almost all the States, elect by districts. In neither is there the least responsibility of the members of any one State to the Legislature or people of any other State. They are, as far as their responsibility may be concerned, solely and exclusively under the influence of the States and people who respectively elect them. Not so the President. The votes of the whole are counted in his election, which makes him more or less responsible to every part—to those who voted against him, as well as those to whom he owes his election; which he must feel sensibly. If he should be an aspirant for a re-election, he will desire to gain the favorable opinion of States that opposed him, as well as to retain that of those which voted for him. Even if he should not be a candidate for re-election, the desire of having a favorite elected, or maintaining the ascendency of his party, may have, to a considerable extent, the same influence over him. The effect in either case, would be to make him look more to *the interest of the whole*—to soften sectional feelings and asperity—to be more of a patriot than the partisan of any particular interest; and, through the influence of these causes, to give a more general character to the politics of the country, and thereby render the collision between sectional interests less fierce than it would be if legislation depended solely on the members of the two Houses, who owe no responsibility but to those who elected them. The same influence acts even on the aspirants for the Presidency, and is followed to a very considerable extent by the same softening and generalizing effects. In the case of the President, it may lead to the interposing of his veto against oppressive and dangerous sectional measures, even when supported by those to whom he owes his election. But, be the cause of interposing his veto what it may, its effect in all cases is, to require a greater body of constituency, through the legislative organs, to put the Government in action against it—to require another key to be struck, and to bring out a more full and perfect response from the voice of the people.

There is still another impediment, if not to the enactment of laws, to their execution, to be found in the Judiciary Department. I refer to the right of the courts, in all cases coming before them in law or equity, where an act of Congress comes in question, to decide on its constitutionality; which, if decided against the law in the Supreme Court, is, in effect, a permanent veto. But here a difference must be made between a decision against the constitutionality of a law of Congress and of a State. The former acts as a restriction on the powers of this Government, but the latter as an enlargement.

Such are the various processes of taking the sense of the people through the divisions and organization of the different departments of the Government; all of which, acting through their appropriate organs, are intended to widen its basis and render it more popular, instead of less, by increasing the number necessary to put it in action,—and having for their object to prevent one portion of the community from aggrandizing or enriching itself at the expense of the other, and to restrict the whole to the sphere intended by the framers of the constitution. Has it effected these objects? Has it prevented oppression and usurpation on the part of the Government? Has it accomplished the objects for which the Government was ordained, as enumerated in the preamble to the constitution? Much—very much—certainly has been done, but not all. Many instances might be enumerated, in the history of the Government, of the violation of the constitution—of the assumption of powers not delegated to it—of the perversion of those delegated to uses never intended—and of their being wielded by the dominant interest, for the time, for its aggrandizement, at the expense of the rest of the community;—instances that may be found in every period of its existence, from the earliest to the latest, beginning with the bank and bank connection at its outset, and ending with the Distribution Act at the late extraordinary session. How is this to be accounted for? What is the cause?

The explanation and cause will be found in the fact, that, fully as the sense of the people is taken in the action of the Government, it is not taken fully enough. For, after all that has been accomplished in that respect, there are but two organs through which the voice of the community acts directly on the Government; and which, taken separately, or in combination, constitute the elements of which it is composed: the one is the majority of the States, regarded in their corporate character as bodies politic, which, in its simple form, constitutes the Senate; and the other is the majority of the people of the States, of which, in its simple form, the House of Representatives is composed. These combined, in the proportions already stated, constitute the Executive Department; and that department and the Senate appoint the judges, who constitute the Judiciary. But it is only in their simple form in the Senate and the other House that they have a steady and habitual control over the legislative acts of the Government. The veto of the Executive is rarely interposed—not more than about twenty times during the period of more than fifty years that the Government has existed. Their effects have been beneficially felt,—but only casually, at long intervals, and without steady and habitual influence over its action. The same remarks are substantially applicable to what, for the sake of brevity, may be called the veto of the Judiciary—the right of negativing a law, for the want of constitutionality, when it comes in question, in a case before the courts.

The Government, then, of the Union, being under no other habitual and steady control but of these two majorities, acting through this and the other House, is, in fact, placed substantially under the control of the portion of the community which the united majorities of the two Houses represent for the time, and which may consist of but fourteen States, with a federal population of less than ten millions, against a little more than six, as has been already explained. But, large as is the former, and small as is the latter,—the one is not large enough, in proportion, to prevent it from plundering, under the forms of law,—nor the other small enough to be secure from the plundering process; and hence the many instances of violation of the constitution—of usurpation, of powers perverted and wielded for selfish purposes, which the history of the Government affords. They furnish proof conclusive that the principle of plunder, so deeply implanted in all governments, has not been eradicated in ours, by all the precautions taken by its framers.

But, in estimating the number of the constituency necessary to control the majority in the two Houses of Congress at something less than ten millions, I have put it altogether too high, regarding the practical operation of the Government. To form a correct conception of its practical operation in this respect, another element, which has, in practice, an important influence, must be taken into the estimate, and which I shall next proceed to explain.

Of the two majorities, which, acting either separately or in combination, control the Government, the numerical majority is by far the most influential. It has the exclusive control in the House of Representatives, and preponderates more than five to one in the choice of the President,—assuming that the ratio of representation will be fixed at sixty-eight thousand under the late census. It also greatly preponderates in the appointment of judges,—the right of nominating having much greater influence in making appointments than that of advising and consenting. From these facts, it must be apparent that the leaning of the President will be to that element of power to which he mainly owes his elevation,—and on which he must principally rely to secure his re-election, or maintain the ascendency of the party and its policy, of which he usually is the head. This leaning of his must have a powerful effect on the inclination and tendency of the whole Government. In his hands are placed, substantially, all the honors and emoluments of the Government; and these, when greatly increased, as they are and ever must be when the powers of the Government are greatly stretched and increased, must give the President a corresponding influence over, not only the members of both Houses, but also public opinion,—and, through this, a still more powerful indirect influence over them; and thus they may be brought to sustain or oppose, through his influence, measures which otherwise they would not have opposed or sustained,—and the whole Government be made to lean in the same direction with the Executive.

From these causes, the Government, in all its departments, gravitates steadily towards the numerical majority,—and has been moving slowly towards it from the beginning; sometimes, indeed, retarded, or even stopped or thrown back,—but, taking any considerable period of time, always advancing towards it. That it begins to make near approach to that fatal point, ample proof may be found in the oft-repeated declaration of the mover of this resolution, and of many of his supporters at the extraordinary session,—that the late Presidential election decided all the great measures which he so ardently pressed through the Senate. Yes, even here—in this Chamber,—in the Senate,—which is composed of the opposing element,—and on which the only effectual resistance to this fatal tendency exists which is to be found in the Government—we are told that the popular will, as expressed in the Presidential election, is to decide, not only the election, but every measure which may be agitated in the canvass in order to influence the result. When what was thus boldly insisted on comes to be an established principle of action, the end will be near.

As the Government approaches nearer and nearer to the one absolute and single power,—the will of the greater number,—its action will become more and more disturbed and irregular; faction, corruption, and anarchy, will more and more abound; patriotism will daily decay, and affection and reverence for the Government grow weaker and weaker,—until the final shock occurs, when the system will rush into ruin, and the sword take the place of law and constitution.

Let me not be misunderstood. I object not to that structure of the Government which makes the numerical majority the predominant element: it is, perhaps, necessary that it should be so in all popular constitutional governments like ours, which excludes classes. It is necessarily the exponent of the strongest interest, or combination of interests, in the community; and it would seem to be necessary to give it the preponderance, in order to infuse into the Government the necessary energy to accomplish the ends for which it was instituted. The great question is,—How is due preponderance to be given to it, without subjecting the whole, in time, to its unlimited sway? which brings up the inquiry, Is there anywhere, in our complex system of governments, a guard, check, or contrivance, sufficiently strong to arrest so fearful a tendency? Or, to express it in more direct and intelligible language,—Is there any where in the system a more full and perfect expression of the voice of the people of the States, calculated to counteract this tendency to the concentration of all the powers of the Government in the will of the numerical majority, resulting from the partial and imperfect expression of their voice through its organs?

Yes, fortunately, doubly fortunately, there is; not only a more full and perfect, but a full and perfect expression to be found in the constitution, acknowledged by all to be the fundamental and supreme law of the land. It is full and perfect, because it is the expression of the voice of each State, adopted by the separate assent of each, by itself, and for itself; and is the voice of all by being that of each component part, united and blended into one harmonious whole. It is not only full and perfect, but as just as it is full and perfect; for, combining the sense of each, and therefore all, there is nothing left on which injustice, or oppression, or usurpation can operate. And, finally, it is as supreme as it is just; because, comprehending the will of all, by uniting that of each of the parts, there is nothing within or above to control it. It is, indeed the *vox populi vox Dei;* the creating voice that called the system into existence,—and of which the Government itself is but a creature, clothed with delegated powers to execute its high behests.

We are thus brought to a question of the deepest import, and on which the fate of the system depends. How can this full, perfect, just and supreme voice of the people, embodied in the constitution, be brought to bear, habitually and steadily, in counteracting the fatal tendency of the Government to the absolute and despotic control of the numerical majority? Or—if I may be permitted to use so bold an expression—how is this, the Deity of our political system, to be successfully invoked, to interpose its all-powerful creating voice to save from perdition the creature of its will and the work of its hand? If it cannot be done, ours, like all free governments preceding it, must go the way of all flesh; but if it can be, its duration may be from generation to generation to the latest posterity. To this all-important question I will not attempt a reply at this time. It would lead me far beyond the limits properly belonging to this discussion. I descend from the digression nearer to the subject immediately at issue, in order to reply to an objection to the veto power, taken by the Senator from Virginia on this side the chamber, (Mr. Archer).

He rests his support of this resolution on the ground that the object intended to be effected by the veto has failed; that the framers of the constitution regarded the Legislative Department of the Government as the one most to be dreaded; and that their motive for vesting the Executive with the veto, was to check its encroachments on the other departments: but that the Executive, and not the Legislature had proved to be the most dangerous; and that the veto had become either useless or mischievous, by being converted into a sword to attack, instead of a shield to defend, as was originally intended.

I make no issue with the Senator, as to the correctness of his statement. I assume the facts to be as he supposes; not because I agree with him, but simply with the view of making my reply more brief.

Assuming, then, that the Executive Department has proved to be the more formidable, and that it requires to be checked, rather than to have the power of checking others,—the first inquiry, on that assumption, should be into the cause of its increase of power, in order to ascertain the seat and the nature of the danger; and the next, whether the measure proposed—that of divesting it of the veto, or modifying it as proposed—would guard against the danger apprehended.

I begin with the first; and in entering on it, assert, with confidence, that if the Executive has become formidable to the liberty or safety of the country, or other departments of the Government, the cause is not in the constitution, but in the acts and omissions of Congress itself.

According to my conception, the powers vested in the President by the constitution are few and effectually guarded, and are not of themselves at all formidable. In order to have a just conception of the extent of his powers, it must be borne in mind that there are but two classes of powers known to the constitution; namely—powers that are expressly granted, and those that are necessary to carry the granted powers into execution. Now, by a positive provision of the constitution, all powers necessary to the execution of the granted powers are expressly delegated to Congress, be they powers granted to the Legislative, Executive, or Judicial Department; and can only be exercised by the authority of Congress, and in the manner prescribed by law. This provision will be found in what is called the residuary clause, which declares that Congress shall have the power "to make all laws which shall be necessary and proper to carry into execution the foregoing powers" (those granted to Congress), "and all other powers vested by this constitution in the Government of the United States, or in any department or officer thereof." A more comprehensive provision cannot be imagined. It carries with it all powers necessary and proper to the execution of the granted powers, be they lodged where they may; and vests the whole, in terms not less explicit, in Congress. And here let me add, in passing, that the provision is as wise as it is comprehensive. It deposits the right of deciding what powers are necessary for the execution of the granted powers where, and where only, it can be lodged with safety—in the hands of the law-making power; and forbids any department or officer of the Government from exercising any power not expressly authorized by the constitution or the laws—thus making ours emphatically a Government of *law and constitution.*

Having now shown that the President is restricted by the constitution to powers expressly granted to him, and that if any of his granted powers be such that they require other powers to execute them, he cannot exercise them without the authority of Congress, I shall now show that there is not one power vested in him that is in any way dangerous, unless made so by the acts or permission of Congress. I shall take them in the order in which they stand in the constitution.

He is, in the first place, made commander-in-chief of the army and navy of the United States, and the militia, when called into actual service. Large and expensive military and naval establishments, and numerous corps of militia, called into service, would no doubt increase very dangerously the power and patronage of the President; but neither can take place but by the action of Congress. Not a soldier can be enlisted, a ship of war built, nor a militiaman called into service, without its authority; and, very fortunately, our situation is such, that there is no necessity, and, probably, will be none, why his power and patronage should be dangerously increased by either of those means.

He is next vested with the power to make treaties, and to appoint officers, with the advice and consent of the Senate. And here again his power can only be made dangerous by the action of one or both Houses of Congress. In the formation of treaties, two-thirds of the Senate must concur; and it is difficult to conceive of a treaty that could materially enlarge his powers, which would not require an act of Congress to carry it into effect. The appointing power may, indeed, dangerously increase his patronage, if officers be uselessly multiplied and too highly paid; but if such should be the case, the fault would be in Congress, by whose authority, exclusively, they can be created or their compensation regulated.

But much is said, in this connection, of the power of removal, justly accompanied by severe condemnation of the many and abusive instances of the use of the power, and the dangerous influence it gives the President; in all of which I fully concur. It is, indeed, a corrupting and dangerous power, when officers are greatly multiplied and highly paid,—and when it is perverted from its legitimate object to the advancement of personal or party purposes. But I find no such power in the list of powers granted to the Executive, which is proof conclusive that it belongs to the class necessary and proper to execute some other power, if it exists at all, which none can doubt; and for reasons already assigned, cannot be exercised without authority of law. If, then, it has been abused, it must be because Congress has not done its duty in permitting it to be exercised by the President without the sanction of law, and guarding against the abuses to which it is so liable.

The residue of the list are rather duties than rights—that of recommending to Congress such measures as he may deem expedient; of convening both Houses on extraordinary occasions; of adjourning them when they cannot agree on the time; of receiving ambassadors and other ministers; of taking care that the laws be faithfully executed, and commissioning the officers of the United States. Of all these, there is but one which claims particular notice, in connection with the point immediately under consideration; and that is, his power as the administrator of the laws. But whatever power he may have in that capacity depends on the action of Congress. If Congress should limit its legislation to the few great subjects confided to it; so frame its laws as to leave as little as possible to discretion, and take care to see that they are duly and faithfully executed, the administrative powers of the President would be proportionally limited, and divested of all danger. But if, on the contrary, it should extend its legislation in every direction; draw within its action subjects never contemplated by the constitution; multiply its acts, create numerous offices, and increase the revenue and expenditures proportionally,—and, at the same time, frame its laws vaguely and loosely, and withdraw, in a great measure, its supervising care over their execution, his power would indeed become truly formidable and alarming. Now I appeal to the Senator and his friend, the author of this resolution, whether the growth of Executive power has not been the result of such a course on the part of Congress. I ask them whether this power has not, in fact, increased or decreased just in proportion to the increase or decrease of that system of legislation which has been described? What was the period of its maximum increase, but the very period which they have so frequently and loudly denounced as the one most distinguished for the prevalence of Executive power and usurpation? Much of that power certainly depended on the remarkable man then at the head of the department; but much—far more—on the system of legislation which the author of this resolution had built up with so much zeal and labor,—and which carried the powers of the Government to a point far beyond that to which it had ever before attained,—drawing many and important ones into its vortex, of which the framers of the constitution never dreamed. And here let me say to both of the Senators,—and the party of which they are prominent members,—that they labor in vain to bring down Executive power, while they support the system they so zealously advocate. The power they complain of is but its necessary fruit. Be assured, that as certain as Congress transcends its assigned limits, and usurps powers never conferred, or stretches those conferred beyond the proper limits; so surely will the fruits of its usurpation pass into the hands of the Executive. In seeking to become master, it but makes a master in the person of the President. It is only by confining itself to its allotted sphere, and a discreet use of its acknowledged powers, that it can retain that ascendency in the Government which the constitution intended to confer on it.

Having now pointed out the cause of the great increase of the Executive power on which the Senator rested his objection to the veto power; and having satisfactorily shown, as I trust I have, that, if it has proved dangerous in fact, the fault is not in the constitution, but in Congress,—I would next ask him, in what possible way could the divesting the President of his veto, or modifying it as he proposes, limit his power? Is it not clear that, so far from the veto being the cause of the increase of his power, it would have acted as a limitation on it, if it had been more freely and frequently used? If the President had vetoed the original bank, the connection with the banking system, the tariffs of 1824 and 1828, and the numerous acts appropriating money for roads, canals, harbors, and a long list of other measures not less unconstitutional,—would his power have been half as great as it now is? He has grown great and powerful, not because *he used* his veto, but because *he abstained* from using it. In fact, it is difficult to imagine a case in which its application can tend to enlarge his power, except it be the case of an act intended to repeal a law calculated to increase his power,—or to restore the authority of one which, by an arbitrary construction of his power, he has set aside.

Now let me add, in conclusion, that this is a question, in its bearings, of vital importance to that wonderful and sublime system of governments which our patriotic ancestors established, not so much by their wisdom,—wise and experienced as they were,—as by the guidance of a kind Providence, who, in his divine dispensation, so disposed events as to lead to the establishment of a system wiser than those who framed it. The veto, of itself, important as it is, sinks into nothing compared to the principle involved. It is but one, and that by no means the most considerable, of those many wise devices which I have attempted to explain, and which were intended to strengthen the popular basis of our Government, and resist its tendency to fall under the control of the dominant interest, acting through the mere numerical majority. The introduction of this resolution may be regarded as one of the many symptoms of that fatal tendency,—and of which we had such fearful indications in the bold attempt at the late extraordinary session, of forcing through a whole system of measures of the most threatening and alarming character, in the space of a few weeks, on the ground that they were all decided in the election of the late President; thus attempting to substitute the will of a majority of the people, in the choice of a Chief Magistrate, as the legislative authority of the Union, in lieu of the beautiful and profound system established by the constitution.

Chapter *XXI.*

"Speech on the Treaty of Washington," 19 August 1842

In this speech, Calhoun explained his long-held conviction that the free exchange of economic goods promotes peaceful relations among countries. In other words, unhindered trade and tolerance could avoid conflict and promote mutual prosperity and peace.

Mr. Calhoun said, that his object in rising was not to advocate or oppose the treaty, but simply to state the reasons that would govern him in voting for its ratification. The question, according to his conception, was not whether it was all we could desire, or whether it was liable to this or that objection; but whether it was such an one that, under all the circumstances of the case, it would be most advisable to adopt or reject. Thus regarded, it was his intention to state fairly the reasons in favor of and against its ratification; and to assign to each its proper weight, beginning with the portion relating to the Northeastern boundary, the settlement of which was the immediate and prominent object of the negotiation.

He was one of those who had not the slightest doubt that the boundary for which the State of Maine contended was the true one, as established by the treaty of peace in 1783; and had accordingly so recorded his vote, after a deliberate investigation of the subject. But, although such was his opinion, he did not doubt, at the time, that the boundary could only be settled by a compromise line. We had admitted it to be doubtful at an early period during the administration of Washington; and more recently and explicitly, by stipulating to submit it to the arbitration of a friendly power, by the treaty of Ghent. The doubt, thus admitted on our part to exist, had been greatly strengthened by the award of the King of Holland, who had been mutually selected as the arbiter under the treaty. So strong, indeed was his (Mr. C.'s) impression that the dispute could only be settled by a compromise or conventional line, that he said to a friend in the then Cabinet (when an appropriation was made a few years since for a special mission to England on the subject of the boundary, and his name, among others, was mentioned for the place), that the question could only be settled by compromise; and for this purpose, some distinguished citizen of the section ought to be selected; and neither he, nor any other Southern man, ought to be thought of. With these previous impressions, he was prepared, when the negotiation opened, to expect if it succeeded in adjusting the difficulty, it would be (as it has been) on a compromise line. Notwithstanding, when it was first announced that the line agreed on included a considerable portion of the territory lying to the west of the line awarded by the King of Holland, he was incredulous, and expressed himself strongly against it. His first impression was, perhaps, the more strongly against it, from the fact that he had fixed on the river St. John, from the mouth of Eel River, taking the St. Francis branch (the one selected by the King of Holland) as the natural and proper compromise boundary, including in our limits all the portion of the disputed territory lying north of Eel River, and west and south of the St. John, above its junction; and all the other within that of Great Britain. On a little reflection, however, he resolved not to form his opinion of the merits or demerits of the treaty on rumor or imperfect information; but to wait until the whole subject was brought before the Senate officially, and then to make it up on full knowledge of all the facts and circumstances, after deliberate and mature reflection; and this he had done with the utmost care and impartiality. What he now proposes was, to give the result, with the reasons on which it rests, and which would govern his vote on the ratification.

He still believed that the boundary which he had fixed in his own mind was the natural and proper one; but as that could not be obtained, the question for them to decide was—Are the objections to the boundary as actually agreed on, and the stipulations connected with it, such as ought to cause its rejection? In deciding it, it must be borne in mind that as far as this portion of the boundary is concerned, it is a question belonging much more to the State of Maine than to the Union. It is, in truth, but the boundary of that State; and it makes a part of the boundary of the United States, only by being the exterior boundary of one of the States of our Federal Union. It is her sovereignty and soil that are in dispute, except the portion of the latter that still remains in Massachusetts; and it belongs in the first place to her, and to Massachusetts, as far as her right of soil is involved, to say what their rights and interests are, and what is required to be done. The rest of the Union is bound to defend them in their just claim; and to assent to what they may be willing to assent, in settling the claim in contest, if there should be nothing in it inconsistent with the interest, honor, or safety of the rest of the Union. It is thus the controversy has ever been regarded. It is well known that President Jackson would readily have agreed to the award of the King of Holland, had not Maine objected; and that to overcome her objection, he was prepared to recommend to Congress to give her, in order to get her consent, one million of acres of the public domain, worth, at the minimum price, a million and a quarter of dollars. The case is now reversed. Maine and Massachusetts have both assented to the stipulations of the treaty, as far as the question of the boundary affects their peculiar interest, through commissioners vested with full powers to represent them; and the question for us to decide is— Shall we reject that to which they have assented? Shall the Government, after refusing to agree to the award of the King of Holland, because Maine objected, now reverse its course, and refuse to agree to that which she and Massachusetts have both assented to? There may, indeed, be reasons strong enough to authorize such a course; but they must be such as will go to prove that we cannot give our assent consistently with the interests, the honor, or the safety of the Union. These have not been assigned, and, he would add, if there be any such, he has not been able to detect them.

It has, indeed, been said that the assent of Maine was coerced. She certainly desired to obtain a more favorable boundary; but when the alternative was presented of another reference to arbitration, she waived her objection, as far as she was individually concerned, rather than incur the risk, delay, uncertainty and vexation of another submission of her claims to arbitration; and left it to the Senate, the constituted authority appointed for the purpose, to decide on the general merits of the treaty, as it relates to the whole Union. In so doing, she has, in his opinion, acted wisely and patriotically—wisely for herself, and patriotically in reference to the rest of the Union. She has not got, indeed, all she desired; and has even lost territory, if the treaty be compared with the award of the King of Holland; but, as an offset, that which she has lost is of little value, while that which she retains has been greatly increased in value by the stipulations contained in the treaty. The whole amount lost, is about half a million of acres. It lies along the eastern slope of the highlands, skirting the St. Lawrence to the east, and is acknowledged to be of little value for soil, timber, or any thing else—a sterile region, in a severe, inhospitable clime. Against this loss, she has acquired the right to navigate the river St. John; and that, not only to float down the timber on its banks, but all the productions of the extensive, well-timbered, and, taken as a whole, not a sterile portion of the State that lies on her side of the basin of that river and its tributaries. But this is not all. She also gains what is vastly more valuable—the right to ship them on the same terms as colonial productions to Great Britain and her colonial possessions.

These great and important advantages will probably double the value of the extensive region, and make it one of the most populous and flourishing portions of the State. Estimated by a mere moneyed standard, these advantages are worth, he would suppose, all the rest of the territory claimed by Maine without them. If to this be added the sum of about $200,000 to be paid her for the expenses of defending her territory, and $300,000 to her and Massachusetts in equal moieties, in consequence of their assent to the boundary and the equivalents received, it must be apparent that Maine has not made a bad exchange in accepting the treaty, as compared with the award, as far as her separate interest is concerned. But be this as it may, she is the rightful judge of her own interests; and her assent is a sufficient ground for our assent, provided that to which she has assented does not involve too great a sacrifice, on the part of the rest of the Union, of their honor or safety. So far from this, as far as the rest of the Union is concerned, the sacrifice is small and the gain great. They are under solemn constitutional obligations to defend Maine, as one of the members of the Union, against invasion, and to protect her territory, cost what it may, at every hazard. The power, claiming what she contended to be hers, is one of the greatest, if not the greatest on earth; the dispute is of long standing, and of a character difficult to be adjusted; and, however clear the right of Maine may be regarded in the abstract, it has been made doubtful, in consequence of admissions, for which the Government of the Union is responsible. To terminate such a controversy, with the assent of the party immediately interested, by paying the small sum of half a million,—of which a large part (say $200,000) is unquestionably due to Maine, and would have to be paid to her without the treaty,—is indeed a small sacrifice, a fortunate deliverance. President Jackson was willing to allow her, as has been stated, more than twice as much for her assent to the award; and in doing so, he showed his wisdom, whatever might have been thought of it at the time. Those, at least, who opposed the treaty, will not charge him with being willing to sacrifice the interest and honor of the Union in making the offer; and yet the charge which they make against this portion of the treaty does, by implication, subject what he was ready to do to a similar one.

But it is said that the territory which England would acquire beyond the boundary of the awarded line, would greatly strengthen her frontier, and weaken ours; and would thereby endanger the safety of the country in that quarter. He did not profess to be deeply versed in military science; but, according to his conception, there was no foundation for the objection. It was, if he did not mistake, the very last point on our whole frontier, from the mouth of the St. Croix to the outlet of Lake Superior, on which an expedition would be organized on either side to attack the possessions of the other. In a military point of view, our loss is as nothing in that quarter; while in another, and a much more important quarter, our gain by the treaty is great, in the same point of view. He referred to that provision by which we acquire Rouse's Point, at the northern extremity of Lake Champlain. It is among the most important military positions on the whole line of our eastern and northern frontier,—whether it be regarded in reference to offensive or defensive operations. He well remembered the deep sensation caused among military men in consequence of its loss; and he would leave the question of loss or gain, in a military point of view (taking the two together), to their decision, without the least doubt what it would be.

But if it should be thought by any one that these considerations, as conclusive as they seemed to be, were not sufficient to justify the ratification of this portion of the treaty, there were others, which appeared to him to be perfectly conclusive. He referred to the condition in which we would be left, if the treaty should be rejected. He would ask—if, after having agreed at Ghent to refer the subject to arbitration, and, after having refused to agree to the award made under that reference, by an arbitrator of our own selection, we should now reject this treaty, negotiated by our own Secretary of State, under our own eyes, and which had previously received the assent of the States immediately interested—whether there would be the slightest prospect that another equally favorable would ever be obtained. On the contrary, would we not stand in a far worse condition than ever, in reference to our claim? Would it not, indeed, be almost certain that we should lose the whole of the basin of the St. John, and Great Britain gain all for which she ever contended, strengthened as she would be by the disclosures made during this discussion?* He was far from asserting that the facts disclosed established

*The following extract from the speech of Mr. Rives, the Chairman of the Committee on Foreign Relations, will show what the disclosures were:—

It appears to the committee, therefore, in looking back to the public and solemn acts of the Government, and of successive administrations, that the time has passed, if it ever existed, when we could be justified in making the precise line of boundary claimed by us the subject of a *sine qua non* of negotiation, or of the *ultima ratio*—of an assertion by force. Did a second arbitration, then, afford the prospect of a more satisfactory result? This expedient seemed to be equally rejected by all parties—by the United States, by Great Britain, and by the State of Maine. If such an alternative should be contemplated by any one as preferable to the arrangement which had been made, it is fit to bear in mind the *risk and uncertainty,* as well as the inevitable delay and expense, incident to that mode of decision. We have already seen, in the instance of the arbitration by the King of the Netherlands, how much weight a tribunal the claim of Great Britain, or that the map exhibited is the one to which Franklin referred, in his note to the Count de Vergennes, the French Minister; but it cannot be doubted that the conformity of the line delineated on the map with the one described in his note, would have the effect of strengthening not a little the claims of Great Britain in her own estimation and that of the world. But the facts stated, and the map exhibited by the Chairman of the Committee on Foreign Relations (Mr. Rives), are not the only or the strongest disclosures made during the discussion. The French map, introduced by the Senator from Missouri (Mr. Benton), from Mr. Jefferson's collection in the Congress library, in order to rebut the inference from the former, turned out to be still more so. This was made in the village of Passy, in the year after the treaty of peace was negotiated, where Franklin (who was one of the negotiators) resided, and was dedicated to him; and

of that sort is inclined to give to the argument of *convenience,* and a supposed *intention* on the part of the negotiators of the treaty of 1773, against the literal and positive terms employed by the instrument in its description of limits. Is there no danger, in the event of another arbitration, that a farther research into the public archives of Europe might bring to light some embarrassing (even though apocryphal) document, to throw a new shade of plausible doubt on the clearness of our title, in the view of a sovereign arbiter? Such a document has already been communicated to the committee; and I feel it (said Mr. R.) to be my duty to lay it before the Senate, that they may fully appreciate its bearings, and determine for themselves the weight and importance which belong to it. It is due to the learned and distinguished gentleman (Mr. Jared Sparks, of Boston), by whom the document referred to was discovered in the archives of France, while pursuing his laborious and intelligent researches connected with the history of our own country, that the account of it should be given in his own words, as contained in a communication addressed by him to the Department of State. I proceed, therefore, to read from that communication:—

"While pursuing my researches among the voluminous papers relating to the American Revolution in the *Archives des Affaires Etrangères,* in Paris, I found in one of the bound volumes an original letter from Dr. Franklin to Count de Vergennes, of which the following is an exact transcript:—

"PASSY, *December* 6, 1782.

"SIR: I have the honor of returning herewith the map your Excellency sent me yesterday. I have marked with a strong red line, according to your desire, the limits of the United States, as settled in the preliminaries between the British and American plenipotentiaries.

"With great respect, I am, &c.,

"B. FRANKLIN."

"This letter was written six days after the preliminaries were signed; and if we could procure the identical map mentioned by Franklin, it would seem to afford conclusive evidence as to the meaning affixed by the commissioners to the language of the treaty on the subject of the boundaries. You may well suppose that I lost no time in making inquiry for the map, not doubting that it would confirm all my previous opinions respecting the validity of our claim. In the geographical department of the Archives are sixty thousand maps and charts; but so well arranged with catalogues and indexes, that any one of them may be easily found. After a little research in the American division, with the aid of the keeper, I came upon a this has the boundary line drawn in exact conformity to the other, and in the manner described in the note of Dr. Franklin—a line somewhat more adverse to us than that claimed by Great Britain. But, striking as is this coincidence, he was far from regarding it as sufficient to establish the claim of Great Britain. It would, however, be in vain to deny that it was a corroborating circumstance, calculated to add no small weight to her claim.

It would be still further increased by the fact that France was our ally at the time, and, as such, must have been consulted and kept constantly advised of all that occurred during the progress of the negotiation, including its final result. It would be idle to suppose that these disclosures would not weigh heavily against us in any future negotiation. They would, so much so—taken in connection with the adverse award of the King of Holland, and this treaty, should it be

map of North America, by D'Anville, dated 1746, in size about eighteen inches square, on which was drawn a *strong red line* throughout the entire boundary of the United States, answering precisely to Franklin's description. The line is bold and distinct in every part, made with red ink, and apparently drawn with a hair pencil, or a pen with a blunt point. There is no other coloring on any part of the map.

"Imagine my surprise on discovering that this line runs wholly south of the St. John, and between the head waters of that river and those of the Penobscot and Kennebec. In short, it is exactly the line now contended for by Great Britain, except that it concedes more than is claimed. The north line, after departing from the source of the St. Croix, instead of proceeding to Mars Hill, stops far short of that point, and turns off to the west, so as to leave on the British side all the streams which flow into the St. John, between the source of the St. Croix and Mars Hill. It is evident that the line, from the St. Croix to the Canadian highlands, is intended to exclude *all the waters* running into the St. John.

"There is no positive proof that this map is actually the one marked by Franklin; yet, upon any other supposition, it would be difficult to explain the circumstances of its agreeing so perfectly with his description, and of its being preserved in the place where it would naturally be deposited by Count de Vergennes. I also found another map in the Archives, on which the same boundary was traced in a dotted red line with a pen, apparently copied from the other.

"I inclose herewith a map of Maine, on which I have drawn a strong black line, corresponding with the red one above mentioned."

I am far from intimating (said Mr. Rives) that the documents discovered by Mr. Sparks, curious and well worthy of consideration as they undoubtedly are, are of weight sufficient to shake the title of the United States, founded on the positive language of the treaty of peace. But they could not fail, in the event of another reference, to give increased confidence and emphasis to the pretensions of Great Britain, and to exert a corresponding influence upon the mind of the arbiter. It is worth while in this connection, to turn to what Lord Ashburton has said, in one of his communications to Mr. Webster, when explaining his views of the position of the highlands described in the treaty:—

"My inspection of the maps, and my examination of the documents," says his Lordship, "lead me to a very strong conviction that the highlands contemplated by the negotiators of the treaty were the only highlands then known to them—*at the head of the Penobscot, Kennebec, and the rivers west of the St. Croix;* and that they did not precisely know how the north rejected—as to render hopeless any future attempt to settle the question by negotiation or arbitration. No alternative would be left us but to yield to the full extent of the British claim, or to put Maine in possession by force,—and that, too, with the opinion and sympathy of the world against us and our cause. In his opinion, we would be bound to attempt it, in justice to Maine, should we refuse to agree to what she has assented. So much for the boundary question, as far as Maine is concerned.

Having now shown—satisfactorily, he hoped—that Maine has acted wisely for herself in assenting to the treaty, it remained to be considered whether we, the representatives of the Union on such questions, would not also do so in ratifying it, as far at least as the boundary question is involved. He would add nothing to what had already been said of the portion in which Maine was immediately interested. His remarks would be confined to the remaining portion of the boundary, extending from the northwestern corner of that State to the Rocky Mountains.

line from the St. Croix would strike them; and if it were not my wish to shorten this discussion, I believe a very good argument might be drawn from the words of the treaty in proof of this. In the negotiations with Mr. Livingston, and afterwards with Mr. McLane, this view seemed to prevail; and, as you are aware, there were proposals to search for these highlands to the west, where alone, I believe, they will be found to answer perfectly the description of the treaty. *If this question should unfortunately go to a further reference, I should by no means despair of finding some confirmation of this view of the case."*

It is for the Senate to consider (added Mr. Rives) whether there would not be much risk of introducing new complications and embarrassments in this controversy, by leaving it open for another litigated reference; and if the British Government—strongly prepossessed, as its minister tells us it is, with the justice of its claims—would not find what it would naturally consider a persuasive "confirmation of its view of the case" in documents such as those encountered by Mr. Sparks in his historical researches in the archives of France.

A map has been vauntingly paraded here, from Mr. Jefferson's collection, in the zeal of opposition (without taking time to see what it was), to confront and invalidate the map found by Mr. Sparks in the Foreign Office at Paris; but, the moment it is examined, it is found to sustain, by the most precise and remarkable correspondence in every feature, the map communicated by Mr. Sparks. The Senator who produced it, could see nothing but the microscopic dotted line running off in a northeasterly direction; but the moment other eyes were applied to it, there was found, in bold relief, a strong red line, indicating the limits of the United States, according to the treaty of peace, and coinciding, minutely and exactly, with the boundary traced on the map of Mr. Sparks. That this red line, and not the hardly visible dotted line, was intended to represent the limits of the United States according to the treaty of peace, is conclusively shown by the circumstance that the red line is drawn on the map all around the exterior boundary of the United States; through the middle of the Northern Lakes, thence through the Long Lake and the Rainy Lake to the Lake of the Woods; and from the western extremity of the Lake of the Woods to the River Mississippi; and along that river, to the point where the boundary of the United States, according to the treaty of peace, leaves it; and thence, by its easterly course, to the mouth of the St. Mary's, on the Atlantic.

Throughout this long-extended line, every question has been settled to our satisfaction. Our right has been acknowledged to a territory of about one hundred thousand acres of land in New Hampshire, which would have been lost by the award of the King of Holland. A long gore of about the same amount, lying in Vermont and New-York, and which was lost under the treaty of Ghent, would be regained by this. It includes Rouse's Point. Sugar Island, lying in the water connection between Lakes Huron and Superior, and heretofore in dispute, is acknowledged to be ours; it is large, and valuable for soil and position. So also is Isle Royale, near the northern shore of Lake Superior, acknowledged to be ours—a large island, and valuable for its fisheries. And also, a large tract of country to the north and west of that lake, between Fond du Lac and the River St. Louis on one side, and Pigeon River on the other—containing four millions of acres. It is said to be sterile, but cannot well be more so than that acquired by Great Britain, lying west of the boundary awarded by the King of Holland. In addition, all the islands in the River St. Lawrence and the lakes, which were divided in running out the division line under previous treaties, are acquired by us under this; and all the channels and passages are opened to the common uses of our citizens and the subjects of Great Britain.

Such are the provisions of the treaty in reference to this long line of boundary. Our gain—regarded in the most contracted point of view, as mere equivalents for the sum assumed to be paid by us to Maine and Massachusetts for their assent to the treaty—is vastly greater than what we have contracted to pay. Taking the whole boundary question together, and summing up the loss and gain of the whole, including what affects Maine and Massachusetts, and he could not doubt that, regarded merely as set-offs, our gain greatly exceeds our loss—vastly so, compared to what it would have been under the award of the King of Holland,—including the equivalent which our Government was willing to allow Maine for her assent. But it would be, indeed, to take a very contracted view to regard it in that light. It would be to overlook the vast importance of permanently establishing, between two such powers, a line of boundary of several thousand miles, abounding in disputed points of much difficulty and long standing. The treaty, he trusted, would do much to lay the foundation of a solid peace between the countries—a thing so much to be desired.

It is certainly much to be regretted, after settling so large a portion of the boundary, that the part beyond the Rocky Mountains should remain unadjusted. Its settlement would have contributed much to strengthen the foundation of a durable peace. But would it be wise to reject the treaty, because all has not been done that could be desired? He placed a high value on our territory on the west of those mountains, and held our title to it to be clear; but he would regard it as an act of consummate folly, to stake our claim on a trial of strength at this time. The territory is now held by joint occupancy, under the treaty of Ghent, which either party may terminate by giving to the other six months' notice. If we were to attempt to assert our exclusive right of occupancy at present, the certain loss of the territory must be the result; for the plain reason that Great Britain could concentrate there a much larger force, naval and military, in a much shorter time, and at far less expense, than we could. This will not be denied; but it will not be always the case. Our population is steadily—he might say rapidly—advancing across the continent, to the borders of the Pacific Ocean. Judging from past experience, the tide of population will sweep across the Rocky Mountains, with resistless force, at no distant period; when what we claim will quietly fall into our hands, without expense or bloodshed. Time is acting for us. Wait patiently, and all we claim will be ours; but if we attempt to seize it by force, it will be sure to elude our grasp.

Having now stated his reasons for voting to ratify the articles in the treaty relating to the boundary, he would next proceed to assign those that would govern his vote on the two relating to the African slave trade. And here he would premise, that there are several circumstances, which caused no small repugnance on his part to any stipulations whatever with Great Britain on the subject of those articles; and he would add, that he would have been gratified if they, and all other stipulations on the subject, could have been entirely omitted; but he must, at the same time, say, he did not see how it was possible to avoid entering into some arrangement on the subject. To understand the difficulty, it will be necessary to advert to the course heretofore taken by our Government in reference to the subject, and the circumstances under which the negotiations that resulted in this treaty had commenced.

Congress at an early day—as soon, in fact, as it could legislate on the subject, under the constitution—passed laws enacting severe penalties against the African slave trade. This was followed by the treaty of Ghent, which declared it to be irreconcilable with the principles of humanity and justice, and stipulated that both of the parties—the United States and Great Britain—should use their best endeavors to effect its abolition. Shortly after, an act of Congress was passed declaring it to be piracy; and a resolution was adopted by Congress, requesting the President to enter into arrangements with other powers for its suppression. Great Britain, actuated by the same feelings, succeeded in making treaties with the European maritime powers for its suppression; and, not long before the commencement of this negotiation, had entered into joint stipulations with the five great powers to back her on the question of search. She had thus acquired a general supervision of the trade along the African coast; so that vessels carrying the flag of every other country, except ours, were subject on that coast to the inspection of her cruisers, and to be captured, if suspected of being engaged in the slave trade. In consequence, ours became almost the only flag used by those engaged in the trade, whether our people or foreigners; although our laws inhibited the traffic under the severest penalties. In this state of things, Great Britain put forward the claim of the right of search as indispensable to suppress a trade prohibited by the laws of the civilized world, and to the execution of the laws and treaties of the nations associated with her by mutual engagements for its suppression. At this stage, a correspondence took place between our late minister at the Court of St. James and Lord Palmerston on the subject, in which the latter openly and boldly claimed the right of search, and which was promptly and decidedly repelled on our side. We had long since taken our stand against it, and had resisted its abuse, as a belligerent right, at the mouth of the cannon. Neither honor nor policy on our part could tolerate its exercise in time of peace, in any form—whether in that of search, as claimed by Lord Palmerston, or the less offensive and unreasonable one of visitation, as proposed by his successor, Lord Aberdeen. And yet we were placed in such circumstances as to require that something should be done. It was in such a state of things that the negotiation commenced—and commenced, in part, in reference to this subject, which was tending rapidly to bring the two countries into collision. On our side, we were deeply committed against the traffic, both by legislation and treaty. The influence and the efforts of the civilized world were directed against it—and that, too, under our lead at the commencement; and with such success as to compel vessels engaged in it to take shelter, almost exclusively, under the fraudulent use of our flag. To permit such a state of things to continue, could not but deeply impeach our honor, and turn the sympathy of the world against us. On the other side, Great Britain had acquired, by treaties, the right of supervision, including that of search and capturing, over the trade on the coast of Africa, with the view to its suppression, from all the maritime powers except ourselves. Thus situated, he must say that he saw no alternative for us but the one adopted—to take the supervision of our own trade on that coast into our own hands, and to prevent, by our own cruisers, the fraudulent use of our flag. The only question, in the actual state of things, as it appeared to him, was, whether it should be done by a formal or informal arrangement? He would have preferred the latter; but the difference between them was not, in his opinion, such as would justify, on that account, the rejection of the treaty. They would, in substance be the same, and will differ but little, probably, in the expense of execution. Either was better than the other alternatives—to do nothing; to leave things in the dangerous state in which they stood; or to yield to the right of search or visitation.

It is objected that the arrangement entered into is virtually an acknowledgment of the right of search. He did not so regard it. On the contrary, he considered it, under all the circumstances, as a surrender of that claim on the part of Great Britain; a conclusion, which a review of the whole transaction, in his opinion, would justify. Lord Palmerston, in the first place, claimed the unqualified right of search, in which it is understood he was backed by the five great powers. Lord Aberdeen, with more wisdom and moderation, explained it to mean the right of visitation simply; and, finally, the negotiation is closed without reference to either, simply with a stipulation between the parties to keep up for five years a squadron of not less than eighty guns on the coast of Africa, to enforce, separately and respectively, the laws and obligations of each of the countries for the suppression of the slave trade. It is carefully worded, to make it mutual, but at the same time separate and independent: each looking to the execution of its own laws and obligations, and carefully excluding the supervision of either over the other, and thereby directly rebutting the object of search or visitation.

The other article, in reference to the same subject, stipulates that the parties will unite in all becoming representation and remonstrance, with any powers, within whose dominions markets are permitted for imported African slaves. If he were to permit his feelings to govern him exclusively, he would object to this more strongly than any other provision in the treaty,—not that he was opposed to the object or the policy of closing the market to imported negroes; on the contrary, he thought it both right and expedient in every view. Brazil and the Spanish colonies were the only markets, he believed, still remaining open, and to which this provision would apply. They were already abundantly supplied with slaves, and he had no doubt that sound policy on their part required that their markets should be finally and effectually closed. He would go further, and say that it was our interest they should be. It would free us from the necessity of keeping cruisers on the African coast, to prevent the illegal and fraudulent use of our flag, or for any other purpose but to protect our commerce in that quarter—a thing of itself much to be desired. We would have a still stronger interest, if we were governed by selfish considerations. We are rivals in the production of several articles, and more especially the greatest of all the agricultural staples—cotton. Next to our own country, Brazil possesses the greatest advantages for its production, and is already a large grower of the article; towards the production of which, the continuance of the market for imported slaves from Africa would contribute much. But he would not permit such considerations to influence him in voting on the treaty. He had no objection to see Brazil develope her resources to the full; but he did believe that higher considerations, connected with her safety, and that of the Spanish colonies, made it their interest that their market should be closed against the traffic.

But it may be asked, why, with these impressions, should he have any objection to this provision of the treaty? It was, because he was averse to interfering with other powers, when it could be avoided. It extends even to cases like the present, where there was a common interest in reference to the subject of advice or remonstrance; but it would be carrying his aversion to fastidiousness, were he to permit it to overule his vote in the adjustment of questions of such magnitude as are involved on the present occasion.

But the treaty is opposed, not only for what it contains, but also for what it does not; and, among other objections of the kind, because it has no provision in reference to the case of the Creole, and other similar ones. He admitted that it is an objection; and that it was very desirable that the treaty should have guarded, by specific and efficient provisions, against the recurrence of such outrages on the rights of our citizens, and indignity to our honor and independence. If any one has a right to speak warmly on the subject, he was the individual; but he could not forget that the question for us to decide is, Shall we ratify or reject the treaty? It is not whether all has been done which it was desirable should be done, but whether we shall confirm or reject what has actually been done;—not whether we have gained all we could desire, but whether we shall retain what we have gained. To decide this as it ought to be, it is our duty to weigh, calmly and fairly, the reasons for and against the ratification, and to decide in favor of the side which preponderates.

It does not follow that nothing has been done in relation to the cases under consideration, because the treaty contains no provisions in reference to them. The fact is otherwise. Much, very much, has been done;—in his opinion, little short, in its effect, of a positive stipulation by the treaty to guard against the recurrence of such cases hereafter. To understand how much has been done, and what has been gained by us, it is necessary to have a correct conception of the state of the case in reference to them, before the negotiation commenced, and since it terminated.

These cases are not of recent origin. The first of the kind was that of the brig Comet, which was stranded on the false keys of the Bahamas, as far back as 1830, with slaves on board. She was taken into Nassau, New Providence, by the wreckers, and the slaves liberated by the colonial authorities. The next was the

Encomium, which occurred in 1834, and which, in all the material circumstances, was every way similar to that of the Comet. The case of the Enterprise followed. It took place in 1835, and differed in no material circumstance from the others, as was acknowledged by the British Government, except that it occurred after the act of parliament abolishing slavery in the colonies had gone into operation, and the others prior to that period.

After a long correspondence of nearly ten years, the British Government agreed to pay for the slaves on board of the two first, on the ground that they were liberated before the act abolishing slavery had gone into operation; but refused to pay for those belonging to the Enterprise, because they were liberated after it had. To justify this distinction, Lord Palmerston had to assume the ground, virtually, that the law of nations was opposed to slavery—an assumption that placed the property of a third of the Union without the pale of its protection. On this ground, he peremptorily refused compensation for the slaves on board the Enterprise. Our Executive, under this refusal, accepted the compensation for those on board the Comet and Encomium, and closed the correspondence, without even bringing the subject before Congress. With such perfect indifference was the whole affair treated, that, during the long period the negotiation was pending, the subject was never once mentioned, as far as he recollected, in any Executive message; while those of far less magnitude—the debt of a few millions due from France, and this very boundary question—were constantly brought before Congress, and had nearly involved the country in war with two of the leading powers of Europe. Those who are now so shocked that the boundary question should be settled, without a settlement also of this, stood by in silence, year after year, during this long period, not only without attempting to unite the settlement of this with that of the boundary, but without ever once naming or alluding to it as an item in the list of the dispute between the two powers. It was regarded as beneath notice. He rejoiced to witness the great change which has taken place in relation to it; and to find that those who were then silent and indifferent, now exhibit so much zeal and vehemence about it. He took credit to himself for having contributed to bring this change about. It was he who revived our claim when it lay dead and buried among the archives of the State Department—who called for the correspondence—who moved resolutions affirming the principles of the law of nations in reference to these cases, and repelling the presumptuous and insulting assumption on which it was denied by the British negotiator. Such was the force of truth, and so solid the foundation on which he rested our claim, that his resolutions received the unanimous vote of this body; but he received no support—no, not a cheering word—from the quarter which now professes so much zeal on the subject. His utmost hope at the time was to keep alive our right, till some propitious moment should arrive to assert it successfully. In the mean time, the case of the Creole occurred, which, as shocking and outrageous as it is, was but the legitimate consequence of the principle maintained by Lord Palmerston, and on which he closed the correspondence in the case of the Enterprise.

Such was the state of the facts when the negotiations commenced in reference to these cases; and it remains now to be shown in what state it has left them. In the first place, the broad principles of the law of nations, on which he placed our right in his resolutions, have been clearly stated and conclusively vindicated in the very able letter of the Secretary of State, which has strengthened our cause not a little, as well from its intrinsic merit as the quarter from which it comes. In the next place, we have an explicit recognition of the principles for which we contend, in the answer of Lord Ashburton, who expressly says, that "on the great general principles affecting this case" (the Creole) "they do not differ;" and that is followed by "an engagement that instructions shall be given to the governors of Her Majesty's colonies on the southern borders of the United States, to execute their own laws with careful attention to the wishes of their Government to maintain good neighborhood; and that there shall be no officious interference with American vessels driven by accident or violence into their ports. The laws and duties of hospitality shall be executed." This pledge was accepted by our Executive, accompanied by the express declaration of the President, through the Secretary of State, that he places his reliance on those principles of public law which had been stated in the note of the Secretary of State. To all this it may be added, that strong assurances are given by the British negotiator, of his belief that a final arrangement may be made of the subject by positive stipulations in London. Such is the state in which the negotiation has left the subject.

Here again he would repeat, that such stipulations in the treaty itself would have been preferable. But who can deny, when he compares the state of the facts, as they stood before and since the close of this negotiation, that we have gained—largely gained—in reference to this important subject? Is there no difference, he would ask, between a stern and peremptory denial of our right, on the broad and the insulting ground assumed by Lord Palmerston, and its explicit recognition by Lord Ashburton?—none in the pledge that instructions should be given to guard against the recurrence of such cases, and a positive denial that we had suffered no wrong or insult, nor had any right to complain?—none between a final closing of all negotiation, and a strong assurance of a final adjustment of the subject by satisfactory arrangement by treaty? And would it be wise or prudent on our part to reject what has been gained, because all has not been? As to himself, he must say that, at the time he moved his resolutions, he little hoped, in the short space of two years, to obtain what has already been gained; and that he regarded the prospect of a final and satisfactory adjustment, at no distant day, of this subject, so vital in its principles to his constituents and the whole South, as far more probable than he then did this explicit recognition of the principles for which he contended. In the mean time he felt assured the engagement given by the British negotiator would be fulfilled in good faith; and that the hazard of collision between the countries, and the disturbance of their peace and friendship, has passed away, as far as it depends on this dangerous subject. But if in this he should unfortunately be mistaken, we should stand on much more solid ground in defence of our rights, in consequence of what has been gained; as there would then be superadded broken faith to the violation of the laws of nations.

Having now said what he intended on the more important points, he would pass over, without dwelling on the provision of the treaty for delivering up to justice persons charged with certain crimes; the affair of the Caroline; and the correspondence in reference to impressment. The first is substantially the same as that contained in Jay's treaty on the same subject. On the next, he had nothing to add to what had already been said. As to the last, he did not doubt that the strong ground taken in the correspondence against the impressment of seamen on board of our merchant vessels, in time of war, would have a good effect. It will contribute to convince Great Britain that the practice cannot be renewed, in the event of another European war, without a certain and immediate conflict between the two countries.

I (said Mr. Calhoun) have now stated my opinion fully and impartially on the treaty with the connected subjects. On reviewing the whole, and weighing the reasons for and against its ratification, I cannot doubt that the former greatly preponderate. If we have not gained all that could be desired, we have gained much that is desirable; and, if all has not been settled, much has been— and that not of little importance. It is not of little importance to have the Northeastern boundary settled—and this, too, with the consent of the States immediately interested; a subject which has been in dispute almost from the origin of the Government, and which had become more and more entangled, and adverse to our claim, on every attempt heretofore made to settle it. Nor is it of little importance to have the whole line of boundary between us and the British dominions, from the source of the St. Croix to the Rocky Mountains, settled—a line of more than three thousand miles, with many disputed points of long standing, the settlement of which had baffled all previous attempts. Nor is it of little importance to have adjusted the embarrassments relating to the African slave trade, by adopting the least objectionable of the alternatives. Nor to have the principles of the law of nations for which we contended, in reference to the Creole and other cases of the kind, recognized by Great Britain; nor to have a solemn pledge against their recurrence, with a reasonable assurance of satisfactory stipulations by treaty. Nor is it of little importance to have, by the settlement of these inveterate and difficult questions, the relation of the two countries settled down in amity and peace,—permanent amity and peace, as it may be hoped,—in the place of that doubtful, unsettled condition, between peace and war, which has for so many years characterized it, and which is so hostile to the interests and prosperity of both countries.

Peace (said Mr. C.) is the first of our wants, in the present condition of our country. We want peace, to reform our own Government, and to relieve the country from its great embarrassments. Our Government is deeply disordered; its credit is impaired; its debt increasing; its expenditures extravagant and wasteful; its disbursements without efficient accountability; and its taxes (for duties are but taxes) enormous, unequal, and oppressive to the great producing classes of the country. Peace settled and undisturbed, is indispensable to a thorough reform, and such a reform to the duration of the Government. But, so long as the relation between the two countries continues in a state of doubt between peace and war, all attempts at such reform will prove abortive. The first step in any such, to be successful, must be to reduce the expenditures to the legitimate and economical wants of the Government. Without that, there can be nothing worthy of the name; but in an unsettled state of the relations of the two countries, all attempts at reduction will be baffled by the cry of war accompanied by insinuations against the patriotism of those who may be so hardy as to make them. Should the treaty be ratified, an end will be put to this, and no excuse or pretext be left to delay the great and indispensable work of reform. This may not be desirable to those who see, or fancy they see, benefits in high duties and wasteful expenditures; but, by the great producing and tax-paying portions of the community, it will be regarded as one of the greatest of blessings. These are not the only reasons for wanting peace. We want it, to enable the people and the States to extricate themselves from their embarrassments. They are both borne down by heavy debts, contracted in a period of fallacious prosperity, from which there is no other honest and honorable extrication but the payment of what is due. To enable both States and individuals to pay their debts, they must be left in full possession of all their means, with as few exactions or restrictions on their industry as possible on the part of this Government. To this, a settled state of peace and an open and free commerce are indispensable. With these, and the increasing habits of economy and industry now every where pervading the country, the period of embarrassment will soon pass away, to be succeeded by one of permanent and healthy prosperity.

Peace is, indeed, our policy. A kind Providence has cast our lot on a portion of the globe sufficiently vast to satisfy the most grasping ambition, and abounding in resources beyond all others, which only require to be fully developed to make us the greatest and most prosperous people on earth. To the full development of the vast resources of our country, we have political institutions most happily adapted. Indeed, it would be difficult to imagine a system more so than our Federal Republic—a system of State and General Governments, so blended as to constitute one sublime whole; the latter having charge of the interests common to all, and the former those local and peculiar to each State. With a system so happily constituted, let a durable and firm peace be established, and this Government be confined rigidly to the few great objects for which it was instituted; leaving the States to contend in generous rivalry, to develope, by the arts of peace, their respective resources; and a scene of prosperity and happiness would follow, heretofore unequalled on the globe. I trust (said Mr. C.) that this treaty may prove the first step towards such a peace. Once established with Great Britain, it would not be difficult, with moderation and prudence, to establish permanent peace with the rest of the world, when our most sanguine hopes of prosperity may be realized.

Chapter XXII.

Much more than a response to the questions of a colleague, this letter presents a comprehensive view of politics and society as well as Calhoun's vision of the role of constitutions. According to Calhoun, "Constitutions stand to governments, as laws do to individuals. As the object of laws is, to regulate and restrain the actions of individuals, so as to prevent one from oppressing or doing violence to another, so, in like manner, that of constitutions is, to regulate and restrain the actions of governments, so that those who exercise its powers, shall not oppress or do violence to the rest of the community."

Fort Hill, *July 3rd,* 1843.

Dear Sir:—It is necessary, before replying to the several questions on which you ask my views, and the reasons and principles on which I rest them, that I should make a remark explanatory of what I understand to be your desire.

Your questions are all couched in general terms, without reference to any particular case, except the sixth and last, which refers to that of Rhode Island. I understand them all, however, to grow out of it, and to have relation to this case; and that, the more fully my answers meet and cover it, the more fully will your object, in propounding the questions, be met.

With this understanding, I shall proceed to reply to your inquiries,—taking them in the order in which they stand in your letter.

Your first question is:—"When the Federal Union was formed by the adoption of our present Constitution, did, or did not, each member thereof possess such a republican form of government as satisfied the Constitution, and which, it is declared, the United States shall guarantee to every State of the Union?"

I answer, yes,—most certainly it did; and that, to suppose the contrary,—that any State was admitted into the Union, whose government, at the time, was not republican, within its meaning, would be absurd in the extreme. The Constitution provides, in express terms,* that—"The United States shall guarantee to every State in the Union, a republican form of government; and shall protect each of them against invasion; and, on application of the Legislature, or of the Executive (when the Legislature cannot be convened), against domestic violence." To suppose, under the first of these provisions, that any State, whose government was not republican, within the meaning of the guarantee, would ratify the Constitution and enter into the Union, and that the other States would accept the ratification and admit her, is too absurd for belief. It would be to suppose, that the State, so ratifying, stipulated for the suppression of the very government under which it entered the Union, and that the Government of the State called the Convention for ratifying the Constitution, with the design that it should be suppressed; or that she was ignorant of what she was doing. It would also be to suppose, that the other States, in accepting the ratification, and admitting her into the Union, permitted that to be done, which was directly opposed to the guarantee; and which, under the duty it imposed on them, they would be bound to suppress; or that they, too, were ignorant of what they were doing. Absurdity could not go further.

On this ground I rest my answer to your first question. Others might be added; but this is deemed sufficiently strong of itself.

Your second question is in the following words: "When a State has been admitted into the Union, and shall call on the Federal Executive for protection, in the manner, and for the purpose prescribed in the section quoted, can he pause to inquire and judge whether such State has, or has not a republican form of government; and according to his opinion thereon, grant or withhold the aid demanded?"

Your question, as I understand it, presupposes a case of domestic violence, within the meaning of the Constitution; and also that the State has made application, in the form it prescribes, for protection; and that your object is, to know if, in my opinion, the Federal Government has a right to determine whether the Government of the State is republican or not; and if it be not, whether the fact would take the case out of the guarantee, and make it the duty of the Federal Government to withhold the protection? With this understanding, I shall proceed to reply to it.

---

*Const. of the U. S. Art. 4, Sec. 4.

I answer, yes; but to explain the reasons and principles on which my answer rests, and the restrictions to which the high and delicate right involved is subject, it will be indispensable to enter fully into the nature and object of the section quoted;—and which, for brevity, I shall call the *guarantee section,*—with the duties it imposes, and the rights it confers on the Federal Government. There is not another in the whole instrument more important; or, on the right understanding of which, the success and duration of our political system more depend.

The section contains three distinct stipulations and guarantees,—that of a republican form of government, to every State of the Union,—that of protection to each against invasion,—and that against domestic violence, on the application of the Legislature, or the Executive, when the Legislature cannot be convened. The States themselves are the parties,—that is, the people of the several States,—as forming distinct, sovereign communities,—and organized under their respective governments. Such is clearly the meaning of the words in the section; and it is in this sense I shall use the words, *States, and People,* in this communication, unless otherwise explained. The language of the section is,—"The United States shall guarantee;" followed by the three stipulations, or guarantees.

In order to ascertain the intention of the parties, in entering into them, we must turn to the preamble of the Constitution, which declares the objects for which it was ordained and established. Among them we shall find three specified;—"to insure domestic tranquility,—provide for the common defence,—and to secure the blessings of liberty to ourselves and our posterity"—which have direct reference to the three guarantees; and to which they clearly stand as *means* to an *end.*

The framers of the Constitution were deeply versed in the history of free and confederated States; and knew well the dangers to which they are exposed from external and internal causes; and devised ample guards against them,—among which these three guarantees are not the least efficient. In order to form a true conception of the mode in which they were intended to act, and to place a correct construction on the guarantees, it will be necessary to inquire, what are the quarters from which the peace, safety, and liberty of the States may be endangered, and against which the guarantees are intended to protect them. They may be, in the first place, from force or violence from within; against which, the guarantee of protection against domestic violence is clearly intended. They may be, in the second place, from hostile attacks from without; and against which, the guarantee of protection against invasion is as clearly intended. And finally, they may be from the ambition and usurpation of their governments, or rather rulers; against which, the guarantee of a republican form of government is intended, as I hold and shall hereafter show, as a protection.

Such being the quarters, from which the peace, safety, and liberty of the States may be endangered or destroyed, and against which the guarantees were intended to secure them, that construction of the *guarantee section,* which shall most fully meet, and most effectually guard against the dangers from these various quarters, and which may not be inconsistent with a fair interpretation of the language of the section, may justly be assumed to be the true one. Guided by this rule, I shall now state what I believe to be its true construction; beginning with the guarantee to protect each State against domestic violence.

I hold, that its object is, to protect the *Governments* of the States, by placing that of each under the protection of the united power of all the States, against such domestic violence or force, as might endanger or destroy it from *within.* It is clearly one of the means, by which the peace, safety, and liberty of the State itself may be endangered or destroyed; and hence it clearly falls within the class of objects, to which the guarantees stand, as means to an end,—as has been stated. If to this be added, that it is difficult, if not impossible, to conceive how force or violence, from within, could be brought to bear against the State, except by being directed against its Government, it would seem conclusive that its protection is the immediate object of this guarantee. Any other would be violence offered by individuals against individuals; and would fall within the jurisdiction of the local authorities and Courts.

But if any doubt should still remain, that the protection of the *Government* of the State is the object, the wording of the guarantee would suffice to remove it. It expressly provides, that the protection shall be on the application of the Legislature of the State, or its Executive, if its Legislature cannot be convened; and thus vests in the *Government of the State,* and not the Federal Government, the right to determine whether there has been a case of domestic violence or not; and also of the necessity and propriety of applying for protection. It is only on such application that the Federal Government has any right whatever to interfere. This provision, of itself, would strongly indicate that the *Government* was the object of protection: but as strong as the indication is, of itself, it will be greatly strengthened by adverting to the reasons for inserting it, deduced from the character of our system of government.

In our complex system, the objects for which governments are instituted, are divided between the Federal and State Governments. The former is the common government of all the States; and to it is specifically delegated the powers necessary to carry into effect all the objects in which they have a common interest. The latter are the separate and peculiar governments of each; and to them and the people, all the other powers are reserved. Among them are embraced those that refer to the internal peace and safety of each State; to the governments of which, it exclusively belongs to determine what may endanger or destroy them; and the measures proper to be adopted to protect them. It is in strict accordance with this distribution, that protection, in case of domestic violence, should be on application of the Government of the State against which it is directed. What adds to the force of the reasoning is, that the provision is omitted in the other two guarantees, when the cause of inserting it does not exist. That it does not in the case of invasion, is clear; as all that appertains to the foreign or exterior relations of the States, belongs, in the distribution, to the Federal Government; and is accordingly embraced among the delegated rights. Hence, it is made its duty, to act, in that case, without waiting the application of the Government of the State invaded. The reason of its omission, in the case of the guarantee of a republican form of government—though less obvious, is not less strong, as I shall show when I come to consider it.

Such are my reasons for believing, that the immediate object of this guarantee, is the protection of the *Government* of the State, against force or violence from *within,* directed against it with a view to its subversion.

The next guarantee is, protection to each State against invasion. Its object is so clear, and it is so slightly connected with the objects of your inquiry, that I shall pass it over, without adding to the remarks I have made, incidentally, in reference to it, in considering the preceding guarantee.

I come now to the last, in the order in which I am considering them; but the first as they stand in the section; and the one immediately involved in the question under consideration,—I mean the guarantee of a republican form of government to every State in the Union.

I hold that, according to its true construction, its object is the reverse of that of protection against domestic violence: and that, instead of being intended to protect the *Governments* of the States, it is intended to protect each *State* (I use the term as explained) against its Government; or, more strictly, against the ambition or usurpation of its rulers. That the objects of the Constitution, to which the guarantees refer,—and liberty more especially,—may be endangered or destroyed by rulers, will not be denied. But, if admitted, it follows as a consequence, that it must be embraced in the guarantees, if not inconsistent with the language of the section. But if embraced, it must be in the guarantee under consideration, as it is not in the other two. If it be added that, without this construction, the guarantees would utterly fail to protect the States against the attempts of ambition and usurpation on the part of rulers, to change the forms of their governments, and to destroy their liberty,—(the danger, above all others, to which free and popular governments are most exposed), it would seem to follow irresistibly, under the rule I have laid down, that the construction which I have placed on the provision, as to the object of the guarantee, is the true one. But if doubts should still remain, the fact, that it fully explains why the provision which requires the application of the State, in case of the guarantee against domestic violence, is omitted, would place it beyond controversy; for it would be a perfect absurdity to require, that the party, against which the guarantee is intended to protect, should make application to be protected against itself.

There remains, indeed, one other quarter, from which the liberties of the States (one of the leading objects of the guarantees) can be destroyed: I mean the people themselves, constituting the several States, and acting in their political character, as citizens, and according to constitutional and legal forms. They may, acting in this character, if they choose, subvert the republican form of government, under which they entered the Union, and establish one of another form; and, thereby, abandon their liberty. I say, abandon it,—for, according to the exalted conception of our ancestors, nothing was worthy of the name of liberty, but that which was enjoyed under free popular governments. Against this danger, there is, and can be no guarantee. The reason requires but little explanation. The States themselves are parties to the guarantee; and it would be absurd to suppose that they undertook to enter into a guarantee against themselves.

Besides, liberty, from its nature, cannot be forced on a people. It must be voluntarily embraced. If the people do not choose to embrace it, or continue it, after they have, it cannot be forced on them. The very act of doing so, would destroy it; and divest the State of its independence and sovereignty, and sink it into a dependent province. But, if it had been possible for it to be otherwise, even in that case, there would have been no guarantee against it. To provide one, would have been regarded as a superfluous precaution; for it was not in the heart of our free and brave ancestors, to conceive that any State of the Union would voluntarily abandon its liberty, by substituting for its republican government, one of a different form. Had such a proposition been made, it would have been regarded as an insult.

Such is the construction I put on the immediate objects of the three guarantees; with my reasons for it. As strong as they are, when the guarantees are considered separately, they are still more so, when viewed in connection as a whole. Thus viewed, according to my construction, they fully meet, and effectually guard against (as far as in the nature of things can be done) every danger, by which the peace, safety, and liberty of the States may be jeopardized or destroyed.

If lawless force, or violence of individuals, under whatever pretext, should be turned against the Government of the State, or its authority, from *within,* with the view of subverting them, the guarantee, to protect each from domestic violence, meets the case; if the attack should be from *without,* that against invasion meets it; and, finally, if the rulers should attempt to usurp power, and subvert the republican form of government, under which the State was admitted into the Union, the guarantee of a republican form of government to every State of the Union meets it. Thus, every door, through which danger may enter, that can in the nature of things be closed, would be closed, if the Federal Government should faithfully enforce the guarantes. Under no other construction, would it be the case; which is proof conclusive that the construction which I place upon the section, is the one intended by the framers of the Constitution.

Having now explained my views of the nature and character of the guarantee section, it will not be difficult to assign my reasons for the answer I have given to the question under consideration. In determining what its duties are, under the section, the Federal Government must look to the whole; and take care that, in enforcing one of the guarantees, it does not violate its duties under another. It has been shown that the objects of the guarantee against domestic violence is, the protection of the *Government* of the State; but when the Government of a State ceases to be republican, it loses its right to protection. This, it has been shown, may take place, by the usurpation of rulers, or by the voluntary act of the people. It is clear that, in either case, the Government of the States should withhold it; and of course it must have the right, in every case, to determine whether the application of a State for protection, be one of such cases or not. In the case of the usurpation of its rulers, it would be the duty of the Government, not only to withhold protection, but to unite its power with the people of the State, to suppress the usurpation. What would be its duty, in addition to withholding protection, in the other, I shall explain in the proper place, when I come to consider what would be the effect of a voluntary change of government, on the part of the people, from a republican to any other, on the relation of the State with the rest of the Union. But, while I admit the right, I also admit, that it is a high and delicate one; the highest and most delicate of any conferred on the Federal Government: and, I would add, the most dangerous, if I did not regard it subject to such restrictions, as left but little discretion in its exercise. What they are, I shall next proceed to consider.

The first, which I consider the foundation of all others, is to be found in my answer to your first question,—that the Federal Government, in determining whether the Government of a State be, or be not republican, within the meaning of the Constitution, has no right whatever, in any case, to look beyond its admission into the Union. From this fundamental restriction, another, deduced from it, necessarily follows, of no little importance,—that no change made in its Government, after its admission, can make it other than republican, which does not essentially alter its form, or make it different in some essential particular, from those of the other States, at the time of their adoption. In other words, the forms of the Governments of the several States, composing the Union, as they stood at the time of their admission, are the proper standard, by which to determine whether any after change, in any of them, makes its form of government other than republican.

But I take higher ground in reference to subsequent changes; and lay it down as a rule, that none such can fairly present the question, if the Federal Government should faithfully perform its duties under the guarantees,—except such as may be made voluntarily by the people of the State, consistently with constitutional and legal provisions; and that, I have shown, would not be a case within the guarantees. So long as it performs faithfully its duties, it is manifest, from what has been stated, that no change in the form of Government of a State, can be made by force or violence from without or within,—from invasion, or from domestic violence; unless it be such, as the united resistance of the Federal Government and that of the State, cannot overcome; and which, of course, would admit of no question under the guarantees.

The only remaining change that could be made, except by the voluntary act of the people, as stated, is that by the usurpation of the rulers of the State, for the time being;—and this the ballot-box would put down,—unless they should resort to force; when it would become, and not before, the duty of the Federal Government to enforce the guarantee, and suppress the usurpation. But this would be a case which would speak for itself, and admit of little doubt in determining; and would rarely, if ever, occur,—if the Federal Government should do its duty, under the formidable difficulties which the guarantees oppose to such cases.

The remaining mode, in which a change of the form of government of a State may be made, from the republican to some other, is, by the voluntary act of the people of the State themselves, acting in their political character, and consistently with constitutional and legal provisions; and this, as I have shown, would not come within the guarantees. But, as it is intimately connected with the subject of your questions, I deem it proper to state what would be the effect of such an act, and the relation in which it would place the State, in reference to the others.

It would, in my opinion, be a clear case of secession,—as clear as it would be for the State to do an act inconsistent with a fundamental principle of the Union; and to assume a character not compatible with her remaining in it. She would, in fact, be a foreign State; and would stand in the same relation to the others, as one foreign State does to another; and, of course, would have no right to claim any protection under the guarantees; or, if she did, the Federal Government would be under no obligation to grant it. There might, indeed, on such application, be a question,—whether, in fact, the change was such, as to make the Government of the State other than republican,—which would have to be decided under the restrictions I have stated. But, if doubt should still remain, the decision should be in favor of the State, when the consequence of deciding against her would be, to withhold protection, and place her out of the Union.

With these restrictions, this high and delicate power would be safe in the hands of the Federal Government; but without them, none could be more dangerous. Give to the Federal Government the right to establish its own abstract standard of what constitutes a republican form of government, and to bring the Governments of the States, without restriction on its discretion, to the test of this standard, in order to determine whether they be of a republican form or not, and it would be made the absolute master of the States. A standard more uncertain, or a greater or more dangerous power, could not be conceived. The Governments of one half of the States of the Union would not stand the test, which would be adopted by a large portion of the other half; and not one, that which many would adopt. The consequence would be, that, instead of tranquillity, safety, and liberty,—anarchy, insecurity, and despotism would universally prevail; and the object of the guarantees be utterly defeated. Nothing but the most rigid adherence, in all cases, to the restrictions laid down, can avert it. To relax in any, even the strongest, would open wide the door of unlimited discretion, and leave the Federal Government, without restriction, to fix on such a standard, as the caprice, ambition, party influence, or party calculations of those who, for the time being, might hold the reins of power, might dictate.

With this answer to your second question, I shall now proceed to reply to your third. It is in the following words:—"After a State has been admitted into the Union, has the numerical majority of the people of such State the right to alter or abolish the Constitution, regardless of the mode prescribed for its amendment,— if any; and where there is none, of the refusal or assent of such State?"

596   JOHN C. CALHOUN: SELECTED WRITINGS AND SPEECHES

I answer—no; neither after, nor before admission. If the right exist at all, it must be either a natural or acquired right. It cannot be the former; because all such rights belong to man in what is called the state of nature,—that is, in the state which is supposed to precede the existence of government,—or, what is called, the political state. Although the human race cannot exist without society, nor society without government, yet, in the order of things, man must have existed before society, and society before government. And hence it has not been unusual for elementary writers on morals and politics, in treating of the rights and duties of man, to regard him in each of these states. In his natural state, he is considered simply as an individual, with no superior; and his rights and duties are deduced from those faculties and endowments, physical, intellectual, and moral,—which are common to the race. Regarded in this state, all are equal in rights. In it, each individual is the sole master of his own actions; and there are neither majorities nor minorities,—nor the rights of majorities and minorities. In the other, or political state, he ceases to be regarded in this isolated and independent character, and is viewed as a member of a body politic, or a State;—that is, a society organized under a government, which represents its sovereign will, and through which it acts. It is in this state, and this only, that majorities and minorities are known, or have, as such, any rights. Whatever rights they possess, are political rights,—the whole class of which are acquired,—and are called conventional; that is, rights derived from agreement or compact, expressed or implied. How absurd, then, is it, to suppose the right of a majority to alter or abolish the Constitution is a natural right,—a right belonging to man regarded as existing in a state of nature,—when, in that state, majorities and minorities are unknown.

If, then, the right of the majority exist at all, it must be as a conventional right; and fortunately for the decision of the question, if it really exists in that character in our system, there will be no difficulty in finding it. The provident foresight of our ancestors has not left to conjecture or implication, in whom the right to abolish constitutions, or forms of government, resides; or how, for the most part, it is to be exercised. In every case (including the Federal Constitution) except New Jersey and Virginia,—and recently Rhode Island,—the authority by which it is to be exercised, and in what manner, is designated in the constitutions themselves. In all, if my memory be correct, the agency of the Government, in some form, is required, to alter or amend the Constitution. In a few, it may be done by the State Legislatures, according to the forms prescribed, without the express sanction of the people; but in all such cases, more than a mere numerical majority of the members is required. The most common form is, through a Convention of the people of the State,—to be called by the Legislature thereof; and in the far greater number, two thirds of the Legislature are necessary to call a Convention;—and, in all, the right of voting for the members of the Convention, or on the ratification of the Constitution, when submitted to the people, is restricted to those having the right of suffrage under the existing Constitutions. In one State, the votes of two thirds of the qualified voters are necessary to make the change. These various provisions clearly indicate the sense of the people of the United States, that the right of altering or changing constitutions is a conventional right, belonging to the body politic, and subject to be regulated by it. In not a single instance, is the principle recognized, that a mere numerical majority of the people of a State, or any other number, have the right to convene, of themselves, without the sanction of legal authority,—and to alter or abolish the Constitution of the State.

Now, as the right, if it exists at all, must exist as a conventional right,—that is, a right founded on express agreement or compact, or, in the absence of such an one, implied, it follows, from the statement, that it does not exist by express agreement or compact, in any of the cases, where provision is made for amending the Constitution: nor can it exist by implication, in any State, unless in the only two where Constitutions make no provisions on the subject.

That the right does not exist by implication in these States (New Jersey and Virginia), I hold to be equally certain. The fact, that their Constitutions do not provide for their amendment, cannot, by any force of reason, imply the right of the majority, to alter or abolish their Constitutions, without the consent of their respective Governments. Government, as has been stated, is the representative of a State, in its sovereign character, and the organ through which it acts. As such, it is vested with all powers necessary to the performance of its high functions, and which are not prohibited or expressly withheld by its Constitution, and among them, the most important of all, that of self-preservation. In our complex political system, the powers belonging to Government, as has been stated, are divided,—a portion being delegated to the Federal Government, as the common representative of all the States in their united character;—and the residue expressly reserved, to be exercised by the States, in their separate and individual character. Of this portion, the State Governments are the representatives and organs; and as such, are invested with all the powers not delegated, which properly appertain to Government, and which are not prohibited by their own, or the Federal Constitution. But they do not comprehend the power to make, alter or abolish constitutions, which, according to our political theory, belongs exclusively to the people; and cannot be exercised by Government, unless specially delegated by the Constitution. With these exceptions, the Governments of the States possess all others; and among them, that of proposing amendments to their Constitutions, and calling conventions of the people, for the purpose of amending, or proposing amendments, to be ratified by the people. That this power properly appertains to the functions of Government, and may be exercised without being delegated, will not be contested or denied. It has been uniformly exercised, and has never been questioned; and it is through its authority, whenever the Constitution provides for its amendment, that conventions are called, or propositions submitted for the purpose, are made. But being a power appertaining to government, it belongs to it exclusively; for government is not only the representative and organ of a State, in its sovereign character, but its sole and exclusive representative and organ; and it has, accordingly, ever been regarded, at every period of history, and under governments of every description, among the highest crimes, for unauthorized individuals to undertake to exercise powers properly belonging to it;—and as such, it has been prohibited under the severest penalties.

If I do not mistake, your Legislature has made the exercise of the very power in question,—that of calling a Convention to amend the Constitution, without its authority, a high penal offence. If I mistake, you can correct me. But whether mistaken or not, surely none will deny, that it is within its competency, or that of the Legislature of any other State, to make it so.

But, it may be asked, if it be a power belonging to Government, and may be exercised without being specially delegated, why have the Federal, and all the State Constitutions,—the two mentioned excepted,—made provisions for their alteration and amendment? Why was it not left to the discretion of Congress, and the State Legislatures, to call conventions, or propose amendments to the people for their ratification? It is not because the power of doing either was doubted, but because those who framed them, while they were too wise not to see that amendments would become necessary, were, at the same time, too deeply impressed with the danger of frequent changes in the fundamental law of a State, to permit amendments to be made with too much facility. To meet the one, it was necessary that they should be left open to amendments; and to guard against the other, that restrictions should be imposed on the amending power; or, without them, the numerical majority of the Legislature might call conventions, or propose amendments at pleasure,—to be adopted by a like majority of the people. The consequence would be, that Constitutions might be changed with almost the same facility as ordinary acts of the Legislature. It is to restrain this facility, that in all cases, where the Constitution provides for its amendment, it imposes restrictions on the power of amending, which would not otherwise exist. To impose such restrictions, was indeed the great object which their framers had in view, in prescribing the mode of amending; and it may be fairly doubted, whether without this, it would not have been left with the Government,—as in the case of Virginia and New Jersey,—to propose amendments and prescribe the forms for their adoption.

In denying, however, the right of the numerical majority, as such, to alter or abolish the Constitution of a State, regardless of the forms prescribed, or, where there are none, without the consent of the Government, I am far from denying that the people are the source of all power; and that their authority is paramount over all. But when political, and not natural rights are the subject, the people, as has been stated, are regarded as constituting a body politic, or State; and not merely as so many individuals. It is only when so regarded, that *they possess any political rights.* Viewed individually, as the elements of which the body politic is formed, they possess none but natural rights. Taken in either light, the people may alter or abolish their Constitution; but with this difference,—that, in the former, they can only do it by acting according to the prescribed forms, where there are such,—and when there are none, through the agency of its representative and organ—the Government of the State;—while, in the latter, they act individually, and on individual responsibility. The one is a political, and the other a natural right;—or as usually called, in such cases, *the right of revolution;*—and can be resorted to, rightfully, only where government has failed in the great objects for which it was ordained,—the security and happiness of the people; and then only where no other remedy can be applied. In such cases, the individuals who compose the community rightfully resume their natural rights; which, however restricted or modified they may be, in the political state, are never extinguished. But as a natural right, it is the right of individuals, and not that of majorities; although it may not be so safely and prudently exercised by one man, or a minority as a majority, it belongs to one as well as the other.

Such is my answer to your third inquiry,—and my reasons for entertaining the opinions I do on the question, in the general terms in which it is expressed. But I am of the impression that a more specific answer is required, to meet fully your intention in propounding it. Your question, as I conceive, presupposes a case of domestic violence, and of application, in due form, by the Government of the State, for protection; and that the precise point, on which you desire my opinion, is, whether the fact, that the violence was under the assumed authority of the numerical majority, to alter or abolish the Constitution, would take it out of the guarantee, and make it the duty of the Federal Government to withhold its protection? And it is, as I understand it, with the view of obtaining an answer to it, in this form, that you have limited your question, as to the supposed right of a numerical majority to alter or abolish its Constitution, to the case of a State after its admission into the Union. With this understanding of your object, I shall proceed to answer.

Whether the fact, that the violence was offered under the assumed authority of the majority, would take the case out of the guarantee, must obviously depend on the fact, whether it has the right assumed. If it has the right to alter or abolish the Constitution of the State, and to establish another in its place, the necessary consequence would be, that the one abolished would cease to be, and the one established would actually become rightfully the Constitution. It would, also, be a necessary consequence, after establishing the new, that those who might assume to exercise the functions of government under the old and abolished Constitution, against the new and actual, would be exercising it without constitutional or legal authority; and that, if the new government should undertake to put down the old by force or violence, and it should apply to the Federal Government for protection, it would be its duty to withhold it. I go farther. If the old should resort to force or violence to suppress the new, and this should apply to the Federal Government for protection, it would be its duty to grant it, and suppress the old. But, on the contrary, if the numerical majority has not the right, all this, of course, would clearly be reversed; and it would be the duty of the Federal Government to grant protection to the old, instead of the new; and, on its application, to put down those who might attempt to subvert it, under the authority of the new. They would, in fact, be a mere body of individuals, acting without constitutional or legal authority; and with no more right to resort to violence against the Government of the State, than any other number of individuals, acting without pretext, against the authority of either.

That the numerical majority has not the right, in either of the cases supposed in your question, I have, I trust, established beyond controversy;—and if so, it is no less unquestionable that, the fact of the violence being offered under its authority, cannot possibly take the case out of the guarantee, and make it the duty of the Federal Government to withhold its protection. Fatal, indeed, would be such a right. Its admission would be the death-blow to republican forms of government, or, what is the same thing, constitutional democracy.

Constitutions stand to governments, as laws do to individuals. As the object of laws is, to regulate and restrain the actions of individuals, so as to prevent one from oppressing or doing violence to another,—so, in like manner, that of constitutions is, to regulate and restrain the actions of governments,—so that those who exercise its powers, shall not oppress or do violence to the rest of the community. Without laws, there would be universal anarchy and violence in the community; and, without constitutions, unlimited despotism and oppression. This is true, be the form of government what it may. If the government of one man, or that of a few, would abuse its authority, if not restrained,—as is admitted,—there is no reason why that of the many would not do the same, if not also restrained. If, in a community of one hundred persons, forty-nine cannot be trusted with unlimited power over fifty-one,—on what principle can fifty-one be trusted with unlimited power over forty-nine? If, unrestrained, the one will abuse its powers, why will not the other also? Can the transfer of a single individual, from the side of the fifty-one to that of the forty-nine, have the magic effect of reversing the character of the two, and making that unsafe, which before was trustworthy?

The truth is,—the Government of the uncontrolled numerical majority, is but the *absolute and despotic form* of *popular governments;*—just as that of the uncontrolled will of one man, or a few, is of monarchy or aristocracy; and it has, to say the least, it has a strong a tendency to oppression, and the abuse of its powers, as either of the others. Hence it is, that it would be the death-blow of constitutional democracy, to admit the right of the numerical majority, to alter or abolish constitutions at pleasure,—regardless of the consent of the Government, or the forms prescribed for their amendment. It would be to admit, that it had the right to set aside, at pleasure, that which was intended to restrain it,—and which would make it just no restraint at all; and this would be, to attribute to the simple numerical majority, an inherent, absolute, and paramount power, derived, not from agreement, compact or constitution, either expressed or implied, but a higher source. It would be, in short, to attribute to it the same divine right to govern, which Sir Robert Filmer claimed for kings; and against which, Locke and Sydney so successfully combated. The argument, in both cases, is drawn from the same source, and leads to the same consequence. Admit political power to be *inherent,*—it matters not whether in a dynasty, or in a numerical majority,—and the consequence is inevitable,—that it is absolute, and cannot be subject to constitutional restraints. It is only on the opposite theory,—that all political rights are derived from assent or compact, expressed or implied, and are conventional,—that government, be its form what it may, can be subject to constitutional restraints; and it is, accordingly, to this source, that Locke, Sydney, and other writers on the side of liberty, traced them. Fortunately for us, their doctrines became the creed of our ancestors, and the foundation of our free, popular, and glorious system of Governments, in which laws derive their authority from constitutions; and these, *from the free and united assent of the whole community, given expressly, or by a cheerful acquiescence.* Admit the opposite doctrine,—the inherent and absolute right of the numerical majority,—and all the restrictions which the Federal and State Constitutions impose on their respective Governments, and on the mode prescribed for their amendment, would be idle and delusive attempts to prevent the abuse of power, and to give a stability to our political system, inconsistent with the principles on which it would rest,—and would prove utterly worthless in practice. There is, and always must be, a majority in, or out of power. If the one has a right to alter or abolish the Constitution, the other must have an equal right to do so. If the majority out of power have the right to call, at their pleasure, a caucus or convention (the name is immaterial), and to alter or abolish the existing Constitution or Government, and establish others which would place them in power,—surely the majority in power have the same right, by the same process, to alter or abolish all the restrictions which the Constitution may place on their power, and make themselves absolute. And when it is remembered how irksome restraints are, who can doubt, if the right be admitted, but that it would soon become the established practice, when the tedious and cumbrous forms, which both the Federal and State Constitutions prescribe for their amendment, would be dispensed with. Once commenced, it would soon supersede entirely the prescribed forms; and when this was done, in a short time, the ceremony of calling a caucus or convention of the major party, be it out of, or in power, would be regarded as too tedious and troublesome,—and the ordinary elections, or some still less certain evidence, would be regarded as sufficient to infer the will of the majority, and to supersede the Constitution; when the will of the numerical majority would take the place of Constitution and laws, and become the sole and absolute power.

This fatal process would be greatly accelerated, if the right of the numerical majority to alter or abolish constitutions, at pleasure, should be admitted, by the very guarantees, which were intended to secure the blessings of liberty, and give stability to our popular constitutional system. I have already shown that, if the right really exists, it would be the duty of the Federal Government, under the guarantee to protect the State against domestic violence, to aid always the side of the numerical majority to suppress the other. If it should be the majority *in power,* seeking to free itself from the restrictions imposed on the Government by the Constitution, it would be its duty to aid it, and to put down those who might attempt to resist the change; or, if it be the majority, *out of power,* seeking to alter or abolish the Constitution and Government, and substitute another, which would give them the power, the Federal Government would be equally bound to take its side, and put down those who might attempt to uphold the authority of the Constitution and Government. The consequence would always be, to add the power and authority of the Federal Government to that of the majority in the State, seeking a change of Constitution and Government, be it in or out of power; and thus, instead of giving stability to the system, the guarantees would become the means of incessant changes and revolutions, and utterly destructive of the ends they were intended to effect.

Having now stated the reasons and principles on which I rest my answer to your third question, I shall proceed to reply to your fourth. It is in the following words:—

"If one of the States of this Union, through her Government, should deny the right of a numerical majority of her people, to alter or abolish her Constitution at pleasure, and such majority should resort to force to effect its object,— and the proper authority, under the Constitution proposed to be suppressed, should call on the Federal Government for protection,—what would you regard as your duty, if President of the United States?"

My answer, after what I have already stated, is a matter of course. I would enforce the guarantee, and protect the State, to the extent of the authority vested in the President of the United States by the Constitution, and Acts of Congress made in conformity to it;—provided (which, I presume, you assumed to be the fact) that the case, in all other respects, is within the provisions of the guarantee.

Your fifth question is,—"If it should be deemed the right of the numerical majority to supersede the existing form of the Government of a State, at pleasure,—and such majority should seek to establish another form of government, other than republican, what would be the remedy, and what the duty of the Federal Government?"

As I do not deem it to be the right of the numerical majority, it will not be expected that I should answer the question: but I have, in answer to your second inquiry, stated what would be the effect if the people of a State, acting constitutionally and legally, should abolish their present republican form of government, and establish another of a different form, which will show what would be my opinion, if I thought the numerical majority had the right. If they had, it would make the numerical majority, in fact, the State;—that is (as explained), the people,—to the exclusion of the rest of the community; and, of course, would give to its act, abolishing the republican form of the government of a State, and establishing one of another form, the same effect, as if done by the people of the State themselves, acting constitutionally and legally.

I come now to your sixth and last question, which is in the following words:—

"As these inquiries have grown out of the Rhode Island question, and that controversy out of the right of suffrage, I ask your opinion on the right of suffrage involved in the controversy."

As I understand the case, the question of suffrage involved was,—whether the freehold suffrage, which existed under their form of government, should not be superseded, and the right be extended to the great mass of the community? It was, to express it in general terms, whether the right of suffrage should be restricted to freeholders, or be placed on a more liberal and enlarged basis?

My opinion is, and ever has been in favor of placing the right of suffrage on an extended basis. One of my first public acts was, to vote, as a member of our State Legislature, for an amendment of the State Constitution, to enlarge the right, and place it on the very liberal basis on which it now stands. The practical operation of the alteration has been good; and I have never had cause to repent my vote, or to change my early opinion. Thus thinking, my opinion and sympathy were on the side of, what has been called, the Suffrage Party, in Rhode Island, as far as the enlargement of the right was involved. The same remark is applicable to the other question involved in the controversy,— whether the old form of government, under the Charter, should not be changed to one more analogous to that of the other States. But I regarded both as strictly domestic questions; and, as such, belonging to the State. Thus regarded, I hold that, so long as the controversy was confined to discussion and agitation, the Federal Government could take no cognizance of it; nor even, on a resort to force, until the Government of the State applied, in due form, for protection: and then, only, to determine whether the case came within the guarantee; and if so, to fulfill its duties. It had, even then, no right to take cognizance of the original cause of the controversy, or to be influenced by its opinion, in reference to it;—unless, indeed, it should incidentally become necessary in determining whether the case came within the guarantee or not,—which could scarcely be possible. Under this impression, I could not permit my individual opinion and sympathy, in reference to the original subjects of the controversy, to control or influence me, in deciding in my official character, on what would be the duty of the Federal Government, in a case involving so many, and such high and solemn constitutional questions, when viewed in, what may be called, the Federal aspect of the subject,—in contradistinction to its domestic.

Having, now, answered your several questions, I deem it due, both to myself and the occasion, to state, in conclusion, what, according to the opinion I entertain, would be the effects of these guarantees, on the supposition that the Federal Government shall faithfully discharge the duties they impose.

The great and leading effect would be, to put an end to all changes in the form of government, and Constitutions of the States, originating in force or revolution; unless, indeed, they should be effected, against the united resistance of the State and the Federal Government. It would give to the Government and Constitution of each, the stability of the whole; so that no one could be subverted without subverting, at the same time, the whole system: and this, I believe to have been the intention of the framers of the Federal Constitution in inserting the guarantee-section. They were experienced and wise men, and did their work effectually. They had carried the country successfully through, by their wisdom and patriotism, the most remarkable political revolution on the records of history, and firmly established the Constitutions and Governments of the States, composing the Union, on the great principles of popular liberty, in which it originated. Nothing was left undone to perfect their great and glorious task, but to reconstruct, on more correct and solid principles, the common Constitution and Government of all the States, and bind them into one compact and durable structure. This was their crowning work; and how well it was performed, the Federal Constitution and Government will stand, more durable than brass, an everlasting monument of their wisdom and patriotism.

But very imperfect, indeed, would their task have been left, if they had not adopted effectual means to guard all the parts against the lawless shocks of violence and revolution. They were too deeply read in the history of free and confederated States, not to know the necessity of taking effectual guards against them; and for this purpose, inserted in the Constitution the guarantee-section, which will effectually and for ever guard against those dangerous enemies of popular and constitutional governments, if the Federal Government shall faithfully do its duty. They would, in such case, effectually close the doors, on every side, against their entrance,—whether attempted by invasion from *without,*—domestic violence from *within,*—or through the lawless ambition and usurpation of rulers.

But while the framers of the Federal Constitution thus carefully protected the system against changes by the rude hand of violence and revolution, they were too experienced and wise to undertake to close the door against all changes. They well knew, that all the works of man, whatever may be their skill, are imperfect of themselves, and liable to decay; and that, in order to perfect and perpetuate what they had done, it was necessary to provide a remedy to correct its imperfections, and repair the injuries of time, by making such changes as the one or the other might require. They also knew that, if such changes were not permitted, violence and revolution would, in time, burst open the doors which they had so carefully closed against them, and tear down the whole system, in their blind and unskillful attempts to repair it. Nor were they ignorant that, in providing for amendments, it would be necessary, in order to give sufficient stability to the system, to guard against hasty and thoughtless innovations; but, at the same time, to avoid such restrictions as would not leave sufficient facility for making the requisite changes. And this, too, is executed with the same wisdom and skill, which characterized every other part of their work, in the various provisions contained in the Federal Constitution for amendments;—which, while they afford sufficient guards against innovations, afford at the same time sufficient facility for the objects contemplated. But one thing still remained to perfect their work.

It might be, that the party in power would be opposed to all changes, and that, in consequence of the door being thus closed against force and revolution, and the restrictions imposed on the amending power, in order to prevent hasty innovations,—they might make successful resistance against all attempts to amend the Constitution, however necessary, if no adequate provision were made to prevent it. This they foresaw, and provided against it an ample remedy; after explaining which, I shall close this long communication.

The framers of the Federal Constitution were not only experienced and wise men, but firm believers, also, in the capacity of their fellow-citizens for self-government. It was in the full persuasion of the correctness of this belief, that, after having excluded violence and revolution, or physical force, as the means of change, and placed adequate guards against innovation, they opened wide the doors,—never to be closed,—for the free and full operation of all the moral elements in favor of change; not doubting that, if reason be left free to combat error, all the amendments which time and experience might show to be necessary, would, in the end, be made; and that the system, under their salutary influence, would go on indefinitely, purifying and perfecting itself. Thus thinking,—the liberty of the press,—the freedom of speech and debate,—the trial by jury,—the privilege of *Habeas Corpus,*—and the right of the people peaceably to assemble together, and petition for a redress of grievances,—are all put under the sacred guarantee of the Federal Constitution, and secured to the citizen against the power both of the Federal and State Governments. Thus it is, that the same high power, which guarantees protection to the Governments of the States against change or subversion by physical force, guarantees, at the same time, to the citizens protection against restrictions on the unlimited use of these great moral agents for effecting such changes as reason may show to be necessary. Nor ought their overpowering efficacy to accomplish the object intended, to be doubted. Backed by perseverance, and sustained by these powerful auxiliaries, reason in the end will surely prevail over error and abuse, however obstinately maintained;—and this the more surely, by the exclusion of so dangerous an ally as mere brute force. The operation may be slow, but will not be the less sure. Nor is the tardiness an objection. All changes in the fundamental laws of the State, ought to be the work of time, ample discussion, and reflection; and no people, who lack the requisite perseverance to go through the slow and difficult process necessary at once to guard against improper innovations, and to insure wise and salutary changes,—or who are ever ready to resort to revolution, instead of reform, where reform may be practicable,—can preserve their liberty. Nor would it be desirable, if it were practicable, to make the requisite changes, without going through a long previous process of discussion and agitation. They are indispensable means,—the only school (if I may be allowed the expression,) in our case, that can diffuse and fix in the mind of the community, the principles and doctrines necessary to uphold our complex, but beautiful system of governments. In none that ever existed, are they so much required; and in none were they ever calculated to produce such powerful effect. Its very complication—so many distinct, sovereign, and independent States, each with its separate Government, and all united under one—is calculated to give a force to discussion and agitation, never before known,—and to cause a diffusion of political intelligence heretofore unknown in the history of the world,—if the Federal Government shall do its duty under the guarantees of the Constitution, by thus promtly suppressing physical force, as an element of change,—and keeping wide open the door for the full and free action of all the moral elements in its favor. No people ever had so fair a start. All that is lacking is, that we shall understand, in all its great and beautiful proportions, the noble political structure reared by the wisdom and patriotism of our ancestors, and to have the virtue and the sense to preserve and protect it: and happy shall I be, if what I have written in answer to your inquiries, should contribute, in the least, to a better knowledge of it, and through this, in any degree, to its perfection and preservation.

With great respect, I am, &c., &c.,

J. C. CALHOUN.

Hon. W. SMITH.

Chapter XXIII.

Calhoun proposed an alternative and peaceable resolution to the troublesome joint occupation of the expansive Oregon territory by the United States and Britain. In the end, the territory was divided in accord with the plan Calhoun had urged while secretary of state (April 1844–March 1845) but more fully explained below, making this, therefore, one of Calhoun's most remarkable speeches.

[Mr. CALHOUN, being entitled to the floor, rose and addressed the Senate:— (Crallé)]

THE question under consideration is, whether notice shall be given to Great Britain that the convention of joint occupancy between us and her, in reference to the Oregon Territory, shall terminate at the end of the year. To that question, and those immediately growing out of it, I shall confine my remarks. I shall say nothing in reference to the title to Oregon. Having been connected with the negotiation in its early stages, it would be indelicate on my part to discuss the subject of title. I shall abstain from all personalities and every thing calculated to wound the feelings of others; but shall express myself freely, fully, and candidly, on all the subjects on which I may touch in the course of my remarks. With these prefatory observations, I shall proceed at once to the discussion of the question of notice.

There is one point on which all must be agreed;—that a great change has taken place since the commencement of this session in reference to notice, in its bearings upon the question of peace and war. At that time, notice was a question of the first magnitude, on the decision of which, to all appearance, depended

the question of peace or war; but now it is one of comparatively minor importance, and may be decided any way, without any decisive effect on either. The
cause of this change will be explained in the course of my remarks. So great,
indeed, has been the change, that it not only rendered inapplicable the reasons
urged in the message, recommending notice to be given, but has altered materially the position of the Executive, and that of the several parties in the Senate
to which it has given origin, as I shall next proceed to show.

That the recommendation of the message was founded on the conviction
that there was no hope of any compromise of the difficulties growing out of the
Oregon question, is too clear to admit of any rational doubt. Its language is
express. It states in so many words the conviction, that no compromise could
be effected which ought to be accepted. On this conviction, it announces that
the offer, which had been made to the British Minister to settle the controversy
on the 49th parallel of latitude, had been withdrawn after its rejection, and our
title to the whole asserted. On the same conviction, it recommends to Congress
to give the notice in order to annul the convention, with the view to remove
all impediments to our assertion of our right to the whole of the territory.
Assuming, then, that there would be no compromise, it informs us that, at the
expiration of the twelve months, a period would arrive when our title to the
territory must be abandoned or firmly maintained; and that neither our honor
nor our interest would permit us to abandon it; in other words, that we must
then assert our exclusive sovereignty to the whole, to the exclusion of that of
Great Britain, unless the latter should, in the interval, abandon its claims to the
territory. Throughout the whole recommendation there is not the slightest intimation that any compromise is expected. On the contrary, the very opposite is
constantly assumed.

But it is alleged that the reason for believing there could be no compromise
was derived from the evidence which the negotiation itself furnished, and especially by the rejection of the offer of compromise on 49∞. Such I admit to be
the case,—and also that it may be fairly inferred, if England should renew, on
her part, the proposition rejected by her Minister, or one substantially the same,
our Executive would accept the offer, and settle by compromise the conflicting claims of the territory. But the message intimates nowhere the slightest
expectation that such an offer would be made,—or, if made, that any compromise could be effected.

Such is the view which I have been constrained to take, after a most careful
and candid examination of the portion of the message recommending notice;
and such, I infer, is the view taken by the portion of the Senate who believe our

title to the whole territory to be clear and unquestionable. On no other view can their warm and decided support of notice be explained. They not only believe that our title is clear and unquestionable to the whole, but also that the honor of the country demands that it should be asserted and maintained by an appeal to arms, without the surrender of any part. Acting on this conviction, it is manifest that they can only support notice on the belief that it would not lead to compromise. On the opposite, they would be compelled to oppose it.

Such, also, would seem to be the view taken of the message by the community at large at the time, if we may judge from the tone of the public press, or what perhaps is a still truer index—the conduct of our intelligent business men. The message had the most decided effect in this respect. Stocks of every description fell, marine insurances rose, commercial pursuits were suspended, and our vessels remained inactive at the wharves.

Such, also, was the view taken by a great majority of that portion of the Senate who were opposed to giving notice,—among whom I include myself. We opposed it on grounds directly the reverse of those on which they who believed our right to the whole territory to be clear and unquestionable supported it. They supported notice because they believed there neither ought to be, nor would be any compromise. We, on the contrary, opposed it because we believed there might be, and ought to be compromise. They opposed compromise because, as has been stated, they believed our title to be perfect to the whole; while we supported it because we believed the title of neither to the whole to be clear and indisputable; and that the controversy might be adjusted by a fair partition of the territory. With such impressions, we believed that two such powerful and enlightened countries as the United States and Great Britain would not resort to arms to settle a controversy which might be peacefully and honorably settled by negotiation and compromise.

Entertaining this opinion, we were compelled to oppose notice, because it was necessary to prevent an appeal to arms, and to insure the peaceful settlement of the question. By defeating it, a breathing time would, at least, be afforded to both parties for calm and mature reflection, under the influence of which, it was hoped, that negotiation might be renewed, and the difference honorably compromised. Or, in case that should fail, things might remain as they have been without a resort to force. In this case, the territory would be left open to emigration, and the question, to whom it should ultimately belong, would be decided by settlement and colonization, unless Great Britain should give notice on her part, in order to prevent it. If she should, we would, at least, gain the advantage of transferring the responsibility from us to her, should war ensue.

Another portion of the Senate appeared to be in favor both of compromise and notice. Their views were not explicitly expressed; but, as far as they were developed, they, too, seemed to think that our title was not so perfect as to exclude an honorable compromise; and appeared to anticipate it, in opposition to the message, in recommending it on the three following grounds: first, on the ground of the general declaration of the President in the latter part of the message, that he hoped an amicable arrangement might be made of the question in dispute, in connection with a declaration of Mr. Buchanan to the same effect, in one of his letters to Mr. Pakenham. It is impossible for me, with every disposition to support the recommendation of the President in favor of notice, to concur in the opinion that a mere general expression of the kind, and inserted in another portion of the message,—even when backed by a similar declaration of the Secretary of State,—could be fairly construed to overrule the opinion,—clearly and explicitly expressed by the message in recommending notice,—that no compromise which ought to be accepted could be effected. I cannot admit of such a construction,—not only because I think it unreasonable, but because I regard the duty of the President, imposed by the constitution, to recommend measures to Congress, as one of a solemn character, and that it ought to be performed with the utmost candor and sincerity. Being addressed to a coordinate department of the Government, it ought to express plainly and explicitly his reasons and motives for recommending the measure, omitting none which he regards as material, and inserting none but such as he believes ought to have an influence upon the deliberations of Congress. It ought to be free from the suspicion of being diplomatic. To admit the contrary, would destroy all confidence between the Legislative and Executive Departments, to the great detriment of the Government. With these impressions, it would be to disparage the character of the President for me to concur in the construction.

The next ground taken by a portion of the Senate referred to is, that notice is recommended to be given by the message, not with the view of giving power to the President to assert our rights to the whole territory, but as a moral weapon, to enforce compromise.

To this construction I have the same difficulty in assenting as to the preceding. There is nothing in the language of the recommendation to authorize it. On the contrary, every word it contains looks expressly, as has been stated, to the enforcement of our rights to the territory on the expiration of the notice. To give a contrary interpretation would be to give a diplomatic character to the message, and be subject to all the objections which have been just suggested. But admitting that it was intended, as alleged, as a moral weapon to effect compromise, I would ask, how could that be effected, but by using it as the means to intimidate Great Britain—to intimidate, by telling her that she must quit the territory within the year, or be expelled at its expiration by force? And what would this be but an appeal to her fears, with the hope of extorting concessions which her reason had refused to yield? Such an appeal, in case of a feeble nation, would be hazardous; but in that of one as great and powerful as England, instead of a weapon to enforce a compromise, it would be one calculated to defeat it.

The remaining reason for voting notice on the part of the Senators referred to, is of a very different character. It objects to the convention itself; and condemns the policy of entering into either that of 1818 or 1827, on the ground that, instead of being the means of securing and perpetuating our rights in the territory, they have had the very reverse effect,—to weaken instead of to strengthen our title to the territory. My opinion, I must say, is precisely the opposite. It would, indeed, have been desirable to have settled it then by a compromise on the 49th parallel of latitude; but that, as is well known, was impossible at the time. The offer, in fact, was made on our side, but rejected on the part of Great Britain. The rejection left no other alternative but an appeal to arms, or a surrender of our rights to the territory, or to enter into the convention. To do nothing would have been to acquiesce in the claims of Great Britain, whose subjects were then in actual possession. Her possession, being adverse to ours, would have been gradually maturing, through the long intervening period, into a title too perfect to be opposed by ours. To avoid this, we were compelled to resort to force, or enter into a convention to preserve our rights. We wisely preferred the latter;—and the conventions of 1818 and 1827 were the consequences of that preference. They were entered into for the twofold objects,—as substitutes for war, and as the means of preserving our rights to the territory, as they then stood, unimpaired. To appreciate the wisdom of the policy, it must be borne in mind that, at the time, our means of asserting our rights to the territory of acquiring possession were exceedingly limited, compared with those of Great Britain, but that they were steadily and rapidly increasing. Those who had the management of affairs, at the period, wisely relied upon time and the rapid spread of population in a western direction, as the means ultimately of acquiring possession of the territory, and entered into the convention with a view of preserving our rights unimpaired until they could operate with full effect.

It is but too common, of late, to condemn the acts of our predecessors, and to pronounce them unjust, unwise, or unpatriotic, from not adverting to the circumstances under which they acted. Thus to judge, is to do great injustice to the wise and patriotic men who preceded us. In this case, it is to condemn such men as Monroe, Rush, Clay, and Gallatin—all of whom had an agency in directing or conducting the negotiations which terminated in the adoption of these conventions. It would be hard to pronounce men like these to have been unwise or unpatriotic in what they did, or to pronounce President Jackson and others after him so, because they acquiesced for many years under the operation of the convention of 1827, when they could have terminated it, at any time, by giving a year's notice. I have not named the most prominent individual concerned in directing these negotiations, because his course, on this occasion, has, in my opinion, cancelled any previous credit to which he would have been otherwise entitled.

Such was the state of things at the commencement of the session, when the President recommended notice to be given to terminate the joint occupancy; and such the position and grounds assumed by the several portions of the Senate in reference to the notice. Since then, as has been stated, there has been a great change, which has materially affected the question of notice, and the position taken by the different portions of the body in reference to it, as I shall next explain.

Public opinion has had time to develope itself, not only on this; but on the other side of the Atlantic; and that opinion has pronounced most audibly and clearly in favor of compromise. The development has been going on, not only in the community, but also in this body; and I now feel that I hazard nothing in saying, that a large majority of the Senate is in favor of terminating the controversy by negotiation, and an honorable compromise. And what is very material, the opinion of the British Government on the subject of compromise has been more clearly and specifically developed than when the message was transmitted to Congress; so much so, that there is ground to hope it is prepared to adjust the difference in reference to the territory substantially on the basis which was offered by the President. It seems to me impossible that any other construction can be given to what Sir Robert Peel said in reply to the question put to him by Lord John Russell. His declaration was made under circumstances calculated to give it great weight. The object of making it was clearly not to censure the able and very faithful representative of Great Britain in this country, but to use the occasion to give assurance that he is ready to make a compromise, as it may be inferred, substantially on the basis of the rejected offer. I trust sincerely that such is the interpretation which our Government has put upon it; and that, regarding it as a direct step towards compromise, it has met it, with a step on our part, by suitable instructions to our Minister in that country. It is to be hoped that a communication has already been transmitted, which

may have the effect of removing what would seem to be the only material difficulty in the way of an adjustment; that is, which shall make the first step towards
resuming the negotiation.

As things now stand, I no longer consider it as a question, whether the controversy shall be pacifically arranged or not, nor even in what manner it shall be
arranged. I regard the arrangement now simply a question of time, and I trust
that, in concluding it, there will be no unnecessary delay. The business of both
countries, and of commerce generally, requires that it should be concluded as
promptly as possible. There is still another and a higher reason why it should be
speedily settled. The question is one of a momentous and delicate character, and
like all such, should be settled, in order to avoid adverse contingencies, with the
least practicable delay. A further inducement for dispatch in settling the Oregon question is, that upon it depends the settlement of the question with Mexico. Until the former is settled, there is but slender prospect that the latter can
be; for so long as the Oregon question is left open, Mexico will calculate the
chances of a rupture between us and Great Britain, in the event of which, she
would be prepared to make common cause against us. But when an end is put
to any such hope, she will speedily settle her difference with us. I trust that when
we come to settle it, we will deal generously with her, and that we will prove
ourselves too just and magnanimous to take advantage of her feeble condition.

It is this great change in favor of the prospect of settling the controversy in
reference to Oregon honorably, by negotiation and compromise, which has
occurred since the commencement of the session, that has made the great difference in the importance of the bearing of notice on the question of peace and war.
What then was apparently almost hopeless, may be now regarded as highly probable, unless there should be some great mismanagement; but just as compromise
is more hopeless, notice becomes more important in its bearing on the relations
of peace and war; and, on the other hand, just as the chances of compromise are
increased, notice becomes less important; and hence its importance at the commencement of the session, and its comparatively little importance now.

I shall next proceed to inquire what bearing the increased prospect of compromise has on the position of the Executive, and that of the several portions of
this body, in reference to notice, and the Oregon question generally. That it is
calculated to affect materially the position of the Executive must be apparent.
That he should recommend giving notice to terminate the convention of joint
occupancy of the territory, with a view of asserting our exclusive sovereignty to
the whole, according to his view of our title, when there was little or no hope
of compromise, is not at all inconsistent with his being prepared to adjust the

difference by compromise, substantially on the ground offered by himself, now when there is a reasonable prospect it may be effected. Measures of policy are necessarily controlled by circumstances; and, consequently, what may be wise and expedient under certain circumstances, might be eminently unwise and impolitic under different circumstances. To persist in acting in the same way under circumstances essentially different, would be folly and obstinacy, and not consistency. True consistency, that of the prudent and the wise, is to act in conformity with circumstances, and not to act always the same way under a change of circumstances. There is a prevalent error on this point. Many think that the very essence of consistency is to act always the same way—adhering to the same party, or to the same measures of policy, without regard to change of circumstances. Their consistency is like that of a physician, who, in the treatment of a highly inflammatory fever, would administer emetics and calomel, not only at the beginning, but at every subsequent stage of the disease. It is the consistency of a quack, which would be sure to kill the patient. The public man who would be consistent in the same way would be but a political quack, and in dangerous cases, his prescription would be not less fatal. If, then, the Executive is now really in favor of compromise,—notwithstanding the strong language used in his message recommending notice (of which I have no information that is not common to all),—it ought not to subject him to the charge of inconsistency, but should be put down to the change of circumstances to which I have adverted.

That it is also calculated to alter the positions taken by different portions of the Senate, in reference to notice, is no less certain; and this my friends (for such I will call them), who go for the whole of Oregon, must, I am sure, feel to be the case with them. They cannot, I am confident, have the same interest in notice now, when there is great reason to believe that the difference will be compromised with or without notice, as they had when there was no hope of compromise. It is clear that, under such change of circumstances, the reason for giving notice with them has, in a great measure if not altogether, ceased, so that I should not be surprised to find their votes cast against it.

But I trust that the change has gone further, and that they, by this time, begin to see that there are some doubts as to our title to the whole of Oregon being clear and unquestionable. It cannot, at least, be regarded as unquestionable, after it has been questioned so frequently and with such ability during this discussion. But if their opinion remains unchanged as to the clearness of our title, I put it to them whether there is not some deference due to the opinion of the great majority of the Senate who entertain different views? Is there not something due to the fact, that the majority even of their own political friends, whose patriotism and intelligence they cannot regard as inferior to their own, think that our title is not so clear but that a compromise might be honorably effected? To put a still stronger question, I ask them, as patriots and friends of Oregon, whether the fact, itself, of so great a division, even among ourselves, does not afford strong reason why the controversy should not be settled by an appeal to force? Are they willing, as wise and patriotic men, desirous of securing the whole of Oregon, to place the country in conflict with so great a power as England, when the united support and zealous co-operation of all would be indispensable to support the country in the contest? I appeal to them, in the humbler character, as party men, whether they are justified in persisting to push a course of policy which, whether it should end in war or not, must terminate in the division and distraction of their party?

Without pursuing this branch of the subject further, I shall conclude what I had to observe in reference to it, by saying that I, for one, feel and acknowledge the change. Nothing could have induced me to vote for notice, in any form, while there was apparently no hope of compromise; but now that there is, I am disposed to do so, if it should be properly modified.

I am thus brought to the question under consideration, to which all the preceding remarks were but preliminary—Shall notice be given to Great Britain to terminate the convention of joint occupancy? After what has been said, a few words will suffice to dispatch it.

The question is not free from doubt. After a review of the whole ground, I can discover but two reasons in favor of giving it. The first is,—to put an end to the agitation of the Oregon question,—which, without it, may run into the next presidential election, and thereby become more difficult of adjustment than ever. The other is,—the apprehension that the Government of Great Britain may wait the final action of Congress in reference to notice before it will move on the subject. Were it not for such apprehension, I would be disposed to postpone notice for the present.

The next question is,—In what form should it be given, if given at all? I, for one, can, under no circumstances, vote for absolute notice, although I admit it would be less dangerous now than when recommended by the message. I cannot consent to give a vote which might be construed to imply, that there was no hope of compromise, and which might, if given in that form, leave a doubt in the public mind as to the real opinion of the Senate in reference to compromise.

Nor can I vote for notice in the form which has been sent to us from the other House. I object to it as equivocal. If the resolution means simply to declare that the President may settle the controversy by compromise, it means nothing, as the President has that right under the constitution, and can neither be clothed with, nor divested of it by the authority of Congress. But if it be intended as a hint to him to settle the question by negotiation and compromise, I object to it for not plainly saying so. I am utterly opposed to all equivocation, or obscure expressions, in our public acts. We are bound to say plainly what we mean to say. If we mean negotiation and compromise, let us say it distinctly and plainly, instead of sending to the President a resolution on which he may put whatever interpretation he pleases.

If we give notice at all, it seems to me, for the reasons just stated, it should be substantially as has been proposed by the gentleman from Georgia (Mr. Colquitt), which plainly expresses the desire of the Senate that it should be settled by negotiation and compromise. For it I am inclined to vote, as at present advised; but regarding notice in all its forms as subordinate to settling the controversy without resort to arms, I reserve my decision until I am called upon to vote; and then I shall decide in the affirmative or negative, according as I shall judge that one or the other is best calculated to advance the end I have in view.

I have thus stated my reasons for supporting a compromise, and for favoring, at present, the giving of notice. I have been governed, as to both, by the circumstances under which I find myself placed, but for which I am no ways responsible. I am doing the best I can, where I find myself; and not what I would under different circumstances. So far from being responsible for the present state of things, I early took my stand against that line of policy which has placed us where we are. I refer to 1843. Then the Oregon question, for the first time, assumed a dangerous aspect. After having been long and frequently brought to the notice of Congress, without exciting attention, I then saw, or thought I saw, that it was destined, at no distant period, to become an absorbing and dangerous question, and accordingly felt it to be my duty, before I decided on my course in reference to it, to examine it in all its bearings with care and deliberation. After much reflection, I came to the conclusion, which I, on the occasion, explained in a speech delivered on the subject. I then saw that there were two distinct lines of policy, which might be pursued: one was,—to adhere to the convention of 1827; oppose every attempt to annul it, and strictly observe its provisions. I saw that, although for a time the convention had operated beneficially for Great Britain, a period was at hand when our turn would come to enjoy its benefits. Its operation had, theretofore, thrown into her hands the whole fur-trade of the region; and we had looked on, while she reaped the rich harvest, when it was in our power at any time to annul the convention by giving the year's notice. But I saw that our forbearance would be compensated by the advantages which the convention was about to confer on us, if we should have the wisdom to adopt the proper line of policy to secure them. The increase of our population, and its progress westward were rapidly extending our settlements towards the Rocky Mountains, through which a pass had been discovered but a few years before, which greatly increased the facility of colonizing the territory.

In this state of things, it was clear to my mind that if we adhered to the convention, and respected its provisions, the progress of events would ultimately give us possession of the whole territory; as our power to settle the territory, and thereby obtain possession, was far greater than that of Great Britain. Its distance from us was far less, and the approach through an open, grassy country affording great facility to the active and hardy pioneers of the West, who emigrate with their families and herds, with little expense or fatigue. Very different was the case with Great Britain. The distance to Oregon, by water, from her shores cannot be much less than twenty thousand miles—a distance but little short of the entire circumference of the globe; while her approach to it through her American possessions opposes great difficulties to emigration on a large scale. Of all the spots on the globe now open to colonization, and susceptible of being colonized, it is the most remote from her, and the most difficult of access. She has many colonies much nearer to her, to which there is much greater facility of access, with equal soil and climate, as yet very partially settled. Even New Zealand in all these respects is superior to it. With these advantages in our favor in settling the territory, and which were yearly rapidly increasing, it was clear to my mind that all we had to do was to adhere to the convention; to observe all its provisions with the most scrupulous fidelity, in order to obtain the actual occupation and possession of the whole country.

As far as I could perceive, there was but one impediment in the way, and that was, that Great Britain, in order to prevent us from obtaining possession by settlement, might give notice herself to terminate the convention of joint occupancy. But of this I entertained but little apprehension. I had read the correspondence of former negotiations with attention, and my interference was, that she placed but little value on Oregon, as a place for a permanent settlement, and that she had, in a great measure, made up her mind, from its geographical position, that it would ultimately pass into our hands. But be this as it may, I could not but see that there were great impediments in her way of giving such notice, as would preclude us from the right of settling. She has, indeed, the same right to terminate the convention of 1827 that we have, as it is expressly provided that either may give it. But there is another convention which she claims to be still in existence, and to which we, holding under Spain, are parties with her. I refer to the Nootka Sound convention. It is strictly analogous with that of 1827, though dissimilar in its language. But unlike the latter, it contains no provision for giving notice, and can only be annulled by violation. Under it, we, according to her own showing, have equal rights with herself to joint occupancy and settlement, of which we cannot be deprived on the ground on which she places her rights to the territory, without a breach of faith.

It seemed then to me clear, that our true policy was such as I have stated; to adhere to the convention, and let settlement determine to whom the territory should belong;—affording in the mean time whatever facilities we might think proper to our people emigrating to the territory, not inconsistent with the provisions of the convention, and extending our laws over them in like manner, and to the same extent that Great Britain had by an act of Parliament. To me it seemed clear that we ought not to go beyond, and that we should by no means extend our laws over it territorially. The necessary effects of this would be to extend our tariff acts to the territory, under an express provision of the constitution, which requires that all duties and taxes shall be laid uniformly throughout the United States. The restrictions imposed by our high tariff duties, on the infant commerce of the territory, would go far, not only to diminish the inducement to emigration, but to alienate the affections of its people. To enjoy the blessings of free trade over the broad Pacific, with its numerous islands and widely-extended coast, will prove, in the end, to be the strongest inducement to emigration; and to impose high duties, would do more to check emigration, to alienate its inhabitants, and separate them from our Union, than any other cause. Oregon will be to the Pacific what New England was to the Atlantic in its colonial state; and its people will contend as earnestly for the unrestricted enjoyment of the trade of the Pacific as the New Englanders did for that of the Atlantic before the Revolution. It was, indeed, one of the principal causes which led to the Revolution. Should we restrict, by our high tariff duties, their infant trade, they might readily find a power prepared to extend to them all the advantages of free trade, to be followed by consequences not difficult to be perceived. Influenced by these considerations, I came to the conclusion that our true policy was to let our people emigrate and govern themselves for the present, with as little interference as possible on our part. In this respect they possess great capacity from their origin and their native instincts. I would let them go there and settle the country in their own way, giving them all the aid, countenance, and support which we could, without extending our authority over them territorially, until it could be properly and safely done. But, be it done when it may, great judgment and caution will be required;—for there lies the great difficulty of reconciling the interest on the eastern side of the Rocky Mountains with that of the western side.

The other line of policy looked to the termination of the convention by giving notice and taking adverse possession of the territory. The bill of 1843, already alluded to, was intended as the first step. I opposed it, not only because I believed that some of its provisions violated the convention, but because I believed the course it indicated was highly impolitic. It seemed to me, indeed, to require little reflection to perceive that, if the bill should pass, and the policy it indicated be adopted, negotiation or war would necessarily follow; and that, if the former should be resorted to in the first instance to prevent war, it would terminate either in compromise or war. There could be no other result. Nor was it more difficult to perceive that, if the question was compromised, it must be on the basis of the 49th parallel. The past history of the affair,—the fact that it had been frequently offered by us substantially as an ultimatum, added to the fact that 49∞ was the boundary on this side of the Rocky Mountains, left no doubt in my mind that, if settled by compromise, it must be on that basis. It is true that our offer heretofore on this basis had been rejected, and that it might thence be inferred that Great Britain could not accede to it consistently with her honor. I am not of that impression. Things have greatly changed since our offers were made and rejected by her. Then, the advantages under the convention were all in her favor; but now they have turned in favor of us. Then, our capacity to settle the country was small; but now, for reasons already stated, they are great; and what is far from being immaterial, this increased capacity to settle and colonize strengthens the foundation of our claims to the territory. The capacity to settle and colonize a contiguous open region, not capable of being settled or colonized by any other power, goes back to the original principles on which all claim to territory is founded.

Seeing that such would necessarily be the consequence of the line of policy indicated by the bill, and wishing to avoid both compromise and war, I took a decided stand against it. I was very ably seconded in my opposition; so much so that, notwithstanding the apparently large majority in its favor when the discussion commenced, it passed this body by an equivocal majority of one. I say equivocal, because one of the Senators felt himself constrained by accidental causes to vote for the measure, after he had avowed his opinion against it. Since then, session after session, measures have been introduced to give notice and extend our authority over the territory, with a view ultimately of taking possession of the whole. As anticipated, negotiation, in order to avoid war, followed;

and now we are brought to the alternative of compromise or fighting, as ought to have been foreseen from the beginning. I again repeat, that I am in no way responsible for the present state of things; and if I am compelled in consequence to vote for compromise and notice, the responsibility rests on my friends behind me, whose course has forced the Government into it by the line of policy they have pursued. I do not impeach their patriotism; but I cannot but think that they permitted their zeal in behalf of the territory, and the impatience of those they represent to occupy it, to get the control of their better judgment.

Having been thus brought, by the line of policy to which I was opposed, to choose between compromise and war, I, without hesitation, take the former. In making the choice, I am actuated by no unmanly fear of the consequences of war. I know that, in the existing state of the world, wars are necessary—that the most sacred regard for justice and equity, and the most cautious policy, cannot always prevent them. When war must come, I may appeal to my past history to prove that I shall not be found among those who may falter; but I shall take care never to contribute by my acts to precipitate the country into a war, when it can be fairly avoided. I am, on principle, opposed to war, and in favor of peace, because I regard peace as a positive good, and war as a positive evil. As a good, I shall ever cling to peace, so long as it can be preserved consistently with the safety and honor of the country; and as opposed to war, I shall ever resist it, so long as it may be resisted consistently with the same considerations. I am emphatically opposed to it in this case, because peace, in my opinion, can be preserved consistently with both, and war avoided without sacrificing either. I am opposed to it for the additional reason, that it would be, in my opinion, highly impolitic—a consideration never to be overlooked when a question of the kind is under consideration. I regard it as highly impolitic in this case, because I believe that, should we resort to it, we would lose, instead of securing, the two objects for which it would be avowedly declared, as I shall now proceed to show.

The first is, to secure what is claimed to be our rights to the whole of Oregon, under the cry of *"all of Oregon or none."* Those who would go into it for that object will, in my opinion, find in the end that *"none"* is much more probable than *"all."* In coming to this conclusion, I concede to my countrymen the highest bravery, energy, patriotism, and intelligence, which can be claimed for them. But these cannot overcome the great obstacles we would have to encounter, compared with what Great Britain would have in a contest for Oregon. As long as she has a large force in the East, and remains mistress of the Pacific, she will be able to place there a much more efficient force, and at far less expense, than we possibly can at present, which would there decide the contest in her favor.

But were it otherwise, from the nature of the contest, Oregon, though the cause of the war, would be speedily forgotten. The struggle once begun, would soon cease to be for Oregon. Higher and far more powerful motives would soon guide the contest. It would speedily become a struggle for mastery between the greatest power in the world on one side, against the most growing on the other. Actuated by all the feelings belonging to such a struggle, both sides would put forth all their vigor, energy and resources,—and, overlooking minor points, would aim to strike the most vulnerable,—and where each might have the greatest advantage,—leaving Oregon to be won or lost as the contingencies of so mighty a contest might decide.

The next object, as is alleged, is to protect our citizens in Oregon. What has just been said is enough to prove how utterly it must fail. Instead of protection, war would most certainly sacrifice them; and this is a strong reason, with me, for opposing it. I feel our obligation to protect them as citizens, and brethren, and kindred. We have encouraged them to emigrate, and I will not give a vote which, in my opinion, would abandon and ruin them. But what war would fail to effect, would be certainly accomplished by compromise on the line offered by the President. There are none of our citizens, if I am correctly informed, settled north of 49∞. Establish that line, and we at once give our citizens in Oregon peace and security, and with them full opportunity to realize their object in emigrating.

But passing from Oregon, I take broader ground, and oppose war for reasons looking to the whole. I see nothing to hope from war, be its result what it may. On the contrary, I believe that the most successful and triumphant war that could be waged—one in which all would be accomplished which its most extravagant advocate could dare hope for—in which we should conquer the Canadas, New Brunswick, and Nova Scotia—in which we should drive the British flag from the continent, and compel Great Britain to yield the whole by treaty, in the short space of ten years, would be disastrous to us. I allude not to its ravages or devastations—to the oceans of blood that must flow, and the manifold losses and miseries which would accompany the war. They are common to all wars; but however vividly painted, they have but little effect in deterring a brave people from a resort to it. No doubt these inflictions would be very great in a contest between two nations of such immense power, and so situated as to be able to do each other the greatest harm in war and the greatest good in peace. But great as the devastation and destruction of life would be in such a struggle, they are of a nature to be speedily repaired on our side. The indomitable industry and enterprise of our people, with the great resources of the country, would soon repair the former, while our rapidly increasing population would speedily repair the latter. War has far heavier calamities for a free people than these, though less visible—calamities in their nature not easily remedied. I refer to permanent and dangerous social and political changes, which often follow in its train, in the character of the people and their institutions. A war between us and Great Britain, such as has been described, in which every nerve and muscle on either side would be strained to the utmost, and every dollar put in requisition which could be commanded, could not fail, under present circumstances, to work most disastrous, and, I fear, incurable changes in the social condition of our people, and in their political institutions. To realize the consequences in this respect which must follow, it is necessary to look at the immense extent to which it would rage. It would, in all probability, prove a Mexican, and an Indian war, as well as a war with Great Britain; and as such would extend to every portion of our entire frontier, including the Atlantic and Pacific, the inland and exterior, constituting a circuit of probably not less than 7,000 miles. It would require, in order to conduct it with the energy necessary to bring it, in so short a time, to the successful termination supposed,—especially in a war for mastery,—immense exertions on land and water. Two navies—one on the Atlantic and the other on the lakes—and six or seven armies, would be required for the purpose, even on the supposition that Oregon would be abandoned. One army would be required on the Mexican frontier; and let no one sneer at the mention of such a power. Feeble as it now is, when paid and supported by British gold, and trained and commanded by British officers, Mexico would prove a formidable enemy. See what British skill and training have made of the feeble Sepoys. The Mexicans are a braver and a hardier people, and, what is no small point, would constitute the cheapest of all armies. There must be, in addition, one to guard the Gulf frontier; another to guard the southern; another the northern frontier on the Atlantic; another to assail the north-eastern frontier on the side of Nova Scotia and New Brunswick; and another to assail the Canadian; and, finally, another to protect our widely extended Indian frontier. All these, in so mighty a struggle against the greatest of all powers, putting forth her utmost strength, would require a force, including the two navies, of not less, I would suppose, than 200,000 men continually in pay. The expense would be enormous. One of the most venerable and experienced of our citizens, Mr. Gallatin, has estimated it at sixty-five or seventy millions of dollars annually, if my memory serves me. My impression is that it falls far short of the actual cost, and that $100,000,000 would not be an over estimate. Supposing the sum of $50,000,000 could be annually raised by taxation,—a sum far greater than he estimates, and in my opinion much beyond what could be effected,—it would leave $50,000,000 annually to be raised by loans, or a forced paper circulation. Now, allowing the war to continue for ten years, there would be incurred a debt, in the time, of $500,000,000, according to these estimates. Even this, it is probable, would fall much short of the reality, assuming the sum stated to be annually required. It would be difficult to obtain loans in Europe; for owing to the conduct of some of the States in reference to repudiation, and other causes not necessary to state, the feeling of Europe would, I fear, be generally against us; while our own resources would not be sufficient to raise the sum required without a great depreciation of our credit, with a loss of 20, 30, or even 40 per cent., before the termination of the war, in contracting loans, or in consequence of the depreciation of our paper circulation. Including all, our public debt would, at the end of the struggle, be probably not less than six or seven hundred millions of dollars. But this is not all.

We would be plunged into the paper system as deeply as we were in the days of the Revolution; and would terminate the war with a mortgage of six or seven hundred millions of dollars on the labor of our people;—for on labor the whole must fall ultimately, while a large portion of this vast amount would go into the pockets of those who struck not a blow, nor lost a drop of blood in the contest, and who acquired their gains by seizing upon the distress of the Government to drive hard and usurious bargains. In addition, we should have the difficult task to perform of restoring to a sound state a greatly depreciated paper circulation, or of extricating ourselves from it whatever way we might—a task which cannot be performed without great distress to the country and ruinous effect to that large and usually the enterprising portion of the community, the debtors. The effects of all this would be highly injurious to the social relations of the people. A powerful artificial class would be created on one side, and a poor and dependent one on the other.

Nor would its effect on our political institutions be less disastrous. Such a war would obliterate the line of distinction, in a great measure, between the Federal and State Governments, by conferring on the former vastly increased power and influence. We would hear no more of State Rights. The Federal Government would then become a great national consolidated Government. Our very success would give a military impulse to the public mind and to the character of the Government which it would be hard, if possible, to overcome,—and which would seek conquest after conquest until a spirit would be engendered totally inconsistent with the genius of our system. It would then be in the straight and downward road, which leads to—where so many free States have terminated their career—a military despotism. In the mean time, we would have to provide for three or four successful generals, who would soon be competing for the Presidency; and before the generation which waged the war would have passed away, they might possibly witness a contest between hostile generals, for that supreme office,—a contest between him who might conquer Mexico, and him who might conquer Canada,—terminated by the sword.

I appeal to the gentlemen who are the warm advocates for "all of Oregon or none," regardless of this mighty hazard, and whose separation from us on this question I regret, and solemnly put the question to them—Is it for you—you, who assume to be democrats *par excellence*—you who are the enemies of the paper system, and of all artificial classes in society—is it for you to support a course of policy which might lead to such disastrous consequences?

But I oppose war, not simply on the patriotic ground of a citizen looking to the freedom and prosperity of his own country, but on still broader grounds, as a friend of improvement, civilization, and progress. Viewed in reference to them, at no period has it ever been so desirable to preserve the general peace which now blesses the world. Never in its history has a period occurred so remarkable as that which has elapsed since the termination of the great war in Europe, with the battle of Waterloo, for the great advances made in all these particulars. Chemical and mechanical discoveries and inventions have multiplied beyond all former example,—adding, with their advance, to the comforts of life in a degree far greater and more universal than all that was ever known before. Civilization has, during the same period, spread its influence far and wide, and the general progress in knowledge, and its diffusion through all ranks of society, has outstripped all that has ever gone before it. The two great agents of the physical world have become subject to the will of man, and have been made subservient to his wants and enjoyments; I allude to steam and electricity, under whatever name the latter may be called. The former has overcome distance both on land and water, to an extent which former generations had not the least conception was possible. It has, in effect, reduced the Atlantic to half its former width, while, at the same time, it has added three-fold to the rapidity of intercourse by land. Within the same period, electricity, the greatest and most diffuse of all known physical agents, has been made the instrument for the transmission of thought, I will not say with the rapidity of lightning, but by lightning itself. Magic wires are stretching themselves in all directions over the earth, and when their mystic meshes shall have been united and perfected, our globe itself will become endowed with sensitiveness,—so that whatever touches on any one point, will be instantly felt on every other. All these improvements—all this increasing civilization—all the progress now making, would be in a great measure arrested by a war between us and Great Britain. As great as it is, it is but the commencement—the dawn of a new civilization, more refined, more elevated, more intellectual, more moral, than the present and all preceding it. Shall it be we who shall incur the high responsibility of retarding its advance, and by such a war as this would be?

I am, in this connection, opposed to war between the United States and Great Britain. They are the two countries furthest in advance in this great career of improvement and amelioration of the condition of our race. They are, besides, the two most commercial,—and are diffusing, by their widely extended commerce, their blessings over the whole globe. We have been raised up by Providence for these great and noble purposes, and I trust we shall not fail to fulfil our high destiny. I am, besides, especially opposed to war with England at this time; because I hold that it is now to be decided whether we are to exist in future as friends or enemies. War, at this time, and for this cause, would decide supremacy;—we shall hereafter stand in the attitude of enemies. It would give birth to a struggle in which one or the other would have to succumb before it terminated; and which, in the end, might prove ruinous to both. On the contrary, if war can be avoided, powerful causes are now in operation, calculated to cement and secure a lasting—I hope a perpetual peace between the two countries, by breaking down the barriers which impede their commerce, and thereby uniting them more closely by a vastly enlarged commercial intercourse, equally beneficial to both. If we should now succeed in setting the example of free trade between us, it would force all other civilized countries to follow it in the end. The consequence would be, to diffuse a prosperity greater and more universal than can be well conceived, and to unite by bonds of mutual interest the people of all countries. But in advocating the cause of free trade, I am actuated not less by the political consequences likely to flow from it, than the advantages to be derived from it in an economical point of view. I regard it in the dispensation of Providence as one of the great means of ushering in the happy period foretold by inspired prophets and poets, when war should be no more.

I am finally opposed to war, because peace—peace is pre-eminently our policy. There may be nations, restricted to small territories, hemmed in on all sides, so situated that war may be necessary to their greatness. Such is not our case. Providence has given us an inheritance stretching across the entire continent, from East to West, from ocean to ocean, and from North to South, covering by far the greater and better part of its temperate zone. It comprises a region not only of vast extent, but abundant in all resources; excellent in climate; fertile and exuberant in soil; capable of sustaining, in the plentiful enjoyment of all the necessaries of life, a population of ten times our present number. Our great mission, as a people, is to occupy this vast domain; to replenish it with an intelligent, virtuous, and industrious population; to convert the forests into cultivated fields; to drain the swamps and morasses, and cover them with rich harvests; to build up cities, towns, and villages in every direction, and to unite the whole by the most rapid intercourse between all the parts. War would but impede the fulfilment of this high mission, by absorbing the means and diverting the energies which would be devoted to the purpose. On the contrary, secure peace, and time, under the guidance of a sagacious and cautious policy, "a wise and masterly inactivity," will speedily accomplish the whole. I venture to say "a wise and masterly inactivity," in despite of the attempt to cast ridicule upon the expression. Those who have made the attempt would seem to confound such inactivity with mere inaction. Nothing can be more unlike. They are as wide apart as the poles. The one is the offspring of indolence, or ignorance, or indifference. The other is the result of the profoundest sagacity and wisdom,—a sagacity which looks into the operations of the great causes in the physical, moral, and political world; which, by their incessant operation, are ever changing the condition of nations for good or evil; and wisdom, which knows how to use and direct them when acting favorably, by slight touches, to facilitate their progress, and by removing impediments which might thwart or impede their course—and not least, to wait patiently for the fruits of their operation. He who does not understand the difference between such inactivity and mere inaction— the doing of nothing—is still in the horn-book of politics, without a glimpse of those higher elements of statesmanship by which a country is elevated to greatness and prosperity. Time is operating in our favor with a power never before exerted in favor of any other people. It is our great friend; and under the guidance of such a policy, it will accomplish all that we can desire. Our population is now increasing at the rate of about 600,000 annually,—and is progressing with increased rapidity every year. It will average, if not impeded, nearly a million during the next twenty-five years; at the end of which period our population ought to reach to upwards of forty millions. With this vast increase, it is rolling westwardly with a strong and deep current, and will by the end of that period, have spread from ocean to ocean. Its course is irresistible. The coast of the Pacific will then be probably as densely populated, and as thickly studded with towns and villages, in proportion to its capacity to sustain population, as that of

the Atlantic now is. At the same rate, we shall have increased to upwards of
80,000,000 of people at the end of another twenty-five years; when, with one
foot on the Atlantic and the other on the Pacific, and occupying a position
between the eastern and the western coasts of the old continent, we shall be better able to control the commerce of both oceans, and to exert an influence over
both continents, than any other country in the world. If we avoid war, and
adhere to peace, all this will be effected—effected, I trust, without the loss of
our free popular institutions. I am aware how difficult is the task to preserve free
institutions over so wide a space, and so immense a population; but we are
blessed with a constitution admirably calculated to accomplish it. Its elastic
power is unequalled,—which is to be attributed to its federal character. The
hope of success depends on preserving that feature in its full perfection, and
adhering to peace as our policy. War may make us great; but let it never be forgotten that peace only can make us both great and free.

With a few remarks relating to myself personally, I shall conclude. I have
been charged with being more strongly inclined to secure the annexation of
Texas, than our rights to Oregon. It has been attributed to my greater partiality to the South than to the West. But I am yet to learn why Texas should be
considered as belonging to the South rather than to the West. I always thought
that it formed a part, and not an unimportant part, of the valley of the Mississippi; and on that account, as well as for giving greater security to the Southern
portion of the valley, the West desired its annexation. Besides, I have yet to learn
that Texas is confined to a southern latitude. I had supposed that it extended far
north and west, up to the latitude of 42∞ in the neighborhood of the great pass
of the Rocky Mountains, on which the value of Oregon to us so much depends.
I had supposed that what are called the Southern States had not so direct and
deep an interest in its annexation as the West; but it would seem, from language
held on this occasion, that, in all this I was mistaken, and that the annexation of
Texas was purely a Southern question, and only supported by the West under
the expectation of obtaining in return the support of the South to the whole of
Oregon up to 54∞ 40, and, if necessary, at the certain hazard of a war.

But, passing by all this, and assuming that Texas was purely a Southern, and
Oregon a Western question, I repel the charge of partiality, and shall now proceed to show that, if a different line of policy was pursued by me in reference
to the two, it was because it was right and proper it should be. I treated both
questions in the manner best calculated to effect the object in view, and indeed
the only one by which both could be secured. The circumstances of the two
cases were entirely different. In the case of Texas, time was against us,—in that

of Oregon, time was with us; and hence the difference in my course of policy in reference to them. To understand the difference it is necessary to premise, that Texas had reached that period in her history when it was clear that she would be compelled to form intimate and dependent relations either with us or England, if she continued independent. But it was manifest, if left alone, without any movement on our part, that her connection must be with England and not with us. She could extend to Texas commercial advantages far greater than we possibly could; and afford her greater facilities in obtaining means to relieve her from her great pecuniary embarrassments. England saw this, and had actually commenced her movements to avail herself of its advantages. We, too, perceived it; and also that annexation afforded the only means of counteracting her movements, and preventing Texas from being placed exclusively under her control. In this emergency, I was called to the State Department, with a view of taking charge of the pending negotiation for annexation. I saw that the time had arrived when immediate and decided action was required; that time was against us, and that, to resist the effects of its operation, boldness and decision were indispensable. I acted accordingly, and success proved the soundness of my policy. It was not a case for masterly inactivity. Not so the case of Oregon,—where time was with us;—and hence the different line of policy which I adopted in reference to it, and which would have secured the whole, had my advice been followed, as has been explained.

In one particular my policy was the same in both cases. I aimed in each to avoid war and preserve peace. I clearly perceived that, in annexing Texas, there was no danger of a war with England, if managed judiciously. She was an independent state, and had been so acknowledged by England, France, and other powers. She had a right, as such, to dispose of herself, and to unite her destinies with ours, if she saw proper, without any right on the part of England to resist it, or ground or pretext to make war in consequence. I also perceived that there were no just grounds to apprehend a Mexican war in consequence. She was not in a condition to make war, without the aid of England, and there was no reason to apprehend that she would be aided or countenanced in it by the latter; unless, indeed, the Oregon question should terminate in a war between us and her,—in which event, I regarded a Mexican war as inevitable, as has been stated. Thus far my anticipations have been realized—Texas annexed, and peace preserved, by the policy which I pursued. A different line of policy—one which would have permitted England to obtain the ascendency over Texas, which she would have acquired without annexation,—would have inevitably led to a state of things, involving us and England finally in war. It would have been impossible to prevent feelings of jealousy and enmity from growing up between us and Texas. The very similarity of our character and pursuits, and the rivalry which they would give birth to, would necessarily lead to that result; while the long and ill-defined boundary between the two countries, extending for more than a thousand miles through forests, prairies, and navigable rivers, without a natural boundary in any part, would produce frequent collisions between our people and those of Texas. Controversies and conflicts would have been the result. Texas, as the weaker power, would throw herself upon Great Britain for support; and wars, frequent and bloody wars, between us and her would have followed. Annexation has fortunately removed these causes of war. Should the Oregon controversy terminate in peace, every cause of war between the two countries would be removed, leaving the prospect of lasting peace between them.

Chapter XXIV.

Though the circumstances of this speech involved the admission of Iowa, which threat-
ened to upset in the Senate the equilibrium between slave and free states, Calhoun's
greatest concern was with the "principle" of the matter. According to Calhoun, the fed-
eral government, especially the legislature, could not constitutionally treat the territories
differently from existing states. Calhoun addressed important questions, still asked
today, about the nature of self-government and the tensions between individual and com-
munal liberty.

Mr. Calhoun rose and said: Mr. President, I rise to offer a set of resolutions
in reference to the various resolutions from the State legislatures upon the subject of, what they call, the extension of slavery, and the proviso attached to the
House bill, called the Three Million Bill. What I propose before I send my resolutions to the table, is to make a few explanatory remarks.

Mr. President, it was solemnly asserted on this floor some time ago, that all
parties in the non-slaveholding States had come to a fixed and solemn determination upon two propositions. One was,—that there should be no further admission of any States into this Union which permitted, by their constitutions, the
existence of slavery; and the other was,—that slavery shall not hereafter exist in
any of the territories of the United States; the effect of which would be to give
to the non-slaveholding States the monopoly of the public domain, to the entire
exclusion of the slaveholding States. Since that declaration was made, we have
had abundant proof that there was a satisfactory foundation for it. We have
received already solemn resolutions passed by seven of the non-slaveholding

States—one-half of the number already in the Union, Iowa not being counted—using the strongest possible language to that effect; and no doubt, in a short space of time, similar resolutions will be received from all of the non-slaveholding States. But we need not go beyond the walls of Congress. The subject has been agitated in the other House, and they have sent up a bill "prohibiting the extension of slavery" (using their own language) "to any territory which may be acquired by the United States hereafter." At the same time, two resolutions which have been moved to extend the compromise line from the Rocky Mountains to the Pacific, during the present session, have been rejected by a decided majority.

Sir, there is no mistaking the signs of the times; and it is high time that the Southern States—the slaveholding States, should inquire what is now their relative strength in this Union, and what it will be if this determination should be carried into effect hereafter. Already we are in a minority—I use the word "we" for brevity's sake—already we are in a minority in the other House,—in the electoral college,—and I may say, in every department of this Government, except, at present, in the Senate of the United States—there for the present we have an equality. Of the twenty-eight States, fourteen are non-slaveholding and fourteen are slaveholding,—counting Delaware, which is doubtful,—as one of the non-slaveholding States. But this equality of strength exists only in the Senate. One of the clerks, at my request, has furnished me with a statement of what is the relative strength of the two descriptions of States, in the other House of Congress and in the electoral college. There are 228 representatives, including Iowa, which is already represented there. Of these, 138 are from non-slaveholding States, and 90 are from what are called the slave States—giving a majority, in the aggregate, to the former of 48. In the electoral college there are 168 votes belonging to the non-slaveholding States, and 118 to the slaveholding, giving a majority of 50 to the non-slaveholding.

We, Mr. President, have at present only one position in the Government, by which we may make any resistance to this aggressive policy which has been declared against the South; or any other that the non-slaveholding States may choose to adopt. And this equality in this body is one of the most transient character. Already Iowa is a State; but owing to some domestic difficulties, is not yet represented in this body. When she appears here, there will be an addition of two Senators to the representatives here of the non-slave-holding States. Already Wisconsin has passed the initiatory stage, and will be here the next session. This will add two more, making a clear majority of four in this body on the side of the non-slaveholding States, who will thus be enabled to sway every branch of this Government at their will and pleasure. But, if this aggressive policy be followed—if the determination of the non-slaveholding States is to be adhered to hereafter, and we are to be entirely excluded from the territories which we already possess, or may possess—if this is to be the fixed policy of the Government, I ask what will be our situation hereafter?

Sir, there is ample space for twelve or fifteen of the largest description of States in the territories belonging to the United States. Already a law is in course of passage through the other House creating one north of Wisconsin. There is ample room for another north of Iowa; and another north of that; and then that large region extending, on this side of the Rocky Mountains, from 49 degrees down to the Texan line, which may be set down fairly as an area of twelve and a half degrees of latitude. That extended region of itself is susceptible of having six, seven, or eight large States. To this, add Oregon which extends from 49 to 42 degrees, which will give four more, and I make a very moderate calculation when I say that, in addition to Iowa and Wisconsin, twelve more States upon the territory already ours—without reference to any acquisitions from Mexico—may be, and will be, shortly added to these United States. How will we then stand? There will be but fourteen on the part of the South—we are to be fixed, limited, and for ever—and twenty-eight on the part of the non-slaveholding States! Double our number! And with the same disproportion in the House and in the electoral college! The Government, Sir, will be entirely in the hands of the non-slaveholding States—overwhelmingly.

Sir, if this state of things is to go on—if this determination, so solemnly made, is to be persisted in, where shall we stand, as far as this Federal Government of ours is concerned? We shall be at the entire mercy of the non-slaveholding States. Can we look to their justice and regard for our interests? I ask, can we rely on that? Ought we to trust our safety and prosperity to their mercy and sense of justice? These are the solemn questions which I put to all—this and the other side of the Chamber.

Sir, can we find any hope by looking to the past? If we are to look to that— I will not go into the details—we will see, from the beginning of this Government to the present day, as far as pecuniary resources are concerned—as far as the disbursement of revenue is involved, it will be found that we have been a portion of the community which has substantially supported this Government without receiving any thing like a proportionate return. But why should I go beyond this very measure itself? Why go beyond this determination on the part of the non-slaveholding States,—that there shall be no further addition to the slaveholding States,—to prove what our condition will be?

Sir, what is the entire amount of this policy? I will not say that it is so designed. I will not say from what cause it originated. I will not say whether blind fanaticism on one side,—whether a hostile feeling to slavery entertained by many not fanatical on the other, has produced it; or whether it has been the work of men, who, looking to political power, have considered the agitation of this question as the most effectual mode of obtaining the spoils of this Government. I look to the fact itself. It is a policy now openly avowed as one to be persisted in. It is a scheme, which aims to monopolize the powers of this Government and to obtain sole possession of its territories.

Now, I ask, is there any remedy? Does the Constitution afford any remedy? And if not, is there any hope? These, Mr. President, are solemn questions—not only to us, but, let me say to gentlemen from the non-slaveholding States, to them. Sir, the day that the balance between the two sections of the country—the slaveholding States and the non-slaveholding States—is destroyed, is a day that will not be far removed from political revolution, anarchy, civil war, and wide-spread disaster. The balance of this system is in the slaveholding States. They are the conservative portion—always have been the conservative portion—always will be the conservative portion; and with a due balance on their part may, for generations to come, uphold this glorious Union of ours. But if this scheme should be carried out—if we are to be reduced to a handful—if we are to become a mere ball to play the presidential game with—to count something in the Baltimore caucus—if this is to be the result—wo! wo! I say, to this Union!

Now, Sir, I put again the solemn question—Does the constitution afford any remedy? Is there any provision in it by which this aggressive policy (boldly avowed, as if perfectly consistent with our institutions and the safety and prosperity of the United States) may be confronted? Is this a policy consistent with the Constitution. No, Mr. President, no! It is, in all its features, daringly opposed to the constitution. What is it? Ours is a Federal Constitution. The States are its constituents, and not the people. The twenty-eight States—the twenty-nine States (including Iowa)—stand, under this Government, as twenty-nine individuals, or as twenty-nine millions of individuals would stand to a consolidated power! No, Sir. It was made for higher ends. It was so formed that every State, as a constituent member of this Union of ours, should enjoy all its advantages, natural and acquired, with greater security, and enjoy them more perfectly. The whole system is based on justice and equality—perfect equality between the members of this republic. Now, can that be consistent with equality which will make this public domain a monopoly on one side—

which, in its consequences, would place the whole power in one section of the Union to be wielded against the other sections? Is that equality?

How, then, do we stand in reference to this territorial question—this public domain of ours? Why, Sir, what is it? It is the common property of the States of this Union. They are called "the territories of the United States." And what are the "United States" but the States united? Sir, these territories are the property of the States united; held jointly for their common use. And is it consistent with justice—is it consistent with equality, that any portion of the partners, out-numbering another portion, shall oust them of this common property of theirs—shall pass any law which shall proscribe the citizens of other portions of the Union from emigrating with their property to the territories of the United States? Would that be consistent—can it be consistent with the idea of a common property, held jointly for the common benefit of all? Would it be so considered in private life? Would it not be considered the most flagrant outrage in the world—one which any court of equity would restrain by injunction, or any court of law in the world would overrule.

Mr. President, not only is that proposition grossly inconsistent with the constitution, but the other, which undertakes to say that no State shall be admitted into this Union, which shall not prohibit by its constitution the existence of slaves, is equally a great outrage against the constitution of the United States. Sir, I hold it to be a fundamental principle of our political system, that the people have a right to establish what government they may think proper for themselves; that every State about to become a member of this Union has a right to form its government as it pleases; and that, in order to be admitted there is but one qualification, and that is, that the Government shall be republican. There is no express provision to that effect, but it results from that important section, which guarantees to every State in this Union a republican form of government. Now, Sir, what is proposed? It is proposed, from a vague, indefinite, erroneous, and most dangerous conception of private individual liberty, to overrule this great common liberty which a people have of framing their own constitution! Sir, the right of framing self-government on the part of individuals is not near so easily to be established by any course of reasoning, as the right of a community or State to self-government. And yet, Sir, there are men of such delicate feeling on the subject of liberty—men who cannot possibly bear what they call slavery in one section of the country—although not so much slavery, as an institution indispensable for the good of both races—men so squeamish on this point, that they are ready to strike down the higher right of a community to govern themselves, in order to maintain the absolute right of individuals, in every possible condition to govern themselves!

Mr. President, the resolutions that I intend to offer present, in general terms, these great truths. I propose to present them to the Senate; I propose to have a vote upon them; and I trust there is no gentleman here who will refuse it. It is manly, it is right, that such a vote be given. It is due to our constituents that we should insist upon it; and I, as one, will insist upon it that the sense of this body shall be taken; the body which represents the States in their capacity as communities, and the members of which are to be their special guardians. It is due to them, Sir, that there should be a fair expression of what is the sense of this body. Upon that expression much depends. It is the only position we can take, that will uphold us with any thing like independence—which will give us any chance at all to maintain an equality in this Union, on those great principles to which I have referred. Overrule these principles, and we are nothing! Preserve them, and we will ever be a respectable portion of the Union.

Sir, here let me say a word as to the compromise line. I have always considered it as a great error—highly injurious to the South, because it surrendered, for mere temporary purposes, those high principles of the constitution upon which I think we ought to stand. I am against any compromise line. Yet I would have been willing to acquiesce in a continuation of the Missouri compromise, in order to preserve, under the present trying circumstances, the peace of the country. One of the resolutions in the House, to that effect, was offered at my suggestion. I said to a friend there, "Let us not be disturbers of this Union. Abhorrent to my feelings as is that compromise line, let it be adhered to in good faith; and if the other portions of the Union are willing to stand by it, let us not refuse to stand by it. It has kept peace for some time, and, in the present circumstances, perhaps, it would be better to be continued as it is." But it was voted down by a decided majority. It was renewed by a gentleman from a non-slaveholding State, and again voted down by a like majority.

I see my way in the constitution; I cannot in a compromise. A compromise is but an act of Congress. It may be overruled at any time. It gives us no security. But the constitution is stable. It is a rock. On it we can stand, and on it we can meet our friends from the non-slaveholding States. It is a firm and stable ground, on which we can better stand in opposition to fanaticism, than on the shifting sands of compromise.

Let us be done with compromises. Let us go back and stand upon the constitution!

Well, Sir, what if the decision of this body shall deny to us this high constitutional right, not the less clear because deduced from the entire body of the instrument, and the nature of the subject to which it relates, instead of being specially provided for? What then? I will not undertake to decide. It is a question for our constituents, the slave-holding States—a solemn and a great question. If the decision should be adverse, I trust and do believe that they will take under solemn consideration what they ought to do. I give no advice. It would be hazardous and dangerous for me to do so. But I may speak as an individual member of that section of the Union. There is my family and connections; there I drew my first breath; there are all my hopes. I am a planter—a cotton-planter. I am a Southern man and a slaveholder—a kind and a merciful one, I trust—and none the worse for being a slaveholder. I say, for one, I would rather meet any extremity upon earth than give up one inch of our equality—one inch of what belongs to us as members of this great republic! What! acknowledged inferiority! The surrender of life is nothing to sinking down into acknowledged inferiority!

I have examined this subject largely—widely. I think I see the future. If we do not stand up as we ought, in my humble opinion, the condition of Ireland is prosperous and happy—the condition of Hindostan is prosperous and happy—the condition of Jamaica is prosperous and happy, compared with what must be that of the Southern States.

Mr. President, I desire that the resolutions which I now send to the table be read.

[The resolutions were read as follows:—

"*Resolved,* That the territories of the United States belong to the several States composing this Union, and are held by them as their joint and common property.

"*Resolved,* That Congress, as the joint agent and representative of the States of this Union, has no right to make any law, or do any act whatever, that shall directly, or by its effects, make any discrimination between the States of this Union, by which any of them shall be deprived of its full and equal right in any territory of the United States, acquired or to be acquired.

"*Resolved,* That the enactment of any law, which should directly, or by its effects, deprive the citizens of any of the States of this Union from emigrating, with their property, into any of the territories of the United States, will make such discrimination, and would, therefore, be a violation of the constitution and the rights of the States from which such citizens emigrated, and in derogation of that perfect equality which belongs to them as members of this Union,—and would tend directly to subvert the Union itself.

"*Resolved,* That it is a fundamental principle in our political creed, that a people in forming a constitution have the unconditional right to form and adopt the government which they may think best calculated to secure their liberty, prosperity, and happiness; and that, in conformity thereto, no other condition is imposed by the Federal Constitution on a State in order to be admitted into this Union, except that its constitution shall be republican; and that the imposition of any other by Congress would not only be in violation of the constitution, but in direct conflict with the principle on which our political system rests" (Crallé).]

I move that the resolutions be printed. I shall move that they be taken up to-morrow; and I do trust that the Senate will give them early attention and an early vote upon the subject.

Chapter XXV.

*Considered by many to be Calhoun's most important speech, it expressed his deep
concern about the neglect of the founding principles of the regime during a national crisis.
Urging restraint against the Polk Administration's efforts to increase the size of the army
and to intensify the conflict with Mexico, Calhoun was a voice of moderation in a political sea of extremist responses. The administration was eventually dissuaded by Calhoun
(and others) from annexing Mexico. In the course of the debate, Calhoun linked the
importance of liberty to the policy decisions of the day, noting "It is harder to preserve than
to obtain liberty."*

Resolutions.

"*Resolved,* That to conquer Mexico, and to hold it, either as a province or
to incorporate it in the Union, would be inconsistent with the avowed object
for which the war has been prosecuted; a departure from the settled policy of
the Government; in conflict with its character and genius; and, in the end, subversive of our free and popular institutions.

"*Resolved,* That no line of policy in the further prosecution of the war should
be adopted which may lead to consequences so disastrous."

Mr. Calhoun said: In offering, Senators, these resolutions for your consideration, I am governed by the reasons which induced me to oppose the war,
and by which I have been governed since it was sanctioned by Congress. In
alluding to my opposition to the war, I do not intend to touch on the reasons
which governed me on that occasion further than is necessary to explain my
motives on the present.

I, then, opposed the war, not only because it might have been easily avoided; not only because the President had no authority to order a part of the disputed territory in possession of the Mexicans to be occupied by our troops; not only because I believed the allegations upon which Congress sanctioned the war untrue; but from high considerations of policy—because I believed it would lead to many and serious evils to the country, and greatly endanger its free institutions. But, after the war was declared, by authority of the Government, I acquiesced in what I could not prevent, and which it was impossible for me to arrest; and I then felt it to be my duty to limit my efforts to give such direction to the war as would, as far as possible, prevent the evils and danger with which it threatened the country and its institutions. For this purpose, at the last session, I suggested to the Senate the policy of adopting a defensive line;—and for the same purpose I now offer these resolutions. This, and this only, is the motive which governs me on this occasion. I am moved by no personal or party considerations. My object is neither to sustain the Executive nor to strengthen the opposition;—but simply to discharge an important duty to the country. In doing so, I shall express my opinion on all points with the freedom and boldness which becomes an independent Senator, who has nothing to ask from the Government or from the People. But when I come to notice those points on which I differ from the President, I shall do it with all the decorum which is due to the Chief Magistrate of the Union.

I suggested a defensive line because, in the first place, I believed that the only certain mode of terminating the war successfully was to take indemnity into our own hands by occupying defensively, with our military force, a portion of the Mexican territory, which we might deem ample for indemnity; and, in the next, because I believed it would prevent a great sacrifice of life and property; but, above all, because I believed that it was the only way we could avoid the great danger to our institutions against which these resolutions are intended to guard. The President took a different view. He recommended a vigorous prosecution of the war—not for conquest—that was emphatically disavowed—but for the purpose of conquering peace—that is, to compel Mexico to sign a treaty ceding sufficient territory to indemnify the claims of our citizens and of the country for the expenses of the war. I could not approve of this policy. I opposed it, among other reasons, because I believed there was no certainty that the object intended to be effected would be accomplished let the war be ever so successful. Congress thought differently, and granted ample provisions, in men and money, for carrying out the policy recommended by the President. It has now been fully tested under the most favorable circumstances. It has been as successful as the most sanguine hope of the Executive could have anticipated. Victory after victory followed in rapid succession, without a single reverse. Santa Anna repelled and defeated with all his forces at Buena Vista—Vera Cruz, with its castle, captured—the heights of Cerro Gordo triumphantly carried—Jalapa, Perote, and Puebla occupied—and, after many triumphant victories under the walls of Mexico, its gates opened to us, and we put in possession of the capital. But what have all these splendid achievements accomplished? Has the avowed object of the war been attained? Have we conquered peace? Have we compelled Mexico to sign a treaty? Have we obtained indemnity? No. Not a single object contemplated by the campaign has been effected; and what is worse, our difficulties are greater now than they were at the commencement,—and the objects sought more difficult to be accomplished. To what is this complete failure to be attributed? Not to our army. It has done all that skill and gallantry could accomplish. It is to be attributed to the policy pursued. The Executive aimed at indemnity in a wrong way. Instead of taking it into our own hands, when we had territory in our possession ample to cover the claims of our citizens and the expenses of the war, he sought it indirectly through a treaty with Mexico. He thus put it out of our own power, and under the control of Mexico, to say whether we should have indemnity or not, and thereby enabled her to defeat the whole object of the campaign by simply refusing to treat with us. Owing to this mistaken policy, after a most successful and brilliant campaign, involving an expenditure of not less, probably, than $40,000,000, and the sacrifice, by the sword and by disease, of many valuable lives, probably not less than six or seven thousand, nothing is left but the glory which our army has acquired.

But, as an apology for this, it is insisted that the maintenance of a defensive line would have involved as great a sacrifice as the campaign itself. The President and the Secretary of War have assigned many reasons for entertaining this opinion. I have examined them with care. This is not the proper occasion to discuss them,—but I must say, with all due deference, they are, to my mind, utterly fallacious; and to satisfy your mind that such is the case, I will place the subject in a single point of view.

The line proposed by me, to which I suppose their reasons were intended to be applied, would be covered in its whole extent—from the Pacific Ocean to the Paso del Norte, on the Rio Grande—by the Gulf of California and the wilderness peopled by hostile tribes of Indians, through which no Mexican force could penetrate. For its entire occupancy and defence, nothing would be required but a few small vessels of war stationed in the gulf, and a single regiment to keep down any resistance from the few inhabitants within. From the

Paso del Norte to the mouth of the river, a distance of a few hundred miles, a single fact will show what little force will be necessary to its defence. It was a frontier between Texas and Mexico, when the former had but an inconsiderable population—not more than an hundred and fifty thousand at the utmost, at any time—with no standing army, and but very few irregular troops; yet for several years she maintained this line without any, except slight occasional intrusion from Mexico, and this too when Mexico was far more consolidated in her power, and when revolutions were not so frequent, and her money resources were far greater than at present. If, then, Texas alone, under such circumstances, could defend that frontier for so long a period, can any man believe that now, when she is backed by the whole of the United States,—now that Mexico is exhausted, defeated, and prostrated—I repeat, can any man believe that it would involve as great a sacrifice to us of men and money, to defend that frontier, as did the last campaign? No. I hazard nothing in asserting, that, to defend it for an indefinite period would have required a less sum than the interest on the money spent in the campaign, and fewer men than were sacrificed in carrying it on.

So much for the past. We now come to the commencement of another campaign, and the question recurs, What shall be done? The President, in his message, recommends the same line of policy—a vigorous prosecution of the war—not for conquest, that is again emphatically disavowed; not to blot Mexico out of the list of nations; no, he desires to see her an independent and flourishing community—and assigns strong reasons for it—but to obtain an honorable peace. We hear no more of conquering peace, but I presume that he means by an honorable peace the same thing: that is, to compel Mexico to agree to a treaty, ceding a sufficient part of her territory, as an indemnity for the expenses of the war, and for the claims of our citizens.

I have examined with care the grounds on which the President renews his recommendation, and am again compelled to dissent. There are many and powerful reasons—more so, even, than those that existed at the commencement of the last campaign—to justify my dissent. The sacrifice in money will be vastly greater. There is a bill for ten additional regiments now before the Senate, and another for twenty regiments of volunteers has been reported, authorizing, in all, the raising of an additional force of something upwards of thirty thousand. This, in addition to that already authorized by law, will be sufficient to keep an effective army in Mexico, of not much, if any, less than seventy thousand men, and will raise the expenses of the campaign to probably not less than sixty millions of dollars.

To meet so large an expenditure would involve, in the present and prospective condition of the money market, it is to be apprehended, not a little embarrassment. Last year money was abundant, and easily obtained. An unfortunate famine in Europe created a great demand for our agricultural products. This turned the balance of trade greatly in our favor, and specie poured into the country with a strong and steady current. No inconsiderable portion of it passed into the treasury, through the duties, which kept it full, in spite of the large sums remitted to meet the expenses of the war. The case is different now. Instead of having a tide flowing in, equal to the drain flowing out, the drain is now both ways. The exchanges now are against us,—instead of being in our favor,—and instead of specie flowing into the country from abroad, it is flowing out. In the mean time, the price of stocks and treasury notes, instead of being at or above par, have both fallen below, to a small extent. The effects of the depreciation of treasury notes will cause them to pass into the treasury in payment of the customs and other dues to the Government, as the cheaper currency, instead of gold and silver; while the expenses of the war, whether paid for by the transmission of gold and silver direct to Mexico, or by drafts drawn in favor of British merchants or other capitalists there, will cause whatever specie may be in the vaults of the treasury to flow from it, either for remittance direct, on account of the ordinary transactions of the country, or to pay the drafts which may be drawn upon it, and which, when paid, in the present state of exchanges, will be remitted abroad. But this process of paying in treasury notes instead of gold and silver, and gold and silver flowing out in both directions, cannot continue long without exhausting its specie, and leaving nothing to meet the public expenditure, including those of the war, but treasury notes. Can they, under such circumstances, preserve even their present value? Is there not great danger that they will fall lower and lower, and finally involve the finances of the Government and the circulation of the country in the greatest embarrassment and difficulty?

Is there not great danger, with this prospect before us, and with the necessity of raising by loans near forty millions, of a commercial and financial crisis—even possibly a suspension by the banks. I wish not to create panic; but there is danger, which makes a great difference in a financial and moneyed point of view between the state of things now and at the commencement of the last session. Looking to the future, it is to be apprehended that not a little difficulty will have to be encountered in raising money to meet the expenses of the next campaign, if conducted on the large scale which is proposed. Men you may raise, but money will be found difficult to obtain. It is even to be apprehended that loans will have to be negotiated on very disadvantageous terms for the public. In the present state of things, if they grow no worse, there can be no resort to treasury notes. They cannot be materially increased, without a ruinous depreciation, and a resort must be had, exclusively, or almost entirely so, to borrowing. But at the present prices of stocks, to borrow so large a sum as will be necessary, can only be done at a greatly increased rate of interest on the nominal amount of stock. In a recent conversation with a gentleman, well informed on this subject, he said that in his opinion, if forty millions are required, a loan could not be had for more than ninety for one hundred, which would be about at the rate of seven per cent.

These are formidable objections; but they are not the only ones that are more so than they were at the commencement of the last campaign. I hold that the avowed object for the vigorous prosecution of the war is less certain of being realized *now,* than it was then; and if it should fail to be realized, it will leave our affairs in a far worse condition than they are at present. That object, as has been stated, is to obtain an honorable treaty; one which, to use the language of the President, will give indemnity for the past and security for the future—that is, a treaty which will give us a cession of territory, not only equal to our present demand for indemnity, but equal to the additional demand—equal to the entire expenses to be incurred in conducting the campaign; and a guaranty from the Government of Mexico for its faithful execution. Now, Senators, I hold that whether the war is successful or unsuccessful, there is not only no certainty that this object will be accomplished, but almost a certainty that it will not be. If the war be unsuccessful; if our arms should be baffled, as I trust and believe they will not be; if, from any unfortunate accident, such should be the case, it is clear that we shall not be able to negotiate a treaty that will accomplish the object intended. On the contrary, if the war should be successful, it is almost equally certain that, in such case, the avowed object for prosecuting the war vigorously, will not be accomplished. I might take higher ground, and maintain that the more successfully the war is prosecuted, the more certainly the object avowed will be defeated, while the objects disavowed would as certainly be accomplished.

What is the object of a vigorous prosecution of the war? How can it be successful? I can see but one way of making it so, and that is,—by suppressing all resistance on the part of Mexico,—overpowering and dispersing her army, and utterly overthrowing her Government. But if this should be done; if a vigorous prosecution of the war should lead to this result, how are we to obtain an honorable peace? With whom shall we treat for indemnity for the past and security for the future? War may be made by one party, but it requires two to make peace. If all authority is overthrown in Mexico, where will be the power to enter into negotiation and make peace? Our very success would defeat the possibility of making peace. In that case the war would not end in peace, but in conquest; not in negotiation, but in subjugation; and defeat, I repeat, the very object you aim to accomplish,—and accomplish that which you disavow to be your intention, by destroying the separate existence of Mexico,—overthrowing her nationality, and blotting out her name from the list of nations,—instead of leaving her a free Republic, which the President has so earnestly expressed his desire to do.

If I understand his message correctly, I have his own authority for the conclusion to which I come. He takes very much the same view that I do, as to how a war ought to be prosecuted vigorously, and what would be its results,—with the difference as to the latter resting on a single contingency, and that a remote one. He says that the great difficulty of obtaining peace results from this,—that the people of Mexico are divided under factious chieftains, and that the chief in power dare not make peace, because for doing so he would be displaced by a rival. He also says, that the only way to remedy this evil and to obtain a treaty, is to put down the whole of them, including the one in power, as well as the others. Well, what then? Are we to stop there? No. Our generals are, it seems, authorized to encourage and to protect the well disposed inhabitants in establishing a republican government. He says they are numerous, and are prevented from expressing their opinions and making an attempt to form such a government, only by fear of those military chieftains. He proposes, when they have thus formed a government, under the encouragement and protection of our army, to obtain peace by a treaty with the government thus formed, which shall give us ample indemnity for the past and security for the future. I must say I am at a loss to see how a free and independent republic can be established in Mexico under the protection and authority of its conquerors. I can readily understand how an aristocracy or a despotic government might be, but how a free republican government can be so established, under such circumstances, is to me incomprehensible. I had always supposed that such a government must be the spontaneous wish of the people; that it must emanate from the hearts of the people, and be supported by their devotion to it, without support from abroad. But it seems that these are antiquated notions—obsolete ideas—and that free popular governments may be made under the authority and protection of a conqueror.

But suppose the difficulties surmounted, how can we make a free government in Mexico? Where are the materials? It is to be, I presume, a confederated government like their former. Where is the intelligence in Mexico for the construction and preservation of such a government? It is what she has been aiming at for more than twenty years, but so utterly incompetent are her people for the task, that it has been a complete failure from first to last. The great body of the intelligence and wealth of Mexico is concentrated in the priesthood, who are naturally disinclined to that form of government; the residue, for the most part, are the owners of the haciendas, the larger planters of the country, but they are without concert and destitute of the means of forming such a government. But if it were possible to establish such a government, it could not stand without the protection of our army. It would fall as soon as it is withdrawn.

If it be determined to have a treaty, it would be a far preferable course, it appears to me, to abstain from attacking or destroying the government now existing in Mexico, and to treat with it, if indeed it be capable of forming a treaty which it could maintain and execute. Upon this point I do not profess to have any information beyond that derived from conversations with those who have been in Mexico; but from all that I can hear, it may be doubted, whether we have not already pushed what is called a vigorous prosecution of the war so far, as not to leave sufficient power and influence in the Government to enter into a treaty which would be respected, when our forces are withdrawn. Such I know to be the opinion of intelligent officers. They concur in thinking that the existing Government at Queretaro, if it should enter into a treaty in conformity with the views expressed by the Executive, would be overthrown, and that we should be compelled to defend that portion of Mexico which we require for indemnity defensively, or be compelled to return and renew the prosecution of the war. If such is its weakness, it may be apprehended that even now, without pushing the vigorous prosecution of the war further, we are greatly exposed to the danger which these resolutions are intended to guard against, and that it requires great discretion and prompt action on our part to avoid it.

But before leaving this part of the subject, I must enter my solemn protest, as one of the Representatives of a State of this Union, against pledging protection to any government established in Mexico under our countenance or encouragement. It would inevitably be overthrown as soon as our forces are withdrawn; and we would be compelled, in fulfilment of plighted faith, implied or expressed, to return and reinstate such Government in power, to be again overturned and again reinstated, until we should be compelled to take the government into our own hands, just as the English have been compelled again and again to do in Hindostan, under similar circumstances, until it has led to its entire conquest. Let us avoid following the example which we have been condemning, as far back as my recollection extends.

The President himself entertains doubt, whether the plan of forming a government in the manner which I have been considering, and treating with it for indemnity, may not fail. In that case, he agrees that the very course to which I have said the vigorous prosecution of the war will inevitably lead, must be taken. He says, after having attempted to establish such a government—after having employed the best efforts to secure peace—if all fail, "we must hold on to the occupation of the country. We must take the full measure of indemnity into our own hands, and enforce such terms as the honor of the country demands." These are his words. Now, what is this? Is it not an acknowledgment, that if he fail in establishing a government with which he can treat, in Mexico—after putting down all resistance under the existing Government, we must make a conquest of the whole country, and hold it subject to our control? Can words be stronger? "Occupy the whole country"—"take the full measure of indemnity"—no defensive line—no treaty, and, "enforce terms." Terms on whom? On the Government? No, no, no. To enforce terms on the people individually. That is to say, to establish a government over them in the form of a province.

The President is right. If the vigorous prosecution of the war should be successful, and the contingency on which he expects to make a treaty fail, there will be no retreat. Every argument against calling back the army and taking a defensive line will have double force, after having spent $60,000,000, and acquired the possession of the whole of Mexico;—and the interests in favor of keeping possession would be much more powerful then than now. The army itself will be larger—those who live by the war, the numerous contractors, the merchants, the sutlers, the speculators in land and mines, and all who are profiting directly or indirectly by its prosecution, will be adverse to retiring, and will swell the cry of holding on to our conquests. They constitute an immense body of vast influence, who are growing rich by what is impoverishing the rest of the country.

It is at this stage that the President speaks of taking the indemnity into our own hands. But why delay it until the whole country is subdued? Why not take it now? A part of Mexico would be a better indemnity now, than the whole of Mexico would be at the end of the next campaign, when $60,000,000 will be added to the present expenditures. We would indeed acquire a control over a much larger portion of her population, but we would never be able to extort from them, by all the forms of taxation to which you can resort, a sum sufficient to pay the force necessary to hold them in subjection. That force must be a large one,—not less, certainly, than 40,000 men, according to the opinion of the Senator from Mississippi (Mr. Davis), who must be regarded as a competent judge upon this point. He stated in debate the other day, that the army now there, exceeding that number, are in danger; and urged, on that account, the immediate passage of the bill to raise ten regiments. On this subject, it is as well to speak out plainly at once. We shall never obtain indemnity for the expenditures of the war. They must come out of the pockets of the people of the United States; and the longer the war is continued, and the more numerous our army, the greater will be the debt, and the heavier the burden imposed upon the country.

If these views be correct, the end of the policy recommended by the President—whether contemplated or not—will be, to force the Government to adopt one or the other alternative alluded to in these resolutions. With this impression, I cannot support the policy he recommends, for the reasons assigned in the first resolution. The first of these is, that it would be inconsistent with the avowed object for which the war has been prosecuted. That it would be so, is apparent from what has already been said. Since the commencement of the war until this time, the President has continually disavowed the intention of conquering Mexico, and subjecting her to our control. He has constantly proclaimed that the only object was indemnity, and that the war is prosecuted to obtain it by treaty. And yet, if the results should be as I have stated, the end will be, that what was disavowed will be accomplished, and what has been avowed to be its object, will be defeated. Such a result would be a deep and lasting impeachment of the sincerity or the intelligence of the Government—of its sincerity, because directly opposed to what it has continually and emphatically disavowed; of its intelligence, for not perceiving what ought to have been so readily anticipated.

We have heard much of the reputation which our country has acquired by this war. I acknowledge it to the full amount, as far as the military is concerned. The army has done its duty nobly, and conferred high honors on the country, for which I sincerely thank them; but I apprehend that the reputation acquired does not go beyond this,—and that, in other respects, we have lost instead of acquiring reputation by the war. It would seem certain, from all publications from abroad, that the Government itself has not gained reputation in the eyes of the world for justice, moderation, or wisdom. Whether this be deserved or not, it is not for me to inquire at present. I am now speaking merely of reputation; and in this view it appears that we have lost abroad, as much in civil and political reputation as we have acquired for our skill and valor in arms. But much as I regard military glory—much as I rejoice to witness the display of that indomitable energy and courage which surmounts all difficulties—I would be sorry indeed that our Government should lose any portion of that high character for justice, moderation, and discretion, which distinguished it in the early stages of our history.

The next reason assigned is, that either holding Mexico as a province, or incorporating her into the Union, would be unprecedented by any example in our history. We have conquered many of the neighboring tribes of Indians, but we have never thought of holding them in subjection, or of incorporating them into our Union. They have been left as an independent people in the midst of us, or been driven back into the forests. Nor have we ever incorporated into the Union any but the Caucasian race. To incorporate Mexico would be the first departure of the kind; for more than half of its population are pure Indians, and by far the larger portion of the residue mixed blood. I protest against the incorporation of such a people. Ours is the government of the white man. The great misfortune of what was formerly Spanish America, is to be traced to the fatal error of placing the colored race on an equality with the white. This error destroyed the social arrangement which formed the basis of their society. This error we have wholly escaped; the Brazilians, formerly a province of Portugal, have escaped also to a considerable extent, and they and we are the only people of this continent who made revolutions without anarchy. And yet, with this example before them, and our uniform practice, there are those among us who talk about erecting these Mexicans into territorial governments, and placing them on an equality with the people of these States. I utterly protest against the project.

It is a remarkable fact in this connection, that in the whole history of man, as far as my information extends, there is no instance whatever of any civilized colored race, of any shade, being found equal to the establishment and maintenance of free government, although by far the largest proportion of the human family is composed of them; and even in the savage state, we rarely find them any where with such governments, except it be our noble savages; for noble I will call them for their many high qualities. They, for the most part, had free institutions, but such institutions are much more easily sustained among a savage than a civilized people. Are we to overlook this great fact? Are we to associate with ourselves, as equals, companions, and fellow-citizens, the Indians and mixed races of Mexico? I would consider such association as degrading to ourselves, and fatal to our institutions.

The next remaining reasons assigned, that it would be in conflict with the genius and character of our Government, and, in the end, subversive of our free institutions, are intimately connected, and I shall consider them together.

That it would be contrary to the genius and character of our Government, and subversive of our free popular institutions, to hold Mexico as a subject province, is a proposition too clear for argument before a body so enlightened as the Senate. You know the American constitution too well,—you have looked into history, and are too well acquainted with the fatal effects which large provincial possessions have ever had on the institutions of free states,—to need any proof to satisfy you how hostile it would be to the institutions of this country, to hold Mexico as a subject province. There is not an example on record of any free state holding a province of the same extent and population, without disastrous consequences. The nations conquered and held as a province, have, in time, retaliated by destroying the liberty of their conquerors, through the corrupting effect of extended patronage and irresponsible power. Such, certainly, would be our case. The conquest of Mexico would add so vastly to the patronage of this Government, that it would absorb the whole powers of the States; the Union would become an imperial power, and the States reduced to mere subordinate corporations. But the evil would not end there; the process would go on, and the power transferred from the States to the Union, would be transferred from the Legislative Department to the Executive. All the immense patronage which holding it as a province would create,—the maintenance of a large army, to hold it in subjection, and the appointment of a multitude of civil officers necessary to govern it,—would be vested in him. The great influence which it would give the President, would be the means of controlling the Legislative Department, and subjecting it to his dictation, especially when combined with the principle of proscription which has now become the established practice of the Government. The struggle to obtain the Presidential chair would become proportionably great—so great as to destroy the freedom of elections. The end would be anarchy or despotism, as certain as I am now addressing the Senate.

Let it not be said that Great Britain is an example to the contrary; that she holds provinces of vast extent and population, without materially impairing the liberty of the subject, or exposing the Government to violence, anarchy, confusion, or corruption. It is so. But it must be attributed to the peculiar character of her government. Of all governments that ever existed, of a free character, the British far transcends all in one particular,—and that is, its capacity to bear patronage without the evils usually incident to it. She can bear more, in proportion to population and wealth, than any government of that character that ever existed:—I might even go further, and assert than despotism itself in its most absolute form. I will not undertake to explain why it is so. It will take me further from the course which I have prescribed for myself, than I desire; but I will say, in a few words, that it results from the fact that her Executive and the House of Lords (the conservative branches of her Government) are both hereditary, while the other House of Parliament has a popular character. The Roman Government exceeded the British in its capacity for conquest. No government ever did exist, and none probably ever will, which, in that particular, equalled it; but its capacity to hold conquered provinces in subjection, was as nothing compared to that of Great Britain; and hence, when the Roman power passed beyond the limits of Italy, crossed the Adriatic, the Mediterranean, and the Alps, liberty fell prostrate: the Roman people became a rabble; corruption penetrated every department of the Government; violence and anarchy ruled the day, and military despotism closed the scene. Now, on the contrary, we see England, with subject-provinces of vastly greater territorial extent, and probably of not inferior population (I have not compared them); we see her, I repeat, going on without the personal liberty of the subject being materially impaired, or the Government subject to violence or anarchy! Yet England has not wholly escaped the curse which must ever befall a free government which holds extensive provinces in subjection; for, although she has not lost her liberty, or fallen into anarchy, yet we behold the population of England crushed to the earth by the superincumbent weight of debt and taxation, which may one day terminate in revolution. The wealth derived from her conquests and provincial possessions may have contributed to swell the overgrown fortunes of the upper classes, but has done nothing to alleviate the pressure on the laboring masses below. On the contrary, the expenses incident to their conquest, and of governing and holding them in subjection, have been drawn mainly from their labor, and have increased instead of decreasing the weight of the pressure. It has placed a burden upon them which, with all their skill and industry,—with all the vast accumulation of capital and power of machinery with which they are aided,—they are scarce capable of bearing, without being reduced to the lowest depths of poverty. Take, for example, Ireland,—her earliest and nearest conquest,—and is it not to this day a cause of heavy expense, and a burden, instead of a source of revenue?

On the contrary, our Government, in this particular, is the very reverse of the British. Of all free governments, it has the least capacity, in proportion to the wealth and population of the country, to bear patronage. The genius of the two, in this particular, is precisely opposite, however much alike in exterior forms and other particulars. The cause of this difference, I will not undertake to explain on the present occasion. It results from its federal character and elective chief magistrate; and so far from the example of Great Britain constituting a safe precedent for us to follow, the little she has gained from her numerous conquests and vast provincial possessions, and the heavy burdens which it has imposed upon her people to meet the consequent expenses, ought to be to us a warning never to be forgotten; especially when we reflect that, from the nature of our Government, we would be so liable to the other and greater evils from which she, from the nature of her Government, is, in a great measure, exempted. Such and so weighty are the objections to conquering Mexico, and holding it as a subject province.

Nor are the reasons less weighty against incorporating her into the Union. As far as law is concerned, this is easily done. All that is necessary is to establish a territorial government for the several States in Mexico,—of which there are upwards of twenty,—to appoint governors, judges, and magistrates,—and to give to the population a subordinate right of making laws—we defraying the cost of the government. So far as legislation goes, the work will be done; but there would be a great difference between these territorial governments, and those which we have heretofore established within our own limits. These are only the offsets of our own people or foreigners from the same countries from which our ancestors came. The first settlers in the territories are too few in number to form and support a government of their own, and are under obligation to the Government of the United States for forming one for them, and defraying the expense of maintaining it; knowing, as they do, that when they have sufficient population, they will be permitted to form a constitution for themselves, and be admitted as members of the Union. During the period of their territorial government, no force is necessary to keep them in a state of subjection. The case will be entirely different with these Mexican territories; when you form them, you must have powerful armies to hold them in subjection, with all the expenses incident to supporting them. You may call them territories, but they would, in reality, be but provinces under another name, and would involve the country in all the difficulties and dangers which I have already shown would result from holding the country in that condition. How long this state of things would last, before they would be fitted to be incorporated into the Union as States, we may form some idea, from similar instances with which we are familiar. Ireland has been held in subjection by England for many centuries;—and yet remains hostile, although her people are of a kindred race with the conquerors. The French colony in Canada still entertain hostile feelings towards their conquerors, although living in the midst of them for nearly one hundred years. If we may judge from these examples, it would not be unsafe to conclude that the Mexicans never will be heartily reconciled to our authority. The better class have Castilian blood in their veins, and are of the old Gothic stock—quite equal to the Anglo-Saxons in many respects, and in some superior. Of all the people upon earth, they are the most pertinacious; they hold out longer, and often when there would seem to be no prospect of ever making effectual resistance. It is admitted, I believe, on all hands, that they are now universally hostile to us, and the probability is, will continue so.

But suppose this difficulty removed. Suppose their hostility should cease, and they should become desirous of being incorporated into our Union. Ought we to admit them? Are the Mexicans fit to be politically associated with us? Are they fit not only to govern themselves, but for governing us also? Are any of you, Senators, willing that your State should constitute a member of a Union, of which twenty odd Mexican States, more than one-third of the whole, would be a part, the far greater part of the inhabitants of which are pure Indians, not equal in intelligence and elevation of character to the Cherokees, Choctaws, or any of our Southern Indian tribes?

We make a great mistake in supposing all people are capable of self-government. Acting under that impression, many are anxious to force free governments on all the people of this continent, and over the world, if they had the power. It has been lately urged in a very respectable quarter, that it is the mission of this country to spread civil and religious liberty over all the globe, and especially over this continent—even by force, if necessary. It is a sad delusion. None but a people advanced to a high state of moral and intellectual excellence are capable in a civilized condition, of forming and maintaining free governments; and among those who are so far advanced, very few indeed have had the good fortune to form constitutions capable of endurance. It is a remarkable fact in the political history of man, that there is scarcely an instance of a free constitutional government, which has been the work exclusively of foresight and wisdom. They have all been the result of a fortunate combination of circumstances. It is a very difficult task to make a constitution worthy of being called so. This admirable federal constitution of ours, is the result of such a combination. It is superior to the wisdom of any or all of the men by whose agency it was made. The force of circumstances, and not foresight or wisdom, induced them to adopt many of its wisest provisions.

But of the few nations who have been so fortunate as to adopt a wise constitution, still fewer have had the wisdom long to preserve one. It is harder to preserve than to obtain liberty. After years of prosperity, the tenure by which it is held is but too often forgotten; and I fear, Senators, that such is the case with us. There is no solicitude now about liberty. It was not so in the early days of the republic. Then it was the first object of our solicitude. The maxim then was, that "Power is always stealing from the many to the few;" "The price of liberty is perpetual vigilance." Then no question of any magnitude came up, in which the first inquiry was not, "Is it constitutional?"—"Is it consistent with our free, popular institutions?"—"How is it to affect our liberty?" It is not so now. Questions of the greatest magnitude are now discussed without reference or allusion to these vital considerations. I have been often struck with the fact, that in the discussions of the great questions in which we are now engaged, relating to the origin and the conduct of this war, their effect on the free institutions and the liberty of the people have scarcely been alluded to, although their bearing in that respect is so direct and disastrous. They would, in former days, have been the great and leading topics of discussion; and would, above all others, have had the most powerful effect in arousing the attention of the country. But now, other topics occupy the attention of Congress and of the country—military glory, extension of the empire, and the aggrandizement of the country. To what is this great change to be attributed? Is it because there has been a decay of the spirit of liberty among the people? I think not. I believe that it was never more ardent. The true cause is, that we have ceased to remember the tenure by which liberty alone can be preserved. We have had so many years of prosperity— passed through so many difficulties and dangers without the loss of liberty—that we begin to think that we hold it by right divine from heaven itself. Under this impression, without thinking or reflecting, we plunge into war, contract heavy debts, increase vastly the patronage of the Executive, and indulge in every species of extravagance, without thinking that we expose our liberty to hazard. It is a great and fatal mistake. The day of retribution will come; and when it does, awful will be the reckoning, and heavy the responsibility somewhere.

I have now shown, Senators, that the conquest of Mexico, and holding it as a subject province, or incorporating it into our Union, is liable to the many and irresistible objections assigned in the first resolution. I have also shown that the policy recommended by the President, if carried out, would terminate, in all probability, in its conquest, and holding it either in one or the other mode stated; and that such is the opinion of the President himself, unless, in the mean time, peace can be obtained. Believing, then, that this line of policy might lead to consequences so disastrous, it ought not, in my opinion, in the language of the second resolution, to be adopted. Thus thinking, I cannot give it my support. The question is then presented—What should be done? It is a great and difficult question, and daily becoming more so. I, who have used every effort in my power to prevent this war, might excuse myself from answering it, and leave it to those who have incurred greater responsibility in relation to it. But I will not shrink from any responsibility where the safety of the country or its institutions are at stake.

The first consideration in determining what line of policy, in the present state of things, ought to be adopted, is to decide what line will most effectually guard against the dangers which I have shown would result from the conquest of Mexico, and the disastrous consequences which would follow it.

After the most mature reflection which I have been able to give to the subject, I am of opinion now, and have been from the first, that the only one by which it can be certainly guarded against, is to take the question of indemnity into our own hands—to occupy defensively, and hold subject to negotiation, a portion of the territory of Mexico, which we may deem ample to cover all proper claims upon her, and which will be best suited to us to acquire, and least disadvantageous to her to lose. Such was my impression when the message of the President of the United States recommended to Congress the recognition of the existence of a war with Mexico. My view, at that time, as to the proper course to be pursued, was to vote the supplies, to rescue General Taylor and his army from the dangers which surrounded them, and take time to determine whether we should recognize the war or not. Had it been adopted, I would have insisted on raising a provisional army, to be collected at some proper point, and to be trained and disciplined: but to postpone the declaration of war until the Congress of Mexico, in which, according to her Constitution, the war-making power resided, should be allowed time to disavow the intention of making war on us, and to adjust all differences between the two countries. But if she refused, even then I would have advised to seize, by way of reprisal, the portion of her territory which we might select, and hold it defensively, as I have just stated, instead of declaring war formally against her; and that mainly for the purpose of avoiding the very dangers against which these resolutions are intended to guard. But such was the urgency which was supposed then to exist, that no time was allowed to present or press these views upon the Senate. Such a course, besides the saving of an immense sacrifice of men and money, and avoiding the many other evils to which the course adopted has already subjected the country, would have effectually prevented our being entangled in the affairs of Mexico, from which we find it now so difficult to extricate ourselves. This consideration alone gives it decisive advantages over the course adopted, and makes it vastly superior, even if it should involve the same sacrifice of men and money to maintain a defensive line, as would, to use the usual phrase, the vigorous prosecution of the war. Mexico is to us as a dead body, and this is the only way that we can cut the cord which binds us to the corpse.

In recommending this line of policy, I look not to the interests of Mexico, but to those of our own country, and to the preservation of its free popular institutions. With me, the liberty of the country is all in all. If this be preserved, every thing will be preserved; but if lost, all will be lost. To preserve it, it is indispensable to adopt a course of moderation and justice towards all other countries; to avoid war whenever it can be avoided; to let those great causes which are now at work, and which, by the mere operation of time, will raise our country to an elevation and influence which no country has ever heretofore attained, continue to work. By pursuing such a course, we may succeed in combining greatness and liberty—the highest possible greatness with the largest measure of liberty—and do more to extend liberty by our example over this continent and the world generally, than would be done by a thousand victories. It may be, in expressing these sentiments, that I find no response in the breasts of those around me. If so, it must be attributed to the fact that I am growing old, and that my principles and feelings belong to a period of thirty or thirty-five years anterior to the present date. It is not, however, the first time I have ventured in their maintenance to stand alone on this floor. When General Jackson, some years since, during the latter part of his administration, recommended to Congress to issue letters of marque and reprisal against France, I stood alone in my place here, and raised my voice against it, on the ground that there was no just cause of war with her; that, in entering into the treaty to indemnify our citizens for old claims against her, the King of France and his Ministers declared to our Minister, that it required a vote of the Chambers to make the appropriation to carry it into effect; and that they were no further responsible than to use their best efforts to induce them to do so. This was all communicated to our Executive, and the treaty accepted and ratified, with this condition attached. And yet the President, although he admitted that the King and his Ministers had fully redeemed their pledge to use their best efforts to obtain the necessary appropriation, recommended the adoption of the measure to which I have alluded, and which would have been tantamount to war. Fortunately the Government of Great Britain, by her interposition, prevented it. This example, I fear, has contributed much to give the strong tendency, which we have since witnessed, to resort to menace and force in the settlement of our differences with other powers.

According to my opinion, all parties are interested in adopting a line of policy which will with certainty disentangle us from the affairs of Mexico, and avoid the great sacrifices of men and money, and the many other evils to which the war exposes us. Let me say to my friends, who support the administration in their policy, that if you persist, and if peace by some good fortune should not be obtained, the war will go on from year to year, and you will be utterly overthrown as a party. Do you not see that its effect, in reference to our internal affairs, is to drive you into a course of policy directly contrary to that which you have professed to support, and in favor of that which you have charged your opponents with supporting. You have ever professed to oppose, as a party, a national debt, and charged your opponents with being its advocates. But what,

I ask, is the effect of the war in this respect? Is it not to create an immense national debt, greater than that which the party to which you are opposed could possibly have created by any other policy, had they been in power? This campaign, on which you look so lightly, will add to it a sum more than half as great as the entire debt of the Revolution. You have been opposed to the extension of the patronage of the Executive, at least in profession. But this war is doing more to enlarge his patronage than any other policy which your opponents could have adopted. You profess to be in favor of a metallic currency. Do you not see that with the increase of stocks and treasury notes, you are in danger of being plunged again into the lowest depths of the paper system? You, as a party, have advocated the doctrine of free trade. Do you not see that, by the vast increase of the expenditures of the country, and the heavy interest which you will have to pay on the public debt, you are creating a necessity for increasing the duties on imports to the highest point that revenue will admit, and thus depriving the country of all the practical benefits of free trade, and preventing the Government from making any material reduction, until the whole debt is paid, which cannot be expected during this generation? What could your opponents have done more, or even as much, to destroy a system of policy which you claim to distinguish you from them, and to establish that which you allege to be the reason why they should be excluded from power? Has not, and will not, this war policy, if persisted in, effectually and finally obliterate the line of policy which you have insisted on as distinguishing you from them? Why, then, to save yourselves from such a result, do you hesitate to adopt the course of policy I have suggested, as the only certain means of preventing these and other evils, and the danger to which our institutions are exposed? The pride of opinion may resist. I know the difficulty, and respect it, with which we yield measures that we have advocated, even when time has shown them to be wrong. But, true magnanimity and the highest honor command that we should abandon them, when they threaten to be injurious instead of beneficial to the country. It would do great credit to the party in power to adopt the policy now, in reference to the war, of taking indemnity into our own hands, by assuming a defensive position, which, it can hardly be doubted they would have done when the war was recognized, if they had foreseen the difficulties and dangers to which it has led. It would be a noble sacrifice of individual pride to patriotism.

In asserting that the only alternative is between the policy recommended by the President and the adoption of a defensive position, I have put out of the question the policy of taking no territory. I have done so, because I believe the voice of the country has decided irrevocably against it, and that to press it as the

alternative, would render almost certain the final adoption of the policy recommended by the President, notwithstanding the disasters which it threatens.
Let me say to my friends on the other side of the Chamber (for as such I regard
them, for political differences here do not affect our personal relations), that they
have contributed by their course to fix the determination not to terminate the
war without some suitable indemnity in territory. I do not refer to your vote
recognizing the existence of war between the Republic of Mexico and the
United States. I well know that you voted with a view to furnish immediate
support to General Taylor and his army, then surrounded by imminent danger,
and not with the intention of recognizing the war; and that you remonstrated
and protested against that interpretation being put upon your votes. But since it
passed, and the war was recognized, most of you have continued to vote for
appropriations to prosecute the war, when the object of prosecuting it was
avowed to be to acquire territory as an indemnity. Now, I cannot see how the
two can be reconciled—how you can refuse to take indemnity in territory,
when you have voted means for the express purpose of obtaining such indemnity. The people are not able to understand why you should vote money so profusely to get indemnity, and refuse to take it, when obtained; and hence public
opinion has been brought so decidedly to the conclusion not to terminate the
war without territorial indemnity. But if such indemnity is to be had without
involving the hazard of conquering the country, with all the dangers to which
it would expose us, we must decide whether we shall adopt a defensive position
or not, now—this very session. It will, in all possibility, be too late at the next.

I have now, Senators, delivered my sentiments with freedom and candor,
upon all the questions connected with these resolutions. I propose nothing now.
But if I find that I will be supported, I will move to raise a Committee to deliberate upon the subject of the defensive line.

The opportunity is favorable, while there are so many officers from Mexico
now in the city, whose opinion would be of great value in determining on the
one to be adopted. If the course of policy which I have suggested should be
adopted, we may not get peace immediately. The war may still continue for
some time; but be that as it may, it will accomplish the all-important object—
will extricate the country from its entanglement with Mexico.

Chapter XXVI.

Written during a period of intense political debate, Calhoun—with great precision—explained why slavery could not be excluded from the Oregon territory, basing his argument on the inherited American political tradition, while criticizing the excesses of the tradition itself.

There is a very striking difference between the position on which the slaveholding and non-slaveholding States stand, in reference to the subject under consideration. The former desire no action of the Government; demand no law to give them any advantage in the territory about to be established; are willing to leave it, and other territories belonging to the United States, open to all their citizens, so long as they continue to be territories,—and when they cease to be so, to leave it to their inhabitants to form such governments as may suit them, without restriction or condition,—except that imposed by the constitution, as a prerequisite for admission into the Union. In short, they are willing to leave the whole subject where the constitution and the great and fundamental principles of self-government place it. On the contrary, the non-slaveholding States, instead of being willing to leave it on this broad and equal foundation, demand the interposition of the Government, and the passage of an act to prevent the citizens of the slaveholding States from emigrating with their property into the territory, in order to give their citizens and those they may permit, the exclusive right of settling it, while it remains in that condition, preparatory to subjecting it to like restrictions and conditions when it becomes a State. The 12th section of this bill is intended to assert and maintain this demand of the non-slaveholding States, while it remains a territory,—not openly or directly,—

but indirectly, by extending the provisions of the bill for the establishment of the Iowa Territory to this, and by ratifying the acts of the informal and self-constituted government of Oregon, which, among others, contains one prohibiting the introduction of slavery. It thus, in reality, adopts what is called the Wilmot proviso, not only for Oregon, but, as the bill now stands, for New Mexico and California. The amendment, on the contrary, moved by the Senator from Mississippi, near me (Mr. Davis), is intended to assert and maintain the position of the slaveholding States. It leaves the territory free and open to all the citizens of the United States, and would overrule, if adopted, the act of the self-constituted Territory of Oregon and the 12th section, as far as it relates to the subject under consideration. We have thus fairly presented the grounds taken by the non-slaveholding and the slaveholding States,—or, as I shall call them for the sake of brevity,—the Northern and Southern States, in their whole extent for discussion.

The first question which offers itself for consideration is—Have the Northern States the power which they claim, to prevent the Southern people from emigrating freely, with their property, into territories belonging to the United States, and to monopolize them for their exclusive benefit?

It is, indeed, a great question. I propose to discuss it calmly and dispassionately. I shall claim nothing which does not fairly and clearly belong to the Southern States, either as members of this Federal Union, or appertain to them in their separate and individual character; nor shall I yield any thing which belongs to them in either capacity. I am influenced neither by sectional nor party considerations. If I know myself, I would repel as promptly and decidedly any aggression of the South on the North, as I would any on the part of the latter on the former. And let me add, I hold the obligation to repel aggression to be not much less solemn, than that of abstaining from making aggression; and the party which submits to it when it can be resisted, to be not much less guilty and responsible for consequences than that which makes it. Nor do I stand on party grounds. What I shall say in reference to this subject, I shall say entirely without reference to the Presidential election. I hold it to be infinitely higher than that and all other questions of the day. I shall direct my efforts to ascertain what is constitutional, right and just, under a thorough conviction that the best and only way of putting an end to this, the most dangerous of all questions to our Union and institutions, is to adhere rigidly to the constitution and the dictates of justice.

With these preliminary remarks, I recur to the question—Has the North the power which it claims under the 12th section of this bill? I ask at the outset, where is the power to be found? Not, certainly, in the relation in which the Northern and Southern States stand to each other. They are the constituent parts or members of a common Federal Union; and, as such, are equals in all respects, both in dignity and rights, as is declared by all writers on governments founded on such union, and as may be inferred from arguments deduced from their nature and character. Instead, then, of affording any countenance or authority in favor of the power, the relation in which they stand to each other furnishes a strong presumption against it. Nor can it be found in the fact that the South holds property in slaves. That, too, fairly considered, instead of affording any authority for the power, furnishes a strong presumption against it. Slavery existed in the South when the constitution was framed, fully to the extent, in proportion to the population, that it does at this time. It is the only property recognized by it; the only one that entered into its formation as a political element, both in the adjustment of the relative weight of the States in the Government, and the apportionment of direct taxes; and the only one that is put under the express guaranty of the constitution. It is well known to all conversant with the history of the formation and adoption of the constitution, that the South was very jealous in reference to this property; that it constituted one of the difficulties both to its formation and adoption; and that it would not have assented to either, had the convention refused to allow to it its due weight in the Government, or to place it under the guaranty of the constitution. Nor can it be found in the way that the territories have been acquired. I will not go into particulars, in this respect, at this stage of the discussion. Suffice it to say, the whole was acquired either by purchase, out of the common funds of all the States,—the South as well as the North,—or by arms and mutual sacrifice of men and money;—which, instead of giving any countenance in favor of the power claimed by the North, on every principle of right and justice, furnishes strong additional presumption against it.

But, if it cannot be found in either,—if it exists at all,—the power must be looked for in the constitutional compact, which binds these States together in a Federal Union; and I now ask, can it be found there? Does that instrument contain any provision which gives the North the power to exclude the South from a free admission into the territories of the United States with its peculiar property, and to monopolize them for its own exclusive use? If it in fact contains such power, expressed or implied, it must be found in a specific grant, or be inferred by irresistible deduction, from some clear and acknowledged power. Nothing short of the one or the other can overcome the strong presumption against it.

That there is no such specific grant may be inferred, beyond doubt, from the fact that no one has ever attempted to designate it. Instead of that, it has been assumed—taken for granted without a particle of proof—that Congress has the absolute right to govern the territories. Now, I concede, if it does in reality possess such power, it may exclude from the territories whom or what it pleases, and admit into them whom or what it pleases; and of course may exercise the power claimed by the North to exclude the South from them. But I again repeat, where is this absolute power to be found? All admit that there is no such specific grant of power. If, then, it exists at all, it must be inferred from some such power. I ask where is that to be found? The Senator from New-York, behind me (Mr. Dix), points to the clause in the constitution, which provides that "Congress shall have power to dispose of and make all needful rules and regulations respecting the territory and other property belonging to the United States." Now, I undertake to affirm and maintain, beyond the possibility of doubt, that, so far from conferring absolute power to govern the territories, it confers no governmental power whatever; no, not a particle. It refers exclusively to territory, regarded simply as public lands. Every word relates to it in that character, and is wholly inapplicable to it considered in any other character than property. Take the expression "dispose of" with which it begins. It is easily understood what it means when applied to lands; and is the proper and natural expression regarding the territory in that character, when the object is to confer the right to sell or make other disposition of it. But who ever heard the expression applied to government? And what possible meaning can it have when so applied? Take the next expression, "to make all needful rules and regulations." These, regarded separately, might, indeed, be applicable to government in a loose sense, but they are never so applied in the constitution. In every case where they are used in it, they refer to property, to things, or some process, such as the rules of Court, or of the Houses of Congress for the government of their proceedings,—but never to government, which always implies persons to be governed. But if there should be any doubt in this case, the words immediately following, which restrict them to making "rules and regulations respecting the territory and other property of the United States," must effectually expel it. They restrict their meaning, beyond the possibility of doubt, to territory regarded as property.

But if it were possible for doubt still to exist, another and conclusive argument still remains to show that the framers of the constitution did not intend to confer by this clause governmental powers. I refer to the clause in the constitution which delegates the power of exclusive legislation to Congress over this District and "all places purchased by the consent of the legislature of the State in which the same may be for the erection of forts, magazines, arsenals, dockyards, and other needful buildings." The places therein referred to are clearly embraced by the expression, "other property belonging to the United States," contained in the clause I have just considered. But it is certain, that if it had been the intention of the framers of the constitution to confer governmental powers over such places by that clause, they never would have delegated it by this. They were incapable of doing a thing so absurd. But it is equally certain, if they did not intend to confer such power over them, they could not have intended it over territories. Whatever was conferred by the same words, in reference to one, must have been intended to be conferred in reference to the other, and the reverse. The opposite supposition would be absurd. But, it may be asked why the term—territory—was omitted in the delegation of exclusive legislation to Congress over the places enumerated? Very satisfactory reasons may, in my opinion, be assigned. The former were limited to places lying within the limits and jurisdiction of the States, and the latter to public land lying beyond both. The cession and purchase of the former, with the consent of the State within which they might be situated, did not oust the sovereignty or jurisdiction of the State. They still remained in the State, the United States acquiring only the title to the place. It, therefore, became necessary to confer on Congress, by express delegation, the exercise of exclusive power of legislation over this District and such places, in order to carry out the object of the purchase and session. It was simply intended to withdraw them from under the legislatures of the respective States within which they might lie, and substitute that of Congress in its place,—subject to the restrictions of the constitution and the objects for which the places were acquired,—leaving, as I have said, the sovereignty still in the State in which they are situated, but in abeyance, as far as it extends to legislation. Thus, in the case of this District,—since the retrocession to Virginia of the part beyond the Potomac,—the sovereignty still continues in Maryland in the manner stated. But the case is very different in reference to territories, lying as they do beyond the limits and jurisdictions of all the States. The United States possess not simply the right of ownership over them, but that of exclusive dominion and sovereignty; and hence it was not necessary to exclude the power of the States to legislate over them, by delegating the exercise of exclusive legislation to Congress. It would have been an act of super-erogation. It may be proper to remark in this connection, that the power of exclusive legislation, conferred in these cases, must not be confounded with the power of absolute legislation. They are very different things. It is true that absolute power of legislation is always exclusive, but it by no means follows that exclusive power of legislation or of government is likewise always absolute. Congress has the exclusive power of legislation, as far as this Government is concerned, and the State legislatures as far as their respective governments are concerned;—but we all know that both are subject to many and important restrictions and conditions which the nature of absolute power excludes.

I have now made good the assertion I ventured to make, that the clause in the constitution relied on by the Senator from New-York, so far from conferring the absolute power of government over the territory claimed by him, and others who agree with him, confers not a particle of governmental power. Having conclusively established this, the long list of precedents, cited by the Senator to prop up the power which he sought in the clause, falls to the ground with the fabric which he raised; and I am thus exempted from the necessity of referring to them, and replying to them one by one.

But there is one precedent, referred to by the Senator, unconnected with the power, and on that account requiring particular notice. I refer to the ordinance of 1787, which was adopted by the old Congress of the Confederation while the convention that framed the constitution was in session, and about one year before its adoption,—and of course on the very eve of the expiration of the old Confederation. Against its introduction, I might object that the act of the Congress of the Confederation cannot rightfully form precedents for this Government; but I waive that. I waive also the objection that the act was consummated when that Government was *in extremis,* and could hardly be considered *compos mentis.* I waive also the fact that the ordinance assumed the form of a compact, and was adopted when only eight States were present, while the articles of confederation required nine to form compacts. I waive also the fact, that Mr. Madison declared that the act was without shadow of constitutional authority;—and shall proceed to show, from the history of its adoption, that it cannot justly be considered of any binding force.

Virginia made the cession of the territory north of the Ohio, and lying between it and the Mississippi and the lakes, in 1784. It now contains the States of Ohio, Indiana, Illinois, Michigan, Wisconsin, and a very considerable extent of territory lying north of the latter. Shortly after the cession, a committee of three was raised, of whom Mr. Jefferson was one. They reported an ordinance for the establishment of the territory,—containing, among other provisions, one, of which Mr. Jefferson was the author, excluding slavery from the territory after the year 1800. It was reported to Congress, but this provision was struck out. On the question of striking out, every Southern State present voted in favor of it; and, what is more striking, every Southern delegate voted the same way, Mr. Jefferson alone excepted. The ordinance was adopted without the provision. At the next session, Rufus King, then a member of the old Congress, moved a proposition, very much in the same shape as the sixth article (that which excludes slavery) in the ordinance as it now stands, with the exception of its proviso. It was referred to a committee, but there was no action on it. A committee was moved the next or the subsequent year, which reported without including or noticing Mr. King's proposition. Mr. Dane was a member of that committee, and proposed a provision the same as that in the ordinance as it passed, but the committee reported without including it. Finally, another committee was raised, at the head of which was Mr. Carrington of Virginia, and of which Mr. Dane was also a member. That committee reported without including the amendment previously proposed by him. Mr. Dane moved his proposition, which was adopted, and the report of the committee thus amended became the ordinance of 1787.

It may be inferred from this brief historical sketch, that the ordinance was a compromise between the Southern and Northern States, of which the terms were,—that slavery should be excluded from the territory upon condition that fugitive slaves, who might take refuge in the territory, should be delivered up to their owners, as stipulated in the proviso of the sixth article of the ordinance. It is manifest, from what has been stated, that the South was unitedly and obstinately opposed to the provision when first moved; that the proposition of Mr. King, without the proviso, was in like manner resisted by the South, as may be inferred from its entire want of success, and that it never could be brought to agree to it until the provision for the delivery up of fugitive slaves was incorporated in it. But it is well understood that a compromise involves not a surrender, but simply a waiver of the right or power; and hence in the case of individuals, it is a well-established legal principle, that an offer to settle by compromise a litigated claim, is no evidence against the justice of the claim on the side of the party making it. The South, to her honor, has observed with fidelity her engagements under this compromise; in proof of which, I appeal to the precedents cited by the Senator from New-York, intended by him to establish the fact of her acquiescence in the ordinance. I admit that she has acquiesced in the several acts of Congress to carry it into effect; but the Senator is mistaken in supposing that it is proof of a surrender, on her part, of the power over the territories which he claims for Congress. No, she never has, and I trust never will, make such a surrender. Instead of that, it is conclusive proof of her fidelity to her engagements. She has never attempted to set aside the ordinance, or to deprive the territory, and the States erected within its limits, of any right or advantage it was intended to confer. But I regret that as much cannot be said in favor of the fidelity with which it has been observed on their part. With the single exception of the State of Illinois—be it said to her honor—every other State erected within its limits has pursued a course, and adopted measures, which have rendered the stipulations of the proviso to deliver up fugitive slaves nugatory. Wisconsin may, also, be an exception, as she has just entered the Union, and has hardly had time to act on the subject. They have gone further,—and suffered individuals to form combinations, without an effort to suppress them, for the purpose of enticing and seducing the slaves to leave their masters, and to run them into Canada beyond the reach of our laws—in open violation, not only of the stipulations of the ordinance, but of the constitution itself. If I express myself strongly, it is not for the purpose of producing excitement, but to draw the attention of the Senate forcibly to the subject. My object is to lay bare the subject under consideration, just as a surgeon probes to the bottom and lays open a wound, not to cause pain to his patient, but for the purpose of healing it.

I come now to another precedent of a similar character, but differing in this—that it took place under this Government, and not under that of the old Confederation; I refer to what is known as the Missouri Compromise. It is more recent and better known, and may be more readily despatched.

After an arduous struggle of more than a year, on the question whether Missouri should come into the Union with or without restrictions prohibiting slavery, a compromise line was adopted between the North and the South; but it was done under circumstances which made it nowise obligatory on the latter. It is true, it was moved by one of her distinguished citizens (Mr. Clay); but it is equally so, that it was carried by the almost united vote of the North against the almost united vote of the South; and was thus imposed on the latter by superior numbers in opposition to her strenuous efforts. The South has never given her sanction to it, or assented to the power it asserted. She was voted down, and has simply acquiesced in an arrangement which she has not had the power to reverse, and which she could not attempt to do without disturbing the peace and harmony of the Union—to which she has ever been averse. Acting on this principle, she permitted the Territory of Iowa to be formed, and the State to be admitted into the Union, under the compromise, without objection; and this is now quoted by the Senator from New-York to prove her surrender of the power he claims for Congress.

To add to the strength of this claim, the advocates of the power hold up the name of Jefferson in its favor, and go so far as to call him the author of the so-

called Wilmot proviso, which is but a general expression of a power of which
the Missouri compromise is a case of its application. If we may judge by his
opinion of that case, what his opinion was of the principle, instead of being the
author of the proviso, or being in its favor, no one could be more deadly hostile to it. In a letter addressed to the elder Adams in 1819, in answer to one from
him, he uses these remarkable expressions in reference to the Missouri question:

> "The banks, bankrupt law, manufactures, Spanish treaty, are nothing.
> These are occurrences, which, like waves in a storm, will pass under the
> ship. But the Missouri question is a breaker on which we lose the Mis-
> souri country by revolt, and what more, God only knows."

To understand the full force of these expressions, it must be borne in mind
that the questions enumerated were the great and exciting political questions of
the day, on which parties divided. The banks and bankrupt law had long been
so. Manufactures, or what has since been called the protective tariff, was at the
time a subject of great excitement, as was the Spanish treaty, that is, the treaty
by which Florida was ceded to the Union, and by which the western boundary
between Mexico and the United States was settled, from the Gulf of Mexico to
the Pacific ocean. All these exciting party questions of the day Mr. Jefferson
regarded as nothing, compared to the Missouri question. He looked on all of
them as in their nature fugitive; and, to use his own forcible expression, "would
pass off under the ship of State like waves in a storm." Not so this fatal question. It was a breaker on which it was destined to be stranded. And yet his name
is quoted by the incendiaries of the present day in support of, and as the author
of, a proviso which would give indefinite and universal extension of this fatal
question to all the territories! It was compromised the next year by the adoption of the line to which I have referred. Mr. Holmes of Maine, long a member of this body, who voted for the measure, addressed a letter to Mr. Jefferson,
inclosing a copy of his speech on the occasion. It drew out an answer from him
which ought to be treasured up in the heart of every man who loves his country and its institutions. It is brief. I will send it to the Secretary to be read. The
time of the Senate cannot be better occupied than in listening to it:

> "*To John Holmes.*
> "MONTICELLO, *April* 22, 1820.
> 'I thank you, dear sir, for the copy you have been so kind as to send me
> of the letter to your constituents on the Missouri question. It is a perfect

justification to them. I had for a long time ceased to read newspapers, or pay any attention to public affairs, confident they were in good hands, and content to be a passenger in our bark to the shore from which I am not far distant. But this momentous question, like a fire-bell in the night, awakened and filled me with terror. I considered it at once as the knell of the Union. It is hushed, indeed, for the moment. But this is a reprieve only, not the final sentence. A geographical line, coinciding with a marked principle, moral and political, once conceived and held up to the angry passions of men, will never be obliterated; and every new irritation will mark it deeper and deeper. I can say, with conscious truth, that there is not a man on earth who would sacrifice more than I would to relieve us from this heavy reproach, in any *practicable* way. The cession of that kind of property (for so it is misnamed) is a bagatelle, which would not cost me a second thought, if in that way a general emancipation and *expatriation* could be effected; and gradually, and with due sacrifices, I think it might be. But, as it is, we have the wolf by the ears, and we can neither hold him nor safely let him go. Justice is in one scale, and self-preservation in the other. Of one thing, I am certain, that as the passage of slaves from one free State to another would not make a slave of a single human being who would not be so without it, so their diffusion over a greater surface would make them individually happier, and proportionally facilitate the accomplishment of their emancipation, by dividing the burden on a greater number of coadjutors. An abstinence, too, from this act of power, would remove the jealousy excited by the undertaking of Congress to regulate the condition of the different descriptions of men composing a State. This certainly is the exclusive right of every State, which nothing in the constitution has taken from them, and given to the General Government. Could Congress, for example, say that the non-freemen of Connecticut shall be freemen, or that they shall not emigrate into any other State?

"I regret that I am now to die in the belief that the useless sacrifice of themselves by the generation of 1776, to acquire self-government and happiness to their country, is to be thrown away by the unwise and unworthy passions of their sons, and that my only consolation is to be, that I shall not live to weep over it. If they would but dispassionately weigh the blessings they will throw away against an abstract principle, more likely to be effected by union than by scission, they would pause before they would perpetrate this act of suicide on themselves, and of treason against the hopes of the world. To yourself, as the faithful advocate of the Union, I tender the offering of my high esteem and respect. "THOMAS JEFFERSON."

Mark his prophetic words! Mark his profound reasoning!

> "It [the question] is hushed for *the moment*. But this is a *reprieve only, not a final sentence*. A geographical line coinciding with a marked principle, moral and political, *once conceived, and held up to the angry passions of men, will never be obliterated, and every new irritation will mark it deeper and deeper*."

Twenty-eight years have passed since these remarkable words were penned, and there is not a thought which time has not thus far verified, and, it is to be feared, will continue to verify until the whole will be fulfilled. Certain it is, that he regarded the compromise line as utterly inadequate to arrest that fatal course of events, which his keen sagacity anticipated from the question. It was but a "reprieve." Mark the deeply melancholy impression which it made on his mind:

> "I regret that I am to die in the belief that the useless sacrifice of themselves by the generation of 1776, to acquire self-government and happiness for themselves, is to be thrown away by the unwise and unworthy passions of their sons, and that my only consolation is to be, that I shall not live to weep over it."

Can any one believe, after listening to this letter, that Jefferson is the author of the so-called Wilmot proviso, or ever favored it? And yet there are at this time strenuous efforts making in the North to form a purely sectional party on it, and that, too, under the sanction of those who profess the highest veneration for his character and principles! But I must speak the truth: while I vindicate the memory of Jefferson from so foul a charge, I hold he is not blameless in reference to this subject. He committed a great error in inserting the provision he did in the plan he reported for the government of the territory, as much modified as it was. It was the first blow—the first essay "to draw a geographical line coinciding with a marked principle, moral and political." It originated with him in philanthropic, but mistaken views of the most dangerous character, as I shall show in the sequel. Others, with very different feelings and views, followed, and have given to it a direction and impetus, which, if not promptly and efficiently arrested, will end in the dissolution of the Union, and the destruction of our political institutions.

I have, I trust, established beyond controversy, that neither the ordinance of 1787, nor the Missouri compromise, nor the precedents growing out of them, nor the authority of Mr. Jefferson, furnishes any evidence whatever to prove that Congress possesses the power over the territory, claimed by those who advocate the 12th section of this bill. But admit, for the sake of argument, that I am mistaken, and that the objections I have urged against them are ground-less—give them all the force which can be claimed for precedents—and they would not have the weight of a feather against the strong presumption which I, at the outset of my remarks, showed to be opposed to the existence of the power. Precedents, even in a court of justice, can have but little weight, except where the law is doubtful, and should have little in a deliberative body in any case on a constitutional question,—and none, where the power to which it has been attempted to trace it does not exist, as I have shown, I trust, to be the case in this instance.

But, while I deny that the clause relating to the territory and other property of the United States, confers any governmental, or that Congress possesses absolute power over the territories, I by no means deny that it has any power over them. Such a denial would be idle on any occasion, but much more so on this, when we are engaged in constituting a territorial government, without an objection being whispered from any quarter against our right to do so. If there be any Senator of that opinion, he ought at once to rise and move to lay the bill on the table, or to dispose of it in some other way, so as to prevent the waste of time on a subject upon which we have no right to act. Assuming, then, that we possess the power, the only questions that remain are—whence is it derived? and, what is its extent?

As to its origin, I concur in the opinion expressed by Chief Justice Marshall, in one of the cases read by the Senator from New-York, that it is derived from the right of acquiring territory; and I am the more thoroughly confirmed in it from the fact that I entertained the opinion long before I knew it to be his. As to the right of acquiring territory, I agree with the Senator from New-York, that it is embraced, without going further, both in the war and treaty powers. Admitting, then, what has never been denied, and what it would be idle to deny in a discussion which relates to territories acquired both by war and treaties, that the United States have the right to acquire territories, it would seem to follow, by necessary consequence, that they have the right to govern them. As they pos-sess the entire right of soil, dominion, and sovereignty over them, they must necessarily carry with them the right to govern. But this Government, as the sole agent and representative of the United States—that is, the States of the

Union in their federal character—must, as such, possess the sole right, if it exists at all. But, if there be any one disposed to take a different view of the origin of the power, I shall make no points with him,—for whatever may be its origin, the conclusion would be the same, as I shall presently show.

But it would be a great error to conclude that Congress has the absolute power of governing the territories, because it has the sole or exclusive power. The reverse is the case. It is subject to many and important restrictions and conditions, of which some are expressed and others implied. Among the former may be classed all the general and absolute prohibitions of the constitution; that is, all those which prohibit the exercise of certain powers under any circumstances. In this class is included the prohibition of granting titles of nobility; passing *ex post facto* laws and bills of attainder; the suspension of the writ of *habeas corpus,* except in certain cases; making laws respecting the establishment of religion, or prohibiting its free exercise; and every other of like description, which conclusively shows that the power of Congress over the territories is not absolute. Indeed, it is a great error to suppose that either this or the State Governments possess, in any case, absolute power. Such power can belong only to the supreme ultimate power, called sovereignty,—and this, in our system, resides in the people of the several States of the Union. With us, governments, both federal and State, are but agents, or, more properly, trustees, and, as such, possess, not absolute, but subordinate and limited powers; for all powers possessed by such governments must, from their nature, be trust powers, and subject to all the restrictions to which that class of powers are.

Among them, they are restricted to the nature and the objects of the trust; and hence no government under our system, federal or State, has the right to do any thing inconsistent with the nature of the powers intrusted to it, or the objects for which it was intrusted: or to express it in more usual language, for which it was delegated. To do either would be to pervert the power to purposes never intended, and a violation of the constitution,—and that in the most dangerous way it could be made, because more easily done and less easily detected. But there is another and important class of restrictions which more directly relate to the subject under discussion. I refer to those imposed on the trustees by the nature and character of the party, who constituted the trustees and invested them with the trust powers to be exercised for its benefit. In this case it is the United States, that is, the several States of the Union. It was they who constituted the Government as their representative or trustee, and intrusted it with powers to be exercised for their common and joint benefit. To them in their united character the territories belong, as is expressly declared by the constitution. They are

their joint and common owners, regarded as property or land; and in them, severally, reside the dominion and sovereignty over them. They are as much the
territories of one State as another—of Virginia as of New-York; of the Southern as the Northern States. They are the territories of all, because they are the
territories of each; and not of each, because they are the territories of the whole.
Add to this the perfect equality of dignity, as well as of rights, which appertain
to them as members of a common federal Union,—which all writers on the subject admit to be a fundamental and essential relation between States so united,—
and it must be manifest that Congress, in governing the territories, can give no
preference or advantage to one State over another, or to one portion or section
of the Union over another, without depriving the State or section over which
the preference is given, or from which the advantage is withheld, of their clear
and unquestionable right, and subverting the very foundation on which the
Union and Government rest. It has no more power to do so than to subvert the
constitution itself. Indeed, the act itself would be subversion. It would destroy
the relation of equality on the part of the Southern States, and sink them to mere
dependants of the Northern, to the total destruction of the federal Union.

I have now shown, I trust, beyond controversy, that Congress has no power
whatever to prevent the citizens of the Southern States from emigrating with
their property into the territories of the United States, or to give an exclusive
monopoly of them to the North. I now propose to go one step further, and
show that neither the inhabitants of the territories nor their legislatures have any
such right. A very few words will be sufficient for the purpose; for of all the
positions ever taken, I hold that which claims the power for them to be the most
absurd. If the territories belong to the United States—if the ownership, dominion and sovereignty over them be in the States of this Union, then neither the
inhabitants of the territories, nor their legislatures, can exercise any power but
what is subordinate to them: but if the contrary could be shown, which I hold
to be impossible, it would be subject to all the restrictions, to which I have
shown the power of Congress is; and for the same reason, whatever power they
might hold, would, in the case supposed, be subordinate to the constitution,
and controlled by the nature and character of our political institutions. But if
the reverse be true—if the dominion and sovereignty over the territories be in
their inhabitants, instead of the United States—they would indeed, in that case,
have the exclusive and absolute power of governing them, and might exclude
whom they pleased, or what they pleased. But, in that case, they would cease
to be the territories of the United States the moment we acquired them and permitted them to be inhabited. The first half-dozen of squatters would become

the sovereigns, with full dominion and sovereignty over them; and the conquered people of New Mexico and California would become the sovereigns of the country as soon as they became the territories of the United States, vested with the full right of excluding even their conquerors. There is no escaping from the alternative, but by resorting to the greatest of all absurdities, that of a divided sovereignty—a sovereignty, a part of which would reside in the United States, and a part in the inhabitants of the territory. How can sovereignty—the ultimate and supreme power of a State—be divided? The exercise of the powers of sovereignty may be divided, but how can there be two supreme powers?

We are next told that the laws of Mexico preclude slavery; and assuming that they will remain in force until repealed, it is contended that, until Congress passes an act for their repeal, the citizens of the South cannot emigrate with their property into the territory acquired from her. I admit the laws of Mexico prohibit, not slavery, but slavery in the form it exists with us. The Puros are as much slaves as our negroes, and are less intelligent and well treated. But, I deny that the laws of Mexico can have the effect attributed to them. As soon as the treaty between the two countries is ratified, the sovereignty and authority of Mexico in the territory acquired by it becomes extinct, and that of the United States is substituted in its place,—carrying with it the constitution, with its overriding control, over all the laws and institutions of Mexico inconsistent with it. It is true, the municipal laws of the territory not inconsistent with the condition and the nature of our political system would, according to the writers on the laws of nations, remain, until changed,—not as a matter of right, but merely of sufferance,—and as between the inhabitants of territory, in order to avoid a state of anarchy, before they can be brought under our laws. This is the utmost limit to which sufferance goes. Under it the peon system would continue; but not to the exclusion of such of our citizens as may choose to emigrate with their slaves or other property, that may be excluded by the laws of Mexico. The humane provisions of the laws of nations go no further than to protect the inhabitants in their property and civil rights, under their former laws, until others can be substituted. To extend them further and give them the force of excluding emigrants from the United States, because their property or religion are such as are prohibited from being introduced by the laws of Mexico, would not only prevent a great majority of the people of the United States from emigrating into the acquired territory, but would give a higher authority to the extinct power of Mexico over the territory than to our actual authority over it. I say the great majority, for the laws of Mexico not only prohibit the introduction of slaves, but of many other descriptions of property, and also the

Protestant religion, which Congress itself cannot prohibit. To such absurdity would the supposition lead.

I have now concluded the discussion, so far as it relates to the power; and have, I trust, established beyond controversy, that the territories are free and open to all of the citizens of the United States, and that there is no power, under any aspect the subject can be viewed in, by which the citizens of the South can be prevented from emigrating with their property into any of them. I have advanced no argument which I do not believe to be true, nor pushed any one beyond what truth would strictly warrant. But, if mistaken,—if my arguments, instead of being sound and true, as I hold them beyond controversy to be, should turn out to be a mere mass of sophisms,—and if in consequence, the barrier opposed by the want of power, should be surmounted, there is another still in the way, that cannot be. The mere possession of power is not, of itself, sufficient to justify its exercise. It must be, in addition, shown that, in the given case, it can be rightfully and justly exercised. Under our system, the first inquiry is: Does the constitution authorize the exercise of the power? If this be decided in the affirmative, the next is: Can it be rightfully and justly exercised under the circumstances? And it is not, until this, too, is decided in the affirmative, that the question of the expediency of exercising it, is presented for consideration.

Now, I put the question solemnly to the Senators from the North: Can you rightly and justly exclude the South from territories of the United States, and monopolize them for yourselves, even if, in your opinion, you should have the power? It is this question I wish to press on your attention with all due solemnity and decorum. The North and the South stand in the relation of partners in a common Union, with equal dignity and equal rights. We of the South have contributed our full share of funds, and shed our full share of blood for the acquisition of our territories. Can you, then, on any principle of equity and justice, deprive us of our full share in their benefit and advantage? Are you ready to affirm that a majority of the partners in a joint concern have the right to monopolize its benefits to the exclusion of the minority, even in cases where they have contributed their full share to the concern? But, to present the case more strongly and vividly, I shall descend from generals to particulars, and shall begin with the Oregon Territory. Our title to it is founded first, and in my opinion, mainly on our purchase of Louisiana; that was strengthened by the Florida treaty, which transferred to us the title also of Spain; and both by the discovery of the mouth of the Columbia river by Capt. Gray, and the exploration of the entire stream, from its source down to its mouth, by Lewis and Clark. The purchase of Louisiana cost fifteen millions of dollars; and we paid

Spain five millions for the Florida treaty; making twenty in all. This large sum was advanced out of the common funds of the Union: the South, to say the least, contributing her full share. The discovery was made, it is true, by a citizen of Massachusetts; but he sailed under the flag and protection of the Union, and of course, whatever title was derived from his discovery, accrued to the benefit of the Union. The exploration of Lewis and Clark was at the expense of the Union. We are now about to form it into a territory; the expense of governing which, while it remains so, must be met out of the common fund, and towards which the South must contribute her full share. The expense will not be small. Already there is an Indian war to be put down, and a regiment for that purpose, and to protect the territory, has been ordered there. To what extent the expense may go we know not, but it will, not improbably, involve millions before the territory becomes a State. I now ask, Is it right, is it just—after having contributed our full share for the acquisition of the territory, with the liability of contributing, in addition, our full share of the expense for its government—that we should be shut out of the territory, and be excluded from participating in its benefits? What would be thought of such conduct in the case of individuals? And can that be right and just in Government, which every right-minded man would cry out to be base and dishonest in private life? If it would be so pronounced in a partnership of thirty individuals, how can it be pronounced otherwise in one of thirty States?

The case of our recently acquired territory from Mexico is, if possible, more marked. The events connected with the acquisition are too well known to require a long narrative. It was won by arms, and a great sacrifice of men and money. The South, in the contest, performed her full share of military duty, and earned a full share of military honor; has poured out her full share of blood freely, and has and will bear a full share of the expense; has evinced a full share of skill and bravery, and if I were to say even more than her full share of both, I would not go beyond the truth; to be attributed, however, to no superiority in either respect, but to accidental circumstances, which gave both its officers and soldiers more favorable opportunities for their display. All have done their duty nobly, and high courage and gallantry are but common attributes of our people. Would it be right and just to close a territory thus won against the South, and leave it open exclusively to the North? Would it deserve the name of free soil, if one half of the Union should be excluded and the other half should monopolize it, when it was won by the joint expense and joint efforts of all? Is the great law to be reversed—that which is won by all should be equally enjoyed by all? These are questions which address themselves more to the heart than the head. Feeble must be the intellect which does not see what is right and just, and bad must be the heart, unless unconsciously under the control of deep and abiding prejudice, which hesitates in pronouncing on which side they are to be found. Now, I put the question to the Senators from the North: What are you prepared to do? Are you prepared to prostrate the barriers of the constitution, and in open defiance of the dictates of equity and justice, to exclude the South from the territories and monopolize them for the North? If so, vote against the amendment offered by the Senator from Mississippi (Mr. Davis), and if that should fail, vote against striking out the 12th section. We shall then know what to expect. If not, place us on some ground where we can stand as equals in rights and dignity, and where we shall not be excluded from what has been acquired at the common expense, and won by common skill and gallantry. All we demand is to stand on the same level with yourselves, and to participate equally in what belongs to all. Less we cannot take.

I turn now to my friends of the South, and ask: What are you prepared to do? If neither the barriers of the constitution nor the high sense of right and justice should prove sufficient to protect you, are you prepared to sink down into a state of acknowledged inferiority; to be stripped of your dignity of equals among equals, and be deprived of your equality of rights in this federal partnership of States? If so, you are wofully degenerated from your sires, and will well deserve to change condition with your slaves;—but if not, prepare to meet the issue. The time is at hand, if the question should not be speedily settled, when the South must rise up, and bravely defend herself, or sink down into base and acknowledged inferiority; and it is because I clearly perceive that this period is favorable for settling it, if it is ever to be settled, that I am in favor of pressing the question now to a decision—not because I have any desire whatever to embarrass either party in reference to the Presidential election. At no other period could the two great parties into which the country is divided be made to see and feel so clearly and intensely the embarrassment and danger caused by the question. Indeed, they must be blind not to perceive that there is a power in action that must burst asunder the ties that bind them together, strong as they are, unless it should be speedily settled. Now is the time, if ever. Cast your eyes to the North, and mark what is going on there; reflect on the tendency of events for the last three years in reference to this the most vital of all questions, and you must see that no time should be lost.

I am thus brought to the question, How can the question be settled? It can, in my opinion, be finally and permanently adjusted but one way,—and that is on the high principles of justice and the constitution. Fear not to leave it to them. The less you do the better. If the North and South cannot stand together on their broad and solid foundation, there is none other on which they can. If the obligations of the constitution and justice be too feeble to command the respect of the North, how can the South expect that she will regard the far more feeble obligations of an act of Congress? Nor should the North fear that, by leaving it where justice and the constitution leave it, she would be excluded from her full share of the territories. In my opinion, if it be left there, climate, soil, and other circumstances would fix the line between the slaveholding and non-slaveholding States in about 36° 30'. It may zigzag a little, to accommodate itself to circumstances—sometimes passing to the north, and at others passing to the south of it; but that would matter little, and would be more satisfactory to all, and tend less to alienation between the two great sections, than a rigid, straight, artificial line, prescribed by an act of Congress.

And here, let me say to Senators from the North;—you make a great mistake in supposing that the portion which might fall to the south of whatever line might be drawn, if left to soil, and climate, and circumstances to determine, would be closed to the white labor of the North, because it could not mingle with slave labor without degradation. The fact is not so. There is no part of the world where agricultural, mechanical, and other descriptions of labor are more respected than in the South, with the exception of two descriptions of employment—that of menial and body servants. No Southern man—not the poorest or the lowest—will, under any circumstance, submit to perform either of them. He has too much pride for that, and I rejoice that he has. They are unsuited to the spirit of a freeman. But the man who would spurn them feels not the least degradation to work in the same field with his slave; or to be employed to work with them in the same field or in any mechanical operation; and, when so employed, they claim the right—and are admitted, in the country portion of the South—of sitting at the table of their employers. Can as much, on the score of equality, be said of the North. With us the two great divisions of society are not the rich and poor, but white and black; and all the former, the poor as well as the rich, belong to the upper class, and are respected and treated as equals, if honest and industrious; and hence have a position and pride of character of which neither poverty nor misfortune can deprive them.

But I go further, and hold that justice and the constitution are the easiest and safest guard on which the question can be settled, regarded in reference to party. It may be settled on that ground simply by non-action—by leaving the territories free and open to the emigration of all the world, so long as they continue so,—and when they become States, to adopt whatever constitution they please, with the single restriction, to be republican, in order to their admission into the Union. If a party cannot safely take this broad and solid position and successfully maintain it, what other can it take and maintain? If it cannot maintain itself by an appeal to the great principles of justice, the constitution, and self-government, to what other, sufficiently strong to uphold them in public opinion, can they appeal? I greatly mistake the character of the people of this Union, if such an appeal would not prove successful, if either party should have the magnanimity to step forward, and boldly make it. It would, in my opinion, be received with shouts of approbation by the patriotic and intelligent in every quarter. There is a deep feeling pervading the country that the Union and our political institutions are in danger, which such a course would dispel, and spread joy over the land.

Now is the time to take the step, and bring about a result so devoutly to be wished. I have believed, from the beginning, that this was the only question sufficiently potent to dissolve the Union, and subvert our system of government; and that the sooner it was met and settled, the safer and better for all. I have never doubted but that, if permitted to progress beyond a certain point, its settlement would become impossible, and am under deep conviction that it is now rapidly approaching it,—and that if it is ever to be averted, it must be done speedily. In uttering these opinions I look to the whole. If I speak earnestly, it is to save and protect all. As deep as is the stake of the South in the Union and our political institutions, it is not deeper than that of the North. We shall be as well prepared and as capable of meeting whatever may come, as you.

Now, let me say, Senators, if our Union and system of government are doomed to perish, and we to share the fate of so many great people who have gone before us, the historian, who, in some future day, may record the events ending in so calamitous a result, will devote his first chapter to the ordinance of 1787, lauded as it and its authors have been, as the first of that series which led to it. His next chapter will be devoted to the Missouri compromise, and the next to the present agitation. Whether there will be another beyond, I know not. It will depend on what we may do.

If he should possess a philosophical turn of mind, and be disposed to look to more remote and recondite causes, he will trace it to a proposition which originated in a hypothetical truism, but which, as now expressed and now understood, is the most false and dangerous of all political errors. The proposition to which I allude, has become an axiom in the minds of a vast many on both sides of the Atlantic, and is repeated daily from tongue to tongue, as an established and incontrovertible truth; it is,—that "all men are born free and equal." I am not afraid to attack error, however deeply it may be intrenched, or however widely extended, whenever it becomes my duty to do so, as I believe it to be on this subject and occasion.

Taking the proposition literally (it is in that sense it is understood), there is not a word of truth in it. It begins with "all men are born," which is utterly untrue. Men are not born. Infants are born. They grow to be men. And concludes with asserting that they are born "free and equal," which is not less false. They are not born free. While infants they are incapable of freedom, being destitute alike of the capacity of thinking and acting, without which there can be no freedom. Besides, they are necessarily born subject to their parents, and remain so among all people, savage and civilized, until the development of their intellect and physical capacity enables them to take care of themselves. They grow to all the freedom of which the condition in which they were born permits, by growing to be men. Nor is it less false that they are born "equal." They are not so in any sense in which it can be regarded; and thus, as I have asserted, there is not a word of truth in the whole proposition, as expressed and generally understood.

If we trace it back, we shall find the proposition differently expressed in the Declaration of Independence. That asserts that "all men are created equal." The form of expression, though less dangerous, is not less erroneous. All men are not created. According to the Bible, only two—a man and a woman—ever were—and of these one was pronounced subordinate to the other. All others have come into the world by being born, and in no sense, as I have shown, either free or equal. But this form of expression being less striking and popular, has given way to the present, and under the authority of a document put forth on so great an occasion, and leading to such important consequences, has spread far and wide, and fixed itself deeply in the public mind. It was inserted in our Declaration of Independence without any necessity. It made no necessary part of our justification in separating from the parent country, and declaring ourselves independent. Breach of our chartered privileges, and lawless encroachment on our acknowledged and well-established rights by the parent country, were the real causes,—and of themselves sufficient, without resorting to any other, to justify the step. Nor had it any weight in constructing the governments which were substituted in the place of the colonial. They were formed of the old materials and on practical and well-established principles, borrowed for the most part from our own experience and that of the country from which we sprang.

If the proposition be traced still further back, it will be found to have been adopted from certain writers on government who had attained much celebrity in the early settlement of these States, and with those writings all the prominent actors in our revolution were familiar. Among these, Locke and Sydney were prominent. But they expressed it very differently. According to their expression, "all men in the state of nature were free and equal." From this the others were derived; and it was this to which I referred when I called it a hypothetical truism;—to understand why, will require some explanation.

Man, for the purpose of reasoning, may be regarded in three different states: in a state of individuality; that is, living by himself apart from the rest of his species. In the social; that is, living in society, associated with others of his species. And in the political; that is, living under government. We may reason as to what would be his rights and duties in either, without taking into consideration whether he could exist in it or not. It is certain, that in the first, the very supposition that he lived apart and separated from all others would make him free and equal. No one in such a state could have the right to command or control another. Every man would be his own master, and might do just as he pleased. But it is equally clear, that man cannot exist in such a state; that he is by nature social, and that society is necessary, not only to the proper development of all his faculties, moral and intellectual, but to the very existence of his race. Such being the case, the state is a purely hypothetical one; and when we say all men are free and equal in it, we announce a mere hypothetical truism; that is, a truism resting on a mere supposed state that cannot exist, and of course one of little or no practical value.

But to call it a state of nature was a great misnomer, and has led to dangerous errors; for that cannot justly be called a state of nature which is so opposed to the constitution of man as to be inconsistent with the existence of his race and the development of the high faculties, mental and moral, with which he is endowed by his Creator.

Nor is the social state of itself his natural state; for society can no more exist without government, in one form or another, than man without society. It is the political, then, which includes the social, that is his natural state. It is the one for which his Creator formed him,—into which he is impelled irresistibly,—and in which only his race can exist and all its faculties be fully developed.

Such being the case, it follows that any, the worst form of government, is better than anarchy; and that individual liberty, or freedom, must be subordinate to whatever power may be necessary to protect society against anarchy within or destruction without; for the safety and well-being of society is as paramount to individual liberty, as the safety and well-being of the race is to that of individuals; and in the same proportion the power necessary for the safety of society is paramount to individual liberty. On the contrary, government has no right to control individual liberty beyond what is necessary to the safety and well-being of society. Such is the boundary which separates the power of government and the liberty of the citizen or subject in the political state, which, as I have shown, is the natural state of man—the only one in which his race can exist, and the one in which he is born, lives, and dies.

It follows from all this that the quantum of power on the part of the government, and of liberty on that of individuals, instead of being equal in all cases, must necessarily be very unequal among different people, according to their different conditions. For just in proportion as a people are ignorant, stupid, debased, corrupt, exposed to violence within, and danger from without, the power necessary for government to possess, in order to preserve society against anarchy and destruction, becomes greater and greater, and individual liberty less and less, until the lowest condition is reached,—when absolute and despotic power becomes necessary on the part of the government, and individual liberty extinct. So, on the contrary, just as a people rise in the scale of intelligence, virtue, and patriotism, and the more perfectly they become acquainted with the nature of government, the ends for which it was ordered, and how it ought to be administered, and the less the tendency to violence and disorder within, and danger from abroad,—the power necessary for government becomes less and less, and individual liberty greater and greater. Instead, then, of all men having the same right to liberty and equality, as is claimed by those who hold that they are all born free and equal, liberty is the noble and highest reward bestowed on mental and moral development, combined with favorable circumstances. Instead, then, of liberty and equality being born with men,—instead of all men and all classes and descriptions being equally entitled to them, they are high prizes to be won, and are in their most perfect state, not only the highest reward that can be bestowed on our race, but the most difficult to be won,—and when won, the most difficult to be preserved.

They have been made vastly more so by the dangerous error I have attempted to expose,—that all men are born free and equal,—as if those high qualities belonged to man without effort to acquire them, and to all equally alike, regardless of their intellectual and moral condition. The attempt to carry into practice this, the most dangerous of all political errors, and to bestow on all—without regard to their fitness either to acquire or maintain liberty—that unbounded and individual liberty supposed to belong to man in the hypothetical and misnamed state of nature, has done more to retard the cause of liberty and civilization, and is doing more at present, than all other causes combined. While it is powerful to pull down governments, it is still more powerful to prevent their construction on proper principles. It is the leading cause among those which have placed Europe in its present anarchical condition, and which mainly stands in the way of reconstructing good governments in the place of those which have been over-thrown,—threatening thereby the quarter of the globe most advanced in progress and civilization with hopeless anarchy,—to be followed by military despotism. Nor are we exempt from its disorganizing effects. We now begin to experience the danger of admitting so great an error to have a place in the declaration of our independence. For a long time it lay dormant; but in the process of time it began to germinate, and produce its poisonous fruits. It had strong hold on the mind of Mr. Jefferson, the author of that document, which caused him to take an utterly false view of the subordinate relation of the black to the white race in the South; and to hold, in consequence, that the latter, though utterly unqualified to pos-sess liberty, were as fully entitled to both liberty and equality as the former; and that to deprive them of it was unjust and immoral. To this error, his proposition to exclude slavery from the territory northwest of the Ohio may be traced,—and to that the ordinance of 1787,—and through it the deep and dangerous agitation which now threatens to ingulf, and will certainly ingulf, if not speedily settled, our political institutions, and involve the country in countless woes.

CHAPTER XXVII.

In his final speech, Calhoun explored the problem of how to preserve the Union. In surveying the dilemma, he identified three things that pitched the issue into a crisis: legislation that kept slavery from the territories; placing too heavy a tax burden on one section of the country and not the others; and, most poignantly, disregard for the vision of the Founders—the "original character" of the country. The transition from a "federal republic" into a "great national consolidated democracy" had corrupted the vision, according to Calhoun, who concluded that a crisis was unavoidable.

I HAVE, Senators, believed from the first that the agitation of the subject of slavery would, if not prevented by some timely and effective measure, end in disunion. Entertaining this opinion, I have, on all proper occasions, endeavored to call the attention of both the two great parties which divide the country to adopt some measure to prevent so great a disaster, but without success. The agitation has been permitted to proceed, with almost no attempt to resist it, until it has reached a point when it can no longer be disguised or denied that the Union is in danger. You have thus had forced upon you the greatest and the gravest question that can ever come under your consideration—How can the Union be preserved?

To give a satisfactory answer to this mighty question, it is indispensable to have an accurate and thorough knowledge of the nature and the character of the cause by which the Union is endangered. Without such knowledge it is impossible to pronounce, with any certainty, by what measure it can be saved; just as it would be impossible for a physician to pronounce, in the case of some dangerous disease, with any certainty, by what remedy the patient could be saved, without similar knowledge of the nature and character of the cause which produced it. The first question, then, presented for consideration, in the investigation I propose to make, in order to obtain such knowledge, is—What is it that has endangered the Union?

To this question there can be but one answer,—that the immediate cause is the almost universal discontent which pervades all the States composing the Southern section of the Union. This widely-extended discontent is not of recent origin. It commenced with the agitation of the slavery question, and has been increasing ever since. The next question, going one step further back, is—What has caused this widely diffused and almost universal discontent?

It is a great mistake to suppose, as is by some, that it originated with demagogues, who excited the discontent with the intention of aiding their personal advancement, or with the disappointed ambition of certain politicians, who resorted to it as the means of retrieving their fortunes. On the contrary, all the great political influences of the section were arrayed against excitement, and exerted to the utmost to keep the people quiet. The great mass of the people of the South were divided, as in the other section, into Whigs and Democrats. The leaders and the presses of both parties in the South were very solicitous to prevent excitement and to preserve quiet; because it was seen that the effects of the former would necessarily tend to weaken, if not destroy, the political ties which united them with their respective parties in the other section. Those who know the strength of party ties will readily appreciate the immense force which this cause exerted against agitation, and in favor of preserving quiet. But, great as it was, it was not sufficient to prevent the wide-spread discontent which now pervades the section. No; some cause, far deeper and more powerful than the one supposed, must exist, to account for discontent so wide and deep. The question then recurs—What is the cause of this discontent? It will be found in the belief of the people of the Southern States, as prevalent as the discontent itself, that they cannot remain, as things now are, consistently with honor and safety, in the Union. The next question to be considered is—What has caused this belief?

One of the causes is, undoubtedly, to be traced to the long-continued agitation of the slave question on the part of the North, and the many aggressions which they have made on the rights of the South during the time. I will not enumerate them at present, as it will be done hereafter in its proper place.

There is another lying back of it—with which this is intimately connected—that may be regarded as the great and primary cause. This is to be found in the fact that the equilibrium between the two sections, in the Government as it stood when the constitution was ratified and the Government put in action, has been destroyed. At that time there was nearly a perfect equilibrium between the two, which afforded ample means to each to protect itself against the aggression of the other; but, as it now stands, one section has the exclusive power of controlling the Government, which leaves the other without any adequate means of protecting itself against its encroachment and oppression. To place this subject distinctly before you, I have, Senators, prepared a brief statistical statement, showing the relative weight of the two sections in the Government under the first census of 1790 and the last census of 1840.

According to the former, the population of the United States, including Vermont, Kentucky, and Tennessee, which then were in their incipient condition of becoming States, but were not actually admitted, amounted to 3,929,827. Of this number the Northern States had 1,997,899, and the Southern 1,952,072, making a difference of only 45,827 in favor of the former States. The number of States, including Vermont, Kentucky, and Tennessee, were sixteen; of which eight, including Vermont, belonged to the Northern section, and eight, including Kentucky and Tennessee, to the Southern,—making an equal division of the States between the two sections under the first census. There was a small preponderance in the House of Representatives, and in the Electoral College, in favor of the Northern, owing to the fact that, according to the provisions of the constitution, in estimating federal numbers five slaves count but three; but it was too small to affect sensibly the perfect equilibrium which, with that exception, existed at the time. Such was the equality of the two sections when the States composing them agreed to enter into a Federal Union. Since then the equilibrium between them has been greatly disturbed.

According to the last census the aggregate population of the United States amounted to 17,063,357, of which the Northern section contained 9,728,920, and the Southern 7,334,437, making a difference, in round numbers, of 2,400,000. The number of States had increased from sixteen to twenty-six, making an addition of ten States. In the mean time the position of Delaware had become doubtful as to which section she properly belonged. Considering her as neutral, the Northern States will have thirteen and the Southern States twelve, making a difference in the Senate of two Senators in favor of the former. According to the appointment under the census of 1840, there were two hundred and twenty-three members of the House of Representatives, of which the Northern States had one hundred and thirty-five, and the Southern States (considering Delaware as neutral) eighty-seven, making a difference in favor of the former in the House of Representatives of forty-eight. The difference in the Senate of two members, added to this, gives to the North, in the electoral college, a majority of fifty. Since the census of 1840, four States have been added to the Union—Iowa, Wisconsin, Florida, and Texas. They leave the difference in the Senate as it stood when the census was taken; but add two to the side of the North in the House, making the present majority in the House in its favor fifty, and in the electoral college fifty-two.

The result of the whole is to give the Northern section a predominance in every department of the Government, and thereby concentrate in it the two elements which constitute the Federal Government,—majority of States, and a majority of their population, estimated in federal numbers, Whatever section concentrates the two in itself possesses the control of the entire Government.

But we are just at the close of the sixth decade, and the commencement of the seventh. The census is to be taken this year, which must add greatly to the decided preponderance of the North in the House of Representatives and in the electoral college. The prospect is, also, that a great increase will be added to its present preponderance in the Senate, during the period of the decade, by the addition of new States. Two territories, Oregon and Minnesota, are already in progress, and strenuous efforts are making to bring in three additional States from the territory recently conquered from Mexico; which, if successful, will add three other States in a short time to the Northern section, making five States; and increasing the present number of its States from fifteen to twenty, and of its Senators from thirty to forty. On the contrary, there is not a single territory in progress in the Southern section, and no certainty that any additional State will be added to it during the decade. The prospect then is, that the two sections in the Senate, should the efforts now made to exclude the South from the newly acquired territories succeed, will stand, before the end of the decade, twenty Northern States to fourteen Southern (considering Delaware as neutral), and forty Northern Senators to twenty-eight Southern. This great increase of Senators, added to the great increase of members of the House of Representatives and the electoral college on the part of the North, which must take place under the next decade, will effectually and irretrievably destroy the equilibrium which existed when the Government commenced.

Had this destruction been the operation of time, without the interference of Government, the South would have had no reason to complain; but such was not the fact. It was caused by the legislation of this Government, which was appointed, as the common agent of all, and charged with the protection of the interests and security of all. The legislation by which it has been effected, may be classed under three heads. The first is, that series of acts by which the South has been excluded from the common territory belonging to all the States as members of the Federal Union—which have had the effect of extending vastly the portion allotted to the Northern section, and restricting within narrow limits the portion left the South. The next consists in adopting a system of revenue and disbursements, by which an undue proportion of the burden of taxation has been imposed upon the South, and an undue proportion of its proceeds appropriated to the North; and the last is a system of political measures, by which the original character of the Government has been radically changed. I propose to bestow upon each of these, in the order they stand, a few remarks, with the view of showing that it is owing to the action of this Government, that the equilibrum between the two sections has been destroyed, and the whole powers of the system centered in a sectional majority.

The first of the series of acts by which the South was deprived of its due share of the territories, originated with the confederacy which preceded the existence of this Government. It is to be found in the provision of the ordinance of 1787. Its effect was to exclude the South entirely from that vast and fertile region which lies between the Ohio and the Mississippi rivers, now embracing five States and one territory. The next of the series is the Missouri compromise, which excluded the South from that large portion of Louisiana which lies north of 36° 30', excepting what is included in the State of Missouri. The last of the series excluded the South from the whole of the Oregon Territory. All these, in the slang of the day, were what are called slave territories, and not free soil; that is, territories belonging to slaveholding powers and open to the emigration of masters with their slaves. By these several acts, the South was excluded from 1,238,025 square miles—an extent of country considerably exceeding the entire valley of the Mississippi. To the South was left the portion of the Territory of Louisiana lying south of 36° 30', and the portion north of it included in the State of Missouri, with the portion lying south of 36° 30', including the States of Louisiana and Arkansas, and the territory lying west of the latter, and south of 36° 30', called the Indian country. These, with the Territory of Florida, now the State, make, in the whole, 283,503 square miles. To this must be added the territory acquired with Texas. If the whole should be added to the Southern section, it would make an increase of 325,520, which would make the whole left to the South, 609,023. But a large part of Texas is still in contest between the two sections, which leaves it uncertain what will be the real extent of the portion of territory that may be left to the South.

I have not included the territory recently acquired by the treaty with Mexico. The North is making the most strenuous efforts to appropriate the whole to herself, by excluding the South from every foot of it. If she should succeed, it will add to that from which the South has already been excluded, 526,078 square miles, and would increase the whole which the North has appropriated to herself, to 1,764,023, not including the portion that she may succeed in excluding us from in Texas. To sum up the whole, the United States, since they declared their independence, have acquired 2,373,046 square miles of territory, from which the North will have excluded the South, if she should succeed in monopolizing the newly acquired territories, about three-fourths of the whole, leaving to the South but about one-fourth.

Such is the first and great cause that has destroyed the equilibrium between the two sections in the Government.

The next is the system of revenue and disbursements which has been adopted by the Government. It is well known that the Government has derived its revenue mainly from duties on imports. I shall not undertake to show that such duties must necessarily fall mainly on the exporting States, and that the South, as the great exporting portion of the Union, has in reality paid vastly more than her due proportion of the revenue; because I deem it unnecessary, as the subject has on so many occasions been fully discussed. Nor shall I, for the same reason, undertake to show that a far greater portion of the revenue has been disbursed at the North, than its due share; and that the joint effect of these causes has been, to transfer a vast amount from South to North, which, under an equal system of revenue and disbursements, would not have been lost to her. If to this be added, that many of the duties were imposed, not for revenue, but for protection,—that is, intended to put money, not in the treasury, but directly into the pocket of the manufacturers,—some conception may be formed of the immense amount which, in the long course of sixty years, has been transferred from South to North. There are no data by which it can be estimated with any certainty; but it is safe to say, that it amounts to hundreds of millions of dollars. Under the most moderate estimate, it would be sufficient to add greatly to the wealth of the North, and thus greatly increase her population by attracting emigration from all quarters to that section.

This, combined with the great primary cause, amply explains why the North has acquired a preponderance in every department of the Government by its disproportionate increase of population and States. The former, as has been shown, has increased, in fifty years, 2,400,000 over that of the South. This increase of population, during so long a period, is satisfactorily accounted for, by the number of emigrants, and the increase of their descendants, which have been attracted to the Northern section from Europe and the South, in consequence of the advantages derived from the causes assigned. If they had not existed—if the South had retained all the capital which has been extracted from her by the fiscal action of the Government; and, if it had not been excluded by the ordinance of 1787 and the Missouri compromise, from the region lying between the Ohio and the Mississippi rivers, and between the Mississippi and the Rocky Mountains north of 36° 30'—it scarcely admits of a doubt, that it would have divided the emigration with the North, and by retaining her own people, would have at least equalled the North in population under the census of 1840, and probably under that about to be taken. She would also, if she had retained her equal rights in those territories, have maintained an equality in the number of States with the North, and have preserved the equilibrium between the two sections that existed at the commencement of the Government. The loss, then, of the equilibrium is to be attributed to the action of this Government.

But while these measures were destroying the equilibrium between the two sections, the action of the Government was leading to a radical change in its character, by concentrating all the power of the system in itself. The occasion will not permit me to trace the measures by which this great change has been consummated. If it did, it would not be difficult to show that the process commenced at an early period of the Government; and that it proceeded, almost without interruption, step by step, until it absorbed virtually its entire powers; but without going through the whole process to establish the fact, it may be done satisfactorily by a very short statement.

That the Government claims, and practically maintains the right to decide in the last resort, as to the extent of its powers, will scarcely be denied by any one conversant with the political history of the country. That it also claims the right to resort to force to maintain whatever power it claims, against all opposition, is equally certain. Indeed it is apparent, from what we daily hear, that this has become the prevailing and fixed-opinion of a great majority of the community. Now, I ask, what limitation can possibly be placed upon the powers of a government claiming and exercising such rights? And, if none can be, how can the separate governments of the States maintain and protect the powers reserved to them by the constitution—or the people of the several States maintain those which are reserved to them, and among others, the sovereign powers by which they ordained and established, not only their separate State Constitutions and Governments, but also the Constitution and Government of the United States? But, if they have no constitutional means of maintaining them against the right claimed by this Government, it necessarily follows, that they hold them at its pleasure and discretion, and that all the powers of the system are in reality concentrated in it. It also follows, that the character of the

Government has been changed in consequence, from a federal republic, as it originally came from the hands of its framers, into a great national consolidated democracy. It has indeed, at present, all the characteristics of the latter, and not one of the former, although it still retains its outward form.

The result of the whole of these causes combined is—that the North has acquired a decided ascendency over every department of this Government, and through it a control over all the powers of the system. A single section governed by the will of the numerical majority, has now, in fact, the control of the Government and the entire powers of the system. What was once a constitutional federal republic, is now converted, in reality, into one as absolute as that of the Autocrat of Russia, and as despotic in its tendency as any absolute government that ever existed.

As, then, the North has the absolute control over the Government, it is manifest, that on all questions between it and the South, where there is a diversity of interests, the interest of the latter will be sacrificed to the former, however oppressive the effects may be; as the South possesses no means by which it can resist, through the action of the Government. But if there was no question of vital importance to the South, in reference to which there was a diversity of views between the two sections, this state of things might be endured, without the hazard of destruction to the South. But such is not the fact. There is a question of vital importance to the Southern section, in reference to which the views and feelings of the two sections are as opposite and hostile as they can possibly be.

I refer to the relation between the two races in the Southern section, which constitutes a vital portion of her social organization. Every portion of the North entertains views and feelings more or less hostile to it. Those most opposed and hostile, regard it as a sin, and consider themselves under the most sacred obligation to use every effort to destroy it. Indeed, to the extent that they conceive they have power, they regard themselves as implicated in the sin, and responsible for not suppressing it by the use of all and every means. Those less opposed and hostile, regard it as a crime—an offence against humanity, as they call it; and, although not so fanatical, feel themselves bound to use all efforts to effect the same object; while those who are least opposed and hostile, regard it as a blot and a stain on the character of what they call the Nation, and feel themselves accordingly bound to give it no countenance or support. On the contrary, the Southern section regards the relation as one which cannot be destroyed without subjecting the two races to the greatest calamity, and the section to poverty, desolation, and wretchedness; and accordingly they feel bound, by every consideration of interest and safety, to defend it.

This hostile feeling on the part of the North towards the social organization of the South long lay dormant, but it only required some cause to act on those who felt most intensely that they were responsible for its continuance, to call it into action. The increasing power of this Government, and of the control of the Northern section over all its departments, furnished the cause. It was this which made an impression on the minds of many, that there was little or no restraint to prevent the Government from doing whatever it might choose to do. This was sufficient of itself to put the most fanatical portion of the North in action, for the purpose of destroying the existing relation between the two races in the South.

The first organized movement towards it commenced in 1835. Then, for the first time, societies were organized, presses established, lecturers sent forth to excite the people of the North, and incendiary publications scattered over the whole South, through the mail. The South was thoroughly aroused. Meetings were held every where, and resolutions adopted, calling upon the North to apply a remedy to arrest the threatened evil, and pledging themselves to adopt measures for their own protection, if it was not arrested. At the meeting of Congress, petitions poured in from the North, calling upon Congress to abolish slavery in the District of Columbia, and to prohibit, what they called, the internal slave trade between the States—announcing at the same time, that their ultimate object was to abolish slavery, not only in the District, but in the States and throughout the Union. At this period, the number engaged in the agitation was small, and possessed little or no personal influence.

Neither party in Congress had, at that time, any sympathy with them or their cause. The members of each party presented their petitions with great reluctance. Nevertheless, small and contemptible as the party then was, both of the great parties of the North dreaded them. They felt, that though small, they were organized in reference to a subject which had a great and a commanding influence over the Northern mind. Each party, on that account, feared to oppose their petitions, lest the opposite party should take advantage of the one who might do so, by favoring them. The effect was, that both united in insisting that the petitions should be received, and that Congress should take jurisdiction over the subject. To justify their course, they took the extraordinary ground, that Congress was bound to receive petitions on every subject, however objectionable they might be, and whether they had, or had not, jurisdiction over the subject. These views prevailed in the House of Representatives, and partially in the Senate; and thus the party succeeded in their first movements, in gaining what they proposed—a position in Congress, from which agitation could be extended over the whole Union. This was the commencement of the agitation, which has ever since continued, and which, as is now acknowledged, has endangered the Union itself.

As for myself, I believed at that early period, if the party who got up the petitions should succeed in getting Congress to take jurisdiction, that agitation would follow, and that it would in the end, if not arrested, destroy the Union. I then so expressed myself in debate, and called upon both parties to take grounds against assuming jurisdiction; but in vain. Had my voice been heeded, and had Congress refused to take jurisdiction, by the united votes of all parties, the agitation which followed would have been prevented, and the fanatical zeal that gives impulse to the agitation, and which has brought us to our present perilous condition, would have become extinguished, from the want of fuel to feed the flame. *That* was the time for the North to have shown her devotion to the Union; but, unfortunately, both of the great parties of that section were so intent on obtaining or retaining party ascendency, that all other considerations were overlooked or forgotten.

What has since followed are but natural consequences. With the success of their first movement, this small fanatical party began to acquire strength; and with that, to become an object of courtship to both the great parties. The necessary consequence was, a further increase of power, and a gradual tainting of the opinions of both of the other parties with their doctrines, until the infection has extended over both; and the great mass of the population of the North, who, whatever may be their opinion of the original abolition party, which still preserves its distinctive organization, hardly ever fail, when it comes to acting, to co-operate in carrying out their measures. With the increase of their influence, they extended the sphere of their action. In a short time after the commencement of their first movement, they had acquired sufficient influence to induce the legislatures of most of the Northern States to pass acts, which in effect abrogated the clause of the constitution that provides for the delivery up of fugitive slaves. Not long after, petitions followed to abolish slavery in forts, magazines, and dockyards, and all other places where Congress had exclusive power of legislation. This was followed by petitions and resolutions of legislatures of the Northern States, and popular meetings, to exclude the Southern States from all territories acquired, or to be acquired, and to prevent the admission of any State hereafter into the Union, which, by its constitution, does not prohibit slavery. And Congress is invoked to do all this, expressly with the view to the final abolition of slavery in the States. That has been avowed to be the ultimate object from the beginning of the agitation until the present time; and yet the great body of both parties of the North, with the full knowledge of the fact, although disavowing the abolitionists, have co-operated with them in almost all their measures.

Such is a brief history of the agitation, as far as it has yet advanced. Now I ask, Senators, what is there to prevent its further progress, until it fulfills the ultimate end proposed, unless some decisive measure should be adopted to prevent it? Has any one of the causes, which has added to its increase from its original small and contemptible beginning until it has attained its present magnitude, diminished in force? Is the original cause of the movement—that slavery is a sin, and ought to be suppressed—weaker now than at the commencement? Or is the abolition party less numerous or influential, or have they less influence with, or control over the two great parties of the North in elections? Or has the South greater means of influencing or controlling the movements of this Government now, than it had when the agitation commenced? To all these questions but one answer can be given: No—no—no. The very reverse is true. Instead of being weaker, all the elements in favor of agitation are stronger now than they were in 1835, when it first commenced, while all the elements of influence on the part of the South are weaker. Unless something decisive is done, I again ask, what is to stop this agitation, before the great and final object at which it aims— the abolition of slavery in the States—is consummated? Is it, then, not certain, that if something is not done to arrest it, the South will be forced to choose between abolition and secession? Indeed, as events are now moving, it will not require the South to secede, in order to dissolve the Union. Agitation will of itself effect it, of which its past history furnishes abundant proof—as I shall next proceed to show.

It is a great mistake to suppose that disunion can be effected by a single blow. The cords which bound these States together in one common Union, are far too numerous and powerful for that. Disunion must be the work of time. It is only through a long process, and successively, that the cords can be snapped, until the whole fabric falls asunder. Already the agitation of the slavery question has snapped some of the most important, and has greatly weakened all the others, as I shall proceed to show.

The cords that bind the States together are not only many, but various in character. Some are spiritual or ecclesiastical; some political; others social. Some appertain to the benefit conferred by the Union, and others to the feeling of duty and obligation.

The strongest of those of a spiritual and ecclesiastical nature, consisted in the unity of the great religious denominations, all of which originally embraced the whole Union. All these denominations, with the exception, perhaps, of the Catholics, were organized very much upon the principle of our political institutions. Beginning with smaller meetings, corresponding with the political divisions of the country, their organization terminated in one great central assemblage, corresponding very much with the character of Congress. At these meetings the principal clergymen and lay members of the respective denominations, from all parts of the Union, met to transact business relating to their common concerns. It was not confined to what appertained to the doctrines and discipline of the respective denominations, but extended to plans for disseminating the Bible—establishing missions, distributing tracts—and of establishing presses for the publication of tracts, newspapers, and periodicals, with a view of diffusing religious information—and for the support of their respective doctrines and creeds. All this combined contributed greatly to strengthen the bonds of the Union. The ties which held each denomination together formed a strong cord to hold the whole Union together; but, powerful as they were, they have not been able to resist the explosive effect of slavery agitation.

The first of these cords which snapped, under its explosive force, was that of the powerful Methodist Episcopal Church. The numerous and strong ties which held it together, are all broken, and its unity gone. They now form separate churches; and, instead of that feeling of attachment and devotion to the interests of the whole church which was formerly felt, they are now arrayed into two hostile bodies, engaged in litigation about what was formerly their common property.

The next cord that snapped was that of the Baptists—one of the largest and most respectable of the denominations. That of the Presbyterian is not entirely snapped, but some of its strands have given way. That of the Episcopal Church is the only one of the four great Protestant denominations which remains unbroken and entire.

The strongest cord, of a political character, consists of the many and powerful ties that have held together the two great parties which have, with some modifications, existed from the beginning of the Government. They both extended to every portion of the Union, and strongly contributed to hold all its parts together. But this powerful cord has fared no better than the spiritual. It resisted, for a long time, the explosive tendency of the agitation, but has finally snapped under its force—if not entirely, in a great measure. Nor is there one of the remaining cords which has not been greatly weakened. To this extent the Union has already been destroyed by agitation, in the only way it can be, by sundering and weakening the cords which bind it together.

If the agitation goes on, the same force, acting with increased intensity, as has been shown, will finally snap every cord, when nothing will be left to hold the States together except force. But, surely, that can, with no propriety of language, be called a Union, when the only means by which the weaker is held connected with the stronger portion is *force*. It may, indeed, keep them connected; but the connection will partake much more of the character of subjugation, on the part of the weaker to the stronger, than the union of free, independent, and sovereign States, in one confederation, as they stood in the early stages of the Government, and which only is worthy of the sacred name of Union.

Having now, Senators, explained what it is that endangers the Union, and traced it to its cause, and explained its nature and character, the question again recurs—How can the Union be saved? To this I answer, there is but one way by which it can be—and that is—by adopting such measures as will satisfy the States belonging to the Southern section, that they can remain in the Union consistently with their honor and their safety. There is, again, only one way by which this can be effected, and that is—by removing the causes by which this belief has been produced. Do *this,* and discontent will cease—harmony and kind feelings between the sections be restored—and every apprehension of danger to the Union removed. The question, then, is—How can this be done? But, before I undertake to answer this question, I propose to show by what the Union cannot be saved.

It cannot, then, be saved by eulogies on the Union, however splendid or numerous. The cry of "Union, Union—the glorious Union!" can no more prevent disunion than the cry of "Health, health—glorious health!" on the part of the physician, can save a patient lying dangerously ill. So long as the Union, instead of being regarded as a protector, is regarded in the opposite character, by not much less than a majority of the States, it will be in vain to attempt to conciliate them by pronouncing eulogies on it.

Besides this cry of Union comes commonly from those whom we cannot believe to be sincere. It usually comes from our assailants. But we cannot believe them to be sincere; for, if they loved the Union, they would necessarily be devoted to the constitution. It made the Union,—and to destroy the constitution would be to destroy the Union. But the only reliable and certain evidence of devotion to the constitution is, to abstain, on the one hand, from violating it, and to repel, on the other, all attempts to violate it. It is only by faithfully performing these high duties that the constitution can be preserved, and with it the Union.

But how stands the profession of devotion to the Union by our assailants, when brought to this test? Have they abstained from violating the constitution? Let the many acts passed by the Northern States to set aside and annul the clause of the constitution providing for the delivery up of fugitive slaves answer. I cite this, not that it is the only instance (for there are many others), but because the violation in this particular is too notorious and palpable to be denied. Again: have they stood forth faithfully to repel violations of the constitution? Let their course in reference to the agitation of the slavery question, which was commenced and has been carried on for fifteen years, avowedly for the purpose of abolishing slavery in the States—an object all acknowledged to be unconstitutional—answer. Let them show a single instance, during this long period, in which they have denounced the agitators or their attempts to effect what is admitted to be unconstitutional, or a single measure which they have brought forward for that purpose. How can we, with all these facts before us, believe that they are sincere in their profession of devotion to the Union, or avoid believing their profession is but intended to increase the vigor of their assaults and to weaken the force of our resistance?

Nor can we regard the profession of devotion to the Union, on the part of those who are not our assailants, as sincere, when they pronounce eulogies upon the Union, evidently with the intent of charging us with disunion, without uttering one word of denunciation against our assailants. If friends of the Union, their course should be to unite with us in repelling these assaults, and denouncing the authors as enemies of the Union. Why they avoid this, and pursue the course they do, it is for them to explain.

Nor can the Union be saved by invoking the name of the illustrious Southerner whose mortal remains repose on the western bank of the Potomac. He was one of us—a slaveholder and a planter. We have studied his history, and find nothing in it to justify submission to wrong. On the contrary, his great fame rests on the solid foundation, that, while he was careful to avoid doing wrong to others, he was prompt and decided in repelling wrong. I trust that, in this respect, we profited by his example.

Nor can we find any thing in his history to deter us from seceding from the Union, should it fail to fulfil the objects for which it was instituted, by being permanently and hopelessly converted into the means of oppressing instead of protecting us. On the contrary, we find much in his example to encourage us, should we be forced to the extremity of deciding between submission and disunion.

There existed then, as well as now, a union—that between the parent country and her then colonies. It was a union that had much to endear it to the people of the colonies. Under its protecting and superintending care, the colonies were planted and grew up and prospered, through a long course of years, until they became populous and wealthy. Its benefits were not limited to them. Their extensive agricultural and other productions, gave birth to a flourishing commerce, which richly rewarded the parent country for the trouble and expense of establishing and protecting them. Washington was born and grew up to manhood under that union. He acquired his early distinction in its service, and there is every reason to believe that he was devotedly attached to it. But his devotion was a rational one. He was attached to it, not as an end, but as a means to an end. When it failed to fulfil its end, and, instead of affording protection, was converted into the means of oppressing the colonies, he did not hesitate to draw his sword, and head the great movement by which that union was for ever severed, and the independence of these States established. This was the great and crowning glory of his life, which has spread his fame over the whole globe, and will transmit it to the latest posterity.

Nor can the plan proposed by the distinguished Senator from Kentucky, nor that of the administration save the Union. I shall pass by, without remark, the plan proposed by the Senator, and proceed directly to the consideration of that of the administration. I however assure the distinguished and able Senator, that, in taking this course, no disrespect whatever is intended to him or his plan. I have adopted it, because so many Senators of distinguished abilities, who were present when he delivered his speech, and explained his plan, and who were fully capable to do justice to the side they support, have replied to him.

The plan of the administration cannot save the Union, because it can have no effect whatever, towards satisfying the States composing the southern section of the Union, that they can, consistently with safety and honor, remain in the Union. It is, in fact, but a modification of the Wilmot Proviso. It proposes to effect the same object,—to exclude the South from all territory acquired by the Mexican treaty. It is well known that the South is united against the Wilmot Proviso, and has committed itself by solemn resolutions, to resist, should it be adopted. Its opposition *is not to the name,* but that which it *proposes to effect.* That, the Southern States hold to be unconstitutional, unjust, inconsistent with their equality as members of the common Union, and calculated to destroy irretrievably the equilibrium between the two sections. These objections equally apply to what, for brevity, I will call the Executive Proviso. There is no difference between it and the Wilmot, except in the mode of effecting the object; and in that respect, I must say, that the latter is much the least objectionable. It goes to its object openly, boldly, and distinctly. It claims for Congress unlimited power over the territories, and proposes to assert it over the territories acquired from Mexico, by a positive prohibition of slavery. Not so the Executive Proviso. It takes an indirect course, and in order to elude the Wilmot Proviso, and thereby avoid encountering the united and determined resistance of the South, it denies, by implication, the authority of Congress to legislate for the territories, and claims the right as belonging exclusively to the inhabitants of the territories. But to effect the object of excluding the South, it takes care, in the mean time, to let in emigrants freely from the Northern States and all other quarters, except from the South, which it takes special care to exclude by holding up to them the danger of having their slaves liberated under the Mexican laws. The necessary consequence is to exclude the South from the territory, just as effectually as would the Wilmot Proviso. The only difference in this respect is, that what one proposes to effect directly and openly, the other proposes to effect indirectly and covertly.

But the Executive Proviso is more objectionable than the Wilmot, in another and more important particular. The latter, to effect its object, inflicts a dangerous wound upon the constitution, by depriving the Southern States, as joint partners and owners of the territories, of their rights in them; but it inflicts no greater wound than is absolutely necessary to effect its object. The former, on the contrary, while it inflicts the same wound, inflicts others equally great, and, if possible, greater, as I shall next proceed to explain.

In claiming the right for the inhabitants, instead of Congress, to legislate for the territories, the Executive Proviso, assumes that the sovereignty over the territories is vested in the former: or to express it in the language used in a resolution offered by one of the Senators from Texas (General Houston, now absent), they have "the same inherent right of self-government as the people in the States." The assumption is utterly unfounded, unconstitutional, without example, and contrary to the entire practice of the Government, from its commencement to the present time, as I shall proceed to show.

The recent movement of individuals in California to form a constitution and a State government, and to appoint Senators and Representatives, is the first fruit of this monstrous assumption. If the individuals who made this movement had gone into California as adventurers, and if, as such, they had conquered the territory and established their independence, the sovereignty of the country would have been vested in them, as a separate and independent community. In that case, they would have had the right to form a constitution, and to establish a government for themselves; and if, afterwards, they thought proper to apply to Congress for admission into the Union as a sovereign and independent State, all this would have been regular, and according to established principles. But such is not the case. It was the United States who conquered California and finally acquired it by treaty. The sovereignty, of course, is vested in them, and not in the individuals who have attempted to form a constitution and a State without their consent. All this is clear, beyond controversy unless it can be shown that they have since lost or been divested of their sovereignty.

Nor is it less clear, that the power of legislating over the acquired territory is vested in Congress, and not, as is assumed, in the inhabitants of the territories. None can deny that the Government of the United States has the power to acquire territories, either by war or treaty; but if the power to acquire exists, it belongs to Congress to carry it into execution. On this point there can be no doubt, for the constitution expressly provides, that Congress shall have power "to make all laws which shall be necessary and proper to carry into execution the foregoing powers" (those vested in Congress), "and all other powers vested by this constitution in *the Government* of the United States, or in *any department* or *officer* thereof." It matters not, then, where the power is vested; for, if vested at all in the Government of the United States, or any of its departments, or officers, the power of carrying it into execution is clearly vested in Congress. But this important provision, while it gives to Congress the power of legislating over territories, imposes important limitations on its exercise, by restricting Congress to passing laws necessary and proper for carrying the power into execution. The prohibition extends, not only to all laws not suitable or appropriate to the object of the power, but also to all that are unjust, unequal, or unfair,—for all such laws would be unnecessary and improper, and, therefore, unconstitutional.

Having now established, beyond controversy, that the sovereignty over the territories is vested in the United States,—that is, in the several States composing the Union,—and that the power of legislating over them is expressly vested in Congress, it follows, that the individuals in California who have undertaken to form a constitution and a State, and to exercise the power of legislating without the consent of Congress, have usurped the sovereignty of the State and the authority of Congress, and have acted in open defiance of both. In other words, what they have done is revolutionary and rebellious in its character, anarchical in its tendency, and calculated to lead to the most dangerous consequences. Had they acted from premeditation and design, it would have been, in fact, actual rebellion; but such is not the case. The blame lies much less upon them than upon those who have induced them to take a course so unconstitutional and dangerous. They have been led into it by language held here, and the course pursued by the Executive branch of the Government.

I have not seen the answer of the Executive to the calls made by the two Houses of Congress for information as to the course which it took, or the part which it acted, in reference to what was done in California. I understand the answers have not yet been printed. But there is enough known to justify the assertion, that those who profess to represent and act under the authority of the Executive, have advised, aided, and encouraged the movement, which terminated in forming, what they call a constitution and a State. General Riley, who professed to act as civil Governor, called the convention—determined on the number, and distribution of the delegates—appointed the time and place of its meeting—was present during the session—and gave its proceedings his approbation and sanction. If he acted without authority, he ought to have been tried, or at least reprimanded, and his course disavowed. Neither having been done, the presumption is, that his course has been approved. This, of itself, is sufficient to identify the Executive with his acts, and to make it responsible for them. I touch not the question, whether General Riley was appointed, or received the instructions under which he professed to act from the present Executive, or its predecessor. If from the former, it would implicate the preceding, as well as the present administration. If not, the responsibility rests exclusively on the present.

It is manifest from this statement, that the Executive Department has undertaken to perform acts preparatory to the meeting of the individuals to form their so called constitution and government, which appertain exclusively to Congress. Indeed, they are identical, in many respects, with the provisions adopted by Congress, when it gives permission to a territory to form a constitution and government, in order to be admitted as a State into the Union.

Having now shown that the assumption upon which the Executive, and the individuals in California, acted throughout this whole affair, is unfounded, unconstitutional, and dangerous; it remains to make a few remarks, in order to show that what has been done, is contrary to the entire practice of the Government, from the commencement to the present time.

From its commencement until the time that Michigan was admitted, the practice was uniform. Territorial governments were first organized by Congress. The Government of the United States appointed the governors, judges, secretaries, marshals, and other officers; and the inhabitants of the territory were represented by legislative bodies, whose acts were subject to the revision of Congress. This state of things continued until the government of a territory applied to Congress to permit its inhabitants to form a constitution and government, preparatory to admission into the Union. The act preliminary to giving permission was, to ascertain whether the inhabitants were sufficiently numerous to authorize them to be formed into a State. This was done by taking a census. That being done, and the number proving sufficient, permission was granted. The act granting it, fixed all the preliminaries—the time and place of holding the convention; the qualification of the voters; establishment of its boundaries, and all other measures necessary to be settled previous to admission. The act giving permission necessarily withdraws the sovereignty of the United States, and leaves the inhabitants of the incipient State as free to form their constitution and government as were the original States of the Union after they had declared their independence. At this stage, the inhabitants of the territory became, for the first time, a people, in legal and constitutional language. Prior to this, they were, by the old acts of Congress, called inhabitants, and not people. All this is perfectly consistent with the sovereignty of the United States, with the powers of Congress, and with the right of a people to self-government.

Michigan was the first case in which there was any departure from the uniform rule of acting. Hers was a very slight departure from established usage. The ordinance of 1787 secured to her the right of becoming a State, when she should have 60,000 inhabitants. Owing to some neglect, Congress delayed taking the census. In the mean time her population increased, until it clearly exceeded more than twice the number which entitled her to admission. At this stage, she formed a constitution and government, without a census being taken by the United States, and Congress waived the omission, as there was no doubt she had more than a sufficient number to entitle her to admission. She was not admitted at the first session she applied, owing to some difficulty respecting the boundary between her and Ohio. The great irregularity, as to her admission, took place at the next session—but on a point which can have no possible connection with the case of California.

The irregularities in all other cases that have since occurred, are of a similar nature. In all, there existed territorial governments established by Congress, with officers appointed by the United States. In all, the territorial government took the lead in calling conventions, and fixing the preliminaries preparatory to the formation of a constitution and admission into the Union. They all recognized the sovereignty of the United States, and the authority of Congress over the territories; and wherever there was any departure from established usage, it was done on the presumed consent of Congress, and not in defiance of its authority, or the sovereignty of the United States over the territories. In this respect California stands alone, without usage or a single example to cover her case.

It belongs now, Senators, to you to decide what part you will act in reference to this unprecedented transaction. The Executive has laid the paper purporting to be the Constitution of California before you, and asks you to admit her into the Union as a State; and the question is, will you or will you not admit her? It is a grave question, and there rests upon you a heavy responsibility. Much, very much, will depend upon your decision. If you admit her, you indorse and give your sanction to all that has been done. Are you prepared to do so? Are you prepared to surrender your power of legislation for the territories—a power expressly vested in Congress by the constitution, as has been fully established? Can you, consistently with your oath to support the constitution, surrender the power? Are you prepared to admit that the inhabitants of the territories possess the sovereignty over them, and that any number, more or less, may claim any extent of territory they please; may form a constitution and government, and erect it into a State, without asking your permission? Are you prepared to surrender the sovereignty of the United States over whatever territory may be hereafter acquired to the first adventurers who may rush into it? Are you prepared to surrender virtually to the Executive Department all the powers which you have heretofore exercised over the territories? If not, how can you, consistently with your duty and your oaths to support the constitution, give your assent to the admission of California as a State, under a pretended constitution and government? Again, can you believe that the project of a constitution which they have adopted has the least validity? Can you believe that there is such a State in reality as the State of California? No; there is no such State. It has no legal or constitutional existence. It has no validity, and can have none, without your sanction. How, then, can you admit it as a *State,* when, according to the provision of the constitution, your power is limited to admitting new *States.* To be admitted, it must be a State,—and an existing State, independent of your sanction, before you can admit it. When you give your permission to the inhabitants of a territory to form a constitution and a State, the constitution and State they form, derive their authority from the people, and not from you. The State, before it is admitted is actually a State, and does not become so by the *act of admission,* as would be the case with California, should you admit her contrary to the constitutional provisions and established usage heretofore.

The Senators on the other side of the Chamber must permit me to make a few remarks in this connection particularly applicable to them,—with the exception of a few Senators from the South, sitting on the other side of the Chamber.—When the Oregon question was before this body, not two years since, you took (if I mistake not) universally the ground, that Congress had the sole and absolute power of legislating for the territories. How, then, can you now, after the short interval which has elapsed, abandon the ground which you took, and thereby virtually admit that the power of legislating, instead of being in Congress, is in the inhabitants of the territories? How can you justify and sanction by your votes the acts of the Executive, which are in direct derogation of what you then contended for? But to approach still nearer to the present time, how can you, after condemning, little more than a year since, the grounds taken by the party which you defeated at the last election, wheel round and support by your votes the grounds which, as explained recently on this floor by the candidate of the party in the last election, are identical with those on which the Executive has acted in reference to California? What are we to understand by all this? Must we conclude that there is no sincerity, no faith in the acts and declarations of public men, and that all is mere acting or hollow profession? Or are we to conclude that the exclusion of the South from the territory acquired from Mexico is an object of so paramount a character in your estimation, that right, justice, constitution and consistency must all yield, when they stand in the way of our exclusion?

But, it may be asked, what is to be done with California, should she not be admitted? I answer, remand her back to the territorial condition, as was done in the case of Tennessee, in the early stage of the Government. Congress, in her case, had established a territorial government in the usual form, with a governor, judges, and other officers, appointed by the United States. She was entitled, under the deed of cession, to be admitted into the Union as a State as soon as she had sixty thousand inhabitants. The territorial government, believing it had that number, took a census, by which it appeared it exceeded it. She then formed a constitution, and applied for admission. Congress refused to admit her, on the ground that the census should be taken by the United States, and that Congress had not determined whether the territory should be formed into one or two States, as it was authorized to do under the cession. She returned quietly to her territorial condition. An act was passed to take a census by the United States, containing a provision that the territory should form one State. All afterwards was regularly conducted, and the territory admitted as a State in due form. The irregularities in the case of California are immeasurably greater, and offer much stronger reasons for pursuing the same course. But, it may be said, California may not submit. That is not probable; but if she should not, when she refuses, it will then be time for us to decide what is to be done.

Having now shown what cannot save the Union, I return to the question with which I commenced, How can the Union be saved? There is but one way by which it can with any certainty; and that is, by a full and final settlement, on the principle of justice, of all the questions at issue between the two sections.

The South asks for justice, simple justice, and less she ought not to take. She has no compromise to offer, but the constitution; and no concession or surrender to make. She has already surrendered so much that she has little left to surrender. Such a settlement would go to the root of the evil, and remove all cause of discontent, by satisfying the South, she could remain honorably and safely in the Union, and thereby restore the harmony and fraternal feelings between the sections, which existed anterior to the Missouri agitation. Nothing else can, with any certainty, finally and for ever settle the questions at issue, terminate agitation, and save the Union.

But can this be done? Yes, easily; not by the weaker party, for it can of itself do nothing—not even protect itself—but by the stronger. The North has only to will it to accomplish it—to do justice by conceding to the South an equal right in the acquired territory, and to do her duty by causing the stipulations relative to fugitive slaves to be faithfully fulfilled—to cease the agitation of the slave question, and to provide for the insertion of a provision in the constitution, by an amendment, which will restore to the South, in substance, the power she possessed of protecting herself, before the equilibrium between the sections was destroyed by the action of this Government. There will be no difficulty in devising such a provision—one that will protect the South, and which, at the same time, will improve and strengthen the Government, instead of impairing and weakening it.

But will the North agree to this? It is for her to answer the question. But, I will say, she cannot refuse, if she has half the love of the Union which she professes to have, or without justly exposing herself to the charge that her love of power and aggrandizement is far greater than her love of the Union. At all events, the responsibility of saving the Union rests on the North, and not on the South. The South cannot save it by any act of hers, and the North may save it without any sacrifice whatever, unless to do justice, and to perform her duties under the constitution, should be regarded by her as a sacrifice.

It is time, Senators, that there should be an open and manly avowal on all sides, as to what is intended to be done. If the question is not now settled, it is uncertain whether it ever can hereafter be; and we, as the representatives of the States of this Union, regarded as governments, should come to a distinct understanding as to our respective views, in order to ascertain whether the great questions at issue can be settled or not. If you, who represent the stronger portion, cannot agree to settle them on the broad principle of justice and duty, say so; and let the States we both represent agree to separate and part in peace. If you are unwilling we should part in peace, tell us so, and we shall know what to do, when you reduce the question to submission or resistance. If you remain silent, you will compel us to infer by your acts what you intend. In that case, California will become the test question. If you admit her, under all the difficulties that oppose her admission, you compel us to infer that you intend to exclude us from the whole of the acquired territories, with the intention of destroying, irretrievably, the equilibrium between the two sections. We would be blind not to perceive in that case, that your real objects are power and aggrandizement, and infatuated not to act accordingly.

I have now, Senators, done my duty in expressing my opinions fully, freely, and candidly, on this solemn occasion. In doing so, I have been governed by the motives which have governed me in all the stages of the agitation of the slavery question since its commencement. I have exerted myself, during the whole period, to arrest it, with the intention of saving the Union, if it could be done; and if it could not, to save the section where it has pleased Providence to cast my lot, and which I sincerely believe has justice and the constitution on its side. Having faithfully done my duty to the best of my ability, both to the Union and my section, throughout this agitation, I shall have the consolation, let what will come, that I am free from all responsibility.

INDEX

Aberdeen, Lord, 579, 580

abolitionists, 213, 530

absolute government: conservative principle of, 21–23; constitutional vs., 7, 25, 94–104, 147–48, 181; force and, 21–23; numerical majority and, 17, 20; right of suffrage and, 8; veto power and, 21. *See also* General Government

absolute majority. *See* numerical majority

act of 1828. *See* Bill of Abominations

Adams, John, 193, 198, 201, 471–72, 669

Adams, John Quincy, 199, 243, 244, 472

Africa, slave trade in, 578–82

Alabama, 399

Alien and Sedition acts, 193, 293; constitutionality of, 197, 376; report to the Virginia Legislature and, 61; Virginia & Kentucky resolutions and, 193–99

alliances, Confederacy and, 65

A Manual of Parliamentary Practice (Jefferson), 243, 250

amending power: Constitution and, 77–78, 87, 95–96, 116–17, 157, 292, 351–52, 371, 377, 408–9, 553–54; division of powers and, 116; General Government and, 171–73; majority and, 553–54, 595–600; nature and character of, 156–66; Senate and, 103; States and, 595–99; State vs. General government and, 301–2, 327–28

American people. *See* people

American political tradition: *Federalist* and, 61; fundamental law and, 61; right of interposition and, 343; slavery and, 661; Virginia & Kentucky resolutions and, 61

American System. *See* Tariff System

Ames, Fisher, 460

anarchy, 288; destructiveness of, 4; government of majority and, 22, 218, 445–50; liberty and, 30–31

Anio, 52

appointments: President and, 117, 121, 552, 561–62; Senate and, 97, 100, 117, 121, 463, 476–77, 552

appropriations: Congress and, 116, 200, 325; for fortifications, 486–87, 490; House of Representatives and, 113; objects of, 426; State vs. General government and, 333; Tariff system and, 284–86, 333, 404–5; taxation and, 200, 357–58

Archer, Mr., 564

Archives des Affaires Etrangères, 574n

aristocracy: compromise and, 45–46; General Government vs., 63; people and, 14, 45–46

Arkansas, 689

army: appropriations for, 490; common defense and, 223–31; increase in size of, 641; President and, 117, 122, 182, 475–76, 565; raising and supporting, 113

NOTE ON THE EDITORS

H. LEE CHEEK, JR., teaches political science at Lee University in Cleveland, Tennessee. He received his bachelor's degree from Western Carolina University, his M.Div. from Duke University, his M.P.A. from Western Carolina University, and his Ph.D. from The Catholic University of America. He is the editor of *Political Philosophy and Cultural Renewal: Francis Graham Wilson, Collected Essays* (Transaction, 2001; with Kathy B. Cheek), *Calhoun and Popular Rule* (University of Missouri Press, 2001), and *Order and Legitimacy* (Transaction, 2002). He has also published many journal articles in publications like the *Journal of Politics*, *Methodist History*, *International Social Science Review*, *Telos*, and is a regular commentator on American politics. As a senior minister in the United Methodist Church, Dr. Cheek presides over worship and leads seminars on the Wesleyan tradition throughout the Southeast.

Conservative Leadership Series editor CHRISTOPHER B. BRIGGS holds degrees from Bowdoin College (summa cum laude) and The Catholic University of America. Assistant editor of *Humanitas,* a journal of the humanities published in Washington, D.C., he lives in northern Virginia.